The World Today Series®

Stryker-Post Publications, Harpers Ferry, WV • USA

Africa

J. Tyler Dickovick

44th edition

Next Edition: August 2010

2009

About the Author . . .

J. Tyler Dickovick is an Assistant Professor of Politics at Washington and Lee University in Lexington, Virginia. He received his Ph.D. in Public Affairs from the Woodrow Wilson School of Public and International Affairs at Princeton University. He also holds a Master in Public Affairs and an MA from Princeton, and a Bachelor of Science in Economics from the Wharton School of Business and a Bachelor of Arts in International Relations from the College of Arts and Sciences at the University of Pennsylvania. He was a 2003 recipient of the Africanist Doctoral Fellowship at the Woodrow Wilson International Center for Scholars in Washington, D.C. His courses include International Development, African Politics, and International Political Economy. He has conducted research in Senegal and South Africa, among other countries, and his publications on the issues of democratization and decentralization appear in such journals as *The Journal of Modern African Studies*, *Publius: the Journal of Federalism*, *Latin American Research Review*, and *Third World Quarterly*. In addition to research in Africa, he served as a Peace Corps Volunteer in Togo from 1995 to 1997.

First appearing as *Africa 1966*,
this annually revised book is published by

Stryker–Post Publications
P.O. Drawer 1200
Harpers Ferry, WV 25425
Telephones: 1–800–995–1400 (U.S.A. and Canada).
Other: 1–304–535–2593
Fax: 1–304–535–6513
www.strykerpost.com
VISA–MASTERCARD–AMERICAN EXPRESS

International Standard Book Number: 978-1-935264-00-2

International Standard Serial Number: 0084-2281

Library of Congress Catalog Number 67-11537

Cover design by nvision graphic design

Cartographer: William L. Nelson

Typography by Barton Matheson Willse & Worthington
Baltimore, MD 21244

Printed in the United States of America
by United Book Press, Inc.
Baltimore, MD 21207

The World Today Series has thousands of subscribers across the U.S. and Canada. A sample list of users who annually rely on this most up-to-date material include:

Public library systems
Universities and colleges
High schools
Federal and state agencies
All branches of the armed forces & war colleges
National Geographic Society
National Democratic Institute
Agricultural Education Foundation
Exxon Corporation
Chevron Corporation
CNN

Photographs used to illustrate *The World Today Series* come from many sources, a great number from friends who travel worldwide. If you have taken any which you believe would enhance the visual impact and attractiveness of our books, let us hear from you.

CONTENTS

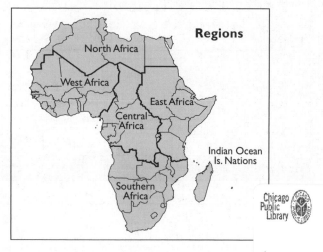

Regions

North Africa
West Africa
East Africa
Central Africa
Indian Ocean Is. Nations
Southern Africa

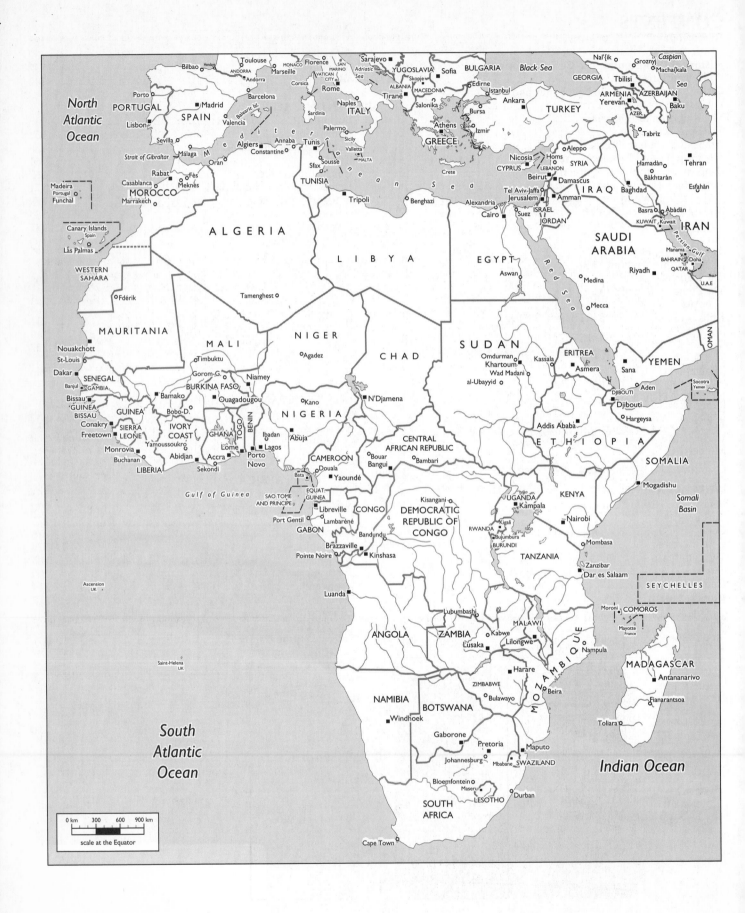

iv

For my family

ACKNOWLEDGMENTS

Too numerous to mention are the people who have supported the work that has gone into this volume. First and foremost among these are four research assistants who did exceptional work in helping to improve the substance and tone for this edition. Three of these worked under the auspices of the R.E. Lee Scholars program. Maya Reimí helped update and improve chapters on an impressive 13 francophone countries in west and central Africa. Grant Russell offered extensive enhancements for the lengthy chapters on South Africa and Zimbabwe, as well as Namibia. Morten Wendelbo helped with significant improvements on Ghana, Nigeria, and Somalia, as well as modifications to chapters on Equatorial Guinea, The Gambia, Liberia, and Malawi; he also assembled the Quick Reference chart at the end of the opening essay. Rachel Mourão was supported by a NASDAQ/SunTrust grant at Washington and Lee, and she worked on the chapters on Angola, Cape Verde, and Rwanda. They made it possible to bring the work more up-to-date, and they helped immensely in improving the writing itself. I also owe continued thanks, of course, to Charles Cutter, whose many years of work on editions of this book up to 2007 continue to form the backbone of much of the historical writing. I am also thankful to many faculty at Princeton University during my graduate work and my colleagues at Washington and Lee University for their support, as well as Annette Seegers at the University of Cape Town and Howard Wolpe at the Woodrow Wilson International Center for Scholars for their hospitality during my research periods at their respective institutional homes. Thanks also to Rachel Beatty Reidl for her collaborations with me in the study of Africa. I also would like to extend my thanks to Wayne Thompson and David Wilt of Stryker Post Publication for giving me the opportunity to continue work on this book. Finally, I owe thanks to Washington and Lee University and to the Lenfest Grant for support for the project. As always, I conclude with thanks and love for Alessandra, Carolina, Gabriela, and the rest of my family for their patience with long days and nights (and occasionally even weeks, when I find myself in Africa) away from home.

✳ ✳

CHARLES H. CUTTER
(1938–2008)
Author, scholar, friend

Foreword to the 44th edition

This 44th edition of *Africa: The World Today Series* is a newly revised edition, though it retains much of the content from earlier editions. I have made numerous changes I deemed necessary, but I have necessarily retained some of the historical content from the 2008 edition and from work in previous years by Charles Cutter.

Several major changes in structure occurred in the 2008 edition, including the reorganization of the regions, and the inclusion of five identically-named sections for each country (Basic Facts; Land and People; The Past: Political and Economic History; The Present: Contemporary Is-

sues; The Future). For the 2009 edition, revisions have focused on updating the empirical material and altering some of the tone. I am convinced, as noted in the subsequent essay, that select countries in Africa are moving along a more positive trajectory than the book suggested in the past. This necessitated a more nuanced outlook for some countries, and this set of changes is something that will continue into the future as events merit. This volume also expands somewhat the treatment of national cultural phenomena, including leading artistic and cultural representations highlighted in the Land and

People sections. The opening essay is almost entirely new, reflecting the changes in Africa in the last year. Finally, we have added a "Quick Reference" chart to the opening essay, to allow the reader to garner a great deal of information about African countries from a cursory glance.

The *Africa* volume is always a work-in-progress, much like the continent itself. Such work benefits from suggestions, corrections, and critiques. Please feel free to contact the author directly at Department of Politics, Huntley Hall, Washington and Lee University, Lexington VA 24450.

Majestic elegance, the cattle of Uganda   Photo by Pat Crowell

NATO Forces patrolling in the Strait of Gibraltar

Photo by Seaman Laura Pons, courtesy NATO

The World and Africa in 2009

In the second half of 2008 and in 2009, since the last volume of this book appeared, Africa and the world have been entwined in a curious tango. On one hand, the advanced, industrialized countries have long viewed Africa as a source of instability and uncertainty. The stories out of Africa are legion, and the facts are sometimes stranger than fiction. In Somalia's collapsed state, modern-day pirates repeatedly venture off the coast to attack shipping vessels using automatic weapons and motorized rubber speedboats. Sudan, the one-time hideout of Osama bin Laden, is run by the genocidal leader Omar al-Bashir, a man now virtually unable to leave his own country because he is a fugitive from international justice. And Zimbabwe's megalomaniacal Robert Mugabe and his incompetent underlings may have had the dubious distinction of setting a world record in 2008: the worst hyperinflation ever. (Whether Zimbabwe actually supplanted Hungary's 1946 hyperinflation remains ambiguous. When inflation is estimated somewhere in the quintillion or sextillion percent range, the numbers get a bit sketchy.) On a continent characterized by such disasters, western governments have lamented the poor state of African governance and economic management, and have made efforts—albeit modest and sometimes misguided—to promote order, stability, and prosperity on the continent. To casual observers,

Africa seems to be a producer and exporter of trouble, but a ravenous importer and consumer of foreign aid and charity.

It takes two to tango, however, and there is another side to the story. In late 2008 and 2009, the global financial crisis brought disruption and instability onto the African continent, courtesy of Wall Street and its derivatives traders, and America's Main Street homeowners and their subprime mortgages. The mechanisms of the crisis in Africa were not the same as those in the United States and elsewhere, since most Africans have less access to credit and benefited little from the global run-up in property values. Rather than foreclosures, collapsed housing markets, and the tightening of credit, Africans have experienced the global recession as a dramatic drop-off in international trade, plummeting prices for export commodities such as oil and copper, and fluctuations in food prices depending upon exchange rate volatility. Together, these elements of the crisis cast a pall over a continent that had recently begun to witness an economic turnaround and recovery. The crisis has slowed Africa's annual economic growth from a robust rate of around 5% to an estimated 1% in 2009, according to the World Bank. This growth rate is better than many countries, but is insufficient to bring millions of Africans out of poverty.

The arrival of problems originated overseas is not new to Africa, of course. After all, this is the continent whose early

economic exchanges with the world were based upon the slave trade. Moreover, during the Cold War, Africa was a central battlefield in the proxy wars for power between a First World led by the United States and the Second World of the Soviet Bloc. The corrupt and vile dictatorships that dotted the continent for 30 years were of Africa's own making, but were aided and abetted by international powers. In short, western countries have a long history of bringing social, political, and economic disruption to Africa, alongside the genuine opportunities, new ideas, and constructive investment they also brought. Colonial history, trade, development aid, policy advice, political interventions, military engagement, and multinational enterprise have constructed a web of interactions between the west and Africa that have had ambiguous consequences for the continent.

To be clear, the crisis of 2009 does not suggest that Africa would be better off reversing its integration with the international economy. The assessment of the situation must be considerably more complex and varied, much as the continent itself must be understood as complex and varied. Rather than offering simplistic lessons, the events of 2009 suggest a dynamic interrelationship between the "globalized" world and the continent that is often seen as the least touched by globalization. Economically, Africa and the world share a mutual dependence that

Africa in 2009

brings benefits and costs to each. Take for instance the massive Chinese investment in Africa in recent years, which would seem an unambiguous boost to African economies. China has supported mineral extraction and exploration, heavy industrial investment, construction of public venues such as sports stadiums, and even provision of artemisinin, the leading anti-malarial drug. On the downside, however, Chinese investment has arguably helped to prop up dictatorships, since China (an authoritarian regime itself) stands by the principle of non-intervention in domestic affairs. Certainly, rotten governments such as those in Sudan and Zimbabwe will appreciate the Chinese investment and willingness to "look the other way" on human rights issues, but large segments of the populations are likely to suffer the consequences.

Africa's interaction with the United States and Europe also has pros and cons. Consider international impacts on African public health. On one hand, the continent has benefited from increasing international support for programming to help control HIV/AIDS. Yet in the last year the swine flu also reached Africa, conveyed from Mexico (almost certainly via the United States and/or Europe) by the vehicles of globalization: air travel and trade. While the pandemic has not caused large numbers of deaths in Europe or America, the strain is likely to spread (and likely mutate) and will be more lethal in a place where larger numbers of people are immuno-compromised. Africa, then, benefits from many of its interactions with the world, but also is susceptible to global complications. On a continent where so many confront HIV/AIDS in precarious

economic circumstances, it may be said in a literal sense that when the world coughs, Africa catches a fever.

Africa in the World in 2009

Much as the world affects Africa, so too does Africa increasingly occupy a prominent place in our collective imaginations, and not only for the reasons seen from the 1970s up through the early 1990s: famine and genocide, poverty and conflict, death and destruction and disease. Rather, contemporary Africa has a whole set of different meanings for most living in the developed world, representing both challenges and opportunities. It is a continent where a several civilizations collide, from Arab to Bantu to Indian to Dutch. It is a continent that is, for some, is ominous and foreboding—"the Dark Continent"—but for many others has the inexorable appeal of vivacity and resilience in the face of humanity's greatest challenges. Most importantly, in a practical sense, it is a continent that increasingly shapes the way of life of many countries beyond the continent itself.

The first reason why Africa is of growing strategic importance to the rest of the world is because of its *weak states*. The most prominent example of this in Africa today is Somalia. In the past year, pirates have attacked ships off the coast of Somalia, affecting vessels and merchant mariners from France, Denmark, and the United States, among other countries. The very idea of piracy immediately invokes lawlessness, but usually sounds outdated, a relic of the past. The basic phenomenon, however, is not historically restricted, but rather depends upon a government's inability to perform the essential tasks of

governing, such as enacting and enforcing laws. As political scientist Jeffrey Herbst has put it, African states too often fail to broadcast their power and authority over their own territory.

A recurring problem in Africa is the failure of "states" to live up to even the basic definition of statehood. While a country may have a plaque and a seat at the United Nations, it may have little internal control; or, as political scientists and sociologists would characterize the phenomenon, they may lack a monopoly on the legitimate use of force in their territory. Put more concretely, many African regimes have proven historically incapable of governing outside the confines of just a few square miles in a capital city. The most striking examples of this phenomenon came from the "warlord states" of the 1990s, when clans of roving bandits—often including child soldiers wielding machetes and automatic small arms—brought mayhem to Liberia, Sierra Leone, and Somalia. (It should be noted here that the 1994 genocide in Rwanda was quite different in this regard. It was in fact meticulously coordinated by one of Africa's more organized state apparatuses, and was not, despite common misperceptions, a spontaneous outburst of violence by marauders avenging "ancient tribal hatreds.")

Why do Africa's weak states matter for, say, Americans? Apart from humanitarian concerns, it is tempting for some to believe that American disengagement from the continent could mean that we simply allow for "African solutions to African problems." Indeed, American disengagement from Somalia in 1993 after the deaths of American troops must be understood in light of the unwillingness of the administration and American populace to stand in the middle of an African conflict. And the failure to intervene in the Rwanda genocide of 1994 must be understood with reference to the prior year's events in Somalia. So why should America involve itself in African problems? Setting aside questions of moral imperatives and those about America's historic role on the continent, there are several simple answers to such a question. A first reason is terrorism.

Weak states are likely breeding grounds for terrorism. Al-Qaeda, like other Islamic fundamentalist movements that advocate terrorism, thrives not in countries where they can live above ground, but rather where power itself is scarcely exercised by the government. Terrorism can flourish where the state cannot penetrate. It is for this reason that the U.S. government has, in recent years, poured money into Western Africa. The Trans-Saharan Counter Terrorism (following on its predecessor, the Pan-Sahel Initiative) will infuse a total of about $100 million into Africa in the years

Village in Tanzania

between 2005 and 2010, with the intention of preventing several West and North African countries with large Islamic populations (Algeria, Chad, Mali, Mauritania, Morocco, Niger, Nigeria, Senegal, and Tunisia) from becoming safe havens for Islamic terrorists. While some of these countries, especially Mali and Senegal, are known for their relatively comfortable relations with the West and for their more liberal interpretations of Islam, other countries are dealing with active radical elements that are openly antagonistic towards the United States and western Europe.

The battle has been engaged by Islamist militants, beginning in North Africa but extending south of the Sahara. In the 1990s a radical insurgent group known as the Salafist Group for Preaching and Combat (*Groupe Salafiste pour la Prédication et le Combat*) emerged in Algeria to fight the government in Algiers. After several attacks, kidnappings, and bombings between 2002 and 2006, the organization staged a pair of twin bombings in Algiers in 2007, killing 23 and then 41 people. Between 2003 and 2006, the group also rebranded itself as AQIM: Al-Qaeda in the Islamic Maghreb. It has taken on the al-Qaeda "franchise" and has been approved by the top leadership of al-Qaeda as the terrorist organization's main wing in North Africa. In the last year, signs have emerged that the organization is reaching further into Mali, Niger, and Mauritania, probably both as an offensive strategy and as a defensive tactic, given the response from the Algerian government.

Weak states imply threats to public health and security beyond terrorism as well. Combating terrorism may be the leading strategic objective of the 21st century; fighting the "War on Drugs" is another, and here too Africa is a front in the battle. Much of the world's illicit drug supply (of, say, heroin) is processed or transshipped through countries like Guinea-Bissau, where corruption is rampant and governmental control is thus woefully inadequate. The deterioration of civil-military relations in Guinea-Bissau and the eventual assassination of its president by the military in 2009 was an event half a world away that scarcely registered in the United States. Yet the consequences of these events come home to Americans in the form of heroin on the streets of Atlanta.

Strengthening Africa's states thus again becomes a matter of self-interest for the industrialized nations of the world. Even for beneficial pharmaceuticals, weak states present a difficulty: a government that cannot govern cannot control dangerous processes of counterfeiting and piracy. That improper or dangerous products could find their way into the world commercial market is an added peril of weak states. Finally, other possible threats to public health come from the inability of inept state management of the possible pandemics that threaten to become the new "plagues" of the 21st century.

Beyond concerns with state weakness, Africa is back on the world map as a locus of great power contestation for the coming century, for one principal reason: energy supplies. Not since the Cold War have the world's leading powers *needed* Africa in the way the United States, China, and Europe need Africa today. Already, Africa supplies about as much oil to the United States as the Persian Gulf provides. And Africa's share of the American market is growing. Angola and Nigeria are leading suppliers to the world, with Gabon, Cameroon, and Congo having historically provided major supplies. The gross domestic product of the tiny nation of Equatorial Guinea has skyrocketed in the last decade as oil investment and production have taken off, though little of the wealth has trickled down to the population. Ghana, meanwhile, is an up-and-coming producer.

Great powers typically contest access to resources, and the emerging battle between the United States and China for access to energy supplies in Africa fits this mold. Much of the aforementioned Chinese investment in Africa is linked to investment in the oil industry, though China has also invested in prestige projects across the continent. The rivalry between the U.S. and China takes on difficult overtones as the former tries to push (perhaps selectively) for a recognition of universal human rights, while the latter expresses support for the principle of "non-intervention" in Africa's domestic affairs. The result is a willingness on the part of China to be cozy with some of the continent's worst dictators, though the United States also has a checkered history that blends accommodation and indignation as regards African governance.

In short, then, Africa matters beyond Africa. Nowhere else in the world do several of America's most prominent foreign policy issues intersect: Africa today includes the stories of radical Islam, drugs, oil, and the growing rivalry with China.

Ex Africa semper aliquid novi

"There is always something new out of Africa," goes the ancient saying, and perhaps the newest thing out of Africa is the increasingly obvious variation across the continent. While we may speak of Africa as a whole for some purposes, and while we may feel we know the general parameters of the African story, the tale is not the same everyplace on the continent, nor is it the same from year to year. Indeed, it is increasingly difficult to describe the trajectory of "Africa as a whole." Rather, we must increasingly make reference to the vast differences between African countries and their experiences, and how these change over time. To some degree, it has always been true that Africa is a varied and complex place: Mauritania and Mada-

Moroccan woman

Africa in 2009

gascar would scarcely be confused with one another culturally, though they may occasionally be confused in name by those being introduced to the continent for the first time. Egypt and Zimbabwe may share in common the pride of their ancient civilizations, and may both be contemporary trouble spots, but the countries are radically different on most other counts. And Senegal and Somalia, at the opposite ends of the Sahara Desert, are just as clearly distinct. Yet what was always true—that Africa is a continent of great variety and complexity—is more evident today.

There are now over a half-dozen African countries, including some of the poorest places in the world, that have been stable and largely democratic for nearly twenty years. At first glance, this may sound unremarkable, and the fact may be almost imperceptible to many observers, albeit mildly encouraging in an historical sense. But there is something more to the story: this democratic legacy may be self-reinforcing. African populations are young, with the median age often under 20 years; this means that in many places an entire generation, and sometimes over half the population, has never known military rule, coups, or social strife. If democratic values take time to consolidate, each passing year in a democracy is precious.

Ghana in 2009 was emblematic of what African democratic consolidation could be. In the runoff election between the two top presidential candidates in late 2008, less than half a percentage point separated eventual winner John Atta-Mills from the runner-up Nana Akufo-Addo. In an election that was roughly as close in the popular vote as that between George W. Bush and Al Gore in 2000, the two candidates promptly affirmed the result, and Akufo-Addo attended Atta-Mills' inauguration soon thereafter. International observers—and most Ghanaians themselves—viewed the election as free and fair. The sequence of events is especially noteworthy for two additional reasons. First, the two candidates drew their strongest support from different ethnic regions of the country, with Akufo-Addo dominating in Ghana's Ashanti heartland and Atta-Mills winning elsewhere. Ethnic differences in the vote seem to have had no significant destabilizing impact. Second, Akufo-Addo represented the governing NPP party of outgoing president John Kuffuor, while Atta-Mills was the opposition candidate from the NDC party of previous president Jerry Rawlings. In many ways, Ghana's achievement was special in Africa precisely because the transfer of power from government to opposition was seen as nothing special: most in the country now presume that a government will leave power when defeated in an election. Ba-

rack Obama offered Ghana's quality of governance as the stated reason for selecting it (over his father's homeland of Kenya) as his first African country to visit as president in July 2009. (Incidentally, shoring up American-Ghanaian relations as petroleum investment materializes is a non-trivial commercial interest, though few have remarked on the fact.)

Another encouraging fact is that Ghana now joins its neighbor Benin as a country meeting the "two turnover" criterion for democratic consolidation. The late political scientist Samuel Huntington argued that a democracy reaches a level of genuine consolidation when there are two democratically-elected turnovers of governing power. This implies that a government (or head of state) loses an election, but also that the government that defeated them loses. The premise of the two-turnover logic is that it suggests all significant parties accept that democracy is "the only game in town," and that all recognize the possibility of losing as a fact of political life.

Along with Ghana and Benin, several other west African countries lead the way as exemplars of democratic persistence, though poverty, social problems, and government ineffectiveness and corruption have not been eliminated. The independent non-governmental organization Freedom House also rates Senegal and Mali as "Free," and Cape Verde receives the very highest rating of 1 for both political and civil liberties. São Tomé e Príncipe is also "free," as are the Indian Ocean nation of Mauritius and the southern African nations of Botswana, Namibia, and South Africa. The persistence of stability and democratization makes for less dramatic news coverage than conflict and disorder, and slow improvement thus does not frequently make the front pages, but in many ways it is the most intriguing of stories in contemporary Africa.

Achievements in several other countries are perhaps more modest, but no less momentous, given the atrocities of recent decades. Sierra Leone and Liberia appear to have reemerged from their horrendous civil wars to create new and hopeful polities with improvements in civil and political rights. Across the continent, Rwanda too appears to have stabilized after the genocide of 15 years ago. Rwanda even is a world leader in the proportion of women in its parliament.

Other countries can claim an even subtler achievement: the persistence of economic and social stability, combined with a creeping sense that politics is liberalizing and possibly democratizing. As noted in 2008, Burkina Faso is an example here. This landlocked country on the Sahelian belt south of the Sahara Desert has never

fully democratized, nor has it witnessed any sort of economic boom. It has, however, slowly moved up the Freedom House rankings in terms of civil liberties, has avoided instability and coup attempts, and has increasingly open elections (though the ruling party and the incumbent president have massive advantages). It has also grown at or about the African average in recent years. This is far from European-caliber democracy and equally far from China-caliber economic growth, but it is also far from the bad old days of coups and decline.

This slow accumulation of "respectability" may be one of the more underreported stories in Africa in recent years. In part, these facts are underappreciated because there is little spectacular to report: moderate improvements make little news, as contrasted with the death and destruction of entire societies in Sudan and Zimbabwe (to be discussed hereafter). Yet it seems clear that, in another generation, young Africans will look back to note that the Africa of the 1990s and this first decade of the new millennium is a very different—and many ways, much improved—place from the continent of the 1970s and 1980s: the founding fathers of independence have largely died or faded from public life, taking with them in most cases the sense that one might be ordained by divine right to be president for life. Dictatorship persists in many cases, but is increasingly embarrassing to Africa's own leaders, who are increasingly (albeit unevenly) willing to stand up for democracy and openness. This is not to suggest problems have evaporated, but it is rather to note that the kind of rule exhibited in Zimbabwe by Robert Mugabe has become more the exception than the rule.

Challenges of leadership and power

This is not to say that all is well in Africa, of course. The continent's powerhouse, South Africa, is one country where the quality of leadership continues to be a curious and complex question. In elections in 2009, South Africa inaugurated a new president, Jacob Zuma, who was elected convincingly as president after leading the ANC to victory in parliamentary elections in 2009 with just under two-thirds of the national vote. Zuma is a Zulu, and his rise to prominence is especially noteworthy in a political party long dominated by the Xhosa people. While Zuma brings a new face to the former liberation movement, he also represents for many the problems of contemporary South Africa. Zuma has faced criminal proceedings on counts of corruption, stemming from the illegal actions taken by some of his closest advisors. Zuma was not convicted, but the trials themselves raised significant questions about political interference in the judiciary, given the prominence of the accused. Previously, Zuma also faced charges of rape. Though eventually acquitted before the law, the spectre of political interference in the subsequent corruption trials continues to cast a cloud over these criminal proceedings as well.

Beyond the concerns about criminal activity are worries that Zuma may exacerbate a trend towards a different tone in the ANC's politics. The years of Nelson Mandela's "Rainbow Nation" have been replaced with greater animosity between races and between political groups. In part, political tension is a consequence of increasing social tension in South Africa, where inequality and crime rates are among the highest in the world. Also contributing, however, is the sense that the ANC must increasingly rely on more divisive appeals to garner electoral support. Zuma's rallies in 2008 and 2009 often featured the singing of "Bring me my machine gun!" in Zulu. While this call has roots in the ANC's history as an armed resistance movement, and it would be an overstatement to claim this was an incitement to violence, the call still raised many eyebrows.

Yet Africa's highly personalized forms of leadership also offer the opportunity for individuals to effect positive change. Again using the South African example, there are also certain improvements that can come with changes in leadership. One is that Zuma may take a harder line towards Zimbabwe's tyrannical Robert Mugabe. Zuma is relatively close to Mugabe's nemesis Morgan Tsvangirai and the Zimbabwean trade union movement, while the opposite was true of Zuma's South African predecessor, Thabo Mbeki. Additionally, under Mbeki and his Health Minister Manto Tshabalala-Msimang, the South African government notoriously botched its response to the HIV/AIDS epidemic in the country, delaying the provision of lifesaving anti-retroviral drugs for reasons that are still unclear. Recent years have seen a corrective on that issue, albeit too late for many millions of South Africans.

Finally, South Africa's political party system has the prospects to grow slowly more competitive as some erstwhile leaders of the ANC grow frustrated with the party's politics. A splinter group of the ANC called the COPE (Congress of the People) ran against the ANC and presented for the first time a potential challenge to the party's hegemony among the black majority. The ANC easily outlasted the COPE—and COPE in fact came in behind the long-standing opposition of the Democratic Alliance led by the dynamic Helen Zille—but the split may indicate more fractious politics and the prospect for more competitiveness in future elections.

Can Power be Shared in Africa?

Another change at the top came in two countries that experimented in 2008 and 2009 with power-sharing. Unfortunately, power-sharing has a poor track record on a continent where political rule has historically been associated with the ability of a leader to provide preferential treatment for "his" people, usually conceived of as an ethnicity, or a conspicuous subset of the whole population. The experiences in Kenya and Zimbabwe seem to confirm the dilemma. The crisis in Kenya included post-election ethnic violence that killed several hundred people in 2008, but mercifully abated when the two leading contenders, President Mwai Kibaki and Prime Minister Raila Odinga, agreed to a government of national unity. While this has held in tenuous fashion, Odinga pulled his Orange Democratic Movement out of cabinet meetings in 2009, claiming that Kibaki was violating the terms of the arrangement.

Zimbabwe, by contrast, remains in disastrous shape. Robert Mugabe has adopted an increasingly paranoiac style as challenges to his rule have grown stronger. Politically, Mugabe orchestrated violence and launched conspiracy-laden tirades against "international imperialists." Zimbabwe endured several years of food shortages, social strife, mass hysteria and violent crime, but the climax was the hyperinflation (peaking a several quintillion or sextillion percent per year) that rendered the currency worthless. Mugabe faced a tough election battle in 2008 as former trade union leader Morgan Tsvangirai presented a unifying alternative to Mugabe's record of economic and social devastation.

The presidential election was riddled with irregularities and Mugabe claimed victory in the end, backed implicitly by the force of the military. On August 16, 2008, Tsvangirai agreed to the post of prime minister in a power-sharing arrangement, and conceded the presidency to Mugabe. In the past year, Tsvangirai has gamely attempted to wield and build an independent power base from his prime ministerial post. He has traveled to international summits and made his case for foreign aid, while subtly making his own case by appearing to be the responsible adult at the wheel in the country. Tsvangirai was set back in 2009, sadly, by another irresponsible person at the wheel in Zimbabwe: a truck driver who plowed into his car on a highway, killing his wife and injuring the prime minister himself. While Tsvangirai initially claimed he believed there was no foul play, many in the MDC remain skeptical, given the numerous previous attempts on his life by Mugabe supporters.

The pattern of governance in Zimbabwe may be less bad than it was a year ago, but it is difficult to call this "improvement." A truly positive turn may need to await the passing from the scene of the 85 year-old president. Mugabe's unwillingness to leave power is a common story in Africa, given the lengthy tenure of the many African leaders who seem to leave power "horizontally" after dying in office.

Nothing is Certain Except Death

It is said that nothing is certain except death and taxes, but given the parlous state of tax collections in Africa, it seems

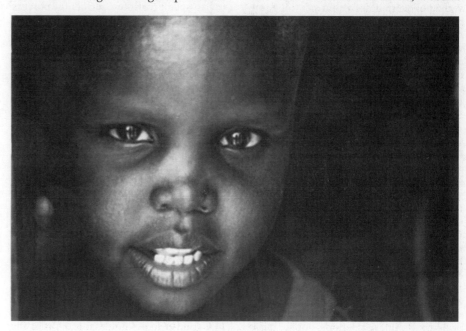

Sudanese boy

Africa in 2009

the saying must be truncated for this continent. To many less-fortunate Africans, even the prospect of death for many of Africa's longest-standing rulers must have seemed uncertain, some of whom rule nearly as long as the life expectancy of certain African countries. The last year, however, has witnessed the passing from the scene of many heads of state, and the resulting changes in the different countries reveal much about the variety of directions African countries are taking.

Omar Bongo's death was one of the most notable among African rulers this year. Bongo ruled Gabon for over 40 years, from 1967 to his death in 2009, by repressing opposition and manipulating electoral politics as necessary. Yet his consummate political skill was using the country's considerable oil wealth to coopt any possible opposition and to ensure his continued dominance of the political scene. Oil production in Gabon under his rule allowed him to preside over increases in wealth that made Gabon one of Africa's wealthiest countries, and also greased the wheels of authoritarianism. Bongo left behind a country with a functioning economic base, but with political and legal institutions that have suffered for years from official neglect. Gabon is not a top candidate for political development, though the passing of the dictator does create an opening.

In two countries that neighbor one another in West Africa, the deaths of presidents forebode greater upheaval. The death of Lansana Conté in Guinea-Conakry and the assassination of Nino Vieira in Guinea-Bissau leave behind countries that seem to be moving in the direction of military-dominated state failures. The case of Conté is the now common African story of a military man who declared a national emergency, seized power in a coup, and then retained power for decades, ruling with an iron fist and indulging in corruption as a means of political control. Like Bongo in Gabon, his death leaves a power vacuum because nearly all political activity was channeled through the president's networks of patronage. The situation in Guinea is worsened, however, by the dysfunctional and devastated economy over which Conté presided. As for Vieira, his assassination at the hands of military personnel clearly came as a form of retaliation for the prior assassination of the military chief of staff. Army soldiers believed Vieira was to blame for the killing and executed him in his home, whereupon the army seized power. The military professes that it will hold elections and return power to civilians, but will also presumably hold a virtual veto over the civilian authorities. The uncertainty in the country is rooted in tenuous civil-military relations, but is exacerbated by a weak state (which makes the

President Robert Mugabe

Prime Minister Morgan Tsvangirai

capital of Bissau a major transshipment point for drugs, as mentioned above).

As contrasted with Bongo or Conté, rather more tears were shed for Zambian president Levy Mwanawasa, who featured among a new generation of African leaders that moved modestly in the direction of better governance. Mwanawasa was a civilian who was narrowly elected president in 2001 with all the advantages of the dominant party, the Movement for Multiparty Democracy (MMD). Despite the irregular poll, Mwanawasa grew relatively popular, despite apologizing for his inability to reduce poverty in Zambia. He was reelected in 2006 and became a leading critic of Zimbabwe, for which he earned international praise an African leader willing to speak truth to continental powers. Even Zambia's opposition leader praised Mwanawasa upon learning of his death. These deaths matter for the stature of the people who have left the scene, but the aftermath in each case has also been illustrative. Whereas Gabon faces an uncertain future and the Guineas seem destined for more instability, Zambia exhibits some of the tendencies of a country tentatively following a better trajectory towards a democratic future.

Development and Change in 2009

The 2008 edition of *The World Today Series* noted that economic growth in Africa was estimated at over 6% per year, facilitating poverty reduction and improvements in social indicators. Commodity prices influenced Africa's boom for several years, as did reconstruction in post-conflict countries like Sierra Leone and Liberia and improved governance and policymaking in countries from Tanzania to Cape Verde. As noted at the top of this essay, the economic crisis of 2008–2009 has

dramatically altered the picture. More Africans are sliding back into poverty and growth has stalled in many countries.

Poverty remains a reality in much of sub-Saharan Africa, of course, and will not be eliminated quickly. The strong performance in a recent handful of years should not be mistaken for long-run improvements, nor should it gloss over the dramatic decline most of Africa has witnessed since the independence era. Even the encouraging signs of recent years are subject to reversal, especially as HIV/AIDS continues to affect ever larger numbers of Africans despite efforts by many countries to combat the epidemic. The question is whether improvements in recent years can be sustained in such a way as to improve basic social indicators of health, education, and incomes. While the story is not wholly positive, it is more so than it has been in many years.

It is important to end neither on a positive note, nor with an overly pessimistic tone. Avoiding naïveté is crucial: we can recall how the excessive optimism of the 1960s independence era was misplaced, and soon gave way to the coups, economic ruin, and heightened poverty of the 1970s and 1980s. But so too does the Afro-pessimism of the 1970s and 1980s seem increasingly dated. Such pessimism is deserved for the countries, like Sudan, that lead the news headlines out of Africa. But the happier story is the quieter one; the countries that are truly advancing may not yet be a silent *majority*, but they are a silently growing number.

The last 25 years have seen more human beings come out of poverty than at any period in history. Of course, the economic growth of China and India—not Africa—drives these numbers. In their success, however, these countries have left relatively straightforward lessons that Africa is capable of adopting: the likelihood of economic success is increased by allowing private economies to run on the basis of market forces, combined with a healthy and enhanced role for governments in supporting human capital and protecting the vulnerable. Reforming the state and improving the capacity of governments is trickier than getting the government out of the way of the market, but is no less important. The task is arduous, but a variety of African countries are showing the way, albeit slowly.

Factors within Africa are the primary drivers of the continent's economic and political outcomes, but international factors also matter immensely. International trade benefits economies, but dependence on external markets also carries its risks, particularly for economies that are dependent upon international demand for a single export product. The promise of Africa's economy is in large part conditioned upon the policies of the advanced, industrialized countries of Europe and North America. With a comparative advantage in labor-intensive agricultural production, many countries in Africa would stand to benefit from free and open trade with the United States and other leading economies. Such trade would result in increased returns to agriculture, which would bring more robust employment opportunities to the rural areas where most poor Africans live. Burkina Faso, for instance, produces high-quality cotton and its farmers would gain substantially from greater trade with the United States. However, US government subsidies to American farmers undercut such opportunities. While African products may be allowed into the United States tariff-free, the gains for Africa from such trade are severely restricted by American domestic politics and policies.

Emblematic of the diversity of experiences within Africa is the following chart, which shows the diversity across Africa in levels of economic development, political and civil freedoms, and human development. The GDP/capita figures, taken from the World Bank, give an average income per person in dollars, including all economic activity in the national territory. (This will greatly "overstate" the wealth of the average person in a country like Gabon or Nigeria, where multinational oil companies extract a good portion of the economic value generated within the borders.) The second column provides the assessment from Freedom House, a rating that combines evaluations of both political rights and civil liberties. Finally, the Human Development Index from the United Nations ranges from a low of 0.00 to a high of 1.00 and reaches a level of over 0.950 for many countries in Europe

and North America, as well as Japan and Australia. The index calculates a single number to give an overall view of social indicators including health (such as life expectancy), education (such as literacy rates), and incomes. Africa is poorer, more authoritarian, and has lower levels of human development than other regions of the world, but the three rankings together also show the range of experiences across the continent. Recognizing the variations within Africa is the prerequisite to analyzing politics, economics, and society on the continent. This is the point of departure for the individual case studies that comprise the bulk of this book.

Quick Reference Table			
Country	GDP/capita	Freedom Ranking	HD
Algeria	4,922	Not Free	0.728
Angola	5,809	Not Free	0.439
Benin	856	Free	0.428
Botswana	8,929	Free	0.570
Burkina Faso	856	Partly Free	0.342
Burundi	114	Partly Free	0.384
Cameroon	1,290	Not Free	0.506
Cape Verde	3,665	Free	0.722
Central African Republic	479	Partly Free	0.353
Chad	936	Not Free	0.368
Comoros	855	Partly Free	0.556
Democratic Republic of Congo	206	Not Free	0.391
Republic of Congo	3,658	Not Free	0.520
Côte d'Ivoire	1,250	Not Free	0.421
Djibouti	1,240	Partly Free	0.494
Egypt	2,109	Not Free	0.702
Equatorial Guinea	16,262	Not Free	0.653
Eritrea	295	Not Free	0.454
Ethiopia	317	Partly Free	0.371
Gabon	10,941	Partly Free	0.633
Gambia	478	Partly Free	0.479
Ghana	786	Free	0.532
Guinea	433	Not Free	0.445
Guinea-Bissau	257	Partly Free	0.349
Kenya	891	Partly Free	0.491
Lesotho	674	Free	0.494
Liberia	235	Partly Free	N/A
Libya	17,468	Not Free	0.798
Madagascar	481	Partly Free	0.509
Malawi	299	Partly Free	0.400
Mali	657	Free	0.338
Mauritius	6,392	Free	0.800
Mauritania	1,196	Partly Free	0.486
Morocco	2,902	Partly Free	0.640
Mozambique	472	Partly Free	0.390
Namibia	3,805	Free	0.626
Niger	387	Partly Free	0.311
Nigeria	1,490	Partly Free	0.448
Rwanda	420	Not Free	0.450
Sao Tome and Principe	1,000	Free	0.607
Senegal	1,110	Free	0.460
The Seychelles	9,440	Partly Free	0.842
Sierra Leone	335	Partly Free	0.335
Somalia	N/A	Not Free	N/A
South Africa	6,170	Free	0.653
Sudan	1,631	Not Free	0.516
Swaziland	2,903	Not Free	0.500
Tanzania	519	Partly Free	0.430
Togo	454	Partly Free	0.495
Tunisia	4,032	Not Free	0.766
Uganda	469	Partly Free	0.502
Zambia	1,223	Partly Free	0.407
Zimbabwe	340	Not Free	0.491

Japan Internet suicide deaths soar

TOKYO – The number of Japanese killing themselves in groups after meeting through the Internet – strangers afraid to die alone – soared to a record 91 last year, nearly double that of 2004, police said yesterday. No religious prohibitions exist against taking one's own life in Japan, where suicide was once a form of ritual atonement for samurai warriors and in modern times is a way to escape failure or save loved ones from embarrassment or financial loss. Suicides surged by 35 per cent in 1998 as Japan's economy was mired in stagnation and have exceeded 30,000 every year since then. Group suicides make up only a small fraction of the total, but the steady annual increase, along with the widespread media coverage most get, has experts increasingly worried.

The Egyptian Gazette

ذی اجبشیان جازیت

Mohamed Abul Hadeed
Board Chairman

Ramadan A. Kader
Editor-in-Chief

gazette@eltahrir.net.eg
Established 1880

J'salem museum stirs anger

TEL AVIV – A senior Muslim cleric said yesterday he asked Israel's Supreme Court to stop construction of a museum dedicated to human rights and tolerance in Jerusalem, after bones from an old Muslim cemetery were found during foundation work. "We adhere to our legitimate right to protect the Ma'man Allah graveyard and all other Muslim cemeteries. This is the oldest Muslim graveyard in Palestine," said Irkima Sabri, the Grand Mufti of Jerusalem and the Palestinian Territories. A petition to halt construction of the museum had been presented to the Supreme Court, he said. A spokesman for the Simon Wiesenthal Centre, an international Jewish human rights group behind the Museum of Tolerance, said the court would hear the appeal next week.

127th Year • Issue No • 40,903 8 Pages Friday • February 10 • 2006 LE1 http://www.eltahrir.net

PRESIDENT Hosni Mubarak and FBI chief Robert S. Mueller during their talks in Cairo yesterday.

Egypt and US discuss security cooperation

PRESIDENT Hosni Mubarak and FBI chief Robert S. Mueller held talks in Cairo yesterday on security cooperation between Egypt and the US and the fight against terrorism, the Middle East News Agency (MENA)said.

Following the talks, Mueller told MENA that he expressed condolences to the Egyptian leader over the ferry disaster in which more than 800 people perished.

"It is regrettable that Egypt is suffering from this disaster," Mueller said.

He said that he had discussed with President Mubarak means to enhance security cooperation between Egypt and the US now that the whole world is combatting terrorism, cyber crime and drug trafficking.

Egypt and the US are exchanging information and expertise on handling cases of terrorism, Internet crime and drug trafficking, the American official told MENA.

It is essential that all countries boost cooperation in fighting these crimes, said Mueller, who held similar talks in Morocco and Algeria.

Earlier in the day, President Mubarak received the speaker of the interim Arab parliament, Mohamed Jassim al-Saqr, MENA said.

Al-Saqr, a Kuwaiti national, is attending a preliminary meeting to approve the bylaws of the Arab world's first regional parliament, which held its inaugural meeting in Cairo in December last year.

The new parliament is based in Syria and will meet twice a year.

The concept of the Arab parliament was part of a package of institutional changes promoted by Arab League (AL) chief Amr Moussa to make the AL a stronger and more effective institution.

The new interim parliament has five years to draft the arrangements for a permanent Arab parliament.

Contacts to free Egyptian diplomat in Gaza

THE Egyptian government is trying to secure the rapid release of a diplomat, who was kidnapped yesterday in Gaza Strip, the Foreign Ministry said in a statement in Cairo.

"The Egyptian authorities are following closely, and in coordination with the Palestinian side, the kidnapping of Egyptian diplomat Hossam Musseli, in order to determine its circumstances and secure his release quickly," the statement, carried by the Middle East News Agency (MENA), said.

Musseli is an adviser at the Egyptian embassy in Gaza, MENA said.

Three masked gunmen in a car opened on Musseli's vehicle and forced him to get into their car, eye witnesses told MENA correspondent in Gaza.

The motive for the abduction of Musseli was not clear and no one immediately claimed responsibility.

In a statement, President Mahmoud Abbas said the kidnappers had broken ranks with the Palestinian people and that he would not allow anyone to harm good relations with Egypt, which twice helped broker a truce between activists and Israel. Gaza borders Egypt.

PALESTINIAN police officers checking the car of Egyptian diplomat Hossam Musseli after he was kidnapped by gunmen in Gaza City.

Witnesses told Reuters that gunmen shot out a tyre of the car in which Musseli was travelling and put another bullet in its fender, forcing it to stop. They then dragged him to their vehicle and sped away.

Gaza has seen a rash of kidnappings since Israel's pullout in September, but foreigners seized by activists with grudges against the Palestinian Authority have been released quickly.

"We strongly reject this act," Palestinian Prime Minister Ahmed Qurie said. "What is left when an Egyptian brother, who is here to help us, is kidnapped? Strict orders have been issued to the security services to search for him."

All Palestinian factions say they have good relations with Egypt.

Hamas leaders from the Palestinian territories and those in exile held talks in Cairo on Wednesday on establishing a new government following the Islamic resistance group's crushing victory over the long-dominant Fatah in a Jan 25 election.

It was not known whether Musseli's kidnap was linked to those talks. A power struggle among factions, gangs and security forces has intensified in Gaza and in the occupied West Bank since the Israeli withdrawal.

In Gaza City, about 100 gunmen from the Popular Army of Fatah blocked a government compound to demand payment of salaries due for work guarding greenhouses in evacuated Jewish settlements.

Dozens of armed activists from the Fatah-affiliated al-Aqsa Martyrs Brigades, gunmen who also serve in Palestinian security forces, mounted a similar protest at the Interior Ministry in the West Bank city of Hebron.

Qurie told a meeting of the Palestinian cabinet in the West Bank city of Ramallah that wages were paid yesterday to Palestinian Authority employees.

Israel agreed on Sunday to hand over to the Palestinians tax revenues it froze after Hamas' election win, but said it would no longer make automatic monthly transfers — a threat to cut off the money if the activist group dedicated to its destruction comes to power.

At the Erez border crossing between Gaza and Israel, Israeli soldiers killed two Palestinian gunmen who threw hand grenades and opened fire at troops, an army spokeswoman said in Tel Aviv.

In a separate incident near Erez, Israeli soldiers fired at two Palestinians who appeared to have been planting a bomb, the spokeswoman said. Palestinian medics said a Palestinian farmer was killed.

Hamas seeks Arab and Muslim aid

DOHA – Hamas will ask Arab and Muslim states for political and financial support to counter threats from the West to halt Palestinian aid, a top official said yesterday.

Khaled Meshaal, politburo chief of the Palestinian resistance group, told state-run Qatar News Agency (QNA) that Hamas would also travel to several other countries to drum up support, adding that the Palestinians "were not begging from anyone".

On Wednesday, US Secretary of State Condolezza Rice said that international aid could not flow to Hamas unless it recognises Israel's right to exist. Israel's foreign minister also urged the world to isolate a Hamas-led government.

"We are confident that Arab and Muslim countries will stand by Hamas and support the Palestinian people to respond to calls for punishing them," Meshaal told QNA, during a visit to staunch US ally Qatar.

"We know that Qatar will be at the forefront of these (Arab and Muslim) countries and all other countries we will visit," he added, without giving any details about the tour.

Hamas, which won a landslide victory against the mainstream Fatah movement in last month's parliamentary polls, is expected to form a new Palestinian government soon.

The United States and the European Union have called on Hamas to renounce violence and disarm activists.

Tomorrow in the **Egyptian Mail**

- Emergence of independent journalism (report)
- Fun & Tears – the most bizarre happenings of the week.
- Eight days a week: a guide to the entertainment events of the week ahead
- ME crystal ball (interview with Abdul Raouf el-Reedi, Egypt's ex-ambassador to the US)

Inside

Egypt shares end down

EGYPTIAN shares fell for a second successive day yesterday, with EFG-Hermes and MobiNil among the most heavily sold stocks.

One trader said MobiNil results announced after trade on Wednesday were below expectations.

Shares in MobiNil, which said its 2005 net profit had climbed 65 per cent, dipped 13.81 Egyptian pounds ($2.41) to 187 pounds.

The benchmark Hermes index ended down 1,660.78 points, or 2.5 per cent, at 64,381.26 points. The broader CIBC index fell 6.42 points, or 2.4 per cent, to 265.44 points. Both indices are near record levels.

"Major profit-taking has been going on for the last few days. At the end of the last 15 or 20 minutes there was buying," Hashem Ghoneim of El Nour Securities told Reuters.

Mass grave for 44 unidentified ferry victims

FORTY four unidentified victims of the Al Salam Boccaccio 98 ferry were buried yesterday in a mass grave in the Red Sea resort town of Hurghada, 450 kilometres southeast from Cairo. About 400 of the 1,400 passengers were confirmed to have been rescued after the ferry went down last Friday about 80km (50 miles) off the Egyptian coast during an overnight journey from Diba in Saudi Arabia to Safaga.

Danish envoy regrets cartoon offence

DENMARK'S ambassador to Egypt yesterday expressed regret over the publication of cartoons deemed offensive to Muslims.

The ambassador apologised for the offense caused by caricatures of the Prophet Mohamed in the September 30 edition of *Jyllands-Posten*.

He denied the existence of what might be described as anti-Islamic feeling in his country.

The Danes are a peaceful and tolerant nation, the envoy said following a meeting with Minister of Waqfs (Religious Endowments) Mahmoud Hamdi Zaqzouq.

Muslims account for 4 per cent of the Danish population, the ambassador said, adding: "In Denmark there are 19 Muslim societies that are free in their activities."

The Danish ambassador presented documents to Zaqzouq expressing the Danes' regret over the fury caused by the publication of the caricatures.

The documents included the apology by the newspaper and the Danish Prime Minister's statement as well as the transcript of his interview with Al-Arabiya satellite television channel.

The Danish diplomat also delivered a letter of apology from Denmark's bishop to the Grand Imam of Al-Azhar Sheikh Mohamed Sayed Tantawi.

The Middle East News Agency (MENA) reported last night that the latest Arabic issues of the German magazines *Der Spiegel* and *Fox* were barred from markets because they had reprinted the offensive cartoons.

33 Shi'ites killed in Pakistan

KOHAT – A suspected suicide bombing and gunfire killed at least 29 Shi'ite Muslims in northwestern Pakistan yesterday and gunmen killed at least four more people in an attack on a bus, officials said.

The bombing targeted a procession in the town of Hangu in North West Frontier Province (NWFP) to mark Ashura, the holiest day for Shi'ites. Officials reported several blasts.

Abdul Rashid, medical superintendent at the Hangu hospital, said 29 people had been confirmed dead there.

Bush: Qaeda planned attack on LA

WASHINGTON – The United States and its allies thwarted an Al Qaeda plot after the Sept 11 attacks to use bombs hidden in shoes to breach the cockpit door of an airplane and fly it into the the tallest building in Los Angeles, President George W. Bush said yesterday.

"The plot was derailed in early 2002 when a southeast Asian nation arrested a key Al Qaeda operative," Bush was quoted by Reuters as saying.

WEATHER

TODAY'S EXPECTED TEMPERATURES (IN CENTIGRADE)

	MAX	MIN
Cairo	19	09
Alexandria	17	08
Luxor	22	09
Aswan	23	10
Quena	22	09
New Valley	20	05
Tanta	17	08
Assuit	20	07
Hurghada	18	10
Sharm el-Sheikh	20	12
Rafah	17	08
Matrouh	18	07
Ismailia	19	08
Menya	20	06
Arish	17	09

(See world weather on Page 8)

SUPER Eagles win the bronze: Nigeria's Garba Lawal (L) and Taye Taiwo (R) go for the ball against Senegal's Souleymane Camara during their African Cup of Nations third place match. Nigeria won 1-0.

Egypt eyes 5th ACN title

Ahmed Atef
Gazette staff

EGYPT will attempt to win a record fifth ACN title when their team of home-based players faces Côte d'Ivoire's impressive array of European exports in today's final.

President Mubarak, who visited the team before their semi-final match against Senegal, has promised to attend the final match if they won.

Meanwhile, huge crowds gathered on Wednesday and yesterday to buy tickets for the final match of the African Cup of Nations (ACN)

Egypt will be meeting Côte d'Ivoire at Cairo International Stadium on 6pm today.

Officials of the Local Organising Committee (LOC) asked for the assistance of security personnel to control the thousands of fans who gathered outside the ticket windows at Cairo International Exhibition Centre in Nasr City.

Fans have harshly criticised the LOC because they were unable to find the assigned ticket sale points and because they were surprised to find tickets in the hands of touts.

LOC officials denied the accusations, saying that tickets have been available in post offices nationwide since last August 2005.

Nobody seemed interested in buying them at that time because fans did not think the National Team would reach the ACN final.

Ticket prices sky-rocketed during the quarter-finals and semi-finals.

Third class tickets, which should cost LE15, have been selling for LE60 on the black market.

Mubarak and president of the Confederation Africaine de Football (CAF), Issa Hayatou will hand the Cup and the gold medals for the first place team and the silver medals to the second placed.

Prime Minister Ahmed Nazif and the country's high ranking officials will attend the match and the final ceremony of the most successful ACN to date.

The Egyptian team, who on paper possesses only an average team, have been swept to the final on a wave of patriotic fervour after overcoming initial skepticism among their own public.

Côte d'Ivoire, meanwhile,

have got steadily better throughout the tournament, eliminating any doubt about their World Cup credentials as they prepare for their first finals appearance in Germany next June.

Egypt have won the title four times on 1957, 1959, 1986 and 1998 and hope to win it for the fifth while Cote d'Ivoire won it once on 1992.

(Editorial on P.3)

HISTORICAL BACKGROUND

A Fanti Chief, Coastal Ghana

Photo by Isabelle Forter

PREHISTORIC AFRICA

As advances in archeology, population genetics and linguistics continue to flesh out our understanding of human evolution, it is clear that the ancestral home of humankind is Africa. Recent DNA research suggests the Vasikela Kung of the northwestern Kalahari Desert of southern Africa are a population that lies close to the root of modern humans' origins. Similarly, the Turkana people of Kenya show the greatest genetic diversity of any known human group, and high diversity is usually indicative of a species' place of origin. Regardless of the specific place of origin, it is clear that *Homo sapiens*, modern humans, evolved in sub-Saharan Africa and, in a later split, migrated out of Africa some 50,000 years ago to populate the rest of the world. And this wasn't the first migration of hominids out of Africa, as recent findings date such occurrences back well over one million years ago.

Archeologists, like population geneticists, continue to add to our store of knowledge of human development. In the Republic of Georgia, scientists have discovered a 1.7 million-year-old hominid skull that shows clear linkages with African fossils. Tools found with the Georgian skulls resembled tools found in the Olduvai Gorge of Tanzania and dated at about 1.8 million years. Discoveries of the migration routes of early hominids now allow scientists to trace the incredible journeys out of Africa.

Early African peoples also adopted signature human customs earlier than once thought. A cave site in Zambia has revealed pigment and paint-grinding equipment that dates back 400,000 years, suggesting the ancestors of *Homo sapiens* were decorating themselves much earlier than ever thought. A recently discovered site along the Red Sea coast of Eritrea appears to be 125,000 years old and documents the utilization of marine re-

sources—clams, crabs and oysters. These are some of the tantalizing discoveries that will form the basis of a fuller understanding of human development in Africa, just as archeological remains testify to the richness of African civilization. Such richness could be seen in its full splendor long before the arrival of European explorers on the continent, as the rest of this brief historical survey will demonstrate.

EARLY CIVILIZATIONS OF THE NILE VALLEY AND MEDITERRANEAN SEA

The Nile Valley was settled and agricultural skills developed by 5000 B.C. This population was able to form one of the first centrally organized societies of the western world by about 3000 B.C., the beginning of the Egyptians. Under the control of the succession of kings (Pharaohs), the social organization of the people permitted rapid evolution and development

1

Historical Background

of writing, architecture, religion and the beginning of scientific thought.

The Egyptians' early religious efforts were varied; they conceived of a god represented by a variety of animal forms. Under the rule of the dynasties, these individual symbols were gradually discarded in favor of the obelisk (a tall, usually pointed four-sided structure with ornate carvings and frescoes which was used as a symbol of *Re*. It is probable that *Re* was associated with local gods which the people were accustomed to worship, but this concept of God led to the development of the first-known beliefs in life after death. The development of writing, first in hieroglyphics (illustrations portraying a variety of thoughts and concepts) and later in abstract symbols (an early "alphabet") in turn enabled the development of a highly stylized literature. A calendar of 365 days was adopted. The religious concept of life after death led in turn to invention of embalming methods to preserve the human body after death. This further resulted in the combination of early geometry with architecture, which permitted the construction of obelisks and elaborate and immense pyramids, the burial tombs of the pharaohs.

The Egyptians under the pharaohs reached their period of greatest power in the 2nd millennium before the Christian era, and gradually declined in strength and organization until they were invaded by a succession of other Mediterranean powers—the Assyrians in the 7th century B.C., the Persians and finally the Greeks under Alexander in the 4th century B.C.

CARTHAGINIAN EMPIRE
c. 300 B.C.

Phoenician traders on the northern coastline of the African continent combined over many centuries with the small number of other people of Middle East origin, emerging into the unified society of Carthage in the 9th century B.C. in what is now Tunisia and part of Algeria. The Carthaginians fought with the inhabitants of Sicily and Sardinia for about four hundred years, eventually winning control of the two islands after many changes in the fortunes of war in the 2nd century B.C. Carthaginian control was brief—the powerful Roman Empire was able to completely conquer Carthage by 122 B.C.

As early as 1000 B.C. the Phoenicians established themselves along the coastline of present-day Libya, founding what later became the city of Cyrene. Three coastal cities to the west were given the name *Tripolitania,* or *three cities,* by the Romans—Sabratha, Leptis Magna and Oea. The first two are now ruins. Oea became Tripoli. Ruins of imperial structures throughout Libya are intermixed with those of earlier temples and buildings dating back to 1000 B.C. In Tripoli, Marcus Aurelius constructed a great arch as a monument to Roman power. After the fall of the Roman Empire, Libya was successively invaded and ruled by Vandals, Byzantines and Greeks. A massive Arab invasion from the east subdued the people in the 8th century, bringing Islam to the native Berber people.

So too in Morocco, many centuries before the birth of Christ, the Phoenicians established trading posts and settled numerous people in the land. From the 1st century B.C. until the 5th century A.D. Morocco was a Roman province, providing foodstuffs for the people of the empire. After the fall of the Roman Empire, there was a quick succession of Vandals, Visigoths, and Byzantine Greeks who conquered Morocco. In the 9th century Arab forces arrived, bringing Islam to the people whom they subdued. The Berbers of inland Morocco were readily converted to this religion. The first rulers of the country claimed to be direct descendants of the Prophet Mohammed. The next centuries were a period of strife between the Muslim-Berbers and the Arab invaders.

After achieving some degree of unity in the 12th century, Morocco began to expand. Its borders ultimately reached from the Atlantic to Egypt and as far as Timbuktu to the south. After consolidating this immense territory, the Moors (the name given to mixed Arab-Berber peoples) conquered almost all of Spain, which became a Moroccan province, and advanced into present-day France. The slow decline of this vast empire culminated in the first part of the 16th century.

South along the upper Nile, the ancient history of Sudan, one of the oldest civilizations in the world, revolves around the pharaohs of Egypt and the Nubian peo-

Roman Imperial Ruins, Sabratha, Libya

Photo by Pat Crowell

2

ple. Gigantic formations of stone in the Nile area to the north furnished the material from which many of the picturesque temples and burial grounds of ancient Egypt were carved and built. In the 8th century B.C. Kushite kings from Nubia, now northern Sudan, conquered Egypt and created the 25th Dynasty. At the beginning of the Christian era, Sudan split into a collection of small, independent states. There were some conversions of people to Christianity in the 6th century, but much of the country remained pagan until there was widespread adoption of Islam, primarily in the north, at the end of the 13th century.

THE KINGDOM OF ETHIOPIA

By tradition, the Ethiopian kingdom dated back to a visit by the Queen of Sheba (a city in Yemen also known as Saba or Sabah) at the court of Solomon. Menelik I, son of Solomon and the Queen, founded the Ethiopian monarchy. There are other indications that the Ethiopians had progressed at a relatively early date in African history. Herodotus, a Greek writer of the 5th century B.C. described Ethiopia; Homer refers to the Ethiopians as a "blameless race" in his writing of about 800 B.C., but for the ancient Greeks, "Ethiopian" referred generally to "the most remote of men," most likely Nubians whose descendents live in modern Sudan, not present-day Ethiopia. There are forty-five references to Ethiopia in the Bible, but again, they point to the lands south of Egypt, Nubia, rather than the area of modern Ethiopia.

Little else is known of the history of Ethiopia at the beginning of the Christian era. The Coptic Christian Church established outposts in Ethiopia and Eritrea in the 4th century, and Islam arrived most probably as a result of continued contact with Arabs by the first part of the 8th century. The capital was moved from the ancient city of Axum to Addis Ababa and the distinctive Amharic language of the Ethiopians slowly evolved. The Christian Church in Ethiopia was established as a branch of the Coptic Christian Church headed by the Patriarch of Alexandria in Egypt. Contact with other Christians was later severed by the Islamic-Arab conquest of North Africa in the mid-10th century.

Although tradition holds that the ancestors of the Somali people, of Cushitic origins, lived in present-day Somalia more than 2,000 years ago, the earliest traces of people date to the 7th century A.D. The Koreishite Kingdom was established at that time by a group of people from nearby Yemen.

THE SPREAD OF ISLAM

The teachings of Mohammed, a religious prophet of the neighboring Arabian

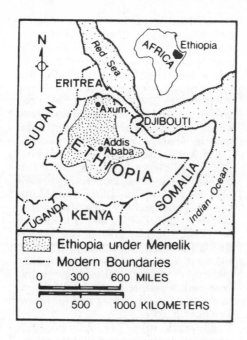

Ethiopia under Menelik
Modern Boundaries

| 0 | 300 | 600 MILES |
| 0 | 500 | 1000 KILOMETERS |

peninsula, were the basis for the religion known to billions today as Islam. The writings of Mohammed, together with his teachings, are gathered together in the Koran. He envisioned his prophecy to be supplemental, adding to and completing previous revelations, including those of Judaism and Christianity, of a single God. Preaching a belief in *Allah*, a single, all-powerful God, Mohammed was supposed to be the last prophet of God. He preached the Last Judgment, a duty to donate to the poor, and an obligation to engage in a daily system of prayer. A line of Islamic rulers established themselves in Damascus in Syria, and from that base other Muslim leaders conquered most of North Africa within a century, even going further to seize most of Spain.

Islam spread southward from the 8th century AD, converting most of the semi-arid regions south of the sands of the Sahara. Because of this contact with Islamic Arabs whose faith was based on a written text and who employed writing in their commercial transactions, we have much more extensive materials on which to build a history of this area. Al Umari, Ibn Khaldun and especially Ibn Battuta who visited the Mansa of Mali in the 14th century, have all left important materials to supplement local oral traditions.

Islam reached the western end of the Sahara as well as the eastern end. The first inhabitants of Mauritania were West African peoples, dating back to the Neolithic period. In historical times, both sub-Saharan peoples and Berbers have inhabited the area. It was the Berbers who founded the austere Almoravid movement and spread its version of Islam throughout the area in the 11th century A.D. An influx of Arabs, following commercial caravan routes, produced the mixed Arab-Berber culture known as Moorish. Federations of Moorish nomadic tribesmen came to dominate sedentary African farmers, many of whom adopted the Islamic faith of their conquerors.

ARABS AND TRADERS IN EAST AFRICA

From the 8th to the 10th centuries A.D. the Arabs penetrated the shoreline of East Africa in increasing numbers, establishing trading posts at Mogadishu (Somali Republic) and Mombasa (Kenya) and in what is now Mozambique. Ivory and African slaves were the basis of a brisk trade, as well as gold, shipped primarily to India. This continued in one form or another until control of the area was seized by European colonial powers in the last part of the 19th century. Persian, Arabic, Indian and Portuguese traders engaged in lively trade with various coastal peoples in and around present day Tanzania, including the island of Zanzibar, a region that had been settled long before by large numbers of Bantus and smaller groups of Nilotic people. Portuguese mariners landed in Kenya as early as 1498, seeking a sea route to the Far East. In the 19th century, Arab and Swahili caravans in search of ivory and slaves penetrated the interior. Colonial activity in the area was first initiated by Germans, followed by the British.

Islands in the Indian Ocean were also accessed first by maritime traders. Probably during the first millennium of the Christian era, people known as the Hovas settled in the highlands of the island of Madagascar and possibly reached the east coast of Africa. The Comoros were first settled by Arab seafarers about 1,000 years ago. The Arabs brought in slaves from

Historical Background

Africa and established a series of small sultanates on the different islands. It was not until 1527 that the Portuguese cartographer Diego Ribero depicted the Comoros islands on a European map. The Dutch arrived at Mauritius, uninhabited by man prior to the time, in 1598, naming it after a prince of Holland. They remained for a century and started sugar production at the time the last clumsy dodo birds walked upon the island. (Concluding that the island offered no profit, they withdrew, and the French arrived in 1715.) The small group of settlers on Mauritius was augmented by African slaves, who worked the sugar plantations that came to dominate the island. The first recorded landfall on the Seychelles islands was made by an expedition of the British East India company in 1609.

THE EMPIRES AND PEOPLES OF WEST AFRICA

A segment of people living in the area south of the Sahara gathered together in the first "empire" of West Africa in the 4th century A.D., eventually controlling a large area that is now part of Burkina Faso, southern Mali and eastern Senegal. The basis of this early group of people was a lively trade in gold and slaves with the nomadic people to the north. *Ghana*, as this empire is historically known, should not be confused with the modern state bearing that name. Its existence continued until it was conquered by the Islamic Berbers from the north in 1076, who converted the local people to their faith.

West Africa's history after Islam arrived in the sub-Sahara dry regions is one of conflict between various tribes and kingdoms, all located within the same general area. The Songhai Empire based in western Niger, which had controlled the region since the 7th century, adopted Islam, as did the Mandingo Empire which arose in Mali. Initially, most of West Africa from about 1000 to 1200 A.D. was divided between the Songhai and Mandingo rulers, with the exception of areas closer to the coast in what are now parts of Guinea, Côte d'Ivoire, Ghana and Burkina Faso.

Trade with the Arabs to the north and east was lively for several centuries, with caravans linking Timbuktu, Gao (Mali), Kano (Nigeria) and the Lake Chad region with the Middle East by way of the Sudan and Egypt. The more affluent Islamic people journeyed on traditional pilgrimages to Mecca from this area of West Africa. Other trading was conducted with the Arab-Berber people of the North where Morocco, Algeria, Tunisia and Libya are now located.

The Mande rulers gradually acquired more territory at the expense of the neighboring ethnic groups after 1200 A.D. A brief domination by the Sosso people of Guinea, led by Sumanguru Kanté, was ended when the kingdoms of the savannah were rallied to overthrow Sosso's oppression in the early 13th century. The leader of this liberation struggle, Sundiata Keita, became the first of the Mansas or Emperors of Mali. Timbuktu, located in a remote part of what is now Mali, became a center of culture and progress fabled throughout West Africa, and was visited by many Arab merchants and travelers. The Empire of Mali disintegrated in the 15th century when Timbuktu was invaded and sacked by desert Tuaregs. A genera-

tion later, in 1468, the Songhai rulers were able in turn to expel the Tuaregs. The Songhai reached their greatest power in the following six decades, at a time when the first Portuguese explorers began to penetrate the area.

Several initially non-Muslim kingdoms arose along the southern coast of West Africa at about the same time the Islamic empires of the upper Niger River were powerful. The Fulani, also known as Peulh, established several states from what is now Senegal to Nigeria, occupying an area between the Muslim empires and the coastal lands, and gradually were converted to Islam. Closer to the coastline, the Mossi created two distinct states within what is now southern Burkina Faso and Ghana, also adopting Islam.

The Ashanti became established in what is now central Ghana, as did the Soso in Guinea, the Yorubas in Dahomey and southwestern Nigeria and the Ibos in southeastern Nigeria. Togolese oral history indicate that in the 15th to 17th centuries Ewe clans from Nigeria and the Ane from Ghana and Ivory Coast settled in the region, which was already occupied by Kwa and Voltaic peoples. Coastal Sierra Leone was thinly populated by the Sherbro, Temne, and Limba peoples who had probably lived in the area for thousands of years by the time the Portuguese explorer, Pedro de Cintra, visited the coastal area in 1460. Impressed by the beauty of the mountains of the southeast, he named the territory Sierra Leone—"Lion Mountains." Already established by this time were Mande-speaking peoples who settled inland. Islam was introduced by Muslim traders and took root initially in the north, but later spread throughout the area.

Early migrations of peoples from the east were long-established in and around Senegal and Gambia rivers by the time of the first European explorations in the 15th century. Paleolithic and Neolithic artifacts have been found near Dakar (Senegal), and early copper and iron objects have been found elsewhere. Berbers from the north established a Muslim monastery in the Senegal River region in the 11th century, converted local populations to Islam, and began a military expansion that ultimately resulted in the conquest of both Ghana and Morocco and the invasion of Spain. The region was strongly influenced by Islamic revival movements from the later 17th century well into the 19th century.

Some of the most important archeological work in Africa has been done in Nigeria, producing evidence of human habitation that goes back thousands of years. The oldest evidence of a widespread organized society is associated with the Nok

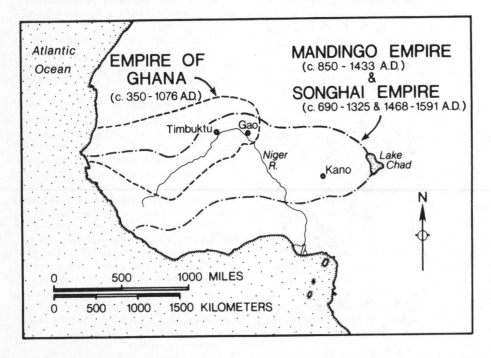

4

Royal Enclosure, 17th-Century, Gondar, Ethiopia Photo by Judi Iranyi

culture (c. 500 BC–200 AD). Yoruba peoples were established in the southern coastal region by the 11th century, and by the 14th and 15th centuries the Yoruba empire was a regional power. Hausa kingdoms were gradually formed after the 12th century in the north and began to undergo conversion to Islam by the 14th century. Fulani (Peulh) nomadic herdsmen became rulers in the Hausa regions of the North as a consequence of an Islamic reformist jihad in the late 19th century. In the densely forested southeast region Ibo peoples organized themselves in small-scale political units centuries before the arrival of the first Europeans.

Farther south, archeological evidence suggests that Cameroon has been occupied for at least 50,000 years. Originally populated by pygmies, who are now found only in small numbers along the southern border, Cameroon was successively invaded by other groups. There is evidence of early state-building societies, the most important of which is Sao, centered in the Lake Chad area. In 1472, a Portuguese explorer, Fernão do Pó (Fernando Po in Spanish) arrived on the coast of what is now Cameroon.

PEOPLES OF CENTRAL AND SOUTHERN AFRICA

Humans have inhabited the area of the present-day Central African Republic for

at least 8,000 years, as polished flint and quartz tools testify. Huge stone megaliths near Bouar date back 2,500 years and suggest a relatively large-scale society with specialized labor. A wide variety of Niger-Congo and Nilo-Saharan languages suggest widespread migrations into the area, dating back to the 10th century. Oral tradition also conveys the story of the mighty Kingdom of the Kongo, probably founded in the 14th century. It was not until 1482 that the first European, the Portuguese navigator Diogo Cão, explored the coastal areas of present-day Congo-Brazzaville. Little is known of the precolonial period of present day Equatorial Guinea; the Fang and other Bantu people settled thinly in Rio Muni and the Bubis settled on Bioko Island.

In Rwanda and Burundi, the original inhabitants were the Twa, a pygmy hunting and gathering people. The Twa were followed by the Hutu who established themselves as farmers. In the 14th century the pastoral Tutsi appeared and imposed their dominance over the mass of Hutu agriculturalists by military power. The Hutu were reduced to serfdom, each choosing a Tutsi lord protector who gave them the use (but not ownership) of cattle, the most important status symbol and source of wealth among the Tutsi. In the 15th century a Tutsi kingdom was founded near Kigali, which by the late

19th century had rounded out its borders to become a unified state whose Mwami (king) ruled through a centralized military bureaucracy. Local chiefs and military captains received tribute from Hutu communities.

Moving towards southern Africa, it becomes more difficult to trace with any precision the migrations of the Bantu people whose descendants live in countries such as Uganda, Malawi, and Zambia today. It is not possible to determine the exact time when the Nilotic groups came to northern Uganda. It seems that before the waves of Bantu migration arrived many centuries ago, the region around Malawi and Zambia was probably scantily settled. Restive Bantu peoples from the north expanded slowly southward from about the 10th century onward, sending successive waves of transients through this country on their journey to the south. Some stayed as permanent settlers, forming into distinct tribes based on common ancestry. As far south as Swaziland, it seems lands were thinly inhabited by a variety of Bantu groups who migrated to the area from what is now Mozambique about 1750.

Regardless of the timing of the migrations, it is clear the Bantu people emerged into rather powerful societies in what is now Uganda and the Congo River basin. The Kabaka, king of a Bantu state in Uganda, who was deposed in 1966, claimed to be the 37th monarch in an uninterrupted rule of a single family. Since there was a lack of the written word during the early centuries, our knowledge of the area's history is dependent on oral sources. In many societies specialists, like the *griots* of West Africa, memorized the history and traditions of their peoples and passed them on to their sons. Spoken and sung, very much like the epics of Homer, these histories provided inspiration and identity for families and communities. Today, they remain an important source for historians attempting to reconstruct an African past.

The Bantu and Sudanic groups expanded at a relatively rapid rate during the first millennium of the Christian era, perhaps as early as the 4th century A.D. There was an initial expansion of Bantu peoples into the eastern regions of Africa, into what is now Tanzania, Zambia and Zimbabwe. The imposing stone constructions at Great Zimbabwe, located in the southwestern part of the nation now bearing that name, suggest a wealthy and privileged elite in control of a powerful state. The site was the capital of a Bantu kingdom that stretched from eastern Zimbabwe over parts of Botswana, Mozambique, and South Africa. The first known permanent settlement was established around the 11th century and building con-

Historical Background

tinued into the early 15th century. The large quantities of stone used to build on the site suggest control over considerable labor. The state's prosperity was based on trade in gold with Swahili speakers on the eastern African coasts. The Zimbabwe ruins, the only pre-European remnant of architecture found below the Sahara in Africa, are attributed to people known as the Monoma and are dated sometime between the 9th and 13th centuries, A.D. The Shona settled at an unknown time in the region; the Zulu and Barotse passed

through during their migration to the south, and the Ndebele, a branch of the Zulu that split off from Chaka Zulu, migrated to the area in the 19th century.

Zimbabwe is the Anglicized version of the Shona word *Dzimbahwe,* meaning stone houses—later understood as graves, or dwellings, of chiefs. The significance must run far deeper. Built in a gentle valley, it is believed to be a sacred place where a person could communicate with his ancestors. Stone huts attached to portions of the ruins indicate that it later became a home for the living. Zimbabwe was abandoned in the early 19th century when fierce Zulu warriors destroyed the Shona confederation.

The Bantu expansion farther southward continued at a slower rate. As it pushed more deeply into the south, it encountered Khoisan speaking pastoralists. When European sailing ships, mainly Dutch and English, began to make regular voyages around the Cape in the 16th century, they too encountered Khoisan pastoralists, eager to sell their surplus animals in exchange for iron, copper, tobacco, and beads. The original inhabitants of Botswana were the San people (Bushmen). Bantu peoples of central and east Africa migrated into the area in the 16th century; during the following centuries, intermarriage and population growth of the Ban-

tus reduced the number of pure Bushmen to a handful. The Tswana remained split into hundreds of tribes and clans until they gathered together under Khama III, chief of the powerful Bamangwato tribe; this was a loose federation which emerged in the last half of the 19th century. Bushmen groups also settled in what is now Namibia, followed by several Bantu tribes. Ovambos and Damara-Hereros became the most numerous groups.

EUROPEAN DISCOVERY AND EXPLORATION

The first exploration of the African coastline started early in the 15th century when Portuguese navigators reached Senegal, Guinea and the islands lying adjacent to the West African coast. By 1492 Fernão do Pó reached the island off the coast of Cameroon, which ultimately came to bear his name, translated into Spanish—Fernando Po (now Bioko Island of Equatorial Guinea). Fifteen years later, Bartolomeu Dias, usually referred to in English as Bartholomew Diaz, was blown by a storm in a southerly direction to the bottom of the continent. Turning eastward, he became the first European to navigate around the Cape of Good Hope.

In 1497, shortly after Columbus' second voyage to America, Vasco da Gama sailed around the African cape in search of a way

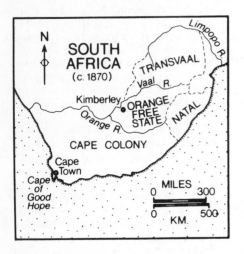

The Imperial Family of Ethiopia, 1930

6

to India, using the primitive navigation information supplied by Diaz. He stopped at Mozambique, Mombasa and Malinda on the east coast of Africa, and was able to obtain the information necessary to proceed onward to India from the Arabs who were already established along the African coast.

With the arrival of increasing numbers of Portuguese vessels, quarrels with the Arab traders intensified. Francisco de Almeida was sent with a squadron to control Arab interference with Portuguese shipping; he took Mombasa in 1505 and ultimately demolished the Arab fleet in 1509, establishing Portuguese supremacy in the eastern coastal area of the continent.

In spite of this rather rapid navigational discovery, there was to be almost no penetration inland by the Europeans for more than three hundred years. With the exception of a Dutch settlement at the Cape of Good Hope, the sub-Sahara inland African regions remained the same dark, forbidding land that was first seen by the Portuguese. Following the precedent of the Arabs of East Africa, the Europeans started a lively West African trade in human cargo—slaves to perform the tasks of labor needed to colonize other parts of the world.

It was an easy task, with little exception, to acquire slaves along the so-called Gold and Ivory Coasts of West Africa. Anchoring their slave ships in natural harbors, the Europeans negotiated with the chiefs of the more powerful ethnic groups that lived inland. When a suitable price (in terms of value, almost nothing) was agreed upon, the men and sometimes the women of a weaker neighboring tribe would be brought to the coast in bondage after a brief skirmish. They were delivered as promised to the slave traders. It was in this manner that black Africans, tempted by their desires for the wealth offered by the white slave traders, sold the bodies of other black Africans into slavery. Africans were split in their views on trade; along with obvious resistance to plunder, some viewed themselves as disposing of undesirable social elements that they believed represented a threat to them, their families and their tribe.

Packed shoulder to shoulder in quarters on the slave ships that were so cramped no one could stand, the cargo of humans, regarded as animals, was transported across the sea, usually to the Western Hemisphere. Those unable to survive were dumped overboard at suitable intervals following their death. The remaining survivors were sold at a handsome profit compared to the sum paid for them along the African coastline—a profit possible even if more than one-half of the ship's cargo died during the trip to the "new world." The fact that an individual slave had survived this journey was testimony to his hardiness and stamina as compared to his less fortunate brethren who had perished. Arriving at a particular destination in the Western Hemisphere where he was sold, the slave was to begin a new and incredibly difficult life in a totally strange surrounding where he would be judged by his physical ability to perform long, long hours of hard manual labor.

EARLY ETHIOPIAN-EUROPEAN CONTACT

In the late dark ages of Europe, a letter from a supposed Christian king of Africa received widespread acclaim as possibly being from an unknown people dating from Biblical times. Inspired by this, a Roman Catholic Pope dispatched several Dominican brothers in the 14th century to locate this Christian kingdom. The results of these efforts are not clear, but an Ethiopian emissary did reach Venice in 1402, arriving later at Lisbon and Rome. In turn, European kings and the Pope sent emissaries to Ethiopia, hoping to enlist help in the continuing "crusades" against the Islamic people of the Middle East and North Africa. This diplomatic effort continued unevenly for four centuries, and there was no other significant contact between this region of Africa and Europe during the passage of those years.

Increased penetration of Ethiopia by Europeans occurred in the 19th century. Although Ethiopia was not formally colonized by any European power, it became subject to a variety of "spheres of influence" of the British, French and Italians in the latter part of the century. The succession to the Ethiopian throne was irregular—every time a king died there was usually a two- or three-way contest for the throne. The somewhat weak character of the nation was further complicated by periodic skirmishes and quarrels over territory with the neighboring Sudanese who were led by religious-political figures with the title *Mahdi*. The Somalis to the east, who were Islamic, also claimed Ethiopian territory, sometimes with the assistance of the French or the Italians. The borders of the kingdom changed countless times during this period.

The modern history of the country begins with the reign of Emperor Menelik II, the first monarch to choose that name since the reign of the son of Solomon and Sheba. It was under the second Menelik that Ethiopia began to have regular contact with the outside world. Although he was at first forced to acknowledge an Italian protectorate over Ethiopia, by 1896 he had consolidated his power sufficiently to send a military force that decisively defeated the Italians. Lidj Yassu, the grandson of Menelik II succeeded to the throne in 1913, but was deposed in 1916. Zauditu, Menelik's daughter, was installed as empress. Her cousin, Ras Tafari Makonnen ascended the throne in 1930, taking the name *Haile Selassie,* which means "the power of the Trinity" in Amharic.

THE ARABS AND OTTOMAN TURKS IN NORTH AFRICA

The Arab-Berber rulers of North Africa who came to power with the spread of Islam were known first as the Almavorid and subsequently the Almohad dynasty. Initially these Muslim kingdoms were characterized by a centralized power, but in the 13th to the 16th centuries there was gradual division into countless numbers of local rulers. Just as Christianity had split into numberless sects, so also had Islam been divided. Although the internal unity of the Arabs diminished, they were usually able to unite against non-Arabs on the infrequent occasions when outsiders threatened their territory.

The Muslim rulers of the Turkish Ottoman Empire gained control of most of Egypt and Libya at the beginning of the 16th century; their power in this area was not absolute since both regions quickly became no more than tribute-paying vassal states of the empire. The Ottoman rulers were almost continuously occupied in wars with Europe and had insufficient resources to bring North Africa directly within the Empire as was done in Syria and Iraq. It was not long before most of North Africa was within the Ottoman sphere.

With the exception of Egypt, the remainder of North Africa continued under the loose control of the Ottoman Empire until World War I. Egypt remained under the Ottomans until the invasion by Napoleon in 1798. The Turks sent Mohammed Ali from an Ottoman military family (probably of Albanian origin) as commander of forces opposing the French; together with the British under Lord Nelson, they were finally able to expel the invaders in the summer of 1799.

Mohammed Ali quickly established his personal rule in Egypt as an Ottoman *Pasha.* Although he and his successors were able to avoid absolute domination by the Ottoman rulers, in reality Egypt continued to be a tributary vassal of the Empire for about 75 years until the British influence became paramount. Khedive Ismail, grandson of Mohammed Ali, ruled as king but under the authority of the sultan and caliphs of the empire; he had received a European education for several years. The Suez Canal was under construction principally in order to provide the British with a shorter route to their possessions in India and the Far East, al-

Historical Background

though the construction effort was in the name of a cooperative effort of most of the European nations and Egypt. In anticipation of the revenues expected from the canal which opened in 1869, Ismail borrowed large sums of money at extremely high interest rates from European banks. When he was unable to repay the loans on schedule, the British used this as a pretext to assert their authority in Egypt, initially with Egyptian cooperation, in order to bring areas bordering the Red Sea waterway and in the Sudan under control. By 1876 Khedive Ismail had been forced to sell all Egyptian shares in the Suez Canal, and Egypt was placed under the supervision of British and French financial controllers. That is considered the start of the colonial period in Egypt; although the Khedives continued to be the nominal power, they were little more than the instrumentality through which the British ruled.

EUROPEAN SETTLERS IN SOUTH AFRICA

Holland, seeking a food and fuel station for its ships sailing to the Dutch East Indies, established a small station on the Cape of Good Hope (near Africa's southernmost tip) in 1652. A fort was constructed to guard against the Hottentots and Bushmen found in small numbers in the area. This outpost developed rapidly,

with the outlying farms worked by slaves brought from the East.

There was a slow expansion of this Dutch community into the interior, though such was not actively pursued by the Dutch East India Company. A substantial number of Huguenot religious refugees from France arrived in 1688, adopting the Dutch social patterns. Further settlement of the interior by the Dutch *Burghers* continued for the next hundred years, since there was little opposition to their desire for additional farmland. It was not until the Dutch had penetrated 200 miles to the northeast that they first encountered the Bantu people who were then in a process of migration from the southeast lake region of Africa. Bitter frontier warfare between the two groups of migratory people continued for the next 75 years, with large numbers of casualties on both sides.

The British took possession of Cape Town in 1795 in the name of the Prince of Orange, who then reigned in Holland and in England when his nation was overrun by the French. The British handed the area over to the Batavian Republic, a puppet state of France, in 1803 (all of this was a product of shifting alliances in Europe involving Napoleon's activities). But in 1806 the British returned; the Cape Colony was officially ceded to it in 1814 and it became a Crown Colony. A substantial migration

of British settlers arrived in the succeeding 30 years, which by 1834 caused widespread unrest among the Dutch farmers of the Eastern Cape, who resented British rule.

Led by hardy souls like Andries Pretorius, for whom Pretoria is named, the Voortrekkers, or pioneers, journeyed in covered wagons to the northeast, overcoming severe hardships and fighting fierce Bantu peoples. In 1839 they founded a new republic called Natal, but were later pushed even farther into the interior by the arrival of British military forces. Crossing the Drakensburg (Dragon Mountains), they went into the Orange Free State and Transvaal. In each area, a Boer republic was proclaimed. Thus, toward the end of the 19th century, there were two Boer republics and two British colonies in what is now the Republic of South Africa. Discovery of a huge 84 carat diamond on the banks of the Orange River by an African shepherd boy in 1869 set off the South African diamond rush. Fortune hunters from all over the world flocked to South Africa. In 1886 the world's largest goldfields were discovered on the Witwatersrand, adding to the influx of non-Boers. With these discoveries South Africa was transformed. From an economic backwater it became a major supplier of precious minerals to the world economy.

Nigeria dances for Queen Elizabeth and Prince Philip, 1956

The Colonial Period

This chapter details Africa during the colonial period, from settlement to the waves of decolonization in the 1960s and thereafter. The organization is according to the European country that colonized and ruled in each territory, reflecting the shared colonial experiences of many countries.

THE PORTUGUESE

Coastal West Africa: Portuguese Guinea

Inching their way down the African coast under the inspiration of Prince Henry—known as "The Navigator"—Portuguese mariners reached the Senegal coast around 1444; they established trading posts at the mouth of the Senegal River, on the island of Gorée, and at Rufisque, all in the region of present-day Senegal that would later come under French control. The Portuguese explored the coastline of Guinea as early as 1446, and this area remained a slave trading coastal region for about the next 450 years. Portuguese control of the area occurred only because it was permitted by the other, more aggressive colonial powers; Portuguese Guinea was deemed somewhat poor territory—what was left after the French and British had colonized West Africa.

The final boundaries of Portugal's African dominions were delineated only in 1905, after both Britain and France had appropriated parts of Portuguese Guinea. Penetration by the Portuguese into the continent's interior was negligible until about 1912; in the years prior the Portuguese had only sporadic control of the region, which was still theoretically a part of European Portugal. It was declared independent on September 10, 1974, with the mainland territory coming to be known as Guinea-Bissau and the islands off the Atlantic coast of Senegal becoming Cape Verde (Cabo Verde).

Equatorial West Africa: Angola and Cabinda, São Tomé e Príncipe

Portuguese navigators discovered the uninhabited islands of São Tomé and Príncipe in the late 15th century. By the mid-16th century the colonial power had imported slaves and converted the islands into a major exporter of sugar. A slave-based plantation economy characterized the islands well into the 20th century, whereupon coffee and finally cocoa emerged with the decline of sugar exports. The rich volcanic soils of São Tomé proved especially well-suited to cocoa trees, and by 1908 the island had become the world's largest producer of cocoa. The crop was grown on extensive plantations called *roças*—owned by Portuguese companies or absentee landlords—that occupied all productive farmland. The *roças*

system inevitably led to abusive treatment of African farm workers, and the history of the islands is filled with slave revolts and resistance to labor demands. Local dissatisfaction with working conditions on the plantations led to an outbreak of riots in 1953. In what became known as the "Batepa Massacre," over 1,000 *Forros* (the descendants of freed slaves) were shot by Portuguese troops for refusing to work the *roças*. The massacre is seen as the beginning of the nationalist movement in those islands. Príncipe is a small and poor island barely supporting the handful of descendants of freed slaves. These islands became independent on July 5, 1975 as The Democratic Republic of São Tomé and Príncipe.

Angola was first explored in 1482 by Diego Cao, who found this region of Africa controlled by the Bacongo people, led by a mighty King of the Congo. A scattering of Portuguese immigrants arrived during the following decades, but they were restricted to the coastal areas by the native Africans as a result of a series of bloody clashes. The King was overthrown, but later reestablished by the Portuguese in 1570.

During the 17th and 18th centuries, Angola was the prime source for slaves deported to Brazil to work the huge coffee plantations in that Portuguese Latin American colony. The Portuguese also established an infamous penal colony there. During the late 19th and early 20th centuries, a multitude of treaties between Portugal and the British, French, Belgians and Germans gradually fixed the boundaries of Angola and Cabinda (an enclave separated from Angola by the Congo River delta). The colony was given a form of internal autonomy in 1914, but this was strictly under White minority rule. Economic development under the Portuguese consisted of agriculture in the form of coffee and cotton production and mineral extraction based on diamonds in northeast Angola.

Periodic uprisings in Portuguese Africa occurred in the 20th century. In its Africa policy, Portugal had almost exclusively favored the Portuguese immigrants and their descendants. After a protracted battle for independence that occasioned the fall of the dictator António de Oliveira Salazar in Lisbon, Angola too gained its independence in 1975. Having received Cuban assistance for a Soviet-backed rebel group, Angola became a Marxist state upon decolonization.

Southern Africa: Mozambique (Moçambique)

The Portuguese presence along the coast of Mozambique dates back to the voyage of Vasco da Gama in 1498. He found a number of trading posts that had

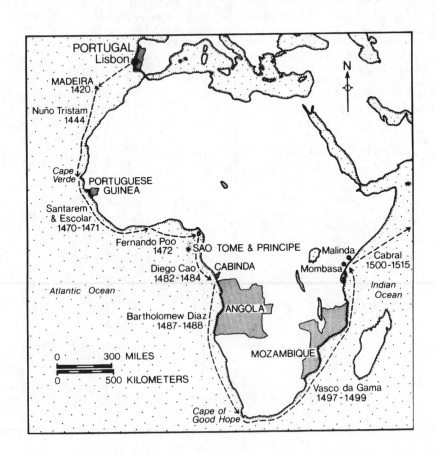

been established by the Arabs, who offered little resistance to Portuguese construction of settlements and forts during the next century. These stations were intended more as an aid to Portuguese efforts in India and the Far East and were little more than stopping places for commercial vessels bound to and coming from those areas.

Shortly after Africa was partitioned at the Berlin Conference of 1885, both the French and Germans recognized Portuguese supremacy in Mozambique; Britain, preoccupied with its own colonial ambitions, largely ignored the Portuguese. Five years later, after expanding into neighboring Nyasaland (now Malawi), the British reached an agreement recognizing Portuguese claims. At the same time, the Mozambique Company was chartered to manage and invest in the colony, backed by substantial amounts of British capital. A massive uprising of Africans at the close of the 19th century hampered economic development in the territory. An early attempt was made in 1907 to establish a legislative council with membership restricted to White settlers in the colony.

As a result of the German defeat in World War II, the Portuguese added a small piece of German East Africa to Mozambique. The colonial period was relatively eventless between the two world wars, apart from the establishment of railroad lines from the port of Beira to Nyasaland (Malawi), Southern Rhodesia (Zimbabwe), Northern Rhodesia (Zambia) and as far as the southeastern province of Katanga (Shaba) in the Belgian Congo, now DR Congo. Though Portugal resisted attempts on the part of the native African majority to obtain independence during the postwar period, the revolution in

Portugal itself brought independence (as with elsewhere in Portuguese Africa) in mid-1975.

THE BRITISH
Coastal West Africa: (The) Gambia

The claimant to the throne of Portugal granted English merchants, in exchange for an undisclosed sum of money, the exclusive right to trade with the people along the Gambia River. Queen Elizabeth I confirmed this sale by granting letters patent to English businessmen, and in 1618 James I granted a charter to the Royal Adventurers of England, giving the company trade franchises in Gambia and in the Gold Coast.

At the same time the British merchants were developing trade in the river area, French interests were expanding in Senegal, and the Gambia River was the best route to the interior of Senegal. Hence, an intense rivalry arose between the two nations in this area of colonial Africa. Their disputes were partially resolved by the Treaty of Versailles in 1783 which granted Gambia to the British, but reserved for the French a small enclave across the water from Bathurst. There had been little exploration or penetration up the river to the interior until after 1860 when British explorers went inland and negotiated treaties with the local chief to obtain additional territory. The city of Bathurst remained a separate entity for the next two decades, sometimes administered from Sierra Leone, otherwise governed as a separate colony.

The present boundaries of The Gambia were delineated by a British-French agreement in 1889. Although the exportation of slaves had been prohibited, it was not until 1906 that the local practice of slavery within Gambia was abolished by

British decree. From the turn of the century until after World War II, there were few significant historical events in Gambia. Periodic efforts of the French to acquire control of the area were unsuccessful. With the exception of Bathurst, no Europeans here.

During World War II, Gambia not only served as an important naval base for military convoys, but contributed soldiers who fought valiantly in the Burma campaign of General Stilwell against the Japanese. The postwar period saw the birth of nationalist sentiment in Gambia. The governor-general granted increasing powers of self government to the Africans of the country and established an advisory council.

In the late 1950s, Gambian leadership gathered into four political parties: the Progressive Peoples Party; the United Party; the Democratic Congress Alliance; and the Gambian Congress Party. The leaders of these groups actually had few differences, except with regard to possible association or federation with Senegal. Ultimately, internal self-government was granted to The Gambia in 1963, followed by explorations of the possibility of union with Senegal. A UN recommendation for unity between the two was turned down.

Coastal West Africa: Sierra Leone

The people of the European mercantile powers, particularly in England, had felt increasing antipathy toward the principle of slavery by the end of the 18th century after the American Revolution. A Society for the Abolition of Slavery was formed under the leadership of Granville Sharp, which planned to establish a colony in Sierra Leone for the slaves that were to be set free. In 1788, the Temne King, Naimbana and his subordinate chiefs, sold a portion of the coastal area of Sierra Leone to the Society, which was then settled initially by a group of 300 Africans freed as a reward for their service in the British armed forces in the battles of the American Revolution, joined by some former Jamaican slaves. The diminutive settlement was administered by the Sierra Leone Company and was immediately burdened by the task of fending off attacks from neighboring groups and French warships.

The area of Freetown, the capital, was originally sold to the British by the Temne ruler, King Tom, as a trading post. Controversial from the start, the sale provoked local skirmishes, which were not subdued until 1808 when Britain began using the harbor as a naval base in its operations against the slave trade, outlawed in 1807. British ships patrolling the Atlantic would capture slaving ships and return them to the Freetown base where the captives would be liberated. Between 1807 and

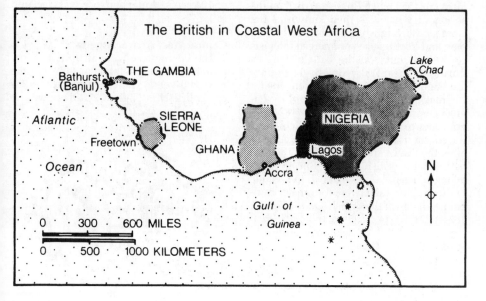

The British in Coastal West Africa

The Colonial Period

1864 more than 50,000 captives were resettled. Much like Americo-Liberians, these resettled former slaves formed a culture separate from hinterland peoples. They were a heterogeneous lot, coming from all over western Africa, but had in common the English language and Christianity. With British encouragement they were turned into a more homogenous Christian community, known as Creoles (or Krios), by the efforts of Protestant missionaries and the black pastors of Freetown churches.

There was little growth—the burden of defense, development and settlement proved to be severe for the Company—and in 1808 Sierra Leone was taken over by the British as a Crown Colony. The English Parliament had abolished slave trade in 1807. Freetown, the name of the Company settlement, became a base for a squadron of ships which sailed the shores of West Africa searching for and intercepting the privateer slave ships. The first slave ship found was quickly condemned in 1808; its human cargo, so recently abducted from other African areas, was released at Freetown. As further slave ships were captured in the succeeding years, thousands of Africans of great diversity in origin were released, most of whom elected to remain in Sierra Leone, settling largely in the areas closest to the coast.

Coastal Creoles had privileged access to European education in the Sierra Leone colony. Fourah Bay College was founded in 1846 by the Church Missionary Society to train teachers and missionaries. Given full degree-granting status by affiliation with Durham University in England only ten years later, Fourah Bay is sub-Saharan Africa's oldest university, proudly earning Freetown the title of "the Athens of Africa." Through access to university education, Creoles prospered, entered the professions, and qualified as doctors and lawyers, becoming an educated elite.

British influence gradually extended inland from the coastline, and in 1895 a protectorate was proclaimed over the colony's hinterland. In the protectorate, the British preference for indirect rule prevailed. Local chiefs ruled under the direction of district commissioners. It was not a system that encouraged the transformation of tradition. In general, the protectorate lagged behind the colony in social and economic development.

The period of the 19th century was one of gradual development by the British in Sierra Leone, with the establishment of a flourishing trade, schools, a college and Christian church missions. The former slaves, called Creoles, isolated from their native peoples and traditions, adopted many English customs which prevail today among their descendants, now num-

Kwame Nkrumah

bering more than 125,000. In 1896 a British protectorate was established over the territory, which by then had definite boundaries with the adjacent French territories as a result of treaties signed in 1861.

The roads to democracy and independence were ones of relatively peaceful development of responsibility and unity among the Creoles and the inland groups, with the first elections for local office being held in 1924. Sir Milton Margai, a Creole leader, was appointed to successive offices in 1954 and the following years, becoming the first prime minister in 1960.

Coastal West Africa: Ghana (Gold Coast)

The Portuguese initially landed in Ghana as early as 1470; they were followed in 1553 by an English arrival on the shores of what was then known as the Gold Coast. English, Danish, Dutch, German and Portuguese commercial interests controlled ports on the Gulf of Guinea during the next 250 years. By 1750, only the English, Dutch and Danes remained.

Great Britain assumed control of English commercial settlements in 1821, negotiating treaties with the local chiefs in the southern areas in 1844. Shortly thereafter, the Danes and Dutch ceded their interests to the British. English forces fought a long series of battles against the Asante of the interior; there were four major campaigns in which the British subdued them: 1824–27, 1873–74, 1893–94 and 1895–96. It was only in 1901 that colonial authority spread through the entire country. After seizing Togoland (Togo) from the Germans during World War I, the British administered it from Accra. With the excep-

tion of the commercial activity in the south coastal area, there was little economic development during the colonial period.

Following World War II, there was a sharp rise of nationalism among the Africans of higher education in Gold Coast, as the colony was called. The United Gold Coast Convention, led by J.B. Danquah, exerted continuous pressure for autonomy and independence. Political developments quickly came to revolve around one person: Kwame Nkrumah. After receiving college educations in the United States and Great Britain, obtaining several degrees in advanced courses of study, he returned to the Gold Coast from England in 1947. As Secretary of the UGCC, he assisted in promoting riots and strikes in early 1948. Both he and Danquah were exiled to a remote northern village by the British Governor; the British accused Nkrumah of being a communist.

Under continuing pressure, the British in 1949 promulgated a new constitution and released the exiled leaders. Nkrumah, restless under the leadership of Danquah, formed his own political party, the Convention Peoples Party (CPP). Further civil disobedience under Nkrumah's leadership resulted in his arrest, conviction and sentence to a two-year jail term. Constitutional reforms in 1951 provided for election of a greater number of Africans to a legislative council and Nkrumah was freed from prison to head the new government.

A new constitution of 1954 established a cabinet composed entirely of African representatives. The subsequent elections again resulted in a majority for the *CPP*. Two years later, Nkrumah, as prime minister, demanded independence. The British held new elections in 1956, which perpetuated the majority of the *CPP* (71 out of 104 seats). Independence was declared in 1957.

Central West Africa: Nigeria

The Portuguese were also the first explorers to land at Nigeria in 1472. For the next 300 years, traders from all nations called briefly in Nigeria, but there was no

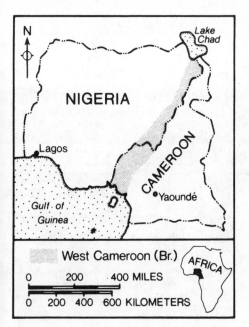

NIGERIA

West Cameroon (Br.)

settlement. The principal purpose of their visits was to obtain human cargo to work in the colonies of the Western Hemisphere. The hundreds of Nigerian tribes periodically attacked each other, and the victor carried off the defeated to be sold into slavery for never more than the equivalent of $10.00 each. Transported across the ocean, they brought prices of up to $300.00. Slavery was not outlawed internally in Nigeria until 1901.

British penetration into the interior of Nigeria following the Napoleonic wars was slow. The British annexed coastal Lagos in 1861 as part of its continuing efforts to suppress the slave trade, but they were unwilling to incur the costs of maintaining an administration in Nigeria. To keep costs down, Lagos was first administered from Sierra Leone. Only in 1886 did Lagos become a separate colony. Later, two other protectorates were declared, one over the Oil Rivers and the other over the Lagos hinterland. In 1894 both entities were merged into the Niger Coast Protectorate. Twenty-three years later, the Niger River Delta was established as a British Protectorate and British influence in Nigeria was formally recognized at the conference of European powers at Berlin in 1885. The British continued to expand in Nigeria through the Royal Niger Company, but in 1900 the territory came under the control of the British Colonial Office.

The people of northern Nigeria were believers in Islam; the Hausa and Fulani, as they are known, were feudally governed by a variety of rulers known as emirs (also spelled amirs). In the north the first British High Commissioner, Frederick Lugard, set about controlling the emirs.

Some were deposed, some defeated in battle, and others collaborated. By 1903 Lugard's conquest of the emirates was complete. Though defeated, the emirates were not dismantled. To spare the British treasury administrative costs, Lugard developed a policy of "indirect rule," relying on existing administrative structures of the emirates. Much of the north's traditional feudal structure was thus maintained. In 1914 northern and southern administrative areas were consolidated into Nigeria, and the difficult tasks of balancing regional interests and identities would dominate Nigerian colonial history.

Even after penetrating into areas of Nigeria, the British had difficulty in controlling the people; there were widespread disturbances and revolts in southern Nigeria in 1904 and an uprising in the Sokoto region of northern Nigeria in 1906. It was not until 1914 that northern Nigeria was fully brought under control, at which time the Colony and Protectorate of Nigeria was formally established. Shortly after World War I, African legislators were included in the Council governing Lagos and southern Nigeria. The British enlarged tin mines on the Jos Plateau and improved the roads, schools and port facilities of Nigeria during the succeeding decades. Following World War II, the Colonial Office adopted successive constitutions which expanded African participation in Nigerian administration on a representative, federal basis. Three political parties evolved on a regional basis: the Nigerian Peoples Congress (North), the National Convention of Nigerian Citizens (Southeast) and the Nigerian National Democratic Party (Southwest). The latter two of these parties pressed energetically for full independence, but the Nigerian Peoples Congress advocated a lesser nationalistic outlook because it feared domination by a combination of the other two parties.

Discussions were held in London in 1957, at which time there were demands by 15 ethnic groups that they become individual and independent nations within the territory of Nigeria. The British resisted these demands and established a central parliamentary government with many powers reserved to the individual provinces; independence was granted in 1960.

Central West Africa: Cameroons

The British had early colonial ambitions in Cameroon and dispatched an emissary to negotiate treaties with the local chieftain in 1884. He arrived on the coast five days too late—the German representative had already concluded agreements with the coastal people, and Cameroon was to remain a German colony until 1916.

The British and French waged a protracted campaign against the German forces in Cameroon during the First World War. The fighting ended with the surrender of the Germans in 1916 (in Cameroon) and under the Treaty of Versailles Britain was awarded the smaller West Cameroon territory and France obtained East Cameroon. The fact that there were two colonies where there had been one gave rise to the plural name *Cameroons* for the area, creating confusion, which persisted after they were again joined together in 1961.

The British held a mandate over its part from the League of Nations and subsequently under a trusteeship from the United Nations. Because of the language difference between the colonial powers of the two countries, there was wide divergence of opinion among the people of West Cameroon as to the political future of the territory in the late 1950s. The British conducted a plebiscite under UN supervision in 1961 to determine whether the people of West Cameroon desired to become a part of the English-speaking Nigeria to the northwest, or to join the French-speaking East Cameroon in a federation. Rather than conduct the plebiscite on the basis of all votes cast in the entire territory, it was decided to count the votes of the northern and southern portions separately. The North voted to become part of Nigeria and the South opted for federation with the former French Cameroon. The voting procedure was strongly opposed by East Cameroon, with considerable numbers of Cameroonians believing that the vote should have been counted as a whole. Had this been done, it seems certain no part of West Cameroon would have merged into Nigeria.

South Africa

The complex history of South Africa's colonial period is addressed in detail in the chapter on that country. In addition, however, the British maintained continuous control over three territories in the South African orbit: Botswana (or Bechuanaland, pronounced Beh-*kwa*-na-land), Lesotho (called Basutoland, pronounced Ba-*soo*-toe-land) and Swaziland (*Swah*-zee-land). During the colonial period, which ended in 1967–68, all three were economically dependent upon what is now the Republic of South Africa, though they were colonies of Great Britain.

Southern Africa: Botswana (formerly Bechuanaland)

The Tswana, as the majority of the people of Botswana are called, remained split into hundreds of tribes and communities until Khama I, Chief of the powerful Bamangwato tribe, consolidated them into a loosely constituted group in the last half

The Colonial Period

of the 19th century. As the *Boers* of South Africa were pushed northward from the Cape by the British, they attempted to penetrate into what is now Botswana, and battles erupted between the two peoples. Khama I, a Christianized native, appealed to the British for assistance, and the country was proclaimed to be under British protection. Khama I reigned over the loosely united country until his death at the age of 93 in 1923, and was succeeded by his son, Sekgoma, who died three years later in 1926.

The British did little more than maintain peace in Bechuanaland during the period of the protectorate, although in later years they provided an annual grant to assist the colony's economy. In 1920 they set up two advisory councils—one for the native African people and one for the European settlers and their descendants who had come in small number to the area. Later, in 1934, they established a constitution which granted authority to the local chieftains and native courts.

The native rule of the Bamangwato passed to Seretse Khama, then the four-year-old son of Sekgoma, under the regency of Tshekedi Khama, brother of the dead ruler. The British had difficulty in controlling Tshekedi—at one time he was deposed as regent for a short time after having had a Briton flogged. Seretse Khama left for England in 1945 to pursue higher education; while studying law he met a young English woman, Ruth Williams, and married her. This interracial marriage of 1949 infuriated the white population of South Africa, and the embarrassed British Government removed Seretse Khama from office and forced him to remain in England until 1956.

After obtaining a renunciation of his chieftainship, the British permitted him to return to Bechuanaland in 1956 as "Mr. Khama." Many of the lesser chiefs opposed his return, as did his uncle, Tshekedi. The British established a Legislative Council in 1958 composed of 35 members equally divided between the races to advise and consent to the acts of the British High Commissioner, who was also executive authority in Swaziland, Basutoland and Ambassador of Great Britain to South Africa. Tshekedi was removed as regent-chief in 1959; the avowed purpose of establishing the council was to prepare Bechuanaland for independence.

Political parties emerged rapidly after the first council meetings—K.T. Motsete formed the Bechuanaland People's Party in 1960, demanding immediate independence and removal of political power from the white settlers. The British tacitly permitted Seretse Khama to enter politics because of his popularity, which had grown since his return from exile. He

Seretse Khama and his wife shortly before Botswana's independence

formed the Bechuanaland Democratic Party, with membership from both races, and advocated a policy of non-racism in government, a move toward internal self-government by 1965 and independence as soon thereafter as possible.

The British reviewed the status of Bechuanaland in 1963 and established a new constitution in consultation with the representatives of the political parties. The first elections in 1965 under the new system were won by Khama's Democratic Party and he was named prime minister. Further negotiations led to an agreement for full independence which became effective on September 20, 1966; Bechuanaland took the name Botswana—land of the Tswana.

Southern Africa: Lesotho (formerly Basutoland)

The people of what is now Lesotho, although composed almost entirely of what are now referred to as South Sotho people, were organized in a multitude of sub-groups and tribes in the early 19th century. Raids from neighboring Zulus and Matabeles had depleted their number, and the remainder were gathered together in a loosely united kingdom by Moshoeshoe I, a chieftain from the northern re-

gion of Lesotho. The land was mountainous, hilly and generally regarded as unsuited for farming by *Boer* descendants of the original settlers of South Africa who had been driven from the Cape region into the interior of South Africa by British pressures.

But pressures for more land led to a 12-year war between the whites of the Orange Free State and the Sothos between 1856 and 1868, which weakened the latter; they lost a substantial portion of their territory, still referred to as the "Conquered Territory." Facing total defeat, the Sothos appealed to the British for protection in 1868. The land area of the protectorate was poorly defined; the British resisted further *Boer* expansion, but had difficulty establishing control in what was considered a remote (from the Cape) land.

Basutoland was annexed to the British Cape Colony in 1871, an act which was resented by the Basutos at the time because the English were just as eager for expansion in southern Africa as were the *Boers*. The unstable union was plagued by disturbances within Basutoland; the British, faced with a state of near anarchy among the people, placed the colony directly under the control of Her Majesty's Government in 1884. The British High Commis-

The Colonial Period

Southern Africa at the Outbreak of World War I

■ British Possessions
▨ British Commonwealth Membership

was charged to the British High Commissioner for South Africa. A proclamation was issued in 1944 by the Commissioner which recognized the Paramount Chief and Council as native authority for internal matters.

The British agreed in 1967 that Swaziland was to be independent after September 6, 1968. Internal self-government was established in April 1967 and elections were held shortly thereafter. The Imbokodvo National Movement (also known as The Grindstone Movement), led by Prince Makhosini Dlamini, won all 24 seats in the National Assembly. King Sobhuza II ascended the throne at the time of independence. Dr. Ambrose Zwane, leader of the opposition Ngwane National Liberation Council, pressed charges that the elections were rigged before the Organization of African Unity and in the UN. Both organizations listened, but did nothing.

Southern Africa: Rhodesia, Zambia, Malawi

A steady, but small procession of traders and missionaries of many European nations established themselves in Mozambique after the Portuguese in the 16th century, yet there was no real colonial effort until almost 400 years later, when diamonds and gold were discovered in the former *Boer* states of South Africa, Transvaal and Orange Free State. Transvaal had been successful in maintaining its independence. In an effort to surround the people of Dutch ancestry, the British commissioned the British South Africa Company in 1889, giving it all rights to an area north of Transvaal without limit.

Under the leadership of Cecil Rhodes, the town of Salisbury was founded in 1890 in what was then known as Mashonaland, inhabited by Matabele (Bantu) people; the city would later come to be known as Harare. Leander Jameson, a close friend of Rhodes, was appointed administrator of the thinly settled area which included what is now Zambia and the name Rhodesia was adopted in 1895. Since the most valuable of the natural resources of this part of Africa were then believed to be only in South Africa, the settlement of Rhodesia was slow. For decades, Salisbury was a rural town with wooden sidewalks and was the only urban settlement in what was a vast agricultural area. In the early 20th century, Zambia was recognized as a distinct state called Northern Rhodesia; both areas were granted full internal autonomy in 1923, when Rhodesia was declared to be a Crown Colony instead of the property of the British South Africa Company.

The white Rhodesians were few in number, but steadily grew into an indus-

sioners spent most of their time in Basutoland settling tribal differences and settling the ever contentious question of who was Paramount Chief; since the reign of Moshoeshoe I the land had been governed by about 22 lesser chiefs, who were in turn superior to approximately 2,000 minor chieftains. Little was done to improve and modernize the lives of the people living in the remote wilderness of the highlands.

The Basutoland Council was informally constituted in 1903 to provide direction in internal matters, and it was recognized officially by the British in 1910 as a legislative body to be consulted on internal affairs of the colony. The Council requested further reform in 1955 in order that its decisions might be conclusive on all internal questions. After a period of negotiation a revised constitution was adopted in 1959, to take effect the following year, which granted the wishes of the Legislative Council.

Pressures for total independence slowly gathered momentum, and Britain decided on a course of action in early 1965. Elections were held in April of that year to determine the popular will with respect to leadership of the colony. The Basutoland National Party of then-moderate Chief Leabua Jonathan gained 31 of the 60 parliamentary seats. The opposition party, the Panafricanist Congress Party, led by Ntsu Mokhele, a leftist, received 25 seats,

and the right-wing Maramatlou Freedom Party, which supported the aspirations for power of Moshoeshoe II, hereditary Paramount Chieftain, won 4 seats. One delegate from the Maramatlou party defected to the National Party shortly after the election. Although Chief Leabua Jonathan, who conducted his campaign from a helicopter provided by the Republic of South Africa, had received a minority of 44% of the popular vote, he negotiated for independence with the British in London.

An independence agreement was reached on June 18, 1966 whereby Basutoland was to become independent and was to be called *Lesotho*, indicating the lowlands of the Sotho—the area they traditionally occupied.

Southern Africa: Swaziland

The Swazis came to their present territory during one of the many Bantu migrations southward through Africa. In the 18th century, Zulu raids into their country forced the tribal chieftain of Mawati to seek British assistance through the Agent General in Natal, who mediated a peaceful relationship between the two groups. For a time, the Transvaal Republic (now a province of South Africa) protected and administered Swaziland. After the *Boer War* (see the Republic of South Africa), control of the territory passed to the British. In 1907, administration of Swaziland

15

The Colonial Period

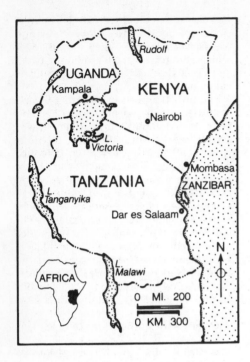

Jomo Kenyatta

trious, conservative society. The African people, with the exception of a few missionary efforts, were largely ignored, and restricted to the poorer lands in the ensuing decades. Salisbury emerged as a cosmopolitan and large city by the end of World War II, which was the beginning of a period of migration of more thousands of white Europeans—principally British—to Rhodesia.

The African people of Rhodesia became increasingly restless after 1960 as many colonies of Africa were granted independence under African leadership, but the resulting limited political effort was unsuccessful because of the power of the white minority which was firmly established. Southern Rhodesia was joined with Northern Rhodesia (Zambia) and Nyasaland (Malawi) into the Federation of Rhodesia and Nyasaland in 1953, but this crumbled because of the overwhelming opposition of the African majorities in what are now Zambia and Malawi. Although there were earlier visits by traders and missionaries, the first significant penetration of Malawi was by the intrepid Scotch missionary, Dr. David Livingstone, on September 15, 1859. For almost 15 years he explored southeastern Africa to proselytize and bring Christianity to the native people. Formal annexation of the area occurred in 1883 when a representative of the British government accredited to the kings and chief of central Africa appeared and negotiated treaties with them. In reality, this was no more than an effort to exclude Portugal and Germany from the area. The British energetically and successfully ended slave trade of Arab raiders.

During the colonial period, particularly after the discovery of gold and diamonds in South Africa and copper in Rhodesia (Northern), the men usually spent several years working in the mines of those territories, bringing their limited wages back home to Nyasaland. Because of this, and the prevalence of the Christian faith among the people, there was no rapid surge of nationalism. This changed in 1953 when Nyasaland was joined into the Federation of Rhodesia and Nyasaland—the Nyasas greatly feared the white supremacy movements that were strong in the other two members of the federation. In an effort to suppress opposition, the British tried to arrest the chief of the Angoni tribe who advocated a passive resistance to the federation. The attempted arrest was unsuccessful, but was the source of an even higher level of mistrust of the British and other white people by the Nyasas. There was a gradual transition to internal autonomy from 1961 to 1963 based upon elections in which the Malawi Congress Party of Dr. Hastings Kamuzu Banda won an overwhelming victory. The despised federation was dissolved in 1963 and independence was granted the following year.

East Africa: Kenya, Uganda, Tanzania (Tanganyika & Zanzibar), and the Indian Ocean

The first British efforts in East Africa occurred in 1823 when Admiral William Owen entered the coastal area, supposedly in an attempt to end the Arab slave trade that had been going on for centuries along the coast. In theory, the Sultan of Muscat on the Arabian coast was the ruler of the region, and his authority was exercised by a viceroy (Sayyid) on the island of Zanzibar. The British, using a combination of threats and treaties, gradually established their control about the turn of the century.

German exploration and annexation of Tanganyika and part of southern Uganda from 1878 to 1885, in turn, aroused the interest of the British in Kenya and Uganda. The Sultan of Zanzibar granted the British East Africa Company a 50-year lease of what is now Kenya in 1887; this in turn was changed to the East Africa Protectorate, governed by a commissioner, by the British government in 1895.

The last quarter of the 19th century in the eastern region of Africa was turbulent. There were efforts by both the British and Germans to enter Uganda, which was divided into four semi-autonomous kingdoms—Buganda, Busoga, Butoro and Bunyoro, of which Buganda was the most powerful. King Mwanga of Buganda, who reigned from 1884 until he was captured and exiled in 1899, tried to play the British off against the Germans by alternating his allegiance. In addition to this swirl of activity on behalf of Germany and Great Britain, there were roving remnants of Arab slave traders and religious conflicts involving and between Catholic and Protestant missionaries and believers, as well as those of Islamic faith.

The borders of this region were adjusted countless times, and not generally along the lines of actual colonial power. By a process of bargaining and trading, accompanied by line-drawing, particularly in Berlin in 1885, the eventual boundaries of the German, British and Portuguese territories, as well as those of King Leopold of Belgium were fixed. The almost straight line that now separates Kenya and Tanzania cuts almost through the center of the territory inhabited historically by the Masai people.

The British encouraged immigration of white settlers to Kenya after the turn of the century, and they established immense plantations in the most select parts of the colony. The tribes people of Kenya, particularly large numbers of the Kikuyu (referred to as "kooks" by the British) were relegated to the poorer, tsetse-fly-infested farmlands. White immigrants entered Uganda only in very small numbers.

At the start of World War I, 300,000 British, South African and colonial Indian troops invaded German East Africa, renamed Tanganyika following the establishment of British control after the war. A force of slightly more than 200 German officers, commanding native troops numbering between 2,500 and 4,000 fended off the massive force for four years under the brilliant leadership of General Paul Von Lettow-Vorbeck. After the war, the British sent the German settlers from Tanganyika, confiscating their lands; a small number were permitted to return within a few years. Kenya was completely dominated by the white farmers and a substantial number of Indians who were descendants of workers brought in to complete a railroad between Nairobi and Mombasa, which had opened in 1895. Uganda was governed through the local kings, and the cultivation of cotton and coffee quickly rose to be the source of the leading exports, permitting Uganda to become the richest British colony in Africa.

Government in Kenya was through a variety of commissioners sent from Britain; it was at a relatively late date that local councils were permitted, and initially even these consisted of people appointed by the commissioners. The white farmers of Kenya requested a regional council for Kenya, Uganda and Tanganyika as early as 1926, but were turned down since it was felt that this was merely an effort of theirs to preserve and extend their power, which excluded the African majority from sharing in government.

Following World War II, the ability of the British to rule effectively in Kenya and Uganda sharply decreased. The population of Kenya was stratified into three groups: the rich, landowning white (a small minority), the Indian and Arab merchant class, and (at the bottom) the huge majority of Africans. The African population had doubled in 25 years, creating tremendous pressure for expansion into the lands exclusively held by white farmers. The white population, instead of recognizing the needs of the Africans, instituted progressively more strict and severe laws directed against the majority.

From the mid-19th century, British interest in the region grew and in 1895 Kenya was declared a protectorate. Railroad construction from the port of Mombassa to Lake Victoria encouraged development of trade and settlement, and in 1920 Kenya became a crown colony administered by a British governor.

Africans were not permitted representation on the colony's legislative council, so developed their own pressure groups. Most active in these developments were members of the Kikuyu tribe, who supplied the bulk of labor used on European farms. By the 1930s there were several organizations to represent the tribe's grievances, among which were low wages and exclusion from profitable coffee growing.

Anti-British Africans formed a terrorist organization, the *Mau Mau*, to achieve their goals. Dreadful brutality became commonplace. The *Mau Mau* attacked whites and mercilessly slaughtered those of their own people who were servile to and worked for the whites. White retalia-

tion was equally brutal. Jomo Kenyatta, the political leader of the majority of African people, educated in Europe, was arrested, tried and convicted for participating in the *Mau Mau* conspiracy and was sentenced to seven years in jail. In 1957 Kenya erupted in a total state of civil anarchy, as *Mau Mau* terrorism had spread into almost every area of the country. Africans suspected of participating in this secret society were shot on the spot by Whites. Even long-trusted house servants had by this time joined the secret organization. It became increasingly apparent that in order to bring stability to Kenya, the British would have to accede to the demands of the *Mau Mau*. Most of the British farmers departed, and in 1960 an agreement was reached in London which gave the Africans a majority in the Legislative Council.

Dissension and political quarrels among the Africans in Kenya retarded the goal of full independence. Kenyatta, released from jail, headed the Kenya-African National Union (KANU), which represented the larger tribes of the country. The Kenya African Democratic Union drew its support from the many smaller tribes. After prolonged discussion in London, a complicated constitution was adopted providing for a loose, federal system of government.

The election conducted in May 1963 resulted in an overwhelming victory for KANU. Under pressure from the majority, the constitution was amended to strengthen the authority of the central government. The British recognized the

independence of Kenya in December 1963.

Uganda was not without disturbance during the postwar period, although not as bloody as that in Kenya. In 1953, with the intent of establishing a central government, the British commissioner informed the kabaka (king) of Buganda that there were to be reforms in administration which would undermine his authority. Edward Mutesa II, the kabaka, adamantly refused to accept these regulations and he forthwith was dismissed as king and put on a plane for London. The Buganda people regarded this as nothing short of an outrage. The British had to constitute a form of martial law to control the people throughout Uganda, and the economy suffered a steep decline.

The British attempted to solve this state of affairs by proposing that the *Lukiko*, the Ugandan tribal assembly, be permitted to vote on whether a new king should be chosen; the Assembly would not listen to the proposal. Kabaka Edward Mutesa was subsequently returned and the British set up a ministerial system of government, increasing African membership in the Legislative Council. The United Kingdom of Uganda was granted full independence in October 1962.

The movement toward independence was relatively tranquil in Tanzania (Tanganyika). The British had received a mandate from the League of Nations to administer the former German colony. This continued under a UN trusteeship. A gradual development of internal self-government was undertaken by the British, starting with a Legislative Council appointed by the government in 1926. Subsequent elections were held in 1958 and again in 1960, the latter of which was won by the Tanganyikan African National Union of Julius Nyerere, who was president of Tanzania until 1985. He retired in that year, but is still a figure of power in the country. Full independence was granted in December 1961.

Britain also seized several French possessions in the Indian Ocean and was the colonial power for Mauritius and the Seychelles for most of the 19th and 20th centuries. On the Seychelles, the abolition of slavery and the shift to small-scale agricultural production in the 19th century triggered an influx of Asians—Chinese, Indians, and Malays. Over the years the populations intermarried, producing the islands' present mixed population, in which descendants of former slaves have remained an underclass.

Northeast Africa: Egypt and the Sudan

During the first half of the 19th century, interest in European technology and education grew rapidly in Egypt, ruled by the

17

The Colonial Period

King Farouk at 16 in 1936

Gemal Abdel Nasser

khedives (kings) nominally subject to the control of the Turkish Ottoman Empire's sultan. The basis for the construction of the Suez Canal lay in this interest, coupled with British and French desires for a shorter route to India and the Far East.

After negotiation with Khedive Ismail, European powers, working through their financial institutions, began construction of the canal, which was completed and opened amid great fanfare in 1869 with a multitude of European royalty present; they later heard the first performance of the opera *Aida,* by Giuseppe Verdi, erroneously said to have been written for the occasion. Egypt had been enriched by the demand for cotton created by the United States Civil War, but had also heavily borrowed at high interest rates to help finance the construction of the canal. From 1870 to 1883, the British succeeded in conquering most of the Sudan, penetrating as far as Uganda, supposedly in partnership with Egypt. The prime interest initially in this area was to end the oppressive slave trade that was firmly entrenched.

A financial crisis compelled the khedive to sell all of the Egyptian shares in the Suez Canal to Great Britain in 1876, giving the British a majority interest. Further financial deficits and inability to repay European loans were the basis of increasing British control of Egypt. The khedives rapidly became figurehead kings, totally subject to British control, which led to an early rise of Egyptian nationalist desires. An army revolt, coupled with a popular nationalist uprising was the excuse used to invade Egypt, and absolute British control of the region resulted.

Although the khedives were retained as the nominal rulers, their power quickly became almost nonexistent in the face of

growing pressures of the nationalist leaders. Eventually, a scheme of rule was devised under the so-called Organic Law which included a legislative council and cabinet with advisory powers. The khedive was controlled by a "Resident and Consul-General" of the British; all high Egyptian ministers had a British "advisor."

In the Sudan, Mohammed Ahmed, a leader known as Mahdi, quickly achieved wide popularity following 1880—in addition to his political military support, he was regarded by his followers, the dervishes, as a modern-day prophet of Islam. By 1884, he had all but completely demolished British and Egyptian forces within the territory. An expedition sent by the British offered the Mahdi some concessions, which were flatly rejected; the Mahdi immediately laid siege to Khartoum where General Charles Gordon and his forces were located.

After several months, the Mahdi entered the city and the British were slaughtered; General Gordon was impaled by a dervish spear. A relief force sent to help arrived in Khartoum three days later, but was greeted only by smoking rubble and the stench of death. Fearful of also being wiped out by the fanatical Sudanese, the rescue force beat a hasty retreat. The control of the Sudan remained with the Mahdi and his successor for ten years. The British, faced with the growing French expansion on the western side of the Nile River in the Sudan, sent a large force under General Sir Horatio Hubert Kitchener to reconquer the territory in 1896–98. The Mahdi had died and the dervishes were disorganized; in the ensuing battle almost

10,000 Sudanese lost their lives and were only able to claim that of 50 British and Egyptians in return. One of the young lieutenants in the British force was none other than Winston Churchill, destined to lead Britain through World War II.

Kitchener was later entitled Lord Kitchener of Khartoum in recognition of his leadership. Entering Khartoum, he emptied the revered tomb of the original Mahdi and dumped the corpse into the river, and then quickly captured and killed the *Khalifa,* successor of the Mahdi. Kitchener marched rapidly southward, meeting the French at Fashoda (now Kodak) in an effort to reassert British power. The result was the Fashoda Crisis (discussed under *The French)* that was finally ended by agreement on areas of control which roughly defined the boundaries between what is now the Sudan, Central African Republic and Chad.

Great Britain and Egypt set up a joint administration of the Sudan; although they were nominally equal partners, the British were in fact the dominant power. After World War I, the British had to institute increasingly harsh measures to maintain their control in Egypt and the so-called Anglo-Egyptian Sudan. At the start of World War I, the Ottomans in Turkey demonstrated sympathy for the German cause, and as a result, the British declared war against them. Although the Ottoman control in Egypt was little more than imaginary, the British used the war as a pretext to proclaim a protectorate status over Egypt, which aroused a great deal of local opposition. The Nationalist, or Wafd Party, quickly became dominant, opposing both the British and the khedives.

A multitude of successive administrations under a semidemocratic constitution ruled following World War I. Ahmed Fuad, the khedive, repeatedly dissolved nationalist governments and announced new elections, in all of which the nationalists scored tremendous victories and returned to power. The nationalist movement was not genuinely popular, however; its primary support came from the wealthy, land-owning *pashas* who had become established during the Ottoman era. The protectorate status was withdrawn in 1922 and Egypt achieved internal autonomy as a result of Wafd efforts.

There were some efforts at economic development during the period between the two world wars based upon the opening of dams along the Nile to partially control the age-old flood and drought cycle of the river. Constitutional reforms gave increasing power to the Egyptian *pashas.* The worldwide depression of the 1930s further lessened British control, and upon the death of King Fuad I in 1936, his hand-

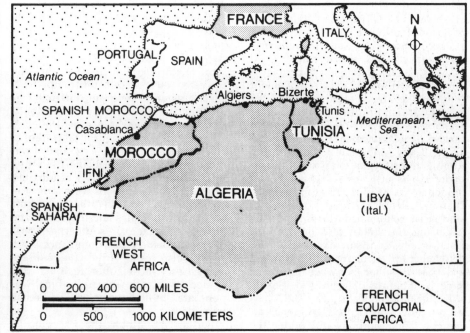

pated at the age of 32, was overthrown and exiled by the military in July 1952; a new era began in Egypt which is now generally thought of as the beginning of true independence in the modern age.

Prior to the defeat of Farouk, the British offered the Sudan a plan of internal self-government which was condemned by Egypt. The colonial government was able to work out a compromise arrangement with the military junta that succeeded Farouk, which provided that the Sudanese should decide whether they were to be independent or part of a federation with Egypt. In 1953 an overwhelming number of the Sudanese voted for independence, which was granted in 1956.

THE FRENCH
North Africa: Algeria, Morocco and Tunisia

With the exception of Morocco, all of Arabic-speaking North Africa was, at the turn of the 18th century, part of the vast Ottoman Empire; the area consisted of a number of small principalities ruled by Turkish military men who had titles of Bey or Dey, depending upon the location. Commerce consisted of trade with regions to the south, and piracy of European shipping in the Mediterranean Sea. The booty seized from the vessels consisted not only of cargo, but the crew as well, which was sold into slavery.

After other nations had sent expeditionary forces against the Arab raiders,

some 16-year-old son, Farouk, came to power. Colorful and pleasure seeking, he was at first very popular. With the consent of the British and other European powers, Egypt became nominally independent in 1936 and was admitted to the League of Nations a year later. British military control was limited to the Suez Canal area.

The king dissolved the *Wafd* government in 1938, and the election that followed was a complete victory for the new pro-king party. Initially arming itself for World War II, Egypt maintained a passive neutrality during the conflict, although it was the scene of battles between the Allied and Axis powers.

Following World War II, the Egyptians sought to end the last vestiges of British domination. Weakened by the war, England was in no position to offer opposition to this demand. The picture was further complicated by the presence of the new state of Israel, carved out of a portion of Palestine, opposed by the Arabs, which led to a brief Egyptian-Israeli battle in 1948, won by the Israelis.

The Wafd Party again returned to power in 1950 after several changes of government reflecting the desires of the nationalists and unrest among the army leadership. Egypt demanded withdrawal of British troops from the Canal Zone and from the Sudan. Great Britain immediately retaliated with a plan for Sudanese independence; this appeared realistic in view of the traditional hatred for and distrust of Egyptians by the Sudanese. Events moved swiftly—the UN requested that Egypt lift its embargo forbidding use

of the Suez Canal by ships bound for or coming from Israel. Egypt replied by abrogating its treaties with the British of 1899 and 1936 and the British navy attacked Port Said and landed forces in the area. Riots erupted in Cairo and there were two rapid changes of government. King Farouk, having grown fat and dissi-

Habib Bourguiba celebrates Tunisian independence

19

The Colonial Period

France sent a force into Algiers in 1830, deposing the dey and seizing a few of the coastal towns. Another dey was selected by the local people, who promptly marshaled attacks upon the French. Eventually the occupying forces had to recognize the new dey, Abd el-Kader. He engaged in sporadic warfare for 15 years against the French, who relinquished to him their claim to interior lands initially, but later drove him into Morocco where other French forces invaded and captured him in 1847.

After the conquest of Algeria, France slowly subdued Morocco, which had initially escaped domination by colonial powers, although the major powers had forced a treaty in 1880 that protected the rights of foreigners within the country. After a 13-year-old boy succeeded as sultan in 1894, the internal conditions deteriorated, reducing Morocco to virtual anarchy by the turn of the century. In exchange for concessions in Libya, Italy relinquished any claim it might have had in Morocco and the British later also acknowledged French supremacy in 1904. A nominal French-Spanish control was established in 1906 after a visit to Morocco by German Kaiser Wilhelm II as evidence of a German interest; negotiations led to an acknowledgment of French domination of the country in 1909. This was given by Germany in exchange for some economic guarantees and a section of the French Congo, which became part of Germany's colony of Kameroun (now Cameroon).

The French-Spanish administration quickly gave way to a French Protectorate under the terms of the treaty of Fez in 1912. When Sultan Moulay Yusuf died in 1927 the French chose his younger son, Sidi Muhammad, as sultan. Known for his retiring disposition, the prince turned into a skilled and forceful king as Muhammad V. Around him Moroccan nationalists of all stripes gathered and challenges to French rule mounted. French attempts to divide Berbers and Arabs backfired and nationalists initiated a new national day, the *Fête du Trône* or Throne Day in 1933. It accentuated the monarch's role as symbol of national unity.

Popular enthusiasm for the young king was often accompanied by anti-French demonstrations. Political parties soon emerged seeking greater Moroccan self-rule. The explicit demand for independence logically followed the country's experiences in World War II. Muhammad V urged cooperation with France when war broke out in 1939, and Moroccan troops fought valiantly to defend the colonial ruler. A defeated France shone less brightly, and Vichy's racial laws were offensive to a monarchy that had a large

Jewish population. The Allies, meeting in Casablanca in 1943, expressed little enthusiasm for continued French presence in Morocco, and by 1944 an Independence Party, *Hizb al-Istiqlal*, was formed.

The monarch's willingness to permit existence of the independence movement annoyed the French administrators. He roused further hostility by refusing to countersign decrees of the French resident general, denying them legal validity. Seeking to divide Arabs and Berbers, French administrators began to cultivate Berber leadership as a counter foil to a nationalist monarch. One of the most formidable, Thami al-Glaoui, the feudal overlord of Marrakesh, condemned Muhammad V as not being the sultan of Moroccans as much as he was the sultan of *Istiqlal*.

Together al-Glaoui and France worked to depose the sultan, but when the French removed him from office in 1953, it made Muhammad a nationalist hero. The Algerian uprising in 1954 diverted French attentions from Morocco and under the overwhelming influence of a popular monarch and a strong nationalist party, Morocco became independent in 1956.

Although the French presence in the area now known as Algeria was initially military, efforts were made to settle colonists from France in the 1860s and 1870s when most of what is now Algeria was gradually brought under colonial control. In Tunisia, the French had economic competition from England and Italy. In return for control of Cyprus, the

British acknowledged France's authority in Tunisia. Because of an outbreak of violence, a naval force seized Bizerte in 1881 and forced the Bey of Tunis to accept the status of a French protectorate over the area. The British, Italians, and Turks all protested, but France had the support of Germany in the move, given in exchange for French support of German colonial ambitions elsewhere in Africa.

Though France had juridical control of North Africa by 1910, *de facto* control was much less complete. During the entire colonial period from the 19th century until about 1960, the Arabs were almost in constant rebellion. Riff tribesmen of the Moroccan mountains and the Berber and Tuareg horsemen of southern Algeria never accepted French dominance. Arab unrest also came from the Muslim *Senussi* sect in neighboring Libya that spilled over into Tunisia, which was populated by Italians as well as French immigrants.

Further complicating the peaceful colonization of North Africa, the immigrants to the area from France were principally military personnel and their families—they quickly developed a militant and conservative attitude as evidenced by their armed opposition to French efforts in the 1870s to placate the restless Arabs. Substantial numbers of Arabs went to France during the colonial period, but both in Africa and in France the two ethnic groups—French and Arab—resisted integration with vigor.

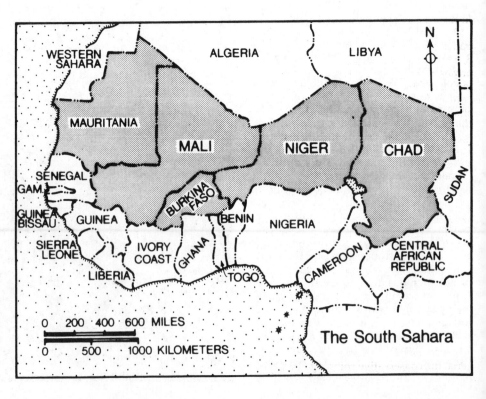

The South Sahara

The Colonial Period

The French colonists assumed the dominant position in North Africa, both economically and in terms of status derived from education. Lower schools were provided for those of French ancestry, but with little exception, no comparable effort was made on behalf of the Arabs. The local rulers were allowed to retain nominal powers, since it was actually easier to rule through them rather than try to depose them.

The earliest signs of Arab nationalism in the region—in Morocco in the 1930s—were partly a response to the world economic depression. Based almost entirely on the agricultural production on farms of European immigrants and their descendants, the whole North African economy was severely impacted by the worldwide economic slowdown. Initial nationalist efforts were the basis of continuing anti-French sentiment among the Arabs, to which was added growing worldwide liberal-nationalistic ideals—only temporarily interrupted by World War II.

Upon installation of a pro-German government under Marshal Henri-Phillipe Pétain in France following the German invasion of that country in World War II, Algeria, Morocco and Tunisia were brought under the nominal authority of the Vichy government which he headed, named after a town in central France from which part of France was administered by his regime in 1940–1944. Although only a relatively insignificant number of French troops loyal to the Axis powers were stationed in the area, the Allies felt that it was necessary to establish Free French control in the area prior to invading Italy.

A combined American-British force invaded Morocco and Algeria on November 8, 1942, and three days later a cease-fire arranged with Admiral Jean François Darlan, the *Vichy* commander, led to Allied control of French North Africa within a short time, with Admiral Darlan achieving the post of Chief of State with Allied approval. Following his assassination shortly afterward, the Anglo-American command tried to install the aging General Henri Giraud as commander of French forces outside France in spite of the more energetic anti-Axis, anti-*Vichy* activities of the Free French led by the younger General Charles de Gaulle. His forces had conducted assaults in and from Brazzaville, French Congo. A brief German offensive in North Africa was repulsed by the Allies in May 1943.

The French were restored to continued colonial control of North Africa following World War II. Their rule was no more effective than the unstable and numerous governments of mainland France. In Algeria, the conservative colonists (*colons*) of French ancestry completely dominated all

phases of government, although Algeria was legally supposed to be an integral part of France. The Communist Party had been outlawed in Morocco, a colony, but this could not be done in Algeria since the communists were not outlawed within France. The *National Liberation Front* quickly rose in power and spearheaded a revolt that started in late 1954 and lasted for seven years. This group was a leftist-socialist-communist Arab party, united in opposition to French colonial rule.

A last-ditch effort of the Secret Army Organization (OAS), composed for the most part of French-descended Europeans, failed to stem the overwhelming tide of revolution in spite of cruel and terroristic anti-Arab measures in 1961. A cease-fire was finally negotiated in March 1962 and President Charles de Gaulle, who had promised the French to end the bloody conflict, recognized Algerian independence on July 3 of that year.

In Tunisia there was also a postwar surge of nationalism. A large middle class of well-educated people had emerged and backed this movement, led by an Arab lawyer educated in France, Habib Bourguiba. His New Constitution Party succeeded the older Constitution Party. Bourguiba's life during the French colonial period alternated between periods of exile and/or imprisonment and periods of nationalistic leadership. Exiled in 1934, he returned in 1936, was rearrested in 1938 and later was freed by the Germans in 1942. He again was arrested when the French returned, but escaped and went into exile. When he returned in 1952, he was arrested, and in 1954 was banished into exile.

By this time Tunisia was in a full state of insurrection requiring the presence of 70,000 French troops to attempt to control

the colony. France granted internal autonomy to Tunisia in 1955, which also provided amnesty for all freedom fighters. Bourguiba was permitted to return, and full independence was achieved on July 20, 1956.

The South Sahara: Mauritania, Mali, Upper Volta (Burkina Faso), Niger, Chad.

Colonization of the southern Sahara region was much slower process than in other areas of the continent because the almost uniformly arid land held little importance to the French. The only reasons for colonization were in order to connect other more valuable colonies and to exclude other foreign colonial effort in the region.

At the Berlin Conference, arranged by Otto von Bismarck of Germany and the French foreign minister in 1884–85, the major world and colonial powers officially decreed that African slavery was to be abolished and that there was to be free navigation of the major rivers of the continent. It was further decreed that colonial power in the area was to be based on presence and actual control. Unofficially, and more important, the representatives took a map of the continent and drew lines indicating areas of interest of the respective powers.

The maps of the continent at that time were uncertain—boundaries differed sometimes more than a thousand miles, depending on the map and the nationality of the cartographer. In their effort to connect the West African and Equatorial African colonies, the French, in 1896–98 sent an expedition under Jean Baptiste Marchand that pushed rapidly northeastward as far as Fashoda (later named Kodak) on the Nile River. At the same time, having defeated the Sudanese, suppos-

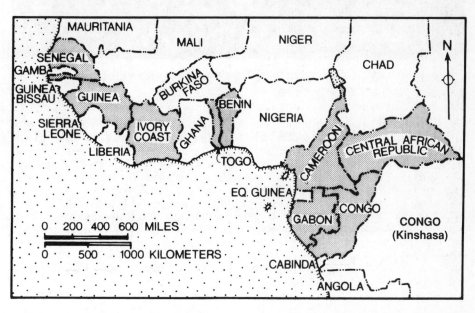

21

The Colonial Period

A contemporary artist interprets the black elite that emerges in the colonial period
Photo by Judi Iranyi

barren land by the end of the 19th century, the nomadic people who lived in the south Sahara region refused fully to submit to foreign rule for several years afterwards. In the final analysis, France was compelled to rule this part of Africa through local tribal leaders who possessed a large measure of autonomy. This permitted nominal French control without large-scale military forces, which would have been necessary for direct rule.

The region was administered as a whole as part of French West Africa. Mali, Niger, Chad and southern Algeria were also known as French Sudan, the French spelling of which was Soudan.

The lives of the people were hardly disturbed by colonial rule. There was virtually no immigration of Europeans such as occurred in North Africa; the only French presence was essentially military. Occasional revolts occurred, which were contained, rather than defeated by the French.

Although there was some sporadic German penetration in World War II during the North African campaigns of 1942–43 in the Mali, Niger and Chad regions, the local people were not involved in the battles. Free French forces under General Jean LeClerc fought several engagements with the Germans in the northern Chad area. With little exception, there was no political movement toward independence from France following World War II in the south Sahara. Niger shared in the development of the Democratic African Rally Party, but in this respect was dominated by the members from the Ivory Coast under Félix Houphouët-Boigny. As a result of unrest of the Muslim Mossi people in what was then called Upper Coast, the area now constituting Upper Volta (Burkina Faso) was separated after World War II from Ivory Coast, taking the French name Haute Volta.

Following the election of Charles de Gaulle as President of France, the French Community was established in 1958—a plan whereby France's colonies in Africa were granted internal autonomy. This was an effort to satisfy independence movements in areas of French Africa outside the south Sahara. It proved to be unsatisfactory in many respects, not the least of which was continued opposition to French authority over foreign relations by a multitude of African nationalists within the Community. Because of this, France granted independence to the remaining south Sahara and West African colonies, numbering 13, in 1960. Thus, without any substantial internal effort to promote independence, the south Sahara region was freed of French authority (which in reality had never been firmly established).

edly on behalf of Egypt, British Lord Horatio Herbert Kitchener was leading his forces southward along the Nile from Omdurman, and a second British expedition was pushing north on the river from Uganda. Further complicating the picture was the imminent arrival of an Ethiopian army on the right bank of the Nile at Fashoda, accompanied by another group of French forces.

The result was the Fashoda Crisis in which the British and French were eyeball-to-eyeball on the brink of total war.

However, France was preoccupied with a complicated political scandal involving top military figures in Paris (the Dreyfuss Affair) which had political and religious overtones. The French blinked first, ending the crisis with an agreement on the lines of French and British authority in the area, which approximately fixed the present eastern borders of Chad and the Central African Republic with the Sudan.

Although the major powers of the world recognized French authority in this

Coastal West and Equatorial Africa: Senegal, Guinea, Ivory Coast, Togo, Dahomey, East Cameroon, Central African Republic, Gabon, Congo

France initially had no colonial ambitions along coastal Africa—scattered missionary stations were established in the 17th and 18th centuries and slave trade was also prevalent at the time. Following the abolition of slave trade in 1815, France maintained very small "factories" (trading posts) along the various parts of the coast.

Colonial interest quickened during the mid-19th century when the major European powers feared that one or another of them would obtain some valuable territory available to all nations, with a potential discovery of valuable metal ores and gems. In reality, with the exception of widely scattered and exaggerated tales brought to Europe by occasional explorers, almost nothing was known of the interior coastal lands of West and Equatorial Africa.

Senegal was the first area of increased French activity—General Louis Faidherbe headed an armed force in 1854, which was immediately resisted by the natives and their Tukuler ruler, El Hajj Omar Tall, but it was gradually able to subdue most of the area. The most commercially important region of Senegal—the Gambia River Basin—had been seized by the British decades prior to the arrival of the French. Under French rule, the trading sites of St. Louis, Gorée, Dakar and Rufisque were granted special political rights. Regardless of race, inhabitants of the "Four Communes," as they were called, were French citizens with the right to elect a representative to parliament in Paris. Initially these representatives were French or mulattos, but in 1914 electors chose the first African, Blaise Diagne, as the Communes' Deputy to the National Assembly. Diagne was given the rank of governor-general to assist in recruiting African soldiers to aid France in World War I. Some 200,000 were eventually recruited from all of French West Africa.

At about the same time a military mission was sent to Guinea, but because of the fierce resistance of the people of the region, penetration into the interior was slow. A local chieftain, Samory Toure, initially signed a treaty that permitted him to claim additional territory to the northwest. This peace was short-lived; further French military efforts were necessary in 1885–86, and a dire threat to the French was mounted when Toure united with the Tukuler people previously driven from Senegal into Mali.

The French offensive was on two fronts—north and east in Guinea and north and west in Ivory Coast, which finally resulted in the defeat of Toure in 1898. He was exiled to Gabon after his capture, where he died two years later. Penetration from southern Ivory Coast had also been slow. Although treaties were signed with the coastal chieftains of the Grand-Bassam and Assime regions, the Agnis and Baoules, two groups closely related to the warlike Ashanti people of Ghana to the west, offered fierce resistance to drives into the interior. Farther north, the Mandingo people of Samory Toure and the Tukuler Africans prevented progress; Ivory Coast was not fully conquered by the French until about 1915.

As a result of a treaty signed with the French in 1851 by Ghezo, ruler of Abomey (Dahomey) a small commercial effort was initiated in that country. Coutonou was ceded as a trading post in 1868. The colonization of Dahomey was not uncontested—the Portuguese and British attempted to encourage intertribal rivalries in order to unseat the French from the coastal area, but without success.

Dahomey, with the exception of its narrow coastal strip, was left virtually untouched until 1890 when Benhazin, the last powerful king of Abomey, refused to sign additional treaties with France. Military occupation of Coutonou was ordered, swiftly followed by a violent uprising, which continued with periodic interruptions until 1894, when Benhazin surrendered. The interior of Dahomey was slowly subdued during the following decades.

Togo was not gained by the French until World War I. The larger part of this former German colony was occupied by French troops in 1916; this control was converted into a mandate by the League of Nations, which divided the colony between France (East) and Britain (West). The British area was joined with the Gold Coast (Ghana). The East Cameroon region was also acquired from Germany in a similar fashion in 1916, also resulting in a League of Nations mandate.

Count Pierre Savorgnan De Brazza of France entered the northern side of the Congo River region of coastal Africa at about the same time that the British-American explorer Henry Stanley was claiming the southern side of the river region on behalf of King Leopold of Belgium in the first part of the 1880s. An Italian count and later French citizen and naval officer, de Brazza signed treaties of protection with a number of African chiefs of the once mighty Kingdom of the Congo, a Bantu empire that at its peak had extended from Gabon to Angola including an area several hundred miles inland from the coast. After exploring most of Congo (Brazzaville), De Brazza went into Gabon and established a small coastal outpost, founded the city of Brazzaville, and governed the area from 1886 to 1897. When horrific reports of abuse of African workers by companies holding concessions in the colony became insistent enough to require action, de Brazza was sent to investigate in 1905. Two years later France restricted the use of forced labor by concessionaires. In 1910 the French joined Moyen-Congo (Middle Congo), as the colony was known, with three others to form French Equatorial Africa (AEF). Brazzaville served as the capital of AEF.

The area that is now the Central African Republic was not penetrated by the French until about 1889, when an outpost

Tirailleurs sénégalais (Senegalese riflemen) training. France employed significant numbers of African troops in both World Wars I and II.

The Colonial Period

Leopold II of Belgium

was established at Bangui, the present capital. The French named this territory Ubangi-Shari after its two principal rivers. It was not until after the turn of the century that effective French control was imposed on Congo, Gabon and the Central African Republic, all of which were combined in 1910 to form French Equatorial Africa, a distinctive administrative area. Upon receiving a mandate from the League of Nations over East Cameroon, a section of the former German colony (Kameroun) was made a part of French Equatorial Africa.

Mauritania, Senegal, Guinea, Ivory Coast, Dahomey, Mali, Upper Volta and Niger had been joined together as French West Africa in 1904; the entire territory was administered from Dakar, Senegal. The part of former German Togoland acquired after World War I was joined into this vast colony.

A variety of local councils were permitted by the French, giving the Africans a limited voice in their local affairs during the colonial period. European-style education was introduced, but never achieved widespread enrollment due to a shortage of trained teachers willing to live in Africa. Small numbers who did obtain secondary education usually went to France if they desired higher level studies.

Roads and railroads were constructed to the extent necessary to commercially develop this area of the continent, such as in Ivory Coast to permit export of agricultural products and in Gabon to support wood production.

After obtaining the necessary medical education, Dr. Albert Schweitzer, world-renowned German philosopher and musician, received permission to establish a Protestant Christian medical mission and hospital at Lamborene in the interior of Gabon. He labored among the people from 1913 until his death in 1965. He adapted medical methods to harmonize with the customs of the Africans.

Other than medical facilities provided principally for Europeans living in West and Equatorial Africa, almost none were established for the benefit of the African people during the colonial years, but there was some improvement in the post-World War II period. Boundaries were stabilized over a number of years by agreements with the British, Belgians and Liberians; the map of colonial Africa underwent no substantial change in West Africa after 1920.

The World Depression of 1929 and the following years had great impact in the coastal colonies of French West and Equatorial Africa, where agricultural products usually were the sole exports. The sharp drop in prices paid for foodstuffs meant a corresponding decrease of income, and accompanying lower living standards, which had not really been much more than marginal.

When France fell to the overwhelming might of the German Nazi military machine, a puppet, pro-German administration was established in France—the *Vichy* government (1940), named for its location in central France. It quickly dispatched administrators and personnel to take control of French Africa; they were generally disliked by the French living in the colonies. Their policies tended in many cases to be openly racist and repressive. French General Charles de Gaulle led a force, aided by British vessels, which attempted to seize Dakar, Senegal in 1940, but it was repulsed. A month later, he was able to capture Douala, Cameroon; Brazzaville was also occupied and a powerful transmitter was erected in order to make daily Free French broadcasts heard in distant areas.

Following World War II, colonial rule continued, but there was a rapid upsurge of nationalism among native Africans. France itself had been economically devastated by the war and only slowly recovered with great amounts of foreign assistance provided by the United States. Political extremism, both rightist and leftist (communist) was rampant, making or-

derly French government all but impossible. Félix Houphouët-Boigny, a nationalist leader in Ivory Coast, organized the Democratic African Rally (RDA) with associated parties in most of France's West African colonies; the allied party succeeded in electing almost all of the area's deputies to the Assembly in Paris between 1947 and 1950. The relatively small number of African delegates allowed by the constitution allied themselves with the communist deputies during this period in an effort to gain support for their nationalist viewpoint, but that allegiance was discontinued in 1950.

France was severely drained by the communist rebellion within its Indochinese colonies, including Vietnam, during the postwar period which ended in a military disaster for the French in 1954. Immediately, a second total rebellion was mounted by the Algerian National Liberation Front which resulted in devastating warfare within that colony for seven more years, with accompanying additional strain upon the French economy. Principally for those reasons, the French were in no position effectively to oppose nationalist demands of their African colonies.

The Overseas Reform Act *(Loi Cadre)* of 1956 gave the African colonies internal autonomy, leaving matters of defense and foreign policy to France in an effort to quiet the demands for total independence. After Charles de Gaulle assumed almost absolute powers in France in 1958, he announced the creation of the French Community, the first step towards granting total independence to the colonies. Guinea, led by Sékou Touré, rejected the plan and that colony gained immediate independence.

Senegal and Mali were joined into the Federation of Mali in 1959 and France made some other minor changes, but granted full independence to all its remaining colonies in West and Equatorial Africa in 1960.

East Africa and the Indian Ocean: Madagascar, French Somaliland, and Indian Ocean Islands

The immense island of Madagascar was known to navigators since the 15th century, but there was no attempt at colonization. The Hindu Merina (Hova) people of Indonesian and Malaysian descent lived in the central highlands; persons of Arab and African heritage inhabited the coastal areas. There was only a brief period when the island was under single control during the 16th century, established by Sakalava (Arab) rulers.

The Merina Kingdom became dominant in the 18th century under King Andrianampoinamerina (1787–1810); he and his successors alternately encouraged the

The Colonial Period

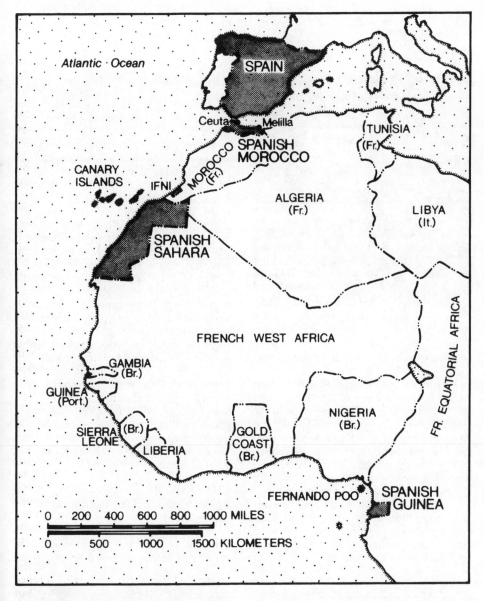

tional uprising suppressed only after months of bitter fighting, which resulted in the deaths of more than 10,000 people of the island. Subsequent constitutional reform in France lessened the tensions in Madagascar, and led to the establishment of the Malagasy Republic within the French Community in 1958. The Republic became fully independent in 1960.

France also colonized smaller islands chains in the Indian Ocean, including the Comoros and the Seychelles, as well as the island of Mauritius. Elsewhere, France colonized Mayotte in the Comoros islands in 1843 and extended its influence to the whole archipelago. In 1912 the four Comoros islands formally became a French colony administered from Madagascar. At French settlements in Mauritius, some intermarriage between French and Africans resulted in the evolution of a stable group of people now known as Creoles. France colonized the Seychelles in the 18th century, but lost them to Britain as a consequence of the Napoleonic Wars.

The tiny, sun-blistered colony of French Somaliland came into existence when treaties were signed with local chieftains in 1862. This colonization, as well as that of the British and Italians in the area, was to secure the regions south of the Suez Canal, then under construction, in order to prevent any disruption of shipping. The only asset of the territory was a deep, natural harbor facing the Gulf of Aden. At the turn of the century, a railroad from Addis Ababa, Ethiopia to Djibouti was completed and was thereafter the prime source of revenue. This colony achieved independence from France in June 1977 and is now known as the Republic of Djibouti.

French and British in their tentative efforts at colonization so that neither would gain the upper hand. Between 1775 and 1824, the island was a stronghold of marauding pirates, including John Avery, Captain Mission and William Kidd. The pirates even formed a republic called Libertalia, which was of brief duration.

Other nations of the world later established commercial relations with the Malagasy people; a treaty of peace, friendship and commerce between the United States and Madagascar was signed in 1881. During this period, British influence in the interior became strong. In 1869, Merina Queen Ranavolona I and her Court were converted to Protestantism. French interests continued to dominate the coastline.

At the Berlin Conference of 1885, as a result of concession by the French to the British in other parts of Africa, Great Britain supported the establishment of a French Protectorate over Madagascar. This status led to the end of the Merina Kingdom. General Joseph Simon Galliene, the first French governor, with the aid of French troops, unified the entire island.

The people—particularly the Merinas—had little use for French rule. In 1916 they rose unsuccessfully in bloody rebellion. The differences between the pro-French coastal inhabitants and those of the interior was expressed in this movement for independence, which was limited to the people of the highlands. After the fall of France in World War II, Madagascar, first administered by the Vichy (pro-Nazi) government of France, was occupied in 1942 by the British to prevent possible Japanese seizure of the strategic island. The Free French gained control in 1943. By 1947, an independence movement had become overwhelming and there was a na-

Kaiser Wilhelm II of Germany

The Colonial Period

THE AMERICANS

For detail on the role of the United States in Africa's colonial period, see Liberia, under *The Past: Political and Economic History*.

KING LEOPOLD AND THE BELGIANS
The Belgian Congo, Ruanda-Urundi

The Belgian efforts at colonization in the Congo region of West Africa call to mind the name of one man: Henry Stanley. Following his birth in Wales, he migrated to the United States where he became an author, soldier and adventurer, fighting on both sides in the American Civil War. Seeking new adventure, he turned to Africa and went to locate the Scottish missionary, Dr. David Livingstone, who had disappeared while exploring central Africa. After locating Dr. Livingstone on the shores of Lake Tanganyika in 1871, he explored the lake regions of the continent and then proceeded westward to the Congo River region. It took him three years to traverse the length of the river; he arrived on the Atlantic coast in 1877 and departed for Europe.

Stanley was immediately summoned by King Leopold II of Belgium, who saw in this explorer a means to compete in the scramble for colonial territory in Africa. Stanley accepted the offer of employment and returned to the Congo, entering into treaties on behalf of King Leopold with the native chieftains. The curious thing about this colonization is that it was not on behalf of the Belgian nation—this was Leopold's personal project.

At the Berlin Conference of 1885, when great portions of Africa were divided between the European colonial powers, King Leopold had personally been awarded the area south of the Congo River as far as Portuguese possessions in the Angola region. Although the area was referred to as "The Congo Free State," the years which followed were harsh. King Leopold used forced labor and torture were to wring production and wealth from the colony; it is estimated that up to 8 million Africans lost their lives during the 23 years of Leopold's exploitation. By 1904, knowledge of these repressive conditions had become known in Europe and the United States; in response to pressure from Britain, Germany and the U.S., King Leopold sent a commission to investigate conditions. The report of the commission, issued in late 1905, indicated that the actions of Leopold's administrators were scandalously cruel and improper. Bowing to continued international pressure, the Belgian parliament passed an act in 1908 annexing the Congo State of Belgium.

During the period at the turn of the century, there was friction between the British, French and King Leopold over control

Benito Mussolini

of the upper (southern) Nile area in the region near Lake Albert. As a result of a compromise, the Congo Free State received a small portion of territory known as the Lado enclave, which reverted to the Sudan (Anglo-Egyptian Sudan) at the death of Leopold in 1910. There were a variety of treaties between the several colonial powers that gradually and firmly demarcated the borders of the Congo region.

Under Leopold, the copper-rich Katanga (now Shaba) area had been opened up, and economic development based on that region's wealth proceeded forward under Belgian administrators. The general approach was that the native Africans should not be given too many privileges lest they become restless. Due to efficient administration, however, the per capita income rose to be one of the highest in colonial Africa.

Belgian forces moved to occupy the northwestern part of German East Africa at the start of World War I. This region, consisting of what is now Rwanda and Burundi, was then called Ruanda-Urundi and became a mandated territory assigned to Belgium in 1923; it was joined administratively with the Congo, which was given a wide degree of autonomy at the same time. Between the two world wars, Belgium made substantial capital investments in the Congo, including construction of railways connecting Kinshasa (then called Leopoldville) to the mineral wealth of Shaba (then called Katanga).

Nationalist pressures on the part of the native Africans mushroomed after World War II. Belgium, prostrated by the battles and German occupation of the war, was actually in no position to resist this movement. In a completely unexpected change, Belgium announced in January 1960 that it would grant independence to the Congo as of June 30th of the same year. It is highly probable that the Belgians hoped that a quick grant of independence would result in chaos to a degree that would justify continued colonial control. This hope, motivated by the desire for further wealth, was almost realized.

THE SPANISH
Spanish Sahara, Spanish Guinea, Ifni, Ceuta, Melilla

The colonization and division of Africa between the major powers in the 19th century was during a period when Spain,

Haile Selassie enters Addis Ababa in 1941

having formerly been a powerful colonial nation, was in a state of decline. The result was that Spain succeeded in claiming Spanish Sahara (also called Spanish Morocco, Rio de Oro), a barren desert area, and Spanish Guinea, a small section of oppressive jungle on the west coast at the Equator, which included the island of Fernando Poo. The enclaves of Ifni, Ceuta and Melilla along the coast of Morocco were holdovers from the time when both Morocco and Spain were controlled by Moorish Arabs. The areas in which Spain was able to lay claim were available largely because of lack of interest in them on the part of other stronger colonial nations.

Although Spain was technically supposed to be in partnership with the French in Morocco during the colonial period, the actual control was by the French. Spain ceded its theoretical protectorate right to Morocco in 1956 when the French granted it independence; a small part of southern Morocco was relinquished in 1958. The enclave of Ifni was returned to Morocco in 1968; Ceuta and Melilla, coastal cities along the coast where Spain and Morocco are closest, remain under Spanish control with the tacit consent of the king of Morocco.

Wind-swept and arid, Spanish Sahara is inhabited by a handful of nomadic Berber-Bedouin tribesmen who had been left to themselves by the Spanish. There had been almost no interest in this area on the part of the rest of the world prior to 1966 when extensive and rich deposits of phosphate were located. After withstanding pressures from the UN, Morocco and Mauritania for a decade, Spain vacated the territory in 1976 (see Western Sahara).

In 1778, Portugal ceded the island of Fernando Pó to Spain. (The Treaty of Tordesillas of 1494, by which the Pope settled territorial claims between Spain and Portugal stemming from the discovery of the New World, had given gave the Portuguese exclusive rights in Africa.) In the 19th century, however, Fernando Pó was used by the British navy in its efforts to suppress the slave trade. Many of the freed slaves were settled on the island and the British assumed responsibility for its administration. The island was abandoned for this purpose when the British shifted their operations to Sierra Leone in 1843. Spain reoccupied the island in 1844 and by 1879 was using it as a penal settlement for Cubans considered too dangerous to be kept on that island. Economic development only began after the Spanish-American war of 1898, when Fernando Pó and its neighboring coastal enclave became Spain's last significant tropical colony. The two provinces were collectively known as Spanish Guinea.

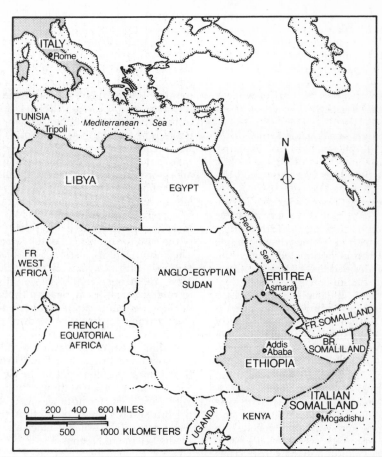

The Italians in Africa

There was no significant nationalist movement reported during the postwar period and no effort was made to prepare the colony for independence. The mainland portion of present-day Equatorial Guinea consisted of an undesirable, oppressively hot and humid area acquired at the Berlin Conference in 1885, which was joined administratively to form a single colony with Fernando Pó.

In the mid-1960s, Spain began to bring increasing pressure on the British to cede the Gibraltar peninsula on the ground that it, lying at the entrance to the Mediterranean Sea, belonged to Spain by virtue of natural geography. In order to reinforce its arguments, Spain granted Spanish Guinea independence in 1968, giving little prior indication of its intention to do so.

THE GERMANS
West Africa: Togo, Cameroon

Although there was some German missionary and trading activity on the coasts of Togo and Cameroon from 1845 onward, these areas also were open to religious and commercial efforts of the remaining European nations. German missionaries arrived as early as 1847, followed soon by

German traders. In the rush to acquire colonies during the 1880s, Gustav Nachtigal negotiated treaties with the Ewe chiefs of the region at Togoville, located on the banks of Lake Togo. The most powerful of them was King Mlapa III.

During the thirty years that followed the announcement of a German protectorate in Togo, there was slow penetration into the interior. The borders with the surrounding colonies were adjusted several times by treaty. The rule of the German administrators was harsh and exploitive; there was no effort to provide any benefit to the people of the region, since the only interest was commercial. Large numbers of Togolese were jailed and forced to labor for the Germans. At the outbreak of World War I, British and French troops invaded Togo from their respective neighboring colonies, Gold Coast and Dahomey. German forces surrendered unconditionally, and Britain and France occupied separate areas of the territory. Germany renounced its colonial territories in the Treaty of Versailles, which concluded the war. In 1922 the newly created League of Nations charged France and Britain with the administration of their re-

The Colonial Period

spective spheres of occupation as part of the League Mandate system. The territory was jointly administered for five years, but was then split into two areas with the British in a smaller, western portion and the remainder controlled by the French. The British area became part of what is now Ghana, formerly known as Gold Coast.

The Portuguese navigator, Fernão do Pó (Fernando Pó in Spanish) had explored the coast of Cameroon in 1472; the prolific shrimp in the River Wouri inspired the sailors to christen the river *Rio dos Camarões*, meaning "River of Shrimp" in Portuguese. There was a variety of commercial activity during the 19th century precolonial period, a time when no single European nation dominated Cameroon. The British decided in 1884 to annex Cameroon and sent an emissary to sign treaties with the local inhabitants. He arrived just days too late—spurred by the rush for colonies, a German consul had already visited Douala, the seaport, and obtained the signatures of the chieftains on treaties annexing Cameroon to Germany; the area was named Kameroun, a Germanization of the original Portuguese name.

The colonial rule of the Germans was similar to that in Togo—exploitative and often cruel. There was some penetration into the interior but control was not established in the northern regions by the Germans. Throughout the colony it became difficult to locate the tribal chieftains, who went into hiding to avoid possible punishment or being held hostage by the colonial administrators. In exchange for support of French claims in Morocco, Germany was granted about 100,000 square miles of Congo (Brazzaville).

Cameroon was the scene of an extensive campaign early in World War I. British and French forces wrested control from Germany, and by the terms of the Treaty of Versailles, Cameroon was split between the two powers. Kamerun, as it was then called, was stripped from Germany and made a mandate of the League of Nations in 1922; administrative responsibilities for the mandate were shared by Britain and France. Modern Cameroon results from the merger of the French and a portion of the English areas.

South Africa: South West Africa

The Germans first entered the region of South-West Africa in the 1840s in a strictly missionary effort, similar to British efforts in South Africa among the native Africans. This outpost, called the Bethany Mission, slowly expanded during the following decades, and numbers of Germans went into the interior from Walfish (Walvis, Walvisch) Bay. The German missionaries twice asked for the British to assume pro-

tection of the Bay area, and in 1877 this request was granted.

There was substantial German migration into South-West Africa during the last quarter of the 19th century. After quarreling with the British for several months, the Germans proclaimed a protectorate over the area in 1884; administration initially was by the German Colonial Company, but in 1892 South-West Africa came under the control of the German government. The migrants to the area were principally farmers and herdsmen who occupied the scarce and choice lands suitable for cultivation and grazing. Discovery of mineral wealth led to further measures designed to exploit the wealth of the land for the benefit of the Germans. The Bantu Hereros, also known as Damaras, rose in bloody revolt from 1904 to 1908, requiring 20,000 German troops to finally defeat them. Several thousand of these people fled to neighboring Botswana (then Bechuanaland) during the revolt.

Within a year of the start of World War I, a combined British and South African *Boer* army was able to defeat the German force of about 3,500 stationed in South-West Africa. The territory was assigned to the British-*Boer* Union of South Africa as a mandate by the Allied Council and later by the League of Nations.

East Africa: Tanzania
(German East Africa)

Initial exploration of the East African coast area occurred in 1860–1865 when Karl von der Decken entered the region, but it was not until 1884, when Karl Peters signed a series of treaties with native kings that the colonial effort actually started. The agreements provided for a sale of land to the Germans for a very small fraction of its probable value. The German status in the area was recognized at the Berlin Conference of 1885, and the German East Africa Company was created to administer the colony.

In the early colonial period, the Germans also acquired lands in adjacent Uganda and coastal Kenya by signing treaties in the former, and coercing the Arab viceroy in Zanzibar to surrender lands in the latter. These were given up by treaties to the British in exchange for a somewhat worthless island in the North Sea and other minor concessions; treaties were also entered into with King Leopold of Belgium and the Portuguese which fixed the border of German East Africa. Penetration into the interior was slow and difficult. The native Africans resisted the German movement; there was a violent uprising of the Muslim Arabs along the coast (1888–90), a revolt of the Wahehe (Wahaya) people (1891–93) and a combined Muslim-

Angoni rebellion (1903–05). The Angonis, a Bantu group related to the warlike Zulus of South Africa, were all but exterminated during this conflict, known as the Maji-Maji Rebellion, in which the Germans ruthlessly destroyed crops and villages, rendering a large area completely desolate.

In 1914, 300,000 British, South African *Boer* and Indian troops invaded German East Africa. A force of slightly more than 200 German officers, commanding native troops numbering between 2,500 and 4,000 fended off the massive attack for four years under the spirited and brilliant leadership of General Paul Von Lettow-Vorbeck.

With great effort, the allies slowly pushed Lettow-Vorbeck from German East Africa into Mozambique and Rhodesia. The Germans refused to stop fighting, and the battles ceased only when their commander was informed that the Armistice of November 11, 1918 had been signed, ending World War I, and providing for the evacuation of Germans from German East Africa.

The British received a mandate from the League of Nations to administer the former German colony, which was renamed Tanganyika. Substantial numbers of German immigrants who had established large, prosperous farms and plantations, were deported to Germany; a few were later permitted to return to the British colony.

In 1890 the Tutsi kingdoms of Ruanda and neighboring Urundi were incorporated into German East Africa. During World War I Belgians occupied the area, and in 1923 Belgium was granted a League of Nations mandate to administer Ruanda-Urundi. It administered the mandate through existing Tutsi political structures. As a consequence, the Tutsi remained a privileged and dominant minority in Ruanda after World War II. These colonies would later become present-day Rwanda and Burundi.

THE SOUTH AFRICANS
Namibia (German South West Africa, South-West Africa)

The Union of South Africa received a mandate from the League of Nations in 1919 over what had been German South-West Africa. After The UN came into existence, it exerted pressures to grant the people of Namibia their independence, a goal that was finally achieved only on March 21, 1990.

THE ITALIANS
The Eastern Horn: Somalia, Ethiopia, and Eritrea

In comparison to other European nations, Italian colonial efforts were relatively weak and delayed, largely because

Italy itself was a weakly defined nation through much of the 19th century. Following agreement among the stronger powers in 1885, the Italians signed treaties during the next four years with the three Muslim sultans in the "horn" region of East Africa. Although Italian Somaliland was acquired as a colony, full control was not established in the area until as late as 1927. The bleak, uniformly hot and dry region was considered to be valueless as a colony and the nomadic Cushites and Somalis who lived in the region, including part of Kenya and Ethiopia, were difficult to control.

Eritreans continued to live a life of localized independence until swept into the maelstrom of events set off by two contending forces in the late 19th century: Italian efforts to colonize the area and efforts of Menelik II, king of Ethiopia, to assemble, by conquest, modern Ethiopia. British and French Somaliland, both areas somewhat more desirable, separated Somaliland from Eritrea, a semiarid expanse given to the Italians by a lack of interest on the part of more powerful colonial nations. Benito Mussolini, the fascist dictator, came to power in Italy in 1922. He began to flex colonial muscles, eyeing with envy the vast territories taken without resistance by the rest of Europe in Africa and elsewhere.

From bases in Eritrea, Italian forces invaded ancient Ethiopia in 1936; Emperor Haile Selassie begged for assistance at the League of Nations, but his plea fell on deaf ears. The fate of Ethiopia had been decided earlier in Paris, when the British and French gave the Italians wide authority over Ethiopia in an effort to appease Mussolini. The figurehead King of Italy proclaimed himself Emperor of Ethiopia, a title recognized at once by Austria and Germany and in 1938 by Great Britain and France.

Ethiopia was joined with Somaliland and Eritrea to form Italian East Africa; initially there was some effort at economic development and road building. However, an attempt was made to assassinate the Italian governor at Addis Ababa in 1937. A reign of terror followed, with widespread arrests and summary executions in an attempt to terrorize the population. Further unrest became intense, and by 1940 the Italians were besieged from within by Ethiopian terrorists and from without by British forces. Exactly five years after the first entry of Italian troops, Haile Selassie entered Addis Ababa at the head of a British-Ethiopian force and Italian rule was ended.

During the postwar period, a plan whereby Eritrea was to become a part of Ethiopia was promulgated at the UN; following its acceptance, the two were joined. The UN granted a trusteeship over Somalia to Italy in 1949; this area had been occupied by the British since the early years of World War II. The trusteeship provided for complete independence within ten years, which was achieved in 1960.

North Africa: Libya

Although many Italian immigrants had settled in North Africa, particularly in Libya and Tunisia, there was no effort to colonize the area until the 20th century. The ambition had been present for decades—when the British and French settled the Fashoda Crisis (see *The French*), the Italians protested since they did not share in the division of the Sahara region of the African continent. Using a short-term ultimatum to provoke a conflict, Italian forces invaded Libya in 1911 in an attempt to seize control from the Ottoman Turks. After taking a few coastal towns, a protectorate status was proclaimed by the Italians.

The Muslim *Sanusi* sect immediately organized a revolt that continued until about 1931 at various places within Libya. Because the Arab-Berber people were given only the poorest parts of the land in which to live, the people of Libya, though eventually subdued, continued to have a smoldering hatred for the Italians.

Italian rule was ended in the two years following 1940. Extensive campaigns were waged by the Allies throughout the land against the Nazis, who had gained control of North Africa when it became apparent that Italy could not act with military authority in the area. The country, historically divided into three provinces of Cyrenaica, Tripolitania and Fezzan, was split between Allied powers at the end of World War II. Fezzan was occupied by the French, and the remaining two provinces were under British administration. Libya's status was submitted to the United Nations, which adopted a resolution providing for independence by the end of 1951.

Ethiopia's Emperor Haile Selassie aboard a U.S. warship with President Franklin D. Roosevelt, then on his way home from the 1945 conference in the Crimea.

NORTH AFRICA

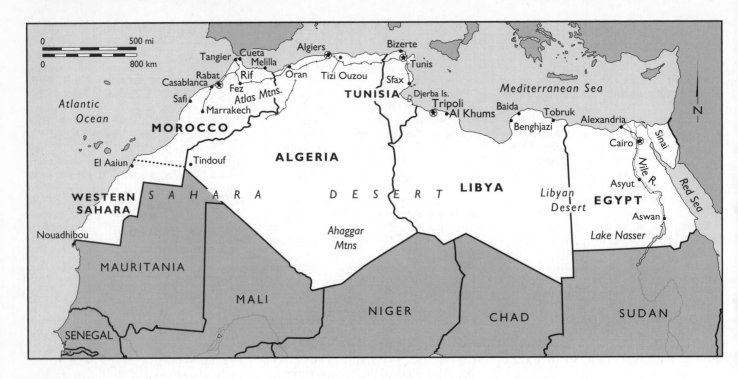

The Democratic and Popular Republic of Algeria

BASIC FACTS

Area: 2,460,500 sq. km. = 950,000 sq. mi. (almost as large as the U.S. east of the Mississippi River)

Population: 33,900,000 (UN 2007 est.)

Capital City: Algiers

Climate: In the coastal region, temperate Mediterranean weather prevails. Inland, it is temperate and cooler in the high altitudes of the mountains. South, in the Sahara Desert, it is hot and dry.

Neighboring Countries: Morocco (northwest); Tunisia and Libya (east); Niger (southeast); Mali, Mauritania (southwest)

Official Language: Arabic

Other Principal Languages: Berber languages, including Kabyle, Tamazight, Taznatit, Tumzabt; Tamahaq, spoken by Tuaregs, and French

Ethnic Groups: Arab-Berber 99%, European less than 1%

Principal Religions: Sunni Muslim (state religion) 99%, Christian and Jewish 1%.

Principal Commercial Products: Petroleum and natural gas 97%

GNI Per Capita: $2,730 (World Bank 2006)

Currency: Algerian dinar

Former Colonial Status: French Colony (1831–1870); integral part of France (1870–1962)

National Day: Revolution Day, November 1st

Chief of State: Abdelaziz Bouteflika, President (since March 1999)

National Flag: Two vertical stripes, green and white, with a red crescent enclosing a five-pointed star in the center.

Land and People

Algeria was a seat of civilization long before recorded history. Its ports and commerce were the lifeblood of early times. The dazzling white city of Algiers, founded about 1,000 years ago, is a cosmopolitan crossroads of the East and West, climbing the Atlas Mountains from the blue Mediterranean. South of the fertile coastal regions and the mountainous areas stretches the vast Sahara Desert, where caravans still cross the arid wastelands. Gleaming modern highways now lead to green oases and oil fields.

Algeria has a 620-mile coastline on the Mediterranean. Two Atlas Mountain chains cross the country horizontally, dividing Algeria into three geographic zones: the northern Mediterranean zone, the high arid plateau between the ranges, and the Sahara. The northern zone, known as the Tell, is a sun-bathed coastal area where vineyards, and orange, fig, and olive trees flourish in valleys and on hillsides. The high plateau is primarily the home of grazing herds of goats, sheep, and camels. South of the Sahara, the immense Ahaggar Mountains are the territory of the Tuaregs, a Berber group with singular customs—the men, not the women, are veiled.

Struggling to maintain its own language and identity is Algeria's Berber-speaking minority. Representing 20% to 30% of the population, Berbers are the original inhabitants of North Africa. They fled to the mountains to resist successive waves of invaders—Romans, Arabs, Turks and French—and preserved both language (*tamazight*) and customs despite conversion to Islam. Berber women, for example, go without the veil. The singer Lounès Matoub, who was assassinated in an ambush in 1998, gave musical voice to Berber nationalism.

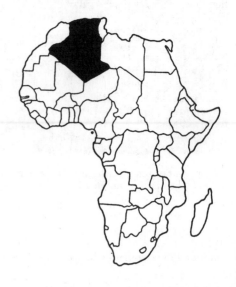

30

A workman with wire for new railway signal lines

The Past: Political and Economic History

For early history, see *Historical Background* and *The Colonial Period: The French*.

After a bitter eight-year struggle against Arab nationalists from 1954 to 1962, France granted independence to Algeria four months after a cease-fire had been negotiated. More than one million French citizens and other European residents had fled the country.

Ahmed Ben Bella, a prominent member of the National Liberation Front (FLN), which had led the fight for independence, headed the new government. A wide range of reforms was undertaken, including the redistribution of land. Closer ties were established with the European communist-bloc nations. Internal tensions within the FLN led to the quiet removal of Ben Bella in 1965. He was placed under house arrest, but was never charged or tried for any crime.

Colonel Houari Boumedienne was installed as chief of state with widespread support of the party leadership. Boumedienne, the former defense minister, established a 26-man Revolutionary Council to assist in governing the nation. He continued in power, weathering a 1967 attempt to oust him and a 1968 assassination plot.

In 1967, the Algerian government began creating new political institutions, beginning with communal and provincial assemblies. A new constitution, openly Marxist, was adopted in late 1976, and President Boumedienne was reelected with a 99% majority. A new National Assembly was elected in 1977. The 261 members were selected from a list of 783 candidates, all of whom were FLN members. President Boumedienne died in late December 1978, the victim of a rare blood disease. In early 1979 elections were held in which there was but one candidate: Colonel Chadli Bendjedid, a former commander and informal coordinator of defense during Boumedienne's illness. He also became secretary-general of the FLN, the two positions being closely interwoven in the one-party governmental structure.

In early 1980 Algeria was shaken by riots led by Muslim fundamentalists who sacked hotels, cafes and restaurants where alcohol—a violation of Islamic teachings—was served. Algeria had always been one of the most secular nations of the Arab world, keeping religion *strictly* out of government, but the successful Islamic revolution in Iran sparked a wave of back-to-Koranic-basics movements throughout Islamic lands. The rioters also attacked several "pleasure houses" provided for Algerian troops stationed near the border with Tunisia.

President Bendjedid was elected to a third five-year term in 1989. But in a decade, Algeria had changed drastically, as the consequences of lavish, but nonproductive spending by the FLN finally hit home. Algeria's external debt was impossibly high—$28 billion—and required 80% of export earnings to pay principal and interest on it. There was little left for social services and productive investment.

The FLN leadership had squandered oil royalties in "window-dressing" projects that sustained its popularity (at least on the surface), but failed to produce economic development. Widespread corruption in the government added insult to injury. By the 1990s the unemployment rate of skilled people exceeded 30%. Young people, raised with expectations of a better life, faced a bleak prospect. With their dreams shattered, they had one of two alternatives: emigration, or Islamic fundamentalism. The first choice was unavailable.

Islamic fundamentalism offered an alternative to the FLN, and *any* alternative would be better, they reasoned. The message of Islamic fundamentalists throughout North Africa and the Middle East was quite simple: anti-Westernism. This program would bring Algeria's fundamentalists into violent conflict with the secular and westernizing elements of the FLN regime.

In response to external and internal pressures, President Bendjedid legalized political parties in 1989, and the first to register was the Islamic Salvation Front (FIS). It had already been clandestinely exploiting discontent among young people. As the movement gathered steam, President Bendjedid firmly warned against "all attempts to return Islam to the era of charlatanism and political opportunism," but it didn't work. FIS candidates won clear majorities in municipal and provincial elections in 1990, and set the stage for an energetic campaign in the forthcoming parliamentary elections.

The government declared a state of siege, arrested and jailed two FIS leaders—Abassi Madani and Ali Belhadj—and postponed the elections. When the elections were finally held in December 1991, the first round produced a striking victory for the FIS. It won 188 seats outright, and seemed virtually certain to obtain an absolute majority in the second round.

Before the runoffs could take place in January 1992, however, President Bendjedid resigned and the army intervened

Algeria

to cancel the elections. A five-member Higher State Council, chaired by Mohamed Boudiaf, imposed military rule. The regime declared a state of emergency, disbanded the FIS and dissolved all 411 FIS-controlled local authorities. On June 29 President Boudiaf was assassinated by a member of his own bodyguard with alleged links with Islamists. Violence increased and Algeria descended into civil war. The Armed Islamic Group (GIA: *Groupe Islamique Armé*) was identified as the main group behind the violence.

Brig. Gen. Liamine Zéroual was subsequently chosen as interim president. Armed fundamentalist forces, principally the GIA and the Islamic Salvation Army (AIS: *Armée Islamique du Salut*), were well equipped with modern weaponry supplied by Iraq and Iran via Sudan. Murder, massacre, and destruction became common.

The military embarked on an antiterrorist campaign in 1994–5. Violent rebels were interned in camps in the remote desert. In rural areas, informal militias were armed as self-defense forces. To legitimize military rule, General Zéroual held presidential elections in 1995, and won a comfortable majority of 64.5%. According to official figures, 75% of the electorate turned out for the election.

The victorious military proposed a new constitution in November 1996. Even though it proclaimed Islam as the state religion, it provided that no party or candidate could have a religious affiliation as a basis for candidacy. Infuriated Islamists opposed it, and the GIA vowed to slit the throat of any person who left home to vote. The government mustered some 300,000 military and police to safeguard the election, and 85% of the electorate approved the proposed changes.

The first parliamentary elections under the new constitution were held in 1997 and resulted in Algeria's first multiparty legislature. A new party to support President Zéroual was created. Benefiting from massive administrative support, the National Democratic Rally (RND: *Rassemblement National et Démocratique*) was the big winner, taking 156 seats (out of 380) with 38% of the vote. Coming in a distant second was the moderate Islamic party, Movement of Society for Peace (MSP), which won 69 seats. The FLN, once Algeria's only party, came in third, taking 64 seats. Two rival secular Berber-based parties, the Socialist Forces Front (FFS) of Hocine Aït-Ahmed and the Rally for Culture and Democracy (RCD) of anti-Islamist Saïd Sadi, each won 19 seats. Some 300,000 security forces were again deployed around the country to guard against attacks by Islamist militants.

Despite comfortable majorities in parliament and in the government, President Zéroual surprised his countrymen by re-signing his office in September 1998, effective with the selection of a successor in April 1999 elections.

In the shadowy world of Algerian politics, characterized more by opacity than transparency, Zéroual had lost the confidence of Algeria's real rulers, the army. With the president's resignation, hopes that new elections could help national reconciliation and move Algeria beyond its current impasse abounded. Zéroual himself had promised free and fair elections, but they were not to be.

By January 1999 it was clear the army had rallied to a consensus candidate, the former foreign minister, Abdelaziz Bouteflika. In March, seven candidates were in the running, but when President Zéroual refused to meet with them to discuss charges of electoral fraud, six withdrew, leaving Abdelaziz Bouteflika the sole candidate. The election was held; Bouteflika was "elected," and once again Algerian hopes were dashed.

Given the dubious nature of his election, President Bouteflika needed to prove he was more than a creature of the generals. In July he launched a "civil concord" initiative, putting his credibility on the line almost immediately. To achieve stability he offered amnesty to all but the worst offenders in Algeria's eight-year civil war. They would have to lay down their arms by mid-January 2000; if not they would be wiped out.

The results of the amnesty are debatable at best. The government formalized a deal with the Islamic Salvation Army (AIS), the largest rebel group and military wing of the banned Islamic Salvation Front (FIS). The two most notorious armed movements—the Armed Islamic Group (GIA) and the Salafist Group for Preaching and Combat (GSPC)—rejected the amnesty and stepped up their attacks. In 2000, 9,000 more Algerians were killed. Organized into small cells, the militants proved difficult to eradicate. Violence remained as intractable as ever, though, for the most part, significantly diminished.

In early 2001 the governing coalition, which included the National Liberation Front (FLN), National Democratic Rally (RND), Rally for Culture and Democracy (RCD), Movement of Society for Peace (MSP), National Republican Alliance (ANR), and the Ennahda (Renaissance) Movement, criticized the president for failing to deal with the nation's social and economic crisis. Almost 40% of Algeria's 30 million people lived below the poverty line. Official figures put unemployment at 40%. Housing stock was inadequate, and there had been riots over the government's allocation of apartments.

The disillusionment and discontent felt by average Algerians burst into ugly anti-regime violence in the spring of 2001. Riots in Kabylia, the Berber heartland, showed the disaffection of Berber youth. Their shouted slogans laid bare Algeria's social and economic crisis: "You cannot kill us," they screamed at the national police, "we are already dead." "Give us work and housing and hope and there will be calm." The targets of their destructive rage were the symbols of government presence and occupation.

Violence in Kabylia persisted through the legislative elections of 2002. By then, security forces had killed more than 100 young people; the regime seemed utterly incapable of resolving the crisis. In March 2002 President Bouteflika announced that Tamazight, the Berber language, would be recognized as a national language, and in April the National Assembly amended the constitution to this effect.

The gesture was symbolic and partial, a palliative that did not placate. It did, however, bring out the darker side of Berber nationalism: intransigence, inflexibility, and a totalitarian willingness to use violence to impose uniformity of action. Berber leaders noted the language was only "national," not "official" and thus not the equivalent of Arabic. They rejected the government's offer and called on Berbers to boycott the May elections.

Both Kabyle-based parties, Saïd Sadi's Rally for Culture and Democracy (RCD) and Hocine Aït-Ahmed's Socialist Forces Front (FFS), boycotted the elections in deference to local opinion. Activists closed virtually every polling place in Kabylia, and where that was impossible, physically prevented the few people who wanted to vote from getting to the polls. In the administrative region of Tizi Ouzou, the Berber capital, voter turn out was 1.8%.

The biggest winner was the FLN, which won 199 seats—an absolute majority—in the National Assembly, but achieved with

President Abdelaziz Bouteflika

Berber cultural claims sometimes erupt in violence

only 35% of the vote. Much of the credit for bringing the party back from the wilderness went to Prime Minister Ali Benflis, the party's new secretary-general. He had campaigned vigorously and suggested both the party's capacity to reform itself and his own desire to do so. During the campaign he openly denounced the party's old guard, declaring they barred younger people from participating and believed in keeping women at home.

The election revealed Algeria's fundamental political pattern of three main ideological blocs. About a third of the electorate could be described as nationalist, supporting the FLN or other government-endorsed party like the RND. An Islamist bloc (MRN, MSP, Ennahda) attracts the loyalty of 15% to 20%, while a Berber bloc (FFS, RCD) can secure the support of 10% to 15%. Given this distribution of sentiment, coalition governments will remain a constant feature of the political system.

Prime Minister Benflis, whose commitment to reform appeared genuine and whose popularity seemed to be growing, was fired by President Bouteflika in early May 2003. The sacking splintered the FLN. When Benflis supporters moved to make the dynamic young leader the party's presidential nominee, Bouteflika loyalists immobilized them in the courts with the acquiescence of compliant jurists.

In the April 2004 election, President Bouteflika ran for a second term against five opponents, one of whom was Ali Benflis. The army promised to remain loyal, but it appears to have encouraged all and backed one. Defying expectations, the race was anything but close. President Bouteflika won by a landslide, taking 84.99% of the votes cast. His nearest opponent, Ali Benflis, the man who many thought stood a chance of beating the incumbent, receiving a humiliating 6.42%. The least skeptical analysis of the outcome is that Algerians supported a man whose policy of national reconciliation had reduced political violence.

"Reduced" is the operative word; Islamist terror groups continued to take their toll. The most violent of these is the Salafist Group for Prayer and Combat (GSPC), which pledged its loyalty to al-Qaeda. The group gained international notoriety in 2003 by kidnapping some 32 European tourists in the Algerian Sahara. The army managed to free 17, but the remaining 15, held by a different GPSC cell, were ransomed by the German government for a reported $6 million.

The sum made the kidnappers' leader, Amari Saïfi, the most powerful regional terrorist and the major buyer of arms from local smugglers and bandits. In the spring of 2004, Saïfi's group became the object of coordinated international action. With American surveillance intelligence, Saïfi's group was flushed from its Algerian sanctuary into Niger, where the Nigerien army pursued remnants of the group into northern Chad. There a GSPC remnant ultimately fell into the hands of Movement for Justice and Democracy in Chad (MDJT) rebels in their Tibesti stronghold. One of the survivors was Saïfi, whom the MDJT seems to have auctioned off to the highest bidder. Libya, ever generous with lubricating funds, won the auction and delivered Saïfi to Algerian authorities in October 2004. The incident proved the growing importance of the Sahel region—from Mauritania to Djibouti—as a potential terrorist training ground.

Closer to home, the government seemed to feel it was winning the war against terrorists and floated the notion of a general amnesty for all involved in the long civil war. In February 2005 President Bouteflika tallied up the cost of that conflict: $30 billion of damage to the country's infrastructure, and 150,000 dead—more than 6,000 of them, according to a government-commissioned report, victims of Algerian security forces.

In September 2005 President Bouteflika submitted his proposed general amnesty—the Charter for Peace and National Reconciliation (CPNR)—the electorate.

Algeria

The charter combined another amnesty offer to all but the most violent participants in the post-1992 killings with an implicit pardon for security forces accused of abuses in the antiterrorist campaign. The project passed overwhelmingly.

In February 2006 parliament enacted legislation to implement charter provisions. Three important aspects stand out: Members and supporters of armed groups are granted exemption from punishment, providing they did not commit collective massacres or rape and did not use explosives in public places. The "disappeared" are recognized as "victims of the national tragedy" and given the same status as "victims of terrorism." Their family members are entitled to compensation.

The law also provides that no legal proceedings may be initiated against members of the defense and security forces for actions taken to protect persons and property, safeguard the nation or preserve the institutions of the state. Significantly, this grant of immunity is coupled with strict punishment for anyone who might criticize the agents of past state terrorism. Those who "damage the respectability of civil servants who have served in a dignified manner" are subject to jail terms of three to five years and hefty fines. The corridors of power in Algeria are murky at best, but it seems clear the army leadership directed its own impunity be implemented, probably as the tradeoff for not opposing President Bouteflika's reelection campaign in 2004.

Those who wanted to take advantage of amnesty provisions in the Charter for Peace had until September 2006 to do so, but as the deadline approached it was clear that GSPC hardliners would remain deaf to the blandishments of national reconciliation. The group defiantly joined al-Qaeda in September 2006; the official announcement of association was symbolically made on September 11, by Ayman Zawahiri, al-Qaeda's second-ranking leader. Two coordinated truck bombs targeting Algiers police stations at the end of October, and an attack on foreign oil workers in December, announced the GSPC's return to violence. In January 2007 the group changed its name to Al-Qaeda of the Islamic Maghreb (AQIM). The rebranding was designed to gain publicity, funding, and recruits by establishing the group as the leader of international jihadism in North Africa.

The United States European Command described AQIM as running mobile training camps for Islamic militants from other North African countries. "They have been doing a lot of training: sort of here today gone tomorrow training in the wadis of northern Mali," said one spokesman. "We are not talking about fixed training sites like we had in Afghanistan. . . . These are meetings of trucks and tents for three days to a week, then they disperse." As militants dispersed to their home countries, there was an upsurge of violence throughout the region.

In Algeria the violence increased as parliamentary elections approached in mid-May 2007. Al Jazeera television ran a recruitment video for AQIM in early May; the tape showed suicide bombers preparing for three simultaneous attacks in Algiers that killed 33 people in April. AQIM urged anyone interested in becoming a suicide bomber to join its ranks.

Increasing violence provided background for the May 17, 2007 National Assembly elections, but AQIM's call for an election boycott probably had less effect on voter intentions than a general disillusionment with parliament and political process. Real power in the Algerian system resides in the murky penumbra of army and security networks that surrounds the presidential office. The electorate was largely indifferent choosing members of a rubber-stamp body. According to official figures (usually inflated), only 35.51% of the electorate made the effort to vote. A three-party alliance joining the FLN, the RND and the MSP in support of President Bouteflika won 249 of the 389 seats in the Assembly, a clear majority. Within the alliance, the FLN suffered the greatest defeat, losing 72 seats as voters registered their frustration with Algeria's basic paradox: an extraordinarily wealthy country seems unable to deliver improvement in the lives of its ordinary citizens.

In August 2008, AQIM struck again, this time in towns to the east of Algiers. In the deadliest attack, AQIM killed 45 people outside a policy academy in Les Issers.

The continued presence of AQIM may call into question the government's ability to provide security, but President Bouteflika has leveraged the country's situation to ensure his continued presence on the political scene. In November 2008, the parliament approved a constitutional change that would allow the president to run for a third term, though the opposition Rally for Culture and Democracy party said this would be "pathetic" and a "national humiliation." Bouteflika promptly won the uncompetitive April 2009 general election with over 90% of the vote.

The Present: Contemporary Issues

The conflict between the army and Islamists in Algeria is a struggle to define the country's identity and future. The army, francophone and secular, is adamantly opposed to Arab-speaking Islamists who advocate an Arab and Muslim identity for Algeria. President Bouteflika treds a narrow path between the two poles of identity.

Lounès Matoub

This was no better illustrated than in his support for an amended Family Code. The original 1984 Code, based in *sharia* law, was fundamentally hostile to women. They needed permission of a *wali*, or male tutor, in order to marry, and could only divorce if they could prove their husband crazy, incarcerated at least five years, or disappeared for at least ten. If a divorce were granted, the family home would go to the husband. The consequence was a growing number of women forced to live on Algerian streets and rummage through garbage for food and cardboard for housing.

The amended Family Code of 2005, strongly supported by President Bouteflika, remains rooted in Islamic law. The noxious provision that requires a woman to have permission from a male *wali* to marry is maintained, though slightly softened by granting a woman the right to chose her own *wali*. Polygamy remains, but a man must henceforth seek the approval of his wives, whose testimony must be verified by a judge, before taking another wife. In a divorce, the mother will keep the family dwelling if she is awarded custody of the children. Proxy marriages, whereby a woman could be married without even knowing it, are prohibited in the new text.

Algeria's Kabyle mountains, the Berber heartland, remain a focal point of opposition to the government. Kabylia is one of the country's poorest and most populous regions. Unemployment is rife, and Berber youth have few future expectations beyond present misery. People there complain of a lack of government assistance and claim they must survive on remittances from relatives who have emigrated to France.

Oil production started in 1957 at Hassi Messouad and Ejelek; it was quickly expanded through pipelines, refineries and additional wells for both petroleum and natural gas made possible by the investment of foreign oil companies. Since that time the hydrocarbon sector has come to dominate Algeria's economy. It accounts for almost 30% of the country's GDP and over 98% of export revenues (2006). It has about 13.3 billion barrels of proven reserves (as of January 2007), but these are likely to increase with new exploration and discovery.

Daily crude oil production averaged 1.37 million barrels a day (bbl/d) in 2006. Despite OPEC-demanded production cutbacks, the government has targeted a crude oil production level of 2 million bbl/d by 2010. As a result of increased production and sharply higher prices, Algeria is sloshing about in oil profits: foreign reserves at the end 2006 were $77.78 billion. In September, the finance minister announced Algeria was paying off $12 billion of its accumulated external debt; that left a mere $5 billion outstanding.

Algeria has some 161.7 trillion cubic feet (Tcf) of proven natural gas reserves—the eighth largest in the world. It is OPEC's largest natural gas producer and Europe's most important supplier of natural gas after Russia, a fact that has sharpened Russia's attention to the country. President Vladimir Putin paid an official visit in March 2006, and several months later, Gazprom, the Russian natural gas and pipeline monopoly that shut the valves on Ukraine and doubled the price of gas to Georgia, signed a memorandum of understanding with Sonatrach, the Algerian state-owned oil and gas corporation. Among other things, the August agreement committed the two to cooperate on "natural gas and oil processing and marketing in Algeria, Russian and third countries." With pipeline agreements with central Asian states and supply contracts with North African gas producers like Algeria and Libya, Gazprom would have, in effect, a gas cartel to squeeze European buyers.

Two important pipelines, with an export capacity of 1.15 trillion cubic feet per year, transport the gas to Europe. The 667-mile Trans-Mediterranean line carries 847.6 billion cubic feet to Italy and ultimately to Slovenia. The Maghreb-Europe Gas line, 1,013 miles long, carries 300.2 billion cubic feet of gas to Spain, Portugal and beyond. Additional pipelines are under consideration, and the government has set a goal of exporting three trillion cubic feet of natural gas a year by 2010.

Despite the financial windfall provided by the hydrocarbon sector, there is little evidence conditions for the bulk of Algeria's population have improved in any way. Fifty-eight per cent of the population is younger than 25, and unemployment stands at 60% among those aged between 20 and 25. More than 200,000 enter the job market every year, but there is insufficient growth to generate the jobs needed for those entering the labor market.

The safety valve for Algeria's unemployed or underemployed is the underground economy. A lively trade and commerce based on smuggling and bribery sustains many. The system is oiled by "*tchipa*," a bribe to police and customs officers. One gets rich in Algeria, said one trader, not by knowing a general, but by knowing a customs officer. Nowadays, the dream of every young Algerian is to work for the customs service.

Besides the pervasive corruption of the black economy, there are two other indicators of social malaise worth mentioning. Suicide and attempted suicide rates have been increasing for the last four or five years (though they remain much lower than European or American rates), and crime has become the biggest worry for Algerians. A May 2003 report by the National Economic and Social Council (CNES) highlighted the emergence of organized gangs specializing in extortion, drug trafficking, and prostitution. Authorities saw crime rising by more than 100% during 2004–2005. To cope with rising crime rates, the government in May 2006 announced that it would nearly double its police force—to 200,000—over the next four years.

These developments should be seen against a background of stagnant economic growth. Economic growth in 2002 was 4.1% hardly enough to reduce growing unemployment. In 2003 GDP growth reached an exceptional 6.8%, the highest rate in five years, but this was caused by higher oil production and prices, plus an exceptionally good year for agricultural production brought on by good weather. In recent years it has turned below 6% once again. In 2005 the government launched an $80 billion five-year plan to stimulate the economy, with the effect being growth rates of between 3% and 6% before the global economic crisis.

The Future

Algeria saw a resurgence in violence in 2007 and 2008, and this casts a pall over the country's future. Tensions remain high even more than 15 years after the beginning of the civil war in 1992 that resulted in about 150,000 deaths. The conflict between Islamists and secularists continues to simmer. As noted above Algeria witnessed its first major suicide bombings during 2007, in Algiers and other cities. By December of 2007, these had resulted in over 100 deaths, with an additional 60 in 2008. There are concerns that the principal force behind the bombings, al-Qaeda in the Islamic Maghreb (AQIM), is growing in strength and possibly reaching its tentacles out into neighboring countries beyond Algeria's southern hinterland.

The country's other worry is the economy, where sluggish growth has denied improved living conditions and stifled hope for Algerians of all ages, especially its young people. Corruption and impunity remain highly sensitive issues, but the criticism of young Berbers—that the regime is corrupt, nepotistic and repressive—resonates especially strongly. President Bouteflika's recent successful campaign for a third term will exacerbate concerns that Algeria is and remains a sclerotic and weak state.

The Sahara's ever-shifting sand dunes hide a tiny fresh-water oasis

The Arab Republic of Egypt

Captain Abdul guides his *falooka* along the Nile   Photo by Rodney McNabb

Basic Facts

Area: 1,000,258 sq. km. = 386,200 sq. mi. (the size of Texas and New Mexico)

Population: 75,500,000 (UN 2007 est.)

Capital City: Cairo

Climate: Dry, semitropical and hot. Temperatures are lower in the north during winter.

Neighboring Countries: Libya (west); Israel (northeast); The Sudan (south)

Official Language: Arabic

Other Principal Languages: Armenian, Domari, (spoken by Muslim Gypsies), Kenuzi-Dongola, and Nobiin. English and French are widely understood by educated classes.

Ethnic Groups: Egyptians, Bedouins, and Berbers 99%, Greek, Nubian, Armenian, other European, primarily Italian and French 1%

Principal Religions: Muslim (mostly Sunni) 94% (official estimate), Coptic Christian and other 6% (official estimate)

Chief Commercial Products: Crude oil and petroleum products, cotton yarn, raw cotton, textiles, metal products, and chemicals

GNI Per Capita: $1,250 (World Bank 2006 est.)

Currency: Egyptian pound

Former Colonial Status: British Protectorate (1914–1922); British exercised domination in various forms over Egypt from 1882 to 1952.

Independence Date: July 23, 1952

Chief of State: Hosni Mubarak, President (since 1981)

National Flag: Three horizontal stripes of red, white and black with the national emblem, a shield superimposed on a golden eagle facing the hoist side above a scroll bearing the name of the country in Arabic, centered on the white stripe. The bird is the golden Eagle of Saladin, Sultan of Egypt and Syria, who expelled the crusaders from Jerusalem in 1187.

Land and People

Strategically occupying the northeast corner of Africa, the land route between Africa and Asia, and commanding the sea route between the Mediterranean and Indian Ocean via the Suez Canal, Egypt is mostly a rainless expanse of desert. The habitable portion of this country has historically been only about 4% of its area. The remainder, within the great Sahara Desert, is a hot, endless landscape of sand dunes dotted with occasional green oases. Only 2.85% of the land, mostly the narrow fringe on either side of the Nile River, is arable, though irrigation projects are slowly transforming desert wasteland into fertile ground in areas near the Nile. From 1960 to 2000 the amount of habitable and cultivatable land rose from 6.1 million to 7.3 million acres, but during the same period total population catapulted from 25 million to 66 million people. As a consequence, Egypt has some of the highest population density in the world, in places well over 4,000 inhabitants per square mile. In the urban megalopolis of Cairo, the figure is a staggering 23,310 per square mile.

The Nile, some 3,470 miles long, is the lifeblood of Egypt, providing water for irrigation and (in former years) fertile silt for the farmlands. Given demographic pressure to create new lands through irrigation, control and use of the Nile and its waters is a central aspect of Egyptian domestic and foreign policy.

A number of peaks in the Red Sea Hills rise to more than 6,000 feet, but Egypt's highest mountains are found in southern Sinai. Of them the highest is Mount Catherine with an elevation of 8,668 feet.

Culturally, ancient Egypt is synonymous with the birth of the history and civilization in the western world. The Great Pyramid at Giza (in the Cairo metropolitan area), the Sphinx, the tomb of King Tutankhamun, and the Valley of the Kings leads Africa's list of famous monuments and historical treasures. Today, the Biblio-

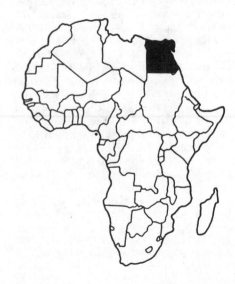

Egypt

The Past: Political and Economic History

Egypt is the oldest cohesive nation in the world, its history dating back before 3000 B.C. Unlike other Middle Eastern and African countries, it has a clear sense of national identity, but part of that identity comes from long periods of subordination to foreign powers. Persia, Macedonia, Rome, Muslim Arabia, Ottoman Turkey, France and England successively exercised dominion. Indeed, following his assumption of power in the 1950s, Gamal Abdel Nasser liked to describe himself as the first Egyptian to rule Egypt since the pharaohs.

The modern Egyptian state begins with the rule of Muhammad Ali, an Albanian soldier in the employ of the Ottoman sultan. Part of the army sent to reassert Ottoman authority following Napoleon's invasion of Egypt in 1798, Muhammad Ali combined forces with the English, defeated the French, and was made governor of Egypt by a grateful sultan in 1805. Ruthless and effective, he set the foundations of the modern state by eliminating remnants of the former Mamluk ruling class (slaughtered when they came as invited dinner guests), crushing peasant rebellions, controlling merchants and Bedouins, and coopting members of the religious class. Muhammad Ali also expropriated landowners, and by 1815 most arable land was state property. Irrigation projects nearly doubled the amount of arable land. The state sent Egyptian cotton to European textile mills and retained the profits.

Muhammad Ali also began the modernization of the Egyptian army. Previously a mercenary force, it became a conscript army, emphasizing Egyptian nationhood, even though officers were usually Turks or other foreigners. The state created Western style schools to train army and bureaucratic personnel and sent educational missions to Europe.

Egyptian forces were initially important in defending Ottoman processions, suppressing rebellion in Arabia and fighting the Greek struggle for independence until European powers intervened and defeated the Ottoman-Egyptian fleet at the battle of Navarino in 1827. Increasingly, however, Muhammad Ali sought greater autonomy from his Turkish suzerain, and even conquered parts of the province of Syria until, once again, European powers intervened. In July 1840 Great Britain, Russia, Austria, and Prussia agreed to end Egyptian rule in Syria. In compensation, Ali and his family were granted hereditary rights to rule Egypt, which remained part of the Ottoman Empire. The dynasty he founded ruled Egypt from his death in 1849 to the middle of the 20th century.

His successors' desires to modernize the country, coupled with personal profligacy,

theca Alexandrina, in Alexandria, which received the distinguished Aga Khan Award for Architecture in 2004, aims to revive the legendary traditions of Alexandria as center of learning and to provide the city with a landmark worthy of its past.

There are an estimated five million Christians in Egypt, members of the Coptic Orthodox Church. Established by the Apostle Saint Mark early in the 1st century, the Coptic Church is one of the oldest Christian churches in existence. Its leader, officially Pope of Alexandria and Patriarch of the See of St. Mark, is selected by an electoral college composed predominantly of laymen. It selects three qualified monks, at least 50 years of age, as candidates for the office of patriarch, and after prayer, the new pope is chosen by lot. The church's present leader, His Holiness Pope Shenouda III, is the 117th Coptic patriarch in a line unbroken from St. Mark. After the Arab conquest of Egypt in the 7th century, Copts ceased speaking Greek, increasing their isolation from other branches of Christianity. Today Arabic is the language of Coptic services with only a few short refrains spoken in Coptic.

Throughout its history the Coptic Church has been subject to periodic repressions. The Roman Emperor Diocletian was so brutal that his horrific executions of 284 A.D. mark the beginning of the Coptic calendar. Although important economically, Copts are frequently discriminated against in terms of employment. One of the country's most skilled diplomats, Boutros Boutros Ghali, was never made foreign minister because, as he was told, a Copt could never represent Egypt at meetings of the Organization of Islamic States. (He went on to become the UN Secretary General.) As a concession to his Coptic citizens, President Mubarak made the Coptic Christmas an official holiday for Egypt in early 2003.

Three Egyptian citizens have been honored as Nobel laureates. The late President Anwar Sadat was the first to receive the Nobel Peace Prize; he was followed by the celebrated novelist Naguib Mahfouz, who won the prize in literature. In 1999, the Egyptian scientist Dr Ahmed Zewail won the Nobel prize in chemistry. Dr. Zewali received his award for studies on the transition states of chemical reactions using spectroscopy.

Egypt

bankrupted the state. Two of them are remembered for overseeing the creation of the Suez Canal. In 1858, Said Pasha granted a canal concession to a French engineer, Ferdinand de Lesseps, and the project was completed under Ismail Pasha in 1869. Inaugurated with much fanfare amid bevies of European aristocrats, including the empress of France, Eugenie, the canal cut 7,250 miles from the London to Bombay journey and heightened Egypt's strategic importance for Europe. Ismail, who obtained the hereditary title of khedive from the Ottoman sultan in 1867, borrowed from European financiers to the point that the state could not repay its debts. To protect creditors' interests, an Anglo-French commission took charge of Egyptian finances in 1876 and the prevailed upon the sultan to depose his Egyptian viceroy in 1879. His son and successor, Tawfik Pasha, had little popular support and his weakness before the European powers roused the ire and contempt of a group of young nationalist army officers led by Ahmad Urabi Pasha.

Born of peasant stock, Urabi was educated at al-Azhar in Cairo, the Middle East's preeminent institution of Islamic learning. Conscripted into the army, he rose to the rank of colonel, early asserting his nationalist credentials by seeking to eliminate the foreigners who monopolized the army's top ranks. In 1881 he led a revolt against that dominance and a year later was named minister of war by Tawfik Pasha. His slogan of "Egypt for Egyptians" expressed Egyptians' near universal discontent with foreign domination and terrified both the khedive and the British.

Fearing Urabi's growing popularity, Twafik requested British and French assistance. A demonstration of naval power in the bay of Alexandria led to riots in the city. In response, the British bombarded Alexandria in July 1882, a senseless act, which only increased Urabi's popular support. In what appeared a revolutionary context, Tawfik fled in fear to British protection. Urabi, calling the khedive a traitor, organized resistance, but his army was defeated, and he was captured, tried, and ultimately exiled to Ceylon. In suppressing the Urabi rebellion, Britain became the master of Egypt. Urabi himself became a nationalist hero and model for successor officers.

When he came to power in 1892, Tawfik Pasha's successor, Abbas II, opposed British power but could do little against the reality of British hegemony. When he called on Egyptians to support Germany in World War I, Britain promptly declared Egypt a protectorate, deposed the khedive and suppressed the title, appointing his uncle as sultan of Egypt.

The peace negotiations which followed the allied victory resonated with rhetori-

Hieroglyphs, Karnac, Upper Egypt   Photo by David Johns

cal idealism. Wilsonian values of "self-determination" gave rise to another powerful expression of Egyptian nationalism in the formation of the *Wafd*. The term, in Arabic, means "delegation," and originated when a delegation of three prominent Egyptian politicians, led by Saad Zaghlul approached the British high commissioner on November 13, 1918. They demanded the protectorate be abolished and replaced by a treaty of alliance, and that they be allowed to travel to London to negotiate such a treaty directly with the British government.

Rejection of these demands resulted in widespread rioting, organized by clandestine *Wafd* cells throughout the country. When Zaghlul and three of his compatriots were arrested in March 1919 and deported to Malta, the disorders only increased. Zughlul was released as a concession to public opinion and he promptly departed for Paris, to present the Egyptian case to the victorious allies meeting to shape the postwar peace. He made little headway there, but in Egypt he became a national hero. For the next couple of years nationalist agitation by Zaghlul and the *Wafd* movement made Egypt virtually ungovernable. Exasperated, General Allenby, the British high commissioner, convinced the British government to issue a unilateral declaration of (limited) independence in February 1922. Britain retained responsibility for the security of the Suez Canal and the defense of Egypt, as well as the protection of foreign interests and minorities.

In 1923 a constitutional monarchy was established with Sultan Fuad as king.

The interior of the Bibliotheca Alexandrina

Saad Zaghlul, who had once again been sent to island exile, this time to the Seychelles, was released to participate in the first elections under the new constitution. The *Wafd*, now a political party, won overwhelmingly. In January 1924 Zaghlul became prime minister, but the forces he had unleashed were ill-contained. Nationalist extremists murdered British officials and Egyptian "collaborators," and in November 1924, the British commander of the Egyptian army was assassinated. Under pressure from the British, Zaghlul resigned from office. In subsequent elections his party still found support, but aged 70, he chose not to lead the new government, opting instead to lead the Chamber of Deputies. Here he was able to exercise some control of the more extreme wing of his party until his death in 1927.

This era of heightened nationalist agitation against British hegemony, and the general disorder that accompanied it, is the background for the formation, in 1928, of the Muslim Brotherhood. Founded by Hassan al-Banna, a charismatic school teacher determined to rid Egypt of British occupation, the Brotherhood (in Arabic, *Al-ikhwan Al-muslimun*) was the first and most important of what would come to be known as Islamic fundamentalist, or Islamist, groups. It advocated a return to the Koran and sayings of the Prophet Mohammad as the foundation of a modern Islamic society and took as its slogan "The Koran is our constitution."

From the late 1920s to the military coup of 1952, little positive change occurred.

King Farouk succeeded to the Egyptian throne in 1936, but provided neither vision nor leadership. British influence waned, and in the same year, the Anglo-Egyptian treaty, restricting British military presence to the Suez Canal zone, was signed. The *Wafd* became increasingly corrupt and bickered with both king and rival parties, all the while bickering within itself. The Muslim Brotherhood became increasingly politicized, rejecting westernization, secularization, and modernization as baleful destroyers of Islamic purity. By the mid-1940s it had organized a terrorist wing and increasingly threatened both the monarchy and the *Wafd* as politics passed into the hands of a more radical generation.

By the end of World War II, in which Egypt was neutral, restiveness of the lower classes rose to feverish heights. The people were governed and exploited by King Farouk and a number of wealthy landowners who controlled almost all the wealth and spent long periods of their time in Europe. Street demonstrations organized by militant nationalists and Islamists became more frequent and more violent, making governance more and more difficult. Concern over the fate of Palestine broadened the scope of Egyptian nationalism, previously focused almost exclusively on domestic concerns. In 1948 Egypt joined with Syria, Jordan and Iraq to dislodge the newly created state of Israel militarily. Defeat in the first Arab-Israeli war revealed the ineptitude of the regime and further eroded what little legitimacy it retained. A group of disillu-

sioned army officers, secretly organized by Gamal Abdel Nasser into the Free Officers Movement, plotted regime change, as they call it nowadays.

The Nasser Years

On July 23, 1952, Nasser led the Free Officers in the *coup d'état* that forced King Farouk to abdicate in favor of his infant son, Fuad II. Major General Mohammed Naguib was chosen head of the government, while Nasser was appointed to the offices of deputy premier and minister of the interior. This situation did not last long. By 1953, the monarchy was ended and a republic proclaimed. In the spring of 1954, power struggles within the ruling military junta were resolved in Nasser's favor: General Naguib was deposed and placed under house arrest. In the same year British troops finally left Egypt following the signing of an evacuation treaty. With an alien dynasty and foreign occupation both ended, there remained only the Palestinian issue to bedevil Egyptian foreign policy.

An assassination attempt by a member of the Muslim Brotherhood in 1954 allowed Nasser to crack down on this element of domestic opposition. Scores of Brotherhood leaders were executed or jailed. Another fundamentalist plot discovered in 1965 proved the Brotherhood had successfully infiltrated both the army and the police, two pillars of Nasser's regime. More arrests and executions followed, the most important of which was Sayyid Qutb, the ideological father of modern Islamic militancy, who was sent to the gallows in 1966.

Nasser declared Egypt a Muslim socialist republic, eliminated political parties and instituted a single mass organization, initially called the National Union, and later the Arab Socialist Union. In January 1956, Nasser promulgated a constitution making Egypt a single-party socialist state with Islam as the official religion; in June 99.8% of the electorate approved it and 99.948% marked their ballots for Nasser, the only candidate, as president.

One month later, the United States and Britain, suspicious of an arms deal Nasser had signed with Czechoslovakia, refused to finance a high dam at Aswan on the Nile River, a key element in Nasser's plans for developing Egypt. In reaction, Nasser defiantly nationalized the Suez Canal Company, declaring its tolls would be used to build the dam. In October Israel invaded the Sinai, destroying Egyptian bases and virtually the entire Egyptian air force. Britain and France soon joined in, flooding the canal zone with thousands of troops. The international community roundly condemned the invasion, and the sides declared a cease-fire in November.

Egypt

The invaders withdrew and UN emergency forces (UNEF) moved in to man the tense Egyptian-Israeli border. Seen as the victim of neocolonialist aggression, Nasser emerged from the brief war with undiminished prestige throughout the Arab world. This encouraged a robust foreign policy engagement with Arab neighbors.

As a first step in creating Arab unity, Nasser joined Egypt with Syria to form the United Arab Republic in 1958. By 1961, however, bitterness had developed between the partners and Syria withdrew. Nasser blamed Syrian "reactionaries" and pushed the Egyptian revolution further to the left. Domestically, "scientific socialism" defined state economic policy, and in 1962, he intervened on the side of republicans fighting to overthrow the monarchy in Yemen. The move antagonized Saudi Arabia, which supported Yemeni royalists, and the United States, which cut off its aid to Egypt in the mid-1960s.

With Egyptian troops bogged down in Yemen, pressures built on Nasser to reengage the issue of Palestine. A decade of relative peace had been established by the presence of UNEF troops on the border with Israel, and Nasser had consistently argued restraint at Arab summit meetings. By 1966, however, Palestinian incursions against Israel were being launched with increasing frequency from bases in Jordan, Lebanon, and Syria. When Israel retaliated, Nasser was taunted with failing the cause of Arab unity and hiding behind the protection of UNEF.

In sympathy with the Syrian government, which was loudly protesting possible Israeli aggression, in 1967 Nasser demanded withdrawal of UN forces stationed along the Israeli border, supposedly to enable Egypt to assist Syria (if necessary). UN Secretary General U Thant ordered the immediate withdrawal of the forces without consulting the Security Council or the General Assembly. Nasser's forces quickly occupied the heights of Sharm-al-Sheikh, a strategic overlook commanding the entrance to the Gulf of Aqaba and announced that all shipping to or from Israel was barred. *Al Ahram*, the semiofficial newspaper of Cairo, published an editorial gleefully declaring that Israel had no choice but to fight if it wished to have access to the Red Sea.

Surrounded and fearing an imminent attack, Israel launched preemptive air strikes against Egypt on June 5, followed by a quick ground offensive against Egyptian, Jordanian and Syrian forces and bombings of Iraqi airfields to eliminate air assistance from that country. The initial air assault on Egypt was from the west, catching almost all Egyptian aircraft (supplied by the Soviets) on the ground. In the ensuing five days of battle, the Arab forces were completely routed. An estimated 10,000 Egyptians died and the Israeli army pushed to the Suez Canal. A UN-imposed cease-fire established an uneasy peace, which continued in effect until the fighting gradually escalated in 1970–1971, requiring another informal cease-fire agreement.

Anwar Sadat

The Six-Day War, as the conflict came to be known, resulted in Israeli control of Sinai, the Golan Heights, the Gaza Strip, East Jerusalem and the West Bank. Both Egyptian arms and the Arab cause were crushed. Nasser resigned from office, but a popular outpouring of support "forced" him to rescind the resignation. To replace $5 billion in lost arms, the USSR supplied almost $7 billion in equipment after 1967, but the radical phase of the Egyptian revolution had ended.

Nasser died unexpectedly in 1970 from a reported heart attack; Egypt and the Arab world were plunged into mourning. Nasser had stimulated Egyptian and Arab pride, despite his poor record in foreign policy adventures. Domestically, his development plans had increased the industrial sector from 10% of GDP in 1950 to 21% in 1970, though any benefits were eroded by rapid population growth. (In deference to Muslim demands, the government did not push birth control policies.) A socialist economy also produced a huge state bureaucracy—the employer of first resort—and an army of state companies that soon became sluggish, cumbersome, and corrupt.

The Sadat Years

Nasser was succeeded by his vice president, Anwar Sadat, another member of the Free Officers. He was thought to be a weak figurehead, but things turned out otherwise. He quickly ousted his rivals and made frequent and dramatic threats to "invade" and "crush" Israel, but until 1973 he did nothing in that direction. When the Soviets criticized Egyptian military prowess, Sadat sent all 20,000 Soviet military advisors packing in 1972, accusing the Soviets of failing to furnish the modern weaponry needed to conquer Israel.

Abu Simbel, Upper Egypt

Photo by David Johns

Israeli control in the Sinai tightened after the 1967 war; there were Israeli settlements, and oil wells appeared. In an effort to wrest occupied areas from Israel, Egypt and Syria launched a two-front attack in October 1973; they had the military and financial support of Arab states and the USSR. The move, made during the Jewish religious festival of *Yom Kippur*, took Israel completely by surprise, and it appeared that Egypt might well be successful in the initial days of conflict.

Israel responded by first driving the Syrians back within shell range of their capital, Damascus, then turned to the Egyptian front. After the largest tank battle in history, the Israelis made daring crossings of the Suez Canal, launching a "pincer" attack that threatened to surround the Egyptians. Within hours the tide of battle had shifted and Cairo itself was threatened.

With Russia threatening intervention, a cease-fire strong-armed the Israelis into giving up all territory west of the canal and enough territory in the Sinai Peninsula to salvage Sadat's reputation; despite defeat, he emerged a modest hero. Additional Sinai territory, including the Abu Rudeis oil field, was ceded to Egypt in late 1976. With U.S. assistance the Suez Canal, closed since the 1967 strife, was back in operation by mid-1975.

While establishing his bona fides on Israel, Sadat changed many of his predecessor's policies. Russian military assistance had already been dispatched before the war, but to lure foreign investment, socialism was also abandoned. Egypt shifted from Soviet support to contributions from Arab oil states (principally Saudi Arabia) and the United States. The monopoly of political space by Egypt's single party was ended, and political parties were permitted to organize and operate. Sadat also re-ordered the relationship between the state and the Muslim faithful.

Calling himself the "Believer President," Sadat introduced *sharia* law in the constitution (as one of the "sources of Egyptian legislation"), lifted restrictions on Muslim fundamentalist organizations, and permitted the proliferation of private mosques, which escaped state supervision and control. This would ultimately facilitate the large-scale introduction of Wahhabi fundamentalism, financed by Saudi Arabia, into Egypt's more mainstream Islam. To counterbalance the weight of the Nasserite left, Sadat encouraged the growing influence of *al-Gama'a al-Islamiyya*, or Islamic Group, which had emerged around 1973 on university campuses, where it violently opposed the student left. (Its spiritual leader was Omar Abdel-Rahman, currently in jail in the USA for the 1993 bombing of New York's World Trade Center.)

Elections in 1976 resulted in an overwhelming victory for Sadat's Arab Socialist Party. The victory gave the president a large political space in which to maneuver, and he proceeded to tackle the major impediment to Egyptian economic reconstruction: peace with Israel. On November 19, 1977, Sadat undertook the most controversial move of his career: he flew to Jerusalem to address a session of the Israeli Knesset. Israelis were stunned and excited at this "breakthrough." Sadat delivered an impassioned plea for a just and lasting peace, but held fast to the proposition that Israel must withdraw from occupied Arab territory and grant Palestinians "their rights." Israeli Prime Minister Begin countered with the Israeli position: we are willing to negotiate, but your price is too high. He insisted that Israel must have "defensible borders."

After much "shuttle diplomacy" and a September 1978 meeting between Sadat, Israeli Prime Minister Menachem Begin, and Jimmy Carter at the presidential retreat of Camp David, a peace treaty between the two countries was signed at the White House on March 26, 1979. When each nation was assured it would be protected from surprise attack, the treaty boiled down to these key points: (1) Israel agreed to withdraw all its armed forces and civilians from the Sinai Peninsula within a period of three years; (2) Egypt guaranteed passage of Israeli ships and cargoes through the Suez Canal; (3) both nations pledged full diplomatic, cultural, and economic relations, and (4) there would be a free movement of people and goods between the two countries. A vast American economic aid program would make Egypt second only to Israel as the recipient of American largess. The Nasserian revolution was virtually turned on its head.

Arab reaction to the treaty was not positive. Islamic fundamentalists declared it an act of treason. Financial aid from the Gulf States and Saudi Arabia was cut, and Egypt was expelled from the Arab League. (It did not rejoin the League until 1989.) At home, a parlous economic situation made Sadat's support fragile at best. In January 1977, well before the dramatic flight to Israel, bread riots had broken out in Egypt's major cities. Some 79 persons were killed, 1,000 wounded and another 1,250 arrested.

Sadat's liberalization of Egyptian economic and political life, limited as it was, ultimately undermined his regime. In August 1981 an alleged plot linking communists and Muslim extremists was discovered; more than 1,500 opponents of the regime, both right and left, were arrested. The Russian ambassador, accused of complicity, was expelled, and a state of emergency was declared. One month later,

while reviewing a military parade, Sadat was gunned down by rebel soldiers belonging to *al-Jihad* (Islamic Jihad or "Holy War"), a clandestine fundamentalist group run by Ayman al-Zawahri, who later went on to become Osama bin Laden's right-hand man. It was the group's spiritual guide, Omar Abdel-Rahman, who reportedly issued the *fatwa* (decree) authorizing Sadat's assassination.

Eight days after the slaying and one day after an overwhelming nationwide referendum, Vice President Hosni Mubarak took the oath as Egypt's fourth president, pledging to continue the policies of the fallen leader. A former bomber pilot and air force chief of staff, Mubarak had been named to the largely honorific post of vice president by Anwar Sadat as a concession to the army, whose "heroes" of the 1973 campaign he had successfully sidetracked. It confirmed the army's continuing political importance as a principal pillar of the regime.

Indeed, the army is a pampered institution, treated with kid gloves. Sadat's economic liberalization allowed the army to enter the economic field, where it became an essential though discreet actor. It owns agricultural land and farm equipment businesses. It controls pharmaceutical businesses as well as construction firms, and at least 20% of Cairo's bread comes from army bakeries. It controls the free trade zones at Port Said and Suez, and benefits from tax exemptions on the import of various goods and equipment. Its businesses are also exempt from labor legislation,

Egyptian Charm

41

Egypt

which gives them a significant competitive advantage. Egypt's army-controlled arms industry is producing mines, light arms, and even Abrams tanks under American license. Retired generals sit on the boards of state corporations and members of the armed forces have access to reserved housing, commissary subsidies, and special vacation sites and opportunities.

The Mubarak Years

The principal challenge faced by President Mubarak has been the threat to state and institutions posed by political Islam—those groups dedicated to overthrowing the regime by violence in the name of Islam. While the assassination of President Sadat is their most notable act of violence, Coptic Christians, secular intellectuals, police and army officials, as well as politicians and cabinet ministers have been targeted by Muslim extremists. In 1995 an attempt was made on the life of President Mubarak while he was attending a meeting in Addis Ababa. *Al-Gama'a al-Islamiyya* even attacked the economic underpinnings of the regime by its bloody assaults on Western tourists, the worst of which came in 1997 when 58 tourists, mostly Swiss, were massacred at Luxor.

President Mubarak diminished Islamist violence through a combination of savage repression and indulgence. After the Sadat assassination, hundreds of militant Islamists were arrested and the regime encouraged their departure to Afghanistan (via Saudi Arabia) where they could fight alongside the Afghan *mujahadin*. The Muslim Brotherhood was even permitted to participate in the elections of 1984 and 1987, but the explosion of Islamic violence in the 1990s required firmer action.

In 1993 Islamic Jihad launched attacks against both the interior minister and the prime minister. Both were unsuccessful, but in the latter attack, the bomb missed its target, injured 21 people and killed a 12-year-old schoolgirl. Her death outraged Egyptians, and when her coffin was carried through the streets of Cairo people cried, "Terrorism is the enemy of God!" In the war against terrorists, mass arrests, torture, extrajudicial executions, and the use of military courts to try civilians have all prompted criticism of the regime's human rights violations.

Given the reality of Islamist terrorism, Egypt complained for years about the absence of cooperation it received from its Arab and Western partners. Only after the Luxor massacre did attitudes change, and after the bombings of American embassies in Kenya and Tanzania by al-Qaeda operatives, the CIA began to work closely with its Egyptian counterparts. Since then, Egypt has obtained the extradition of a number of important militants from places

President Hosni Mubarak

like Albania, Bulgaria, Kuwait, Yemen and even Latin America. Domestically, too, the Luxor massacre changed things. Middle class opinion was appropriately horrified and turned against militant extremism to such an extent that *Gama'a al-Islamiyya's* military wing declared a unilateral ceasefire in 1999, though some cells refused the call. In 2001 the group published four books explaining its abandonment of *jihad* and the armed struggle.

Despite the seeming success of repression, the whole dreary cycle seemed to repeat itself in October 2004, when six years of relative calm were shattered by bloody attacks on tourist sites in Sinai. Terrorists struck the Taba Hilton Hotel and two tourist camps, killing 34 people and wounding 105. The government initially claimed the car bombings were the work of a small, isolated group of Palestinian and Egyptian terrorists who died in the attack, but later focused more on local Bedouin groups. As many as 2,400 people were arrested and held without charges months after the attack.

Terrorists struck again in July 2005, this time hitting at the heart of Egypt's Sinai tourism, Sharm al-Sheikh, at the southern tip of the penninsula. Dubbed the "Red Sea Riviera," the area had been turned into a showpiece by the government. Sharm was a place of broad, clean streets, and world-class resorts for the tourists, and a peaceful refuge that hosted important international summits. On July 23, 2005 it was the site of Egypt's bloodiest terrorist attack yet. At least 88 people, most of them Egyptians, were left dead. A credible claim of responsibility was received from the "Abdullah Azzam Brigades of al-Qaeda in Egypt and the Levant," which also claimed credit for the Taba bombings the year before.

The violence of the attack generated a good deal of soul-searching among intellectuals and in the Egyptian press. *Al-Akhbar* called the perpetrators "a gang of misguided people" who had "nothing to do with Islam," but *Al-Misri al-Yawm* saw

it differently. For it, "scholars and leaders who live in our midst" were to blame. "We have kept silent," the paper commented, "while Wahabite thinking has infiltrated Egypt." Widespread salafist ideology, the paper thought, was the cause of increased terrorism. Egypt's Nobel laureate in literature, Naguib Mahfouz, summed up the sentiment of many: "What revolts me the most is that these crimes have been committed in the name of Islam." In April 2006, bomb attacks in the Red Sea resort of Dahab killed 20 more. Cairo was hit in 2008 when a tourist area was attacked.

The Egyptian political system has many of the trappings of a multiparty democracy, but they remain more decorative than real. Before legislative elections in 1984, Mubarak legalized political parties and guaranteed them freedom of the press. In the elections, somewhat less than half of the 12.4 million registered voters cast ballots, but, with an assist from administrative manipulation, they gave an overwhelming vote of confidence to Mubarak's National Democratic Party (NDP), which had replaced Sadat's Arab Socialist Party. It won 389 out of 448 total seats in the People's Assembly.

The election also saw the participation of the Muslim Brotherhood, presumably to offer an alternative to the rigidly fundamentalist Islamic Jihad. The New Wafd Party, allied with the Muslim Brotherhood, won a total of 59 seats. In the highly disputed legislative elections of 1987, the NDP won 346 seats, while the Islamic alliance won 60, 37 of them from the Muslim Brotherhood. New Wafd, which supports a liberal economy domestically and is anti-Israeli internationally, secured 36 seats.

Legislative elections in 1995 were held against a background of President Mubarak's decision to widen an antiterrorist, anti-Islamist campaign. Widespread arrests occurred, and military tribunals issued death sentences for some and prison terms for a great many more. Enthusiasm for the crackdown greatly accelerated following the attempt on the president's life while he was visiting Addis Ababa in midyear. Cynics claimed all of this was calculated to influence the elections later that year.

Held in November, they resulted in an overwhelming victory for the ruling National Democratic Party (NDP), achieved through unprecedented irregularity and fraud. The Muslim Brotherhood, many of whose candidates had been condemned by military court days before the election, was steamrolled; the other opposition parties were no more successful. The NDP carried 430 seats; New Wafd was reduced to six, and the Muslim Brotherhood man-

Egypt

Cairo modernizes—McDonald's arrives

Photo by David Johns

aged to elect only a single candidate. In all, only 14 opposition representatives sat in the People's Assembly, hardly a glowing endorsement of effective multiparty democracy.

The People's Assembly election of October 2000, the first conducted with the supervision of judges to assure fairness, proved something of an embarrassment for President Mubarak's National Democratic Party. While the party nominally holds 85% of the seats in the Assembly, most of the new MPs representing the party originally ran as independents. The Assembly elections also marked the return of the Muslim Brotherhood, which managed to win 17 seats despite the usual harassment by the authorities. Though the group remains officially banned, individuals affiliated with it ran successfully as "independents."

Egyptian presidential elections are also part of the democratic façade. There are, however, no balloon-dropping political party nominating conventions in Egypt. Instead, the presidential candidate is nominated by parliament—the People's Assembly and the Shura Council—and then approved in a countrywide referendum. Unsurprisingly Hosni Mubarak was nominated to a fourth presidential term in July 1999. In September Egyptian voters marked their ballots—a green circle to approve, a black circle to disapprove—and 93.97% voted to approve Mubarak's nomination.

Given overwhelming single-party dominance of the system one can easily understand how opposition is sometimes expressed in outrageous political violence,

but because of that violence, stability has been privileged over expression. As a consequence the regime is authoritarian and political life is stifled. The search for stability through silence is itself destabilizing. Denied voice in the political arena, Islamist sentiment erupts elsewhere.

The determination to control political life in the name of stability has had a corrosive effect on Egypt's political system. Power is dangerously concentrated in the hands of one man, the president. An aging generation of politicians has been ossified in place, with little intention of giving up the benefits of power. The system has become hermetically sealed off from social reality and desperately needs to be opened up. Its reinvigoration requires new blood and ideas.

Surprisingly, the man chosen to infuse new blood and ideas seems to be not the president, but his son, Gamal. Appointed to the NDP's 25-member secretariat in 2000, Gamal Mubarak is chairman of the party's policy committee, which, in early 2003, proposed the abolition of state security courts and the creation of a national council for human rights. The younger Mubarak has also spoken of the need to "dynamize political life" by modernizing laws governing political parties.

Political Reform

Egypt's September 2005 presidential election President Mubarak made the election special by securing a constitutional amendment allowing, for the first time, competitive candidacies; ten challengers signed up, though none was ever expected to win. The two most prominent

were Numan Gumaa of the Wafd Party and Ayman Nour of the *Al-Ghad* (Tomorrow) Party; at the age of 40, Nour was the youngest of the candidates, a striking contrast to the 77-year-old Mubarak. The campaign was oddly different—Egyptians had never seen their president stand up and ask for their support—but dismally similar. When the final results were reported, Hosni Mubarak won by a landslide: 88.6% of the votes; it would his fifth consecutive six-year term as president. His nearest competitor was Ayman Nour, founder of the Ghad party, who officially received 7.3% of the vote. Voter turnout was appallingly low—a mere 23% of registered voters.

Ayman Nour had already tasted the bitter fruit accorded regime opponents in Egypt: after announcing he planned to run for president against Mr. Mubarak, he was jailed in early 2005 on trumped-up charges of forging some 2,000 signatures to secure registration for his party in 2004. *Al-Ghad* was the first new party permitted in years. The incident prompted Secretary of State Condoleezza Rice to cancel a planned trip to Egypt and Mr. Nour was ultimately released on bail, enabling his presidential campaign. (Mr. Nour would be no beneficiary of "reform" in Egypt. In December he was tried, found guilty, and sentenced to five years in prison on the forgery charge; his appeal against the verdict was rejected in May 2006.)

The November 2006 parliamentary elections saw some 5,000 candidates vying for the 444 elected positions (ten more are appointed by President Mubarak). The ruling NDP put up 444 candidates, but an estimated 2,000 NDP dissidents made up half the 4,000 independent candidates. The National Front for Change, an opposition alliance of 12 political groups, announced an electoral list of 225 candidates. The regime's flirtation with political tolerance extended to the outlawed Muslim Brotherhood. For the first time, its parliamentary candidates openly campaigned as movement members and openly used its controversial slogan, "Islam is the Solution."

The Brotherhood's campaign was successful. Banned but tolerated, it managed to get 88 of its "independent" candidates elected to the People's Assembly—the largest block among the 100 opposition seats in the new legislature. The opposition reduced the NDP majority from 388 to 315, still more than enough to control things, but a clear sign that the rustle of change might at last be heard in Egypt.

Egypt's 2005 election brought to the fore a new set of heroes for reformers. Not the Mubaraks, father and son, nor even the secular opposition, which did miserably in elections for the People's Assembly. (Ay-

43

Egypt

man Nour even lost his seat.) Instead, it was Egypt's judges who, in an extraordinary display of defiance, refused to oversee elections unless parliament passed legislation guaranteeing their independence and became the heroes of the day.

The judges demanded not only independence, but the sole right to monitor elections, which, they charged, were corrupt. Indeed, two of them faced charges for having publicly described the 2005 parliamentary elections as fraudulent. Their disciplinary hearing in April 2006 brought added street theater and chaos to Cairo's streets. Fifty of their colleagues staged a sit-in at the headquarters of the judges' professional association. Fifteen were arrested; most were beaten. The show of force was huge—larger than the one deployed to Sinai after the bombings of tourist sites the same week. It was clear that what everyone called the "Revolt of the Judges" had opened a seam in the country's authoritarian political system and the regime's only response was repression.

President Mubarak chose to close the loopholes constitutionally. Near the end of December 2006, he addressed parliament, and, besides telling members he intended to stay in power as long as his "heart beats in his chest," he asked them to amend 34 articles of the constitution. The first major constitutional change since 1971, the amendments were billed as part of his political reform. The opposition and its civil society supporters would have nothing of it, declaring the whole affair a sham and a backtracking on democracy. The proposals convulsed Egyptian political life for the next several months.

Some of the amendments were housekeeping in nature—getting rid of obsolete references to "socialism," for example. Others clarified the steps to be taken should the president become ill or incapacitated, a rational necessity given the absence of a vice president and the presence of a 79-year-old president. Three other amendments provoked general fulmination.

Article 5 would prohibit political activity and parties based on religion, and candidates would be required to have a party affiliation. In other words, no "independent" candidacies, the way Islamists had entered parliament in the last election, would be allowed. Article 88 removed judicial supervision of elections—no more pesky judges peering into ballot boxes and denouncing fraud. Article 179 set forth special presidential powers to fight terrorism. These included sweeping powers to arrest terrorist suspects, to monitor private communications, and to refer suspects to military and special courts. In many ways the new provisions embedded old procedures formulated under the state's emer-

gency powers. Now they would have constitutional sanction. Amnesty International, never one to avoid hyperbole, called the provisions the "greatest erosion of rights in 26 years."

With his NDP firmly in control of both houses of parliament, there was never a doubt about the outcome. The amendments were approved and sent to the voters in a referendum in late March 2007. NDP members manned the phone banks to mobilize a largely cynical and apathetic electorate. According to the justice ministry, 27% of eligible voters turned out for the poll, and 75.9% of them approved the amendments. The opposition, which had called for an election boycott, estimated that no more than 5% had participated.

Elections to the Shura Council, Egypt's upper legislative house, were set for June 2007, and the Muslim Brotherhood actively campaigned on its very religious platform of "Islam is the Solution." The government turned its back on any political reform, reverting to form by actively repressing Brotherhood leaders and members. The campaign against the Brotherhood has been particularly intense since a military-style parade by young men from the Brotherhood's student affiliate at Al Azhar University in December 2006. Dressed in black uniforms (reminiscent of those worn by the Iranian Republican Guard or Hezbollah in Lebanon) and performing martial arts movements, the young Islamists raised fears that the Brotherhood was providing paramilitary

training to its members and might have secret militias. It was an image completely at odds with that the leadership sought to convey, in tones of mellifluous moderation, to every passing journalist.

The Present: Contemporary Issues

Following the terrorist attacks of September 11 the Egyptian economy experienced its worst crisis in a decade, even worse than that following the local terrorist assault at Luxor in 1997. Tourism, which accounts for 12% of the economy, and one in seven jobs is enormously sensitive to events like these, and that's precisely the reason why terrorists have targeted the sector. In 2000, 5.4 million people visited Egypt and accounted for $4.3 billion in revenues. A year later, following terrorist attacks in the United States and war in Afghanistan, visitors fell to 4.7 million and revenues to $3.8 million. By 2005, worldwide tourism had rebounded generally, and Egypt benefited accordingly. Despite the hideous attacks in Sinai, 8.4 million visitors arrived. Revenues will surpass the $6 billion the sector earned in 2004.

The four main sources of hard currency for Egypt—tourism, oil, fees from the Suez Canal, and workers' remittances—were all affected by the terrorist attacks in New York and Washington. The war in Iraq was a second shock to the Egyptian economy. Iraq was Egypt's number one trading partner, with exports exceeding $1.7 billion in 2002.

Egyptian judges protest disciplinary action against colleagues who spoke out against electoral violations

©Serene Assir/IRIN

His Holiness Pope Shenuda III, head of the Egyptian Coptic Church

As a consequence of these external events, the economy slowed considerably: real GDP grew only 4.2 % in 2004 and, at 4.9%, was not better in 2005. With a population growth of 1.9%, however, those figures suggest stagnation rather than improvement. Unofficial estimates place Egypt's unemployment in the 15% to 25% range (officially it's only 10%); the rate is highest among young job seekers, and each year some 800,000 more of them enter the job market.

Given the government's policy of admitting all high school graduates into the university system (12 government universities, with eight affiliated branches and 20 campuses), the annual number of university graduates is around 195,200. Unfortunately the system fails to provide the skills most relevant to the job market. The market is simply unable to absorb the many university students graduating each year.

In recent years, oil revenues have represented about 40% of Egypt's foreign exchange, but oil production has been declining. The oil fields of the Gulf of Suez and Sinai are mature. Egypt's crude oil production peaked at 922,000 barrels per day (bbl/d) in 1996; it averaged only around 579,000 bbl/d in 2005. Egypt's last major discovery was more than 20 years ago in the Western Desert. Offshore exploration in the Mediterranean is under way, but to date, most discoveries off the Nile Delta have been natural gas.

Foreign oil companies began active exploration for natural gas in the early 1990s, and found significant deposits in the Nile Delta, offshore from the Nile Delta, and in the Western Desert. Over the last five years exploration has resulted in

the discovery of at least 33 major fields—those whose output exceeds 100 million barrels of oil equivalent. Egypt's natural gas production nearly doubled between 1999 and 2003, and in 2004 it had reached 3.6 billion cubic feet per day (Bcf/d); daily production was expected to rise to around five billion cubic feet by 2007. The government estimates Egyptian natural gas reserves at 58.5 trillion cubic feet (Tcf).

Given these resources, natural gas is likely to be the primary engine of growth for the Egyptian economy in the coming years. In a rare example of economic cooperation between Arab states, Egypt and Jordan inaugurated a gas pipeline in July 2003, marking Egypt's first exports of natural gas. The pipeline is expected to move 600,000 tons of natural gas annually, from Egypt to Jordan, and is part of a longer line planned to eventually reach Turkey and the markets of Europe.

For its own electricity needs, which are growing at 7% a year, Egypt has opted for an alternative source: nuclear energy. At a NDP meeting in September 2006, Gamal Mubarak announced that the country was ready to resume its nuclear research program, suspended twenty years earlier after the Chernobyl disaster. President-father Hosni Mubarak later confirmed his son's statement, saying the Egypt must take advantage of new energy sources. Shortly thereafter the energy minister announced construction of a nuclear power plant on the Mediterranean coast, ostensibly to help water desalinization efforts. It

would cost $1.5 billion, produce 1,000 MW of electricity, and could be completed by 2015.

Prior to 1967 the economy was largely dependent on a single crop: cotton. Egyptian long staple and extra-long staple cotton is probably the best in the world. It is stronger and can be spun more finely than nearly any other variety in the world. In America it is associated with the most luxurious bed sheets; in Europe, with the finest shirts, and in India, with the thinnest, most diaphanous saris. Despite its reputation, however, the Egyptian cotton industry is dying. Cotton revenues have fallen below those supplied by petroleum.

The area devoted to cotton cultivation has gradually fallen from 1.3 million acres in 1980–1981 to 780,000 acres. Almost all of this acreage is devoted to extra-long and long staple cotton, but only about a third of total production is exported. Roughly 200,000 tons goes to the domestic market, which cannot adequately process high-end cotton. When Gamal Abdel Nasser nationalized the industry in the 1950s, emphasis was placed on creating jobs and import substitution to clothe the country's poor population. Eastern European-supplied machinery could only process much coarser grades of cotton. Ready-to-wear textile manufacturers today prefer to import cheaper short-fiber cotton than use home-grown material.

Only 2.85% of Egypt's total land mass is arable, basically the narrow strip of land that borders the Nile and its delta. Ag-

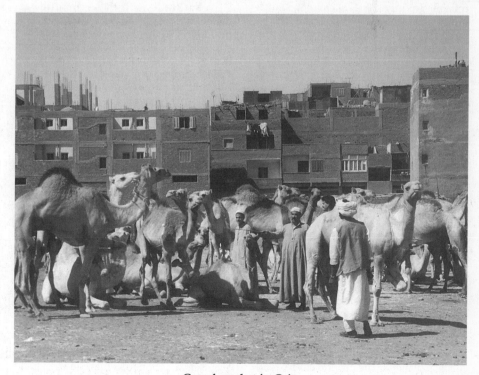

Camel market in Cairo

Egypt

riculture, which is dominated by small landholders, contributed 13.9% to GDP in 2005 and employed about 35% of Egyptian workers. Despite this, Egypt still imports more than half of its food, which includes 10 million tons of grain each year. To sustain the agricultural sector the government has sought to open new farming lands through vast irrigation projects. In many ways they are Hosni Mubarak's Pharaonic legacy to Egypt when he leaves office: two enormous water projects, both involving Nile waters, both designed to create hundreds of thousands of acres of arable soil for land-starved Egyptian farmers, both costing billions of dollars.

In the south, the Toshka project, at an estimated cost of $2 billion, is designed to pump 5 billion cubic meters of water a year from Lake Nasser into the Western Desert to put some 1.04 million acres of land under cultivation. The *Financial Times* of London reported that the bank thought megaprojects like Toshka were "putting an unbearable strain on the government's finances, helping to create unacceptably high interest rates, a deteriorating balance of payments and putting pressure on the currency." In the north a similar irrigation project has started to bring water to the parched Sinai desert through four 42-meter-deep ducts that actually carry Nile waters under the Suez Canal. The project, which is designed to add 544,388 acres of arable land, also has cost estimates in the range of $2 billion. Financing has come mainly from the emir of Kuwait.

There are hopeful signs of economic reform. In July 2004 a cabinet shuffle brought in a new NDP government, reportedly close to Gamal Mubarak and strongly reformist. The new Canadian-educated prime minister, Ahmed Nazif, was the youngest (52 at the time) and most effective member of the outgoing cabinet and a surprise appointment. Within a few weeks of taking office the new government had introduced far-reaching economic changes: customs tariffs were slashed by 40%, a new trade deal with Israel and the United States was signed, income taxes were cut by half, and many bureaucratic impediments to doing business in Egypt were swept away, in an effort to spur foreign investment and revitalize a dormant economy.

Cairo, with all its suburbs, contains more than 16 million people and is the largest city in Africa and the Middle East. Nearly two million automobiles clog its streets. To this cement, iron, chemical and metal factories and smelters, and daily garbage offer their noxious contributions, leaving the city of a thousand minarets veiled in a cloak of yellow-gray haze. Cairo's governor has plans for the chaotic city: extending water, sewage and telephone systems,

Gamel Mubarak, President Hosni Mubarak's son. And successor?

as well as garbage collection; reclaiming the banks of the Nile for public parks. Taxis, minivans and city buses are switching to compressed natural gas—a fuel system in which Cairo is now a world leader.

Foreign Policy Issues

Like Libya, Egypt has turned its attention to sub-Saharan Africa. The interest is both economic and political. Egypt joined the Common Market for Eastern and Southern Africa (COMESA) in 1998 and shortly afterwards, acceded to COMESA's free trade area. Tariffs on imports from COMESA countries have been reduced by 90%, but trade with these countries accounts for only 1.1% of exports and 1.3% of imports (2000). Far more important are strategic necessities. African states represent potential threats for Egypt on the issue of sharing and using the Nile waters. The existing Nile Water Agreement was signed in 1929, ratified in 1952, and barred states from using the waters of Lake Victoria without Egypt's permission. (Sudan and Egypt renegotiated the agreement in 1959 to permit construction of Aswan High Dam.)

The agreement, which benefited only Egypt and Sudan, became outdated as other states on the river and its tributaries made plans to use the waters for their own development. Not being independent in 1929, and thus not themselves signatories to the original agreement, the other riverine states pressed for renegotiation.

Ethiopian proposals to construct a series of dams on the Blue Nile galvanized action, and in June 2001 the Nile Basin Initiative (NBI) was created. It linked ten Nile Basin states: Burundi, the Democratic Republic of Congo, Egypt, Eritrea, Ethiopia, Kenya, Rwanda, Sudan, Tanzania and Uganda.

With $140 million granted by the World Bank and donor governments, seven feasibility studies were undertaken to study possible cooperative development of Nile resources, but frustrated by a lack of progress, Kenya announced its intention to disregard the treaty's provisions in late 2003. Pushing things further, Tanzania precipitated a crisis by diverting water from Lake Victoria in early 2004.

NBI crisis meetings were convened in Uganda the very next month. For Egypt, the issue is critical. Of the Nile's estimated annual allotment of 83 billion cubic meters (Bcm), Egypt has been receiving 55 Bcm under the 1929 treaty. Virtually its entire agricultural sector, especially irrigated developments in the south, is dependent on Nile waters, and the country has repeatedly said it would reject any proposal to lower its quota. It has searched for water alternatives for its neighbors, including financing the digging of wells in Kenya, but it is unlikely these will provide adequate replacement waters.

The war against Iraq brought extraordinary pressure to bear on the government in 2003. Though emergency laws ban public demonstrations, the government sanctioned huge mass rallies to show itself sensitive to popular outrage. President Mubarak viewed the war as completely destabilizing and has deplored what he sees as its consequences: "If there is one bin Laden today, there will be 100 bin Ladens afterward."

Egyptian women are slowly gaining legal protection and rights in a male-dominated society. The tortured course of rules governing female circumcision finally concluded at the end of 1997. In December the country's highest judicial authority, the Council of State, banned the practice of excision, even when the consent of child or parent is given. The court ruled that excision—surgical removal of the clitoris—was physical mutilation as defined in the Penal Code and was therefore punishable by the law. Although there is no Koranic sanction for the practice, female circumcision had long been practiced in Egypt. Indeed the operation has traditionally been seen as a mark of virtue and guarantor of modesty. In 1997 a detailed demographic survey indicated that more than 97% of women and girls had been through the ordeal.

In early 1999 the government introduced a modification of law codes to give women greater divorce rights. Islamic law allows a man divorce by simple repetition of a ritual formula three times—and divorce is immediate. A woman, on the other hand, might have to go through years of litigation if her husband were unwilling to grant divorce. Every year some 20,000 women went before the courts requesting a divorce and if it was not given immediately, the woman remained under the legal tutelage of her husband who could, for example, prevent her from getting a passport.

The new code was finally approved in January 2000 after rousing heated controversy. (Hard-line Muslim clerics had described it as a threat to the stability of society.) The reforms of Egyptian family law are far-reaching. A woman will now be able to divorce her husband, with or without his assent. She is required to return any dowry or its equivalent in cash or property. She will also be able to call on the Egyptian government to garnish her husband's wages if he refuses to provide for her. If he disappears or cannot pay a court-ordered living allowance, she will be able to draw from a special state bank to keep her family afloat. Lost in the politics of compromise was a provision that would have allowed Egyptian women to travel abroad without the permission of their husbands.

Homosexuals are subject to severe repression in Egypt. For years the media and government have pretended homosexuality was a Western "disease" that hardly existed in Egypt. In May 2001, however, the police raided the somewhat appositely named "Queen Boat"—a three-deck floating discotheque moored on the Nile whose Thursday night parties attracted a sizable gay clientele—and arrested dozens of attendees. After releasing foreigners, the Egyptians were jailed. Then, using the detainees' address books and confiscated mobile phones, the police tracked down and arrested dozens more.

Prosecutors argued that their actions defiled Islam and constituted a risk to the state, justifying the trial of 52 gay men in the State Security Court—an institution created by emergency laws passed after Anwar Sadat's assassination in 1981. Human Rights Watch reported they were subjected to humiliating "forensic" examinations, tortured, and given long jail terms for "debauchery." Twenty-three were convicted and jailed for one to five years. There is no appeal from the State Security Court, and there was no intervention on the defendants' behalf by human rights organizations.

The Future
The illiberal nature of the Mubarak regime exacerbates the tensions between Islamists (most particularly the Muslim Brotherhood) and the establishment. The recent arrests of over 800 Brotherhood supporters (and the imprisonment of about 25 of the organization's leaders) has raised the conflict once again. Additionally, the Cairo bombing in February 2009 confirms that Egypt still wrestles with a radical form of Islam that reared its head at Luxor and Sharm al-Sheikh in previous years. Tensions have heightened between the press and the government as well, with the Mubarak regime putting several prominent editors and journalists on trial for their reporting. These accumulated tensions make Egypt's political system look like a tinderbox; Westerners are periodically reminded that it is this political environment that gave rise to movements

such as Islamic Jihad and individuals such as al-Qaeda's Ayman al-Zawahiri.

In 2007, the governing NDP reinforced its position by winning parliamentary elections. Within the NDP, Hosni Mubarak reconfirmed his own position in November of that year by winning a vote that retained him as party leader. The rapid promotion of Gamal Mubarak within the NDP—he is now one of the party's five top leaders—has suggested to some that he is being groomed as a possible successor to his father. Born in 1963, Gamal is seen as the leader of those younger politicians who want change and would likely encounter significant opposition from the army and older party hacks were dynastic ambitions pushed. He would appear to have little if any support outside the hermetic confines of the NDP and has consistently denied presidential ambitions.

Egypt's economy may be growing, but the massive challenges of overcoming extensive poverty and inequality remain. Cairo continues to grow as a city, but this also gives rise to classic urban problems such as overcrowding, congestion and pollution. Another major challenge going forward is the water supply. Egypt relies almost exclusively on the Nile, which originates to the south and flows through Ethiopia and Sudan before reaching Egypt; with water widely predicted to be the resource over which the major wars of the 21st Century will be fought, Egypt must constantly keep an eye on this precious resource.

Socialist People's Libyan Arab Jamahiriya

Modern Tripoli   Photo by Pat Crowell

Basic Facts

Area: 1,758,610 sq. km. = 680,000 sq. mi. (about the size of Alaska plus Arizona)

Population: 6,200,000 (UN 2007 est.)

Capital Cities: Tripoli (pop. 1.5 million, estimated) and Benghazi (pop. 750,000, estimated), co-capitals; Baida is the administrative center; moves are now underway to transfer the administrative sector to Al Jofor.

Climate: Mediterranean, with summer and winter in a narrow 50-mile-wide band along the coast; semiarid in the region adjoining the coastal belt, arid and hot in the remainder within the Sahara Desert.

Neighboring Countries: Algeria and Tunisia (west); Egypt (east); The Sudan (southeast); Chad and Niger (south)

Official Language: Arabic

Other Principal Languages: Berber languages, including Jabal and Zuara; Tamahaq, spoken by Tuaregs; Italian, English, all widely understood in the major cities.

Ethnic Groups: Berber and Arab 97%, Greeks, Maltese, Italians, Egyptians, Pakistanis, Turks, Indians, and Tunisians

Principal Religion: Sunni Muslim 97%

Chief Commercial Products: Crude oil, refined petroleum products, and natural gas.

GNI Per Capita: $5,530 (World Bank 2006 est.)

Currency: Libyan dinar

Former Colonial Status: Turkish Colony (1553–1911); Italian Colony (1911–1943) British-French jurisdiction (1943–1951)

Independence Date: December 24, 1951

Chief of State: Col. Moamer al-Qadhafi, "Leader of the Revolution"

National Flag: A plain green field.

Land and People

Libya covers a vast area of central North Africa, most of which lies within the blistering Sahara Desert. The coastal area is fertile and populous—in reality it is a series of oases in an otherwise dry countryside. Farther inland, mountains rise in plateaus to heights of up to 3,000 feet. There is irregular rainfall in the region due to the perpetual struggle between the moist winds of the Mediterranean and the dry, hot air of the desert.

A short distance inland, rainfall becomes increasingly light. Sudden showers, when they occur, fill otherwise dry river beds to overflowing, sweeping valuable topsoil to the sea. Temperatures in the winter often go below freezing, but they may rise quickly to as high as 80°F. in January because of the *ghibli,* a hot, arid wind from the desert.

The low mountains, with scattered scrub vegetation, provide forage for the Barbary sheep, which need little water to survive. The sands of the Sahara take charge about 50 miles from the sea, where temperatures may soar as high as 137°F. in the shade. In the extreme south, the land rises abruptly to heights of 10,000 feet and more in the majestic and remote Tibesti Mountains.

The Islamic Libyans tend to be basically conservative in their outlook. The lodges of the Islamic Senussi Brotherhood have been the traditional centers of art, religious philosophy and learning, but they are gradually giving way to a system of public education based on more modern concepts and "Qadhafi ideology." Compulsory, free education greatly reduced a pre-1951 illiteracy rate of 90% to less than 50%. High schools and technical colleges emphasize the development of practical skills calculated to contribute to the growth of the economy.

Libya contains a remarkable collection of sites that bear witness to the life that flourished there during prehistoric, Punic, Greek, Roman and Byzantine eras.

One rock art site alone—Tadrart Acacus on the southwest border, east of the city of Ghat—contains thousands of cave paintings in very different styles, dating from 12,000 B.C. to 100 A.D. They catalogue the changing fauna, flora and life styles of the populations that succeeded one another in this Saharan region.

Three sites, Cyrene, Leptis Magna and Sabratha all hold enormous tourist potential. Cyrene, founded in the 7th century B.C., is one of the most complex archaeological sites in the Mediterranean region.

Libya

Cyrenians built the biggest Greek Doric temple in Africa in the 6th century B.C.—the Sanctuary of Zeus, comparable to the Temple of Zeus at Olympia. Leptis Magna was enlarged and embellished by Septimius Severus, who was born there and later became emperor. It was one of the most beautiful cities of the Roman Empire, with its imposing public monuments, market place, storehouses, shops and residential districts. Sabratha, once a Phoenician trading-post that served as an outlet for the products of the African hinterland, was later Romanized and rebuilt in the 2nd and 3rd centuries A.D. Its theater, victory arch and arena all bespeak the efforts of Roman city planners.

The Past: Political and Economic History

For early history, see *Historical Background* and *The Colonial Period: The Italians.*

By the turn of the 20th century, Libya had been historically divided into three provinces—Cyrenaica, Tripolitania and Fezzan. At the close of World War II, the allied powers, the United States, France, Great Britain and the Soviet Union, could not agree on the future of Libya. Italy had renounced all rights to the colony under the terms of the peace treaty it signed in 1947. The provinces of Cyrenaica and Tripolitania were under British control and the French administered Fezzan.

At about the same time that the so-called "Big Four" submitted the question of Libya to the UN, the British recognized Emir El Sayyid Muhammad al-Mahdi el-Senussi as head of state in Cyrenaica; he took the name King Idris. A grandson of the founder of the *Senussi* sect of Islam, he set up a government and proclaimed independence of all Libya. The UN debated for many months, and ultimately passed a resolution providing for Libyan independence by 1951. The National Constituent Assembly met and proclaimed Idris to be King of Libya; a constitution was prepared which came into effect with formal independence in 1951.

Initially a loose federation under the monarch, Libya adopted a new constitution in 1963, which provided for a central government and merged the provinces. The kingdom had a two-chamber legislature; the Senate was appointed by the king and the Chamber of Deputies was elected by the people. There were no political parties.

Because Idris failed to ally Libya firmly enough with the Arab cause against Israel, a group of army officers, headed by 1st Lt. Moamer al-Qadhafi deposed the king in September 1969. Ironically, the king, because of illness, was prepared to announce his abdication the next day. He died in Cairo in 1983.

The government was placed in the hands of a revolutionary council and radical changes were implemented—U.S. military bases were closed and 25,000 Italians either left or were expelled, many of them leaving their property, including $25 million in bank deposits, to be confiscated.

From that point Qadhafi became the darling of the revolutionary left. He yearned for Arab unity, and he spent most of the next years financing various revolutionary movements throughout the world, using Libya's immense oil wealth. He attempted to persuade the leaders and people of virtually every Arab nation, and even tiny Malta, to enter into a union with

King Idris I on his 75th birthday, 1965

Libya. Failure to achieve a single union produced frustration, and Qadhafi has frequently denounced the leadership of states unwilling to join his projects. In the process he increasingly distanced himself from other Arab leaders. Egypt's *El Ahram*, that nation's semiofficial newspaper, once accused Qadhafi of being a "maniac and mere highwayman, even though he may own the gold of Midas."

Ever restless, Qadhafi kept Libya in turmoil through various administrative and structural reforms, while destabilizing other states through a variety of foreign adventures. In 1976 he annexed a 60-mile-wide strip of northern Chad and involved himself in the country's civil war, supporting rebel troops against the central government. The adventure ceased after Chadian troops, with French assistance, routed the Libyans in 1987, capturing about $1 billion of Soviet-manufactured military materiel. An inveterate arms-buyer, Qadhafi bought billions of dollars in military equipment during the 1970s

and 1980s, more indeed, than Libya had troops to use or pilots to fly.

Relations between Libya and the United States have long been tense. In 1979 Libyan mobs sacked the U.S. Embassy. Relations between the two countries came to a standstill while the U.S. insisted Libya take full responsibility for the attack. Qadhafi called it a "spontaneous demonstration by students," and offered neither apology nor admitted responsibility. He heightened the verbal offensive against the United States in 1981 after the U.S. shot down two Libyan jets over the Gulf of Sidra. The U.S. said the incident resulted from an unprovoked attack on U.S. jets, but Qadhafi accused the U.S. of aggression.

Under Qadhafi, things in Libya are very much ad hoc and subject to change. He does not use the title of president; he prefers "Eternal Guide" or "Leader of the Revolution." He decreed that Libya has no central government, just a series of "Basic People's Congresses." Their decisions are carried out by layer upon layer of committees and a general secretariat. He made military training mandatory for both girls and boys in secondary schools. This training program, plus the formation of a "People's Army" containing school and university students, made conservative elements of the military very apprehensive. There have been several attempts on Qadhafi's life.

Terror has been an integral part of Col. Qadhafi's foreign and domestic policy. In 1984–1986, terrorism was primarily directed at Libyan dissidents living in exile. By late 1985, Qadhafi's anti-Americanism had become virulent enough for President Ronald Reagan to urge all Americans living illegally in the country to leave. Travel visas to Libya were forbidden. In response to his anti-American rhetoric, the U.S. sent a naval task force into the Gulf of Sidra, past what Qadhafi had labeled "the line of death," sank two Libyan patrol boats, and conducted air raids against Libyan radar and missile installations on the mainland. Shortly thereafter a bomb ripped a discotheque in West Berlin, killing two U.S. servicemen; irrefutable evidence indicated Libya was responsible. When the trial of those responsible finally took place in November 2001, a German court blamed Libya's intelligence service, and four people, including a former Libyan diplomat, were sentenced to prison terms of 12–14 years.

In April 1986 President Reagan ordered an air strike against Libya, conducted from bases in England. Among the hits made was Qadhafi's residence. An American spokesman curtly stated "We didn't know he was home." He was, and the attack visibly shook him. When he finally appeared on television about five weeks

Libya

Moamer al-Qadhafi

later, he was at times incoherent and appeared to be heavily sedated. For the next 18 months Qadhafi was continuously on the move, fearful of losing his life. His popularity plummeted as basic commodities disappeared from markets, but by 1988 he reemerged and embarked, erratically, on a course to normalize Libya's relations with the rest of the world.

Recognizing the toll UN economic sanctions took, Qadhafi organized a remarkable and ultimately successful campaign to eliminate them. The sanctions had resulted from alleged Libyan complicity in terrorism against two airliners—a Pan American flight, which exploded over Lockerbie, Scotland in December 1988, and a Brazzaville-to-Paris UTA flight, which exploded over Niger in March 1989. In the first, 270 people had been murdered, including a number of American citizens; in the second, 170, largely French citizens, died. When Qadhafi refused to hand over the alleged perpetrators, the UN Security Council ordered air and military embargoes in 1992.

In 1993 the sanctions were tightened to include the freezing of Libyan funds and financial resources in other countries, and a ban on the sale of equipment for oil and gas operations. Libyan sanctions never prohibited the sale of petroleum or froze petroleum investments. Unable to convince the UN on these matters, the United States imposed tougher unilateral sanctions in 1996, applying them to investments in Libya's oil or gas sectors. The lifting of the UN sanctions was conditioned on the two Libyan suspects in the Lockerbie case being turned over to the British and Americans.

By 1998 the sanctions were extracting a severe price from the Libyan economy, and at some point Col. Qadhafi decided to eliminate these two obstacles to Libya's reinsertion into the world community. The

two cases had different velocities and followed different trajectories, both equally improbable. In the UTA case, Qadhafi allowed a French investigating judge to question some 50 members of the Libyan intelligence services in Tripoli in 1996. During this visit, the judge "found" and seized a suitcase at the intelligence service offices. Not only was the suitcase identical to the one believed to have been stuffed with explosives that brought the plane down, but somewhat miraculously, the judge also found timers and detonators similar to those used in the bombing. It was the theater of political calculation: Qadhafi abandoned his officers that the international community might abandon its isolation of Libya.

The French judge drew up charges accusing the second-in-command of the Libyan intelligence services, Abdallah Senussi—Qadhafi's own brother-in-law—of giving the order to bomb the UTA flight. Five others were also named in the indictment, and their trial *in absentia* took place in Paris in March 1999. All were found guilty and sentenced to life in prison. Libya later paid some $31 million as compensation to the victims' families.

Largely marginalized by other Arab states, Qadhafi turned increasingly to his African neighbors. Indeed, solidarity with them became the "priority of priorities" for Libya. In June 1998 the OAU voted to ignore the UN air embargo on Libya, and several African presidents flew into Tripoli to visit the colonel. Libya downgraded its "permanent" status at the Arab League, scrapped its Arab Ministry, and changed the name of its radio from the "Voice of the Arab Nation" to "Voice of Africa." The ever-mercurial Qadhafi told an Arab delegation that "for good or worse, nothing will ever link me to Arabs," and that he wanted "Libya's interests to be in Africa and remain there."

Some of Libya's African friends, including Nelson Mandela, facilitated a resolution of the Lockerbie case. The mechanism was unique, precedent-setting, and diplomatically complex: The two Lockerbie suspects would be tried in the Netherlands, under Scottish law. The duo was transferred in April 2000, and UN sanctions were automatically suspended.

The Lockerbie trial began in April 2000, and the panel of three Scottish judges hearing the case rendered their verdict in late January 2001. They found Abdel Basset al-Megrahi, a Libyan intelligence agent, guilty of murdering 270 people. Al-Megrahi's sentence was life imprisonment in a Scottish jail. His lawyers appealed the verdict, but a panel of Scottish judges denied it in March 2002.

The United States and the United Kingdom, however, still demanded that Libya

take responsibility for the bombing and agree to a compensation package for families of the victims. Secret negotiations to this end were revealed in the spring of 2002. More than a year later, in August 2003, Libya formally took responsibility for the bombing in a letter to the UN Security Council and signed a compensation deal worth $2.7 billion to the families of Lockerbie victims. In September the Security Council permanently lifted its sanctions against the regime. (The French, a bit *retardataire*, saw how badly their compensation negotiations had fared and demanded they be reopened.)

Internationally, Col. Qadhafi presents himself as the new and revised edition, a rogue reformed. No longer the sponsor of terror and destabilization, the colonel is now the sponsor and protector of stability among his African neighbors. The high point of Libya's Africa-first policy came in March 2001, when an extraordinary OAU summit met in Sirte and agreed to the creation of an African Union (AU). The AU was inaugurated in July 2002, with South Africa's Thabo Mbeki the new formation's first president, not the dreamer of unity, Col. Qadhafi. In a strife-torn continent, there continue to be unending opportunities for the "Guide" to offer his services as a diplomatic broker between contending parties. In March and April 2007 Col. Qadhafi became actively involved in the most pressing of the continental crises, Darfur.

As relations with Africa warmed, relations with the Arab League chilled to the point of rupture. At an early March 2003 League summit called to discuss the situation in Iraq, Qadhafi and the Saudi Crown Prince, Abdullah bin Abdul Aziz, traded public insults while embarrassed Egyptian TV operators desperately sought to pull the plug on live transmission. The scene was so envenomed that one Saudi paper, *Okaz*, called for Qadhafi's overthrow. The colonel proceeded to withdraw his ambassador to the kingdom and escalated things by demanding to withdraw from the League. To reporters he said that Libya was "above all an African country . . . the African Union is sufficient enough." The decision to leave the League definitively was announced as "irrevocable" in April 2003, but was never implemented.

Internally, the government has faced continuing opposition, which intensified as economic conditions deteriorated. Violent clashes with militant Islamist opposition groups occurred in 1997, particularly in the eastern region. The government tightened security measures, made hundreds of arrests and conducted military operations in the affected areas. Members and sympathizers of banned Islamic groups were closely monitored; activities at mosques were surveilled.

To deal with its opposition, the government has frequently resorted to the use of terror. In March 1997 the Libyan General People's Congress approved a collective guilt and punishment law. By this law any group, large or small, including towns, villages, local assemblies, tribes or families can be punished in their entirety if accused by the People's Congress or a People's Committee of sympathizing, financing, or in any way helping, protecting or failing to identify perpetrators of crimes against the state. The crimes include "obstructing the people's power, instigating and practicing tribal fanaticism, possessing, trading in or smuggling unlicensed weapons, and damaging public and private institutions and property." The scope of the law is staggering.

During the heyday of socialist economics, members of so-called "Popular Committees" terrorized the bazaars of Tripoli and other cities. Formed in 1996 and made up of volunteers, often students and army officers, the committees were charged by Colonel Qadhafi with purifying cities of the "satanic filthiness of the West." Ambulatory peddlers, selling a few items on the streets in one of the few expressions of a free market to be found in Libya, were subject to the Committees' attention. Imported items were confiscated, sellers fined, and examples made. One Palestinian merchant was accused of "inundating the Libyan market with Israeli aphrodisiac chewing gum," proving how ever-vigilant revolutionary puritanism needs to be. Punishment for deviance is severe: Under laws passed in 1996 any Libyan can be punished by death for speculations in food, currency, clothes or housing during a state of war or blockade—which included the UN sanctions.

Clearly those multilateral sanctions worked, and the social consequences of economic constriction were something the regime ultimately chose not to bear. As Qadhafi's handling of the Lockerbie case showed, pragmatism trumps ideology. The colonel-guide now speaks of free markets and investments, and the revolutionary committees have been marginalized. In September 2000 he articulated his vision of the new Libya: "Now is the era of economy, consumption, markets, and investments. This is what unites people irrespective of language, religion, and nationalities." Despite such globalist geniality, vestigial anti-Americanism remains, as does an implacable opposition to Israel.

Libya's development of a missile program, with Chinese and North Korean assistance, remained a principal U.S. security concern after the Lockerbie file had been closed. Though not part of the Bush administration's "axis of evil," Libya was accused of trying to acquire weapons of mass destruction (WMD), and the Bush administration chose not to lift American sanctions when the Security Council lifted its. Instead, it kept the issue alive and the pressure on.

The invasion of Iraq made implicit threat direct reality, and the light of war clarified the colonel's vision on the utility and danger of WMD. Secret contacts were made with the British and Americans, negotiations conducted, and nine months later, in December 2003, the colonel-guide stunned the world by announcing that Libya would abandon its programs to develop weapons of mass destruction.

The country's nuclear projects were opened to international inspection and the UN's International Atomic Energy Agency (IAEA) indicated there was evidence that Libya had produced a small amount of plutonium. Though it was insufficient to make a bomb, it was clear Libya was close to obtaining nuclear weapons capability.

In terms of nuclear intelligence, Libyan cooperation provided information on the vast procurement network operated by the Pakistani physicist, Dr. Abdul Qadeer Khan, revered as the "father" of Pakistan's nuclear bomb. In his spare time, Dr. Khan ran an international black market in nuclear-weapons materials. To enrich uranium obtained from North Korea, Libya had made some $100 million worth of purchases, primarily centrifuge technology, from the Khan network. In one small step for a less-dangerous nuclear world, the Libyan program has been dismantled and carted away.

Libya's readmittance to the family of nations seemed nearly complete following British Prime Minister Blair's meeting with Qadhafi in March 2004; by the end of 2004 Gerhard Schroeder of Germany, Ital-

Roman Imperial theater at Sabratha   Photo by Pat Crowell

Libya

Libya opens to the world. Thousands view the total eclipse of the sun, March 29, 2006

Photo by Beverly Ingram

ian Prime Minister Silvio Berlusconi, and French President Jacques Chirac had all made official stops in Tripoli to meet with the colonel-guide, and in Washington, President George W. Bush had removed virtually all the U.S. unilateral sanctions, helping Libya attract badly needed foreign investment.

Allegations that Col. Qadhafi had approved a plan to kill Crown Prince Abdullah, Saudi Arabia's ruler, did, however, keep Libya's name on America's list of state sponsors of terrorism.

When Libya and Saudi Arabia reestablished diplomatic relations in late 2005, the U.S. declared the issue closed and opened the doors were open to full recognition of Col. Qadhafi's regime. That came in May 2006, after the Libyan regime renounced terrorism. Final resolution of the Lockerbie compensation question followed in 2008 and then-Secretary of State Condoleezza Rice visited Libya that year (after Libya released foreign health workers in 2007 who stood accused of deliberately spreading HIV/AIDS). Still, Col. Qadhafi continues to be an enigmatic figure from whom the occasional odd outburst is expected.

The Present: Contemporary Issues

Libya's economy is dependent on its petroleum industry. According to the World Bank, in 2005 oil accounted for 95% of foreign earnings, 93% of government revenues, and 72.6% of GDP. UN sanctions hurt the economy and hydrocarbon sector badly. Libya reported estimated losses amounting to nearly $27 billion resulting from them. Economic growth became pinched. Growth of 2% was reported in 1995, but this fell to 0.7% in 1996 and 0.6% in 1997. With the regime's reintegration into the world community following its renunciation of nuclear projects and terrorism, GDP grew at an estimated 3.5% in 2005, down slightly from growth of 4.6% in 2004. Skyrocketing oil prices have boosted government revenues significantly. With its oil bonanza, the government has embarked on an investment program to modernize the sector and expand production.

With sanctions curtailing investment, Libya's oil capacity remained stagnant at 1.3 million–1.4 million barrels per day (bbl/d) for a decade. Petroleum facilities and air and ground infrastructure weren't modernized in years. By 2000 oil production capacity had slipped to around 810,000 bbl/d, down from a peak of 3.3 million bbl/d in 1970. With only internal flights, airport maintenance and upgrading had deteriorated, and road construction languished. The lifting of sanctions opened enormous opportunities for Libya and foreign business investment. Results were soon noticeable.

In 2004 Libyan oil production was estimated at 1.6 million bbl/d, and the government announced ambitious plans to increase production to 2 million bbl/d by 2008–2010, and 3 million by 2015. Libyan officials estimated the country needed $30 billion in investment to achieve these goals. It has begun an aggressive auction of exploration licenses to major oil companies.

The Libyan prize is huge. There are about 39 billion barrels of oil reserves (2005), and Libyan oil is extremely high-quality, low-sulfur content crude.

Low production costs in Libya add incentives. Onshore costs can be as little as $5 a barrel, and given the shallowness of the Mediterranean, even offshore costs are low by world standards.

In 2001 the National Oil Corporation opened more than 322,000 square miles to foreign companies for exploration in production-sharing agreements. About 80% of Libya's known reserves are located in the Sirte basin, but huge areas of the country are unexplored and untested. Oil industry analysts see excellent potential for additional oil discoveries.

When the results of the first exploration license auction were announced in January 2005, U.S. oil companies won 11 of the 15 concessions offered. Occidental Petroleum won nine concession blocks, while ChevronTexaco and Amerada Hess each acquired one block. In October 2005 another 26 licenses were put up for auction and these were won by French, Italian, Norwegian, Russian, Turkish, Japanese, Indian and Malaysian firms. The auction round brought in some $500 million in new investment monies, and Libyan authorities announced they were preparing another 100 licenses for future bidding.

China's CNPC was also a successful bidder in the October round, and in January 2006, Chinese Foreign Minister Li Zhaoxing arrived in Libya to sign a variety of cooperation agreements. Never at a loss for producing surprises, Libyan foreign policy seemed to tred risky ground. On the very day colonel-guide Qadhafi was meeting with Foreign Minister Li, one of his sons was in Taipei, meeting with Taiwan's President Chen Shui-bian. President Chen announced he had accepted an invitation to visit Libya, and the two countries would open trade offices in each other's capitals. Foreign Minister Li called it an insult to China, and Col. Qadhafi seemed more inscrutable than ever.

Natural gas production also has enormous potential and is a high priority for Libya. Proven reserves as of January 2005 were estimated at 52 trillion cubic feet (Tcf), though some industry experts believe them to be even higher. Libya would like to shift to the greater use of gas rather than oil domestically, freeing up more oil for export. It also has great expectations for gas exports to Europe, a market carefully scrutinized by Vladimir Putin's Russia.

Gazprom, the Russian natural gas and pipeline monopoly that shut the valves on Ukraine and doubled the price of gas to Georgia, won a 10% stake in a Libyan offshore exploration block in January 2007; it

plans to invest some $200 million on the project. With pipeline agreements with central Asian states and supply contracts with North African gas producers Algeria and Libya, Gazprom would have, in effect, a gas cartel to squeeze European buyers.

Despite seeming energy wealth, Libya struggles to meet growing domestic demands for power; the city of Tripoli, for example, cannot yet receive gas by pipeline. The country is pushing ahead with plans to set up a nuclear plant for civilian use. The project is dependent on western nations offering technical and financial assistance.

Libya's initial transformation to a free-market economy was overseen by Prime Minister Shukri Ghanem, a professional economist long known for his support of a liberalized economy. Besides open competition for oil exploration concessions, the government began a program of privatizing more than 300 government companies—selling them off to private sector and foreign investors. Shukri Ghanen was replaced in March 2006, however, and appointed head of the national oil company. His replacement, Prime Minister Baghdadi Mahmudi, promised to continue economic reform, and the cabinet shuffle may have had more to do with the regime's somewhat opaque internal politics than economic reform.

Apparently Mahmudi was perceived as a bit less threatening to entrenched interests than Prime Minister Ghanen, but there are strong elements of policy continuity between the two. Each addressed the problem of Libya's hugely inflated public bureaucracy similarly. In May 2005 Ghanen announced a radical diet for the morbid obesity of the civil service: the

government was simply unable to create new jobs in the public sector. The state is Libya's largest employer, having one million workers on its payroll (some of them twice). In January 2007, Prime Minister Mahmudi announced the necessity of budgetary liposuction: 400,000 public employees would have to be laid off.

Both Ghanen and Mahmudi seem at one with the man most associated with the idea of Libya's need for economic reform—Seif al-Islam, Moamar Qadhafi's eldest son. In August 2006 Seif Qadhafi accused public servants of operating like a "mafia" to block essential economic and political changes.

To cushion the blow, each public employee made "redundant" will be given three year's salary and credits up to $43,000 for business startups by the more entrepreneurially minded. Indeed, American advisors are being brought in to teach the fundamentals of private enterprise. In effect, the government is recycling oil revenues into economic diversification. Initially it is emphasizing construction (500,000 housing units over the next five years) and tourism development.

With some 1,340 miles of undeveloped coastline and remarkable architectural ruins, Libya offers enormous opportunities in tourism. The country has five UNESCO World Heritages sites (Leptis Magna, Sabratha, Cyrene, Ghadames, and the southwestern rock art sites of Tadrart Acacus), but only one five-star hotel—the Corinthia Bab Africa Hotel in Tripoli. The Corinthia, which is the first enterprise in Libya to allow customers to use credit cards, is an indication of just how nascent the tourism industry is. Other impediments: the country remains alcohol free and has a notoriously difficult (and expensive) visa process; tourists who have Israeli visas in their passports will be denied entry to Libya.

The Future

The opening of the economy promises jobs for the unemployed—more than 30% of the population—and a chance at improved living standards. The boom in oil prices in recent years places Libya in the fortunate position of receiving a major windfall of foreign exchange.

In recent years, Libya has quietly taken a more respectable place in the "community of nations." Tensions with the United States persist and likely will be for as long as Colonel Qadhafi remains in power. Nonetheless, Libya is no longer the pariah state it once was. This is not to say it is democratic, as personal freedoms, political rights and press freedoms leave much to be desired.

African Unity billboard   Photo by Pat Crowell

The Kingdom of Morocco

The World Heritage site of Ait Benhaddou

Photo by Jinny Lambert

Basic Facts

Area: 458,730 sq. km. = 200,320 sq. mi. (larger than California; the disputed territory of Western Sahara, now a part of Morocco, is another 102,703 sq. mi.)

Population: 31,200,000 (UN 2007 est.)

Capital City: Rabat

Climate: Semitropical and moist along the coastline and inland for 125 miles. Cool, with frost and snow in the high altitudes of the Atlas Mountains. A hot, semiarid plateau on the south side of the Atlas Mountains quickly gives way to the Sahara Desert. The dry season of the coastal regions is from April to October.

Neighboring Countries: Algeria (east, southeast); Mauritania (south); Morocco claims the entire territory of Western Sahara, formerly Spanish Sahara, most of which it occupies.

Official Language: Arabic

Other Principal Languages: Berber languages, including Ghomara, Tachelhit, Tamazight, Tarifit; French, Spanish (largely in the enclaves of Melilla and Ceuta)

Ethnic Groups: Arab-Berber 99.1%, other 0.7%, Jewish 0.2%

Principal Religions: Muslim 98.7%, Christian 1.1%, and Jewish 0.2%

Chief Commercial Products: Food and beverages 30%, semi-processed goods 23%, consumer goods 21%, and phosphates 17%

GNI Per Capita: $1,730 (World Bank 2006 est.)

Currency: Dirham

Former Colonial Status: French Protectorate (1912–1956)

Independence Date: March 2, 1956

Chief of State: King Mohamed VI (since July 1999)

National Flag: A five-pointed star in green outline on a red background.

Land and People

Situated on the northwest corner of Africa, Morocco is the African nation closest to the European continent, separated from Spain by the narrow Strait of Gibraltar. Three ranges of the high, rugged Atlas Mountains extend through the central and eastern portions of the country for more than 500 miles. In the hinterland of Fez, the Middle Atlas meets the Rif Range, which forms a crescent of land 6,000 feet high flanking the Mediterranean. To the south, the Middle Atlas is succeeded by the High Atlas, some of whose peaks reach a height of 13,000 feet. The Atlas, stretching almost the entire length of Morocco, form a natural barrier between the fertile coast and the dry Sahara Desert and give the country three major environmental zones: relatively well-watered coastal lowlands, the mountain highlands, and the eastern deserts.

The coastal region is fertile, with a gentle climate. When ample rainfall arrives intense cultivation of the land is possible, but precipitation is irregular and droughts are not uncommon. White beaches along

Morocco

the seacoast stretch for almost 1,700 miles along the Atlantic Ocean and the Mediterranean Sea, providing ample opportunity for the development of tourism.

Temperatures are cool in the highlands and bitterly cold in the winter. They are often snowcapped in the summer, permitting skiing at the same time bathers relax in the sun along the coast. Rainfall is concentrated in the cooler months from October to May, while summers are dry.

A note on royal names and titles: Moroccan princes are referred to with the title Moulay (master), unless their name is Mohamed. Since the only "Master Mohamed" is the Prophet, princes named Mohamed are addressed as *Sidi* (my lord). Princesses are given the title *Lalla*.

The historic city of Meknès, founded in the 11th century by Almoravid rulers as a military town, is a major tourist attraction. Meknès became a capital under Sultan Moulay Ismaïl (1672–1727), the founder of the Alawite dynasty. The sultan transformed the city into an impressive center of Spanish-Moorish style surrounded by high walls. Monumental entrance doors show the harmonious blending of Islamic and European styles of the 17th-century Maghreb.

The Alawite dynasty has provided the country's sultans since the mid-17th century. Like his predecessors, King Mohamed bears several titles—Commander of the Faithful, Savior, and Shadow of the Prophet on Earth—that reflect the dynasty's claim to be directly descended from the Prophet Mohammed. The claim has been the traditional means by which Moroccan kings have legitimized their rule and, more recently, checked the claims of Islamists.

The Past: Political and Economic History

For early history, see *Historical Background* and *The Colonial Period: the French.*

Power in independent Morocco was concentrated in the hands of the monarch. Sultan Muhammad V (who officially adopted the title of king in August 1957) chose his ministers personally and kept personal control of the all-important army and the police forces. He was assisted, if that be the word, by a Consultative Assembly of 60, which he himself named. His eldest son, Moulay Hassan, became chief of staff and learned the art of politics and power from a skilled practitioner. Royal absolutism was slightly modified by a royal charter issued in May 1958 creating a constitutional monarchy.

When *Istiqlal* split along generational and ideological lines in 1959, the king positioned himself as neutral arbiter, well above the political fray. *Istiqlal*'s main faction, containing older and more traditional

elements, was headed by Muhammad 'Allal al-Fasi. A smaller section headed by Mehdi Ben Barka was formed of younger men, intellectuals who favored socialism and had republican leanings. To pursue these goals, they formed the National Union of Popular Forces (UNFP).

Moulay Hassan was elevated to the throne as King Hassan II upon the unexpected death of his father in 1961. He promptly drafted a new constitution providing a parliamentary government. Elections were held in 1963 and the National Assembly began to function. Both Istiqlal factions were in opposition, while a miscellany of royal supporters coalesced in the Front for the Defense of Constitutional Institutions. Political bickering led to political paralysis. The king dissolved parliament after only a year and resorted to personal rule. Over the years it was clearly Hassan II's preferred form of governance.

The king's most formidable opponent, Mehdi Ben Barka, was forced into exile. Once the king's mathematics instructor, Ben Barka later turned radical, touting a Nasserist "Arab revolution" against Morocco's "reactionary" monarch. His support of revolutionary Algeria led to subsequent charges of high treason, including allegations of plotting against the life of Hassan II. He was sentenced *in absentia* to death. From his home in Paris Ben Barka became leader of the opposition to Hassan—until, that is, he was kidnapped and disappeared in October 1965. Numerous observers have suggested that the Ben Barka plot was managed by General Muhammad Oufkir, the king's minister of the interior.

There followed a period of constitutions and coups, none of which were successful. Army rebels attempted it in 1971, raking the king's birthday party with gunfire and killing 98 guests, one of which was the Belgian ambassador. A year later General Oufkir apparently led a second coup, which almost downed the royal plane. Hassan survived, as he did some eight other attempts on his life. For the faithful, such luck meant he must be a good ruler, gifted with *baraka*—a kind of divine grace.

His opponents were less fortunate. General Oufkir died at the royal palace, supposedly by his own hand. Hundreds of suspects, including members of his family, were imprisoned. It was a tad more genteel than the fate of rebels against his father. While crown prince and army chief in 1958 Hassan had suppressed a rebellion in the Rif mountains. Rebellion ringleaders, so the story goes, were flown out to sea in helicopters and shoved overboard. True or not, it certainly contributed to the prince's image: fear, not love, was a more likely policy. Indeed, force seemed to be respected by Moroccans. Hassan's forceful policies to absorb Spanish Sahara increased his popularity in the mid-1970s.

Hassan turned Western Sahara into a fervent nationalist cause. Good relations with Israel and Washington provided the weaponry to defeat the Polisario Front, a guerrilla insurrection seeking independence for the area. Ultimately the war evolved to a stalemate, with Moroccans hunkering down behind massive walls of sand. Nationalist fervor over Sahara could not for long disguise the country's real social and economic and political problems.

Rissani Suq, Tafilat

Photo by Ross Dunn

Morocco

Constitutional tinkering—and it was frequent—never threatened the king's personal rule. Royal decrees could not be debated, for that would be like challenging the will of God. It was also a crime to question the royal finances. Repressed political energy will always find a way out, and the regime faced not only plots against its ruler, but periodic riots, strikes, and other manifestations of discontent.

By the early 1980s bad harvests, a sluggish economy, and the continuing financial drain of the Sahara war increased domestic strains. Islamic fundamentalism was finessed by the king's claim of descent from the Prophet, but its growing influence among both the educated and the impoverished suggested fundamental weaknesses in the system. International lenders and human rights organizations pressed for reform.

The king responded, as always, with a combination of symbol and reality. There seemed to be a greater liberalization. Amnesties were granted to some long imprisoned in remote places; curbs on the powers of security and police forces were announced. Another constitutional referendum was held in 1992, but its provisions were superseded by yet another constitutional change submitted to referendum in 1996. There would be a new bicameral parliament. It would consist of an indirectly elected upper house and, for the first time since independence, a directly elected popular assembly. It was still change from above—royally directed political reform.

The 1997 elections were Morocco's first direct elections for the lower house of parliament and an effort to spread democracy to rural areas. Three main political groups took almost equal numbers of seats in the Chamber of Deputies. The *Koutla* left-wing opposition block took 102 seats. Its dominant partner, the Socialist Union of Popular Forces (USFP) won 57 seats to become the largest party in parliament. The right-wing *Wifak* block won 100 and a center-right grouping received 97. The relatively equal distribution of seats among the principal forces hinted at stalemate rather than action.

For the first time a fundamentalist religious party, the Islamist Popular Constitutional Democratic Movement (MPCD), won seats (nine) in parliament. The remaining seats in the 325-seat chamber went to a scattering of minor parties. The big loser in the elections was *Istiqlal*. It won only 32 seats, down from 43 in 1993 elections, and blamed its loss on fraud and electoral manipulation by the Interior Ministry.

Though a parliamentary system, the government emerged less from parliament than from the king. Hassan II re-

King Mohamed VI

served the right to appoint and fire ministers. The king asked Aberrahmane Youssoufi, the 73-year-old leader of the USFP, to form a government, but the king retained control over two of the most important ministries. The Interior Ministry assignment went to the king's right-hand man, Driss Basri. Defense remained in the hands of the king as supreme commander of the Royal Armed Forces.

To Moroccans Driss Basri was the most powerful and feared of Hassan's ministers. As minister of the interior for over 20 years, Basri controlled a web of security agents and spies who informed him of the slightest hint of dissent or opposition. He controlled appointments of governors and other regional and local officials. The police were under his control and his jails were places of detention and torture. Even critical foreign-policy questions were under his purview. In many ways the Interior Ministry was a parallel government operating above the law and responding only to the king. Basri was grand vizir of the king's dark side.

After 38 years of less than progressive rule King Hassan died in July 1999. He was succeeded by his unmarried elder son, Crown Prince Sidi Mohamed. Mohamed VI's first speech ignited a spark of optimism brighter than any generated by the halfhearted reforms of his father. He evoked the poverty of his people, the fate of women, and the need for change. Action followed words. Corrupt governors were fired and some 10,000 prisoners released from Moroccan prisons. Victims of human rights abuses and relatives of those who had simply "disappeared" were rec-

ognized and offered compensation by the state. Before a December 1999 deadline, the Moroccan human rights commission received 5,500 requests for compensation from victims of the former regime. In November 1999 King Mohamed confirmed his commitment to change by dismissing the much-feared interior minister, Driss Basri.

Mohamed also began the process of bringing his father's political opponents home from exile or freeing them from house arrest. The most notable of the exiles was the 73-year-old Abraham Serfaty. Head of the Marxist-Leninist *Ila al-Amam* group, Serfaty had been sentenced to life in prison for making statements in favor of self-determination for the Western Sahara. After a 17-year incarceration, he was released from jail and expelled from Morocco after enormous international pressure. He had been living in exile for eight years when the young king allowed him to return, a free citizen once again. The family of Mehdi Ben Barka, who "disappeared" under mysterious circumstances in 1965 while living in France, had their passports restored and were allowed to return to Morocco.

The other notable political opponent restored was the Islamist leader Sheikh Abdessalam Yassine, the most radical of King Hassan's challengers. The 72-year-old Yassine was head of *al-Adl wal-Ihsane* (Justice and Charity). Active mainly on university campuses and in the poor districts of large cities, Justice and Charity is the country's biggest Muslim fundamentalist organization, and advocates the reestablishment of the caliphate and the application of *sharia* law.

Sheikh Yassine had long been a thorn in the side of King Hassan. In the 1970s he had been detained without trial for more than three years for sending a 114-page letter to the royal palace criticizing the king for copying Western values—described as barbarous, materialistic and egoistic—and demanding the application of *sharia* law. Government ministers had long called for his release, but palace officials argued he should first acknowledge the religious authority of King Mohamed VI, who bears the title *Amir al-Mu'minin* or "Commander of the Faithful."

The sheikh, seemingly an inveterate letter writer, persisted in his ways even while under house arrest. In February 2000 he addressed a 35-page letter to the king raising one of the most taboo of subjects—the royal family's wealth. It called on the king to return billions of dollars that Islamists allege his father had stashed abroad. Yassine was finally released from ten years of house arrest in May 2000.

Despite fresh vigor and a new optimism generated by the new king, it is difficult

An olive seller

Photo by Jinny Lambert

to say that much progress has been made on Morocco's most pressing problems. There remain utterly fundamental problems about the source of policy innovation and direction between a democratically elected government and a king possessing extraordinary sources of constitutional power and traditional legitimacy. The weight of authority seems to have swung back to the monarch. It was the king who, drawing upon his religious authority as commander of the faithful, took practical action to deal with two of the country's abiding problems: illiteracy and unemployment. In August 2000 he announced that Morocco's mosques would be used to dispense literacy courses, as well as religious, civic and health education. Women—whose literacy in the rural areas is estimated to be as low as 10%—were a primary target of the program.

The 2002 legislative elections confirmed royal dominance. Certainly the fairest elections ever held, the very honesty of the elections reflects royal will: the king saw the first elections to take place during his reign as a means of regaining the trust of a population grown cynical with previous electoral fraud and falsification.

The election featured several innovations. Proportional representation, with electors voting for a party list rather than individual candidates, was employed. To assure female representation in parliament, voters also selected ten percent of their future MPs from a national list of exclusively female candidates. Among all the Arab states, this set-aside assured Morocco of having the largest contingent of women in its legislature. For the first time

also ballots featured party logos to facilitate recognition by illiterate voters. To dissuade fraud and fixing, more than 50,000 bottles of indelible ink were imported to dab the hands of voters, and prison sentences were introduced for vote-buying by candidates—a great tradition of Moroccan politics.

One obvious consequence of these changes was a greater number of political parties participating. Twenty-six of them nominated 5,873 candidates (269 of them women) on 1,772 lists in 91 electoral districts. In the final results representation in parliament was more fragmented than ever: 22 parties would take seats in the new legislature where only 15 had sat before.

The election produced no seismic change. Retiring Prime Minister Youssoufi's USFP claimed the largest number of seats: 50 in the 325-member House of Representatives. *Istiqlal* took second place with 48 seats, while the moderate Islamist Party of Justice and Development (PJD) made the biggest gain, winning 42 seats to its previous 14. Sheikh Yassine's fundamentalist Justice and Charity party called for an election boycott and ran no candidates, so its popularity remained untested.

Paradoxically, the new government that emerged from Morocco's cleanest, most transparent and most democratic election would not be party based. Following the election the king appointed his current interior minister, Driss Jettou, as prime minister. Unaffiliated with any political party, Jettou was a businessman—a former shoe manufacturer—who heads a team of born-

again democrats. In Moroccan politics the palace remains the final arbiter. The prime minister and four other ministers—including defense, foreign affairs and Islamic affairs—are appointed by the monarch. The king presides over meetings of this select cabinet, which operates in parallel with the prime minister's own cabinet, and takes most of the important policy decisions.

In 2002 Moroccan security forces dismantled an al-Qaeda sleeper cell, directed by three Saudis, with plans to blow up American and British war ships passing through the Strait of Gibraltar. A year later, al-Qaeda-linked terrorists set off five bombs near Western and Jewish targets in Casablanca, killing 43 people (including 12 terrorists) and wounding more than 100. Alawite Morocco, ruled by a descendent of the Prophet, was no longer immune to international Islamic terrorism; May 16, 2003 became the country's 9/11.

Parliament reacted by passing a strict antiterrorism law, but the king, the embodiment of official Islam, remained silent. One Rabat paper, *Al-Alam*, referred to a "savage terrorist aggression with foreign hands," but investigation showed the May 16 perpetrators were largely local. Indigenous Islamic fundamentalism was the major threat to Morocco's developing democracy. Symptomatically, municipal elections were postponed from June to September, giving the government more time to campaign against the possibility of a fundamentalist takeover of the country's biggest cities: Casablanca, Rabat, Fez, and Tangiers.

The September 2003 elections were dominated by the two leading traditional parties: Istiqlal and the socialist USFP together won more than 30% of the vote for 23,000 local seats. The one legal Islamist party, the PJD, won less than 3% of the vote, but only because it discreetly chose to run candidates in only 20% of the constituencies. In Casablanca, Morocco's largest city, the PJD won in all eight districts where it presented candidates; had it chosen to run in the city's other eight districts, Casablanca would have had an Islamist government.

On two of Morocco's most prickly policy issues, Spain and Western Sahara, the king has provided policy initiative. In October 2001 he withdrew, without consulting his government, Morocco's ambassador to Spain, signaling the depth of tensions that had developed between the two countries. Relations had soured over Spain's continued support of the Algerian-backed Polisario Front (PF) and its claims for self-determination in Western Sahara. This was, however, only one of several issues that made the Spanish-relations dossier one of the thickest.

Morocco

Relations With Spain

Wary of the decline of fishing stocks in its Atlantic waters, Rabat has refused to renew its fishing agreement with the EU. The Spanish fishing fleet was by far the worst affected. More than 300 vessels and their crews were idled by the failure to reach a new agreement, and the EU had to come up with funds to effect a re-conversion of fleet and crews.

Morocco's fundamentally stagnant economy has not been characterized by significant job creation. Unemployment among the young is at 30%, forcing thousands of men, educated and uneducated, to migrate in search of employment. Spain, a 90-minute boat ride away, is a natural first stop, and a steady stream of clandestine immigrants arrives on Spanish shores. In 2006 some 47,000 illegal immigrants from West Africa arrived in Spain. In many ways North Africa is to southern Europe as Mexico is to the U.S., with the threat of Islamic fundamentalism thrown in.

The jumping-off spots for many of those seeking clandestine entry into Spain are the two Spanish enclaves of Ceuta (Sebta to Moroccans) and Melilla—microscopic residuals from an earlier era. Ceuta, barely seven square miles in size, is a peninsula across from Gibraltar that is, like Melilla, an autonomous region of the Spanish kingdom. Moroccans have lived and worked and bought duty-free goods in both the enclaves for years. With increased illegal migration (a profitable activity of organized crime groups), Spanish authorities heightened security measures.

They ringed both enclaves with two razor-wire fences, ten and a half feet high. The fences are six feet apart, separated by a no-man's-land, constantly observed by 37 infrared cameras, 230 searchlights and 21 watchtowers. Even that proved insufficient to arrest the floodtide of immigrants. In 2005 the Spanish government raised the fence to a height of 20 feet. Coastal patrols have been increased, and a $120 million radar system was installed to surveil the strait. As a consequence of these heightened security measures, most illegal immigrants now attempt to enter Spain through the Canary Islands.

Relatively large immigrant populations are a continuing source of tension between the two countries. Moroccans are the largest immigrant group in Spain, numbering well over 300,000. To service their spiritual needs, there are an estimated 1,000 mosques, functioning out of sight of outsiders in apartments, garages, or workshops with often radical preachers. From this milieu came the al-Qaeda-linked terrorists responsible for the March 11, 2004 train bombings in Madrid. They killed 191 people, wounded more than 1,500, toppled an incumbent government, and transformed relations between Morocco and Spain.

In the still unfolding investigations, Spanish authorities have identified 14 of 18 so far charged with the bombings as Moroccans. One of the ringleaders, a Tangiers native named Jamal Zougam, had connections to two banned Moroccan groups: *Salafiya Jihadiya*, (SJ: Salafist Jihad) implicated in the 2003 Casablanca bombings, and the *Groupe islamiste combattant marocain* (GICM: Moroccan Islamic Combat Group), which claims to struggle for an Islamic state in the kingdom.

Zougam was a disciple of Muhammad al-Fizazi, the spiritual leader of *Salafiya Jihadiya*. Al-Fizazi, had been preaching a virulently anti-Western brand of Islam from a mosque in Tangiers until he was arrested, tried, and given a 30-year sentence of inciting violence in Morocco in 2003. Unfortunately, in the Madrid killers he found perfect translation of his exhortation to utilize portable telephones as "an arm of Islam": they converted their cell phones into detonators.

Facing a common threat from Islamist militancy, Morocco and Spain now cooperate closely in both legal and security issues concerning illegal immigration, international terror and, increasingly, its ties to drug trafficking and organized criminal networks. A new agreement, signed in May 2004, provides for a Spanish judge to be based in Rabat and a Moroccan judge in Madrid to speed up judicial procedures involving both countries.

That cooperation has become increasingly important as militant Islamists have regionalized their organization of jihadist terror. All across North Africa and across the Mediterranean in Europe governments are in a permanent fight against international terrorism. As one French investigative judge, Jean-Louis Bruguière, warns, there has emerged an "arc of radical Islamism" under the leadership of the AQIM (Al-Qaeda in the Islamic Maghreb, formerly the Algerian GSPC, or *Group Salafiste de Prédication and du Combat*).

Arrest announcements detailing terrorist plots come often in Morocco, and this has dominated the international news out of the country in recent years. In early September 2006, police reported that 56 terror suspects had been swept up in an antiterrorist investigation. The suspects were, police officials said, members of a group calling itself *Ansar al-Mahdi* (Supporters of the *Mahdi*, a figure whose arrival is said to herald the end of the world in Islamic tradition) and had amassed material to make far more explosives than had been used by the Casablanca bombers in 2003. Among those arrested were four women, including the wives of two pilots for the national airline, Royal Air Maroc,

and at least five former soldiers with training in the use of explosives. The interior minister tried to put the best possible spin on the obvious: militant Islamists had penetrated the military and security services in their recruitment. The number of those recruited, said minister Benmoussa, was "very limited and involved isolated and marginal cases."

Nevertheless reaction was swift. Airports throughout the kingdom were placed on high alert. Security control of passengers was tightened and security patrols at airport perimeters intensified. At Mohamed V airport outside Casablanca security cameras were modernized to record all movement at the airport; all female workers were prohibited from wearing the veil.

The king acted promptly to deal with the infiltration of his armed forces. Both the head of military intelligence and the director of national security were fired and the royal security apparatus reorganized. Military conscription was ended.

More Casablanca suicide bombings in March and April 2007, which police initially thought were botched affairs by hapless jihadi whose bombs exploded accidentally, have turned out to be more sophisticated, better funded, and better armed than originally thought. Though government officials played down possible international connections, others were quick to point out the upsurge of similar recent incidents in Algeria and Tunisia, for which the Al-Qaeda of the Islamic Maghreb (AQIM), had claimed credit.

A string of arrests has followed in 2008 and 2009, including 36 people in February 2008 and 35 more in July of that year. An additional 15 arrests followed in August, of alleged members of Fath al-Anadalous (an al-Qaeda-affiliated group). At the same time, the Moroccan justice system was completing convictions against several terror masterminds, including Abdelkader Belliraj, the alleged leader of al-Qaeda in Morocco, who was extradited to Belgium. Forty people were convicted for complicity in bombings of an internet café in Casablanca, and in February 2009, Saad Housseini was convicted and sentenced to 15 years for his role in the 2003 Casablanca bombings that killed 45 people. Also in 2008, two Moroccan men were convicted of participation in the Madrid train bombings.

Western Sahara

Western Sahara, formerly known by the names of its two former subdivisions, Saguia el-Hamra and Rio de Oro, lies within one of the most oppressive parts of the immense Sahara Desert. A narrow band along the coast receives torrential thunderstorms wafted inland by the steady trade winds. The only thing that remains after the rain is more erosion—the water either spills into the short rivers emptying silt into the Atlantic Ocean, or is quickly swallowed up by the scorched land.

This thinly populated desert region became a Spanish colony when no one else wanted it during the scramble for colonies at the close of the 19th century. For details of earlier and colonial history, see *Historical Background* and *The Colonial Period: The Spanish.*

The territory, then known as Spanish Sahara, came under Moroccan-Mauritanian domination as a result of a series of diplomatic and military actions after the Spanish left in 1975.

Morocco, Algeria and Mauritania had joined together in the early 1970s to pressure Spain to relinquish the territory. Spain dragged its feet as long as possible, all the while mining the phosphate deposits, which were the colony's only resource. When guerrilla activity commenced in 1974 and sabotaged phosphate extraction, Spain surrendered the territory. The question, of course, was to whom or what it should be relinquished. Morocco, Mauritania and Algeria had rival claims and positions.

The Algerians supported the Polisario Front (PF: Popular Front for the Liberation of Saguia el-Hamra and Rio de Oro)—an organization that claimed to represent the national ambitions of the people of the former colony. Morocco, then backed by Mauritania, insisted that Spain should "return" the Western Sahara as part of greater Morocco.

Seizing the initiative, King Hassan announced a "green march" into Spanish Sahara. Some 200,000 Moroccan civilians crossed the border and penetrated six miles into the territory. Spain transferred administrative responsibility to Morocco and Mauritania, and the Polisario proclaimed the existence of the Sahrawi Arab Democratic Republic (SADR), which was immediately recognized by Algeria as the former colony's only legitimate government. Armed conflict soon broke out between the various actors.

Moroccan and Mauritanian troops quickly solidified their position in Western Sahara, while Algeria supported Polisario sabotage and violence. Initially Morocco and Mauritania seemed in firm control, but PF guerrilla activities posed substantial problems for both nations. Incursions into Mauritania by PF guerillas threatened the Mauritanian capital. A poor nation with an all but nonexistent military capability, Mauritania folded in August 1978. King Hassan proclaimed Western Sahara the 37th province of Morocco, rallying his subjects to a sense of Moroccan nationalism.

Morocco now controls all but the easternmost portion of Western Sahara, which is walled by a ten-foot-high "berm" intended to keep Sahrawi "rebels" out. Since that time, rebel activity has been irregular. Most Sahrawi—more than 150,000 of them—are sheltered in camps near Tindouf, Algeria, subject to the less than tender mercies of the Polisario Front.

The UN has been trying to hold a referendum that would allow the Sahrawi to determine their own future. Since no one can agree on just who is a Sahrawi and who should be eligible to vote in the referendum, the issue is unresolved.

Former Secretary of State James Baker, Kofi Annan's personal representative for Western Sahara, launched another drive to resolve the dispute in May 2000. In 2002, Baker, faced with consistent intransigence from all parties, submitted four proposals to the UN Security Council. The first was to proceed with referendum plans for the territory without the agreement of both parties on specifics. Second was a proposal to grant significant autonomy to the region as part of Morocco. After five years, the Sahrawi would be given a chance to vote on their status. The third proposal was to partition the territory between the contending parties, and the fourth, indicating the degree of frustration the issue has provoked, was simply to walk away, admitting the UN was unable to solve the problem.

The Security Council met in April 2002 to choose a course of action—and could not. Since then, there are several signs that resolution of the problem may be possible. On the Polisario side, the Front has lost its nearly mythical military commander, Lahbib Sid'Ahmed Lahbib Aouba, better known by his *nom de guerre*, Commandant Ayoub. A cofounder of the PF, Commandant Ayoub broke with PF authorities and defected to Morocco, pledging his personal allegiance to King Mohamed in September 2002.

The possibility of oil off the Western Saharan coast may well be the greatest lubricant of movement on the issue. Both TotalFinaElf, France's largest oil firm, and the Oklahoma City-based Kerr-McGee Corporation, signed exploration contracts with Morocco. When the SADR began offering overlapping and competitive blocks in its own licensing round, Kerr-McGee allowed its Moroccan-granted rights to lapse. Business does not like ambiguity.

After several years of securing little more than frequent-flyer mileage, Ambassador Baker resigned as mediator in June 2004. In September, Morocco received its most significant diplomatic rebuke in years when South African President Thabo Mbeki extended diplomatic recognition to the self-proclaimed Sahrawi Republic. Morocco withdrew its ambassador from South Africa and went through an agonizing period of critical self-appraisal of the failure of its diplomacy.

Years after their cease-fire, Morocco and the Polisario Front remain without agree-

A local vegetable retailer

Photo by Taylor O'Connor

Morocco

ment. In March 2006 King Mohammad VI made his third visit to the territory, consulting with local notables and appointing a royal advisory council of 140 members. As is usual in Moroccan affairs, policy initiative on the Sahara issue may come from the king. The outlines of his policy seem clear: Morocco will not cede "one inch of territory, not one grain of sand," but is willing to discuss a broad grant of autonomy within a framework of Moroccan sovereignty. With nothing better to do, the UN Security Council has invited both sides to face-to-face talks and has asked them to negotiate unconditionally. The dispute is now 32 years old.

Boosting the social and economic status of women was a major policy focus of the Youssoufi government. In a traditional, male-dominated society women are disadvantaged. More than 60% of Moroccan women are illiterate, for example, with the rate rising to 90% in poor rural areas. This limits their ability to contribute significantly to the country's economic development.

In March 1999 the government introduced a series of proposals that would alter the country's traditional Islamic marriage statutes. The plan would ban polygamy and raise the minimum age for marriage from 15 to 18. A system of legal divorce would replace the current norm of simple verbal dissolution through repudiation by the husband. Under the new proposals divorce would be in the hands of a judge. The new statutes also stipulated that a couple's assets must be shared after divorce.

After the government announced its reforms, most political and religious groups expressed passionate reactions. Fundamentalists and modernists staged dueling marches in Casablanca and Rabat. An estimated 500,000 traditionalists demonstrated in Casablanca against the project, dwarfing a demonstration by supporters of the plan, who rallied about 40,000 people in Rabat. The government stayed its hand; reform of the family code languished.

Following the bloody Casablanca bombings, Islamists kept a low profile. In the breathing space provided by quiescence, the king took up the issue of family code reform, something central to his concerns since the beginning of his reign. In October 2003 he announced a new code, "in perfect harmony with the spirit of Islam," and, exercising audacious leadership, helped push the code through parliament. (It was passed unanimously by both chambers, including the Islamic PJD.) The new code, which became effective in February 2004, recognizes the equality of the sexes, suppresses the husband's right of repudiation, raises the age of consent to 18 and renders polygamy virtually impossible to practice.

With the adoption of the *Mudawana*, or Family Code, Morocco becomes a rare exception in the Muslim world, where the status of women remains a battlefield between modernists and radical Islamists.

The Present: Contemporary Issues

Agriculture contributes about 13.3% of Morocco's GDP (2005) and accounts for about 50% of the labor force, but it is highly dependent on rainfall patterns. As a consequence, economic growth tends to be erratic, making the conditions of rural farmers difficult at best. According to government statistics, GDP grew by only 0.9% in 2000, following two successive years of drought. Better rains in the following years brought higher economic growth: 3.5% in 2004, but a year later growth had fallen to 1.7%. Growth levels in this range are far too sluggish to deal with the country's poverty and unemployment problems.

Morocco is considered to have the best agricultural land in North Africa and produces wheat, barley, beans sugar beets and citrus fruits. Much of the arable land remains unused due to a lack of irrigation, one of the priorities in the government's five-year development plan.

There are no government statistics on Morocco's cannabis crop (known locally as *kif*), the amount of which, no doubt, also fluctuates with rainfall conditions. Morocco is among the world's largest producers of cannabis. Its cultivation and sale is the economic basis for much of the Rif Mountains of northern Morocco, where over 200,000 acres are devoted to its production. About two-thirds of the 800,000 people of the Rif, most of them Berbers, depend on cannabis for their income. They produce an estimated 47,400 tons of hashish a year, most of it exported to Algeria, Tunisia, and Europe—smuggled to Spain, Portugal, and France by sea, then by road to other countries in Europe. The total trade is estimated to be worth more than $13 billion, but most of the profits are taken by drug lords, most of them European criminals living on Spain's Costa del Sol.

For most Rif inhabitants, cannabis cultivation is simply a matter of survival: "It keeps us alive, not the government," said one local. The region is isolated, underdeveloped, impoverished, and alienated. Resentments still linger from the brutal repression of a Berber rebellion in 1958. After that, the central government pretty

A nesting stork   Photo by Taylor O'Connor

much abandoned the region to its own; infrastructure investments—roads and schools—were minimal. When an earthquake hit the area in early 2004, it took several days for supplies to reach some villages because of difficult topography and poor infrastructure.

Intensified government attention and unfavorable climatic conditions have recently reduced acreage devoted to cannabis and overall yield. The UN's Office on Drugs and Crime reports that total acreage devoted to cannabis in 2005 was down 40%—from nearly 300,000 acres in 2004 to around 180,000 a year later. Production, according to the agency's *2006 World Drug Report*, declined by 45% in the same period.

The arrest of a talkative drug baron in August 2006 dented the protective shield provided by corrupt Moroccan officials, including the director of security of the royal palaces, Abdelaziz Izzou. The high-profile narcotics and corruption trial of 17 suspects, including Izzou and 11 police officers and interior ministry officials, began in April 2007.

Attempts to diversify have produced a modestly mixed economy. The mining sector remains crucially important. There are about 90 mining companies producing about 20 different mineral products. Phosphates account for 92% of mineral production. Morocco has the largest phosphate reserves in the world—110 billion tons—and produces significant amounts of fertilizers and phosphoric acid. It is the world's number one phosphoric acid exporter, averaging 1.7 million tons of exports annually. Phosphates and their by-products account for 18% of Morocco's total exports.

Heightened demand, largely spurred by China's natural resource needs, have increased phosphate exports and revenues. In September 2005 the Chinese group Sinochem signed an agreement with Morocco's *Office Chérifien des Phosphates* (OCP) to increase phosphate exports to China from 200,000 tons a year to 750,000 tons. It also signed a joint venture agreement to produce phosphoric acid and phosphate fertilizer in Morocco.

A fishing industry is developing, but over-fishing by aggressive industrial fishing fleets has severely reduced the stock of available fish, and Morocco has had to declare an occasional "biological repose" in response. Much of the over-fishing was done by European fishing fleets, and Morocco refused to renew its fishing agreement with the EU until recently. As of April 2007 a total of 119 European boats are authorized to begin fishing in Moroccan waters four a period of four years. For these fishing rights, the EU will pay Morocco $187 million dollars.

Tourism is of growing importance, but subject to sharp fluctuations reflecting world events. The industry was dealt a deadly blow by the terrorist attacks on New York in September 2001. By December an estimated 100,000 hotel reservations had been cancelled. Overall, the number of tourists who arrived in 2002 fell 3%, with heavy declines in the cities of Marrakesh and Agadir, which usually attract more than two-thirds of Morocco's tourists. The next year, with the invasion of Iraq and terrorist attacks in Casablanca, was even worse.

In May 2002 Prime Minister Youssoufi announced a tourism development scheme. Dubbed *Plan Azur*, the program aims to add 40,000–50,000 hotel rooms as part of a plan to attract ten million tourists to the country by 2010. Five coastal sites, including the walled city of Essaouira—known for its close-knit community of Sephardic Jews and particularly its Jewish musicians—have been selected for development. Nearing completion, the coastal site of Saïdia shows the scale of Azur: 29 hotels providing 17,000 rooms, three 18-hole golf courses, a marina to accommodate 700 boats, and a three-mile seaside promenade are just the major elements of the development. The *Ansar el-Mahdi* arrests in September 2006 highlighted just how vulnerable the whole infrastructure of tourism in Morocco is—and how expensive it will be to provide security.

The U.S. and Morocco signed a Free Trade Agreement (FTA) in June 2004 after 13 months of tough negotiations. Morocco's largest exports to the U.S. are semiconductors, minerals, and clothing, while the largest U.S. sales to Morocco are grains and civilian aircraft. Ratified in 2006, the FTA has lifted the total trade between the two countries from around $850 million in 2003 to around $1 billion in 2006. Before trade volume can increase much more, Moroccan ports will have to be brought in line with international security standards. Both the ports of Casablanca and Tangiers, nerve centers of the kingdom's economy, are considered vulnerable. In contrast, Morocco's largest and most modern port, the Tangiers Med, will open in July 2007 with a full range of modern high-tech security devices: thermal image cameras, explosive detectors, bio-metric ID controls and security badges.

Not endowed with the fabulous wealth of some of its neighbors, Morocco's economic growth has been modest, but op-

Ruins of the Roman city of Volubilis. Many of the city's buildings were destroyed to provide building materials to construct the palaces of Moulay Ismail in nearby Meknès.

Morocco

portunity has often been frittered away. A major reason, argues the World Bank, is the country's bloated and heavily unionized administration. It employs some 750,000 people, including security forces and paramilitary forces, under the direct control of the Interior Ministry. The wages of this army of civil servants devour a full 12% of Morocco's GDP, and the share is growing.

The effects are immediate and real: Morocco budgets more for education than its neighbors, but achieves less because of excessive administrative costs. One out of two children of school age do not go to school in Morocco. One in two Moroccans can neither read nor write, a literacy rate worse than India's. The rates are worse in many isolated Berber communities, which only contributes to the sense of abandonment the community already feels.

Unemployment is at least 16% and more in the urban centers—up to 25%. Among young people, unemployment figures rise to at least 30%. The economy needs to create approximately 250,000 jobs a year to accommodate the young who enter the job market annually. Given limited opportunity, many head abroad as illegal immigrants seeking work in Europe. An estimated 100,000 to 200,000 depart every year.

Perhaps the most important potential for the Moroccan economy lies with the discovery of oil in the Talsint region of southeast Morocco. For years Morocco has had to import virtually all of its oil and gas. To encourage exploration and development, it drastically overhauled its investment code: required participation by the state in such endeavors was reduced from 50% to 25%, and companies were offered a ten-year tax abatement once production begins.

In announcing the discovery to the nation, Mohammed VI demonstrated a keen ear for Islamic critics. These riches, he told his audience, would never be allowed "to engulf us in fatalism, indolence and consumerism, paralyzing our energy and our human and natural potentialities." Perhaps more importantly, in terms of Morocco's economic development, he seemed to look to neighboring Algeria as a negative model: "The wealth discovered," he affirmed, "will never constitute an alternative to our agricultural heritage, but rather a tool for its enrichment."

The Future

Morocco's political system remains fragile. The dynamic for change clearly rests more with king than parliament. Proclaimed "King of the Poor," the young monarch owes his adulation as much to reaction against the dark days of his father as to his own personality. With the 2007 elections (in which Abbas El Fassi was designated to form the government), Morocco took one more small step towards political openness. The biggest challenges in the political arena include the continued threat of terrorism that Morocco witnessed in 2003. The wheels continue to turn in the criminal justice system as Morocco seeks to prosecute alleged terrorists, and a steady stream of arrests and verdicts seems likely over the coming years.

Economically, the country remains on a solid trajectory, albeit one that does not presage dramatic economic growth or poverty reduction. Unemployment remains a problem, but inflation is low and the economy is stable and growing at a moderate pace. While dependence upon agriculture is problematic, the economy is not susceptible to major swings from international commodity prices.

The Basilica at the Roman site of Volubilis, north of Meknès

The Roman colosseum at El Djem

Photo by Beverly Ingram

Basic Facts

Area: 164,206 sq. km. = 63,431 sq. mi. (slightly larger than Florida)

Population: 10,300,000 (UN 2007 est.)

Capital City: Tunis

Climate: Warm, Mediterranean in the northern and central parts; hot and dry in the semi-Sahara south-southwest

Neighboring Countries: Algeria (west); Libya (east, southeast)

Official Language: Arabic

Other Principal Languages: French; possibly some Berber languages

Ethnic Groups: Arab 98%, European 1%, Jewish and other 1%

Principal Religions: Muslim 98%, Christian 1%, Jewish and other 1%

Chief Commercial Products: Hydro-carbons, textiles, phosphates and chemicals

Chief Agricultural Products: Olives, olive oil, grain, dairy products, tomatoes, citrus fruit, beef, sugar beets, dates, almonds

GNI per capita: $2,890 (World Bank 2006 est.)

Currency: Dinar

Former Colonial Status: French protectorate (1881–1956)

Independence Date: July 20, 1956.

Chief of State: Zine Abidine Ben Ali, President

National Flag: A white disk bearing a red crescent and a five-pointed star centered on a red background

Land and People

Tunisia, the smallest country of North Africa, lies almost in the center of the Mediterranean Sea coastline, with a seashore almost 1,000 miles long. The coastal belt, with an average of 50 miles in width, is the site of farmland. The coastline extends horizontally for 140 miles in the North and then proceeds irregularly southward for a lineal distance of 300 miles. There are three large gulf areas of gentle warm waters that carve semicircles. The coastal strip is succeeded by a gently rolling tableland with an average altitude of 1,600 feet—an area of grass and forestland. This, in turn, is followed by the semidesert to the south-southwest where there is little rainfall, and shallow salt lakes. Though this sparsely settled territory is within the desert, it is not quite as bleak and hot as the central Sahara.

A variety of well-maintained museums offer testimony to the diverse cultural heritage of Tunisia. The National Museum of the Bardo, located in the old palace of the bey in a Tunis suburb, is the finest archeological museum in the Mahgreb. Its stellar attractions are the mosaic floors from the Roman cities of northern Tunisia, rich evidence of the extraordinary wealth and luxury of Rome's breadbasket province. Further evidence of Tunisia's importance to Rome is the grand amphitheater of El Jem. After the coliseums of Rome and Capua, the one at El Jem was the third largest ever built by the Romans; it accommodated some 30,000 spectators. Dougga, some 70 miles southwest of Tunis is another spectacular Roman site. Its capitol, a temple dedicated to Jupiter, Juno and Minerva, dominates the ruins.

Near Kairouan, the sacred city of Islamic Tunisia, one can visit the national Museum

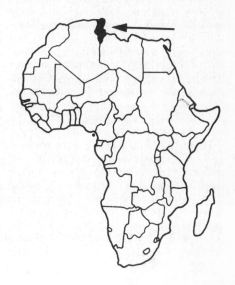

Tunisia

of Islamic Art with its stunning collection of ceramics and calligraphy. In Mahdia, in the heart of the east coast tourist areas and still an important weaving center, one can visit the Textile Museum of the Dar el-Himma. The museum features a fine collection of traditional Tunisian costumes, one of the principal manifestations of women's artistic creativity.

The Past: Political and Economic History

For early history, see *Historical Background* and *The Colonial Period: The French*.

France recognized Tunisian independence on July 20, 1956. The old monarchy was abolished in 1957 when the Constituent Assembly established a republic, naming Habib Bourguiba president. Following adoption of a constitution, the first elections were held in 1959 in which there was only small opposition to the New Constitution Party of President Bourguiba. After being elected to a third term in October 1969, Bourguiba was proclaimed president for life in 1975; he served in that role until November 7, 1987, when advanced age and increasing senility caused his constitutional removal.

A 189-member Chamber of Deputies is elected for terms of five years. The legislature's upper house, called the Chamber of Councillors, was approved by constitutional referendum in May 2002. It consists of 126 members, two-thirds of whom are elected by indirect suffrage; the rest are appointed by the president and all serve a term of six years. The first elections for councillors took place in July 2005.

The Tunisian constitution recognizes Islam as the state religion, but this has always been a tolerant and open society. President Bourguiba did many things to anger Muslim fundamentalists. He permitted wives to institute divorce proceedings against their husbands and encouraged women to enter all trades and professions. He also westernized the court system by abolishing most of the powers of the Muslim religious courts and rabbinical tribunals and turning their functions over to the civil courts. All distinctions between religious and public schools were abolished. He even went further in 1984, and included two women in his cabinet. Islamic fundamentalists saw these moves as cutting the taproots of the Islamic traditions.

Islamic fundamentalists were arrested and refused permission to function as a political party; stiff prison sentences were substituted for death penalties. The straw that broke the camel's back came in June 1981 when fundamentalists raided a beach resort where Europeans, in sometimes scanty attire, lived "the good life;" the resort was all but destroyed. This was a terrible blow to Tunisia's profitable tourist industry and marked the beginning of the crackdown on the zealots.

Besides the creation of a secular state, Habib Bouguiba's other lasting contribution to the development of modern Tunisia came in the emphasis he gave to education. From the beginning, Bourguiba gave it priority. Access to primary, secondary and higher education was made free. Curriculum was modernized. Until universities were established, virtually all Tunisian students benefited from scholarships that allowed them to attend universities in France or elsewhere.

The development of higher education has been particularly remarkable. At independence there were only two universities in Tunisia; today there are 13, scattered throughout the country. In 1955 there were 2,374 students enrolled for university education. In 2005 Tunisian universities enrolled 346,000 students. The government's focus on education has facilitated economic growth and the creation of a significant middle class.

After 30 years in power, Habib Bourguiba, suffering from Parkinson's disease, became visibly senile—he could not remember things he had done the previous day and started taking irrational actions. His persecution of Islamic fundamentalists, whose number had been swollen by migration to the cities from rural areas, reached an intolerable level. Acting swiftly, former Prime Minister Zine Abidine Ben Ali declared Bourguiba incapable of carrying out his office and removed him on November 7, 1987, thus becoming president of Tunisia. The move had widespread support from all elements and factions within Tunisian society. Among his first moves, the new president commuted the sentences of several hundred Islamic fundamentalists and suggested he would dissolve the parliament and hold elections earlier than the scheduled date in 1991. He rescheduled them for November 1989.

When it appeared that he and his party were well ahead of any competitor, President Ben Ali advanced the contest to April 1989. His judgment was correct—the Democratic Constitutional Rally (RCD), the new name of Bourguiba's party, won more than 80% of the vote and all 141 seats in the National Assembly.

By late 1991 the Islamic fundamentalists had again bloomed and seriously threatened a tourist industry that was reaching new heights of prosperity. The government, acting through the military in 1992, brought 171 members and leaders of the outlawed *Nahda* group before the Tunis military court. Thirty-five received life sentences, 142 received sentences of three to 20 years, and four were acquitted.

The firmness with which the Islamists were handled sent a clear message to other political groups in Tunisia. It was clear that President Ben Ali was not a man comfortable with opposition. Repression in one form or another has been extended out from the fundamentalists. Amnesty Inter-

A local artisan embosses souvenir plates

Photo by Beverly Ingram

Habib Bourguiba

national claims that hundreds of political prisoners are held behind bars in Tunisia. The consequence is clear: Tunisia's opposition parties are some of the most restrained in Africa. The press more often than not appears more as lapdog than watchdog.

In the 1994 presidential elections no opposition party was able to put forth a candidate. The Tunisian constitution requires potential presidential candidates to secure the nominating signatures of 30 members of parliament, but with the president's RCD in a monopoly position there, it's hard for any candidate to get his papers signed. Unopposed, Zine Abidine Ben Ali won 99.9% of the vote. In the legislative balloting of the same year, four opposition parties were only able to win 19 seats in parliament, but it was the first time the opposition would be represented there; Ben Ali's RCD won 144 seats. Tunisia remained firmly within the president's iron grip.

In the years since President Ben Ali first came to power the apparatus of surveillance and control has come to dominate Tunisian life. The number of police is four times larger than it was in 1987, and it is aided by a host of additional agencies of surveillance that have been created by authorities. The secretary-general of Amnesty International has spoken of a strategy of "interiorizing fear" within the citizenry and the International Federation for the Rights of Man has called Tunisia a "police state." Membership in the RCD is a political necessity. One's membership card is often a survival tool, the first thing shown police when stopped for questioning. Perhaps apocryphally, but suggestively, the story goes about that Tunisian children, asked to design a new symbol for their country, drew a police van.

Presidential elections were held in October 1999, and new election laws permitted the possibility of multiparty elections

for the first time in Tunisian history. No longer were the signatures of 30 political grandees required. Leaders of political parties who had been in that role for five years, and whose parties were represented in parliament, were eligible to run for the office of president. Only two candidates besides the president met these requirements: Mohamed Belhaj Amor, secretary-general of the *Parti de l'unité populaire* (PUP), and Abderrahmane Tlili of the *Union démocratique unioniste* (UDU).

Official election results were scarcely credible: President Zine el Abidine Ben Ali was reelected by 99.4% of the voters. It was enough to assure Tunisia a place in the Jurassic museum of retrograde political forms.

Despite a network of 132,000 policemen and 5,000 wiretaps on the telephone lines of its citizens, the regime did not anticipate the social unrest that rocked both Tunis and several southern cities in early 2000. Taxi drivers disabled the capital for three days in February, protesting a new driving code with increased fines. In the same month several Tunisian cities witnessed protests against stiff increases in the price of gasoline, transport, and food products, especially bread.

In some places the protest began in secondary schools and colleges. When students went out to protest in the streets, they clashed with police, but were supported by locals, mainly youth and mostly unemployed.

None of these events was, of course, reported in the local press. Censorship is a basic element of a security state, and the Tunisian Press Code allows the government to precensor and ban publications. Any information that might be used to criticize the government is eliminated. Politically sensitive articles are sent to the Interior Ministry for review, and each edition must be registered with the ministry before publication.

A stone carver

President Ben Ali

On the occasion of the 13th anniversary of his accession to power in November 2000, President Ben Ali spoke soothing words to his critics. Stressing his "unshakeable faith in the principles of human rights," he announced the state would pay compensation to any individual unlawfully arrested and detained. This, of course, was merely days after a Paris news conference where four Tunisian students had given graphic accounts of beatings, rape, and torture they endured at the hands of Tunisian security agents. The press conference also announced publication of a 200-page report entitled "Torture in Tunisia," issued by the Committee for the Respect of Freedom and Human Rights in Tunisia (CRLDHT).

In the same November address he announced future amendments to the Press Code to eliminate physical punishment of journalists. He specifically noted punishments for "libel of public order," a crime of infinite breadth and ambiguity the president called "rather murky" and open to "various interpretations."

President Ben Ali was scheduled to end his constitutionally permitted third term in 2004. Instead, a series of constitutional amendments were proposed in 2002, the effect of which was to allow him to run for an unlimited number of terms. The constitutional age limit for candidates was also raised from 70 to 75 years. Government propaganda emphasized the second legislative house (the Chamber of Councillors) to be created and the requirement that there be runoff elections to assure a majority vote for the presidency. Less mentioned were the provisions that increased presidential powers and gave immunity from prosecution, during and after his presidency, for any official acts.

The constitutional amendments easily passed the RCD-dominated legislature and were then submitted to a popular referendum—a first in Tunisian history. When the interior minister announced the results of the May 26, 2002 voting— 99.56% approved—he said they would

Tunisia

"surprise only those who do not know Tunisia." Ninety-five percent of registered voters participated—not unusual in a country where civil servants fetch in those who might have overslept on election day.

Presidential and parliamentary elections took place in October 2004, and the results were less than surprising. The opposition could not produce anything like a clear vision of where they wished to lead the country and could do little more than agree with many of the president's campaign proposals. President Ben Ali won convincingly over three opponents, taking a palindromic 94.49% of the vote; his nearest competitor, Mohamed Bouchiha of the Party of Popular Unity took a mere 3.8%.

In parliamentary elections, the president's RCD took 152 of 189 seats in the Chamber of Deputies; five parties shared the 20% of seats allocated to the opposition. The Movement of Socialist Democrats is the largest parliamentary opposition with 14 deputies. Perhaps the most interesting result of the election is the significant representation of women in parliament. President Ben Ali made the decision to allocate 25% of positions on the party's district slates to female candidates, and as a consequence, 43 newly elected members of parliament are women.

The percentage of women in the Tunisian legislature—22.7%—is the highest in the Arab world, whose legislative bodies average only 6.7%. Internationally it is one of the highest in the world, ranking above the average found in European legislatures—19%—and only below the legislatures of Nordic countries, which contain nearly 40% women.

President Ben Ali's tough-minded regime has spared Tunisians from the worst excesses of Islamic fundamentalism, and Tunisia has become an important ally of the United States in the war on international terror. The most lethal incidents since the attack on the island of Djerba in 2002 occurred in late 2006 and early 2007, the consequence of the Algerian GSPC's (*Groupe Salafiste pour prédication et le combat*) regionalization of jihadi terror as it rebranded itself Al-Qaeda of the Islamic Maghreb (AQIM).

In January 2007 Tunisian authorities announced they had killed 12 Islamic extremists and captured 15 more. Six of them had crossed into the country from Algeria. Their leader, Lassad Sassi, was a former Tunisian policeman who had run a terrorist cell in Milan until May 2001, when he fled to Algeria. In Italy, Sassi was on trial (*in absentia*) for providing military clothing and money to the GSPC and planning and financing suicide bomb attacks in Italy. According to Tunisian authorities, Sassi and five other men—four Tunisians and one Mauritanian—crossed

The Bardo Museum, Tunis, has one of the world's best collections of Roman mosaics.
Photo by Beverly Ingram

from Algeria months before, set up camp, and trained 20 other Tunisian men in the use of automatic weapons and explosives. The clashes left eight policemen and 12 militants dead, including Sassi. Explosives and satellite images of the American and British embassies were found in the group's hideouts, according to the interior minister.

The Present: Contemporary Issues

Historically a granary of the Mediterranean, Tunisia's agricultural sector was eclipsed by its petroleum production, which became, for years, its biggest moneymaker. Oil production, from aging wells, is now declining. According to the U.S. Department of Energy, oil production in 2005 was around 75,000 bbl/d (barrels a day), a 37% decline from the country's peak output of 120,000 bbl/d between 1982 and 1984. Proven reserves are modest—308 million barrels as of January 2006, but a booming economy has meant increased energy demand, only partially met by increased production of natural gas. The government has sought to encourage new exploration with a more liberal hydrocarbon code, but success rates have been low.

Tunisia has 2.8 trillion cubic feet of proven natural gas reserves, most of which is located offshore, and the state-owned *Société Tunisienne de l'Électricité et du Gaz* (STEG) has successfully encouraged a shift to gas as an energy source. According to STEG figures, natural gas consumption accounted for 44% of Tunisia's energy usage in 2005. In 2003 it represented only 14% of the country's energy consumption.

Agriculture employs about 30% of the workforce and accounts for around 12.6% of GDP (2005). Relatively rich and pro-

ductive, around 30% of the land is arable. The minister of environment has noted, however, that desertification destroys some 66,690 acres of fertile land every year, occasioning losses of $15 million. The sector is subject to the visissitudes of nature: In 2002 agricultural production was hit by the most severe drought in most Tunisians' memories, and the agricultural production shrank.

Some 60 million olive trees occupy a third of the country's arable land, and olive oil is Tunisia's most important agricultural export. The country is the world's fourth-ranked producer, after Spain, Italy and Greece. From extensive grape vineyards, mostly in the north, Tunisia produces table grapes and over 60 types of wine.

Tourism replaced oil as Tunisia's biggest foreign exchange earner in 1999, but suffers the consequences of international terrorism, dropping after the 9/11 attacks, and especially after the April 2002 attack on the Ghriba synagogue on Djerba Island. Twenty people were killed, including 13 German tourists, and the attack was linked to al-Qaeda. Built in the 1920s, Ghriba sits on the site of Africa's oldest synagogue, believed to have been built about 2,500 years ago. According to tradition, the first Jews came to Djerba in biblical times, bringing a stone from the First Temple, destroyed by the Babylonians in 586 BC. The stone is kept in a grotto at Djerba's synagogue. The thousands who make an annual *Lag Ba'omer* pilgrimage to the synagogue were down to hundreds in 2002.

The end of the decline in worldwide tourism arrived in 2005. As travelers once again began to sally forth in large numbers, Tunisia received 6.4 million international visitors, up from five million in

2002. In 2005 the tourism sector earned over $2 billion, around 7% of GDP.

With tourism, the textile industry is the most important sector of the Tunisian economy, accounting for 6% of the country's GDP. The industry has generated some 280,000 jobs and some 2,000 companies, but expiration of multilateral textile agreements in 2005 and the opening of markets to a flood of Chinese products have forced some restructuring in the industry.

Job creation has been significant in recent years, but despite this, the unemployment rate remains at about 14%, according to official figures (2004). Unofficially, it is higher, and job creation was President Ben Ali's number one priority in the 2004 election campaign. He reiterated its importance during the 2006 celebrations of Tunisia's 50 years of independence, saying unemployment had to be reduced from 14% to 10% by 2010. The World Bank estimates indicate this would require annual growth rates of 6.5%.

A secular state, Tunisia allows greater freedom to its women than most other Muslim countries. Shortly after becoming president in 1956, Habib Bourguiba initiated the most radical emancipation of women in Islam. The foundation of that emancipation was the 1956 personal status code. It abolished polygamy, divorce by a husband's simple repudiation, and male tutelege of women. In their place, it granted the right of judicial divorce to men and women equally, and provided for divorced husbands to leave the home and pay alimony. Another sign of women's emancipation: One rarely sees a woman dress in the body-covering *chador*. In the cities younger women dress in Western attire, but increasingly one sees women wearing the Islamic scarf to cover their heads.

In addition to the increased usage of the headscarf, sociologists also note an increased and ostentatious attendance at Friday prayers. Both have been seen by some psychologists as a defense mechanism or form of passive resistance against the few opportunities for political expression. President Ben Ali's allocation of female seats in the 2004 legislative elections can be understood in this light, but it is also an expression of independent Tunisia's commitment to women. In comparison to other Arab countries, Tunisia provides greater gender equality and more professional opportunity to women than anywhere else. Women constitute 27% of judges, 31% of lawyers, 40% of higher-education teachers, and 34% of all journalists.

The government pursues a policy of Arabization, the speed and fervor of which often depends on relations with France.

Bilingualism is still tolerated; it is not the intention of the government to eliminate French, but merely to readjust its place in an Arab nation. Shopkeepers have already been forced to remove signs employing the Latin alphabet, and civil servants have been ordered to use the country's official language in all documents since 2001.

In education the problems are greater. First, it is a question of which Arabic to use. A Tunisian's mother tongue is a dialectical Arabic, spoken on a daily basis but not written. At school, the student is introduced to written classical Arabic, the language of instruction. In the larger society an Intermediate Arabic, halfway between the two, has been developing, and for the past few years a fourth alternative has been offered by the daily presence of Arabic-language television broadcasts emanating from the Persian Gulf state of Qatar.

Dialectical differences in Arabic suggest the second problem facing the government's Arabization program—the availability of textbooks. Given the absence of standardized terminology in some of the sciences, for example, there are no university textbooks available.

The Future

The government's economic policies have made Tunisia the most competitive economy in Africa, ranked 30th out of 125 countries evaluated by the World Economic Forum in 2006. That put it well above South Africa, the continent's second most competitive economy, ranked 45th. Tunisia's GDP grew by an estimated 6.3% in 2007, a figure made more impressive by the country's relatively low rates of population growth. Foreign investors, more impressed by political stability than human rights issues, have responded to the government's efforts to liberalize and open the economy. All in all, this makes Tunisia an economic success story.

Tunisians, 60% of whom are middle-class, may be willing to accept economic benefit at the cost of political freedom. For the Ben Ali regime, security and stability are contingent on control; of course, control has weakened potential checks on the government. Secular opposition has been hindered; it is not lost on potential investors that Islamic fundamentalists have thrived most where no meaningful secular opposition exists. (Still, Tunisia has thus far better resisted the advance of al-Qaeda in the Islamic Maghreb than its neighbor Algeria; the lack of news out of the country may be seen as a positive indicator.) Without a free press, corruption can flourish and the rule of law vanish. For Tunisia the tension between political control and economic liberalization will dominate the next few years.

A Tunisian bread seller   Photo by Beverly Ingram

WEST AFRICA

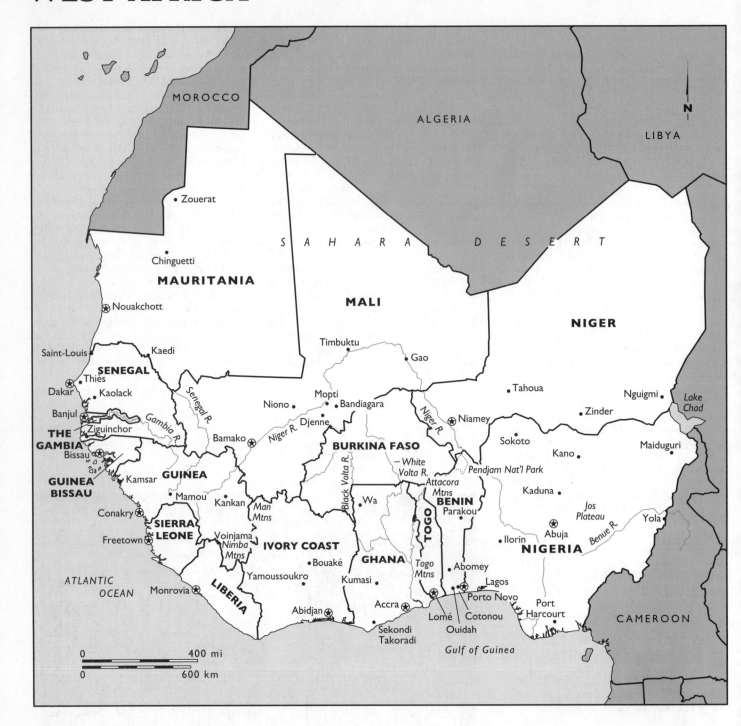

The Republic of Benin (pronounced ben–neen)

Basic Facts

Area: 115,773 sq. km. = 44,483 sq. mi. (slightly larger than Tennessee)

Population: 9,000,000 (UN 2007 est.)

Capital City: Porto Novo

Climate: Hot and humid in the south tempered by sea breezes; tropical in the north, with wet seasons in the south (mid-March to mid-July and mid-September to mid-November. Northern Benin historically had a single wet season (June-October), but more recently has witnessed drought.

Neighboring Countries: Togo (west); Burkina Faso (northwest); Niger (north); Nigeria (north, east).

Official Language: French

Other Principal Languages: Fon, Adja, Yoruba, Bariba

Ethnic Groups: There are 42 distinct ethnic groups in Benin. The Fons, Adjas, Yorubas and Baribas are the largest, constituting more than half the population.

Principal Religions: Indigenous beliefs 50%, Christian 30%, Muslim 20%—estimated

Chief Commercial Products: Cotton, corn, cassava (tapioca), yams, beans, palm oil, peanuts, livestock

GNI Per Capita: $856 (World Bank 2008 est.)

Currency CFA franc (African Financial Community)

Former Colonial Status: French Protectorate (1892–1960)

Independence Date: August 1, 1960

Chief of State: Thomas Yayi Boni, President (since April 2006)

National Flag: A green vertical stripe at the staff with two horizontal stripes of yellow (top) and red (bottom) filling the remaining area

Land and People

Benin lies in a small belt of land stretching from the warm waters of the Atlantic Ocean to a distance of 450 miles inland. The coastline is 78 miles wide, but in the north the width increases to over 200 miles. The coastal area, with palm trees waving gently in the breezes from the ocean, is a region of picturesque lagoons and inlets. A narrow sandbar lies close to the entire coastline; the lagoons open to the sea in only two places. A series of clay plateaus extend further inland for a distance of about 50 miles, terminating at the rocky foothills of the stretch of mountains that divides the north from the south. There usually has been abundant rainfall in this region, as well as along the coast, supporting dense vegetation in the areas not under cultivation. Immediately south of the Attacora Mountains, which rise to a height of 2,300 feet, there is a swampy depression. From these mountains to the north, the land gently descends in a patchy forest with very little undergrowth, to the plains of the Niger River valley. Temperatures north of the mountains are more varied than in the rest of the country. The dry season from November to May has in recent years been transformed to a year-long drought, creating severe conditions for the area.

The Pendjari National Park, next to the borders of Burkina Faso and Niger, is a reserve to protect the country's dwindling numbers of wild game. It extends across the boundary into the two neighboring countries. Although hunting is not permitted within its limits, hunters pursue animals in the surrounding areas.

While Porto Novo is the official capital of the nation, most government offices and embassies are found 20 miles to the west at the port city of Cotonou (*Ko-toe-new*), the country's de facto capital. Cotonou is Benin's chief commercial center and has the country's most developed tourist industry.

The palace site of the Kings of Dahomey at Abomey has been on UNESCO's World Heritage list since 1985. The entire palatial site is vast, extending over approximately 108 acres. Each successive Dahomean king added to the site, making it a visual symbol of his obligation "to make Dahomey ever greater."

The palaces of King Guézo (1818–1858) and his son King Glèlè (1858–1889), with important relief sculptures that document the history and culture of the Dahomean kingdom, have undergone extensive restoration and conservation since 1992. They now house the Abomey Historical Museum, which contains 300 years of royal history.

Arguably the greatest expression of the kingdom's identity and ideology are the royal bas-reliefs of Abomey, lovingly restored with the aid of the Getty Conservation Institute and others. Each of the kings had a series of names; usually associated with a natural creature, these became the subject of palace beliefs. Proud Glèlè compared himself to a lion, while his father chose the buffalo. Near the coastal town of Ouidah modern artists have created concrete representations of these royal symbols. One is a chameleon, the symbol of King Akaba (1685–1708)—who changed his policies to suit the situation; the "Chameleon" would later become a nickname for Benin's foundational president, Mathieu Kérékou.

Culturally, Benin is mostly known for being the home country of the voodoo religion, brought to the Americas through slave trade. The religion was once banned in the country, but today Benin celebrates the world's only Voodoo Day, which draws thousands of participants.

The Past: Political and Economic History

For early history, see *Historical Background* and *The Colonial Period: The French.*

Upon independence in 1960, present-day Benin took the original name Dahomey, from the two words *Dan Home* which literally means "on the belly of Dan." (The name is taken from the legend of Dacko, a contender to the throne of the ancient city of Abomey, who reputedly beheaded, buried and built an edifice over the corpse of his rival Dan.) Independence was achieved on August 1, 1960 and Hubert Maga was elected first president of the Republic of Dahomey in December.

Water dwellers, Ganvie, Benin. The more elaborate house at left is that of the Chief of the Fons.

AP/Wide World Photo

Benin

Former President Mathieu Kérékou

Part of the elite educated at the École William Ponty in Dakar, Maga had represented Dahomey in the French national assembly and was one of the few African politicians to hold a ministerial position in the French fourth republic, as secretary of state for labor from November 1957 to May 1958. A northerner, Maga was one of a triumvirate of nationalist politicians who shaped the early course of Dahomean politics. Caught between the rivalries of the two southern leaders, Sourou Migan Apithy and Justin Ahomadegbé, Maga was soon the target of southern political classes. Trade unions, historically powerful in the country, criticized him for his lavish spending, especially the construction of a sumptuous presidential palace.

After a workers' strike and street demonstrations, Maga was overthrown in a military coup led by Colonel Christophe Soglo in October 1963. The coup ushered in a period of political instability in which military regimes restored authority to civilians, only to topple them once again. Maga, Ahomadegbé and Apithy circulated in and out of office with successive coups in 1965, 1967, and 1969. The military leader of the 1969 coup finally relinquished power to the three leaders collectively, creating a triumvirate in May 1970.

The country's fifth *coup d'état* occurred in October 1972, when Commander Mathieu Kérékou ended the three-man Presidential Council, declaring "that the authority of the State has disappeared everywhere." After arresting several politicians and putting several to death, Kérékou announced a "program of national construction" and established the *National Council of the Revolution* in late 1973. A year later he announced Marxism-Leninism as

the country's official doctrine and scientific socialism its way of development. On November 30, 1975, the name "Dahomey" was replaced by the revolutionary "People's Republic of Benin," which became a single-party state controlled by the *Parti de la révolution populaire du Bénin* (PRPB: Revolutionary Party of the Benin People). Benin would be ruled by a Marxist military dictatorship for 17 years. The PRPB nationalized foreign interests and established ties with the U.S.S.R., China, Cuba and North Korea, though this resulted in little assistance from the Communist world. During the Cold War, these moves inevitably alienated the West.

The PRPB was the only legal party, and the 196-member Revolutionary Assembly was a rubber stamp for the party leader, Mathieu Kérékou, who centralized power and overlapped state and party structures. Kérékou was first elected to a three-year term as president in early 1980, then reelected to an extended five-year term in mid-1984 and yet again in 1989.

Kérékou's Marxist state was an economic disaster, and with the collapse of communist regimes in Eastern Europe, Beninese felt increasingly free to speak out against a repressive regime. By June 1989 the regime was facing a severe financial crisis and growing social unrest, characterized by intensifying strikes and demonstrations by civil servants and students. By the end of that fateful year, the regime had adopted a structural adjustment program and the party had abandoned Marxist-Leninist principles and accepted the separation of state and party.

The popular protests of 1989 led to a National Conference to discuss Benin's problems in early 1990. Kérékou made public confession of his errors and submitted himself to popular will. In a December 1990 referendum, the Beninese adopted a new multiparty constitution by an overwhelming majority (93.2%). "The People's Republic of Benin" became the "Republic of Benin"; thus ended 17 years of Marxist rule.

A transitional parliament organized multiparty, democratic elections in 1991. Kérékou stood for election, but was defeated by Nicéphore Soglo, a French-educated economist with experience at the World Bank in Washington. In democratic Benin multiparty exuberance flourished, but Soglo had difficulty securing legislative majorities.

Soglo was not able to lessen Benin's economic woes despite implementing liberal economic policy. Privatization of state corporations drew the ire of unions and resistance slowed the pace of economic reform. The new president's style brought him additional enemies. A flamboyant politician, Soglo frequently traveled abroad

and installed numerous family members in government jobs. Meanwhile, ex-president Kérékou kept a low profile, lived austerely, found religion, and bided his time. Intriguingly, the Beninese returned the former dictator to office in March 1996 runoff elections, wherein Kérékou received 52.5% of the vote to Soglo's 47.51%.

Kérékou's time in the political wilderness was transformative. He put aside Mao jackets and donned suits and ties. In so doing, he earned a new nickname from his fellow citizens: The Chameleon. Kérékou continued the economic liberalization begun under Soglo, with efforts to privatize or close inefficient state enterprises and to downsize Benin's civil service. These efforts met with resistance: strikes by public employees became common occurrences and contributed to a climate of unrest.

Legislative elections in spring 1999 produced another slender majority in parliament—understandable with over 100 political parties in the country. The opposition won 43 out of 83 seats in the National Assembly, the slimmest of majorities. Soglo's Renaissance Benin (RB) fared best among the opposition parties, winning 27 seats.

Ultimately, though, the presidential party, being the party of power, has inducements with which to encourage opposition members to cross the aisle and enjoy the benefits of power. Where President Kérékou could not get a legislative majority, he could issue a presidential decree to secure the same ends, another feature of Beninois politics.

Benin's reputation as a "laboratory of democracy" was severely tested by presidential elections in early 2001. In the primary, President Kérékou faced three challengers, including ex-President Soglo. In the first round, Kérékou received 47% of the vote while Soglo received about 29%. The third-place finisher, Adrien Houngbédji, president of the National Assembly, garnered 13% while Bruno Amoussou came in a distant fourth with a mere 4% of the ballots. A runoff election was needed, but Soglo refused to run, citing irregularities and fraud. The election was, he said, a "masquerade." The third-place finisher, Houngbédji, similarly rejected the results, leaving only Bruno Amoussou's name to be placed on the ballot as a runoff opponent. As a member of the Kérékou cabinet who had already asked his supporters to vote for the president in the runoffs, Amoussou did no campaigning and conceded the election before the ballots had been counted. President Kérékou earned a dubious victory with 84% of the vote, cast by only 53% of eligible voters.

Local government elections—the first in Benin's history—were held in December

2002, and provided an opportunity for the opposition to test itself before parliamentary elections which would follow in March, 2003. Results demonstrated a focus on "big men" and a regionalization of opposition strength. Nicéphore Soglo's *Renaissance du Bénin* won 36 of 45 seats on the Cotonou city council, allowing him to become mayor of the country's economic capital. The coalition of parties supporting President Kérékou, the *Union pour le Bénin du futur* (UBF), won a paltry four seats. In Porto Novo, Adrien Houngbédji was elected mayor after his Democratic Renewal Party (PRD) swamped the presidential coalition, winning 27 out of 29 seats. Opposition parties also won in Parakou, the most populous city in the north and a traditional stronghold of President Kérékou.

In March 2003 parliamentary elections, a total of 1,162 candidates representing 14 parties or party alliances competed for the National Assembly's 83 seats. Kérékou's UBF won an outright majority of 53 seats, while Soglo's *Renaissance du Bénin* (RB), split by internal factionalism, captured only 15 seats in a humiliating loss. Houngbédji's PRD, which had included RB dissidents on its electoral lists, took 11 seats. The man who assembled the presidential alliance and organized its campaign was none other than Bruno Amoussou, now a minister of state in the Kérékou cabinet.

After more than 30 years in power and twice limited from seeking a third term (a third term was prohibited by the constitution and, additionally, candidates must be less than 70 years of age) President Kérékou announced in mid-2005 that he would not seek to change the constitution to permit further rule. "If you don't leave power," he told his followers, "power will leave you," an insight rarely understood by other African leaders.

Former president Nicéphore Soglo, was similarly barred from the race by age, but

President Thomas Yayi Boni

his eldest son, Léhadi Vinagnon Soglo, bore the family name into the campaign as the candidate of the Benin Renaissance party. Both family and party were divided, however, and Léhadi was opposed by his younger brother, Galiou, on the presidential ballot.

Testifying to the richness of Benin's political life, and the sidelining of the country's two "Big Men," the Constitutional Court certified 26 presidential candidates, including two women. Both Bruno Amoussou and Adrien Houngbédji threw their hats into the ring, but from the very beginning of the campaign, the most-talked-about candidate was an outsider, Thomas Yayi Boni, who had resigned as head of the West African Development Bank (BOAD) to make his first run at office.

A Ph.D. in economics, Boni campaigned on economic policy, highlighting the need for growth, careful management of state funds, and creating a better environment to attract foreign investment. In the March 2006 elections, some 70% of eligible voters turned out and nearly 36% of them supported Boni. His nearest competitors were the old campaigners, Adrien Houngbédji (with 24% of the vote), and Bruno Amoussou (with 17%). Houngbédji and

Boni faced each other in runoffs and Boni played on his outsider's role. "Change is necessary," he said, and "change will come." The electorate handed him a stunning victory with almost 75% of the vote.

April 2007 legislative elections produced a victory for a coalition of parties, collectively known as the *Cauri Forces for an Emerging Benin*, supporting President Boni. The coalition won 35 out of 83 seats, the largest number ever achieved by an electoral coalition. Another coalition supporting former-President Nicéphore Soglo, the Alliance for Dynamism and Democracy, garnered 20 seats, and Adrien Houngbeji's Democratic Renewal Party arrived in third place, with 10 seats.

The Present: Contemporary Issues

Benin's economy remains dependent on cotton exports, as it was at independence. It accounts for 80% of export income and represents 13% of GDP. Given the importance of the cotton industry, one recent minister of rural development encouraged the establishment of five new cotton-processing factories. Benin now has the capacity to process more than 650,000 metric tons of raw cotton, while production has dropped to 250,000 tons. Along with Burkina Faso, Benin has been active in world trade discussions against subsidies granted to cotton farmers in the United States and Europe. Agricultural subsidies to farmers in the developed world are estimated to have cost African producers $300 million dollars from 1999 to 2001 alone.

Benin's port of Cotonou serves as a regional transit hub important for supplying landlocked Niger and Burkina Faso. Cargo handling at the port has been liberalized, and the Benin Port Authority (SOBEMAP) now competes with the Danish company Maersk. With this newly competitive environment, the Autonomous Port of Cotonou (PAC) registered

Palace of the Dahomean Kings at Abomey
Photo of Francesca Piqué, courtesy Getty Conservation Institute

Benin

some increased traffic. It also benefited from political instability in Côte d'Ivoire as shippers shunned the port of Abidjan. Corruption, however, slowed genuine growth in port usage.

A major local problem is pollution in Cotonou, which experiences some of the worst air in West Africa, largely the product of gasoline engine exhaust. Its visibility is frequently zero, with the main producers being old used cars and the city's innumerable motorbikes. (Drivers tend to believe that a vehicle uses less fuel when it's filled with oil, this burning oil adds to pollution.) The motorbikes, or "zemidjans" (literally "take me quickly" in the local language) ferry passengers from place to place during the day, spewing out carbon dioxide, carbonic acid, and other pollutants. The more entrepreneurial owners rent their bikes for a more morbid evening service: transporting the bodies of the dead. For those families unable to afford standard mortuary charges, the motorbike hearse is an affordable alternative. The cadaver is placed on the bike, lashed to the driver and held by a family member as it is whisked to the family home for appropriate ceremonies.

Corruption remains endemic in Benin. According to Finance Ministry figures, the state loses nearly $100 million a year to corruption, embezzlement and the misuse of public funds. The minister of justice claimed that corruption was rife "in the law courts, within the police, the gendarmeries, the private sector, and even strikes the Non-Governmental Organizations." Regional administration was, he said, similarly tainted. From driver's licenses to diplomas, to get what one wants in Benin, one only needs to know how "to place a pebble on the dossier"—the local euphemism for corruption. When he returned to power in 1996 General Kérékou set up an ambitiously titled "public morality unit," vowing to stamp out corruption in the public sector. Despite the fanfare, Kérékou's anticorruption commissions yielded few results. The *Cauri Forces for an Emerging Benin* coalition won the election promising to implement anticorruption reforms, but the effectiveness of those still remains unseen.

Benin has benefited from China's thrust into Africa. The Cotonou Congress Palace was financed with an interest-free loan of $22,244,879, while other Chinese projects include Cotonou's Friendship National Stadium and Lokossa Hospital. In early 2007 Foreign Minister Li Zhaoxing began the annual parade of Chinese dignitaries to Africa in Benin, leaving behind reduced debt obligations, commitments for more than $3 million in loans, and additional aid for infrastructure.

Benin has qualified for a five-year, multi-million-dollar ($307 million) grant from the American Millennium Challenge Account (MCA), which seeks to transform development funding by tying more aid to greater achievement in democracy, transparency, and human rights. The biggest chunk of money—$169 million—will be spent on modernizing the Port of Cotonou by dredging the harbor to accommodate larger ships and improving security measures.

A smaller portion of MCA funds—$36 million—will help Beninese property owners obtain land titles through banks, free of charge. The goal of the initiative is to resolve the problem of land insecurity and provide greater potential capital for local investment: with titles to their property, owners will gain access to bank loans.

The Future

Benin is one of the handful of African countries that democratized at the end of the Cold War and that has remained a democracy ever since. Despite hiccups (especially in the 2001 elections), the country maintains electoral freedoms and civil rights. Political problems in Benin center on the relatively uncertain nature of the party system: with a lack of strong and stable institutions, politics remains quite fluid and open to outsiders. While Yayi Boni is a relative outsider in *Beninois* politics, he has navigated the beginning of his term without major unrest. Each passing year would seem to add additional weight to the likelihood of democracy persisting: by 2008, about half of Benin's young population had never known any political system besides democracy.

The economic future is less encouraging than Benin's recent political achievements. Though economic growth is positive in real terms, it is barely sufficient to keep up with population growth in a country where the average number of births per woman is over 5 children. The lingering effects of Benin's Marxist phase of the 1970s and 1980s—a high degree of centralization and bureaucratization—weigh heavily on economic development. Given the multiplicity of political parties and activist trade unions with capacity to mobilize to oppose reforms, inertia and immobility characterize the political-economic sphere. In addition, corruption is rife, and combating it will be necessary for Boni to manage a turnaround.

Mud-relief sculpture of King Glèlè's "Jar of Unity"

Burkina Faso

Market day, Burkina Faso

Basic Facts

Area: 274,540 sq. km. = 106,000 sq. mi. (slightly larger than Colorado)

Population: 14,800,000 (UN 2007 est.)

Capital City: Ouagadougou (pronounced Wah-gah-doo-goo)

Climate: Cooler and drier (November–March); warm and dry (March–May); warm with variable rainfall (June–October)

Neighboring Countries: Mali (west and north); Niger (east); Benin (southeast); Togo, Ghana, Côte d'Ivoire (south)

Official Language: French

Other Principal Languages: Bissa, Bobo, Fulfulde, Gourmanchéma, Jula, Lobi, Mòoré, Tamajek

Ethnic Groups: Mossi about 47%, Gurunsi, Senufo, Lobi, Bobo, Mande, Fulani, Tuareg

Principal Religions: Indigenous beliefs 40%, Muslim 50%, Christian (mainly Roman Catholic) 10%

Chief Commercial Products: cotton, animal products, gold

GNI Per Capita: $587 (World Bank 2008 est.)

Currency: CFA franc (no longer tied to the French franc)

Former Colonial Status: French Colony (1896–1932); part of Ivory Coast, Niger and French Soudan (1932–1957); French Overseas Territory (1958–1960)

Independence Date: August 5, 1960

Chief of State: Blaise Compaoré, President (since 1987, most recent election 2005)

National Flag: Horizontal red and green stripes with a yellow five-pointed star in center.

Land and People

Burkina has a comparatively pleasant climate, full of gentle hills, with an average altitude of 800 feet. The tall grass of the plains and the green forest grow rapidly during the usual wet season from May to November in years of normal rainfall. Almost daily rains are usually short thunderstorms—the rest of the day during these months is warm and sunny. Toward the end of November, the rains become less frequent and finally almost

cease altogether. The grasses of the plains, which have risen to heights of six feet, turn brown waiting to be consumed by localized brush fires. A drier area is found in the north and northwest, which is a transition zone between the plains and the hot Sahara farther north. It is from this great desert that the *harmattan* (the hot wind of the dry season) comes, covering the whole country. The rivers of Burkina Faso, the Black, Red and White Voltas, and the tributaries of the Niger in the east—are not navigable. Travel to and from land-locked Burkina Faso is principally over the railway from Ouagadougou through Bobo-Dioulasso to Abidjan in Côte d'Ivoire.

Since 1969 Burkina Faso has taken the art of film to heart with gusto and enthusiasm. Indeed, it's probably the only country that's given film-makers their own public monument. Ouagadougou, Burkina's capital and largest city, is the site of the important biennial Pan-African Festival of African Cinema and Television, more simply known as Fespaco. The 20th festival was held in early 2007 and exhibited more than 200 films to eager viewers. The festival's grand prize went to *Ezra*, a Nigerian film. Directed by Newton Aduaka, *Ezra* tells the story of a child soldier caught up in Sierra Leone's decade-long civil war.

The Burkinabé architect Diébédo Francis Kéré won the prestigious Aga Khan Award for Architecture in 2004 for his design of a primary school in Gando. While

Burkina Faso

an architecture student in Berlin, Kéré set up a fund-raising association to ensure a school for his natal village. Local government agencies provided funding to train brick makers in working with compressed stabilized earth, and actual construction of the school was carried out by the village's men, women, and children. The building was honored for designing climatic comfort with low-cost construction, making the most of local materials and the potential of the local community, and adapting technology from the industrialized world to local conditions.

Literature in Burkina Faso is based on the oral tradition, *Maximes, pensées et devinettes mossi* by Dim-Dolobsom Ouedraogo is inspired in the oral tradition. Ouedraogo collected the popular oral tradition relating the story of the Mossi Kingdom and translated it into paper.

The Past: Political and Economic History

For early history, see *Historical Background* and *The Colonial Period: The French*.

France signed a treaty in 1960 granting what was then Upper Volta independence. The country adopted a new constitution, taking effect in that year. Upper Volta was governed by a president elected for a five-year term, and a 75-member National Assembly, both elected by universal suffrage. The constitution provided for a separate judiciary. Maurice Yaméogo's Volta Democratic Union captured all the seats of the Assembly and he became the first president. Although quite popular, a combination of corruption and adverse economic conditions, including high unemployment, led to his downfall. Col. Sangoulé Lamizana assumed charge; Yaméogo was tried and imprisoned in 1969, but was released in 1971.

Col. Lamizana was a burly, imposing figure with tribal scars on his cheeks. A devout Muslim, he made a pilgrimage to the city of Mecca. He appeared to be making progress toward restoring civilian rule, but in 1970 a constitution was adopted providing that he serve for a transition period of four years; thereafter the president would be elected.

When 1974 arrived, President Lamizana dissolved the legislature, appointed himself to the additional positions of prime minister and army chief of staff, and declared Upper Volta a single-party state. In 1977 Upper Voltans voted to return to civilian rule—and for political parties to be allowed to resume their activities. Unsurprisingly, General Lamizana was elected to a seven-year term of office.

During the next two years Upper Volta plunged to economic depths. Corruption was rampant, and persistent drought further impoverished the populace. Opposi-

tion parties were squeezed out of existence, but a powerful labor movement remained. Massive strikes paralyzed the country in 1980. The military looked on with increasing alarm as the government floundered and finally intervened, placing the president under house arrest.

The leader of the bloodless coup was Lamizana's former foreign minister, Colonel Saye Zerbo, who was immediately proclaimed president of the Military Committee for Reformation and National Progress—and chief of state. Rivalries within the army produced two further coups, one in 1982 and one in August 1983 when Capt. Thomas Sankara became president of the National Council for the Revolution (CNR).

Committees for the Defense of the Revolution (CDRs) were organized to implement the CNR's Marxist-Leninist programs. Sankara himself adopted romantic austerity and self-denial as a central part of his self-image. Virtually his only possessions were his guitar and his used car, a tiny Renault 5, which he chose as the official vehicle for his whole government. By word and deed the charismatic Sankara

sought to lead and mobilize, but personal revolutionary idealism alone was insufficient. The CDRs, organized as popular mass organizations, deteriorated into gangs of armed thugs and clashed with several trade unions. Revolutionary People's Courts struck fear into the populace, yet resistance grew. On October 15, 1987, Sankara was deposed and killed in a a coup d'etat this action was directed by his friend and colleague, Blaise Compaoré. The man who had created modern Burkina Faso was unceremoniously buried in a common grave in Ouagadougou. Only later were his remains moved and the grave given a proper headstone. Years afterwards, followers continue to leave flowers, and Sankara has become an icon for youthful Africans who have dubbed him "Che Sankara." Like the famous Che poster, Sankara's thin, mustachioed features grace stickers that appear on motorcycles, taxis and trucks throughout West Africa.

Compaoré, along with two other members of the CNR, Jean-Baptiste Boukary Lengani and Henri Zongo, formed the Popular Front (FP) to continue the revolu-

Ouagadougou's monument to film makers   Photo by Andy Trimlett

74

President Blaise Compaoré

tion; its principal constituent was the leftist Organization for Popular Democracy/Labor Movement (ODP/MT). Recognizing the discontent aroused by the more extreme of Sankara's policies, Compaoré moderated them and opened the Front to non-Marxist organizations. In September 1989, while he was returning from an Asian trip, Lengani and Zongo were accused of plotting the overthrow of the Popular Front government. Arrested, they were swiftly executed the same night.

The Popular Front drafted a new constitution, that of Burkina Faso's Fourth Republic, in 1990; it was ratified by referendum in 1991. Compaoré resigned from the army to contest December's presidential elections. He was elected without opposition, but nearly 75% of eligible voters simply stayed home on election day. The ODP/MT won a majority of legislative seats in 1992 elections, and in February 1996, it merged with several smaller opposition groups to form the Congress of Democracy and Progress (CDP).

In early 1997 the CDP used its parliamentary majority to amend the constitution, eliminating the provision that limited Burkina Faso's president to two terms. The opposition futilely protested the amendment would institute lifelong political power. The deposit required of presidential candidates was also increased, from two million CFA francs ($4,000) to five million CFA francs—about $10,000. Parliament also recognized world changes following the collapse of the Soviet Union by purging the constitution of such Sankara-era terminology as "the people," and "the toiling masses."

Legislative elections held in 1997 resulted in a huge CDP majority—101 out of 111 seats, but only 44% of voters visited their polling places. The October 1998 presidential elections posed few problems for President Compaoré, who was easily returned to office. The opposition boycotted the elections, and the only question was how many voters would even bother to show up. President Compaoré needed a big enough turnout to retain his credibility, especially after the dismal participation rate seven years previously. When the results came in, Compaoré won nearly 88% of the vote. According to official figures, 56% of registered voters participated.

Two deaths that shook the nation

President Compaoré's inauguration in December was darkened by the mysterious death of Burkina Faso's most prominent journalist, Norbert Zongo, the managing editor of the weekly *Independent*. Celebrated for his hard-hitting critiques of the regime, Zongo (actually the pen name of Henri Segbo) was known as "the Incorruptible." His charred body was found, along with three others, in the burned out wreckage of an automobile. The exterior of the auto showed no signs of fire damage; the victims had been shot with 12-caliber bullets and given a *coup de grace* with a 357 Magnum. Zongo's death rocked the nation, prompting a wave of violent protests that continued through the spring. The president was forced to create an independent national commission of inquiry to examine the more than suspicious death. Places on the commission were reserved for representatives of the international press, human rights organizations, and members of the victims' families. Representatives of the ministries of Security, Defense, and Justice joined them. Even before the work of the commission was completed the details began to leak out confirming the widespread belief that Zongo was the victim of a political assassination. Noting "contradictions and incoherence" in the testimony of members of the Presidential Guard, the commission pointed to them as "serious suspects" in the case.

The commission's report linked Zongo's assassination to his exposé of the earlier murder of a chauffeur assigned to President Compaoré's younger brother, François. The evidence indicated that David Ouédraogo, the chauffeur, had been involved, with three others, in the theft of money from François's wife. All four had been taken, on the order of François Compaoré, to a security prison and subjected to the most grotesque of tortures, both psychological and physical. Then, they were taken out and forced to dig their own graves, lined up before a firing squad, and subjected to the terror of mock execution. Ouédraogo himself reportedly died of the effects of torture, which included being roasted alive.

Norbert Zongo's reporting and demand for justice made him a popular hero, but an enemy of the state. His assassination exposed the dark side of the Compaoré regime and generated vociferous demands to end "impunity" for killers.

The controversy forced a presidential transformation. The president developed a kinder, gentler image. Two weeks after

Cotton farming   ©Brahima Ouedraogo/IRIN

Burkina Faso

the commission of inquiry's report was issued, the president appointed a College of Sages to recommend action to end the political crisis. The 16-member council was headed by the Bishop of Bobo-Dioulasso and consisted of three former heads of state, eight religious and traditional leaders, and three "resource persons." Acting with dispatch, the group asked for the arrest of all those implicated in the death of David Ouédraogo. The next day, three members of the Presidential Guard close to President Compaoré were detained in Ouagadougou and charged with murder of François Compaoré's driver.

In August 2000, a military tribunal met to hear the case against five members of the *Régiment de la sécurité présidentielle* (Presidential Guard) charged with David Ouédraogo's murder. Three, including the Guard's former head, Marcel Kafando, were quickly found guilty and sentenced to long jail terms. In addition, the three were ordered to pay a staggering fine of 200 million CFA in damages to the Ouédraogo family—nearly $270,000. Outside the courtroom, more than 3,000 people gathered to denounce the trial as a miscarriage of justice, given the absence of the principal suspect, Francois Compaoré.

In early February 2001 the government acted to quell continuing unrest over the Zongo affair. Burkina Faso's attorney general announced the indictment of Marcel Kafando, the former head of the Presidential Guard, for murder and arson in the journalist's death, but these charges were ultimately dismissed by a Burkinabé judge in July 2006 for "lack of evidence."

To deal with ongoing agitation over the murder, the government orchestrated a "national day of forgiveness" in late March 2001. The event had been recommended by the College of Sages to assuage years of public anger. By any standard of evaluation, it was a remarkable event.

Standing before a crowd of 30,000 Burkinabé in a local stadium, President Compaoré delivered an unprecedented apology for crimes against the populace. "I ask for pardon," he said, "and express deep regret for tortures, crimes, injustices, bullying and other wrongs."

The new mood in Burkinabé politics was manifest in the parliamentary elections of May 2002. They were organized by an Independent National Electoral Commission (CENI), a first for the country. The government agreed to finance political parties, and electoral law was changed to elect members of the legislature by proportional representation. For the first time a single ballot listing all the competing parties was employed, with color photographs. To ensure electoral honesty, transparent ballot boxes, some of which

had to be borrowed from neighboring Benin, were used. The CENI also hired 2,000 observers to supervise the election. The cost of all this was a hefty $9.2 million.

The calls to electoral participation worked. Some 1,740 candidates, representing 30 political parties, entered the competition. Given a fair chance, the opposition scored strongly against the current party. President Compaoré's ruling Congress for Democracy and Progress (CDP) dropped from 101 seats to 57 in Burkina Faso's 111-member parliament.

Of the 54 seats won by the opposition, Hermann Yaméogo's Alliance for Democracy and Federation/African Democratic Rally (ADF/RDA) obtained 17, while the Party for Democracy and Progress/Socialist Party (PDP/PS) of Joseph Ki-Zerbo won ten. The remaining 27 seats went to ten other opposition parties—seven of them to "Sankarist" parties which claimed to uphold the revolutionary ideals of the young army captain.

If the 2002 elections pointed to a difficult time for President Compaoré, the September rebellion in neighboring Côte d'Ivoire that same year changed the president's political fortunes even more. He proved an effective manager of the economic crisis that followed the closing of rail connections between the two countries. The government made successful appeals to international donors, and skillfully handled thereturn of over 300,000 Burkinabé, violently driven from their homes and despoiled of their property in a frenzy of Ivoirian xenophobia. The events solidified both presidential popularity and national identity.

Offended honor produced patriotic sentiment, and Burkinabé rallied around their president. Internal opponents were silenced, and the president emerged more firmly in charge of the domestic scene than he had been in several years.

His active leadership of poor cotton-producing countries, opposing subsidies to American and EU cotton farmers that impoverished African growers, restored him to the good graces of his regional colleagues. His involvement in the lethal exchange of arms for diamonds that fueled destructive conflict in West Africa and Angola, were now things of the past. With those wars ended, an intransigent Laurent Gbagbo, Côte d'Ivoire's president, seemed the greater threat to regional stability.

Compaoré entered the November 2005 presidential elections with huge advantages in the country's highly factionalized political culture. Twenty-eight of the country's 100 political parties supported the president's reelection bid. Fifteen opposition parties coalesced in a loose alliance called *Alternance 2005*, but, unable to unify their views on a single candidate,

the group put up three. One Burkinabé summed up popular reaction to the opposition: "We laugh when we see these opposition leaders on television. If they can't even get on among themselves how are they going to run the country?"

Most observers described Compaoré's campaign as "American style," and there lots of souvenirs—tee shirts, hats, ties, pens, and even bottles of mineral water emblazoned with the presidential visage—for voters to recall the president's name and face. When the last ballot was tallied, Blaise Compaoré was reelected to a third term by a smashing 80.35%. His nearest rival, Bénéwendé Stanislas Sankara, representing the Union for Rebirth/Sankarist Movement (UNIR/MS) party, received support from only 4.88% of the electorate. Fifty-seven percent of eligible voters participated in the poll, and international observers described it as "fair."

Legislative elections in May 2007 swung the pendulum of support back to President Compaoré's CDP. The party won 73 of 111 parliamentary seats, while 12 opposition parties divided the 38 remaining seats, down from 54 in the previous legislature. The biggest loser was Hermann Yaméogo, one of the president's fiercest critics. His *Union nationale pour la démocratie et le développement* (UNDD) failed to win a single seat—a humiliating loss of seven.

The Present: Contemporary Issues

The United Nations estimates that anywhere from 2.7% to 6.5% of adults in Burkina Faso are infected with the AIDS virus (2003), the highest rate in West Africa. Infection rates are much higher in urban centers, and combating the disease is a government priority. At the high end there are an estimated 370,000 AIDS orphans; 42% of all rural households and 45% of all urban ones include an orphan. Life expectancy was only 42.9 years in 2003, but inevitably it could push lower as a consequence of HIV/AIDS.

Burkina Faso is one of 16 African countries that have outlawed female genital cutting (FGC). Anyone removing a girl's clitoris risks a fine of $1,800 and a prison term of three years; if a victim dies as a result of the operation, the prison term can rise to ten years. The government has established a national telephone hotline to fight the procedure and points with pride to statistical results in the ten-year battle: when the anti-FGM law first went into effect, around two-thirds of Burkinabé girls were being circumcised; now probably less than one-third are subjected to the procedure.

Following the assassination of Thomas Sankara, the government began a slow liberalization of a socialist economy. Cumbersome regulations, price controls and widespread government involvement in productive sectors, all of which were a brake on private investment, were eliminated. Some state companies have been privatized and the economy is now more open to market forces. It remains, however, dependent on agricultural production, which represents some 30.6% of GDP (2005). Over 80% of the population is engaged in subsistence agriculture.

Cotton remains the most important cash crop, traditionally accounting for as much as 60% to 70% of export revenues. Around 700,000 people are actively engaged in cotton growing; their work directly sustains another 2.5 million people, about one out of five Burkinabé. Production in 2006 reached record levels: 713,000 tons, compared to 600,000 tons the year before.

There is much concern over the effects of recent U.S. farm policies, which protect American farmers from depressed international market prices. With these protections uneconomic farms can dump raw and ginned cotton onto world markets with impunity, leaving key African producers like Burkina Faso with little market demand and lowered prices. President Compaoré led the public assault on rich-country cotton subsidies at World Trade Organization meetings in Geneva and Cancun, Mexico, in 2003.

Overall, some 3 million Burkinabé lived at one time in Côte d'Ivoire, but recently several thousand have fallen victim to rising antiforeigner sentiment there. Countless Burkinabé homes were destroyed, and Ouagadougou has announced that over 300,000 of its citizens have returned home since September 19, 2002, when a rebel war broke out there. The economic

impact of Ivoirian xenophobia has been significant for Burkina's economy.

The country's commerce was deeply affected. Landlocked, Burkina Faso was dependent on Côte d'Ivoire's ports for 80% of its exports and 60% to 70% of its imports. All basic items such as soap, salt, cooking oil and rice, either imported from or produced in Côte d'Ivoire, transit through the port of Abidjan. Remarkably, Burkina's economy has adjusted quickly. The government cut bureaucratic red tape for transporters to help reduce the cost of truck transport, and goods were reoriented to Lomé (Togo), Tema (Ghana), and Cotonou (Benin).

Ghana and Burkina Faso have inaugurated a joint technical committee to study the feasibility of constructing a railway linking the two countries. The line would help solidify the increased economic relations that have developed since the Côte d'Ivoire crisis began and take a good deal of pressure off of Ghana's battered roads. The line would also facilitate exportation of landlocked Burkina's huge manganese deposits in the northeast, where the proposed line would end. The Indian government has already pledged $500 million partial financing for development of a rail network linking Niger, Burkina Faso, Benin and Togo.

The country is rich in gold reserves and a new mining code, adopted in May 2003, is designed to make investment in the sector more attractive. A number of mining projects are still in the planning stages and could become operating mines within the next five years, or sooner, given the recent spike in gold prices.

Any industrial development in Burkina Faso is utterly dependent on electricity,

water, and good roads, all of which are in short supply. Bobo Dioulasso, the country's second city, has long been its economic capital, but 100% of Bobo's electricity comes from Côte d'Ivoire. It was the only product not affected by the crisis. There are plans to connect Burkina with Ghana's electrical grid by a 127-mile line, but that's not expected to be in operation before 2012.

In April 2002 Burkina Faso was certified by the IMF and World Bank as having completed the requirements for admission to the Heavily Indebted Poor Countries (HIPC) initiative. It meant debt relief for about 50% of the country's stock of debt over the long term, but a great percentage of that—all multilateral debt—was cancelled by the world's richest countries, the G-8, at their 2005 summit meeting.

In 2007, this arid country suffered some of its worst flooding in recent memory. The inundations killed a small number, but they displaced many thousands and destroyed much cropland. In 2008, the country broke into protest against the rising food prices; in March 184 people were arrested as a result of illegal protest in Ouagadougou. Food markets in Burkina Faso are being crowed out by rising international food prices.

The Future

With debt service charges reduced, one should hope to see the government pay greater attention to poverty reduction programs. The country remains desperately poor, ranking 174 out of 177 countries on the UN's 2006 *Human Development Index* (just above Mali, Sierra Leone and Niger). It has long been an important labor reserve for neighboring countries. Burkina Faso's migrant workers, who annually fan out across West Africa in search of employment, traditionally send back remittances that contribute about 5% to GDP. These have been reduced by the crisis in Côte d'Ivoire.

Burkina Faso is not among Africa's most democratic nations, nor among its most economically successful. Nonetheless, it has witnessed some improvements in recent years. The Compaoré government, which originally seized power in the military coup that overthrew the charismatic Thomas Sankara, has slowly decompressed Burkinabé politics. The country's politics may now be seen as reasonably "free," but not "fair"; civil liberties are improving and voting is increasingly open, but the ruling party has considerable political advantages. An additional concern is the increasing restiveness of public sector employees, including those in the army, who in late 2007 demanded improved compensation and work conditions.

Primary school, Gando. Designed by Diébédo Francis Kéré, winner of the Aga Khan Award for Architecture in 2004.
Photo courtesy AKDN

The Republic of Cape Verde (pronounced *Vair*-day)

Mindelo, São Vicente. Cultural and intellectual capital of Cape Verde

Photo by Michael Beguelin

Basic Facts

Area: 4,030 sq. km. = 1,559 sq. mi. (slightly larger than Rhode Island). Ten rather mountainous islands and eight additional islets.

Population: 506,000 (UN 2008 est.)

Capital City: Praia (on São Tiago island)

Climate: Temperate; warm, dry summer; precipitation meager and very erratic, producing prolonged droughts; harmattan winds from the Sahara can obscure visibility.

Official Language: Portuguese

Other Languages: Crioulo (a blend of Portuguese and West African words)

Ethnic Groups: Creole (mulatto) 71%, African 28%, European 1%.

Religions: Roman Catholic (infused with indigenous beliefs); Protestant (mostly Church of the Nazarene)

Principal Commercial Products: Shoes, garments, fish, bananas, hides

GNP Per Capita: $3,665 (World Bank 2007 est.)

Currency: Cape Verdean escudo

Former Colonial Status: Portuguese colony

Independence Date: July 5, 1975 (from Portugal).

President Pedro Pires

Chief of State: Pedro Pires, President (since March 2001)

National Flag: Three horizontal bands of light blue (top, double width), white (with a horizontal red stripe in the middle third), and light blue; a circle of 10 yellow five-pointed stars is centered on the hoist end of the red stripe and extends into the upper and lower blue bands.

Land and People

Cape Verde, 729 miles west of Senegal, is the western end of the drought-prone Sahel. Rain falls, if at all, only two or three months a year, and lack of rainfall shapes the archipelago's precarious economic existence. Its history is dominated by the years of famine and drought, with 1747 still referred to as the worst recorded. At nearly 10,000 feet, the Pico do Fogo volcano is the archipelago's most imposing landmark. Still active, the volcano last erupted in 1995.

Cape Verde had no indigenous people. It was settled by Portuguese, Jews, and Africans in the 15th century; they mingled, creating a Creole culture. A little over 400,000 Cape Verdeans live on the islands of the archipelago. More than 500,000 live in the eastern United States, primarily in Rhode Island and Massachusetts.

Cape Verde has always been a cultural crossroads. Islanders speak Crioulo, a mix of Portuguese and West African languages, and Prime Minister Jose Maria Neves has promised to make Crioulo the Cape Verdean official language.

78

Cape Verde

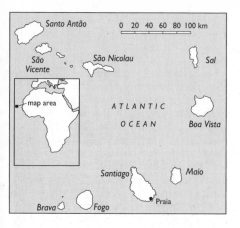

Former Prime Minister Carlos Veiga

The islands' rich musical heritage reflects their isolation and poverty, and their synthesis of intersecting cultures. For generations the islands sent their men abroad to work, manning, in the 19th century, the ships of the American whaling fleet. Longing and loneliness characterize the most famous Cape Verdean musical form, the *morna*. It combines the sadness and longing of the Portuguese *fado* melodic line with a quickness of rhythm that is distinctly African. The singers of *morna* sing of *"saudade,"* a Portuguese word meaning longing and yearning, homesickness and nostalgia. It is the haunting sadness of an island people driven to leave by poverty, but always looking back to home and loved ones. One of the greatest Cape Verdean singers is Cesaria Evora, whose recordings are perennially near the top of World Music charts and whose live performances have captivated an international audience.

The Past: Political and Economic History

For early history, see *The Colonial Period: the Portuguese.*

Under the leadership of Amilcar Cabral, the struggle to free Cape Verde from Portuguese colonial rule began in the early 1960s. Cabral's nationalist party, the African Party for the Independence of Guinea-Bissau and Cape Verde (PAIGC), fought to liberate and unite both colonies. Cabral saw neither; he was assassinated in early 1973. The colonies won independence in 1975 under the leadership of Aristides Pereira.

Efforts continued to unite Cape Verde and Guinea-Bissau, but following the 1980 *coup d'état* in Guinea-Bissau, which resulted in the overthrow of Luis Cabral by Nino Vieira, union was no longer possible. In Cape Verde, the governing party renamed itself the *Partido Africano da Independencia de Cabo Verde,* or PAICV.

Pereira's authoritarian rule lasted until multiparty elections in 1991, won by the

Movimento para a Democracia (MPD) led by Antonio Mascarenhas. President Mascarenhas was reelected in 1996 without much opposition or participation. Only about 40% of the electorate managed to turn out.

The electoral rivalries of the PAICV and MPD continue to divide the community of Cape Verdean immigrants in America. As expected in color-conscious America, the community is also divided over conceptions of race and color. Lighter-skinned, longer-established Cape Verdeans frequently refer to themselves as Portuguese. Others live in the black community and identify themselves as black.

Cape Verde grants voting rights to anyone born in the islands, so many Cape Verdean emigrants participated in the parliamentary and presidential elections of 2006. Absentee ballots are not employed in the process. Instead, polling places are set up in community centers wherever a concentration of islanders lives. There were nine official polling places in Massachusetts, Rhode Island, and Connecticut for this election cycle.

Based largely on diaspora support, the PAICV, which had governed the islands for the first 15 years after independence, retained political power by winning 41 out of 72 parliamentary seats in January 2006 elections. The MPD won 29 seats, and Independent and Democratic Christian Union (UCID) captured the remaining two seats. The MPD leader, Agostinho Lopes, somewhat expansively claimed the election was the "greatest electoral fraud" in the country's history, and even President Pires admitted "small irregularities," but international observers generally credited it with being free and fair.

The two principal parties faced off again in the February 2006 presidential elections. President Pedro Pires was once again the PAICV's standard bearer, while

former Prime Minister Carlos Veiga represented the MPD. At age 71, a veteran of the islands' independence struggle against the Portuguese, Pires secured a comfortable 51% of the vote, far from the cliffhanger of the election in 2001 when a mere twelve votes separated the two men.

The PAICV controls both the executive and legislative branches, but because some financial legislation requires a two-thirds majority, the party faces an opposition possessed of a formidable political weapon with which to force moderation. When the constitutional court declared parts of the 2002–03 budget unconstitutional because it had not received a two-thirds majority, the government began to talk about amending the constitution. That too requires a two-thirds majority: cooperative understanding between the country's two major parties remains a necessity.

In the end of 2007, the World Trade Organization approved Cape Verde's accession to the organization. In July of 2008, the country formally became the 152nd member of the WTO.

The Present: Contemporary Issues

Cape Verde has extremely limited natural resources. An archipelago of ten larger islands, only nine of which are habitable, and eight smaller islets, Cape Verde has little land to cultivate. Only 20% of the land is arable, and the country is subject to persistent periods of drought, interrupted by torrential rains and floods that erode what useful land is available. Although 70% of the population lives in rural areas, agriculture contributes only about 6.8% of GDP. (Some 73% of GDP is from the service sector.) Beans and maize are the most important foodstuffs grown, but production fluctuates with climatic conditions and other crops include bananas, sweet potatoes, yams, manioc, pumpkins, sugarcane, coffee, and groundnuts. Still, the country must import 80% of its food. This results in a large trade deficit. During years of drought and failed crops, the country is dependent on the international community for food.

Cape Verde must import all petroleum products, and the government's budget has been hard hit by recent oil price increases. To prevent water and energy costs from rising beyond the capacity of the poor to pay, the government set aside more than $20 million to subsidize diesel and fuel used to produce electricity. Small butane cylinders, most frequently used by the rural poor, were also subsidized.

HIV/AIDS has made its appearance in Cape Verde, and the government is acting to curb its spread with free distribution of condoms and public information campaigns. Though the infection rate remains low (0.44%), a 2005 study by Nova Uni-

Cape Verde

versity, Lisbon, reported that some 90.9% of the 1,540 young people interviewed "showed a level of ignorance about HIV transmission modes."

According to the UN, Cape Verde has become a major transit point for the shipment of cocaine from South America to Europe. With more than 1,200 miles of ill-patrolled shorelines and an endless supply of "mules" in nearby West Africa, the country is a top target for international drug syndicates and criminal networks. The government has recently committed $6 million to a new law enforcement program that will upgrade air and sea security for the islands. The investment has yielded some results: in 2006 a Guinea-Bissau-registered ship carrying three tons of cocaine was intercepted in Cape Verde waters.

After attaining power in 1991, the MPD government reversed the socialist policies of its predecessor and liberalized the economy. Prices and exchange rates now are independent from government control, and a privatization program is selling off state corporations. These policies have encouraged foreign investors, donors, and lenders. Investors committed $20 million to projects in 2004, in part to make use of Cape Verde's abundance of low-wage employment.

Lenders have approved of Cape Verde's economic policies. In 2005 the World Bank noted that absolute poverty had declined steeply, from 49% in 1988 to 37% in 2002, reflecting "robust growth and effective delivery of services." Economic progress has helped ease Cape Verde's debt and in

April 2002, the IMF extended a low-interest $11 million loan to the country. The credit agreement helps eradicate internal debt, the servicing of which has been one of the main burdens on the state budget. Cape Verde is on the verge of exiting the Least Developed Countries category and becoming a "middle income" state.

GDP growth has been steady in recent years, at 4.4% in 2004 and 5.5% in 2005, largely powered by the development of tourism. With an abundance of good quality beaches and a dry, sunny climate, tourism has strong growth potential. The government has encouraged foreign investment in the industry, which now brings some 170,000 visitors to the islands and contributes 11% of GDP. However, tourism-led growth is asymmetrical: it mostly benefits the capital Praia, the port city of Mindelo (on São Vicente), and the island of Sal, where the international airport is located. Elsewhere poverty has increased, especially in the rural areas of Fogo, Brava and Santo Antão. The consequence is a rural exodus of the young looking for work in tourist centers.

Linkages to the international economy are extremely important to the Cape Verdean economy. An estimated 20% of the GDP—about $100 million annually—is derived from remittances sent home by expatriates, and no visit of a Cape Verdean president to the United States is complete without a stop in Massachusetts and Rhode Island, where the wealthiest of the Cape Verdean diaspora reside. Chinese investment has also been important, with development projects financed by China includ-

ing the construction of a National Stadium, a second hydroelectric dam at Figueira Gorda on the island of São Tiago, and a cement factory, as well as investments in the ceramic and fishing industries. There are also plans for a new National Assembly building, a national library, and a mausoleum for Amilcar Cabral. Finally, the government is also firming its ties to the European Union. The Cape Verdean escudo was once tied to the Portuguese escudo, but with the introduction of the euro, it is now linked to the new currency. The government appears to be preparing to adopt the euro as its currency, much as the microstates of Andorra, Monaco, San Marino and the Vatican have done.

The Future

Cape Verde's outlook, while very limited by climate and geography, remains solid, if unspectacular. The 2006 elections provided the sense of stability and continuity that attract investors. The country has also invested in government transparency through an Internet-based government financial management system. The aim is to attract more investors by providing easy access to information about open bids for goods and services. The system also improve the communications with Cape Verdean citizens that live outside the islands, and this is particularly important given the importance for the country of the Cape Verdean diaspora and its remittances. (Several hundred thousand people of Cape Verdean descent live in Massachusetts and Rhode Island.) The stability and unique location the country provide the aforementioned opportunities for the expansion of investment. Yet rapid growth seems unlikely. Tourism and fishing appear to be the most promising areas of development.

Cape Verde maintains open ties with the international economy. While seeking to maintain close and favorable relations with China, it has also sought tighter association with the United States; the US military has begun training rapid intervention units for Cape Verde.

Together, these phenomena suggest Cape Verde is an African case apart, both literally and figuratively. The small and remote country faces few of the conflicts and menaces that plague other parts of West Africa. This makes for a more peaceful society, but also for greater difficulty in maintaining linkages to the rest of Africa. Indeed, one of the reasons for which Cape Verde diverges from other African countries is its physical separation. In short, there is no reason to expect the country to regress or backslide, but with a small and geographically fragmented domestic market, there are questions about the natural limits to its economic growth.

A gracious town square in Mindelo

Photo by Michael Beguelin

The Republic of Côte d'Ivoire

The government established the French form of *Ivory Coast* as the country's official designation, pronounced *Coat deev-whar.*

Our Lady of Peace, Yamoussoukro—the world's largest Christian church

Basic Facts

Area: 323,750 sq. km. = 125,000 sq. mi. (somewhat larger than New Mexico)

Population: 19,300,000 (UN 2007 est.)

Capital City: Yamoussoukro

Climate: Tropically hot and humid in the south, with two wet seasons (March–July and October–November). Warm and less humid in the north with a single wet season (May–October).

Neighboring Countries: Liberia, Guinea (west); Mali, Burkina Faso (Upper Volta-north); Ghana (east)

Official Language: French

Other Principal Languages: Anyi, Attié, Baulé, Bété, Dan, Guéré, Guro, Jula, and Sénoufo

Ethnic Groups: More than sixty ethnic groups. Prominently, Baulé (15%), Sénoufo (10%), Bété (6%), Lagoon peoples (5%), Agni (Anyi-3%), and a Mandé cluster of groups, including Jula, Bambara, and Malinké (17%). Non-Ivoirian Africans, Lebanese, Asians, and Europeans composed nearly 27% of population before the recent disturbances.

Principal Religions: Muslim 60%, Christian 22%, and indigenous 18% (some of these are also numbered among the Christians and Muslims).

Chief Commercial Products: Cocoa, coffee, tropical woods, petroleum, cotton, bananas, pineapples, palm oil, and fish

GDP Per Capita: $1250 (World Bank 2008 est.)

Currency: CFA franc (African Financial Community)

Former Colonial Status: French Colony (1839–1960)

Independence Date: August 7, 1960

Chief of State: Laurent Gbagbo, President (after disputed elections, October 2000)

National Flag: Three vertical stripes of orange, white and green.

Land and People

The Republic of Côte d'Ivoire occupies an area in the center of the south coast of the West African bulge. The coast, warmed by the waters of the Gulf of Guinea, is 340 miles long; from the border of Ghana for a distance of 185 miles to the west, it is flat and sandy, with many inland lagoons. The remainder of the coast towards Liberia has numerous sharp rocks and is higher. The surf along the entire shoreline is quite heavy, steadily pounding the sand and boulders. Dense forests and jungles spread their green foliage farther inland, covering almost 40% of the country. Tall niagou, samba and mahogany trees struggle against each other for precious sunlight, crowding smaller trees and undergrowth.

Midway to the north, the trees gradually become thinner and are succeeded by low scrub trees, grasses and brush vegetation. This in turn gives way in the extreme northern area to a semiarid climate, which has in the past supported grasslands, occasionally interrupted by taller growth. With the African drought of the past decade, this northern region has become increasingly desolate.

The country is mostly level—only the Man Mountains in the area closest to Liberia and Guinea relieve the monotony of the plains. The southern and central portions of the country have traditionally received ample rainfall and have high humidity. Temperatures are warm in the North, with less (or hardly any) rainfall.

Côte d'Ivoire's population is an ethnic mosaic consisting of some 60 groups, roughly divided into four linguistic families—Akan, Kru, Mandé and Voltaic—having distinct characteristics and regional identifications. Akan speakers dominate the southeast, and the most prominent subgroup, the Baulé, have also settled in savanna regions of central Côte d'Ivoire. Catholic missionaries were first active in the southeast, bringing mission education and literacy, which provided access to employment in the colonial civil service. From that position of privilege, Akan speakers came to dominate Ivoirian politics. Both presidents Houphouët-Boigny and Bédié were Baulé.

The southwestern region is dominated by Kru-speaking peoples. Though Protestant missionaries were active in the southwest, most peoples there practice indigenous religions. Laurent Gbagbo comes from one of the Kru subgroups, the Bété. Southern Mandé speakers are found in the western regions, and General Gueï belonged to the Yacouba subgroup. "Northerners" are almost equally split between Northern Mandé speakers and Voltaic speakers like the Sénoufo. The Northern

Côte d'Ivoire

Mandé include Malinké and Jula (or Dyula), traditionally long-distance traders. Alassane Ouattara hails from this group.

While Southern Mandé practice a variety of indigenous religions and Christianity, Northern Mandé are almost all Muslims and members of their merchant class have settled in most of the major cities of the south. There they have become influential enough to dominate the local politics of several southern cities.

The Past: Political and Economic History

For early history, see *Historical Background* and *The Colonial Period: the French.*

When full independence was gained by Côte d'Ivoire on August 7, 1960, Félix Houphouët-Boigny (*Fay-lix Who-fway Bwa-nyee*) became its first president. A Baulé, with ancestors including a line of chiefs, Houphouët-Boigny had attended the prestigious École William Ponty in Dakar, Senegal. The school brought together the very best students from each of the French West African colonies. It prepared them for positions in the colonial civil service or French commercial enterprises. Houphouët-Boigny was trained as a *médecin africain*. Perhaps even more important for future political developments, Ponty created an educated elite which would ultimately bring the various colonies of the French West Africa to independence.

Houphouët-Boigny traveled the colony extensively as a rural doctor and in 1940 inherited large coffee-producing tracts of land from his father, a wealthy planter and chief. Using modern techniques, he was able to expand their output, becoming a very wealthy man in a relatively short time. By the 1940s he was acknowledged as leader of disgruntled African planters and founded the African Agricultural Union in 1944. The group fought colonial policies that favored French planters and worked to end forced labor of Africans on white-owned plantations.

He formed the *Parti démocratique de la Côte d'Ivoire* (PDCI) in 1945, mobilized African planters, and was elected a deputy to the French National Assembly in 1945 and again in 1946. In the Assembly, Houphouët initially affiliated with the French Communist Party. After long and persistent harassment by colonial officials, he broke with the Communists in 1950 and began to cooperate with the French. In West Africa his PDCI was part of the *Rassemblement démocratique africain* (RDA: Democratic African Rally), a Federation-wide party.

In 1958, when General de Gaulle offered the possibility of immediate independence

President Laurent Gbagbo

to France's colonies, Houphouët campaigned vigorously for self-government within the Franco-African Community. He was an equally vigorous opponent of any large federation of independent states, refusing to see Côte d'Ivoire's wealth used to subsidize French West Africa's poorer states.

Félix Houphouët-Boigny became prime minister of the Côte d'Ivoire in 1959 and in 1960 was elected the first president of the independent state. He was the architect of Côte d'Ivoire's rise from colonial backwater to relatively wealthy republic.

His political base remained with the African planting class, and economic development reflected their interests. Commercial export of coffee and cocoa was encouraged and facilitated by development of roads. The port of San Pedro in the southwest was built to facilitate exports of the two crops. To work the plantations, migrant workers from Côte d'Ivoire's overpopulated and underdeveloped north were encouraged to travel south. Similarly, migrant labor from Mali, and what is now Burkina Faso, was encouraged to travel to the plantations. Land ownership and even citizenship were made possible for the newcomers.

For 30 years the PDCI remained the country's sole political party, and Houphouët-Boigny governed by crafting an alliance between Akan-speaking southerners and largely Muslim northerners. When young northerners complained of unemployment and uneven regional development in the 1970s, a flurry of projects was started in the north, but by the early 1990s northern resentments and frustrations could no longer be so easily bought off.

As elsewhere in Africa, waves of sentiment for multiparty democracy were felt in Côte d'Ivoire in the late 1980s. In response to popular demand, and a bit of pressure from the World Bank, free formation of po-

litical parties was permitted for the first time during the 1990 elections. One of the most critical voices was that of Laurent Gbagbo, a member of the minority Bété community. A former history professor, Gbagbo founded the *Front Populaire Ivoirien* (FPI) in 1990 and ran for president against Houphouët. Gbagbo's FPI gave expression to the frustrations felt by those who had long suffered under a government dominated by Akans. Ominously for the future, Gbagbo charged that Houphouët's power was based on the vote of "foreigners."

Côte d'Ivoire's founding father died in December 1993 and was succeeded by his protégé—another Baulé speaker—Henri Konan Bédié. Less confident and politically skilled than Houphouët, Bédié seemed not to understand the basic pragmatism by which Houphouët had ruled, winning over opponents through co-optation and cooperation, consensus and compromise. As tough economic restructuring began to be implemented, a scapegoat had to be found. It would be Côte d'Ivoire's "foreigners," and more specifically, northerners.

Northern resentments built up. Northerners felt they were not receiving a fair return for political support and economic contributions given over the years. They received fewer political appointments, and economic development of the region was stinted. They were too frequently hassled when trying to obtain national identity cards and complained of being treated not like citizens, but as foreigners. Their answer was to split from the PDCI.

The *Rassemblement des républicains* (RDR: Republican Rally), based mainly in the north, was founded in September 1994 only a few months after Houphouët-Boigny's death. Its leader was Houphouët's prime minister and rival with Konan Bédié as his successor, Alassane Ouattara.

Faced with an increasingly desperate economic situation and deprived of the PDCI's traditional northern support, Konan Bédié resorted to the baser instincts of his countrymen. "Foreigners" were stigmatized; a populist Ivorian ethno-nationalism was generated. It was not the first time the regime had diverted attention from its problems by arguing that foreigners exploited the colony's wealth. Dahomeans (from present-day Benin) had been the object of attack in 1958, but now it was the turn of Burkinabé and Malian migrant laborers. It was easy, by extension, to include Bédié's lapsed allies—northern Muslims.

First articulated by Bédié in an August 1995 speech to the PDCI faithful, the concept of Ivorian identity—*Ivoirité* in French—became central to political discourse in the country and was used to justify what developed into violent xenophobia.

"Ivoirization" was instituted in 1996, a direct reversal of the open borders policy

Côte d'Ivoire

of the country when plantation labor was needed. Now, to officially be a citizen, one had to prove his or her parents and grandparents were born in Côte d'Ivoire. Strict nationality rules for presidential candidates were introduced into the Ivorian electoral code.

Alassane Ouattara, once a prime minister under Houphouët-Boigny, was effectively prevented from running in 1995 because of these rules. He later accepted appointment as IMF deputy director. When, in April 1998, he announced that he would not seek reappointment and would be available to serve his country, the controversy reemerged with a vengeance. One PDCI leader accused him of being a foreigner. "We must close ranks," he told a party audience, "and not let ourselves be distracted by provocations of messiahs coming from other lands."

The virulence of attacks on Ouattara suggested the nervousness and even paranoia of the political class. He was both a northerner and Muslim, the "other" for the Akan-speaking Christian core of PDCI support. Like his predecessor Houphouët-Boigny, President Bédié was a Christian politician in a country increasingly turning to Islam.

Raw statistics describe a situation ripe for xenophobic reaction: Côte d'Ivoire has an estimated three million people officially described as "residents of foreign nationality." Another two million are residents of foreign origin—migrant workers and their descendents, largely Muslim. In short, some 30% of the population could be demagogically defined as "foreign."

Bédié's campaign to promote Ivorian nationalism produced increasing hostility directed at foreigners and ethnic minorities. Smoldering resentment against "foreigners," particularly in the south, erupted in ethnic pogroms in several communities. Anti-ethnic riots and continuing political demonstrations took place against a background of deteriorating economic conditions. The cocoa industry was particularly affected after the European Union agreed to allow chocolate manufacturers to use less cocoa butter in their confections.

Economic problems fueled political tension throughout 1999 as the country approached its presidential election. The government vigorously repressed its critics, imprisoned opposition leaders, and prohibited street demonstrations. The campaign against Ouattara grew increasingly personal. When one judge ruled that Ouattara qualified as a presidential candidate, the Justice Ministry forced that judge to resign and replaced him with a jurist who ruled that Ouattara's identity papers were forged. In early December the government issued a warrant for Ouattara's arrest.

The End of the First Republic

The country's cumulative crises were resolved on Christmas Eve, when General Robert Gueï, a former army chief of staff, assumed leadership of disgruntled soldiers demanding back wages and overthrew the Bédié government. France, with significant commercial interests at stake—20,000 citizens actually resident in the country, and 550 soldiers stationed there—did not act to restore the *ancien régime*. The country at large seemed to greet the coup with an enormous sense of relief.

Military intervention did not, cool political temperatures, however. After the Christmas Eve coup Côte d'Ivoire was plagued by violence and instability. General Gueï moved with military dispatch. A new constitution was written, submitted to voters, and massively approved in July 2000, but it carried into the Second Republic the fertile seeds of division cultivated in the First: Presidential candidates were required to have two Ivorian parents. Bédié's "*Ivoirité*" was given formal constitutional recognition.

Presidential elections were organized for October, and nineteen people submitted candidacy papers. Fourteen were declared ineligible by the Supreme Court. Included among the disqualified were representatives of the largest opposition parties—Émile Constant Bombet (PDCI) and Alassane Ouattara, (RDR). At best, the remaining five candidates, Robert Gueï among them, represented no more than 15% of Côte d'Ivoire's diverse population.

The campaign came down to a battle between General Gueï and Laurent Gbagbo, the former history professor who, as the leader of the socialist *Front Populaire Ivoirien* (FPI), had opposed the governing PDCI since 1990. Security forces engaged in bloody assaults against northerners, judged by dress and religion to be opponents of General Gueï. When the electoral commission proclaimed Gueï the winner in October elections, Gbagbo called out his supporters to protest. People took to the streets in massive demonstrations. The general fled and Laurent Gbagbo proclaimed himself winner and president.

Attacks against "foreigners" did not end. The new regime, like its predecessors, found the ethno-nationalism of "*Ivoirité*" politically useful and played to its supporters' basest instincts. The worst such incident occurred at the Abidjan suburb of Yopougon. There, gendarmes slaughtered 57 individuals and dumped them in a mass grave. Their only crime was to be Muslim or have a "northern" name.

Once installed as president, Laurent Gbagbo refused all suggestions that the election be rerun despite its dubious legitimacy—not only were the major candidates

excluded, but 62% of registered voters boycotted it. He also failed, disastrously, to curtail state-sponsored ethnic violence, and even appeared to encourage it.

In December 2000 legislative elections were organized, and now a Gbagbo court, echoing Konan Bédié's, excluded Alassane Ouattara (a one time ally of Gbagbo) from even running for the National Assembly. Demonstrations followed and many thought the country was on the verge of civil war. The RDR boycotted the election with such success that in some northern areas absolutely no one turned up at the polling stations. Only 33% of registered voters summoned courage or interest enough to vote.

The FPI obtained 96 seats in the 225-seat Assembly—not enough to govern alone—with the former governing Ivory Coast Democratic Party (PDCI) garnering 94 seats. Twenty-two independents would act as swing votes between the contending factions.

Municipal elections in March 2001 were dominated by Ouattara's RDR, now participating on a nationwide basis. By selecting candidates representative of local constituencies, the RDR gained control of all towns in the northern region and some of the largest southern cities, including Gagnoa, Laurent Gbagbo's birthplace. With these elections the RDR proved itself a national party that could be successful in a fair election.

The Politics of Reconciliation

Desperate to end the turbulence that threatened its internal power and external support, the Gbagbo regime convened a National Reconciliation Forum in late 2001, but ultimately regime behavior was little changed. Persecution and discrimination persisted; impunity grew, which only emboldened xenophobes and made

Alassane Ouattara

Côte d'Ivoire

life increasingly insecure for opponents of the regime. (In August 2001 eight gendarmes, for example, were charged with multiple murder in the Yopougon massacre, but were acquitted by a military tribunal for lack of evidence.)

These tensions exploded on September 19, 2002. Dissident divisions of the Ivoirian army mutinied, allegedly over issues of pay and demobilization. In coordinated attacks, the mutineers took control of the northern city of Korhogo and the central city of Bouaké. There was fighting in Abidjan, the commercial capital, but loyalist troops retained control of the city. During the fighting the interior minister was killed and the minister of defense attacked. The government claimed it was an attempted *coup d'état* and used the occasion to eliminate its enemies.

Troops in army fatigues murdered General Guëi—who had just withdrawn his party from the governing coalition and was suspected of planning a coup—along with his wife, aides, and other family members. A similar death squad arrived at Alassane Ouattara's home, but forewarned, he and his wife escaped over a wall into the neighboring German Embassy. He was later given sanctuary in the French Embassy.

The army mutineers soon incorporated civilian elements, named themselves the *Mouvement patriotique de Côte d'Ivoire* (MPCI), and announced their complaints and policy demands: They were fighting a "dictatorship" that treated them like "slaves," as one spokesman put it. They demanded Laurent Gbagbo's resignation and a transitional government that would organize new presidential elections, open to all.

The besieged president lofted his flimsy legitimacy, but it was a banner to which few rallied. Despite defense agreements with the country, France chose to pursue a "neither . . . nor" policy—neither interference nor indifference. In practical terms that meant dispatch of troops to protect French citizens and evacuate them from Korhogo and Bouaké, both controlled by the rebels.

With no outsider willing to fight the rebels, president Gbagbo was forced to rely on his own ill-trained, underequipped, demoralized, and disorganized army. The effort to retake Bouaké was a humiliating failure. To prevent further deterioration, France secured a cease-fire and established a buffer zone between government and rebel forces. The country was effectively divided in half. Rabid anti-French sentiment became the order of the day.

The regime accused hostile neighbors (Burkina Faso and Liberia) of arming and aiding the rebels, and denied responsibility for the acts. To defend itself, the Gbabgo government began to acquire arms and menfrom Eastern Europe and Angola. (Gbagbo had gained Angolan goodwill by breaking Côte d'Ivoire's connections with UNITA on becoming president.)

Much like the Hutu regime in Rwanda, the government whipped up ethnonationalist fervor in the streets and on the airwaves. Muslims, "foreigners," and political opponents became the object of virulent attack, and none more so than Alassane Ouattara who was all three to his detractors. The low point was no doubt reached when one daily, *La National*, proposed a simple word game: by using the letters in the name Alassane Dramane Ouattara, wrote the author, one could spell out the words "Satan," "demon," *"meurtre* (murder)," and "torture."

The wages of hate were not long in being gathered. Mobs demanding Ouattara plagued the French Embassy and nearly broke in. In early October 2002, illustrating the psychological centrality of the Yopougon massacre and its subsequent impunity, MPCI rebels massacred dozens of gendarmes at Bouaké after a chilling reminder: "Remember Yopougon? Now it's your turn." (Members of the Ivoirian regular army kept in the same holding area were not harmed.) Death squads began to roam through Abidjan, selectively assassinating regime opponents and intimidating others into silence by kidnapping and torture. A UN report of February 2003 suggested the death squads were comprised of elements close to the government, the presidential guard, and a Bété tribal militia.

Ivoirian equivalents of the Nazi Nuremberg laws began to be enacted. In Bonoua, only 30 miles from Abidjan, "foreigners" could not be allocated any stall at the local market, or land on which to build. They were also forbidden to work as transporters or to enter into a mixed marriage, and, in the language of the legislation, every family was "strictly forbidden to have recourse to any procedure to integrate a foreigner into our ranks."

Charles Blé Goudé, leader of the Young Patriots, now an "Ambassador of Peace"
©IRIN

As violence and fear intensified in the cities, the war in the countryside took on larger regional dimensions. Two new rebel groups located in Western Côte d'Ivoire announced themselves in November 2002—the *Mouvement populaire ivoirien du Grand Ouest* (MPIGO: Ivorian Popular Movement of the Greater West) and the *Mouvement pour la Justice et la Paix* (MJP). Both claimed to be fighting to avenge the murder of General Guëi and to remove Laurent Gbagbo. Both drew support from President Charles Taylor of Liberia and recruited from his reserve of mercenaries without borders—willing to fight anywhere, at any time, for any booty.

After France had gathered all the various forces together and twisted arms to secure agreement on a government of national union in January 2003, the need for mercenary services diminished significantly. Convincing them to go home proved more difficult. A joint operation by rebels, the Ivory Coast army, and 900 French troops was organized to clear western areas of the Liberian fighters.

Such cooperation was made possible by the Marcoussis peace accords hammered out at the end of January in a Parisian suburb. Those agreements, imposed on a reluctant Laurent Gbagbo, created a government of national unity that included ministers from the rebel groups (now collectively called the "New Forces"). The government was headed by a consensus premier, Seydou Diarra, a northerner.

The Diarra government found itself regularly impeded. Fearing assassination, rebel ministers were hesitant to attend initial cabinet meetings in Yamoussoukro. In Abidjan, the hardliners around Laurent Gbagbo organized public demonstrations of opposition and private acts of terror against those thought to support the New Forces. Foremost among these thuggish forces was the Alliance of Young Patriots headed by Charles Blé Goudé.

Though he periodically swore to uphold the Marcoussis agreement, President Gbagbo consistently delayed, circumvented, and obstructed any constructive progress to a peaceful resolution of the tensions that divided his country. He was received by French President Chirac with all the dignity of a head of state in February 2004, and seemingly emboldened by the recognition, he became even more intransigent. When the opposition proposed to demonstrate against the president's actions, Gbagbo decreed a prohibition on demonstrations through the month of April. Undaunted, opposition parties organized a pacific march in Abidjan to support Marcoussis, and the president responded with brute force. The city was closed down. Helicopters surveilled the participants from above, while below de-

Côte d'Ivoire

fense and security forces crushed the demonstration in blood. A UN report said that the government security forces and the militia killed at least 120 people. When they had completed their work, President Gbagbo congratulated his forces.

The UN report called the deaths "indiscriminate killing of innocent civilians," and noted that individuals from northern Côte d'Ivoire and immigrants from Burkina Faso had been "specially targeted" even though these communities had "little or nothing to do with the march." Following the massacre, New Forces rebels and the four main opposition parties in parliament withdrew their 26 ministers from the government of "national reconciliation" and broke off dialogue with President Gbagbo.

The government also continued to buy arms and hire mercenaries; by November 2004 it decided the time had come to crush the rebellion by military force. Aerial raids were launched against the five rebel strongholds in the north and west. During the last, on November 6, a government plane bombed a French military installation in Bouaké, killing nine French soldiers and one American civilian. France retaliated by destroying virtually the entire Ivoirian air force. Anti-French mobs rioted in Abidjan, largely targeting their mayhem and violence at French property and personnel: shops were fired, women raped, and men beaten.

Angry voices throughout the city fanned ultranationalist and anti-French sentiments. Young Patriots, a target audience for disinformation, were told the French intended to remove President Gbagbo from office. They responded by surrounding the principal sources of regime power: the Presidential Palace and the national radio and television station. In the chaos at least 20 and perhaps as many as 60 Ivoirians were killed.

The UN Security Council issued an immediate arms embargo and gave leaders one month to get the peace process back on track or face a travel ban and a freeze on their personal assets. The usually listless African Union enlisted President Mbeki of South Africa to lead an African mediation effort. The April 2005 Pretoria Agreement emerged from his mediation. It declared the war to be ended, reiterated previous accords, and perhaps most importantly, reaffirmed a determination to organize presidential elections in October 2005. President Mbeki dealt deftly with the central issue of those elections: the candidacy of Alassane Ouattara. The intransigent Laurent Gbagbo was pressured to abandon his demand for a constitutional referendum on the topic, and in late April he announced that he was invoking "exceptional measures" to suspend the normal rules for the next election

to allow Alassane Ouattara to participate in the presidential election of October 2005.

In May Ouattara and Henri Konan Bédié ended their long political feud to join forces against a common enemy, Laurent Gbagbo. The RDR and PDCI (plus two smaller opposition parties) created a new opposition coalition: le Rassemblement des Houphouëtistes pour la démocratie et la paix (RHDP: Rally of Houphouëtistes for Democracy and Peace).

At the end of June, after two days of talks in the South African capital, Pretoria, the government and rebel movement agreed to a new set of agreements, including a calendar for disarmament and a revision of several laws, including the important text on nationality. Deadlines came and went however, and each side accused the other of undermining the agreement. The government refused to act until rebels had begun disarming, and rebels refused to disarm because political reforms had not been implemented.

Given the political paralysis that overtook the country, the international community turned up its rhetoric to shame foot-dragging politicians. UN Secretary General Koffi Annan took the lead. A presidential election in October 2005 wasn't possible, he said in early September, "because political leaders and parties have not cooperated." He went on to accuse them of trying to "destroy" their country and threatened sanctions to bring them to their senses.

The normally somnambulant AU was spurred to action by President Obasanjo of Nigeria and recognized an extension of President Gbagbo's terms for "not more than 12 months." It offered a new peace plan that included an appointed prime minister with "full authority over his cabinet" to lead the country toward elections in October 2006. The UN Security Council quickly endorsed the proposal, which it enshrined as Resolution 1633.

The resolution created an important new body to make sure disarmament and elections took place by the October 31, 2006 deadline: the International Working Group (IWG). Broadly constituted, the IWG was designed to bring the full weight of the international community to bear on the country's fragile peace process. It consists of representatives of the UN, the AU, the European Union, IMF and World Bank, and Francophonie (the international grouping of French-speaking countries), as well as representatives from South Africa, Benin, Ghana, Guinea, Niger, Nigeria, France, the United Kingdom, and the United States.

In November the IWG set forth a road map for translating the Pretoria Accord and UN Resolution 1633 into reality. Three of Africa's most prominent leaders, Oba-

sanjo of Nigeria, Mbeki of South Africa, and Mamadou Tanja of Niger, the current head of the West African regional grouping, ECOWAS, shuttled between the various parties and finally designated Charles Konan Banny, the governor of West Africa's central bank, as Côte d'Ivoire's interim prime minister. His mandate from the UN Security Council was to organize elections by October 2006 and disarm contending forces: northern rebels and southern pro-Gbagbo militias.

Prime Minister Banny was sworn into office in early December, and after much haggling among the parties, presented his cabinet by the end of the month. As usual, the most difficult negotiator was Laurent Gbagbo, who wanted his own men controlling the ministries associated with revenue and force—Economy and Finances; Defense and Security. Banny's cabinet managed the difficult task of bringing on board representatives of the rebels, government, and major opposition parties, but the new prime minister was almost immediately tested.

On January 2, 2006 what appears to have been a minor military mutiny took place in the capital. More seriously, the IWG's recommendation not to extend the mandate of the National Assembly, which had expired in December, mobilized Gbagbo supporters. Protesters took to the streets and condemned UN interference in the country's affairs, generally paralyzing the city and terrorizing UN personnel.

As usual, the master of Ivorian street theater, Charles Blé Goudé, was in the

Ex-Prime Minister Charles Konan Banny
©IRIN

Côte d'Ivoire

thick of things. Some 2,000 of his Young Patriots blockaded the main UN bases in Abidjan and other cities until he told them to go home. (With the installation of the Banny government, some of the traditional funding sources to support groups like the Young Patriots had been squeezed off; with nothing to be paid out, the demonstrators quickly lost interest.) On February 7, 2006 the UN Security Council imposed a 12-month travel ban and assets freeze on Blé Goudé and two others for hampering peace efforts. He was cited for "public statements advocating violence against United Nations installations and personnel . . . direction of and participation in acts of violence by street militias, including beatings, rapes and extrajudicial killings . . ." (In an Orwellian turn, Laurent Gbagbo named Blé Goudé an "Ambassador of Peace" in May 2007.)

With strong international backing and no need to present his policy initiatives before a hostile national assembly, Prime Minister Banny confronted the mine fields of Ivoirian politics. Charged with preparing elections and with disarming rebels in the north and loyalist militias in the south, Banny faced irreconcilable demands posited by the Gbagbo regime and the New Forces. For the government, disarmament was the *sine qua non* of all else; for the New Forces, issuance of identity papers and a resolution of the question of one's Ivoirian identity was paramount.

The political stakes for each side are high. Laurent Gbagbo wants elections without an increased electorate, many of whom would be northerners systematically excluded and abused by his and previous administrations. For northern rebels, the arms they possessed represent the sole trump they

Prime Minister Guillaume Soro

hold. Recognizing both processes—identification and disarmament—were intimately linked, the Banny government committed itself to pursuing each simultaneously. Gbagbo and company resisted.

A pilot scheme registering immigrants to obtain certificates of national and voters cards was denounced by the president for opening the way to "massive fraud" in the areas under the control of the New Forces. Young Patriots took to the streets to protest, while the pro-Gbagbo press mounted vicious attacks on Alassane Ouattara. Prime Minister Banny himself came under attack for being a puppet of France and the UN.

Once the registration scheme expanded, obstructionists reacted even more violently. In July, the president of Gbagbo's FPI, Pascal Affi N'Guessan, demanded the Young Patriots halt registration by all means possible, and Gbagbo himself scathingly denounced the UN as pro-rebel, which only intensified the depredations of loyalist militias. Given this environment, there was no way elections could be held in October.

Indeed, there was a political premium for interfering with Prime Minister Banny's efforts to organize elections: Without elections, the president and his supporters had made clear, Laurent Gbagbo would remain in office until a new president was sworn in.

With peacekeeping costs mounting and results becoming more uncertain, the UN Security Council sought to loosen, if not dislodge, the largest boulder on its roadmap to resolving the Ivoirian conflict— Laurent Gbagbo. In early November, past its original deadline for elections, it unanimously voted Resolution 1721, extending the terms of both Gbagbo and Banny for another year and calling for elections to be organized by the end of October 2007. Prime Minister Banny was to have "all necessary powers" needed to carry out his mandate, including the power to issue laws by decree within governmental and cabinet meetings. The resolution also gave the prime minister authority over the country's army and defense forces.

Resolution 1721 sent Laurent Gbagbo's survival skills into overdrive. With umbrage and vehemence he denounced the grant of enhanced authority to the prime minister as unconstitutional—but said nothing about the equally unconstitutional extension of his own term of office. The Gbagbo-Banny confrontation was not long in coming.

In August, Prime Minister Banny had suspended the chief of Abidjan's port authority after it was revealed that European toxic wastes had been allowed to enter the port and had been distributed in 15 sites around the city; at least ten people had died after being contaminated. A November investigation fingered the port chief, Marcel Gossio, as "an accomplice" of the polluters, but he and two others suspended by the prime minister in the wake of the scandal—Gbagbo men all—were reinstated in early December by the president. Street manifestations multiplied; burning tires, broken windows and thrown rocks—urban guerilla warfare—devastated Abidjan. The confrontations lasted eight days; at least three Ivoirians were killed.

For President Gbagbo, survival skills honed over years in opposition, and years of thwarting political enemies, prompted a multidirectional defense. To his political base he presented himself as a populist nationalist, defending his country against French neocolonialism. To his fellow West African leaders, he argued the dangerous precedent set by Resolution 1721, which superseded, in effect, national constitutions and national sovereignty. But by far the cleverest ploy was to seek to divide the Houphouëtistes by directly sounding out the young Catholic leader of the New Forces, Guillaume Soro. It was an end run around imposed prime ministers and the whole apparatus of conflict resolution created by the international community; and best of all, it could be marketed as an African solution to African problems. Timing favored the great manipulator: his two nemeses, the UN's Kofi Annan and French president Jacques Chirac were both leaving office.

The Gbagbo-Soro discussions were mediated by Burkina Faso's president, Blaise Campaoré, and resulted in a peace accord signed on March 4, 2007. The agreement envisioned restarting the citizen identification process, presidential and legislative elections by October, disarmament and integration of a limited number of northern rebels and loyalist militiamen into the national army, and suppression of the "zone of confidence" separating north and south by gradual withdrawal of both UN and French forces.

Having no alternative, the accord was cautiously accepted by the international community. Equally hesitantly, Guillaume Soro, one-time leader of the country's militant student union, accepted Laurent Gbagbo's proposal to become the Côte d'Ivoire's latest prime minister. Prime Minister Soro seems to have conceded much more than he got in negotiations with the wily Laurent Gbagbo. The President's supporters occupy the two most important ministries in the new cabinet—interior and defense—and constitute the largest voting bloc—11 of 33 members. The FN will hold seven portfolios, while the PDCI and Alassane Ouattara's RDR were given five each, with the remainder going to smaller parties and civil society.

Elections have yet to be held. Initially scheduled for October 2008, they were postponed multiple times over issues of identity cards, candidate's nationality. As a response the UN has extended its embargo on Ivorian diamonds until elections are held.

The Present: Contemporary Issues

The core issue of Ivoirian politics remains the question of citizenship and inclusion on electoral rolls for those systematically excluded by xenophobic jingoism. The Gbagbo-Soro accord spoke only of amending existing rolls, which systematically excluded those considered "foreigners." For President Gbabgo, the possibility of keeping voters' cards out of the hands of potential opponents will be an enormous incentive to push for elections a quickly as possible.

Abidjan, the former capital city, is located on lagoons inland from the coast. The city now has a population of more than 3.5 million—the equivalent of the population of the entire country at independence in 1960. The city is home to most of the French citizens who still remain in the country. Well down from a population of 60,000 in 1978, today's expatriates live in a state of tension and fear, the objects of hostility and attack.

Much of the fear and tension is generated by a steady stream of anti-French invective spewed by Laurent Gbagbo's supporters and applauded at the highest leadership levels. Much of the radical anti-French rhetoric comes from the ranks of the powerful student union—*Fédération étudiante et scolaire de Côte d'Ivoire* (Fesci). Organized into the Association of Young Patriots by the former Fesci leader, Charles Blé Goudé, they have become the regime's storm troopers. Known as "the general of the young," (and to his friends as "the machete") Blé Goudé tools around Abidjan, surrounded by his Kalashnikov-bearing body guards, as the incarnation of what he calls opposition to "the dictates of Paris." There is more than symbolism to the young man. He sees himself as the youth movement's ideologue, and has begun to formulate the notion that decolonization has not yet ended and will only do so with the departure of the last Frenchman.

Côte d'Ivoire's economy is heavily dependent on agriculture. Cocoa coffee, and timber are its principal exports. Together, they produce about 70% of total export earning and contribute 40% of GDP. Côte d'Ivoire is the world's largest cocoa producer, representing about 40% of the world's cocoa output. There are some 620,000 cocoa and coffee farmers out of a population of 16 million, and another three million people depend directly on the commodities for their livelihoods.

One consequence of the reliance on earnings from cocoa, coffee and palm oil, is that vast areas of tropical rainforest have been destroyed to create commodity plantations. Dependent on migrant labor, cocoa plantations, particularly in the western region, have been the scene of vicious antiforeign pogroms. Many of the migrants, often from Burkina Faso and Mali, had lived in the region for years and had even bought property. Hyped up by the government's xenophobic rhetoric, locals chased thousands of northerners from their homes, lands, and livelihoods.

Control of the cocoa-producing areas was the major source of the Gbagbo regime's revenues. There was virtually no transparency, but donor-nation diplomats estimate that as much as 20% of those revenues were siphoned off to buy arms for the regime and to support the thuggish activities of loyalist militias like the Young Patriots.

Additional funding for the Gbagbo regime's support of loyalist militias came from the country's nascent oil sector. Côte d'Ivoire possesses proven oil reserves of some 100 million barrels, most of it located off shore. In 2008, some 55,000 barrels per day (bbl/d) were being produced. Though the books are hardly transparent, it looks as though oil income has replaced cocoa as the principal source of revenue for the state.

The principal economic resource for the New Forces government in the north is the region's cotton industry. A number of factors have compromised the industry's productivity. Planters and cooperatives have not been paid by processors, which has dissuaded many from replanting their fields. The absence of banks in the north impedes the transfer of funds, and cotton processors find it difficult to finance cotton shipments. With the division of the country, transportation costs have risen 40%. As a consequence, stocks accumulate at the factories and run the risk of deteriorating.

The Future

Despite some signs of optimism in the establishment of peace accords between the government and the New Forces, the situation in Côte d'Ivoire remains fragile. Given the bitter words and hardened attitudes that separated contending forces, it would be a miraculous turn if the Gbagbo-Soro team were to manage free, fair, and transparent elections in the near future. Presidential elections are now scheduled for November 29, 2009. The New Forces still control the northern half of the country, but have begun to disarm. In late 2007, rebel troops and government troops began to pull back from the front lines, and UN peacekeepers continued to play a role designed to facilitate the forthcoming elections.

This country was West Africa's economic star for much of the first three decades after independence; this has given Côte d'Ivoire an industrial base and an economic memory that is the envy of many neighbors. But the more recent past weighs more heavily on the future; conflict and uncertainty are likely to continue. In addition to concerns about the peace settlement and reunification of the country, rising food costs led to riots that hit many African countries in 2008; this is suggestive of the economic difficulties facing the country and its neighbors.

Citizenship registration

©IRIN

The Republic of The Gambia

Mothers lined up for food

Photo by Ken Brown

Basic Facts

Area: 10,463 sq. km. = 4,005 sq. mi. (Connecticut is 20% larger)

Population: 1,800,000 (UN 2008 est.)

Capital City: Banjul

Climate: Subtropically warm with a wet summer (May–October) and a dry and somewhat cooler season (November–April).

Neighboring Countries: The Gambia is enclosed on three sides by Senegal.

Official Language: English

Other Principal Languages: Fulfulde, Jola, Mandinka, Soninke, and Wolof

Ethnic Groups: African 99% (Mandinka 42%, Fula 18%, Wolof 16%, Jola 10%, Serahuli 9%, other 4%), non-African 1%

Principal Religions: Muslim 95%, Christian 4%, indigenous beliefs 0.08%

Chief Commercial Products: Peanuts and peanut products, fish, cotton lint, and palm kernels

GNI Per Capita: $320 (World Bank 2008 est.)

Currency: 1 dalasi (D) = 100 butut

Former Colonial Status: British Colony (1816–1965)

Independence Date: February 18, 1965

Chief of State: Yahya A.J.J. Jammeh, President (since 1994)

National Flag: Three horizontal stripes of red, blue, and green; thin white lines separate the stripes. Symbolically, the blue stripe (Gambia River) is between the red and green stripes (sun shining on the river as it flows through the fertile land).

Land and People

The Gambia has the smallest area of any independent nation on the African mainland. Slicing thinly into the northwest coast of Africa and facing the tropical waters of the Atlantic Ocean, this country lies within an area smaller than Jamaica. It was named *The* Gambia by the government to avoid confusion with Zambia.

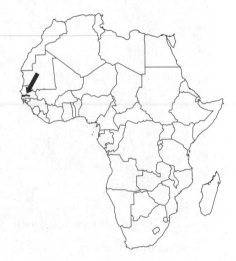

The Gambia is a fingerlike projection into the territory of southern Senegal by which, except for the seacoast, it is surrounded. The country largely follows the Gambia River, which is navigable by oceangoing vessels for 150 miles inland; smaller ships can traverse its entire length. The estuary contains one of the finest natural harbors in Africa.

The entire territory is low-lying, never exceeding a height of 120 feet. On each side of the broad river, thick swamps contain mangrove trees which can reach heights of up to 100 feet. Farther inland from the river is a region of swamps and river flats. This swampy belt is succeeded by round hills and rolling plateaus with thick growths of grass and periodic clumps of trees. There is ample rainfall for cultivation in this long and narrow nation, seldom more than 20 miles in width.

The Past: Political and Economic History

For early history, see *The Colonial Period: The British* and *The Colonial Period: The French.*

Conferences between the British colonial rulers and The Gambia in 1964 led to full independence on February 18, 1965; David K. Jawara was installed as the first prime minister. The Gambia elected to become a republic within the British Commonwealth in 1970 at which time Prime Minister Jawara became president.

Elections held in April 1977 (the first in ten years) resulted in a continuation of control by the People's Progressive Party led by President Jawara, who was elected to a five-year term. In mid-1981, while he was in London attending the wedding of Prince Charles, a force of leftists attempted to overthrow the government, but was unsuccessful. Elections held in May 1982 resulted in a legislature dominated by the PPP, which won 27 of 36 seats.

Presidential elections in 1987 were contested by two other parties competing with the PPP, but despite this, President Jawara was reelected by a comfortable 59% of the vote. President Jawara initially announced that he would not stand for reelection, but in early 1992 he changed his mind. The outcome was not unexpected—he won 59% of the vote; his party elected 25 of the 36 members in the legislature.

Unrest had been bubbling just below the surface for a decade, and finally erupted decisively in mid-1994 when Lt. Yahya Jammeh staged a coup. The basic problem was army personnel who had not been paid while rampant government corruption was obvious. Jammeh established a five-man ruling council. A referendum was held approving the new constitution.

Jammeh resigned his commission and was elected president in September 1996.

Parliamentary elections in January 1997 were contested by Jammeh's party, the Alliance for Patriotic Reorientation and Construction (APRC), the United Democratic Party (UDP) led by Ousainou Darboe, the People's Democratic Organization for Independence and Socialism (PDOIS), the National Reconciliation Party (NRP) and five independents. The APRC, organized to contest every seat, won more than a two-thirds majority—33 seats. The UDP won seven, the NRP two and the PDOIS one. The elections were controversial and most observers thought them neither fair nor free.

Given its origins in a military *coup* and fraudulent elections, it is little surprising that the regime is authoritarian and oppressive. President Jammeh dominates the country and controls the instruments of force and fear. He holds the Ministry of Defense portfolio through which he commands the army. The National Intelligence Agency reports directly to him. Oppositional activity is closely watched and the main opposition group, the United Democratic Party (UDP) is frequently denied permission to hold public rallies. Members of the UDP have been arrested and regularly accuse the police of torture. Members of parliament are prohibited from criticizing the president and denied the right of discussing any matter involving in the courts.

The media is equally subject to abuse and control. In 2003 *The Independent* newspaper came under particular attack; staffers received death threats, its editor-in-chief was detained by the National Intelligence Agency following publication of an article critical of President Jammeh, and its premises were set ablaze by three unidentified men. In May 2004, President Jemmeh took to the airwaves to excoriate journalists who failed to register with the National Media Commission (NMC). "We believe in giving each fool a long rope to hang themselves (sic)," he said. If they failed to register in the remaining three months of grace, he warned, "[t]hey will either register or stop writing or go to hell."

Critical journalism in The Gambia is a life and death profession. In December 2004, Deyda Hydara, the editor of *The Point* newspaper and one of the country's leading journalists, was brutally murdered, shot three times in the head after he had been sharply critical of newly passed press laws. One law made all press offenses, including libel, punishable by imprisonment—six months for the first offense and three years for repeat offenders. In order to continue publishing, media proprietors were required to prove they

could pay the hefty new penalties created by the law if they published such material; owners are required to sign a bond worth $17,000 and use their homes as collateral. In addition they are required to purchase operating licenses five times as expensive as before. The investigation of Hydara's murder seems to have been quietly put to rest. A 23-page intelligence report summarized the government attitude: Hydara was "an instigator who stirred up the anger of a number of people through critical reports in his newspaper."

The government also uses brute force against its citizens. The APRC has traditionally used its youth wings, trained by Libyans, as its storm troopers, breaking up opposition rallies, bullying and beating candidates and opposition supporters. At a UDP meeting in June 2000, things got out of hand and one APRC supporter was killed. The UDP leader, Ousainou Darboe, and some 20 of his followers were promptly arrested and charged with murder. Most were acquitted, but the trial of Darboe and four close associates was long-postponed and not settled until June 2005 with acquittal for all. Implacable in the destruction of his opponents, President Jammeh called the aquittal decision "a disaster to the maintenance of the rule of law," and the state appealed the court's ruling.

President Jammeh won another five-year term in October 2001 elections, beating the UDP's Ousainou Darboe, with a margin of 53%, just enough to avoid a runoff. The election, described as "relatively free and fair" by observers, was not without its quaint charms. Voters indicated their preference by dropping a marble into the drum of their chosen candidate. The marble struck a bell inside the drum—to ensure that multiple voting could be detected. Bicycles were banned from the vicinity of polling stations to avoid confusion with their bells.

President Jammeh celebrated his victory by firing several civil servants from the Finance Ministry, Customs and Excise Department, police force, Gambia International Airlines and social security services for alleged disloyalty. The dismissals came after an explicit campaign threat: "You are supposed to be loyal to the ruling party as civil servants and not opposition forces," Jammeh warned. "Anybody who does not cherish my party will not be working with us. I am ready to sack all opposition sympathizers in my government." After heavy lobbying, most were reinstated, but fear had been made reality.

Legislative elections in January 2002 resulted in a total triumph for Jammeh's ruling APRC after the UDP withdrew, claiming manipulation of the voter lists. Non-APRC candidates won only three seats in the 53-member legislature. With its

overwhelming majority, the APRC-dominated legislature quickly made it even more difficult for future presidential candidates to compete against President Jammeh: Section 48 of the constitution was amended to eliminate the need for runoff elections. Henceforth a candidate could be elected by a mere plurality of votes. The Secretary of State for Justice said the measure would be "cost effective."

One result of the contest was a split in the UDP. The party's former propaganda secretary, Lamin Waa Juwara, openly called for Darboe's resignation, and was promptly expelled from the party, forming his own—the National Democratic Action Movement (NDAM).

As NDAM leader, Juwara became one of the regime's most vigorous opponents, regularly arrested and detained by security forces. In February 2004 he was sentenced to six months in jail for "uttering seditious words"—that is, calling for popular demonstrations to protest the continuing decline of The Gambia's currency, worsening economic conditions, and endemic regime corruption.

Opposition leaders seemed to transcend their differences in 2005. In January, the NDAM's Juwara, along with UDP's Darboe, Hamat Bah of the National Reconciliation Party (NRP), Sidia Jatta and Amie Sillah of the Peoples Democratic Organisation for Independence and Socialism (PDOIS), and Omar Jallow and Alhaji Yahya Ceesay of the Peoples Progressive Party signed a memorandum of understanding establishing an alliance of opposition parties: the National Alliance for Democracy and Development (NADD). The agreement called for a common candidate to challenge Yahya Jammeh in the 2006 presidential election.

Despite this attempt at unity, the opposition remained divided and weak; it was no match for the presidential juggernaut in September 2006 elections. As usual, op-

President Yahya Jammeh

The Gambia

position candidates were harassed and the lives of reporters made difficult; President Jammeh was reelected for a third term with 67.3% of the vote. Ousainou Darboe, the main opposition candidate, secured only 27%, while Halifa Sallah was the third place finisher with a modest 6%.

The president's APRC won a similar landslide victory in the January 2007 legislative elections: 47 seats to the UDP's four. One additional seat went to NADD, and a single, lonely "independent" also took a seat in the legislature. Voter enthusiasm was minimal: only 38% of registered voters participated.

Corruption remains a serious problem, and the government established an anticorruption commission to examine the assets of active and retired ministers and senior military officials, the first instance, it claimed, where a sitting African government has probed itself. The commission submitted a four-volume report detailing tax evasion and fraud in high places and several senior government officials, including cabinet ministers, lost their jobs and forfeited assets to the state. Later, it turned out, some were reappointed after paying a fine.

The regime, as befits its origins and authoritarian nature, has been shaken by several attempted coups, the latest coming in March 2006 and led by the armed forces chief of staff, Col. Ndure Kham. Coming just months before Banjul would host the AU summit, the coup attempt proved embarrassing for the regime. President Jemmeh promised that any attempt to overthrow his government would be "crushed without mercy."

Culture: The Gambia's population is 95% Muslim, and female circumcision is widespread, practiced by varying numbers of Mandinka, Serahuli, Fula, Wolof, and Jola peoples. An estimated 80% of Gambian women have had their clitoris surgically removed. A variety of women's groups have been organized to ban female genital mutilation (FGM), but they receive little support from President Jammeh. In January 1999, Jammeh called those working to eliminate FGM "enemies of Islam" who sought to undermine the religion and African culture. Since then he has begun to speak out publicly against the practice, but his government will not impose a ban.

As elsewhere in West Africa, Islam in Gambia has been traditionally flexible, accommodating a variety of indigenous practices. Having condemned traditional religious leaders, both Christian and Muslim, for supporting the Jawara regime, the young Lt. Jammeh reached out to young Islamist clerics, educated in Saudi Arabia in Wahhabist fundamentalism. Upon returning to The Gambia, they grew their beards, donned long white robes, and followed the more rigid practices of Islam.

Following the events of September 11, 2001, however, the president's relationship with the Islamists cooled. In July 2003, speaking on the ninth anniversary of the *coup* that brought him to power, the president directed his criticism to what he called "the criminal elements of Islam" who believe "that it is the long beard that will take you to heaven." "God will not judge you, by your long beards," he proclaimed. "God will judge you by what you do. You are a disgrace to Islam."

Bizarrely, President Jammeh announced he had discovered a "miracle" treatment for HIV/AIDS in January 2007. Based on medicinal plants and a Koranic verse, the treatment cured the disease within days, said the president. Nearly universal condemnation followed, and when the UN's envoy in The Gambia publicly expressed doubts and suggested it could lead to irresponsible sexual behavior, he was expelled from the country. The president has since used his "treatment" on several individuals, but there has been no evidence that it has helped anyone.

The Present: Contemporary Issues

The Gambia's economy is agriculturally based and largely dependent on groundnut export earnings. Seventy to 80% of the country's workforce is engaged in farming; of generally low productivity, Gambian farmers, 75% of the country's labor force, contribute about 33% of GDP (2005). About 60% of all cultivated land is planted in groundnuts (peanuts). Their export provides nearly 85% of all export earnings. Despite the importance of the agricultural sector, it has not received enough government investment to make it more productive.

A once promising tourism industry is on the verge of collapse. Tourists, harassed by unemployed locals known as "bumsters" and solicited for drugs or sex, have turned their backs on The Gambia.

The Gambia's budget runs regular deficits and to make up some of the shortfall, massive tax increases were introduced to generate operating revenues in 2004. A variety of professions (mechanics, carpenters, hairdressers, welders, butchers, masons, cattle dealers, tailors, and mobile foreign exchange dealers) have been asked to pay around $90 to $313 in income taxes. Buyers of imported water and soft drinks found the beverages newly taxed, though mosquito nets remained tax free.

Under increasing economic pressures, everyday Gambians increasingly see the regime as corrupt and self-serving. President Yahya Jammeh, whose salary was about $100 per month when he overthrew the government in 1994, has boasted on national radio and television that he will never be poor, his children will never be poor and his children's children will never be poor. He now owns a zoo, for which he imports expensive exotic animals from around the world, an expensive mansion in his home village, and reportedly a personal airline.

The country's accumulated debt is enormous—$622 million as of 2004—and debt servicing consumes about a third of the budget. For the cynical, the government's vaunted anticorruption campaigns are only intended to distract the citizenry from the country's economic decline. For the more positively minded, the debt reflects the transformation effected by the Jammeh regime. In ten years it has created a national university, increased access to education, especially for girls, built four new hospitals, paved hundreds of kilometers of roads and introduced national television. President Jammeh has announced that oil had been discovered in commercial quantities in The Gambia's offshore waters, but it will be years before production can begin.

The Future

The Gambia remains a military dictatorship despite its democratic trappings. Neither media nor opposition can flourish in this environment; the regime is fundamentally unaccountable and will continue its repression with impunity. The decline of democracy is all the more striking at a time when many African countries are moving in the other direction, and especially considering The Gambia's relatively robust democracy at one time. The country was one of only three democracies on the continent (along with Botswana and Mauritius) in 1990.

The Gambia remains poor in resources; the country is ranked 155 out of 177 on the UN's 2006 *Human Development Index.* Yet the case can be made that this poverty promotes at least some degree of accountability, for the government is dependent on tax revenues, and thus it must moderate its worst instincts in ways foreign to those dictators that sit upon natural resources. Political change is not entertained by President Jammeh. In April 2006 he counseled anyone who thought to replace him "to wait like a vulture, patiently," because he planned to remain in office for the next 30 years.

The Republic of Ghana

Coastal humidity creates a palpable atmosphere.

Photo by Bianca Scotton

Basic Facts

Area: 239,460 sq. km. = approx 93,000 sq. mi. (slightly smaller than Oregon)

Population: 23,832,495 (CIA World Fact Book July 2009 est.)

Capital City: Accra

Climate: Hot and humid in the southwest; warm and less humid in the north. Wet season (May–September) and dry season (October–April).

Neighboring Countries: Ivory Coast (west); Burkina Faso (Upper Volta—west, north); Togo (east).

Official Language: English

Other Principal Languages: Akan, Twi, Moshi-Dagomba, Ewe, and Ga

Major Ethnic Groups: Akan/Asante 45%, Moshi-Dagomba 15%, Ewe 12%, Ga 8%

Principal Religions: Christian 69%, Muslim 16%, Indigenous beliefs 9%.

Chief Commercial Products: Gold, cocoa, timber, tuna, bauxite, aluminum, manganese ore, and diamonds

GDP Per Capita: $786 (World Bank 2007 est.)

Currency: Cedi (GHC), revalued in 2007 (10,000 old cedis = 1 new cedi)

Former Colonial Status: British Colony (1821–1957)

Independence Date: March 6, 1957

Chief of State: John Evans Atta-Mills, President

National Flag: Three horizontal stripes of red, yellow and green with a five-pointed black star in the center of the yellow stripe.

Land and People

Ghana is situated in the center of Africa's Gulf of Guinea coast, with a 334-mile-long shore washed by the Gulf's warm waters. The coastline is irregular, interrupted by streams and lagoons covered with strand and mangrove growth. In the eastern inland coastal area, the terrain consists of scrub and grassland, interrupted by clumps of bushes and small trees. Inland from the western coast there

is an area of rainforest supporting dense growths of trees towering to heights of 200 feet.

Some 175 miles north from the sea, dense vegetation gives way to grassland areas with less rainfall and shorter, more sparsely distributed trees. The harmattan, a dry wind from the Sahara, penetrates from November to April. Humidity drops during this season, and both grasses and trees turn yellow; the trees lose their leaves within a few weeks. Temperatures in the grassland region are high since there is no cooling breeze from the sea. In the extreme North, rainfall is very scarce causing Northern Ghana to suffer significant desertification in the past few years. There are no true mountains in Ghana—the highest elevation is 2,900 feet in the part closest to the eastern boundary.

Traditional kingdoms continue to flourish in Ghana, and their rulers exercise influence inside and outside the country. The Asantahene, paramount chief of the Asante Federation, occupies the Golden Stool of the Asante. Nana Kwaku Duah, a London-trained accountant and business

executive, aged 48 upon assumption of the throne in 1999, asserted the long continuity of his office in his official name. As Asantahene he is known as Osei Tutu II, after the first Asante king. His coronation, an "enstoolment" among the Asante, took place on the Golden Stool, which is believed to have descended from Heaven in a cloud of white dust, landing on the lap of Osei Tutu I. Asantes believe the stool contains the soul of the Asante nation.

Ghana is home to proud cultural traditions among which Highlife music is one of the great contributions. In literature, the country gave birth to prominent writers such as Ayi Kwei Armah, whose novel *The Beautiful Ones Are Not Yet Born* captured the pathologies and disillusionment of the Ghana's post-independence decline. In more eclectic folk art, the Accra suburb of Teshi has become a major point of attraction for tourists as the home of some of Ghana's most brilliant artistic expressions: fantasy coffins. Coffins made in the form of fish, hens, roosters, leopards, lions, or elephants are readily available. Patrons of the funerary artists often want to bury loved ones in something that reflects their life or work, be it hammers for carpenters, mobile phones for executives, canoes or cocoa beans, or even Coca-Cola bottles or miniature fire engines.

The country is rich in historical sites of interest. As Ghana was the origin of much of the transatlantic slave trade, the country is a leading destination for tourists from the Americas who seek to explore their African heritage. The castles at Elmina and Cape Coast are solemn reminders of the historical injustices perpetrated upon some Africans.

Finally, Ghanaian culture must include the "Black Stars." Ghana's national soccer team had a resounding success at the World Cup finals in Germany in 2006, advancing to the second round after wins over the United States and a powerful

Ghana

Czech Republic team. In 2008, Ghana hosted Africa's top regional tournament, the African Cup of Nations, where the Black Stars took third place.

The Past: Political and Economic History

For early history, see *"Historical Background"* and *"The Colonial Period: The British."*

Independence and the Kwame Nkrumah Years (1957–1966)

For many years, Ghana was one of Africa's greatest disappointments. The early leader, pushing for freedom in the first days of independence, Nkrumah soon became a corrupt dictator. Famously, the country was wealthier than South Korea in 1957, but declined catastrophically while Asian countries (and even neighboring Côte d'Ivoire for a time) seemed to plow ahead.

After Ghana's independence in 1957, President Kwame Nkrumah (Kwah-mi N-kroo-mah) rapidly transformed the government patterned after various communist nations. His Convention People's Party (CPP) became the instrument of all political thought. Nkrumah acquired the power to jail people for ten years without trial, and the press was rigidly censored. Establishing close ties with China and the Soviet Union, Nkrumah regularly accused the Western nations of "neo-colonialism."

Rich by African standards, Ghana began its independence with a relatively full treasury. This allowed Nkrumah to borrow huge sums of money from abroad, which were then squandered on lavish prestige projects of little productive value. Agricultural development was largely ignored, and by 1966, Ghana was in economic meltdown. At the time of independence, Ghana was the world's leading cocoa exporter and its economic prospects were excellent. When Kwame Nkrumah and his Convention People's Party came to power, they sought economic development through rapid industrialization, directed and funded through the state. Investment funds largely came from accumulated surpluses of the Cocoa Marketing Board, a government institution which oversaw and took most of the profits from the trade in cocoa beans. Few of the state enterprises created at this time proved profitable. State budgets were in deficit to such a degree that cocoa surpluses could not cover the budgets, as cocoa prices slipped precipitously on world markets. A huge accumulated debt was Nkrumah's legacy to his political heirs.

Army officers seized power early in 1966, deposing Nkrumah and forming the National Liberation Council. The new regime released almost 1200 political prisoners from jails, but arrested Nkrumah's sympathizers, and expelled Communist technical and political personnel. Nkrumah went to Guinea, where his friend, Sékou Touré, bestowed on him the honor of titular head of state. He died there in 1972.

The Rawlings Regimes (1979–2000)

Successive governments, military and civilian, failed to solve the problems left them by the previous regime. Soaring inflation, corruption, fraud, unemployment, and a heavy debt made it near impossible for the subsequent leaders to turn around the economy. In 1979, Flight Lt. Jerry Rawlings, with a group of young officers, took over the government and oversaw elections for a new civilian government. The newly elected government lasted only until New Year's Eve, 1981, when Lt. Rawlings again appeared on the scene and deposed the elected chief executive, pledging to provide stable democracy for the country. Rawlings, head of a seven-man council, suspended the constitution and abolished all of Ghana's six political parties. Accusing the previous government of failing to provide for the needs of the people, he called upon the citizens to become actively involved in "the decision-making process."

The new government adopted radical rhetoric—Rawlings was an unabashed admirer of Libya's Col. Qadhafi. Following the Libyan model, the Rawlings regime installed "People's Defense Committees" and "Committees for the Defense of the Revolution" in city neighborhoods, rural villages, and industrial plants. The stated purpose of these committees was to act as watchdogs against corruption.

As the economic decline continued, Rawlings eventually rejected leftist approaches and established an Economic Recovery Program with the guidance of the IMF and the World Bank in 1983. The government restored fiscal discipline, improved tax collection, and generated a budget surplus by 1986. In 1986, Rawlings began a second phase of the recovery program with deeper structural adjustments: he scaled down the bloated and costly bureaucracy by firing some 45000 civil servants, he liberalized foreign exchange policy, overhauled the investment code to encourage foreign investment, privatized state enterprises, and adopted a less radical rhetorical style.

Bowing to international pressures in the political arena, Rawlings allowed a multiparty system to develop in the early 1990s. Preparatory to elections scheduled for November 1992, he resigned from the air force (as required by new election laws) and ran for president as a civilian. With multiparty democracy, however, Ghana fell off the straight-and-narrow economic path. As an inducement to civil servants to support his party, Rawlings granted large public employee raises. Rawlings won with 60% of the vote, becoming the first African head of state to make the conversion from military ruler to democratic civilian leader. The economic consequences, however, were the evaporation of five years worth of surpluses, and an increased inflation and domestic debt.

Nonetheless, Rawlings and his National Democratic Council (NDC) won another mandate in 1996, when Rawlings retained the presidency with 57.4 % of the vote. The NDC's nearest rival, John Kufuor, heading an alliance consisting of the New Patriotic Party (NPP) and the People's Convention Party, won a respectable 39.6%. In legislative elections the NDC won 132 seats, an absolute parliamentary majority.

By the time the elections of 2000 rolled around, the country's economic woes had worsened. Prices of Ghana's major exports, gold and cocoa, declined, and petroleum prices soared; the decline in the value of exports and the increasing costs of imports put additional pressure on public accounts. Inflation soared to 60% and interest rates to nearly 50%. Unemployment hovered at about 50% while the value of Ghana's currency, the cedi, collapsed from 2.75/dollar in 1981 to 6,800/dollar in 2000. Per capita income of $410 in 1981 had dropped to $360 by 2000. As a consequence, the NDC paid the price when Ghana's third democratic election was held.

The Kufuor and Atta-Mills Administrations (2000–present)

Constitutionally prohibited from seeking a third term, Rawlings handpicked his vice president, John Evans Atta-Mills, to be his successor. The NPP again nominated John Kufuor, an Oxford-trained lawyer, businessman and long a conservative opponent of the regime. A Roman Catholic from the country's influential Asante tribe, Kufuor campaigned on a platform of "positive change."

Former President John Agyekum Kufuor

Though marred by some violence, the vote count was generally fair. The NPP won 100 of the 200 parliamentary seats. Its presidential candidate, Kufuor, nearly won a first ballot victory, taking a lead of 48.44% to John Atta-Mills' 44.8%. In the runoff, all five minor candidates threw their support to Kufuor, who won with an impressive 57%. When Atta-Mills telephoned his concession speech, Ghanaians sighed in collective relief: the country had successfully achieved a democratic transfer of power.

The transition has not been without its problems and tensions. President Kufuor must regularly deal with the legacy of former President Rawlings. In August 2002, speaking in Kumasi, the heartland of Kufuor's support, Rawlings called for "positive defiance" and reminded his audience that "We don't have to wait for the next election to prevent the rot," implying for some a strong desire for a coup to topple the NPP. Rawlings called the NPP "the worst government the country has ever had," a startling claim in light of the many years of malgovernance in the 1960s and 1970s. Relations between Rawlings and Kufuor remain cold at best and in March 2007 Rawlings even refused to participate in Ghana's celebration of its 50 years of independence, instead issuing a message to Ghanaians, criticizing the government for, among other things, "pervasive corruption at all levels, missed opportunities for genuine progress, nepotism, tribalism and known cases of political torture and killings." Months earlier, the minister of information, with some exasperation, had commented on Rawlings' most recent statements. It was beginning, he said, to look like Rawlings "has eaten the head and brains of a baboon and is having nightmares."

Ghanaians continue to wrestle with its authoritarian past. After 18 months, of hearing about 4,000 petitions, Ghana's National Reconciliation Council (NRC) submitted its 2004 report on human rights abuses during "periods of unconstitutional rule." The Rawlings years of "unauthorized" rule (1979; 1981–1993) featured prominently in the hearings, serving only to erode Rawling's claims of moral legitimacy and to diminish his self-defined legacy. Much like its South African model, the commission's mandate was to discover the truth about past abuses and help those who suffered deal with their pain and move on. It also sought to help the abusers come to terms with the experience and obtain forgiveness. President Kufuor's style is less high-pitched and more mild-mannered than Rawling's. He marked the end of his first year in office by holding an unprecedented public question-and-answer session. Dubbed the "people's assembly," the event featured Kufuor and his entire cabinet hearing complaints and answering questions posed by a capacity audience, which filled Accra's international conference center. The assemblies were commonplace throughout Kufuor's leadership.

Similar efforts have been made to involve the Ghanaian citizens living abroad President Kufuor has held "Peoples' Assemblies" with a cross section of Ghanaian expatriates, in which he explains policies, answers questions and offers thanks for support. (Bank of Ghana figures show that remittances from Ghanaians abroad have topped the one billion dollar mark.) In efforts to continue reform, Kufuor's government has focused on repairing the economy, which has necessitated some political risks, including doubling fuel prices.

The December 2004 elections were a reprise of the matchup in 2000 of the NPP's Kufuor and John Atta-Mills of the NDC. With strong world prices for cocoa and gold pushing Ghana's economic growth to over 5% a year and with substantial debt reduction from the World Bank and major Western donors, economic basics favored the the president. Some 83.2% of eligible voters turned out and President Kufuor won a solid 52.75% against John Atta-Mills, who won a respectable 44.32% of the vote. Observers agreed the election was free and fair, an important consolidation of democracy for the country. Indeed, parliamentary elections saw many MPs, including ministers, lose their seats. Kufuor's NPP garnered 129 seats in the 230-member house, while Atta Mills's NDC took 88; the remaining seats were distributed among smaller parties, including the once dominant CPP, which won just four seats.

Voting in future elections could be greatly changed by the passage, in early 2006, of the Representation of the Peoples Amendment Bill (ROPAB). The new legislation allows Ghanaians living abroad to vote in all public elections and referenda. Vigorously opposed by the NDC, the bill was passed unanimously after the opposition boycotted legislative meetings for two weeks, protesting "growing intolerance and disrespect for minority rights in Ghana's current parliament." More realistically, as the *Accra Mail* put it, they knew the majority of new voters would not vote for their party: "The embedded reason that fuels their own fear is an admission that they played no small part in the exodus of massive numbers of Ghanaians to run from the familiarity of their country for other lands."

The Present: Contemporary Issues

In his 2004 reelection campaign, Kufuor pointed to increased economic growth, reduced inflation, interest rates and government borrowing, as well as a stabilized cedi, the national currency. The achievements came through tough political choices that imposed austerity and caused hardship, such as increased utility rates and school fees, and the elimination of costly gasoline subsidies. To soften the blow, the government provided more public transportation and raised the minimum wage by 26%—to $1.05 a day. The economy saw a growth of 5.2% in 2003, and exceeded 2004 predictions to achieve a growth of 5.8%. According to the World Bank, the number of Ghanaians in poverty was down to 33.4% in 2005 from 39.5 in 2000. Impressed, the bank supported, under the enhanced Heavily Indebted Poor Countries (HIPC) initiative, a $3.7 billion debt-reduction package for Ghana. Debt servicing was reduced by some $200 million, and the money saved has been invested to increase production and promote sustainable livelihoods among Ghana's desperately poor farmers. In June 2005, the world's richest countries, collectively known as the G-8, announced cancellation of the debt owed by 18 countries, including Ghana. Its share of the windfall was estimated at $4.1 billion, about 80% of the country's external debt.

University of Ghana, Legon   Photo by Isabelle Forter

Ghana

Having reduced public debt and eased debt servicing, multilateral lenders evinced concern in 2006 with China's rush to supply new loans to Ghana. In June 2006, Chinese Premier Wen Jiabao visited Ghana, part of a seven-nation African foray. Among the usual bounty distributed on such occasions were concessionary loan agreements worth $108 million; the biggest portion was a $66 million low-interest loan destined to upgrade Ghana's communication network. In September, U.S. Treasury Secretary Henry Paulson called it "irresponsible borrowing," and the usually more discrete World Bank warned of the "time bomb of a cycle of indebtedness" that might threaten the country's economy in the future.

In 2008, Ghanaians witnessed the second peaceful democratic transition of power, as John Evans Atta-Mills of the NDC won the presidential election in his third attempt. Kufuor, allowed only two elections as president by the constitution, passed on the NPP candidacy to Nana Dankwa Akufo-Addo, who lost the election with 49.77% against Atta-Mills' 50.23%. Some initial tensions after the vote quickly dissipated as Akufo-Addo accepted the result and graciously agreed to attend Atta-Mills' inauguration. The election was deemed open and fair, reinforcing Ghana's reputation as one of the most politically free countries on the continent.

The large opposition is worried that Atta-Mills, who was Rawlings' vice-president, is unable to govern without letting Rawlings interfere, and that Rawlings may thus regaining some of the power he lost at the end of his presidency in 2000. Agriculture is the main sector of the economy, accounting for nearly 39% of GDP and employing over 55% of the working population in 2005. Despite its generally dwindling fortunes, cocoa remains the country's biggest industry. Production in the 2005–06 harvest year, was an excep-

tional 740,000 tons, the highest production in the history of the cocoa industry in Ghana. President Kufuor pledged to increase production to one million tons by using science, technology and "best practices." The government has vowed to tackle the issue of abusive child labor on the cocoa farms by 2011, alongside the improvements in output.

Nearly three million acres are planted in cocoa, worked by some 700,000 farmers. Most of the holdings are small, which contributes to Ghanaian cocoa's reputation for high quality. (The smallholder takes the time to sort bad nuts from the cocoa and more carefully tends the fermentation and drying process than large-scale farmers do)

Gold vies with cocoa as the country's biggest foreign exchange earner thanks to a liberalized mining code. Ghana produces around 2.2 million ounces of gold annually, making it Africa's second largest gold producer after South Africa. The income represents about 45% of the country's foreign exchange revenues. To encourage foreign investment, the government has opened protected forest reserves to mining companies. The six companies receiving mining licenses (for gold and bauxite) have committed themselves to invest over $2 billion. Government ministers toured some of the reserves and met with local communities to help them make a decision. Desperate for amenities and secure jobs, many local residents favored the mines.

A coalition of local and international NOGs vigorously opposed some of the developments, especially Newmont Mining's Ahafo project in western Ghana. As described by the company, the $470 million project would develop four open-pit mines capable of generating 500,000 ounces of gold over a 15-year life span. It would create 620 permanent jobs and, depending on the price of gold, generate $300 million to

$700 million in revenues for Ghana. Opponents argued it would displace more than 9,000 people, 95% of whom were subsistence farmers, and employ "significantly less stringent human health or environmental standards" than used in the United States. Of particular concern is contamination of drinking water from mine wastes, including arsenic used in the mining process. In February 2006, the Board of Governors of the International Finance Corporation, the World Bank's investment agency, approved a loan to Newmont Mining to continue the project.

Timber, fishing, oil and tourism all offer potential development opportunities.

The Future

Today, far from being a basketcase, Ghana is one of Africa's success stories. Ghana's political stability is the envy of many neighboring countries, and with the transition from Rawlings to the Kufuor government, Ghanaians have reason to cheer. There are no immediate prospects of a return to military rule, and democracy has slowly consolidated over the past decade. Ghanaians enjoy an increasingly robust democracy, with an improving rule of law and relatively secure civil liberties.

Economically, the country remains deeply impoverished, like most countries in the region. Some 40% of the population still has a per capita income of less than one dollar a day. Yet the direction of change is positive. The discovery of oil off the Ghanaian shores is tremendously promising. With reserves estimated at 10 billion barrels, Ghana will benefit from a massive influx of cash over the next two decades. In an effort to avoid the tragic fate of Nigeria, which has seen its oil revenues disappear with corruption, Ghana's government is seeking expertise on extraction and savings from Norway (which has set aside oil proceeds for long-term use in a fund totaling 322 billion dollars), among other countries. According to the current finance minister Kwabena Duffuor, "In 10 years time, Ghana will be a very prosperous nation."

Due to its relatively strong recent record in governance, the country is regularly included among the "model" African countries that were candidates for debt relief and increases in international aid. *The Economist* magazine called the 2008 election "a fine example for the rest of Africa," especially given the statesmanlike conduct of the two top candidates after Atta-Mills' thin margin of victory. Continued political stability is supporting prospects for economic development. While Ghana faces a continued and prolonged fight with poverty, corruption, and strengthening state institutions, its trajectory is far preferable to many of its African neighbors.

A traditional family compound

Photo by Isabelle Forter

The Republic of Guinea (pronounced *Gih*-nee)

Guinean family outside traditional thatch-roofed home.

Basic Facts

Area: 245,857 sq. km. = 95,000 sq. mi. (about the size of Oregon)

Population: 9,400,000 (UN 2007 est.)

Capital City: Conakry

Climate: In the extreme Southeast and Southwest there are small hot and humid areas of jungle with two rainy seasons (May–July and September–November). The climate gradually changes the terrain to a warm, semiarid region in the North with a single rainy season (April–October).

Neighboring Countries: Guinea-Bissau (west); Senegal, Mali (north); Ivory Coast (east); Liberia, Sierra Leone (southeast)

Official Language: French

Other Principal Languages: Baga, Dan, Fuuta Jalon, Kissi, Malinké, Maninka, Mano, and Susu

Ethnic Groups: Peuhl 40%, Malinké 30%, Soussou 20%, smaller tribes 10%

Principal Religions: Muslim 85%, Christian 8%, indigenous beliefs 7%

Chief Commercial Products: Bauxite, alumina, diamonds, gold, coffee, fish, and agricultural products

GNI Per Capita: $433 (World Bank 2008 est.)

Currency: Guinea franc

Former Colonial Status: French Colony (1894–1958)

Independence Date: October 2, 1958

Chief of State: Capt. Moussa Dadis Camara, Junta Leader (since December 2008)

National Flag: Vertical stripes of red, yellow and green.

Land and People

Facing southwest on the Atlantic Ocean in the western bulge of Africa, Guinea has an irregular, but level coastline. Immediately inland there is a gently rolling area, covered with dense vegetation in the more southern coastal area. Grassy plains, interspersed with trees, are found in the north coastal region. Farther inland the landscape slowly rises in a series of flat plains and table mountains. The Fouta Djallon mountains rise to heights of 6,000 feet in central Guinea and are the source of three large West African rivers: the

Niger, the Gambia and the Senegal. Farther to the northeast, the land slowly descends to flat grassland, which has greater variation in temperatures than the more humid coastal area. These grasslands attain a rich, green color towards the end of March, and vegetation grows rapidly in the rainy season, which lasts until November. In southeast Guinea the terrain becomes somewhat higher, containing dense forests with a pattern of rain quite similar to that of the plains land. As the dry season commences in the latter part of November, the leaves of the trees turn into a panorama of brilliant colors, not because of cold weather, but because of the lack of moisture. This is the equivalent of "winter" in Guinea, and it is not until April that the landscape is again green.

There are more than 16 distinct ethnic groups within the country, the great majority of which profess Islam as religion. Despite the efforts of the former ruling party, traditional values have survived. Female genital cutting (FGC) is still practiced in Guinea, although it was officially banned in 1984. Prior to 1998 more than 90% of Guinean women were circumcised. The circumcisers were generally older, well-respected women in their communities. During the summer season, when schools were not in session, a circumciser would perform as many as 380 operations on young girls aged 8 to 15. In recent years, the government has mounted a campaign to abolish the practice. Didactic plays, and traditional songs and dances of the circumcision ceremony itself, explain the issue and dramatize the consequences of FGC to a largely illiterate audience. The World Bank has provided circumcisers with training in alternative sources of livelihood and access to small business startup funds; several hundred have left the field. As a consequence new circumcisions have been reduced to roughly 20% of young girls nationwide.

The Past: Political and Economic History

For early history, see *"Historical Background"* and *"The Colonial Period: The French."*

In the 1958 constitution of the French Fifth Republic, General Charles De Gaulle inserted a provision giving to France's colonies the choice of full independence or autonomy within the French Community. Under the leadership of the young trade unionist, Ahmed Sékou Touré, Guinea opted to become fully independent—the only French colony to make that choice—and it was proclaimed a nation on October 2, 1958.

Ahmed Sékou Touré became the country's first president, and, deeply imbued with Marxist-Leninist thought, he created

Guinea

a single-party dictatorship. The Democratic Party of Guinea (PDG) was the sole political force in the country. Sékou Touré was its Secretary-General. Membership in the party was said to be as many as 2 million, organized into thousands of local committees. Elections were a simple formality, for the party expressed the will of the people. Opposition was considered tantamount to treason, and critics suffered grievously. The brutality of Touré's repression increased as his paranoia increased, reaching a peak in October 1971 when thousands were killed.

Touré died in a Cleveland hospital in March 26, 1984. Prime Minister Louis Lansana Beavogui, immediately took control of the government, but a group of young military officers, disgusted with what they called a "bloody and ruthless dictatorship," took over the country on April 3, 1984.

A Military Committee for National Redressment (CMRN) was established and immediately began to release some political prisoners from Conakry's notorious Camp Boiro. More than 50,000 people disappeared, or were assassinated at the camp, according to the Association of Child Victims of Camp Boiro.

The new government was initially led by Col. Lansana Conté, president, and Col. Diarra Traoré, prime minister, but rivalry soon led to the latter's demotion in December 1984. Dissatisfied, Traoré and others attempted a coup in July 1985 while President Conté was at a conference out of the country. The president returned to Guinea, restored control with relative ease, and ordered the summary execution of 30 people involved in the attempt, including Traoré. The coup attempt and the crackdown had overtones of ethnic conflict.

After Sékou Touré's death, Guinea embarked on a more liberal economic course. France, which had given Touré the cold shoulder after Guinea opted for independence and socialism, agreed to lend development money, and the International Monetary Fund granted a line of credit to reconstruct the nation's economy. Under the new economic scheme, the government cut the bloated bureaucracy and privatized several government-owned enterprises that were products of Touré's socialism.

Sadly, a change of regimes did not lead to improving Guinea's human rights conditions. Military trials in 1986–7 of about 200 officials of the Touré regime resulted in 60 death sentences, 21 of them *in absentia*. The purpose of the trials was to instill fear, particularly in urban areas, where government popularity had plunged because of desperate economic conditions. Amnesty International described "arbitrary arrests, torture, deaths in detention and death penalty" as "common currency" in Guinea.

Bowing to the winds of change following the collapse of Eastern European communism, the CMRN secured referendum approval of a new constitution in late 1990. It mandated a multiparty system and limited the president to two consecutive terms. The multiparty system was installed in April 1992. Though many parties were formed, the opposition was unable to break the stranglehold of President Conté's Party of Unity and Progress (PUP).

President Conté himself took office in 1994 after multiparty elections in 1993, deemed an "electoral masquerade" and "a comedy" by the opposition. He barely survived a military mutiny in 1996 when army units rebelled, demanding higher pay. They burned down the presidential palace, looted shops and led the president off to an army base. Fifty people were killed in the incident. President Conté was forced to sign a five-point accord with the mutineers before being returned to power. Whatever modicum of liberalism he may have had died with the coup.

Amnesty, apparently, was not part of the agreement. Long-delayed trials began in early 1998 and exposed confessions extracted by torture and ethnic bias against soldiers not of the president's Soussou group. Stiff sentences of 20 years hard labor were handed down on participants. Later, the army was subjected to a major purge, mostly of President Conté's presumed ethnic enemies. (Under Sékou Touré the Peulh ethnic group was singled out for persecution; under Lansana Conté it tended to be the Malinké.)

The Soussou make up only 15% to 20% of the population, but dominated the machinery of repression—the Ministry of the Interior, police and security forces; they also dominated the PUP. Risen to power by coup, terrified by another, President Conté often exhibited a bunker mentality,

viewing other ethnic groups with the greatest of suspicion and withdrawing to the safety of his own.

Presidential elections in December 1998 demonstrated the sharpness of ethnic division in Guinea. Conté faced four opponents, three of whom concluded an electoral alliance aimed at stopping President Conté from winning on the first ballot. Linked together within the Coordination of Democratic Opposition (CODEM) were the Malinké Alpha Condé, the Peulh Mamadou Ba, and Jean-Marie Doré of one of the smaller ethnic groups. If the alliance could force the president into a second ballot, all agreed to support his opponent. However, in dubious balloting, The Ministry of Interior awarded Conté a first-round victory with 56.12%. Ba won a quarter of the vote and Alpha Condé slightly less than 17%.

Two days after his victory, President Conté had his rival Alpha Condé arrested—despite his status as a member of parliament—and charged with state security offenses. Riots broke out in the principal Malinké communities and several people were killed. In Conakry, women bared their breasts—a traditional sign of mourning—in protest and were arrested for assaulting public modesty. Fourteen leading members of the Malinké opposition, including members of parliament, were arrested, charged with threatening public order, found guilty and jailed. Similar treatment of Malinké leadership within the army soon followed, with a major purge of the army in March 1999 in which the armed forces chief of Staff, Col. Oumar Soumah was sacked together with 30 other officers associated with the 1996 army mutiny. Opponents who have fled the country represented a continuing threat. From neighboring Sierra Leone, RUF (Revolutionary United Front) fighters launched deadly border raids on several northern Guinean towns. Guinean officers, some of them former mutineers of 1996, offered the training that lead to the surprising military of the raids.

In this atmosphere of rising tension and violence, the long-delayed trial of Alpha Condé finally concluded in September 2000. The State Security Court convicted Condé of sedition and sentenced him to five years in prison. Kept in virtual isolation, denied audience with his lawyers and family members, Condé was given little opportunity to defend himself.

The deplorable nature of Guinean justice made Condé a focal point of regime criticism nationally and internationally. President Wade of Senegal offered asylum and encouraged his release. Faced with substantial pressure, President Conté ultimately granted Condé a presidential pardon in May 2001.

Former President Lansana Conté

The Guinean coastline

©Photographie Michel Hasson

In November 2001, the government organized a referendum to amend the constitution to permit President Conté a third term. Official results indicated 87% of Guinea's four million registered voters voted, with 98% voting in favor. The opposition, which had boycotted the election, claimed that fewer than 20% of registered voters actually took part.

Long-postponed parliamentary elections were held in June 2002, and this time the opposition was hopelessly divided. The parties of longtime opponents Mamadou Ba and Alpha Condé joined with those of two defectors from the presidential camp—Conté's former prime minister, Sidya Touré, and the former speaker of the National Assembly, El-Hadji Biro Diallo—to form the Front for Democratic Change (FRAD). FRAD opted to boycott the election, while other opponents engaged the *Parti de l'unité et du progrès* (PUP), Guinea's governing party. The result was a massive victory for Conté's PUP, which won 90 of 114 seats.

Constitutional limitations now eliminated, President Conté, reportedly extremely ill from diabetes and heart problems, once again stood for election in December 2003. All major opposition parties boycotted the elections and Conté claimed, once again, 95% of the total vote. Even before the elections signs of restiveness emerged within the army. In early November 2003, speaking on the occasion of the army's 45th anniversary, Conté warned those planning a coup: "If any of you here think you are capable of becoming president," he told his uni-

formed audience, "then form a political party, make yourself candidate and face the electorate." By the end of the month dozens of junior army officers and soldiers had been arrested in a series of swoops on army barracks and private homes throughout the country, including Guinea's current leader Moussa Camara. In November 2005, Conté furthered his purge the nation's strongest institution—the army—by dismissing more than 1,800 officers over the age of 60, many of them ethnic Peulhs. The purge left the state security apparatus firmly in the hands of the president's Soussou confreres.

The government fails in basic public service provision; it does regularly supply electricity and running water. Popular anger increased with spiraling inflation and endemic corruption. (Guinea ranked only one step above Haiti, the most corrupt of 163 countries assessed in Transparency International's 2006 *Corruption Perceptions Index*.) Militant action by students and workers continued relentlessly throughout 2006. In December, when President Conté personally visited the local jail to free two friends and collaborators facing trial for embezzlement of public funds, Guinea's two most powerful labor federations took to the streets to protest corruption and judicial interference.

In early January 2007 Guinea's unions pushed their demands further, successfully calling for "an unlimited general strike" coupled with "acts of civil disobedience" to restore "total republican order." Fourteen of the country's political parties, including the principal opposi-

tion—the RPG and the UFR—supported the call. Shops, offices and markets closed, and public transport shut down on the 10th of January.

Eight days into the strike, protesters upped the ante, demanding the National Assembly declare the presidency vacant because Conté was "physically weakened," "visibly forgetful," and in a "degraded state of health" and therefore unable to carry out the duties of his office. Still, the government repressed the protests violently and arrested the leadership. On January 22; security forces killed 20 protesters and wounded some 150 more. Two days later a weakened president agreed to cede some powers to a consensus prime minister; unions agreed the concessions were sufficient to end the strike, which had resulted in the deaths 59 Guineans over 18 days.

Respite from the tumult of agitation was brief. When Conté appointed Eugène Camara (one of his strongest loyalists) as prime minister in February, unionists relaunched the general strike, and demanded Conté's resignation. The government responded by declaring a state of emergency, with the president noting that "Orders have been given to the heads of the armed forces to take all necessary measures to re-establish public order." In the first day of the emergency, at least 11 more Guineans were killed, including a soldier lynched by protesters. On February 26, 2007, President Conté announced the appointment of Lansana Kouyaté as prime minister. Kouyaté, a former diplomat and UN under-secretary general, was one of five names supplied by unions and opposition parties as acceptable. With Kouyaté's appointment, Guinea's second major general strike in less than two months ended with a casualty total of 137 deaths and another 1,700 wounded. Lansana Conté survived the unrest, barely, by maintaining the loyalty of Guinea's army.

In May 2008 after disagreements on the legitimacy of some members of the cabinet and Kouyaté's decision to allow Libyans to run luxury hotels, President Conté sacked the Prime Minister and appointed Ahmed Tidiane Souaré to the post. Kouyaté's removal was not met with the same amount of civil unrest than his appointment, because there was a general belief that the former Prime Minister had not preformed up to his mandate by not including members of the opposition in the new cabinet or discussions regarding important government issues.

In December 2008, Aboubacar Somparé, the President of the National Assembly, announced on television that Conté had died on December 22 "after a long illness." Following his death, as might have been anticipated, the military organized a

Guinea

new coup d'état, toppling the provisional government and establishing a military junta. The leader of the junta was a junior officer, Capt. Moussa Dadis Camara. Initially, the ousted government rejected Camara and his colleagues, but after seeing the reaction of the populace many former ministers aimed to be incorporated into the new government.

A couple of weeks after the coup the junta appointed a banker, Kabiné Komara, as Prime Minister. He is seen as a political technocrat but politically inexpert; however, the appointment of a civilian as a premier is a hopeful sign, given the newly-instituted junta. Capt. Camara insists that he does not want to hold to power and that he will hold elections in 2010, after the country has been brought back to order. If his promise is fulfilled in 2010, Guinea will see its first free elections.

The Present: Contemporary Issues

Guinea is rich in natural resources—bauxite, iron, gold, and diamonds—and the water to produce the energy needed to process and convert those raw materials. It could produce a rich bounty of agricultural goods, yet Guinea's agriculture languishes, a hangover from the days of socialist collectives that stifled initiative. Ports and roads—the central elements of the infrastructure—are deficient. Schools and health provision are poor, with only 29.5% of the population literate (2004) and a life expectancy of just 53.9 years (2004).

With about one-third of the world's bauxite reserves—the principal ore used in making aluminum—government planners transformed Guinea from an exporter of agricultural products into a major bauxite exporter. But the Marxist economic thinking and state-led development of the Touré years proved an abject failure.

Other state enterprises created bloated bureaucracies whose salaries devoured bauxite profits. With little money invested productively, growth and development languished, while smuggling and the clandestine economy flourished. As the government lost tax revenues, health, social services and infrastructure deteriorated.

Meanwhile, Guinea ultimately had to import food while squandering bauxite resources. The bulk of Guinea's population is engaged in subsistence agriculture, and in many ways Guinea is a vast garden. A broad range of products can be grown year round, watered by abundant rains: rice, tomatoes, onions, coffee, cocoa, bananas, and melons. Yet agricultural productivity remains low, and distribution, is weak because of the dilapidated roads and bridges. Consumers in the capital, Conakry, often pay dearly for mangos while they rot in the countryside. Despite

employing around 67% of the population, farming generates only about 25.6% of GDP (2005).

Guinea's economy is dominated by its mining sector, which generates about 30% of GDP. Bauxite, alumina, gold, and diamonds produce about 90% of export revenues. Bauxite alone accounts for nearly 80% of foreign exchange earnings, and the country produces 14.5 million tons of bauxite annually, making it the world's second largest producer after Australia. In 2004 the government signed with Canada's Global Alumina an agreement to create a refinery in an area previously given in a concession to an American and Canadian joint venture called *Companie des Bauxites de Guinée* (CBG)Under the agreement Global will develop, finance, construct and operate a new refinery. The new plant is designed to refine 8.5 million tons of bauxite annually, producing 2.8 million metric tons of alumina. The total project—refinery, mines, power plant, a dam for water supply, upgrades of railroad lines to transport processed alumina to the coast, and an expansion of facilities at the port of Kamsar—calls for an investment of some two billion dollars, and employment for 10,000 to 12,000 workers over four years.

Capt. Camara has accused foreign mining companies of not providing enough compensation for their operations in Guinea. He has threatened to close companies and is investigating several agreements and contracts signed by the Conté government. Mining companies are worried they are being targeted for political and economic reasons. The result is an uncertain climate for investment.

Guinea's number two bauxite company, the *Société des Bauxites de Kindia* (SBK), was established primarily to supply bauxite to the Nikolaeyev alumina refinery in Ukraine. It produces about 2.5 million tons of bauxite a year. In April 2001, Russian Aluminium (RusAl), announced it would take over management responsibilities of SBK and proposed spending $40 million to upgrade and expand SBK's mining activities. RusAl also received a concession to develop additional deposits at Dian-Dian. The project is estimated to take seven years to build and cost $1.73 billion. When completed, the complex will have the capacity to produce 11 million tons of bauxite and 1.2 million tons of alumina annually. Currently, the government is evaluating the conditions of transfer of SBK to RusAl, it has threatened RusAl with taking over SBK once more.

Gold and diamond mining are both growing. Historically most famously associated with gold (the region gave its name to Britain's first gold coin), Guinea

produced 400,000 oz. in 2001. Commercial diamond production began in 1999 and 90% of Guinea's mined diamonds are gem quality. Overall, Guinea is estimated to have 25 to 30 millions of carats yet to be mined.

Despite these opportunities, the World Bank halted loan disbursements to the country in early 2004, and the government, unable to pay its bills, resorted to the printing press to turn out more Guinean francs. Inflation devastated the few Guineans who had jobs: university-educated government employees had to pay more than half a month's salary for a 50-kilogram bag of rice. On the UN's 2008 *Human Development Index* Guinea ranked 167 out of 179 countries listed.

The Future

The new military junta promises not to stay in power and hold elections in 2010, but there is high degree of unrest and mistrust in the country. Camara seemed modest in his ambitions at the outset, but at the same time claims of attempted coups have been made and the government has been clustering itself around a very tight security belt. There have been several critiques against the government for not speeding the process of handing over the reins of power to a fully civilian government. Additionally, there is the unresolved issue of whether Capt. Camaracan take off his uniform and be a candidate in the 2010 election.

The economy is likely to continue to benefit from global demand for raw materials, including precious metals. At the same time, sustained economic growth will likely require more robust diversification. Despite a wealth of natural resources, Guinea's economic growth has been consistently sluggish. In 2005, for instance, GDP showed a modest rise—3%—but this was barely sufficient to keep up with population growth, estimated at over 2% annually.

As elsewhere in Africa, political stability and economic performance mutually inform one another. For Guinea to leverage its natural resources into growth, development, and poverty reduction, the country must invest its mining proceeds in infrastructure and building human capital. It must exploit its comparative advantage in labor-intensive agriculture. Yet the legacy of bloated state enterprises and state bureaucracy continues to hinder the country, and the political uncertainty makes productive investment all the more challenging. The prospects are for continued underperformance for a country that was an early leader at independence, but which has declined since.

The Republic of Guinea-Bissau

A quiet area near Bissau

Basic Facts

Area: 36,260 sq. km. = 14,000 sq. mi. (the size of Connecticut and Massachusetts; includes the Bijago Archipelago)

Population: 1,700,000 (UN 2007 est.)

Capital City: Bissau

Climate: Very warm and humid with a wet season from May to October and a drier period from November to June.

Neighboring Countries: Senegal (north); Guinea (southeast)

Official Language: Portuguese

Other Principal Languages: Balanta, Crioulo (the lingua franca in much of Guinea-Bissau), Fulfulde, Mandinka, Mandyak, Papel

Ethnic Groups: Balanta 30%, Fula 20%, Manjaca 14%, Mandinga 13%, Papel 7%, European and mulatto less than 1%

Principal Religions: Indigenous beliefs 50%, Muslim 45%, and Christian 5%

Chief Commercial Products: Cashews, fish, peanuts, palm kernels, and sawn lumber

GNI Per Capita: $257 (World Bank 2008 est.)

Currency: CFA franc

Former Colonial Status: Portuguese Colony (1885–1974).

Independence Date: September 10, 1974 (The date on which Portugal recognized independence; unilateral declaration of independence was September 24, 1973.)

Chief of State: Raimundo Pereira, Interim President (Malam Bacai Sanhá, President-elect. Sanhá was elected July 26, 2009 as this book went to press, and will be sworn in, September 8, 2009).

National Flag: Three stripes—red, vertical nearest the staff upon which there is a centered, black star and two horizontal stripes of yellow (top) and green (bottom).

Land and People

Bordering on the waters of the Atlantic, most of Guinea-Bissau is a swampy coastal lowland with about sixty small islands lying close to the shoreline. On its eastern and southern borders it is protected by the Fouta Djallon mountains of Guinea. The level land, coupled with more than adequate rainfall, contributes large quantities of produce with less labor than is found in most areas of Africa.

The Balanta people of the coastal lowlands tend to live by subsistence agriculture; the Mandingas and Fulani of the interior place greater emphasis on the ownership of livestock. Contact between the Portuguese and the Africans was minimal during the colonial period; almost no educational facilities were provided for Africans. A tiny handful of Africans lived as *assimilados*, speaking Portuguese and adopting European customs. Cape Verde Creoles long dominated the business scene in Bissau and always assumed social status than darker-skinned mainlanders. This was the cause of smoldering resentment.

Guinea-Bissau's most famous cultural export is probably "gumbe" music, a style that fuses folk and several West African styles. Manecas Costa, whose song "Fundo di Mato" appears on the Putumayo label's African Odyssey album, is one of the best-known proponents of the style.

99

Guinea-Bissau

The Past: Political and Economic History

For early history, see *"Historical Background"* and *"The Colonial Period: The Portuguese."*

The armed struggle against Portuguese colonial rule in Africa began in 1961 under the leadership of Amilcar Cabral and the *Partido Africano da Independência da Guiné e Cabo Verde* (PAIGC: African Independence Party of Guinea and Cape Verde). The rebellion forced Portugal to maintain some 35,000 troops in the territory—half of whom were African—to oppose some 10,000 rebels who operated as guerrillas: rebels would attack an administrative or military post and then disappear into the dense rain forests. Portuguese forces controlled only the coastal urban enclaves. Rebels dominated the interior and established basic schools and services to govern the area. International support came from Soviet and Chinese arms and Cuban trainers in neighboring Guinea, where the PAIGC established its headquarters.

Cabral was assassinated in early 1973 in Conakry reportedly by agents of the Portuguese dictatorship, and was succeeded as head of PAIGC by his Cape Verdean halfbrother, Luís de Almeida Cabral. By 1974 the liberation struggle reached military stalemate, draining men, material, and morale from colonial Portugal. Disgruntled Portuguese army officers overthrew the Lisbon dictatorship and quickly negotiated independence with the country's colonies.

Guinea-Bissau's independence was recognized on Sept. 10, 1974, and the Portuguese left the country within a month. Luís de Almeida Cabral, became independent Guinea-Bissau's first president. The PAIGC was proclaimed the country's only party, and organized politics along Marxist-Leninist lines. The socialist economy failed to provide growth and development; discontent set in, exacerbated by dominance of party, government and army by a *mestizo* intellectual minority representing a mere 2% of the population. The Cabral regime ruthlessly suppressed political dissent and killed thousands of its enemies. In 1980 a rival war veteran and member of the Papel minority, Joaõ Bernardo Vieira (known as "Nino"), seized power in a military coup.

Within the resistance movement there had always been tension between the Creole leadership from Cape Verde and the less educated indigenous mainlanders, but the anticolonial struggle helped unite the factions. After the Vieira coup, however, the movement split. In Cape Verde, the governing party renamed itself the *Partido Africano da Independência de Cabo Verde,* or PAICV, severing the party links between mainland and islands.

General Vieira was elected to a five-year term as president in 1984 and again in 1989. Marxist rhetoric vanished as Vieira sought to reestablish ties with Portugal and the West. By 1992, however, Guinea-Bissau was still a single-party state, and only grudgingly did the government open political space to multiparty competition. After several delays, the government organized elections in July 1994. President Vieira and his PAIGC triumphed in the country's first multiparty contest, though the losing parties accused the government of election fraud. International observers termed the contest a fair one.

By 1997, the PAIGC was paralyzed by conflicts between two major party factions—one led by Vieira, and another led by a former prime minister, Manuel Saturnino da Costa, the party's national secretary. Vieira's removal of da Costa as prime minister set him at odds with major PAIGC factions. Those factions came to control parliament and ultimately brought Vieira's regime down (for a first time).

Latent hostilities within the political class broke into open conflict with President Vieira's sacking of Army Chief of Staff Ansumané Mané, in June 1998. Mané was charged with insufficient control of cross-border arms trafficking. The army rose in revolt to support its popular leader and soon controlled most of the capital city. President Vieira called upon Senegal and Guinea for assistance against the rebels, but foreign troops were not enough to crush a popular rebellion. The consequences of Vieira's fallout with the Army Chief of Staff foreshadowed Vieira's violent death in 2009.

The army and its civilian supporters controlled the countryside and a good portion of the capital. A bloody impasse resulted, only ending in May 1999 when the army once again rebelled as Senegalese and Guinean troops withdrew. President Vieira fled the burning executive palace to seek sanctuary in exile in Portugal.

Parliament drafted a new constitution and set multiparty elections for both parliament and president. They were held in November and January. The leading contenders for the presidency, Malam Bacai Sanhá and Kumba Ialá, both emerged out of the PAIGC. Sanhá, the parliamentary speaker and leader of one of the anti-Vieira factions in parliament, had been made interim president when Vieira fled to Portugal. His opponent was the product of missionary education, sent to Portugal where he studied philosophy at the University of Lisbon. On his return to Guinea-Bissau, Ialá taught at the national lycée and worked as a PAIGC militant. He ultimately became disaffected and left the party, going into opposition.

The result was a decisive victory for Kumba Ialá, who won 72% of the ballots and thereby ended a quarter-century of PAIGC domination. The new president was a Balanta (the country's largest ethnic group), and never appeared in public without the bright red bonnet of a senior Balanta initiate. For many the bonnet symbolized his ethnic identity and his rejection of imported colonial religions (Islam and Christianity). He made it very clear that he believed the Balanta had provided the bulk of fighting men who brought the country to independence and that they had been treated unjustly by the previous regime. This sense of ethnic identity and grievance led to accusations that he favored Balanta over others in civil and military appointments. Inevitably, ethnic tensions heightened.

In legislative elections that followed, the PAIGC also did poorly, arriving in third place with only 24 seats. Ialá's Party for Social Renewal (PRS) and the Guinea-Bissau Resistance party (RGB) were the principal victors, but neither achieved a parliamentary majority. In February 2000, the PRS and the RGB formed a coalition government, with the PAIGC the principal opposition. The coalition left unresolved the most sensitive issue facing the country: the relationship of army and junta to the new civilian government.

Long-simmering tensions between state and army culminated in November when General Mané canceled army promotions made by the president, declared himself army chief of staff, and once again plunged the country into turmoil. The PAIGC and other opposition parties welcomed Mané's declaration, but the rebellion was short-lived. The general was tracked down and killed in a shootout with loyalist troops. Ialá exacerbated the growing political tensions with erratic leadership. At odds with a fractious parliament with no majority party, Ialá ran through five prime ministers and changed

**Former President
Joaõ Bernando "Nino" Vieira**

ministers so rapidly some embassies gave up on maintaining a current cabinet list. He dismissed judges and appointed their successors without consulting the National Assembly—thus undermining judicial independence—and threatened to fire the bulk of the civil service.

In November 2002 Ialá peremptorily dissolved parliament (which had voted a new constitution curtailing presidential powers) and ruled by decree. He harassed and jailed opponents, and shuttered newspapers and radio stations. The opposition took to the streets, accusing Ialá of trying to turn the country into a dictatorship.

Virtually bankrupt, the government had no money to pay its employees; soldiers were given bags of rice instead of paychecks. Unpaid civil servants began public sector strikes and Ialá's domestic and international support rapidly eroded. In an attempt to end the political paralysis, Ialá succumbed to pressure to hold new parliamentary elections, which were ultimately set for October 2004.

In early September 2004, the prime minister remarked that the country would face troubles if President Ialá's Party for Social Renewal didn't win the October elections. Army leaders, who had already warned the president their restless troops needed to be paid, acted in the early hours of September 14. In less than a half hour, without firing a shot, they deposed Ialá and installed in power a 32-member Military Committee of the Restoration of Constitutional Order and Democracy (CMROCD). Army chief of staff General Verissimo Seabra Correia, announced he would act as interim president until new elections could be held. Under pressure from presidents Obasanjo of Nigeria and Wade of Senegal, he agreed to the appointment of a civilian president. A 17-member ad hoc commission headed by Bissau's highly-respected Roman Catholic Bishop chose a politically unaffiliated Creole businessman close to the church, Henrique Pereira Rosa, as interim president, while the army insisted upon Antonio Arthur Sanhá, general secretary of the PRS as prime minister. The ad hoc commission also recommended creation of a Transitional National Council (TNC)—a broad-based council of civilian and military representatives that would act as a nominated legislature until parliamentary elections could be held.

By the end of September the new government was sworn in, and the TNC, consisting of 56 members headed by General Seabra Correia, was put in place, and elections for a new National Assembly were held in March 2005. Of Guinea-Bissau's 603,000 registered voters, about 75% cast their ballots in what observers described as a free and fair election. The PAIGC won 45 seats in the 102-member legislature, de-

Former President Kumba Ialá campaigns again in the presidential election of June 2005. ©IRIN

spite opposition from eleven other parties and three electoral coalitions. The PRS, still dominated by Kumba Ialá, came in second with 35 seats, followed by the United Social Democratic Party (PUSD) with 17.

In May, parliament appointed the PAIGC's Carlos Gomes Júnior, a businessman who was reportedly the richest man in Guinea-Bissau, as prime minister. His selection represented the political ascendancy of Creoles, culturally more westernized and better educated than other groups within the PAIGC, and his cabinet appointments emphasized the selection of men with advanced technical expertise and skill, something considered a handicap during the days of Kumba Ialá.

Civilian technical expertise proved incapable of controlling military militancy. A contingent of soldiers who had served as UN peacekeepers in Liberia mutinied in October, demanding back wages and benefits and improved living conditions. The mutiny resulted in the brutal murder of head of the armed forces, General Seabra Correia, and several others. To observers, their deaths had ethnic overtones: those killed were Papels; their killers were Balanta. Having decapitated military leadership, the mutineers bullied the government into proposing an amnesty for actions extending back to the military coup of 1980 and imposed their choice of new military commanders. General Tagme Na Wai, a Balanta and a former guerilla fighter who fought in the war of liberation against Portuguese rule, was appointed armed forces chief of staff.

Presidential elections in mid-June 2005 were meant to end the country's transitional period, but seemed to further divide

the country. Three heavyweight contenders entered the electoral ring. The PRS designated Kumba Ialá its candidate, while the PAIGC nominated Malam Bacai Sanhá. Former President Nino Vieira chose to run as an independent, disavowing the PAIGC. An exceptionally high turnout—87% of registered voters—cast their ballots, but gave none of the three candidates a majority. Malam Bacai Sanhá received the most votes, followed by "Nino" Vieira. Forced off the ballot, Kumba Ialá threw his support to Vieira who took 55% of the runoff vote, compared to Sanhá's 45%. The losing PAIGC candidate claimed fraud and said he would not recognize the result.

As prime minister, the PAIGC's Carlos Gomes Júnior adopted the same hard-line position, provoking an institutional confrontation between parliament and the new president. After 14 pro-Vieira dissidents defected from the PAIGC to sit as independents in September, Gomes lost his parliamentary majority and was dismissed by Vieira. Five days later Vieira appointed his close ally and former campaign manager, Aristides Gomes, as the new prime minister. Bitter personal rivalries and ambitions have destabilized thereafter. The PAIGC challenged the dismissal of its prime minister, but lost its appeal to the Supreme Court in January 2006. Rejectionist to the end, the party refused the court's decision and continued an implacable opposition to the government of Aristides Gomes.

Like the PAIGC, Kumba Ialá's Social Renovation Party (PRS) was riven by factional dispute. Ialá himself returned to Bissau in November 2006, and, promising to lead the party to electoral victory in 2008's legislative elections, successfully won the party's presidency. The victory was challenged in court by anti-Ialá forces within the party.

On January 4, 2007 Commander Lamine Sanhá, a former navy chief of staff was shot by unidentified gunmen outside his home in the capital; he died two days later, and his death set off riots in Bissau. Two people were killed in clashes between security forces and demonstrators, and a good deal of property, including a house reportedly belonging to President Vieira, was destroyed. Vieira's onetime ally—and now archenemy—former-Prime Minister Carlos Gomes Júnior, misguidedly sought political advantage from the tragedy. In interviews Gomes recklessly claimed that Vieira was systematically ordering the killing the members of the military junta that overthrew him in 1999.

To preserve public order, it said, the government issued an arrest warrant for Gomes, who promptly fled to the UN Peacebuilding Support Office (UNOGBIS) for protection. The crisis lasted for 17 days,

Guinea-Bissau

during which UNOGBIS successfully secured withdrawal of the warrant. Gomes was allowed to return home with promises from the government that both he and his family would be protected.

The government's arrest warrant seemed to provide a moment of unity for the normally dysfunctional National Assembly. (Gomes had, in theory, immunity from arrest as a member of parliament.) By mid-March 2007 PAIGC loyalists had managed to cobble together enough votes to censure Prime Minister Aristides Gomes and call for a new government of national unity. "There is no valid reason to dissolve the government," said President Vieira's spokesman. In response, the PRS spokesman ominously warned that "if the president refuses to dissolve the government, he will be held responsible for the consequences that spring from this crisis." This time, the president blinked. In April he appointed Martinho N'dafá Cabi of the PAIGC, a former defense minister, to replace Prime Minister Aristides Gomes at the head of a government of national unity (including the PAIGC, the PRS, and the PUSD) for one year. By February 2008, the PAIGC withdrew support from N'dafá Cabi. The government postponed the March 2008 legislative elections, however, and Vieira extended the mandate of the legislature This arrangement lasted until July 2008, when the PAIGC left the government. In August, Vieira dissolved the parliament and appointed Carlos Correia as interim head of government.

Tensions between state and army grew as political instability continued. In November 2008, Nino Vieira narrowly escaped an attack by soldiers at his home, part of an apparent coup attempt. Also that month, the PAIGC prevailed in legislative elections, winning an outright majority, but the focus on the political sphere would soon be redirected to the relationship between state and army.

In early 2009, General Tagme Na Wai accused the presidential guard of attempting to assassinate him by shooting at his car. This signaled continued mistrust between Vieira and the army. On March 1, 2009, Tagme Na Wai was killed in a bomb attack at the military headquarters in Bissau.

The following day, March 2, 2009, elements of the army attacked the presidential residence and killed President Vieira as he attempted to flee. The military leadership assumed control of the country and established a commission to investigate the killings. It named Raimundo Pereira, the speaker of Parliament, as interim head of state. The interim government called for elections within months.

The first round of the presidential elections were held on June 28, 2009, and no candidate received a majority. This necessitates a runoff election for July 26, 2009 between the top two vote-getters, which means a rematch between Malam Bacai Sanhá (of the PAIGC) and Kumba Ialá (of the PRS). Sanhá garnered 40% in the first round and Ialá 29%. Henrique Rosa, who earned 24% of the vote as an independent candidate, will not participate in the runoff and has not yet endorsed either candidate.

The Present: Contemporary Issues

Guinea-Bissau is one of the poorest and least developed countries in the world, ranking 173nd out of 177 on the UN's *Human Development Index* for 2006. Its social statistics make depressing reading: life expectancy is only 46 years. Illiteracy is a whopping 60%, rising to 75% for females. A large majority of the population lives below the poverty line of one dollar a day.

An economy already in crisis was devastated by the civil war earlier this decade that destroyed roads and bridges. The government remains the country's largest employer and 80% of government revenue goes to the public sector payroll. Cash-strapped, however, it has regularly fallen behind in its salary obligations, and striking public workers, demanding months of back pay, are a regular feature of Guinea-Bissau's public life. The country now depends heavily on foreign assistance for its budgetary revenues.

Under normal circumstances Guinea-Bissau's economy is heavily dependent on exports of cashews and timber and the sale of fishing licenses. Agriculture provides jobs for 82% of the population and generates about 70% of GDP and 93% of exports (2004). The main food crop is paddy rice, which is grown on nearly 20% of all cultivated land. With Chinese assistance, Guinea-Bissau has attempted to expand out-of-season rice production through irrigation most notably at Contuboel, about 100 miles east of Bissau. The paddies stretch over 660 acres. Unfortunately, the standing water in the paddies has increased the incidence of malaria in the region.

Cashew nuts account for between 80–90% of Guinea-Bissau's exports, most of which are shipped to India for processing. Guinea-Bissau is currently ranked as the world's fifth-largest producer of cashews. Imaginatively, the government has announced plans to build a series of small thermal plants around the country that would use the dried waste of the cashew fruit to produce electricity.

Coastal fishing resources are extremely rich, but subject to over-exploitation. Guinea-Bissau currently sells the right to fish in its 200-mile Exclusive Economic Zone, and industrial fishing trawlers, rapacious and damaging to the stock of fish, take their catch home for processing. The country signed a fishing agreement with the EU in March 2001 worth around $45 million. Negotiations to renew the agreement collapsed in early 2007, as the government sought a compensation increase of $13 million while EU negotiators wanted a reduction of $8 million.

Guinea-Bissau's unpatrolled islands and inlets have become West Africa's major transit point for drugs moving from South America to Europe. Local police seized millions of dollars of Latin American cocaine in 2005, but the capacity of West African criminal gangs to elude far outpaces the capacity of local authorities to surveil and capture. Experts fear government stability is threatened as drug traffickers extend their influence into ministries, the army and the police.

The Future

Guinea Bissau is one of West Africa's most fragile and unstable countries, as demonstrated by the assassination of President Vieira in 2009. The army, which insists it was not staging a coup when Vieira was killed, in effect maintains a veto over government policy, even as it prepares for upcoming elections. Factional division within and between the country's main political parties mean that even a return to regular civilian rule after runoff elections in July will not guarantee stability. Along with neighboring Guinea-Conakry, which also is subjected to military rule at present, the country's political prospects are among the worst in West Africa.

Guinea-Bissau's economy is also fragile, especially when contrasted with neighboring countries and with the natural potential of the land. The country continues to rely on select cash crops, most notably cashews, for foreign exchange. More recently, however, the emergence of drug transshipment as a major economic activity has raised the question about whether Guinea-Bissau will become a "narco-state." While this promises some quick cash for enterprising outlaws, it also suggests the decay of social order in a society where institutions are already weak.

A child soldier wearing a teddy-bear backpack aims his rifle, once the terror of Liberia   Photo by AFP/George Gobet

Basic Facts

Area: 111,370 sq. km. = 43,000 sq. mi. (Slightly smaller than Pennsylvania)

Population: 3,400,000 (UN 2007 est.)

Capital City: Monrovia

Climate: Warm and humid, with a wet season (April–November) and a drier season (December–May).

Neighboring Countries: Sierra Leone (west); Guinea (north); Côte d'Ivoire (northeast, east)

Official Language: English

Other Principal Languages: Over thirty, including Bassa, Dan, Gola, Grebo, Kisi, Kpelle, Krahn, Loma, Mano, Manya, Vai

Ethnic groups: Kpelle, Bassa, Gio, Kru, Grebo, Mano, Krahn, Gola, Gbandi, Loma, Kissi, Vai, and Bella, Americo-Liberians 2.5% (descendants of immigrants from the U.S. who had been slaves)

Principal Religions: Traditional 70%, Muslim 20%, and Christian 10%

Chief Commercial Products: Diamonds, iron ore, rubber, timber, and coffee.

GDP Per Capita: $500 (CIA World Fact Book 2009 est.)

Currency: Liberian dollar

Former Colonial Status: Liberia has traditionally been an area of United States development.

Independence Date: July 26, 1847

Chief of State: Ellen Johnson-Sirleaf, President (elected November 2005)

National Flag: Eleven horizontal stripes of red and white, with a single white star on a blue rectangle in the upper left-hand corner.

Land and People

Liberia is located on the southern part of the west coast of Africa, facing the warm equatorial waters of the Gulf of Guinea. It is within the tropical region of Africa and as such, has a warm, humid climate. Its forest areas are thickly carpeted with roots, dead leaves and debris, which are quickly made a part of the earth by the rapid rate of decay. From the floor of the jungle, shrubs and small trees entangled with vines rise from 40 to more than 100 feet. Interspersed with this thick growth are the so-called crown trees, which bear foliage only at immense heights, having trunks up to 12 feet in width. The coastal area of Liberia, receiving the most rainfall, is dotted with lagoons, tidal creeks and marshes. During the eight-month rainy season, hardly a day passes without an inch or more of rainfall, including sharp thunderstorms intermingled with a steady, tedious downpour. Six rivers flow from the interior southwest to the Gulf of Guinea; they are not navigable for more than a few miles inland and are bounded by level land suitable for cultivation. Further inland the terrain rises slowly to a level of 1,000 feet in a series of plateaus obscured by the dense undergrowth. Low mountains rise occasionally throughout the country, seldom reaching a height of more than 3,000 feet, with the exception of the Nimba and Wale mountains, which are 4,500 feet high.

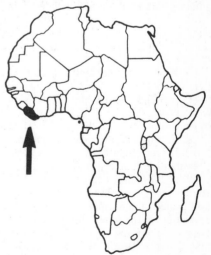

Liberia

Before the revolution of Samuel Doe, there was a basic divergence of cultural traditions in Liberia. The descendants of freed slaves living in the coastal regions were for the most part urban, Christian people. English was the language of choice and they preferred American styles in dress. They particularly valued formal attire, including tuxedos and top hats—notwithstanding the close, tropical climate.

The Past: Political and Economic History

Kru, Gola and other ethnic groups had lived for countless centuries in Liberia before the arrival of Europeans. Portuguese mariners were the first to describe the Liberian coast and identify its commercially valuable products in the 15th century. The area came to be called the Grain Coast because of the grains of the Melegueta pepper, as valuable as gold to a Europe cut off from the Asian spice trade—a consequence of Ottoman conquests.

Easily reached by the ships of slave traders, local chiefs along the Grain Coast willingly sold conquered peoples to them. The market for field labor on the plantations of the southern colonies of America and in the West Indies was immense. Traders often took only the men for heavy work, leaving the women and children to fend for themselves.

The origins of Liberia took vague shape as early as 1691 when the Virginia legislature passed a law requiring that any slave owner granting freedom arrange passage out of the colony for the freedman within half a year. Where they went was not spelled out, but there was a growing feeling that it was dangerous to allow slaves and freed Africans to mingle.

More than a century passed before Virginia lawmakers once again considered the problems caused by slavery. The 1789 slave revolt in Haiti had sent a chill through plantation owners. Thomas Jefferson expressed the view that there should be a plan for colonizing blacks, and the Virginia legislature requested President James Monroe to obtain land outside the United States, preferably in Africa, for this purpose. The idea of a colonization project developed.

The American Colonization Society was founded in 1816. Its object was to transport freeborn blacks and emancipated slaves back to Africa. In Henry Clay's words, such colonization would "draw . . . off" free blacks, lest they incite a slave rebellion.

In 1818 representatives of the American Colonization Society visited the Grain Coast of West Africa. After several failed attempts to secure land for the colonization project, the Society finally signed an agreement with local chiefs granting it possession of Cape Mesurado in 1821. The first American freed slaves landed in 1822.

By 1830 the tiny colonization effort had grown to a thousand people. This new "land of liberty" was named Liberia, from the Latin root for "free." The colony continued to expand, and its trade increased because the settlers preferred American food and goods, which had to be brought in by ship.

The settlers united in 1839 to form the Commonwealth of Liberia under a governor appointed by the American Colonization Society. In 1847 the Free and Independent Republic of Liberia was proclaimed by Governor Joseph Roberts, a freeborn black man who hailed from Virginia. The new nation was recognized within a short time by the European powers, but not by the United States until 1862.

Life for the descendants of the freed slaves was harsh. This was a hostile land— a difficult place in which to survive, since they had little Africa-specific agricultural knowledge, and little interaction with the indigenous tribes. Liberia's economic and political elite of Americo-Liberians remained pretty much in the coastal communities. The government could not exert effective authority for more than 20 miles inland. As a consequence, it was not until the 1930s that there was any real penetration of the interior by the Americo-Liberians.

The state ran up a huge debt, and in 1909 President Theodore Roosevelt appointed a commission to investigate Liberia's finances. The bailout plan involved a loan raised by international bankers, guaranteed by the state's customs revenues. The customs receivership, administered by British, French, German and American officials, brought some stability to Liberia's finances, but the country's financial reorganization was scuttled by World War I. When the Firestone Tire and Rubber Company secured a concession of one million acres to establish a rubber plantation in 1926, the Liberian government arranged a loan through the company to

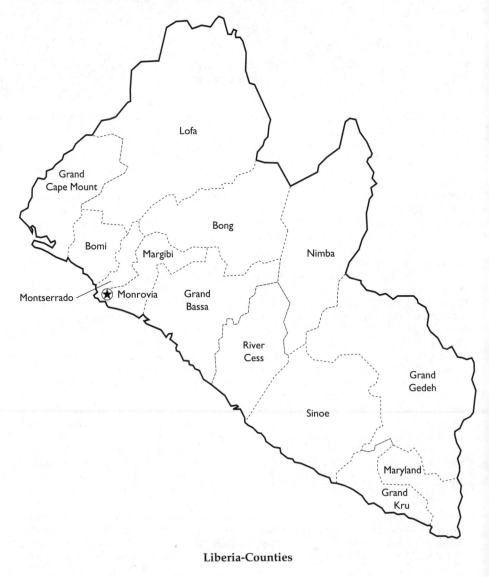

Liberia-Counties

Liberia

consolidate its debts. The loan helped to stabilize the country's finances, but the administration of its customs and internal revenue was placed in the hands of an American advisor. The government was not able to liquidate its external debt until 1952—the first time since it took its first loan in 1871.

Liberia's special relationship with the United States was intensified with the coming of World War II. With most Asian sources of rubber cut off by the Japanese, Liberia was virtually the only source of natural rubber available to the allies. A defense agreement signed in 1942 brought vast infrastructure developments to Liberia. Strategic roads were constructed, along with an international airport and deepwater harbor at Monrovia, Liberia's capital city named after President James Monroe. The American dollar was declared legal tender in 1943.

William V.S. Tubman (b. 1895) was elected to a four-year term of office as president in 1944. Ultimately he would be elected to seven successive terms. Although a descendent of American immigrants, Tubman grew up in poverty, peripheral to the core of the Americo-Liberian elite. A self-made man, he studied the law after work and passed his bar examination at age 23. He joined the True Whig Party, the Americo-Liberian political machine that controlled Liberia economically and politically, and held a variety of public offices. At 35 he was elected to the Liberian Senate, where he became a bit of a gadfly opposing the Americo-Liberian establishment.

To remove the pesky critic, the True Whig leadership booted him "upstairs" with an appointment as an associate justice of the Liberian Supreme Court. From here Tubman unexpectedly announced his candidacy for President in 1943, success-

fully campaigned and won easily. He would dominate Liberian politics for the next 28 years, dying in office in 1971.

Tubman realized the True Whig Party's continued hold on power depended on extending its reach beyond its Americo-Liberian constituency. He was the first president to appoint "country people"—that is, indigenous Africans—to high positions. Tubman made efforts to establish linkages between Americo-Liberians and traditional authorities in the hinterland.

Foreign investment under Tubman led to uneven development, with the hinterlands almost always receiving only crumbs and leftovers. This only exacerbated tensions between the Americo-Liberian elite and indigenous Liberians.

When President Tubman died in 1971 his vice president, William Tolbert, succeeded him. Tolbert was the first Liberian president to speak an interior tribal language, and he attempted to follow through on Tubman's efforts to incorporate indigenous Liberians. For his efforts to expand educational opportunities and bring interior peoples into the elitist government, President Tolbert was criticized by Americo-Liberians for having "let peasants into the kitchen."

By 1979, long-term inequalities, rural poverty, and economic mismanagement had brought the country to a crisis point. When rice supplies dropped because farmers found it more profitable to work as laborers on the large rubber plantations, the government proposed the price be raised from $22 to $26 per hundred pounds to encourage greater production. Since rice is the staple food of the people, the plan touched off populist riots in Monrovia; there was widespread looting. About 50 people were killed and another 500 injured.

Ninety percent of the businesses in the capital were either partially or totally destroyed, with damage said to be about $50 million. President Tolbert imposed a curfew on the city, and Congress granted him emergency powers, but these proved too late to stem the tide of rebellion. Enemies of the establishment surfaced, and on April 12, 1980, a group of noncommissioned officers led by Master Sergeant Samuel K. Doe stormed the Executive Mansion, assassinated President Tolbert (and disemboweled him), seized power and set up a People's Redemption Council (PRC).

Doe and his fellow noncommissioned officers represented a variety of back-country peoples who had traditionally been excluded from power by Americo-Liberians. Members of indigenous ethnic groups could achieve NCO status in the army, but Americo-Liberians, dominated most of the upper ranks. Doe was a member of the Krahn people, while his two principal partners, Thomas Quiwonkpa and Weh Syen, were Gio and Kru respec-

tively. Ten days later the PRC organized the public execution of 13 high officials of the deposed government.

In 1983, Charles Taylor, who was serving as deputy minister of commerce in the Doe government, was charged with corruption. Among other things, he had ordered $1 million worth of bulldozers, which never arrived. The money was stashed in American bank accounts, and when he fled Liberia for his life, Taylor headed straight to the U.S. Arrested and jailed, he managed to escape and made his way back to Africa. In 1988 Taylor, still a fugitive from American justice, was reportedly supported and trained by Moamer al-Qadhafi at a Libyan terrorist base.

Doe set about transforming himself into a civilian ruler, to pacify potential donors who might have any qualms about people who shoot their way into office. A new constitution was approved in July 1984, and in October 1985, general elections were held to implement its provisions. Doe, now head of the National Democratic Party of Liberia (NDPL) was elected president. The NDPL claimed victory by a slender margin—50.9%, but the election was seen as utterly fraudulent by most observers. Under President Doe, Krahns were given most of the authority in the military and the most significant posts in government. Ethnic rivalry intensified as a consequence.

Successive U.S. administrations poured over $400 million into President Doe's eager hands. Liberia became an important listening post and staging base for CIA operations in central and southern Africa, but by 1987 most of the money couldn't be accounted for, and the U.S. was forced to send in the auditors. It was an impossible mission; Doe simply refused to cooperate.

Shortly after the 1985 presidential elections, Thomas Quiwonkpa, the former army commander, returned to Liberia via Sierra Leone and staged a coup against President Doe. It failed. Quiwonkpa was apprehended, killed, and dismembered. According to some reports (and a recurring theme in the Liberian tragedy), part of his body was consumed by his executioners. A nationwide pogrom against Quiwonkpa's Gio people and the closely related Mano ensued. Execution, flogging, castration, dismemberment, and rape became all too common as Liberia sank into bloody civil strife.

Liberia's civil war broke out in earnest in December 1989 when Charles Taylor led an invasion of insurgents from Côte d'Ivoire. They called themselves the National Patriotic Front of Liberia (NPFL) and received support from Libya, Burkina Faso, Côte d'Ivoire and Liberians living abroad. From Libya they received training and money.

M/Sgt. Samuel K. Doe

Liberia

Mano and Gio youth flocked to Taylor's NPFL to avenge the sufferings of their people. General disgust with Doe rallied others, and soon Taylor's forces had overrun most of the country. Control of rich diamond-producing areas supported the rebellion. The violence was grim, the brutality bestial.

By August 1990 anarchy prevailed and other West African states decided to intervene militarily to spare the nation. The military force they created was called ECOMOG, standing for the ECOWAS Monitoring Group. Charles Taylor would long remember the ECOMOG intervention, thinking it cheated him of total victory.

The intervention contributed to a fragmentation of the NPFL and localization of warlord activities. One of Taylor's principal aides, Prince (a relatively common Liberian first name, having nothing to do with royal affiliation) Yormie Johnson, formed his own rebel force, called the Independent National Patriotic Front of Liberia (INPFL), and in September 1990 captured President Doe when he left the besieged Executive Mansion to meet with the head of ECOMOG. Doe was cruelly tortured, mutilated and executed—and the violence preserved on videotape. The video went around the world, shocking the public.

By mid-1995 even Monrovia had become a wasteland in which teenage rebels cruised the streets with loaded automatic weapons and medium artillery. When rebel factions began ambushing ECOWAS forces, Nigeria's military ruler, Sani Abacha, intervened. Abacha summoned faction leaders to Abuja, ordered disarmament, set an election date, and appointed an interim ruler—Ruth Sando Perry, who had been a senator during the Doe period.

Multiparty elections were finally held in July 1997 and Charles Taylor emerged victorious. Seventy-five per cent of the Liberian electorate placed their desire for peace in the hands of the man most responsible for the devastating civil war. His National Patriotic Party (NPP) won an absolute majority in both houses of the legislature.

The extent of the destruction that took place in Liberia's civil war was staggering. More than 5% of the population was killed, and more than half a million Liberians fled the country. Almost 50% of those remaining were displaced from their home villages.

Under Charles Taylor Liberia took on the appearance of a security state. Security agencies, loyal only to president Taylor, were everywhere. The army (AFL), once dominated by President Doe's Krahn, was marginalized and its members reduced to begging for money on street corners or pleading at the Defense Ministry for their

Charles Taylor

unpaid salaries. In effect, the AFL was replaced by militiamen, often little more than bodyguards for President Taylor, kept loyal by regular payments in rice and dollars. State security forces were flagrant abusers of human rights.

Not content with maintaining internal power through repression, President Taylor sought a larger regional role by destabilizing his neighbors. He was the principal patron of the remarkably vicious RUF in Sierra Leone, offering training, weapons, staging grounds for attacks and safe haven for retreat. The effort was paid for by Sierra Leone diamonds mined by the rebels, from which President Taylor exacted a share.

The UN Security Council sought to limit Taylor's destabilizing machinations, and voted unanimously to impose sanctions on all diamond exports in March 2001; it also renewed its arms embargo. These sanctions proved as effective as a colander holding water.

To pay for its arms shipments, the Taylor government diverted money from the Liberian International Ship and Corporate Registry (LISCR). More than 2,000 ships fly the Liberian flag. The U.S.-based LISCR administers the country's maritime registry and normally transmits about $18 million to the Liberian government—a sum that represents about 25% of the country's annual revenues.

The Taylor government justified its illegal arms purchases by the insurgency it faced at home. Rebels seeking the overthrow of his regime came together in a loose coalition calling itself Liberians United for Reconciliation and Democracy (LURD). The only thing that united the rebels was a common antipathy for Charles Taylor. For his part, Taylor (correctly) accused Guinea of aiding and abetting his en-

emies. As the rebel forces became more threatening, President Taylor increased his arms purchases, little impeded by the paper ferocity of UN sanctions.

President Taylor's support of two rebel groups in western Côte d'Ivoire (MPIGO: *Mouvement populaire ivoirien du grand ouest*, and MJP: *Mouvement pour la Justice et la Paix*) also boomeranged. In April 2003 a new rebel group, the Movement for Democracy in Liberia (MODEL)—financed by Côte d'Ivoire's president, Laurent Gbagbo—began to harass Liberian government forces from the southeast.

By June it was clear the Taylor regime was rapidly unraveling. While MODEL forces attacked from the south, fighters from the main rebel group (LURD) swept south in an attempt to capture the capital. Peace talks aimed at ending the two-pronged rebellion were organized in Ghana, but were overshadowed by President Taylor's indictment by the Sierra Leone Special War Crimes Court in March 2003. A ceasefire agreement was reached, but proved short-lived as rebels pressed their advantage, demanding President Taylor's resignation and departure as the price of peace.

Fighting intensified and fatalities mounted. ECOWAS agreed to supply peacekeepers. His options reduced to nil, President Taylor resigned and flew away to exile in Nigeria on August 11; U.S. forces, which had remained at sea, just over the horizon, finally entered Liberia. In Ghana, rebels and representatives of the former Taylor regime signed an agreement formally declaring a ceasefire and end to Liberia's civil war on August 18, 2003. With guns quieted, the UN began what would become one of its largest peacekeeping missions, some 15,000 troops.

As interim president, the Accra conferees chose a politically neutral figure: Gyude Bryant, a little-known businessman without ties to either the former government or the rebels. The interim transitional government's principal task was to organize elections for a new government in October 2005.

The United Nations Mission in Liberia (UNMIL) was assigned the arduous task of disarming combatants and organizing opportunities for reintegration into civil society. By March 2007 some 75,000 out of 100,000 demobilized former combatants have either completed or are currently participating in reintegration programs, including formal education and vocational skills classes. Another 23,000 ex-combatants still await reintegration opportunities funded by the international contributors.

These figures do not cover the thousands of child soldiers enlisted in the various militias that ravaged Liberia during the Taylor years. Some 11,000 former child soldiers were identified as beneficiaries of reintegration programs. Administered by the UN's Children's Fund, the program had provided opportunities to 9,704 former child combatants by early 2007.

The international community has pledged $520 million for Liberia's reconstruction, and the United States has pledged $200 million for reforming the security sector. Thirty-five million dollars were earmarked for recruiting and training a new 4,000-man "state-of-the-art" army. DynCorp International, a privately owned security company headquartered in Virginia, is hired to do the work.

The cause of such costly national reconstruction, Charles Taylor, was given gracious exile in a government guest house by President Obasanjo of Nigeria in 2003. Pressures to extradite Taylor were resisted as Obasanjo indicated he would only re-spond to a specific request from a democratically elected government in Liberia.

The elections that would produce such a government were held in October 2005. Thirty parties entered the fray, fielding over seven hundred candidates for the Senate (30 members) and lower house (64 members); twenty-two candidates vied for the presidency. In the final tally, the leading candidate was George Weah, a popular professional soccer player representing the Congress for Democratic Change (CDC), who won 28.3% of the vote. He was followed by Ellen Johnson-Sirleaf, a Harvard-educated economist who had once worked for the World Bank and the United Nations, the nominee of the United Party (UP) with 19.8%.

Weah and his supporters asserted massive fraud and claimed an astounding 62% of the vote, a position supported by neither international observers nor the NEC (National Elections Commission). With no candidate garnering the required 50%, a runoff election was needed. Results proved Liberian voters valued political and economic experience over soccer fame: Ellen Johnson-Sirleaf obtained 59.4% of the votes, becoming Liberia's—and Africa's—first elected female president.

One of her first challenges was the fate of Charles Taylor. Cossetted in the cushy comfort of a Calabar guest house, the former president remained a vexing problem. With pockets of supporters scattered throughout the country, and a phone to keep in touch, Taylor had already been accused of plotting against his archenemy, Guinea's President Lansana Conté. President Johnson-Sirleaf preferred to get her administration under way without having to deal with the Great Destabilizer. Rebuilding war-battered Liberia, where running water and regular electricity were

Voinjama in the far northeast

©IRIN

Liberia

nonexistent, was her first priority she announced in her inaugural address, demands built up. Taylor's victims, international human rights organizations, and even foreign officials pressured her to request his repatriation. On the eve of her first official state visit to the United States in March 2006, she formally requested his return from Nigeria.

Amply forewarned, Charles Taylor fled Calabar, but was apprehended by Nigerian authorities and immediately whisked off to the prison compound of the International War Crimes Tribunal in Sierra Leone. There, nervous authorities were no more willing to have him present in the country. Appeals were made to have him express delivered to The Hague, where it was expected the Dutch could provide escape-proof detention, allowing Liberia's new government at last to get down to the daunting tasks of reconciliation and rebuilding. Taylor's trial began in June 2007 and is scheduled to last for 18 months. As of June 2009, there has still been no conviction. A US court in Miami, however, has sentenced Taylor's son, a US citizen, for conducting terror under his dad's regime.

In January 2007, marking the one-year anniversary of her election, President Johnson-Sirleaf could present her countrymen a relatively positive balance sheet: peace prevailed; there was progress on economic recovery and growth in public revenues. Electricity and pipe-borne water were being provided to some parts of Monrovia. There was even hesitant movement on the crippling problem of endemic corruption.

Charles Gyude Bryant and several former ministers of the National Transitional Government were implicated in a report on economic crimes prepared by ECOWAS auditors and charged with financial malfeasance. Edwin Snowe, an ally of Charles Taylor who served as Speaker of the House of Representatives until forced to resign in early 2007, was also being investigated—for misappropriation of some one million dollars from the Liberian Petroleum Refinery Company; Snowe had been the company's managing director during the transitional regime.

While the security situation in Liberia remains calm, its neighbors, Guinea and Côte d'Ivoire, are profoundly destabilized; implosion in either could have serious consequences for Liberia. UNMIL has about 11.000 troops remaining in Liberia, down from 15000. As part of its security mission, the force has carries out ground patrols along Liberia's borders.

The Present: Contemporary Issues

Monrovia, the capital city, still suffers the effects of destructive civil conflict. Its power system was knocked out in 1990

President Ellen Johnson-Sirleaf
Photo courtesy White House/Shealah Craighead

and there is little prospect of an early restart for the city's main electricity supply. In its place, the sound of thousands of private generators fills the evening air. The war also stopped the flow of water from the city's taps, and residents are dependent on polluted wells, expensive truck-delivered purified water, or jerry cans of water sold from handcarts on the city streets. Water distribution pipes are so old, rusted, and broken they will have to be ripped up and replaced in order to supply drinking water to residents and the costs tremendous.

Liberia's 14-year civil war destroyed its economy. GDP dropped 25% to 50% of its prewar levels, and per capita income sank to $140—the very bottom of the UN's *Human Development Index* for 2002. Since the Accra Accords of August 2003, however, there has been some economic improvement; after a calamitous decline of 31% in 2003, the country's GDP rose from all-time lows by a modest 2.6% in 2004 and 5.3% in 2005. Results in 2006 seemed even better: in January 2007 President Johnson-Sirleaf announced the country had posted an 8% growth in GDP for the year. In 2008, the country mustered a full 7.5%, before the global financial crisis took a toll on Liberia's growth. Prior to 1990 the economy was primarily based on iron ore, rubber, timber, diamond and gold exports. With substantial investments in rich iron ore deposits, Liberia was once the world's fifth largest exporter, but war completely disrupted the industry. In 2005, Mittal Steel, one of the world's largest steel companies, signed a deal with transitional government authorities to develop some billion tons of iron ore reserves in Nimba County, close to the Guinea border. Over 25 years, the company committed to spending $900

million to develop not only the mines, but also rail and port infrastructure to evacuate the ore. The contract was controversial from the beginning, with charges of a $100,000 bribe having been handed under the table to Transitional Chairman Gyude Bryant. Global Witness, the British NOG committed to exposing the corrupt exploitation of natural resources, also weighed in: Mittal, it noted, was allowed to opt out of human rights and environmental laws in the contract.

When Ellen Johnson-Sirleaf took office, one of her most popular engagements was a promise to review all contracts signed by the interim government. By December 2006, the Mittal contract had been investigated and renegotiated. Mittal's investment was increased to $1 billion and the Liberian government was to retain ownership of rail and port infrastructure.

Before the war the rubber industry generated over $100 million annually in export earnings. Some 50,000 people earned their living through the industry. The Firestone rubber plantation, roughly 188 square miles containing 8 million rubber trees and 670 miles of roads, was the largest rubber plantation in the world. It has yet to recover fully from war damages. Many of its trees were over-tapped by looters and will have to be cut down and replanted. It takes seven years for a rubber tree to mature and be ready for tapping.

In February 2005 the transitional government extended Firestone's land concession for 36 years as part of its efforts to revitalize the economy. For its part, Firestone indicated it planned to invest more that $100 million in the rubber industry. Among other things, the company planned to give 600,000 rubber stumps to small-scale farmers to help them replant their plantations. Elsewhere, Liberia's rubber plantations face a grimmer reality.

In May 2006 a UNMIL report indicated at five out of seven of the country's rubber plantations were plagued by gangs of mostly young men—former fighters from the civil war—who were illegally tapping trees and profitably selling it to local merchants. They could earn anywhere from $60 to $150 a week, a powerful inducement to illegal tapping in a country where 80% of the population is unemployed, and the World Bank estimates that most people live on less than one dollar a day. In August 2006 the government, backed by UN peacekeepers, repossessed the Guthrie plantation in northwestern Liberia from some 500 ex-rebels who had controlled it since the end of the war. The Liberian Rubber Planters Association now oversees the enterprise, with UN soldiers standing guard. Some of the former rebel squatters who once controlled Guthrie are now employed tapping trees.

In 2000, Liberia recorded exports of $61.6 million, led by rubber and timber. The figures represented a 23% increase over 1999 and illustrated the feverish logging activity in Liberia's forests. Like much of Liberia's economic activity, the timber industry was dominated by Charles Taylor. Global Witness examined the importance of timber for President Taylor and concluded it was more financially valuable to him and his security forces than was the diamond trade: revenues from timber constituted 50% of the country's export earnings before the UN Security Council imposed sanctions in July 2003 in an effort to restrict Taylor's regional threat. (Sanctions on the diamond trade had already been voted in 2001.)

After new logging legislation intended to prevent corruption and mismanagement in the timber industry was passed, the UN Security Council lifted its three-year ban on logging in June 2006. Sanctions on the notorious "blood diamonds" were maintained until April 2007.

Liberia's "flag of convenience" ship registry was long a honey pot for the Taylor regime. The registry is second only to Panama's, and includes more than 2,000 vessels. (Thirty-five per cent of the world's tanker fleet and a large number of cruise ships are also covered by the Liberian flag.) Fees brought in about $18 million annually, and helped to pay for President Taylor's arms purchases. Under President Johnson-Sirleaf, the Liberian government plans to renegotiate the management contract for the ship registry to secure more revenues.

As part of its antiterrorism campaign, the U.S. government signed an accord with Liberia in February 2004, which allows the U.S. Navy to board Liberian flagged vessels in international waters to inspect for unconventional weapons. The agreement was the first of its kind and resulted from fears that terrorist networks would use ships to attack the American economy.

The Future

Civil conflict killed more than 200,000 people and displaced at least half the pre-war population of 2.5 million. The legacy of war is appalling. Child soldiers, given drugs to fortify their fighting resolve, pose difficult social problems. Medical experts estimate that up to 70% of all combatants continue to use drugs, and many have become addicts. Unless a place in society (care, support and education) is found for these former combatants, violence could re-ignite at any moment. Moreover, the flow of drugs into Liberia is basically unimpeded. Law enforcement agencies seem unable or unwilling to stop the smuggling of illegal substances. Liberia is believed to have become a transit point for drug trafficking throughout the region.

That said, the future looks brighter for Liberia than it has at most any point in recent memory, in some cases literally: since the arrival of Ellen Johnson-Sirleaf, Monrovia has seen some electricity flow for the first time in 15 years. To say that Liberia is better off today than several years ago may be faint praise, but nonetheless it is clear the country is moving in the right direction. The country is a staunch American ally in the region, and in its post-conflict reconstruction phase it has become a favorite of development agencies. There is a long way for the country to go, but (mercifully) the likelihood of major social strife, civil war, and descent into the anarchy of the 1990s seems less likely with each passing day.

The Republic of Mali

A traditional Dogon granary

Photo by Dan Silver

Currency: CFA franc
Former Colonial Status: Part of French West Africa (1890–1960)
Independence Date: September 22, 1960
Chief of State: Amadou Toumani Touré, President (since May 2002)
National Flag: Three vertical stripes of green, yellow and red.

Land and People

Some 60% of landlocked Mali is covered by the Sahara Desert. This empty land, inhabited by descendants of the Berber tribes who live a nomadic, pastoral life, has virtually no rain. The otherwise flat terrain is broken occasionally by rocky hills. The country becomes more hospitable to the south of fabled Timbuktu, an important emporium on an ancient caravan route of Arab merchants. The Niger River flows north, making a great bend to the south near Timbuktu and then continuing to its eventual meeting with the Atlantic in Nigeria. With its tributary, the Bani River, it forms an inland delta, the rich farming heartland of Mali. The country becomes slightly more temperate south of the Niger, receiving greater rainfall in average years. This section is part of the so-called Guinea Savanna, a brush and low tree belt stretching from the Atlantic coast 3,000 miles inland to the east.

In 2004 UNESCO classified the Tomb of the Askia in Gao a World Heritage site. The 55-foot-high pyramidal structure was built in 1495 by the first of the emperors of Songhai, the Askia Mohamed, and is one of the finest examples of the monumental mud-building traditions of the West African Sahel.

Mali's musical traditions are among the most distinguished in West Africa. Traditionally the preserve of craft specialists called *griots,* music has breached the boundaries of caste in the modern era. One of Mali's greatest musical stars is Salif

Basic Facts

Area: 1,204,350 sq. km. = 545,190 sq. mi. (more than four times the size of Nevada)
Population: 12,300,000 (UN 2007 est.)
Capital City: Bamako
Climate: Hot and dry in the northern two-thirds of the country; increasing rainfall and more temperate in the southern third. Two short rainy seasons have watered the south, but high temperatures cause rapid evaporation.
Neighboring Countries: Senegal (southwest); Mauritania (north, northwest); Algeria (northeast); Niger (east, southeast); Burkina Faso, Côte d'Ivoire, Guinea (south)

Official Language: French
Other Principal Languages: Bambara (or Bamana), spoken by 80% of the population. Bomu, Boso, Dogon, Fulfuldé, Kassonké, Malinké, Senoufo, Songai, Soninké, Tamajeq, Tamashek
Ethnic Groups: Mandé 50% (Bambara, Malinké, Sarakolé), Peul 17%, Voltaic 12%, Songhai 6%, Tuareg and Moor 10%, other 5%
Principal Religions: Muslim 90%, indigenous beliefs 9%, Christian 1%
Chief Commercial Products: Gold, cotton, and livestock
GNI Per Capita: $380 (World Bank 2006 est.)

110

Keita. Born in 1949, Salif was an albino in a culture where albinos are believed cursed. Ostracized by his father, Keita and his mother were only allowed to return to his village when the local Imam predicted great things for him. Limited by sensitive skin and poor eyesight, Keita was unable to become a teacher and when he decided to become a professional musician he was practically disowned. Today he is one of the luminaries of World Music, renowned throughout the world.

Mali's most distinguished scientist is the astrophysicist Cheikh Modibo Diarra. Dr. Diarra worked for NASA and was the mastermind of the Pathfinder mission to Mars. In 1998 he was appointed as the UNESCO Goodwill Ambassador to Africa—the first African and the first scientist to hold that post.

The Past: Political and Economic History

For early history, see *Historical Background* and *The Colonial Period: The French.*

Known as French Soudan, Mali became part of the French Community in 1958, with almost complete internal autonomy. With French permission, Soudan and Senegal joined in 1959 to form the Mali Federation, but this was dissolved in 1960 when Senegal dropped out. After achieving independence in 1960, the government headed by Modibo Keita withdrew from the French Community, which had evolved into a postindependence economic union of former French colonies in association with France.

Keita announced that Mali was a socialist nation and sought assistance from the Soviet Union and later from communist China. Mali received Russian aircraft and weapons, and the Chinese sent technical assistance and some financial aid. Under Keita, Mali's fragile gradually declined over the ensuing years. The ruling Soudanese Union Party, which also controlled the press, labor unions, and state youth organizations, gradually splintered into two groups. One favored a total socialist commitment, while the other saw advantages in economic cooperation with France and its former colonies.

By 1967 the economy was in disarray and the government bankrupt. The pro-French faction prevailed, and in 1967 Mali rejoined the Franc Zone. This had the effect of halving the income of the small segment of Malians who were engaged in the wage economy. Unrest resulted, and Keita dissolved the Political Bureau of the state party because "it ceased to enjoy the confidence of the people."

In this unstable situation a group of young army officers seized control, establishing a Military Committee for National Liberation (CMLN). The military imprisoned Keita in distant, desolate Kidal deep in the Sahara. Lt. Moussa Traoré became Mali's president and dominant political figure. The new military leaders attempted economic reform, but were debilitated by internal political struggles and a disastrous drought. Ultimately corrupt and repressive, the Traoré regime sustained itself in power for years. A new constitution created a single-party state in 1974, and in 1976 Traoré created a new party, the Democratic Union of the Malian People (UDPM). He led the party in sham elections in 1979, winning 99% of the vote. Challenges to his power, by students or from within the military, were brutally suppressed.

Desperate to improve the economy, the government approved plans for economic liberalization and signed an agreement with the IMF. By 1990, the austerity demanded of such plans had begun to pinch all but the ruling clique. The Soviet Union's collapse encouraged demands for multiparty democracy, something Traoré was unwilling to concede. In early 1991, student-led antigovernment demonstrations broke out. In four days of bloody street rioting an estimated 200 people were killed by government forces. On March 26 a military *coup d'état* overthrew the president, suspended the constitution, and set in motion the process by which Mali would return to civilian rule.

A new National Reconciliation Council was headed by Lt. Col. Amadou Toumani Touré, who promised democratic reforms, lived simply, and kept his word. He governed for 14 months, during which he established the processes for multiparty democracy and then stepped down. From January to April 1992 Malians enthusiastically participated in presidential, legislative, and local elections. Twenty-one political parties participated, with eleven of them winning seats in parliament. Alpha Oumar Konaré, an archeologist, defeated nine other candidates for the presidency, and his Association for Democracy in Mali (ADEMA) secured a parliamentary majority.

During his first five-year term Konaré won plaudits for devolution of more governing powers to local authorities. Political expression flourished: some 40 independent newspapers and journals, in French, Arabic, and local languages appeared, often criticizing the government. Fifteen radio stations, a more important source of news in a largely illiterate population, blossomed in Bamako alone; 40 others broadcast elsewhere in the country. For Western states, Mali became a showcase for democracy.

In 1995 Konaré put a temporary end to the long-term Tuareg rebellion that had ravaged the north. There, Tuareg nomads, pastoralists whose flocks had been decimated, whose water holes had dried up, and whose people were on the brink of starvation, had been driven to revolt by a callous and corrupt regime. They took up arms against the military dictatorship of Moussa Traoré in 1990, calling themselves the *Movement populaire de l'Azawad* (MPA), after thousands of tons of food destined for starving nomads had been stolen by the army. When the army proved ineffective in limiting Tuareg raids on farmers along the Niger River, the farmers themselves organized a militia, which they called *Ghanda Koy*—Masters of the Land— to strike back at nomads. Both groups rallied to Konaré's peace and reconciliation program in 1995. The program disarmed the armies, paid some 9,000 fighters $210, and made efforts to integrate some of the former combatants into the army, a task rendered more difficult by the preference of Tuaregs for Arabic language over French. In March 1996, President Konaré symbolically set fire to several thousand weapons to seal the peace.

A committed democrat and by all accounts a most humane leader, Konaré commuted death sentences meted out to Moussa Traoré and several of his cronies to life imprisonment and closed the terrifying prison at Kidal. President Konaré had no trouble in his search for a second five-year term in 1997. Unfortunately, the 1997 presidential and legislative elections proved a logistical disaster. Poorly administered and producing such dubious results that a court threw them out, they had to be repeated. The opposition—and there were now some 62 parties in Mali, many

President Amadou Toumani Touré

Mali

organized around a single personality—screamed foul and took to the streets. Security forces used tear gas to control mobs. The second round of elections was boycotted by the opposition, and thousands stayed away from the polls, fearful for their personal safety. Konaré and ADEMA won handily, but their mandate was weakened by events.

This electoral fiasco produced longstanding political tension in Mali. Municipal elections had to be postponed repeatedly. As a way out of this impasse, President Konaré proposed a National Political Forum to examine Mali's electoral legislation. Regional forums met in December 1998 and discussed constitutional revisions, the organization of future elections, party financing, and the power of the Independent National Electoral Commission (CENI).

At the end of these regional consultations, official delegates met in Bamako in January 1999 to make final recommendations. The final document included, at the suggestion of Konaré himself, a constitutional provision that explicitly limits a president to no more than two terms. The state agreed to find the necessary funding for any political party playing a positive civic role and agreed that journalists should no longer be imprisoned for offending press laws.

For the presidential elections of April 2002, 24 candidates presented themselves to the electorate, but only 38% of eligible voters took the elections seriously enough to participate. The election was held against a backdrop of worsening economic conditions. The cotton sector was in crisis, and export income had fallen nearly 50%. Family incomes shrank while gas and electricity prices soared. Women took to the streets with their pots and pans to complain about the high cost of living.

ADEMA splintered, divided by disputes between reformist youth and political veterans. The younger elements rejected the presidential ambitions of former Prime Minister Ibrahim Boubacar Keïta and drove him from the party. To pursue

The tomb of the Askia in Gao. Named a UNESCO World Heritage site in 2004.

his own presidential candidacy, IBK, as he is known, formed a new party, the Rally for Mali (*Rassemblement Pour Mali*: RPM), which became the country's 74th party.

ADEMA formally endorsed the candidacy of the brilliant and very rich Soumaila Cissé, a former finance minister. This prompted the incumbent ADEMA prime minister, Mandé Sidibé, resigned to run as an independent. Having spawned three candidacies from its ranks, ADEMA stood little chance of winning the election.

The favorite was General Amadou Toumani Touré (ATT to his friends), who ran without party affiliation, but was backed by a coalition of some 28 parties. The man who overthrew the dictatorship of Moussa Traoré had developed an enormous popular following since he returned power to civilian authorities in 1992. With 24 candidates, a runoff was inevitable. General Touré led the vote with 28.7%, followed by the ADEMA candidate Soumaila Cissé with nearly 21.3%—enough to make the runoff. IBK, who had received the backing of Bamako's imams during their pre-electoral Friday sermons, arrived in third place, a mere 4,000 votes behind Cissé, with 21.03%. He protested and claimed fraud, but ultimately accepted the Constitutional Court's results, urging his followers to vote for General Touré.

In the runoff General Touré won a crushing victory, defeating his rival 65% to 35%. Having run without his own party, and having declared he would not create one, ATT promised to work closely with whatever parliamentary majority emerged from Mali's 2002 legislative elections.

The elections gave RPM and ADEMA dominant positions in the National Assembly, but neither achieved a clear majority. Ibrahim Boubakar Keita was, however, overwhelmingly chosen as the parliamentary speaker.

To form a new government, President Touré chose a Tuareg, Ahmed Mohamed Ag Hamani, as prime minister. A technician (a trained statistician) and former ambassador, Ag Hamani, like President Touré, had no party affiliation and formed a cabinet of national unity, including representatives from a broad range of Malian parties. With two nonparty leaders at the helm, Mali entered a period of politics by consensus rather than confrontation.

In early 2004 Mali's desolate northern region became one of the latest international terrorist sites. Algerian Islamists, known in French as the *Groupe armé salafiste pour la prédication and le combat* (GSPC: Salafist Group for Preaching and Combat) had kidnapped 32 European tourists near the Libyan-Algerian border the year before and transported some of them to Northern Mali. To free its citizens, Germany paid a ransom of nearly $6 million,

instantly making the GSPC leader, Ammari Saifi, the most powerful Islamic militant in the region.

Saifi, once an Algeria Special Forces paratrooper, used his hostage booty to buy arms and recruits in Northern Mali. His movements were monitored by American and Algerian intelligence, and when notified of his whereabouts, Malian troops forced him into Niger, from whence he was chased into Chad, where 43 of his men were killed or captured.

American Special Forces have trained some 300 Malian troops as part of the State Department-sponsored Pan-Sahel Initiative (PSI). The program was designed to furnish training and equipment (especially communications materials) to permit rapid response to terrorist threats in the four Sahel countries of Mauritania, Mali, Niger and Chad. The Pan-Sahel Initiative has since been upgraded in name, scope, and budget. Now called the Trans-Saharan Counterterrorism Initiative, it additionally includes Algeria, Morocco, Senegal and Nigeria, among other countries. Its main target is al-Qaeda in the Islamic Maghreb (AQIM), the descendant of the Algerian Islamist group GSPC.

Eastern Mali has long been a lawless area plagued by banditry, smuggling and kidnapping. Despite the 1992 peace agreement with the government, Tuareg factions remained restive and resentful, feelings exacerbated by PSI actives in the region. In May 2006 Tuareg dissidents attacked two military sites in Kidal and another in Menaka, near the Niger border, and held them long enough to abscond with a large supply of weapons.

The leader of the raid was Lieutenant-Colonel Hassan Fagaga, one of the highest ranking Tuaregs to have been integrated into the national army following the Tuareg rebellion of the 1990s. Col. Fagaga had deserted the army in February, demanding better work and living conditions for former rebels who had been integrated into the army and the creation of a new political district in the Kidal region for better representation of Tuareg interests.

A ceasefire was brokered by Algeria in July 2006, and details of a peace settlement were hammered out over the following months. The rebels gave up demands for regional autonomy, and the government agreed to speed up development of the three northern provinces. Details were finalized in February 2007: deserters were permitted to return to the army, and rebels agreed to return stolen arms and munitions. The settlement was festively celebrated in early March. A convoy of some 200 cars brought about 2,000 former rebels to Kidal; thousands lined the streets in welcome and watched them hand back the stolen weapons.

Mali

Peace in the north was an additional triumph in President Touré's reelection campaign. Eight candidates opposed the incumbent, including the redoubtable Ibrahim Boubacar Keita, who represented the RPM. Low turnout—less than 40% participated—suggested voters might be skeptical of politics and politicians, but change, apparently, was not what they wanted. Forty-four parties supported the outgoing president, and he garnered nearly 70% of the electorate's support in 2007, shocking his opponents with a first ballot victory.

Nonetheless, the unrest in the north and east continued into 2008 and 2009. Tuareg rebels attacked a military base in December of 2008, taking hostages and killing about two dozen people. By February 2009, Malian forces had retaliated by assaulting several Tuareg rebel bases and inducing the surrender of several hundred militants.

The Present: Contemporary Issues

As with other Sahel states, Mali's economy is agriculture-based and subject to meteorological caprice. Cotton is the principal cash crop, and it supports nearly a quarter of the population directly or indirectly. It has traditionally accounted for half of Malian export earnings, but the industry is withering.

The cotton sector is plagued by exogenous difficulties. Both China and the United States, the world's biggest cotton producers and exporters, privilege their cotton farmers. The 2002 U.S. Farm Act protects American farmers from depressed international market prices, allowing otherwise uneconomic farms to dump cotton onto world markets at prices that undercut those of Malian farmers.

Oxfam, the British NGO, says that every acre of American cotton receives subsidies of $230, while China provides annual subsidies to its cotton farmers estimated to amount to some $1.2 billion. Mali has joined Burkina Faso, Benin, and Chad in highlighting the devastating effects of rich-country subsidies on African cotton farmers in various world trade meetings.

A variety of domestic factors also make the Malian cotton farmer less productive. Poor quality seeds, expensive fertilizers and insecticides, too small growing plots, land of poor fertility without irrigation, poorly kept roads, and large administrative costs of the state marketing body all reduce production and returns. Where the Malian farmer produces a ton of cotton per hectare, farmers in China and Brazil produce three tons on the same acreage.

Conflict in Côte d'Ivoire shut down Ivoirian ports and increased transportation costs for cotton shippers. Goods had to be reoriented to Ghanaian ports or Lomé, Togo, seriously burdening road infrastructure. In late 2004 the governments of Burkina Faso, Mali and Ghana instituted an axle-load control system for trucks using the important Bamako-Ouagadougou-Accra route. Between 70% and 90% of all vehicles using the route were found to surpass weight limits, accelerating road deterioration and raising maintenance costs to unacceptable levels.

Gold replaced cotton as Mali's biggest income producer in 2000. In 2004 Mali produced some 1.34 million ounces of gold, making it the fourth-largest producer in Africa—after South Africa, Ghana and Tanzania. South African interests jointly own the country's two major mining operations, Morila and Loulo, with the government.

In early 2003 the IMF announced that Mali was to benefit from debt relief amounting to approximately $675 million under the enhanced Heavily Indebted Poor Countries (HIPC) initiative. Additional relief came in 2005, when the leaders of the G-8, the world's richest countries, agreed to cancel the multilateral debt (owed to agencies like the World Bank and IMF) of 19 of the world's poorest countries, Mali included. Mali's accumulated debt, almost all of it owed to multilateral lenders, amounted to $3.129 billion. Debt repayment and service charges can now, in principle, be used to fund anti-poverty programs.

Excision—the removal of the female clitoris—is currently practiced by all of Mali's ethnic groups, with the exception of some Tamashek, Songhai and Dogon groups. A national Demographic and Health Survey conducted in 1996 indicated that 94% of all Malian women had been excised. The same survey concluded that overall, 75% of Malian women were in favor of continuing the practice. Urban women were less supportive than rural, and the more educated the women, the less likely they were to support the practice. In the desert north and east, where Islam has been less influenced by traditional animist belief, FGM is much less common. A 2002 health survey found that only 17% of women in Timbuktu, Gao and Kidal had been subjected to genital cutting.

The Future

Tackling Mali's abysmal poverty is the principal task for Ahmadou Toumani Touré; he has claimed he will create over 50,000 jobs for young people. Mali remains one of the poorest countries in the world, ranked 175 of 177 on the UN's *Human Development Index* for 2006. Economic opportunities are scarce, though recent debt relief should allow the government some breathing space to channel investment into social services and stimulate productive investment.

Mali's other enduring difficulty is the on-again, off-again battle with Tuareg rebels. While the central government seems to have made some progress in recent months, it must be noted that the rebellions were thought to be over as early as 1995. Peace and reconciliation has been Touré's strength, but it is premature to say the internal conflict has subsided. Mali is also increasingly attentive to the southerly movement of the AQIM (al-Qaeda in the Islamic Maghreb) terrorist organization, which thrives in the weakly-governed regions of the Sahara and north-central Africa.

The crushing poverty of this Saharan nation makes its democracy all the more impressive. Mali has spent nearly 20 years in relative freedom after decades of misrule. Civil liberties and personal freedoms are largely respected, and political rights are relatively secure. The variant of Islam found in most of Mali (apart from the small number of extremists) is also quite open and tolerant of western norms of speech, as evidenced by the subdued reaction inside Mali to the uproar over caricatures of the Prophet Mohammed. Given the challenges the country has already faced, there is little reason to suspect any dramatic reversal of the country's relatively strong record of democracy, though corruption, mismanagement, and internal conflict in the hinterland will not be wholly eliminated.

The port of Mopti. Bars of Saharan salt await shipment.

Photo by Abby Silver

113

The Islamic Republic of Mauritania

Crane operator at a mining site near Nouadhibou

casionally intrude and brief but heavy rainfall collects into streams and rivers within a few minutes. Two hours after the end of the storm, there is no sign of moisture. In some places, the water descends to great depths, supporting a few green oases, which stand out in the otherwise empty landscape. Southern regions are subject to sporadic torrential rain showers, which can wreak much damage.

A narrow band of semiarid land stretches from west to east in the southern region of the country. Its rainfall of about four inches per year supports low, sparse scrub vegetation. The most heavily populated area of the country lies along the Senegal River. The rich soil is periodically flooded during normal years by the river, which, when added to the rainfall of 10 to 25 inches, permits cultivation and cattle raising.

At independence in 1960, some 83% of the population was nomadic. Today that figure is about 5%, the consequence of devastating droughts in the 1970s and their periodic reoccurrence. Animal herds were decimated, and traditional family life and the rural economy were virtually destroyed. The result was a massive migration to the principal urban centers. Nouakchott and the port Nouadhibou were among the fastest-growing cities in the world. In the space of 40 years the capital's population grew from 40,000 to today's 1.4 million. Eighty percent of the country's urban population lives in the two cities of Nouadhibou and Nouakchott.

Surrounding both Nouakchott and Nouadhibou today are encampments of the impoverished, mud-built shanty towns from which the poor can view the privileged position of the ruling class. Forty percent of the country's entire population lives in and around the capital. Most live from odd jobs, and their homes have neither electricity nor running water.

Basic Facts

Area: 1,085,210 sq. km. = 419,000 sq. mi. (one and one-half times the size of Texas)

Population: 3,100,000 (UN 2007 est.)

Capital City: Nouakchott

Climate: Hot and arid; drought conditions have existed for the last decade.

Neighboring Countries: Senegal (southwest); Western Sahara (northwest); Algeria (northeast); Mali (east and southeast).

Official Languages: Hasaniya Arabic, Wolof

Other Principal Languages: Fulfulde, Soninke, Zenaga; French

Ethnic Groups: mixed Moor/black 40%, Moor 30%, black 30%

Principal Religion: Islam

Chief Commercial Products: Fish and fish products, iron ore, and gold

GNI Per Capita: $560 (World Bank 2006 est.)

Currency: 1 ouguiya (UM) = 5 khoums

Former Colonial Status: French Colony (1920–1960)

Independence Date: November 28, 1960

Chief of State: Mohamed Ould Abdel Aziz, President (elected July 18, 2009 and sworn-in August 5, 2009 as this book went to press).

National Flag: Green with a yellow five-pointed star above a yellow, horizontal crescent; the closed side of the crescent is down; the crescent, star, and color green are traditional symbols of Islam.

Land and People

Mauritania lies on the upper west coast of Africa, almost wholly within the immense Sahara Desert. The northern two-thirds of the country is totally flat and stony, with virtually no rain. Its *ergs* (huge areas of dunes) are constantly transformed by hot, dry winds, which make the implementation of road infrastructure virtually impossible. Thunderstorms oc-

114

Mauritania

Desert oases, once thriving commercial and cultural centers, are now prey to an advancing Sahara. Chinguetti, the legendary seventh holiest city in Islam, once boasted a population of 3,000; 30,000 camels annually drank its waters. Today it is almost a ghost town. UNESCO has named it part of the world's patrimony in recognition of its spiritual and cultural importance. In Chinguetti eight families guard its greatest treasures: thousands of manuscripts—verses of the *Koran*, treatises on religion, astronomy and traditional medicine, works of poetry. The oldest go back to the 12th century. None have been translated and almost all are in advanced stages of deterioration.

Mauritania's other great treasure is the *Parc National du Banc d'Arguin* (PNBA), which UNESCO made a World Heritage site in 1989. Located on the Atlantic coast, the park provides a unique example of the transition zone between the Sahara Desert and the Atlantic Ocean. It covers an area as large as Lebanon, equally distributed between land and sea and was founded in 1976 mainly for its bird life. More than two million wading birds rest there on their annual migrations, and during breeding season 45,000 pairs of aquatic birds—pelicans, flamingos, spoonbills, herons, cormorants, and others—nest in the park.

The Past: Political and Economic History

For early history, see *Historical Background* and *The Colonial Period: The French*.

Mauritania achieved full independence in 1960; the government adopted the presidential system, with a president elected for a five-year term by all citizens. The first presidential elections were held in 1961 and resulted in victory for the Republic's founder, Moktar Ould Daddah. President Ould Daddah was reelected in 1966, 1971 and 1976. The unicameral National Assembly of 40 members was also elected by universal suffrage. The People's Party was dominant after 1959, holding all seats in the National Assembly.

Mauritania's relations with Morocco and Algeria were quite close. In the heady days of African liberation from colonial rule, they each had an interest in Spain's holdings in Spanish Sahara—rich with a billion tons of phosphate. Wearied of guerrilla activity in its African territories, Spain decided to surrender Spanish Sahara.

Mauritania joined with Morocco to exclude Algeria from the desert wasteland. The end result was a de facto partition of the former Spanish colony, with Mauritania receiving a portion in the south and Morocco receiving a larger northern area. Algeria supported the Polisario Front, Spanish Sahara's independence movement, and Mauritania soon found itself at war.

France pledged to help Mauritania against attacking Polisario guerrillas, and after the guerrillas established the Saharan Arab Democratic Republic in Spanish Sahara and made forays into Mauritania, the French launched air strikes from bases near Dakar, Senegal.

Badly drained by a staggering military budget, which had increased army strength in two years from 1,500 to 15,000 men, the economy sagged noticeably. Things worsened when the Polisario attacked the railroad moving iron ore, the country's principal moneymaker, to the port of Nouadhibou. In these circumstances the army intervened to topple the Ould Daddah government in mid-1978.

In 1979 Mauritania officially ended its role in the desert war over the Western Sahara. Drained by its costly struggle with Polisario guerrillas, it renounced all claims to the territory. In 1983 it officially recognized the Saharan Arab Democratic Republic.

Mauritanian politics have traditionally been dominated by the cultural and ethnic divide that divides the population. An artificial creation of the colonizer, Mauritania joins Moors, northern nomadic peoples of Arab-Berber culture, with southern, sedentary black Africans, agriculturalists concentrated in the Senegal River valley. The Moor segment of the population itself is divided into two groupings: so-called "White Moors," descended from the region's Arab-Berber conquerors, and "Black Moors," black Africans of Arab-Berber culture, traditional servants and slaves of the conquerors. Moors speak Arabic, while the Afro-Mauritanians of the south tend to speak French in addition to their indigenous languages. Virtually all are Muslim, but Moors tend to take a single wife, while Afro-Mauritanians tend to be polygamous. This has resulted in a more rapid population increase among Afro-Mauritanians, now about one-third the population. These racial identities are the historical basis of social tensions.

At independence, White Moors held political power, while Afro-Mauritanians were more numerous within the civil administration. Founding President Moktar Ould Daddah was able to keep the tensions in check, but with the beginning of the Saharan conflict in 1978 power became increasingly concentrated, especially after Ould Daddah's overthrow in 1978, in the hands of White Moors. "Arabization" policies were pursued in schools and workplaces, to the protests of Afro-Mauritanians. Several military regimes followed until Colonel Maouya Ould Sidi Ahmed Taya took power in 1984.

Afro-Mauritanians became fearful when Moors began to invest in southern agricultural lands as early as 1983. Municipal elections of 1986 seemed to increase the power of Moors even further, just as the economic consequences of economic liberalization began to impact Afro-Mauritanians most heavily. There was a failed *coup d'état* in 1987, the core of which was the clandestine Front for the Liberation of Africans in Mauritania (FLAM). Racial incidents in the Senegal River valley in 1989 resulted in massacres of African farmers and retaliatory racial onslaughts against Moors in Senegal. Approximately 95,000 Afro-Mauritanians were expelled or fled from 1989 to 1991. Mali and Senegal received the bulk of those fleeing.

The discovery of another plot against the regime in 1991, the details of which remain obscure to this day, resulted in hundreds of Afro-Mauritanian soldiers being arrested, tortured, maimed, and executed. Parliament passed an amnesty bill in 1993 to preclude any legal pursuit of those involved, but has not acknowledged responsibility or wrongdoing. It has, however, given pensions to the widows of some of those killed.

The appearance of what seemed to be racial purges, coupled with the regime's support of Iraq during the Gulf War, led to international isolation and diminished foreign aid. Col. Taya effected a turnabout by beginning the process of controlled democratization in 1991. After 14 years as head of the military junta, he announced a referendum on a new constitution and general elections. The new constitution was approved and legislation legalizing political parties passed shortly thereafter.

Taya's opponents coalesced to form the *Union des Forces Démocratiques* (UFD) and

Ex-President Sidi Ould Sheikh Abdellahi

Mauritania

the outgoing regime responded by creating the *Parti Républicain et Démocratique et Social* (PRDS), which brought together Col. Taya's supporters—prominently local notables, tribal chiefs and businessmen. In the presidential elections of 1992, the UFD nominated Ahmed Ould Daddah, half brother of Mauritania's first president, to run against Col. Taya. Taya won with 63% of the votes, but Ould Daddah's 33% was more than respectable, given the "irregularities" of the election.

Refusing to accept the results of a fraudulent election, the UFD boycotted parliamentary elections later that year, allowing the PRDS to dominate the legislature. Losses led to defections from the UFD as the pragmatic and opportunistic migrated to the PRDS. As a result of this influx of new supporters, the PRDS became the sole vehicle of meaningful political expression in Mauritania; internal clashes between factions became more important than contests between rival parties in Mauritanian politics.

President Taya showed himself to be a keen political pragmatist by reversing alliances. In October 1995 the Iraqi ambassador was thrown out and Iraqi citizens loyal to the Arab nationalist *Ba'athist* movement of Saddam Hussein were accused of creating secret missions throughout Mauritania. In November, Taya's government recognized the state of Israel, definitively reorienting Mauritania's political direction.

The opposition, given a new issue with the recognition of Israel, regrouped in 1995. One part of it formed Action for Change (AC). The party was led by Messaoud Ould Boulkheir, a "Harratin," or Black Moor descended from slaves, and presented itself as the champion of the oppressed, articulating both the grievances of Black Moors and Afro-Mauritanians. Multiparty legislative elections in 1996 reinforced PRDS power; the party won 70 out of 79 seats in parliament. The AC won only a single seat, the remaining going to independents. Massive fraud on both sides was reported, with the opposition charging the government with running voters from polling station to polling station in minibuses. Still, only 30% of those registered to do so actually voted.

In advance of the presidential elections of December 1997, UFD and AC joined to create a United Opposition Front, but were no more successful than before. President Taya was reelected to a second six-year term winning more than 90% of the vote against four opposition candidates. His main challenger, economist Ch'Bih Ould Cheikh Malaine, did particularly well in Mauritania's two major urban centers. After his victory, President Taya announced that he would "wage war without mercy"

Colonel Ely Ould Mohamed Vall, Chairman of the Military Council for Justice and Democracy

on poverty, but no mention was made of the growing concentration of wealth in the hands of an emerging, but extremely narrow, middle class. During the campaign Malainine revealed that 39 Mauritanians held 70% of the country's wealth, and 27 of them were members of a single tribe, President Taya's own Smassids.

Throughout the period the clandestine Afro-Mauritanian political movement calling itself FLAM continued to call for the autonomy of southern Mauritania and a resolution of the issue of some 70,000 deported black Mauritanians who have been living in Senegal and Mali since 1989. FLAM accused the regime of "Mauritanian apartheid," characterized by exclusion of Afro-Mauritanians from public affairs, generalization of Arabizing policies, and affirmation of the exclusively Arab character of the country.

Igniting a firestorm of controversy within and outside the country, Mauritania agreed to establish full diplomatic relations with Israel in October 1999. With Jordan and Egypt, Mauritania became only the third Arab state to establish diplomatic relations with Israel. The opposition organized regular and ongoing protest demonstrations.

As always, the government's response was repression. Ahmed Ould Daddah's rechristened *Union des forces démocratiques-Ere Nouvelle* (UFD-EN) was banned in October 2000 because, said the government, it was waging a "smear campaign against the country" and calling for violence.

In December 2000, President Ould Taya announced a series of political reforms to give his image a more liberal sheen. Proportional representation, enhancing the opposition's chances to gain representation in parliament, was introduced for multimember districts in the country's three largest cities—Nouakchott, Nouadhibou, and Selibaby. To strengthen politi-

cal parties, the state agreed to fund them on the basis of their showing in forthcoming municipal elections and give them access to state-controlled media. Independent candidacies would be prohibited.

The first elections to take advantage of the new provisions were the parliamentary and municipal polls of October 2001. Eighty-one National Assembly seats were up for grabs. Only President Taya's PRDS presented candidates in each of the 45 electoral districts. The Rally of Democratic Forces (RFD: *Rassemblement des forces démocratiques*), which had emerged from the remains of Ahmed Ould Daddah's UFD-EN after it was banned in October 2000, competed in only 20; Messaoud Ould Boulkheir's Action for Change (AC) presented candidates in just 15.

As additional confidence-building measures, the government issued new tamper-proof identity cards, published voter lists on the Internet, and employed transparent ballot boxes. Participation was up considerably—50% of those registered—from 30% in the 1996 legislative elections.

When the results were tallied, Taya's PRDS won 64 out of 81 seats; six additional seats went to small parties backing the presidential majority. The opposition garnered 11 seats, with four of them going to Action for Change and three to the Rally of Democratic Forces; Cheikh Malainine's FPM won a single seat.

The EU praised the conduct of the elections and called upon Mauritanian parties to maintain a constructive dialogue "so as to strengthen confidence in democratic institutions and create an environment in which all shades of opinion can be freely expressed." President Taya was not, however, a man who has much appreciation for diversity of opinion, especially when it was critical and when presidential elections were approaching.

In January 2002 the government banned Action for Change, accusing it of inciting violence and racial tension. The decision followed a debate on government policy in 2002, during which opposition members repeatedly questioned officials on what would be done to improve race relations and end slavery. AC's leader, Messaoud Ould Boulkheir—himself a descendant of slaves—reacted by succinctly describing the Taya regime: "It is a military government, an undemocratic government that cannot accept a dissenting view, a government that is ready to trample on all rights in order to achieve its objectives."

Despite numerous political parties, Mauritania under President Taya remained more authoritarian than democratic. Taya ruled with an iron fist and any velvet glove was pretty threadbare. Opposition parties that pushed too hard were banned, their leaders subjected to imprisonment;

the press was systematically censured and unions were prohibited from public demonstrations.

The PRDS operated as a political machine for winning elections and distributing the political loaves and fishes—access to political positions and the resources they control. Factional disputes within the party were largely tribal, ethnic, and regional. White Moors from Adrar (President Ould Taya's native region) and Brakna were highly influential; the majority of the Black Moor elite was to be found within the party, along with leading Afro-Mauritanian figures. Frequent ministerial reshufflings allowed an efficient redistribution of spoils to reflect any necessary change or tweaking of influence within the party.

Of all the tribal factions within the PRDS it was President Ould Taya's Smassids who took a lion's share of the spoils. They constituted a virtual financial cartel with significant interests in every economic sector. Thus Ch'Bih Ould Cheikh Malainine's comment that 39 Mauritanians held 70% of the country's wealth, and 27 of them were members of a single tribe. Thus, too, the finding of the UN's Development Program that wealth in Mauritania is very unequally distributed: the richest 20% control 44% of the nation's wealth; the poorest 20% control a mere 6.4%.

Inequality, exclusion, and political repression kept tensions high in Mauritania. The regime's recognition of Israel provided focus for incendiary comment by Arab nationalists and Islamic fundamentalists. The combustibility of the situation was revealed in June 2003, when elements of the armed forces attempted a violent overthrow of the Ould Taya government. Rebels overran the presidential compound, but Ould Taya rallied his personal guard, shot his way out to nearby police headquarters and sustained a 36-hour siege. Loyalist army forces, directed by President Taya himself, suppressed the attempted coup, but it was a close call.

With his vulnerability obvious (and opposition politicians lamenting the coup's failure) Ould Taya decided not to postpone presidential elections scheduled for November. Instead, he boldly appointed a Black Moor, Justice Minister Sghaïer Ould Mbareck, his new prime minister, the first Harratin to occupy the office. The appointment was not without its political implications. Ould Mbareck hailed from Mauritania's far eastern province of Hodh el-Chargui, where many of the rebels had their family roots.

In the November 2003 presidential elections, five opposition candidates challenged Ould Taya's bid for a fresh six-year term. His most formidable opponent was Mohamad Khouna Ould Haidalla, the former military ruler who had been over-thrown by Ould Taya in 1984. Haidalla attracted a heterogeneous group of opportunists to his campaign: liberal reformers, Arab nationalists, and Islamic fundamentalists—all united by a common distaste for the incumbent. When the results were tabulated, President Taya won 67% of the ballots; Ould Haidalla placed second with about 19% of the vote. The opposition rolled out its usual litany of fraud complaints, but hard-to-fake voter cards and transparent ballot boxes did much to undermine the credibility of such charges.

After the 9/11 terror attacks in New York, President Taya committed himself to the war on terror, and Mauritania, with its little-patrolled desert crossings, alleged al-Qaeda cells, and large segments of its Muslim population sympathetic to Osama bin Laden and Saddam Hussein, has received special attention from U.S. planners. The country is one of four initially part of the Pan-Sahel Initiative, designed to train and prepare local armed forces to combat terrorist groups that seek to make the Sahara a new Afghanistan.

Suspected extremist Islamist activity had been on the rise in Mauritania for some time. As part of the government's ongoing struggle with Islamist opposition, police conducted extensive raids against suspected terror cells, including mosques, in April and May 2005. They accused al-Qaeda of pouring vast sums into mosques and Islamic schools to recruit insurgents and send them to the front lines of holy wars in Iraq and Afghanistan. Seventeen alleged members of the Algerian-based GSPC (Salafist Group for Preaching Combat) were charged with plotting acts of terror. In June, an army base in the Sahara was attacked by elements of the GSPC; 15 Mauritanian soldiers were killed, some with their throats slit. On its website, the group claimed the attack "was in revenge for the violence perpetrated against our brothers in prison," referring to the 17 fundamentalists arrested in April raids.

The pressures, internal and external, were building up on President Taya. After three successive coup attempts, he seemed to withdraw to an ivory tower and lose touch with Mauritanian reality. It took only his absence from the country in August, on the occasion of the Saudi monarch's funeral, for his own security forces to set in motion the fourth and final coup against him. On August 3, 2005 troops seized state radio and television buildings, closed the capital's airport, and announced Taya's overthrow.

Army officers calling themselves *Conseil militaire pour la justice et la démocratie* (CMJD) declared the armed forces had unanimously decided to "end the totalitarian practices of the deposed regime." With Colonel Ely Ould Mohamed Vall—the head of national security—as its leader, the CMJD announced it would exercise power for two years to allow time to put "open and transparent" democratic institutions in place.

True to its word, the CMJD organized a referendum on a new constitution in June 2006. The new text, which limited a serving president to two terms in office and cut the presidential terms from six to five years, was approved by 96.9% of Mauritanian voters; a remarkable 76.5% of all eligible voters participated in the foundation of a new state. The constitution provided for a bicameral legislature: a 56-member Senate, elected for six-year terms by municipal leaders, and a 95-member National Assembly, chosen by popular vote to serve five-year terms.

Some 25 political parties submitted lists of candidates for the first round of Assembly elections in November; to these were added numerous independent candidates. Electoral rules set aside 20% of the seats for female candidates, a first for Mauritania. When the runoff elections were completed in December, Mauritanian voters had produced a varied and potentially contentious lower house. Twelve political parties are represented; Arab nationalists will sit with Afro-Mauritanians, and liberals with Islamists.

Ostensibly the Assembly's largest cohesive bloc is represented by former opponents of the Taya regime. Eleven opposition parties joined together as the Coalition of Forces for Democratic Change (CFDC) and won 41 seats; the largest element within the CFDC is represented by the 15 seats of the Ahmed Ould Daddah's Rally of Democratic Forces (RFD). Parties associated with the former presidential majority, most importantly, the Republican Party for Democracy and Renewal (PRDR)—a renamed PRDS—secured 13 seats, but the real power brokers may well be the 41 members elected as "independents." Several of them are Islamists since sectarian parties and movements were banned from electoral participation.

The presidential election, which concluded the 19-month transitional process, took place in March 2007. A record 20 candidates joined the fray, making a first-round victory impossible. Constituent members of CFCD presented four candidates, the most prominent of whom was the RFD's Ahmed Ould Daddah. For the first time a Harratin, Messoud Ould Boulhkeir of the *Alliance populaire progressiste* (APP), was a candidate for the country's highest office. Eighteen parties, generally supportive of the former regime and calling themselves "The Charter," united behind the candidacy of Sidi Ould Cheikh Abdallahi. His credentials were

Mauritania

mixed: a minister under ex-President Taya, he had also been put under house arrest by Taya. "Sidi," as his backers called him, presented himself as a man of consensus and stability. Abdallahi received 25% of the votes in the first round of balloting; Ahmed Ould Daddah arrived in second place with slightly more than 20% of the vote.

In the runoff election, Abdallahi received crucial backing from the third-place finisher, Zeine Ould Zeidane, a former governor of the Bank of Mauritania, and, much to the surprise of the traditional opposition, from the fourth-place finisher, Messoud Ould Boulhkeir, the "Harratin" descendent of slaves. Abdallahi's campaign stressed reconciliation to heal the wounds that still lingered from racial conflicts going back to 1989, and his message prevailed. He won 52.85% to Ould Daddah's 47.15%. Boulhkeir received his political reward when the National Assembly convened in April and elected him its president. Zeine Ould Zeidane was named prime minister, though he later resigned in May 2008.

High in Sidi's priorities was reinforcing the national unity of a country riven by ethnic and socio-economic divisions. He promised special legislation criminalizing slavery (officially abolished in 1981) and rehabilitating the rights of Afro-Mauritanians subject to abuse and expulsion between 1989 and 1991.

The Sidi government did not last long, however. On August 6, 2008, Gen. Mohamed Ould Abdel Aziz and the military overthrew the president in a bloodless coup. They did so in apparent retaliation for Sidi's attempts to dismiss top military brass, most notably the coup perpetrators themselves. Gen. Abdel Aziz himself resigned from the head of the junta in April 2009, in order to be eligible to run in forthcoming elections called by the military. The acting head of state is Ba Mamadou Mbaré, former president of the Senate, until upcoming elections are held on July 18, 2009.

The Present: Contemporary Issues

Mauritania emerged from the terrible drought conditions of the 1970s and 1980s with a few years of decent rain. Animal flocks that had been devastated were gradually reconstituted. Cattle, which had fallen to 7.6 million head in 1973, rose to 11 million head by 1999, but three consecutive years of drought devastated both food and cattle production. More than 100,000 head of cattle died and herders had to lead their herds farther south in search of greener pastures. Only in August 2003 did the rains return, giving hope of abundant pasturage and removing the looming specter of drought and famine.

The agricultural sector traditionally employs 60% of the population and contributes 23.7% of the GDP (2005), but these figures are always subject to the absence of water. In 2002 rainfall was so inadequate peasant farmers were unable to sow sorghum and millet, the principal cereal grains grown. The farmer's life is one of constant struggle: "The land teaches us much," runs the Mauritanian proverb, "because it resists us."

For years Mauritania's principal source of income was iron. The iron ore industry is centered on the open-pit mines of Zouérat in the north. Ores are processed and then transported by train to the coastal port of Nouadhibou, some 400 miles away. Convoys of up to 250 ore-bearing cars, pulled by four engines and extending a mile and a half in length, evacuate the desert's wealth. On their return trip, the trains bring food, water and supplies to Zouérat, a town of 40,000 built to sustain the mines.

The industry is operated by SNIM (*Société Nationale Industrielle et Minière de Mauritanie*), which is 80% state-owned. Kuwaiti and Jordanian investors, along with the Islamic Bank, hold the remaining shares. The company employs some 4,000 workers, but its infrastructure is seriously aging.

In addition to repair and upgrading of the rail connection to the Atlantic, major work on the loading port for iron ore at Nouadhibou will be undertaken. Built in 1963, the port is dilapidated. In 1999 French experts had already declared it might have to shut down because of its failure to comply with safety standards. Upgrades and repairs are more likely given the recent surge in iron prices, largely driven by the Chinese demand for steel. Iron prices doubled between 2003 and 2005, going from $20 to $40 a ton. Production in 2004 rose 14%, to 11 million tons, and the company's 2004 sales amounted to $240 million, 45% higher than the year before. At a rate of 12 million tons a year, Mauritania's proven iron reserves should last another 100 years. They contribute about 12% of GDP.

Waters off the Mauritanian coast are rich fishing areas—perhaps too rich. From 200 ships harvesting the sea in 1996, more than 500 were working the waters in 1998. Both catch and income were reduced as a consequence of industrial-scale fishing techniques. Species like dolphins, sharks and turtles declined dangerously.

The depletion of fishing stock resulted from Mauritania's fishing agreement with the European Union. In exchange for $600 million in cash over six years, EU ships were allowed unrestricted fishing rights. Giant Dutch factory trawlers, for example, could catch and freeze 300 tons of sardines a day. In 1998, the government began the process of declaring a two-month "biological rest" to help fishing stocks renew themselves, but even this proved ineffective. It has occasionally banned all fishing, except traditional nonmotorized fishing by local communities, in the Banc d'Arguin National Park.

Fishing currently accounts for about half of Mauritania's export income and contributes 10% of GDP. Japan is the biggest buyer of Mauritanian fish, and Mauritania maintains a sizable trade surplus with the Asian country.

Mauritania renewed its EU fishing agreement in August 2001, but the new accord was severely criticized by the local

The SNIM train carries iron ore from the desert to the port of Nouadhibou

environmental group, Pechecops, which described signing the agreement as "tantamount to signing the death warrant of Mauritania's national fisheries sector," because it would result in overfishing. Octopus fishing, for instance, has been devastated by commercial overharvesting, with the 2001 catch generated one-third the catch of 1993 from over three times the number of fishing vessels. This major industry in Mauritania is suffering as octopus stocks continue to decline precipitously putting the long-term potential of the Mauritanian fishing sector at risk.

Given its dependence on iron and fish, Mauritania desperately needs to diversify its economy, but diversification requires investment and there is little capital available. International financial aid accounts for 80% of the country's investment budget and international lenders have justifiable concerns. Mauritania has faithfully followed structural adjustment programs; the budget is balanced (with foreign assistance) and inflation is down. There has been reasonable growth but little distribution of its consequences. The staggering inequalities of Mauritanian life are suggested by a simple fact: 80% of Mauritania's value added tax was once paid by a mere 12 individuals.

The country remains deeply impoverished and ranks 153 (out of 177 countries) on the UN Development Program's *Human Development Index* for 2006. About half the population lives in poverty, and 32% of all children under the age of five suffered from malnutrition in 2000; almost half the adult population is illiterate, and life expectancy is 53.7 years (2005). These figures are dire, but Mauritania benefited from debt relief under provisions of the Highly Indebted Poor countries (HIPC) initiative and from decisions in 2005 and 2006 to cancel the multilateral debt of 19 of the world's poorest states, Mauritania included.

Mauritania is now an oil-producing nation. The Australian company Woodside began production at the Chinguetti offshore field in February 2006. Located in the Atlantic some 43 miles from Nouakchott, the field was initially predicted to produce 75,000 bbl/d (barrels a day) for ten years, but actual production has proved disappointing—around 33,000 bbl/d. Woodside cut its estimates of total reserves in the field by 57% in November 2006, to 53 million barrels.

That's only the beginning; at least two other major fields, expected to bring production to 200,000 bbl/d, await development. By 2010 the expectation is that oil revenues will reach $1.5, doubling the country's 2004 GDP. Chinese state petroleum companies have moved with alacrity to stake a claim in Mauritania's oil bonanza. China National Petroleum Corp. (CNPC) bought a 65% stake in offshore Block 20, and agreed to fund all exploration costs. At $8.6 million, it's probably a bargain. Covering nearly 4,000 square miles, the block is considered the most promising portion of Mauritania's Coastal Basin. CNPC operates the adjacent Block 12, providing ample opportunity for logistical and operational efficiencies. To help solidify relations, China's deputy foreign minister in charge of Africa, Qiao Zonghua, dropped a tidy $7 million in assistance on the country in July 2005.

Sensitive to the abject failure of oil revenues to improve the lives of people living in oil-producing countries, the government of President Vall endorsed the Extractive Industries Transparency Initiative (EITI), which is designed to improve transparency and accountability in the use of natural resources. As part of its EITI commitment, the government has appointed a committee to oversee the use of oil and mineral revenues and ensure they are used to benefit all Mauritanians. The committee consists of representatives of government, oil industry, and civil society, including the press, unions and NGOs.

The Future

Though Mauritania has never been fully democratic, there were reasons for optimism in the country under President Abdallahi. General Abdel Aziz's bloodless coup in August 2008 was a setback that illustrated the tenuous nature of democracy in fragile states. Forthcoming elections in July 2009 should store a civilian regime, and there is a good chance the former general Abdel Aziz will become president, which has ambiguous implications for longer-term democratization. An Abdel Aziz victory would mean an elected executive would have the backing of the army, but on the other hand former military rulers in Africa have often held only a dim view of civil liberties and political rights.

The economy may benefit from natural resources, though it will take some time to bring Mauritanians out of grinding poverty, given the country's location near the bottom of international measures of human development. National incomes will depend largely on how and when oil resources come online. In the meantime, high levels of poverty and inequality will remain the norm.

The Monk Seal, one of the world's rarest mammals

The Republic of Niger   (pronounced Nee-*zhair*)

President Tandja Mamadou

Basic Facts

Area: 1,266,510 sq. km. = 489,000 sq. mi. (three times the size of California)
Population: 14,200,000 (UN 2007 est.)
Capital City: Niamey
Climate: Hot and dry desert in the north; semiarid and warm in the south with a wet season from June to September producing 9 to 30 inches of rainfall in normal years.
Neighboring Countries: Burkina Faso (southwest); Mali (west); Algeria (northwest); Libya (north); Chad (east); Nigeria and Benin (south).
Official Language: French
Other Principal Languages: Arabic, Fulfuldé, Hausa, Kanuri, Songai, Tamajek, and Zarma
Ethnic Groups: Hausa 56%, Djerma 22%, Fula 8.5%, Tuareg 8%, Beri Beri (Kanouri) 4.3%, Arab, Toubou, and Gourmantché 1.2%, about 1,200 French expatriates
Principal Religions: Muslim 80%, remainder indigenous beliefs and Christians.
Chief Commercial Products: Uranium ore, livestock products, cowpeas, onions
GNI Per Capita: $240 (World Bank 2006 est.)

Currency: CFA franc
Former Colonial Status: French Colony (1921–1960)
Independence Date: August 3, 1960
Chief of State: Tandja Mamadou, President (since 1999)
National Flag: Three horizontal stripes of orange, white and emerald green. There is an orange globe in the middle of the white stripe.

Land and People

The Republic of Niger covers an immense area in north-central Africa. It is one of the most thinly populated nations of the continent. A huge plateau, the country is desolate but diversified, sometimes rocky and sometimes sandy, furrowed in many places by fossilized beds of ancient Sahara rivers. Hot and dry, it is pockmarked with small basins in the southern area which briefly turn into ponds during the "winter."

A narrow belt of territory in the south stretches along the entire width of the country and is the only fertile region. This area of trees and shrubs, interspersed with cultivated land supported by irrigation or wells, gives way quickly to a transition zone where the trees become smaller, and the lack of moisture supports only sporadic grazing by nomads' animals. In the northern two-thirds of the territory, the shifting sands of the hot desert render human life impossible except in the region of uranium mines, and only sparse, rudimentary animal life is found.

Little more than 2% of the land area is under cultivation, most of which is gathered around the 185-mile-long portion of the Niger River within the country's boundaries. The river floods from June to September, helping to provide moisture for the surrounding vegetation. The climate is exceedingly hot and dry during eight months of the year.

A *National Geographic*-financed expedition into the Niger desert discovered extraordinary rock carvings—huge giraffes carved into desert sandstone 9,000 years ago. The largest stands over 20 feet tall; its proportions are meticulously accurate and its reticulation beautifully created in low relief. Wavy lines come from the mouths of these giraffes and to them are attached small human figures. No one is sure what they mean, but their artistic achievement is undeniable. For preservation purposes the actual site of this Sistine Chapel of rock art remains hidden. Casts will allow worldwide audiences to appreciate the consummate skill of their unknown creators.

The Past: Political and Economic History

For early history, see *Historical Background* and *The Colonial Period: The French.*

Niger became an autonomous member of the French Community in 1958, but opted for independence in 1960. Diori Hamani was chosen the country's first president. Under the first postindependence constitution, the president held office for a term of five years and was elected by universal suffrage. The National Assembly of 60 members, elected in the same manner, sat for five years.

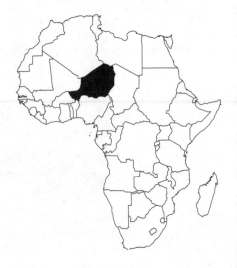

Niger

After independence, Diori's Niger Progressive Party held all seats of the National Assembly and dominated the government. In 1974 the single-party regime was overthrown in a military coup led by Lt-Col Seyni Kountché. Kountché ruled as military dictator until 1987 when he died in Paris of AIDS. He was succeeded by his cousin, Col. Ali Saibou, as chief of state. President Saibou grudgingly agreed to a new constitution, which was approved in 1992. It greatly curtailed the power of the military and mandated multiparty elections, which were held in 1993. A 43-year-old economist, Mahamane Ousmane, of the *Convention Démocratique et Sociale* (CDS: Social Democratic Convention) won a majority.

He quickly alienated most of the National Assembly, and government came to a virtual standstill. The military, led by Brig. Gen. Ibrahim Maïnassara, staged a coup in January 1996, arresting the president and prime minister. A new constitution was adopted, and elections were held in July. Maïnassara, running as an independent, won. The opposition contested the results, and the crisis deepened four months later when the eight main opposition parties boycotted legislative elections. Pro-government parties and sympathizers claimed all 80 seats in the National Assembly.

On a more positive note, the government achieved a resolution of rebellion of Tuareg and Toubou peoples, both of which felt marginalized and excluded from Nigerien society. Two main rebel movements (at one time there were some 15 rebel groups in Niger), the Organization of Armed Resistance (ORA) and the Coordination of Armed Resistance (CRA), signed a peace agreement in April 1995. It called for reintegration of these former rebels into Nigerien society. Some would be integrated into the army or paramilitary ranks, but this process was painfully slow. Parliament finally voted amnesty for all desert guerrilla groups in March 1998. Shortly afterwards, the two main rebel fronts handed over their arsenals of heavy machine guns, rocket-launchers, antitank mines, and ammunition. Tuaregs are now regularly appointed by the prime minister as members of the Cabinet.

From that high point General Maïnassara's difficulties increased. The country was wracked by a continuing series of strikes, protests, mutinies, and rebellions. Salaries to soldiers and civil servants and scholarships to students went unpaid for months. The political opposition found the streets a comfortable place for political theater.

Niger's long political instability reached a climax in early 1999. Local elections were held for the first time, and when early

Ex-President Ibrahim Mainassara Barre

results showed the opposition winning handily, armed men appeared in those polling areas where it seemed most successful. Ballots and official tabulation reports were destroyed, the vote disrupted. The opposition was justifiably outraged. Supporters were called to the streets to protest and widespread unrest ensued; a day later they called upon the president-general to resign.

The next day, April 9, 1999, the president's own security command shot him to death as he was preparing to leave the Niamey airport. Eyewitnesses reported that Presidential Guard members repeatedly shot the president with a truck-mounted large-caliber machine gun, nearly severing his body in two. With Orwellian glibness the commander of the Presidential Guard, Major Daouda Mallam Wanke, emphasized to reporters that Maïnassara's death was totally unpremeditated, merely an "unfortunate accident."

Very quickly the National Assembly and Supreme Court were dissolved, the constitution and political parties suspended, and a National Council for Reconciliation (CRN) put in place. Major Wanke was chosen as president and head of the CRN, which consisted of 14 junior officers.

Expressions of outrage were heard from every part of the world, and France (on whom the Niger economy is largely dependent) suspended all military aid and economic assistance. The new regime had to respond quickly. Major Wanke went on radio and television and announced that the junta would return the country to civilian rule by the end of the year. Elections would be held in November and the new president would be sworn in on December 31. Members of the military and security forces were specifically banned from standing for election. The major also indicated that there would be a referendum on yet another new constitution in

June. The junta's timetable was scrupulously followed.

The new constitution designed a parliamentary regime with a relatively strong president. There would be a single house legislature with executive power shared between the president and the prime minister. The president must name the prime minister from a list of three candidates proposed by the parliamentary majority. Article 141 of the new constitution provided amnesty to those responsible for "the *coups d'état* of January 27, 1996 and April, 9 1999."

The constitution of the Fifth Republic was approved by a nearly 90% majority, a figure made less impressive by the fact that only a little over 30% of the electorate participated. As promised by Major Wanke, multiparty presidential and parliamentary elections followed in October and November.

Seven candidates competed for the presidency. In the runoffs, Tandja Mamadou, the candidate of the National Movement for a Developing Society (MNSD), beat Mahamadou Issoufou, the candidate of the Niger Party for Democracy and Socialism (PNDS) by a margin of nearly 60% to 40%.

Tandja, a retired military officer, had first become prominent when he helped oust Niger's first president, Diori Hamani, in 1974. He served as interior minister for both presidents Kountché and Ali Saibou. Under the latter, he was responsible for the bloody repression of Tuaregs in 1990. An ethnic Kanouri, Tandja profited by a runoff alliance with Mahamane Ousmane, a member of Niger's influential Hausa majority, leader of the *Convention Démocratique et Sociale* (CDS) and the country's last democratically elected president. His younger Hausa opponent, Mahamadou Issoufou, spent lavishly and campaigned vigorously in what Nigerien commentators called "an American style."

In elections for the National Assembly, Tandja's MNSD and CDS alliance won an absolute majority of 55 out of 83 seats. Much to the relief of many, the electoral system eliminated minor parties. Only three other parties would be represented in the new parliament. Issoufou's PNDS won 16 seats, and the Rally for Democracy and Progress (RDP) of former President Maïnassara won eight. The remaining four seats were won by the *Alliance nigérienne pour la démocratie et le progrès* (ANDP).

President Tandja Mamadou faced military mutinies in 2002 (privates earn about $35 a month, equivalent to the price of a 200 pound bag of millet), but as his term of office drew to an end in 2004, it was clear he had brought both stability and credibility to Nigerien democracy. With Prime Minister Hama Amadou, the president had maintained civil peace, achieved a number

Niger

of rural development projects that made rural voters happy, and saw to it that urban civil servants were regularly paid.

Tandja was a candidate to succeed himself in the October 2004 presidential elections and he faced five opponents. His principal rivals from 1999, Mahamadou Issoufou of the PNDS, and Mahamane Ousmane of the CDS headed the opposition, while Moumouni Djermakoye, Cheiffou Amadou, and Hamid Algabid played secondary roles. In first-round balloting President Tandja failed to secure a majority, winning only 40.67% of the votes; his nearest competitor was Mahamadou Issoufou who received 24.6%. The losers urged their voters to support the outgoing president, and in November runoffs, Tandja triumphed convincingly: 65.5% of the vote to his challenger's 34.5%. He became the first elected leader of Niger to have completed his term of office without being assassinated or ousted by coup. In parliamentary elections, Tandja's National Movement for a Developing Society (MNSD) elected 47 deputies, while five other parties supporting the president brought the presidential majority to a comfortable 88 seats. Mahamadou Issoufou's PNDS affirmed its role as the principal opposition party with 25 seats. Niger's fragile democracy seemed to have matured, which would make the chaotic change of 2009 all the more disappointing.

In 2009, Tandja Mamadou's second (and ostensibly final) term as president was drawing to a close. However, Tandja saw an opportunity to seize an unconstitutional third term through political machinations, and has now plunged the country into a constitutional crisis. After long denying any interest in a third term, the president decided that "the people" insisted upon his continued presence. He proposed a referendum to decide the issue, though the Nigerien constitution explicitly forbade any such referendum or any constitutional amendment to extend presidential term limits. Tandja disbanded the legislature and proposed to call new legislative elections for later in 2009, to be followed by a referendum on a new constitution and sub-

sequent presidential elections in which he wished to run (all within a matter of a few months). When the Constitutional Court ruled against Tandja's scheme, the president demanded a reversal of the ruling and then began to rule by decree. This has resulted in the prospect of a general strike and a battle between institutions to ensure a modicum of governance.

Far from the high politics in the capital Niamey, Niger's sparsely populated northern region remains a security problem for the government. It has been the scene of banditry and tourist kidnappings that have forced trans-Saharan traffic to travel in convoys protected by heavily armed soldiers. The presence of armed Islamist radicals, members of the Algerian *Groupe salafiste pour la prédication et le combat* (GSPC: Salafist Group for Preaching and Combat, later renamed AQIM: Al-Qaeda in the Islamic Maghreb) in the same geographical area, has complicated the security situation. In March 2004 one Salafist band, involved in kidnapping over 30 European tourists in Algeria, engaged Nigerien forces and was chased into neighboring Chad, where it was annihilated by Chadian troops.

Niger was a part of the 2002 U.S. State Department-sponsored Pan-Sahel Initiative (PSI) to track and destroy Islamic fundamentalists operating in the region. The program furnished training and equipment (especially communications materials) to permit rapid response to terrorist threats in the four Sahel countries of Mauritania, Mali, Niger and Chad. American surveillance provided the intelligence to pinpoint the GSPC in Niger, where it had been working hand-in-hand with armed bandits, using hideouts and caches left over from the 1990s Tuareg rebellion.

The Pan-Sahel Initiative has since been upgraded in name, scope, and budget. Now called the Trans-Saharan Counter-Terrorism Initiative (TSCTI), it includes a number of north and west African countries. The multiagency initiative will be annually funded at the $100 million level for five years, beginning in 2007. Bat-

talions of 500 soldiers from the eight countries will be trained and equipped with Toyota Land Cruisers, radios, uniforms, global-positioning devices and fuel trailers.

The Present: Contemporary Issues

Like Mauritania, Niger is challenged by the persistence of traditional slavery among its nomadic peoples. Although banned by law, slavery is still practiced. New anti-slavery provisions have been included in the country's penal code to discourage the practice. These provide prison terms of 10 to 30 years and fines of one million to five million CFA francs (about $1,921 to $9,605) for those found guilty of enslavement. "*Timidria*," which means "freedom" in the Tamajek language of the Tuaregs, is an NGO dedicated to fighting the practice and aiding its victims.

Social and religious traditions, coupled with high levels of poverty, produce an extremely high number of early marriages. According to the UN Children's Fund, nearly half of Niger's young women are married by age 15 and 90% are married by age 18. Half of all Nigerien women have their first pregnancy while still teenagers; on average each will bear 7.7 children during her lifetime.

Female genital cutting (FGC) is practiced by a third of the country's population. The practice was outlawed in 2001, but it remains widespread and no one has ever been prosecuted for performing the operation. For many, the removal of the clitoris reduces a woman's sex drive and guarantees marital fidelity. Niger's National Assembly rejected the Maputo Protocol on the protection of the rights of African women in June 2006. Deputies feared sections declaring FGC, polygamy, and marriage of minors violations of human rights would upset their constituents.

Niger's economic predicament is illustrated by 2005 statistics: GDP growth was just 4.5%, while population growth was 3.5%—one of the highest rates in the world. (Since independence in 1960 Niger's population has quadrupled.) The conditions of individual life in Niger are spiraling downwards and poverty is increasing. More than 60% of the population survives on less than $1 per day, and only 28.7% of all adults are literate.

Niger's women bear particular burdens. Not only do they have the highest fertility rate in the world, averaging nearly eight children per woman, but they suffer one of the world's highest infant mortality rates. Out of every 1,000 live births, 150 die (2005); on average, 256 of every 1,000 children will die before they are five. For girls, according to the World Health Organization, the figure is even higher: 265 will die (2003). Only 9.3% of them are literate (2003),

Presidential palace, Niamey

and only 32% of girls eligible for primary school are actually enrolled (2005).

Niger is the world's third largest uranium producer (after Canada and Australia), extracting around 3,000 tons a year; most of this is sold to France and Japan.The uranium is mined in the region of Arlit, some 620 miles north of Niamey, by two French companies (Cominak and Somaïr) employing around 1,600 persons. Raw uranium is transported by truck to the port of Cotonou (Benin) and shipped to Narbonne, in southwestern France, for processing.

The French holding company Areva, which has a controlling interest in both firms, has been the object of protests in Arlit throughout 2006 and 2007. In addition to charges of exploitation and profiteering, the protesters, backed by the French anti-nuclear lobby and environmental groups, have also demanded an investigation of radioactive contamination in mining communities. In April 2007, Tuareg rebels identifying themselves as members of the *Mouvement des Nigériens pour la Justice* (MNJ) attacked a French uranium-prospecting camp in the area, making off with six vehicles and a number of mobile phones.

For years Niger's main source of export revenues, uranium, accounted for 80% of the national budget in the 1980s. Production peaked at 4,360 tons in 1981, and then prices collapsed. For a long while diminished demand and reduced prices seriously affected government revenues. Recently, however, expanding Asian economies have driven the prices of virtually all commodities higher and made mineral

A slave boy draws water for his master. More than 43,000 individuals are estimated to belong to the slave caste in Niger. ©IRIN/G. Cranston

exploration more attractive. In 2004 Niger's uranium ore production increased from below 3,000 tons to 3,334 tons, worth approximately $128.5 million. Taxes and fees generated $12.3 million for the national budget.

Long a monopoly of French interests, Niger's potential uranium deposits have attracted others. The government, hoping to earn more from the surge in uranium prices, has diversified the exploration licenses it has granted. British, Canadian and Chinese firms are all active in the area.

Gold seems the most promising alternative in a desperate effort to diversify away from an uncertain reliance on uranium. Canadian and Moroccan interests are currently developing two neighboring gold mines—Samira Hill and Libiri. Production began at an expected annual rate of 135,000 ounces in 2004. Koma Bangou, located slightly more than 100 miles southwest of Niamey has sparked a gold rush since 2001. More than 15,000 people are reported to have moved into the area after being abandoned by a foreign firm that year.

Surrounded by oil-producing states—Algeria, Libya, and Chad—Niger maintains some speculative hope of productive oil discoveries. Exploration has been going on since 1958 and one reserve of some 300 million barrels has been identified in a permit area operated by Exxon Mobil. In 2004 Petronas, the Malaysian oil giant, began three exploratory wells at Nguigmi in eastern Niger, close to the Chad frontier, and Algeria's Sonatrach has exploration permits in both northeast and central Niger. Given Niger's landlocked geography, the investment necessary to export the oil is simply too great. To be profitable, reserves of at least a billion barrels are necessary.

With its tremendous energy needs, China seems less concerned with commercial reality and may be willing to invest in the difficult and hard to transport. Niger has already granted exploration rights in its Tenere Block to the China National Petroleum Company. That's the same company that built an oil pipeline in Sudan to transport non-optimally located oil to refineries on the Red Sea. In May 2007 an ebullient communications minister spoke of Niger's first barrel of oil flowing somewhere in 2009–2010.

Niger qualified for participation in debt relief programs under the Highly Indebted Poor Countries (HIPC) program and the Multilateral Debt Relief Initiative. As of 2003, its external debt stood at over $2 billion, most of it owed multilateral lenders like the IMF or World Bank, but this was reduced by about $1.3 billion, taking Niger's debt burden from 76% of GDP to under 15%. Niger is one of the 19 countries that has benefitted most cancellation of multilateral debts.

As a profoundly poor state, Niger represents all the social and medical consequences of devastating poverty. The country has been spending three times more on debt payments than on health and education; in 2003, according to the World Health Organization, the government spent only $27 per person on health. The consequence is seen in raw statistics: in Niger, more than 15% of children suffer from severe malnutrition according to a May 2006 UNICEF report; 50% of them suffer stunted growth. Malnutrition often leads to an early death for the children. Their deaths result from long-term starvation diets that weaken the immune system and allow children to be killed by measles, malaria, meningitis and diarrhea. The most horrifying of the child killers is noma, a disease like gangrene that starts as a small black spot on the face and progresses by devouring facial tissue, muscle, and bone.

The Future

Niger's economy has seen little growth and development since independence. The UN Development Program's *Human Development Index* for 2006 ranks Niger as the poorest, least-developed country in the world—177 out of 177 countries ranked. Economic problems are crushing, with little prospect for improvement. The social benefits of Niger's natural resources seem a long way off.

Politically, the country has been "partly free" under Tandja Mamadou, but the constitutional crisis of 2009 has exposed the president's deep authoritarian streak. The executive has exhibited a willingness to overrun countervailing institutions, including the legislative and judicial branches and the existing constitution, in order to ensure an additional term of office. Moreover, the state continues to control much of the media, and there are some threats to civil liberties, though elections seemed to improve after the early 1990s.

Finally, violent conflict in Niger between the government and Tuareg peoples seemed to subside in 2009. As in neighboring Mali, a restive force of dissident Tuaregs appeared in early 2007 by launching attacks on military outposts and mining camps in Niger's insecure north. The group, calling itself the *Mouvement des Nigériens pour la Justice* (MNJ), called for more equitable distribution of the benefits of the region's natural resources and greater political inclusion of marginalized Tuareg peoples into Niger's political life. The government deemed them bandits bent on destabilizing the country. In 2009, the MNJ and the government agreed to cease hostilities, though the final resolution remains unclear.

The Federal Republic of Nigeria

National Mosque—Abuja

Basic Facts

Area: 924,630 sq. km. = 357,000 sq. mi. (A little large than Texas and Oklahoma together)

Population: 150,000,000 (CIA World Fact Book 2009 est.)

Capital City: Abuja (Lagos, while often confused with being the capital, is the center of most commerce and culture.)

Climate: Hot and humid in the coastal belt and southern interior; hot and less humid in the central plains regions; semiarid to arid and hot in the extreme north.

Neighboring Countries: Benin (west); Niger, Chad (north); Cameroon (east).

Official Language: English

Other Principal Languages: There over 450 languages spoken. Prominent are Edo, Fulani, Hausa, Ibibio, Igbo, Ijo, Kanuri, Nupe, Tiv, and Yoruba.

Ethnic Groups: Prominent are the Hausa, Fulani, Yoruba, Ibo, Ijaw, Kanuri, Ibibio, and Tiv.

Principal Religions: Muslim 50%, Christian 40%, indigenous beliefs 10%

Chief Commercial Products: Petroleum and petroleum products 95%, cocoa, rubber

GNI Per Capita: $560 (World Bank 2006 est.)

Currency: 1 naira (N) = 100 kobo

Former Colonial Status: British Colony (1914–1960).

Independence Date: October 1, 1960

Chief of State: Umaru Musa Yar'Adua, President (Since May 2007)

National Flag: Three vertical stripes of green, white and green.

Land and People

Nigeria, the 14th largest country (in area) on the African continent with the largest population of any African nation, lies facing the Gulf of Guinea on the southern coast of West Africa. From the warm waters of the ocean the land has a flat appearance; there is a belt of dense swamp and towering mangrove trees ten to 15 miles wide. This marshy coastal area resembles the bayous of Louisiana, particularly in the delta of the Niger River.

Farther inland, there is a region 50 to 100 miles wide where the vegetation is thick green tropical forest rising from more stable ground. The trees of this warm and humid area reach heights of 200 feet where vines entwine all growth.

This forest area and the coast receive up to 150 inches of rainfall per year.

The land rises slowly in a series of foothills to the Jos Plateau, reaching altitudes up to 1,000 feet. Tall grasses grow rapidly between widely spaced trees. The dry season, from October to April, evaporates moisture from the ground, hardening the earth so that when the spring rains come, the soil erodes into the rivers.

There is a semiarid to arid region in the extreme north, close to Lake Chad and Niger. It is the transition zone lying between the Sahara Desert and the green forests and jungles of the south, receiving 25 inches or less of rain per year. In the last decade, "less" has been the rule. This area is threatened by the expansion southward of the great desert.

During the dry season, particularly in December and January, the *harmattan*, the hot wind blowing from the desert, penetrates to the Gulf of Guinea, lowering the humidity and raising dust storms in the interior.

Nigerians pride themselves on being, in many ways, the "biggest" and the "best" on the continent. Nigeria is the most populous country in Africa. The ruling party, PDP is the largest political party in Africa and the Nigerian Television Authority is the largest television network. Nigeria has given birth to some of the most important African writers, such as Chinua Achebe and Wole Soyinka, whosee books have been bestsellers around the world. Chimamanda Ngozi Adichie is perhaps the most prominent young female author on the continent today. Most of the soap operas shown in English speaking Africa are produced either in South Africa or in Nigeria, in what has been dubbed "Nollywood." Also famous for its music (with the likes of Fela Kuti, Femi Kuti, and King Sunny Adé), Nigeria stands out as one of Africa's cultural powerhouses.

Nigeria can also claim to have the largest number of universities in Africa, but the educational system, from primary through university, is a shambles. For years, if not decades, universities have been easy recruiting grounds for the militant groups.

According to USAID, only 60% of those eligible are enrolled in primary school and nearly half of them eventually drop out before completing primary education; of those who complete sixth grade, only 40% are functionally literate. At Nigeria's once proud universities, the curriculum is outdated and sorely in need of updating, while facilities are in a state of rapid decay. The government's budgetary allocation for education has fallen steeply from 11.2% in 1999, to 1.83% in 2003. UNESCO recommends an allocation of 26% of a country's annual budget to education, but given competing priorities, there is no way the government will reach this level for years, if at all. (With a GDP of $200 billion in 2008, Nigeria is a classic example of the "paradox of poverty." Vast oil wealth has been translated into neither development nor improved living conditions for the bulk of its huge population. On the UN's *Human Development Index* for 2006, Nigeria ranked 159 out of 177 states, mostly due to its low literacy rates.)

The country's health statistics are worsened by events in northern Nigeria. There, obscurantist religion and politics collided with lethal impact in 2003. Claiming that polio vaccines were contaminated and may be responsible for the spread of AIDS, Muslim clerics in four northern states—Bauchi, Kano, Kaduna, and Zamfara—forced a halt in the World Health Organization's program to eliminate the crippling disease in Nigeria. WHO reported that 40% of new cases of polio in 2003 were in Nigeria; and by 2005 the agency had tracked cases directly traceable to the Nigerian strain of the virus in 16 countries—all the way to Indonesia.

In September 2003 Nigeria became the third African country (after South Africa and Algeria) to have a presence in outer space when a Nigerian satellite was launched from the Plesetsk Cosmodrome in Russia. The satellite is designed to survey deforestation and water resources where ground observation would be laborious and difficult. A second Nigerian satellite, this time Chinese-made and Chinese-launched, was sent into space in May 2007. It was expected to offer broadcasting, telecommunications and broadband Internet services for Africa. The project cost $311 million.

The Past: Political and Economic History

For early history, see *Historical Background* and *The Colonial Period: The British.*

In Nigeria's 1947 constitution, the British introduced a federal system of government that entrenched the dominant interests of the colony's three major regions: the northern and mainly Muslim Hausa and Fulanis, the predominantly Catholic Ibo in the east, and the Anglican and Muslim Yoruba in the west. When Nigeria became independent in 1960, regional differences were inevitable. Much of the nationalist agitation that culminated in independence came from southerners, better educated after longer contact with European missionaries and traders.

Balancing regional tensions is a recurring issue in Nigerian history and politics. When Nigeria became a federal republic in 1963, its president was the distinguished

**President Shehu Shagari
(from 1979 through 1983)**

nationalist, Nnamdi Azikiwe, an Ibo. The federal prime minister was a northerner, Sir Abubakar Tafewa Balewa. An initial harmony was entirely superficial. Elections in 1965 only exacerbated tensions and exposed deep-seated corruption within the system.

Resentment against northern domination of the federal system resulted in a bloody *coup d'état* in January 1966. It would be the first military intervention that would come to characterize Nigerian political life. Led by Major-General Johnson Aguiyi-Ironsi, an Ibo, the coup resulted in the brutal murder of the most prominent northern politicians, including Prime Minister Balewa and the Sarduana of Sokoto. Southerners, especially Ibos, who, because of their educational achievements had been employed and posted throughout Nigeria, became the object of bloody reprisals in the north. Ibo families fearing for their lives began a mass exodus to the eastern region.

General Ironsi was killed in a countercoup in July and was replaced by neither a northerner nor a southerner, but a man of the Middle Belt, Lieutenant-Colonel Yakubu Gowon. Conferences to settle the conflict were unproductive and with the leadership of Colonel Odumegwu Ojukwu, an Ibo, three eastern states seceded from the federation in 1967 to form the independent Republic of Biafra.

From 1967 to 1970 Nigeria was consumed by civil war. The world took note when images of starving Biafran children, their bellies swollen in starvation and their hair turned orange by Kwashiorkor—the Ghanaian word for protein deficiency—became nightly features on the televised news. The war ended abruptly in 1970 when Ojukwu fled and the Biafrans surrendered. Between half and two million people died during the war.

The early 1970s were dominated by efforts to rebuild the nation's economy, severely damaged by the war, and to reinte-

Nigeria

Northern Nigeria's ancient Muslim city of Kano at the edge of the Sahara   AP/Wide World Photo

grate the eastern region into the federal system. Some of this work was facilitated by the oil boom of the period. As a consequence of its oil production, Nigeria became one of Africa's wealthiest states, but in many ways, oil has been as much a curse as a boon.

As the country increased its dependence on petroleum, it suffered from price fluctuations—boom in the 1970s, bust in the early 1980s when the price of oil plummeted. Investments in the energy sector diverted money from the development of the agricultural sector, just as petroleum-related jobs drew thousands from their fields, resulting, in part, in the current food crisis in the countries surrounding Nigeria. As Nigeria has grown, the country has increasingly imported food from neighboring countries, rather than relying on its own agricultural sector. In addition, the vast income derived from oil only intensified regional discontent. Producing areas suffered environmental degradation and felt as though "their" resources were siphoned off to the central government,

from which they received few benefits. Oil income also encouraged lavish, often superfluous, construction projects and provided endless possibilities for corruption.

The construction of the new federal capital city at Abuja was a classic example of Nigerian corruption. By the mid-80s, half-completed government buildings and luxury hotels were everywhere, replete with poor quality design, workmanship and materials.

In 1975 General Gowon was overthrown and replaced by Brigadier Murtala Ramat Mohammed who began the process of moving the federal capital to Abuja. Caught in a Lagos traffic jam, Murtala was assassinated in a 1976 coup. His replacement, Lieutenant-General Olusegun Obasanjo, led the effort to introduce a new, American-style presidential constitution. Elections under the new constitution brought a northerner, Alhaji Shehu Shagari, to power in 1979.

Oil revenues, which peaked in 1980, provided prosperity that drew attention away from regional and ethnic tensions.

By 1983, an election year, income from oil had dropped by half. The government responded to popular pressures and expelled more than one million foreigners, mostly Ghanaians, saying they had overstayed their visas and were taking jobs from Nigerians. The act proved popular in Nigeria, and President Shagari was reelected in an election deeply flawed by irregularities.

Fraud, corruption, and waste under the civilian government were massive and economically debilitating. The military, disgusted with rampant corruption, took power under the leadership of General Ibrahim Babangida. After 25 years of turbulence and corruption, a wide variety of Nigerians—intellectuals, the press, businessmen and even former politicians—supported Babangida. The new government instituted military tribunals for officials suspected of corruption and offered public executions of violent criminals as proof of moral rigor.

General Babangida's government was under heavy external and internal pres-

126

A Nok Sculpture from Nigeria's earliest great civilization
Photo Courtesy Galerie al Farahnick, Brussels

sure to return power to civilians by the beginning of the 1990s. Suspicious of any proliferation of parties, Babangida decreed that there be only two. One, the Social Democratic Party, was to be "a little" to the left; the other, the National Republican Convention, was to be "a little" to the right. Such was the military mind at work, simplifying the complex and making choice easier.

Elections were held in June 1993, but were annulled when preliminary results showed victory by Chief Moshood Abiola, a super-rich Yoruba businessman who also happened to have good connections with some northern politicians. Soon thereafter President Babangida resigned from office, and Chief Ernest Shonekan was appointed head of the Interim National Government. The interim was brief. On November 17 Defense Minister Sani Abacha staged yet another coup. With Abacha, Nigeria entered one of its darkest periods.

Infinitely corrupt and sadistically brutal, Abacha flouted both civil and human rights, and violently suppressed any opposition. Political parties were outlawed, their candidates silenced, and labor strikes promptly abolished; state, local and federal government offices were seized. When Abiola proclaimed himself president in 1994, Abacha had him arrested and impris-

oned. The military government worked through local, traditional rulers to maintain control of Nigeria, particularly in the oil-producing regions. What was to become the model for ethnic mobilization in the Delta was founded in 1990 in Ogoniland by the Ogoni playwright Ken Saro-Wiwa. His Movement for the Survival of the Ogoni People (MOSOP) issued an Ogoni Bill of Rights that described local misery and posited a vision of Ogoni autonomy and self-determination—"political control of Ogoni affairs by Ogoni people"—and their right to control and use a fair proportion of Ogoni economic resources. It was, in short, a claim for Ogoni statehood made symbolically concrete in 1993 with an Ogoni national day—January 4—complete with Ogoni flag and anthem. In 1994 Saro-Wiwa and eight other activists decided to dramatize the regional inequalities from which their people suffered. Four traditional Ogoni leaders were gunned down, and the government charged Saro-Wiwa and his cohorts with the murders. A trial, held in secret, by a court selected by Abacha, followed. Death sentences for all nine men were inevitable, and despite international protest, they were carried out.

It was clear that General Abacha was planning to run for the Nigerian presidency later in 1998, but the Abacha era

came to an abrupt end in June when the dictator suddenly died. General Abdusalam Abubakar, chief of the defense staff, succeeded him as head of state and effected a transition to civilian rule. Political detainees were released, including General Obasanjo who had been detained since 1995 as a suspect in an anti-Abacha coup. Chief Abiola, in detention since 1994, suddenly collapsed on July 7. All efforts to save his life failed. His death eliminated a major problem for General Abubakar and facilitated the relatively smooth transition to civilian rule in May 1999.

Elections for a civilian government were organized and successfully carried out. Northern power brokers—the Kaduna mafia—agreed to a shift in power that would bring a southerner to the presidential office for the first time. For the presidency, two Yoruba opposed each other. Olu Falae, a former finance minister, was the standard bearer of the progressive Alliance for Democracy and the more conservative All People's Party (APP). Olusegun Obasanjo, the only military man actually to hand back the reins of government to civilians, represented the centrist People's Democratic Party (PDP). Obasanjo, who clearly had the backing of northern politicians and the army, won 62.8% of the vote to Falae's 37.2%. The PDP also won a clear majority in both houses of parliament.

President Obasanjo's first term was four years of crisis-to-crisis management. The return to democracy placed extraordinary demands on the government. Freed from 15 years of iron-fisted military rule, Nigerians erupted in what appeared at times a volcanic expression of grievance, com-

Former President Olusegun Obasanjo

Nigeria

Natural gas storage sphere, Escravos Project   Photo courtesty Chevron

plaint and demand, often descending into ethnic, regional or sectarian conflicts—most of which went back to the very origin and creation of the state.

At the heart of all current controversies are the nature and definition, if not the existence, of the Nigerian state: What should be the balance of resources and power between the central government and individual states?

Regional Tensions

Regional tensions persist in both north and south. In the south, crisis is centered in the Niger Delta area, source of Nigeria's wealth, but an area in which the processes of extracting that wealth have created an ecological hell. Since 1986, millions of barrels of oil have been spilled on the land and creeks of the Delta region, killing the soil and polluting the waters, depriving local inhabitants of their traditional means

of livelihood. For years, eight million cubic feet of natural gas flared daily, adding deadly illumination to the processes of extractive destruction.

Despite its generation of fabulous wealth, the Niger Delta area remains one of Nigeria's poorest and least developed regions. For residents, a welter of small-scale ethnic communities, there is a near total absence of schools, drinking water, electricity, and medical care. A crescendo of regional complaint has been raised, demanding a greater share of petroleum profits. The most intractable of demands came from young members of the Ijaw community, probably the fourth largest ethnic group in Nigeria.

On December 11, 1998, some 5,000 members of the Ijaw Youth Council (IJC) from the Delta region met in Kaiama, Bayelsa State, and passed what has become known as the Kaiama Declaration.

The declaration gave vent to their frustrations with the leadership of an older generation that had achieved so little in terms of communal and environmental improvement. "We are tired," the resolution said, "of gas flaring, oil spillages, [and] blowouts. . ." In many ways it amounted to a declaration of secession from a Federal Nigeria. The IJC declared that it ceased to recognize all decrees "enacted without our participation and consent."

The declaration went on to claim ownership of all natural resources found in Ijaw territory and demanded that the oil companies stop exploration and exploitation activities. Oil workers were given an ultimatum to vacate Ijaw land or face the consequences. The deadline for cessation of activities and withdrawal of personnel was set for December 30. Then, the declaration said, "Ijaw youths in all communities in all Ijaw clans in the Niger Delta will take steps to implement these resolutions. . ."

To ease tensions, the government agreed to implement a constitutional provision that allocates 13% of oil revenue to each oil-producing region. But the legislation creating a Niger Delta Development Commission (NDDC)—caught in a dispute between legislature and executive—was long delayed, and the basic question of whether the provision covered both offshore and onshore oil production proved difficult to resolve.

Funding of the NDDC remains controversial. By law, the federal government was to contribute 15% of its oil revenues, the state governments 10% of theirs, and oil-producing companies 3% of their budgets to the commission. Oil-producing states have refused to contribute, saying the federal legislature could not statutorily allocate monies constitutionally granted to the states, while both the federal government and companies have been slow to fulfill their allotments.

Ethnic violence, amounting to a virtual rebellion by militant Ijaw youth, surged, forcing oil companies like ChevronTexaco and Royal Dutch Shell to evacuate the region and the federal government to establish a heavy security presence in the regional center of Warri. Given the exclusivity of Ijaw demands, interethnic conflicts have increased as other communities have sought establish subnational identities and assert their claims on Delta resources. The entire area has increasingly become ungovernable, a fact underlined by the emergence of yet another claimant in early 2006—the Movement for the Emancipation of the Niger Delta (MEND).

Unlike previous incarnations of ethnic grievance, MEND seems not to claim nano-national identity and says it rejects secession from Nigeria; it claims to fight for greater regional autonomy and resource control. MEND brought a new level of sophistication to guerilla struggle in the Delta. Speed boats quickly attacked targets in rapid succession; radically improved firepower and combat training made the attacks lethally and destructively successful. MEND's highly mobile units kept both Shell's western-trained private security forces and elite Nigerian units off balance and unable to protect the company's production network. On April 19, 2006 MEND took its guerilla war directly to that security complex, detonating a car bomb at a military barracks in Port Harcourt. It was, said the group's statement claiming responsibility for the attack, "symbolic rather than strategic" and meant to warn "the Nigerian military, oil companies and those who are attempting to sell the birthright of the Niger Delta peoples for a bowl of porridge."

Guerrilla attacks on Delta oil production had already cut output by 550,000 barrels a day, driving oil prices to record highs. MEND promised no let up. "Our aim," it had earlier written, "is to totally destroy the capacity of the Nigerian government to export oil."

Faced with this assault on Nigeria's economy, President Obasanjo offered concessions. Greater employment opportunities for Delta youths in the oil sector, navy, and police were promised, as was a major development plan that involved a $1.8 billion highway through the region generating 20,000 new jobs.

The Ijaw National Council reiterated its claim that denial of Ijaw rights had forced their youths into armed action. Among other things, it demanded immediate demilitarization of the region. When elected IYC president in 2001, Asari, a founding member of the Ijaw Youth Council, changed the group's slogan to "Resource Control and Self Determination By Every Means Necessary." The strategy resulted in the creation of the NDPDF and a damaging guerrilla campaign against the government and oil companies.

For its part, MEND was even more categorical in its rejection of President Obasanjo's Delta Marshall plan. One MEND negotiator told Reuters that the struggle had gone "beyond just development." The inevitable MEND e-mail warned oil companies and workers to "leave while they can," promising to "resume attacks with greater devastation and no compassion on those who choose to disregard our warnings."

Sectarian Tensions

The Obasanjo government faced sectarian crisis after the governor of an obscure northern state decided to implement Sharia law for the state's Muslim population. Sharia imposes a variety of harsh and in many ways brutal punishments. At

independence Nigeria's legal system incorporated aspects of Islamic, Western and customary law. Customary law applied to land and marriage matters in parts of the Christian and animist south, for example, while Islamic law applied strictly to personal matters, not criminal matters in the north.

Under Sharia law some states have banned prostitution, gambling and the consumption of alcohol, while others have introduced single-sex schools and taxis. Sentences include death by stoning for adultery or sodomy, amputation of limbs for stealing, and public flogging for premarital sex or drinking alcohol in public. The introduction of Sharia as applied to criminal matters by the northern states—now some 12 in number—has resulted in destructive sectarian and communal riots in some areas and Sharia Law is an ongoing source of tension.

Nigeria's minister of justice has raised the issue to a constitutional level. In letters to the governors of the northern states that had adopted Muslim law, he described Sharia penalties as unconstitutional. "A Muslim," he wrote, "should not be subjected to a punishment more severe than would be imposed on other Nigerians for the same offense. Equality before the law means that Muslims should not be discriminated against."

President Obasanjo ran for reelection in April 2003, facing nominees from 20 political parties. In practical terms, his principal opponent was another retired general and former president, Muhammadu Buhari, nominated by the All Nigeria People's Party (ANPP), the renamed APP.

As the governing party, the People's Democratic Party (PDP) had significant advantages, and these advantages were reflected in election results. The PDP won majorities in both houses of parliament, the bulk of state governorships (27 out of 36), and its presidential candidate, Olusegun Obasanjo, roundly defeated the ANPP's Buhari—62% to 32%. Constitutionally limited to two terms, President Obasanjo initially worked to amend the constitution to permit a third term. The issue divided administration, party, and country; there was also considerable international pressure on the president to desist in his efforts. The third-term push ended in mid-May 2006 when the Nigerian senate, amid swirling accusations of hugely expensive vote-buying, voted down the proposed amendment.

Plateau State election billboard, 2007, illustrating the careful balance between Christian and Muslim candidates for governor and deputy governor ©David Hecht/IRIN

Nigeria

The ruling People's Democratic Party (PDP) nominated Umaru Musa Yar'Adua, the little-known governor of the impoverished northern state of Katsina personally chosen by President Obasanjo to be his successor. (His older brother, Shehu Yar' Adua, had served as Obasanjo's deputy during his time as military ruler.) Pious and somewhat reclusive, Yar'Adua's governorship was characterized by financial prudence and accountability. He is also one of the few Nigerian governors absolved of corruption by the country's anti-graft agency. As his running mate, Yar' Adua chose Goodluck Jonathan, the Ijaw governor of the Delta's oil-rich, and very corrupt, Bayelsa state. Jonathan had only recently become governor, having replaced Governor Diepreye Alamieyeseigha, who was held on fraud and corruption charges.

In a field of some 25 candidates, the only other nominee who had any meaningful chance at election was the former military ruler, Muhammadu Buhari, who was nominated by the All Nigeria People's Party (ANPP). To his credit, Buhari was known for his relatively successful war against corruption when in office. President Obasanjo's vice president, Atiku Abubakar, who had opposed the third-term amendment, bolted the PDP and secured the nomination of the Action Congress, largely composed of disgruntled former PDP members.

Unsurprisingly, the PDP won another victory in the elections in April 2007. Its well-run and well-funded electoral machine was superior to any other in Nigeria. Umaru Yar'Adua collected 24.6 million votes, 70% of those cast. His nearest rival received only 6.6 million, while former-vice president Atiku came in third with 2.6 million votes.

By every objective standard the election was hopelessly flawed. Ever discreet, former-Secretary of State Madeleine Albright said the process "failed the Nigerian people," and the International Republican Institute said it fell "below acceptable standards." Local election monitors called the voting a "charade."

After two years in office, the current administration has left much to be desired. Some of the worst fighting in decades has broken out between ethnic groups and the government over the mismanagement of oil. Yar'Adua has offered concessions, but none which satisfy the militants. Even during the election, Yar'Adua was flown out of the country for surgery, and lately, his missing appearances and sudden travels abroad seem to bear witness that his health is declining. Nigeria has a delicate power system, in which a sort of gentlemen's agreement alternates between the north and the south, in terms of where the president is from. If Yar'Adua, a Muslim northerner, was to leave his post, Goodluck Jonathan (vice president), a Christian Southerner would take over power, which could result in conflict.

The Present: Contemporary Issues

Nigeria's economy was radically transformed by the advent of oil production. From an agricultural economy, deriving 65% of foreign exchange earnings from food exports, Nigeria moved to become a major oil-exporting nation. The petroleum industry, centered on the Delta region of the Niger River, dominates Nigeria's economy. It accounts for nearly 95% of foreign exchange earnings, 80% of federal government revenues, and a whopping 50% to 55% of GDP.

Nigeria possesses 36.2 billion barrels of proven oil reserves—most of them along the Niger River Delta. In 2005 the country was pumping an average of 2.4 million barrels of crude oil a day. Royal Dutch Shell is the biggest company in the oil patch, accounting for nearly half of Nigeria's total oil production; other major players are the American firms Exxon-Mobil and ChevronTexaco, the Italian company ENI/Agip, and France's TotalFinaElf.

On Transparency International's *Corruption Perception Index* for 2006, Nigeria is just four steps from bottom-ranked Haiti. Pervasive corruption, coupled with colossal economic mismanagement and excessive dependence on oil, are largely responsible for the country's poor economic performance and appalling poverty. Some 66% of the population lives below the poverty line of a dollar a day, compared to only 43% in 1985.

Oil production has been regularly interrupted by local protest and ethnic violence in the Delta region. Sabotage, occupation of oil facilities, hostage taking and kidnapping are all employed by local activists, whose legitimate claims are increasingly drowned out by the violence with which they express their claims. Major oil firms like Chevron and Shell have been compelled to shut down their operations in the area. At the height of the troubles in 2003 Nigeria's oil exports were cut by 40% of normal production. Nigeria has lost billions in oil and gas revenues because of the continuing crisis in the Delta region.

Shell and other oil producers have also suffered staggering daily losses from organized thievery, or "bunkering," by lethally armed criminal networks. Illegal oil bunkering would appear to be Nigeria's most profitable private business. Estimates of daily losses vary widely. The governor of Delta state has said that thieves steal 300,000 barrels of Nigerian crude every day. Shell alone has reported losing 100,000 barrels a day. If one assumes a price of $15 to $20 a barrel—it is illegal after all—the thieves are earning between $2 million and $6 million daily. (With oil at nearly $70 a barrel on the world market, the thieves are truly making off like bandits.) Working with the tacit support of local and foreign business mafias, and abetted by powerful local military or political "godfathers," these criminal networks are important sources of funding for local militias and fueling the Delta's destabilizing arms race.

There are also huge environmental impacts from bunkering. In 2003 there were 582 recorded pipeline vandalizations. Most of these were puncturing to steal oil, but after puncturing the pipelines, the thieves leave them leaking. The resultant spills have damaged wetlands, forests, and farmlands; they are also linked to the deadly fires that occur when local villagers attempt to scoop up the leaked oil. Pipeline fires have claimed more than 2,000 lives. The destroyed land increases food prices in the whole region, causing hunger in neighboring countries as well.

Under-equipped and overwhelmed by the magnitude of bunkering, the government has stepped up patrols of the Niger Delta, aided by seven ships donated by the United States. Royal Dutch Shell, which suffers so much from illegal bunkering, has proposed a system of chemical analysis that would let investigators determine the country of origin of any oil suspected of being stolen. All of this may be too little, too late. The criminalization of Nigeria's oil industry may have transcended the state's capacity to control its most important resource.

China has begun to stake its claims on Nigeria's oil wealth. Shortly before President Hu Jintao's April 2006 visit, China National Offshore Oil Corp (CNOOC), confirmed it had signed a $2.7 billion deal to buy a 45% share of a Nigerian offshore oil field. It was the company's biggest overseas purchase to date. The purchase, Akpo field, now pumps 225,000 barrels a day. At the conclusion of President Hu's visit, it was announced that China would invest some $4 billion in oil and infrastructure projects. Included would be a controlling interest in the 110,000 bbl/d oil refinery at Kaduna and commitments for railroad and power station construction. MEND quickly responded with violence, promising punishing attacks against the Chinese if they entered. As of now, little has been made of that threat.

Nigeria is moving to diversify and decrease its dependence on oil. Natural gas, closely associated with oil, will ultimately replace it as the backbone of Nigeria's economy. The move to gas production comes from the government's desire to curb flaring, the simple burning off of gas associated with oil drilling and pumping. Seventy-five per cent of all associated gas is currently flared, making Nigeria one of the world's worst heat polluters. Most flaring has been eliminated, and using selling the natural gas now brings Nigeria more than 10m dollars in revenues every day.

Gas production in Nigeria faces the same problems of order and stability as the oil industry. Only 30% of Nigeria's gas reserves are offshore. Another 30% are in swamplands, and the rest are on dry land where production is vulnerable to escalating violence.

Nigeria remains an important hub in the international illicit drug trade. Drug traffickers have a preference for repatriation of their profits, and the consequence of this has been the growth of elaborate money-laundering schemes. These are so extensive that the American Secret Service maintains a separate Nigerian fraud squad in metropolitan Washington.

The Future

Nigeria is precariously poised on a knife's edge. On the one hand, the country has managed an improbable run of relatively democratic elections. On the other, regional and sectarian tensions—between north and south, Christian and Muslim—have stretched the national fabric dangerously. Apart from conflicts over *sharia* law, the country witnesses titanic amounts of corruption and a reputation for poor governance. Yar'Adua, has failed to bring about much needed change in government institutions, though his presidency has witnessed some successes. Yar'Adua's seemingly poor health poses a threat to the relative calm the country enjoys at this time.

The economy also gives reason for worry. While recent oil price surges should benefit Nigeria, the country is infamous for failing to parlay its windfalls into productive investment. The oil-producing regions of Nigeria have not reversed their long decline, and conflicts around production of the commodity seem to worsen with each passing year. Nigeria's growth is thus misleading. Industrial and agricultural development will need to stabilize to complement the boon from extractive resources.

Feeding livestock in a Nigerian village

The Republic of Senegal

Presidential palace

Basic Facts

Area: 196,840 sq. km. = 76,000 sq. mi. (about the size of Nebraska)

Population: 12,400,000 (UN 2007 est.)

Capital City: Dakar

Climate: Warm and dry in the north; warmer and more humid in the south, with usually a wet season (July–October) and a dry season (November–June).

Neighboring Countries: The Gambia is a finger-like projection extending eastward from the Atlantic coast to the interior; Mauritania (north); Mali (east); Guinea-Bissau, Guinea (south).

Official Language: French

Other Principal Languages: Over 30. Prominently: Bambara, Pulaar (Peul), Diola (Jola), Malinké, Serere, Soninké, and Wolof, spoken by about 75% of the population.

Ethnic Groups: Wolof 43%, Peul 24%, Serer 15%, Diola 4%, Mandinka 3%, Soninké 1%, European and Lebanese 1%, other 9%

Principal Religions: Muslim 92%, indigenous beliefs 6%, Christian 2% (mostly Roman Catholic)

Chief Commercial Products: Fish, ground nuts (peanuts), petroleum products, phosphates, and cotton

GNI Per Capita: $710 (World Bank 2006 est.)

Currency: CFA franc

Former Colonial Status: French Colony, a part of French West Africa (1895–1960). French commercial interests were active in Senegal prior to the formation of French West Africa.

Independence Date: June 20, 1960

Chief of State: Abdoulaye Wade, President (since March 2000)

National Flag: Three vertical stripes of green, yellow and red, with a green star on the middle yellow stripe.

Land and People

The Republic of Senegal, the westernmost portion of Africa, lies in a transitional zone between the steaming jungles of the Gold-Ivory Coast to the south and the endless, dry Sahara to the north. Its unique position has made it a true "crossroads" of the world—between Europe and Latin America, the United States and the Near and Far East, and finally, between South Africa and the European and American continents.

It is a flat, rolling plains country with characteristic grasslands and low tree vegetation. In the southwest there is a small area of jungle and the coastline is often marsh or swampland. There are no high mountains in Senegal, but there are four large rivers flowing in parallel courses from east to west. These rivers are navigable to a substantial distance inland from the Atlantic, particularly during the wet season.

The strong winds from the Sahara usher in the traditional dry season each November. This wind of dry months, called the *harmattan* by the people, occasionally rises to almost torrential velocity, producing severe dust and sandstorms. All too frequently, the wind is year-round, creating severe drought problems and intrusion of the Sahara at the rate of about four miles per year.

Dakar, the busy seaport and capital of Senegal, has been a pole of attraction for visitors the world over. The city has grown by leaps and bounds, however, and its beauty has been marred by the problems of urban congestion. With more than three million inhabitants Dakar can boast cyber cafés throughout the city, but its transportation system is paralyzed by

132

rush hour gridlock. Massive investment is underway to improve the traffic flow. Dakar's buses are known for air pollution, and the older models are being phased out for newer vehicles. Rubbish collection, too, tests the patience of those living in the capital, and the government struggles to keep up.

Wielding great influence in this Muslim nation are the Sufi orders, or "brotherhoods," which characterize Senegal's Islamic culture. The orders—two major ones and several smaller—are hierarchically organized around several religious lineages. Disciples are organized into associations and owe both loyalty and labor to their *marabouts* (pronounced *mara boos*) or spiritual guides.

The most numerous of these is the *Tijaniyya* order, divided into several branches. Smaller but more cohesive is the *Mouride (Moo*-reed) order, which owns the largest peanut plantations and is generally considered the most influential. Each has its own spiritual leader, or *Caliph General* (pronounced *Khalif*). The authority of this high office is transmitted through family dynasties that formed after the deaths of the orders' founders.

With a rich and vital cultural life, Senegal is famed for its writers, filmmakers and musicians. Senegal's founding president, the poet and philosopher Léopold Senghor, died in December 2001 at the age of 95. Along with Aimé Césaire of Martinique and Léon G. Damas of French Guyana, Senghor was one of the originators in the 1930s and 1940s of the concept of *Négritude*, a notion celebrating the authenticity of African values and the contribution they make to what he called the "civilization of the universal."

In 1984 the poet was elected to membership in the *Académie française*, France's most prestigious cultural society. Founded in 1635 by Cardinal Richelieu, the French

**Senegal's first president, Hon.
Léopold Sédar Senghor**

Academy is limited in membership to 40 members, known as the 40 immortals. Senghor was its first black member.

The Past: Political and Economic History

For early history, see *Historical Background, The Colonial Period: The French.*

With the creation of France's Fourth Republic, Senegal's two socialist deputies, Lamine Guèye and Léopold Sédar Senghor, worked to restore and extend these rights of full French citizenship. Senghor, a brilliant student who achieved the highest academic degrees in the French language, taught the language in French lycées and was essentially the grammarian responsible for the language of the Fourth Republic's constitution, led Senegal to complete independence in 1960. Senghor (b. 1906) dominated Senegalese politics for the first two decades of the country's independent existence. An internationally proclaimed poet, Senghor combined a humanist orientation with refined political skills. A Roman Catholic in an overwhelmingly Muslim country, he collaborated with the grand *marabouts*, leaders of Senegal's major Islamic brotherhoods, and maintained close ties with the former colonial ruler, France. A Serer, he led a predominantly Wolof nation. Under his leadership Senegal developed a more tolerant and pluralist state than most other African states.

In the early period, his Progressive Senegalese Union (UPS) ruled as a single dominant party, but in 1976 Senghor authorized opposition parties. Despite greater political openness, the additional parties had little electoral success; President Senghor was overwhelmingly reelected in 1978 to another five-year term.

In perhaps the most orderly transfer of power seen to that point in Africa, the aging president resigned his office on December 31, 1980, and turned it over to his able prime minister, Abdou Diouf, who completed his predecessor's term of office. In February 1983 President Diouf rolled up an impressive victory in democratic elections; both he and the Socialist Party (PS) received more than 80% of the vote. Seven other parties competed in the contest.

Opposition to the Diouf administration centered around Abdoulaye Wade's Senegalese Democratic Party (PDS), the principal opposition party in the 1983 and 1988 elections. President Diouf won handily in both contests, and after brief but bitter opposition following the 1988 elections, Wade and three other opposition leaders joined the socialists in a coalition government; this lasted until 1992 when they resigned, complaining they had been influential on only trivial issues.

President Abdoulaye Wade

The resignation allowed Wade to compete in early 1993 elections free of administrative ties, but because the opposition remained deeply divided, Diouf and the PS continued to dominate Senegalese political life.

Presidential elections in February 2000 featured eight candidates, but only four had any reasonable expectations of electoral success. The two principal candidates were familiar opponents. President Diouf was the standard bearer of the PS and the longtime opposition leader Abdoulaye Wade represented the *Parti Démocratique Sénégalais* (PDS).

After 40 years in power, the PS had become increasingly dysfunctional as a political family. Two PS defectors, both onetime party heavyweights, entered strong candidacies, made stronger by their ability to criticize Diouf and the PS from inside knowledge. Djibo Leity Kâ, representing the Union for Democratic Renewal (URD), had been part of the PS leadership until he lost favor in 1998. Moustapha Niasse, a former foreign minister, enjoyed an international reputation and access to considerable campaign financing.

At 73 years of age, Abdoulaye Wade was the grand old man of Senegalese opposition, but the darling of the young. His campaign stops drew enthusiastic crowds. Change was in the air and "*Sopi*," the Wolof word for change, was the chant of the crowds. If elected, he promised, he would organize a referendum to dissolve the national assembly and change the constitution.

Change, indeed, was what the Senegalese voters wanted. With a host of international observers watching, the usual mechanisms of electoral manipulation were put aside. Dramatically, President Diouf failed to obtain a majority in the first round of voting. In the runoff, Wade won 58.5% of the vote. Diouf graciously admitted defeat and announced his retirement from politics. (He is now the secretary-

Senegal

general of La Francophonie, largely the international organization of former French colonies and protectorates, basically equivalent to the Commonwealth.)

President Wade quickly drafted a new, more democratic constitution. Among a number of important changes, presidential terms were reduced to five years from seven. The Senate, an ineffective retirement home for faded PS politicians, was abolished and the National Assembly reduced from 140 members to 120. The president was granted the right to dissolve the Assembly (dominated by the PS) after two years of existence. The right to form opposition parties was entrenched; the prime minister's duties were enhanced and the judiciary given more independence. For the first time women were given equal property rights with men.

In early January 2001, 94% of Senegalese approved the new constitution. Elections to choose the members of the new National Assembly were held at the end of April, and a coalition of 40 pro-Wade parties calling itself "Sopi" swept the field, winning 90 of 120 seats. The landslide victory gave President Wade a free hand to effect the changes his constituents demanded.

The victory also highlighted the fragile nature of Wade's coalition. Relations between President Wade and Moustapha

The Khalif of the Mourides

The Khalif of the Tijanis

Niasse, his first premier, had already deteriorated. In the April 2001 legislative elections, Niasse's Alliance of Progressive Forces (APF) campaigned independently, won 11 seats—just ahead of the former ruling *Parti Socialiste*—and became the official opposition.

On September 26, 2002 Senegal experienced great national tragedy when the Joola, a ferryboat run by the Senegalese military and carrying three times as many passengers as allowed, capsized in the Atlantic off the coast of The Gambia while making its way from Zinguinchor to Dakar. The tragedy came just ahead of the end of school holidays, and many of those who drowned were the best and brightest of Casamance's students returning to their academic work in the capital. In the final assessment, 1,863 died—more than the Titanic; only 64 were rescued. The vast majority of them were from Zinguinchor, the regional capital—a terrible toll for a sleepy county seat of only 200,000 people: In Casamance they still speak of a "lost generation."

The Joola sinking also took a political toll. Both the transportation and armed forces ministers resigned, and the country's navy chief was fired. After her initial dismissal of government responsibility for the accident, Prime Minister Mame Madior Boye was also replaced by President Wade. Her cabinet was dissolved and the president appointed a new premier—Idrissa Seck, a close aide of the president who had a strong background in both business and politics.

Prime Minister Seck, who had been instrumental in Wade's electoral success, also ran into difficulties with the chief executive, reportedly over the inclusion of Djibo Leity Kâ, a key opposition figure, in the cabinet. Wade fired the man he called his "son" in April 2004, after Seck had served less than 18 months. Initially accused and questioned about excess spending in a local construction scandal, Seck was later charged with endangering state security. Supporters took to the streets shouting "Idy for President" and had to be dispersed with tear gas. By August, the well-oiled machinery of political repression began to operate. Seck was expelled from the PDS and parliament voted to try him before a special court. Jurists seemed not to want to play their part however. In February 2006 an investigating panel of the Senegalese high court ordered his release and the most serious charges dropped. Seck had spent more than seven months in jail.

To replace Seck, President Wade appointed Macky Sall as prime minister—his fourth since 2000. Sall had earlier served as both minister of mines and interior minister and, apparently less threatening to the president, has managed to

serve longer than any of his predecessors in the office of prime minister.

In October 2005, Senegal reestablished diplomatic relations with the People's Republic of China, "suspended" when it recognized Taiwan in early 1996. In renewing ties with mainland China, Senegal recognized it as the sole representative of the Chinese people and Taiwan as an integral part of the Peoples' Republic. In return, the People's Republic offered development munificence.

New Sino-Senegalese cooperative projects will include road building and the renovation of 11 regional sports stadia. Somewhat more grandiose is construction of the biggest theater in West Africa, seating 18,000 and providing parking for 3,000 cars. The price tag: $35 million.

At eighty years of age, astonishingly vital and still charismatic to his followers, Abdoulaye Wade ran for a second term of office in February 2007. There was much talk of unity within the opposition, but rhetoric did little to restrain political ambitions. Sensing weakness, 14 other candidates submitted papers to campaign for the presidency. The most serious of them were Moustapha Niasse and Idrissa Seck, Wade's former prime ministers; Abdoulaye Bathily, head of the leftwing Democratic League/Movement for the Labor Party, Ousmane Tanor Dieng, who had succeeded Abdou Diouf as the leader of the Socialist Party (PS), and his arch-rival within the PS, Robert Sagna. Significantly, Sagna was mayor of Ziguinchor and had severely criticized Wade's efforts to resolve the Casamance rebellion as "amateurish."

There was much else to criticize in President Wade's seven-year tenure. A marked predilection for *grands travaux*—large-scale public works projects—and grandiose promises (including new highways, tunnels, and a new international airport) have been slow to materialized, though construction is underway. For many there was disillusionment that promises of "sopi" had never arrived. The most damning indictment of Wade's seven years was the flight of young Senegalese men who braved the horrors of rickety fishing boats on the open seas to seek opportunity elsewhere.

Despite a relatively dismal economic record, however, Wade prevailed against a badly divided opposition. When the ballot tabulation was completed, the outgoing president had received 55.9% of the votes. No runoff election would be needed, and the opposition, which had counted on the election going two rounds, could only explain its miscalculation and loss by claiming electoral fraud. ECOWAS election observers disagreed, calling the polling "free and fair." Some 70% of all registered voters participated, a new record for Senegalese elections.

Waiting for the evening catch

Following the defeat, the principal opposition parties announced they would not participate in legislative elections scheduled for June 2007. Voters would be choosing deputies to sit in an enlarged National Assembly; its size had been increased in November 2006 from 120 members to 150. Sixty members of the new assembly would be elected proportionally, from national lists; the remaining 90 would be chosen in single-member districts. In the off-year election with no presidential competition at the top of the ballot, only 38% of the electorate participated.

Local elections in 2009 told a different story, and represented the first major electoral setback for Wade's government. A new opposition coalition called *Benno Siggil Senegaal* (United to Boost Senegal in Wolof, the national *lingua franca*) claimed several large cities, including the big prize, Dakar. Widely interpreted as a referendum on the government's popularity several years out from the 2012 presidential elections, the local elections give a preliminary sign the electorate is seeking further *alternance* after a decade of Sopi and the PDS. While the local elections are not as consequential as national results, the government's relatively statesmanlike acceptance of the defeat bodes well for continued democratic practice.

Casamance

The Movement of Democratic Forces of Casamance (MFDC) has been intermittently fighting some 20 years for the region's independence. Located south of The Gambia, the province has long thought of itself as exploited, virtually colonized by northerners. Unlike most north/south conflicts in Africa, the struggle in Casamance does not pit an Islamic north against an animist south because most of the region's people are Muslims,

including a slight majority of the dominant ethnic group, the Diola. Instead, the conflict is economic.

Casamance produces peanuts, like the rest of Senegal, but also has rich fishing grounds off its coast and has over the years become a tourist mecca for Europeans. It produces cotton for northern factories, and its forests provide charcoal for Dakar. Coastal waters hold the promise of petroleum yet to be found. Despite the region's wealth, however, Casamançais have seen few benefits. They question where the money has gone and deplore the degradation of the region's resources. For them, Dakar represents "northern domination" and "Senegalese neocolonialism."

Industrialized fishing fleets are depleting coastal waters, and forests are shrinking rapidly. They note that traditional rice cultivation, based on natural inundation, was destroyed by the importation of cheap foreign rice. At the same time they point out huge investments in the north to create a rice industry based on much more expensive damming and irrigation. Insufficient development of roads has hampered the marketing of local fruits and vegetables; Casamançais oranges and mangos rot on the ground. Currently, one of the most productive crops is *yamba*, the local name of cannabis. Driven by a huge demand in Dakar, *yamba* has become one of the principal sources for rebel financing; dismantling criminal gangs involved in the *yamba* trade will be one of the major tasks facing the government following any peace agreement.

One factor complicating settlement over the years has been the factional division of the MFDC. The movement's historic leader, Abbé Augustin Diamacoune Senghor, long held a moral authority that kept the group cohesive, but over the years, that authority eroded and Diamacoune's control diminished. Others, more militant, like Sidi Badji, founder of the movement's armed wing, rose to contest Diamacoune. Following the death of Sidi Badji in May 2003, the hard-line dissident faction, now led by Salif Sadio, continued to disrupt the area from villages and bases it controlled in Guinea-Bissau and refused to recognize a peace accord signed by Abbé Diamacoune in December 2004. The accord, representing the pragmatic elements within the movement, renounced armed struggle and agreed to open "serious negotiation" with the government.

In mid-March 2006 the Sadio faction, now little more than armed bandits, engaged in firefights with a rival faction, disrupted the area's cashew harvest, and displacing thousands. The Guinea-Bissau army intervened and by mid-April had destroyed the rebels' primary base of operations, driving them north to the Gambian

border. There Sadio managed to find a new patron for his depredations, Gambia's president, Yahya Jammeh. Jammeh has reportedly introduced Sadio to Libya's "Guide," Moamer al-Qadhafi. This may explain why Salif Sadio, the most radical of the MFDC factional leaders, now also seems to be the best financed and armed among them. The death of Abbé Diamacoune in January 2007 removes from the scene an important tempering and unifying element and increases the likelihood of conflict among MFDC factions and continuing disruption of Casamance.

The Present: Contemporary Issues

Senegal's economy has been dependent upon the production of peanuts for the past three decades; production now exceeds well over one million metric tons a year, made possible by improved methods of cultivation and development of plantations to replace smaller farms. Though surpassed by other exports in terms revenue, groundnuts (as peanuts are referred to outside the U.S.) remain the most important source of employment in Senegal. Forty percent of cultivated land is now used for peanut production. Overall the agricultural sector represents only 17% of Senegal's GDP, but employs 70% of the country's work force.

Under pressure from the IMF, Senegal has engaged in difficult structural reforms to improve economic performance. Until 1994, Senegal's performance was mediocre, but since the devaluation of the CFA Franc in 1994 and adherence to vigorous structural reform programs, economic growth improved, averaging about 5.3% from 1996 to 2000.

When he was elected in 2000, President Wade set out to create annual growth rates of 7% or more, but though there is improvement, economic growth has not been spectacular. In 2004 and 2005, according to World Bank figures, growth was 6.2%. With an annual population growth rate of 2.4%, however, Senegal needs to achieve GDP growth of 8% just to keep pace with demographic increases.

Rice is Senegal's favorite food. The Senegalese eat their way through some 900,000 tons of it every year, but only produce 200,000 tons locally. Rice imports cost a staggering $110 million—about 2.2% of the country's GDP. To reduce rice imports President Wade is trying to persuade his countrymen to eat maize, a grain with more protein than rice that can be grown more widely.

Since the CFA devaluation in 1994, fishing has become Senegal's principal revenue earner. Nutrient-rich cold waters off the Senegalese coast have made an extremely rich fishing area, but since the arrival of foreign trawlers, particularly from

Senegal

the EU, fish stocks have crashed. Several hundred trawlers from Spain, the Netherlands, Portugal and other EU nations have badly over-fished the area. In 1998 Dakar official began to imposed rest periods—temporary fishing bans—on threatened species to help rebuild stocks. Certain types of nets were also banned. Senegal's agreement with the EU expired in 2001, and faced with Morocco's refusal to renew its agreement, the EU pressured Senegal to increase fishing quotas by an unconscionable 61%. Senegalese fisherman point to the EU agreement as the principal source of their collapsing activity. They simply cannot compete with huge European trawlers. Increasingly their tiny craft have been used to transport the desperately poor who flee the country seeking economic opportunity in Europe.

After conceding the critical nature of the situation, the government created a five-year action plan on fishing and aquaculture—fish farming. Costing around $36 million, the plan is designed to produce some 100,000 to 110,000 tons of farmed fish in some 7,500 basins around the country. The UN Food and Agriculture Organization is training 3,000 experts in fish farming to assure successful operation of the farms. The plan runs through 2010.

In the past few years Senegal's tourism sector has developed strongly and has become the second most important earner of foreign exchange after fish. Its touristic resources—miles of beautiful beaches, a rich culture, and important historical sites like St. Louis and the island of Gorée—remain relatively underexploited.

The government would like to reorient the tourist industry to higher-end traffic, which would entail banishing the backpacking tourist. The advantage: it estimates tourist receipts would double without doubling the number of visitors. In 2002 the government set a goal of 1.5 million annual tourists by 2010, and 2.5 million by 2015. In 2005 the country received 350,000 visitors.

Not richly endowed with natural resources, Senegal is making slow progress in developing those that do exist. Mittal Steel announced a $2.2 billion mining investment in February 2007 (shortly before the presidential election). The project involves exploitation of iron reserves, estimated at 750 million tons, in the Faleme region. To evacuate the ore, a railroad will be constructed; to ship it to Mittal refineries in Europe a new port near Dakar will have to be constructed. The company hopes to begin production at the site in 2011.

A number of independent oil companies have shown interest in Senegal's offshore prospects. ROC (Australia) has invested heavily in three blocks known as the Casamance blocks. The concession covers over 8,000 sq. km. and lies north of two oil discoveries made by Houston-based Vanco oil company. Until commercially viable discoveries are made and begin pumping, however, Senegal remains a country without major natural resources.

Basic social statistics reveal the magnitude of the challenges facing the government. Per capita income is $710 and life expectancy at birth is 56 years. The adult literacy rate for men is only 48.1% of those over the age of 15; for women, the figure is a mere 28.7% The fertility rate (births per woman) is five, but infant mortality is 80 per 1,000 births; 137 out of 1,000 children will die by the age of five (2004). In 2000 the country slipped into the category of Least Developed Countries. It ranks 156 out of 177 on the UN's *Human Development Index* for 2006.

The government's biggest economic concern is unemployment. Every year an additional 100,000 young people leave school and enter the job market, but with a lackluster economy, they find no jobs. Many spend their time standing in line for a visa at the Embassies of France, the United States or Italy. Others join the growing exodus of Africans and Asians seeking to reach Europe.

Senegal is a springboard for illegal migration. They board open fishing boats and head for the nearest European footfall—the Spanish-owned Canary Islands, some 930 miles off the southern coast. The International Organization for Migration estimated that 27,000 migrants journeyed by boat to the Canaries in 2006. Spanish authorities estimated that another 500 died at sea.

The Future

The election of Abdoulaye Wade raised expectations of better days ahead for Senegal, now that the sclerotic PS has left power. While some economic progress has been made, development is slow, and Wade's government is witnessing some voter dissatisfaction in turn. The Senegalese economy is growing, but at a measured pace, and citizens are challenged by the increasing costs of food and fuel. With debt relief having helped the country immensely, there is little risk of economic collapse; by the same token, there is little expectation of dramatic achievements. The economy will continue to be helped by foreign assistance, which flows into Senegal by virtue of its stability (at least outside the Casamance) and relatively positive track record in governance.

Politically, the country remains one of Africa's most democratic states, a reputation it has earned over the course of several decades (even when political liberalism was quite circumscribed). The government's defeat in local elections in Dakar and other cities in 2009 may be the first sign of another prospective alternation of power in 2012. Such an alternation, if it occurred, would only confirm Senegal's democratic credentials by virtue of a second governmental turnover. While there is an occasional hint of an authoritarian streak in the Wade regime, abuses are quite limited. Most disagreements over policy are limited to what would be found in other imperfect (yet solid) democracies.

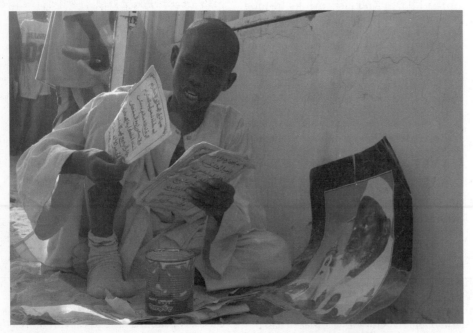

A young Mouride prays before a photo of his Khalif at Touba, Senegal

©IRIN

The Republic of Sierra Leone (pronounced See-*air*-uh Lee-*own*)

Panoramic View of Freetown

Basic Facts

Area: 72,326 sq. km. = 27,900 sq. mi. (slightly larger than West Virginia)
Population: 5,900,000 (UN 2007 est.)
Capital City: Freetown
Climate: Equatorial, very warm and humid.
Neighboring Countries: Guinea (north and northwest); Liberia (southeast)

Official Language: English (regular use limited to literate minority)
Other Principal Languages: Mende (principal vernacular in the south), Temne (principal vernacular in the north), Krio (English-based Creole, a lingua franca and a first language for 10% of the population but understood by 95%).
Ethnic groups: 20 native African tribes 90% (Temne 30%, Mende 30%, other 30%), Creole 10% (descendants of freed Jamaican slaves who were settled in the Freetown area in the late 18th century, refugees from Liberia's recent civil war), small numbers of Europeans, Lebanese, Pakistanis, and Indians.
Principal Religions: Muslim 60%, indigenous beliefs 30%, Christian 10%
Chief Commercial Products: Diamonds, rutile, cocoa, coffee, and fish
GNI Per Capita: $220 (World Bank 2006 est.)
Currency: Leone
Former Colonial Status: British Colony (1808–1961)
Independence Date: April 19, 1961
Chief of State: Ernest Bai Koroma, President (since September 7, 2007)
National Flag: Three equal horizontal stripes of green, white and blue.

Land and People

Sierra Leone lies on the west coast of Africa that extends westward into the Atlantic above the equator. Its climate is almost identical with that of the Congo River basin to the southeast—hot, rainy and oppressively humid. The Freetown area along the seacoast receives 150 inches of rain each year, and the relative humidity seldom drops below 80%. The coastal belt, averaging 60 miles in width, is a region of dense mangrove swamps quite similar to the Florida Everglades.

Stretches of wooded hill country rise from the coastal belt to gently rolling plateaus in the north. Mountains tower to heights of 6,000 feet in the southeast area near the Moa River. Although there is a nominally dry season from November to April, heavy rains, especially in July, August and September, contribute to the dense, jungle growth characteristic of portions of Sierra Leone.

The population is made up of some 18 different ethnic groups, each exhibiting similar cultural features. These include governmental systems based on chieftaincies and patrilineal descent, secret societies, and subsistence agriculture. The Mende, found in the east and south, and

Sierra Leone

the Temne, in the north, are the two largest groups and constitute about 60% of the population. Creoles, descendants of freed blacks who arrived in the 19th century, live mainly in Freetown and the western region. There has been much intermarriage between groups and 11 years of civil war displaced massive numbers of people from their traditional home areas.

Paramount chiefs are the traditional rulers of Sierra Leone, especially in the provincial areas. There are 149 paramount chieftaincies in the country and 63 of the incumbents died during the 11-year civil war. Elections to replace them were held in early 2003. In 13 of the districts there were strong protests and threats of violence where the elections had been politicized. In each, the SLPP was accused of selecting candidates who were party supporters rather than representatives of the traditional ruling houses.

The Past: Political and Economic History

For early history, see *Historical Background* and *The Colonial Period: The British.*

World War II gave rise to much nationalist ferment in West Africa, and following the war Britain began the process that would lead to independence. The privileged status of Sierra Leone's Creole elite was not entrenched. In the constitution of 1951, the notion of majority rule, which privileged hinterland peoples, prevailed. The first government elected under it was led by Milton Margai of the Sierra Leone People's Party (SLPP)—basically a Mende-dominated protectorate party.

Following independence in 1961, the parliamentary government was controlled by the SLPP, led initially by Sir Milton and, after his death in 1964, by his brother, Sir Albert Margai. Elections held in 1967 were hotly contested by a rival party, the All People's Congress (APC), led by Siaka Stevens. Favored by Coastal Creoles, the APC was initially a coalition party of Temnes, Creoles, and Limbas brought together by Stevens to counter the strength of the Mende-dominated SLPP. A pre-election attempt of Margai to outlaw the APC failed. Early returns indicated that the APC had captured 32 seats in the parliament to 28 for the SLPP. Governor General Sir Henry Josiah Lightfoot Boston (a Creole) quickly gave the oath of office to Siaka Stevens, making him prime minister. The military arrested both Stevens and Boston ten minutes later.

A National Reformation Council, established by the officers, continued in power until April 1968, when privates and non-commissioned officers mutinied, imprisoned their officers, and restored parliamentary rule under Stevens and the APC. He ruled with increasing repression, using the army to subdue hinterland supporters of the SLPP. In 1971 he declared Sierra Leone a republic, turned his back on Britain, and set about to consolidate his authority even further. In 1978 he proposed a constitutional referendum to create a single-party state, something he claimed was more authentically African, and generated a huge majority—97.1%—in its favor. When sworn in for a seven-year term under the new constitution he rejoiced in the voters' rejection of "... the worn-out, multiparty (system) ... inherited from our colonial master, Britain."

Much of Sierra Leone's current civil strife began during Siaka Stevens' repressive single-party rule. The notorious Internal Security Unit—groups of unemployed urban youth, fed with drugs and promises of employment—was used to terrorize and intimidate regime opponents. Corruption was institutionalized as Stevens and his cronies looted state resources. The economy declined; the tax base virtually disappeared, and what remained of the economy went underground. The state's ability to supply services collapsed. Rural Sierra Leone was increasingly isolated from the capital (the railroad linking Freetown to the hinterland was dismantled in the 1970s and no roads replaced it) and spiraled into abject poverty.

As his term of office was drawing to an end in 1985, the elderly Stevens designated Army Chief Maj. General Joseph Momoh his successor. Weak and easily manipulated by Stevens, Momoh was expected to protect his extensive business interests.

Faced with the economic chaos that was Stevens' legacy, President Momoh turned to international lenders. Austerity measures insisted on by the IMF lowered the standard of living and raised social tensions. Subsidies of rice and fuel were gradually reduced while anger increased. Government corruption became pathological. When workers were forced to appear personally to pick up their pay in cash, it turned out that 75% of those listed as employees didn't exist.

A rebel insurgency led by Foday Sankoh, aided by Moamer al-Qadhafi and Charles Taylor's National Patriotic Front of Liberia, broke out in 1991. It found willing recruits in the communities of southeastern Sierra Leone that had suffered much from the corruption of the APC regime. Increasingly Momoh had no control over corruption, government, or insurgency. His poor prosecution of the war against Sankoh's Revolutionary United Front (RUF) and failure to support his troops in that effort led junior officers, under Captain Valentine Strasser, to take power in April 1992.

Captain Valentine Strasser

Under Strasser, then 26 years old, the National Provisional Ruling Council (NPRC) had some initial successes. The educational system worked for the first time in years, and teachers were paid on time. Clinics were stocked with medicines and there was a national cleaning day every Saturday to scrub up local communities. Youth took to the streets and picked litter, cleaned out gutters and drains and beautified walls with painted murals. Strasser's own profligate spending roused resentment among the troops, however. Things soon began to spiral out of control as senior officers lost control of their troops: being a soldier became a license to murder and steal. Strasser was finally replaced in a palace coup by an army colleague, Brigadier Julius Bio, on January 16, 1996.

Faced with continuing economic and political instability, Bio agreed to hold elections to restore civilian rule. As testimony to Sierra Leone's fragmented political culture, 13 parties competed and six managed to elect members to the House of Representatives. The largest number of seats, 27, went to the SLPP, followed by 17 seats for the United National People's Party (UNPP).

The SLPP's Ahmad Tejan Kabbah and the UNPP's John Karefa-Smart topped the field of ten presidential contenders, and in the runoff election Kabbah was declared the victor with 59.5% of the vote. A former UN official, he slowly built confidence in his leadership and in late 1996 the RUF agreed to discontinue its rebellion and surrender all arms. A promising beginning ended abruptly in May 1997 when army enlisted men revolted over unpaid wages, threatened cutbacks in their rice rations, and possible reductions in force. President Kabbah fled his capital and the rebellious troops installed Johnny Paul Koroma, a major who had been jailed for treason, as head of an Armed Forces

Sierra Leone

Revolutionary Council (AFRC) to govern Sierra Leone. The country descended into anarchy.

Soldiers looted indiscriminately and within days were joined by fighters of the rebel front eager to share the spoils. Their common experience was poverty, and they expressed their sense of injustice in robbery and mayhem.

ECOWAS foreign ministers met in Conakry in late June to negotiate a return to civilian rule, but diplomacy with the AFRC failed. The army and its allies seemed more interested in plunder than peace. The West African states decided to intervene militarily.

Warfare would be waged for nearly ten months, involving three major components: ECOWAS forces, army mutineers and their guerrilla rebel allies, and a variety of traditional hunter societies, generally referred to by the Mende term, "Kamajors," loyal to the deposed Kabbah. Armed and trained by private security companies guarding Sierra Leone's diamond mines, the Kamajors became a major element in the ensuing struggles and were officially recognized by the government as the Civil Defense Force (CDF).

In February 1998 ECOWAS forces, largely Nigerian troops, drove the military junta from Freetown, and President Kabbah triumphantly returned to his war-ravaged capital in March. Mutineers and rebels had stolen anything of value. Schools and Fourah Bay University were stripped; foreign embassies were sacked before the mutineers withdrew to the countryside where their depredations continued with murderous intensity. Opponents of the AFRC, local supporters of President Kabbah, and members of the Kamajor hunting groups were singled out for particularly vicious reprisals.

Kabbah's ECOWAS-supported government exercised only a tenuous control over the country. In early January 1999 the rebels launched a brutal attack on the capital itself. The cruelty one had come to associate with the rebels seemed to reach new heights. Random killing, mutilation, and rape were horrifically widespread. After nine days of intense fighting, the rebels, who had come close to capturing the city, withdrew. A fifth of all the capital's buildings were destroyed.

Under intense pressure from the international community, government and rebels gathered in Lomé, Togo, and signed a peace accord in July 1999. Its content could not give heart to humanitarians. Violence, fear, and intimidation received their reward. RUF leader Foday Sankoh was put in charge of Sierra Leone's diamond production, and Major Johnny Koroma, head of the Armed Forces Revolutionary Council (AFRC) that overthrew

President Ernest Bai Koroma

President Kabbah, was named Chairman of the Commission for the Consolidation of Peace. For those who elaborated, directed, and implemented a brutal policy of rape, mayhem, murder, and maiming, amnesty would be granted.

UN peacekeepers received little cooperation from RUF leaders. Few rebels surrendered their arms, and peacekeepers were kept out of RUF-controlled areas. Rebel diamond production continued and was easily filtered out through The Gambia, Burkina Faso or Liberia to pay for weaponry.

In May 2000, when the Nigerian-led ECOWAS peacekeeping force announced its departure, the rebels attacked, held several hundred UN peacekeepers captive, and advanced on Freetown. In August a renegade army faction, calling itself the West Side Boys and renown for its brutality, kidnapped 11 British soldiers. Britain's Tony Blair, seeing the moral and political necessity of action, intervened militarily. British Special Forces were sent in, the kidnapped secured, their captors killed or taken prisoner.

Faced with British resolve and might, the RUF returned to the conference table. Along with the capture and imprisonment of Foday Sankoh, the RUF leader, in May 2000, and intensified international pressure on Charles Taylor, the Liberian president, to end his support of the rebels, the British military intervention transformed the situation. RUF representatives signed a ceasefire in November 2000 and slowly began to disarm. By January 2002, 45,000 combatants had handed over their weapons, and UN peacekeepers declared the war over.

President Kabbah's term of office expired in March 2001, but was prorogued

by parliament. With stability restored, the long-postponed presidential elections were held in May 2002. Given an opportunity to choose their leader freely and safely, a remarkable 80% of registered voters turned out. There were nine candidates. Given the credit for bringing in the British and restoring peace by his fellow citizens, Ahmad Tejan Kabbah won a stunning 70.6% of the popular vote, eliminating the need for a runoff with his nearest rival. Alimany Paolo Bangura, the candidate of the RUF, was supported by only 1.7% of Sierra Leone's voters.

By early 2007 one could be guardedly optimistic about this Lazarus of states, returned from the dead. The security situation remained stable, but fragile. The United Nations Mission in Sierra Leone (UNAMSIL) demobilized more than 70,000 former combatants, and after five years on the job, UNAMSIL withdrew its last troops in December 2005. To focus on the country's postwar needs, the Security Council unanimously approved creation of the UN Integrated Office in Sierra Leone (UNIOSL) in January 2006 to help the government reinforce human rights, fulfill development goals, enhance transparency, and conduct free and fair elections in 2007.

Sierra Leone's Truth and Reconciliation Commission (TRC), appointed in May 2002, submitted its final report in October 2004. The main report weighed in, quite literally, at 1,500 pages, with a 3,500-page annex, bearing the testimonies of over 8,000 who had been brutalized by the country's 11-year civil war.

The commissioners coldly dissected the causes of the conflict and concluded that the country's political conflicts were all about power and the benefits it conferred. "Tragically," said the commissioners, "these characteristics persist today in Sierra Leone." Corruption, which had been one of the elements initially prompting Foday Sankoh's rebellion, remained pervasive in their eyes, and if not curtailed, it would sap the country of its life force and provide grounds for further conflict.

Egregious examples of corruption were easy to find. Teachers routinely went without their salaries because school authorities had stolen the funds. Clinics were built, but no drugs were supplied because of what is graciously called "seepage." Schools were constructed, but there was no money for blackboards or desks because so much had been siphoned off in kickbacks and bribes. Huge quantities of desperately needed supplies and materials simply disappeared, presumable stolen and sold for personal gain. One government report found that the Health Ministry had failed to distribute 95% of the medicine and equipment intended for public hospitals.

Sierra Leone

Under considerable outside pressure, an Anti-Corruption Commission (ACC) was set up, but it was not permitted to prosecute suspects. That was the prerogative of the attorney general's office, where files gathered dust and were never acted upon. By late 2005, when not a single prominent official had been convicted, the power to prosecute corruption cases was moved to a three-man team of two foreign prosecutors acting with an official from the attorney general's office; the decision to prosecute is made by a majority vote, depriving the office of its veto power. Progress on prosecutions is hoped for, if not expected.

The UN Security Council has established a War Crimes Court for Sierra Leone to try those who bore the greatest responsibility for human rights abuses during the civil war. Combining both international and local jurists, the court has indicted only 13 individuals and seems likely to fall short of providing a sense of justice for the war's victims. Two of those indicted, Foday Sankoh and his deputy Sam "Mosquito" Bockerie, are dead, and one other—the military junta leader, Johnny Koroma—is in flight. Former Liberian President Charles Taylor, indicted as bearing the greatest responsibility for war crimes and crimes against humanity committed during the war, now rests in a Dutch jail. Given security fears, his trial will take place in The Hague rather than Freetown.

Nine former militia leaders and commanders have been arrested and put in the court's custody. Sam Hinga Norman, once Sierra Leone's minister of internal affairs and the former leader of the pro-government militia known as "Kamajors," faced prosecutors in early 2006. The 66-year-old Norman, a high chief in southern Sierra Leone, was charged with over eight counts of war crimes, including unlawful killings, the use of child soldiers, looting and burning, and terrorizing civilians. To many Sierra Leoneans he was a national hero for leading the Kamajor hunters against the RUF and deserved congratulations, not condemnation. The competing narratives were made moot by Norman's death in February 2007.

Despite statistical economic growth, the general populace has seen little improvement in its life circumstances. Sierra Leone ranks at the very bottom—number 176 out of 177—on the UN's *Human Development Index* for 2006. (Only Niger ranks lower, though it should be noted that there were insufficient data to rank neighboring Liberia.) Fifty-seven percent of its population lives in abject poverty, earning less than a dollar a day; three-quarters of those between the ages of 18 and 35 are unemployed, and life expectancy in 2005 was barely 41 years.

In 2007 Sierra Leone prepared to effect the first transition from one civilian government to another since civil war ravaged the country in the 1990s. The elections were scheduled for August, and the major parties selected their champions. The SLPP selected Vice President Solomon Berewa as its leader, automatically making him its candidate for the presidential election. For its part, the All People's Congress (APC) chose its leader, Ernest Bai Koroma, a Fourah Bay graduate and businessman, as its standard bearer. Defeated in his campaign to become SLPP leader, Charles Francis Margai, son of a former president and nephew of another, testily resigned from the party and announced the formation of yet another opposition group: the People's Movement for Democratic change (PMDC).

Much depended on a successful organization and conduct of this election. The country has few viable political institutions, a population grown cynical with war and corruption, and disillusionment with a self-serving political class. To ensure transparency and effectiveness, UNIOSL has worked to develop operational capacities of the National Electoral Commission and a voter registration taskforce. Election costs are being subsidized by a variety of international actors, but a budgetary deficit of several million dollars is still expected.

The leaders of eight political parties signed an electoral code of conduct in November 2006, but the greatest responsibility in this area rests with the SLPP government. The temptation is strong to exploit the advantages of incumbency and control of state resources to the benefit of electoral victory. Any perception that the political playing field is uneven severely undermines the legitimacy of electoral results. Given the country's fragile stability, that's not a desired outcome. Ernest Bai Koroma and the APC and SLPP emerged victorious.

Failed institutions and a semi-lawless environment have contributed to Sierra Leone's culture of corruption. So widespread is it that a rich vocabulary of terms has developed to detail nuances and differentiate behaviors. "Kavei," for example, means cheating, while "guyu-guyu" refers to shady practices. An opinion survey taken in 2000 showed that 94% of Sierra Leoneans thought corruption was rampant and widespread in most institutions.

The Present: Contemporary Issues

Since the end of conflict in January 2002, the Kabbah government has struggled to regain control over the country's territory and economy, based on agriculture and mining. The bulk of the population is engaged in subsistence farming, with plantation agriculture significant only in certain parts of the country.

The entire sector was seriously disrupted during the civil war. Overall, agriculture traditionally contributed 50% of GDP and employed between 65% and 80% of the population. The most important commercial crops are cocoa and coffee, and the government's goal is to revitalize both commodities and assure food security by boosting domestic production of rice. (Sierra Leone exported rice until the 1980s, but since then has been an importer of the grain.)

Working with a Chinese tractor   Photo by Catherine Bolten

Mining has long been the major bulwark of Sierra Leone's economy, with rutile (an important source of titanium) and diamonds the principal source of government revenues. Sierra Rutile Ltd. (SRL), the world's largest producer of natural rutile until it was closed for security reasons in 1995, was the country's largest taxpayer, private sector employer and foreign export earner. The company shipped its first consignment of the mineral since 1995 in March 2006.

Sierra Leone's alluvial diamond fields lie in areas once controlled by the rebels. The bulk of RUF diamond production was smuggled to Liberia where it was converted to cash with which to buy arms. Arms were sourced in Ukraine or other eastern European states and supplied to the rebels through Liberian or Burkinabé connivance, with Liberia's president reportedly profiting handsomely as middleman in these operations. The international community branded these war diamonds as "blood" or "conflict" diamonds, and ultimately banned their sale.

Under a system of the international controls aimed at ending the illicit trade in "conflict diamonds," the value of Sierra Leone's official diamond exports has increased significantly, from $76 million in 2003 to $127 million in 2004 and $150 million in 2005. The total value of the country's annual diamond production, however, is estimated at between $250 million and $300 million. The difference is smuggled out of the country to finance a variety of (usually) illicit activities.

Sierra Leone's diamond trade, legal and illegal, is controlled by the large Lebanese trading community that dominates the country's commercial sector. In 2004, one Lebanese company, owned by a Sierra Leonean-born Lebanese trader, exported almost half of all officially certified diamonds.

Because of capitalist investment required, deep mining of diamonds buried in kimberlite pipes is insignificant compared to alluvial (surface) mining. Only one industrial mining company has undertaken the task, and the operation produced 78,500 carats worth $13.86 million in 2004, increasing to 116,700 ct, worth $22.5 million in 2005. It is likely more deep mining operations will be undertaken once peace and stability are assured.

Few foreign companies have ventured back into the country, with the notable exception of Chinese concerns. Tolerant of high risk, and aggressive in seeking the economic advantage due the first in, Chinese businesses can be seen in virtually every sector of Sierra Leone's economy—from hotels to building materials. The Chinese government has assisted the navy by the gift of a fisheries patrol vessel.

The Future

There is more to be optimistic about in Sierra Leone than there has been for years, though corruption and popular disillusionment with the pace of progress will temper that optimism and challenge the government. In terms of risks, the country's external debt was about $1.5 billion in 2005, but the IMF and World Bank have provided debt relief under the Heavily Indebted Poor Country (HIPC) initiative. In recent years, 50% of the government's budget has been funded by grants and loans from international financial institutions. Such dependence will likely continue for the near future.

The recent news out of the international tribunals in 2009 has also suggested that some degree of justice may still be meted out to the former rebels and warlords that terrorized the country for years. The trial of Liberia's Charles Taylor has resumed in the Hague, and the UN Special Court for Sierra Leone convicted three former high-ranking officials of the RUF as of April 2009. The court handed down sentences to Issa Sesay (52 year prison sentence), Morris Kallon (40 year sentence), and Augustine Gbao (25 year sentence) for counts of war crimes and crimes against humanity.

Politics in Sierra Leone (like those in neighboring Liberia) seem to have taken a turn towards stability and some degree of promise. The election in 2007 of President Ernest Bai Koroma and the APC and SLPP parties is a good sign. While crime and social problems remain rampant, the likelihood of civil strife and open warfare have subsided. There was some violence in recent local elections, but the violence appears not to have generalized. The country is not yet a full democracy, but its trajectory gives reason to hope that its greatest challenges going forward will not be war and conflict, but the reconciliation and reconstruction needed in its aftermath.

A slightly rundown dormitory, Fourah Bay College.   Photo by Catherine Bolten

The Republic of Togo

A balanced conversation in Lomé   AP/Wide World Photo

Basic Facts

Area: 56,950 sq. km. = 21,988 sq. mi. (half of Mississippi, vertically)

Population: 6,600,000 (UN 2007 est.)

Capital City: Lomé

Climate: Warm, humid and tropical

Neighboring Countries: Ghana (west); Burkina Faso (Upper Volta, north); Benin (east)

Official Language: French

Other Principal Languages: Ewe and Mina (the two major African languages in the south), Kabye (sometimes spelled Kabiye) and Dagomba (the two major African languages in the north), and Gourmanché, also spoken in the north.

Ethnic Groups: Over 30, among the most prominent the Ewe, Mina, and Kabre. 99%; European and Syrian-Lebanese less than 1%

Principal Religions: Indigenous beliefs 70%, Christian 20%, and Muslim 10%

Chief Commercial Products: Phosphates, cotton, coffee, and cocoa.

GNI Per Capita: $350 (World Bank 2006 est.)

Currency: CFA Franc

Former Colonial Status: German Colony (1885–1916), French Colony (1916–1960)

Independence Date: April 27, 1960

Chief of State: Faure Essozima Gnassingbé, President (since disputed elections of April 24, 2005)

National Flag: Green, yellow, green, yellow equal horizontal stripes. A red square at the staff top half with a superimposed white five-pointed star.

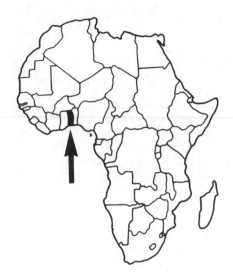

Land and People

Lying almost in the center of the Gold and Ivory coasts, Togo is a long, narrow country stretching 360 miles from the blue Atlantic into the interior. This small nation is only 31 miles wide at the coast and 100 miles in width at its broadest point. As is common to this region of Africa, the climate of Togo is predominantly hot and humid on the coast with a drier and slightly cooler region in the north. Picturesque Lake Togo, with quiet, fresh water, is located in the central coast region, a center of modern recreational facilities. The central section is traversed by the Togo Mountains and is succeeded in the north by a level territory of farms.

The people of the populous southern coast area are better educated and economically better off than those of the sparsely settled north. The Ewe people have dominated cultural life in Togo and extend beyond its borders well into Ghana to the west. There are few communities that lack educational facilities within Ewe country. In spite of this, Togo's literacy rate, as of the year 2004 was 53.2%, though regional and gender disparities exist.

The Koutammakou landscape in northeastern Togo, which extends into neighboring Benin, was made a UNESCO World Heritage site in 2004. Home to the Batammariba people, the landscape is characterized by distinctive architecture: many two-story tower houses and granaries that are almost spherical above a cylindrical base. UNESCO called Koutammakou "an outstanding example of a system of traditional settlement that is still living and dynamic."

The Past: Political and Economic History

For early history, see *Historical Background* and *The Colonial Period: The Germans* and *The Colonial Period: The French*.

In 1956 a UN-sponsored plebiscite allowed the people of British Togoland to vote on joining the Gold Coast, which was rapidly approaching independence. The two were united and became independent as Ghana in 1957. French Togoland became an autonomous republic within the French Union in 1956 and achieved its independence in 1960.

Pre-independence elections installed Nicholas Grunitzky of the Togo Progressive Party (TPP) as premier. Advocating independence, the Togo Unity Party (TUP), led by Sylvanus Olympio, defeated Grunitsky's TPP in 1958 elections, and Olympio went on to become Togo's first president when the country became independent in 1960. Olympio was not a native of Togo, having been brought to Africa from Brazil by his father when he was a small child. He spoke several foreign languages as well as

Togo

Ewe, the predominant language of southern Togo.

Olympio was assassinated in early 1963 outside the U.S. Embassy in Lomé where he had been seeking refuge. Grunitzky returned later and was named prime minister by Sgt. Gnassingbé Eyadéma, who was in the group that killed Olympio. A new constitution was adopted, and four political parties participated in elections held in 1963, which were officially won by Grunitzky's Togo Progressive Party; he became president.

Dissatisfied with a general lack of progress, which he attributed to the bickering of politicians, Gnassingbé Eyadéma, now a Lt. Colonel, seized power in 1967 and abolished all parties. He later formed the Rassemblement du Peuple Togolaise (RPT) and ran in 1972 as the sole candidate for president, receiving about 90% of the vote in a "yes"-or-"no" contest.

President Eyadéma and the military governed Togo for some 38 years, and for three decades assassination, torture, and routine abuse of civil liberties and human rights characterized the regime. Gilchrist Olympio, the son of assassinated President Sylvanus Olympio, was almost killed in a 1993 assassination attempt after he emerged as a potential rival to President Eyadéma. He retreated to exile in France, fearing he would not survive in Togo. The 1993 election was a sham—with as many dead people voting as live ones.

The midsummer presidential elections of 1998 were prepared with care. A new constitutional court created to hear any election disputes was filled with Eyadéma supporters. A new communications authority was established to oversee the media. It too was controlled by Eyadéma appointees. A new electoral code was passed, giving responsibility for organizing and supervising the elections to the Ministry of the Interior. In March 1998 the elections, originally scheduled for August, were advanced to June. Surprise, the president-general knew, is a tactical element.

To the surprise of none, the election proved that political dinosaurs live, sustained by a DNA of fraud. Eyadéma was reelected by a modest 52.13% of the votes cast, just enough to avoid a runoff election. Immediately prior to announcement of election results, the head of the electoral commission resigned, saying she had received telephone calls threatening her life. Four other members of the commission also resigned. Eyadéma's principal rival, Gilchrist Olympio, was allotted a generous 34.1% of the ballots by the interior ministry, which ran the election.

Opposition protests were met with tear gas grenades. Olympio said his own calculations showed he won 59% of the vote and vowed to use all peaceful, legitimate, and constitutional means to have the results annulled, all of which, of course, were of no avail. The president-general, who had already served 31 years as head of state, became Africa's longest serving leader and second only to Fidel Castro in longevity of rule.

The spring 1999 legislative elections were equally farcical. The opposition boycotted, and candidates of Eyadéma's RPT won 79 of 81 parliamentary seats. The Interior Ministry claimed that over 66% of registered voters participated, while the opposition claimed the figure didn't pass 10%. The European Union, which had suspended economic cooperation with Togo after the electoral farce of 1993, called for an "internal dialogue" between the opposition and the regime, but the positions of each were so entrenched the possibility of dialogue seemed remote.

Former President Eyadéma

In May 1999 Amnesty International described Togo as a "state of terror," characterized by executions and extra-judicial executions perpetrated by authorities throughout the political crisis from 1993 to 1998. Hundreds had been killed in the days leading up to the 1998 elections alone. Evidence gathered from Togolese and Beninois fishermen indicated that manacled opponents had been thrown into the sea from Togolese air force planes.

The Togolese army, on which President-General Eyadéma's repression relied, consists of 9,450 men, more than one for every 560 citizens. The army, like the other forces of order, is largely recruited in the north, President-General Eyadéma's region of origin. Four new brigadier generals were appointed in early 1998, and all of them were, like Eyadéma, northerners. Of the nine Togolese generals, five, including the president, are of the same ethnicity (Kabye). The elite Presidential Guard is led by President Eyadéma's son, Colonel Ernest Gnassingbé, while another son, Commandant Rock Gnassingbé, leads a motorized division.

President-General Eyadéma's brutal repression and cavalier attitudes toward democratic processes left Togo in a state of permanent political crisis and economic stagnation. Only in 1999 were there signs that the president-general was willing to compromise with his opponents, and then, only after years of economic sanctions had taken their toll. "National reconciliation" discussions took place in July under the authority of four facilitators appointed by the EU and La Francophonie, the French equivalent of the Commonwealth. On a visit to West Africa President Jacques Chirac of France forcefully announced that only national reconciliation would enable the EU to resume its aid.

After conversations with the president-general, Chirac himself announced that Eyadéma would step down at the end of his presidential term in 2003, respecting the constitution by not presenting himself for a third term. The president-general announced he would dissolve the contested National Assembly and call new parliamentary elections in March 2000. He also agreed to the creation of an independent electoral commission. All parties present affixed their signatures to what was called the Lomé Framework Agreement.

Opposition intransigence, however, scuttled much of the facilitators' effort. Gilchrist Olympio, fearing for his life, refused to participate in the Lomé reconciliation talks for security reasons. Internal opponents of the regime found numerous details to quibble and complain over. In exasperation, the four "facilitators" sent their recommendations directly to the National Assembly, which approved a new election code in March. When the legislature amended the proposed code, the opposition once again objected and withdrew from reconciliation discussions. The elections of 2000 never took place.

On the eve of President Chirac's visit, the Benin League for the Defense of Human Rights confirmed Amnesty International's charges that hundreds had been summarily executed and their bodies dumped into the sea in the run-up to the presidential elections in 1998. The League reported finding more than 100 bodies in coastal villages. Some were headless, handcuffed, or riddled with bullets. They were, said the League, "pushed from low-flying planes and helicopters coming during the night from Togo."

By June 2000 a joint commission between the United Nations and the OAU was set up to investigate the allegations of state-sponsored massacres, no doubt much to the embarrassment of President

143

Togo

Eyadéma who had begun serving a term as OAU chairman.

The inquiry team made clear its belief that individuals linked to Togolese security forces, working in cooperation with the Togolese police and allied militias, had indeed carried out summary executions of the government's political opponents. It was not the first embarrassment with which the president-general had had to deal.

The Fowler Report to the UN Security Council of March 2000 had identified Eyadéma as one of those facilitating the continuing arms supply of Jonas Savimbi's UNITA forces in Angola. A follow-up experts report issued in December accused Togolese authorities of accepting "blood diamonds" from Savimbi in exchange for illegal arms and fuel shipments.

European mediators left Togo at the end of January 2001, admitting that their efforts had "ended in failure." Obstructions and delays have continued to undermine new elections. As the March 2002 elections approached, President-General Eyadéma's government returned to its traditional suppression of civil liberties. Freedom of expression in all its forms was curtailed. Yaovi Agboyibo, the former head of Togo's Bar Association, was jailed in August 2001 for having accused Prime Minister Agbéyomé Kodjo of "complicity with criminals" while heading the Lomé Port Authority. Two call-in radio talk shows, which gave citizens an opportunity to voice their opinions, were suspended for broadcasting "defamatory" programs.

In February 2002, the government rushed a series of self-serving amendments to the elections code to the legislature, which, having no opposition members, passed them unanimously. Under the changes, presidential candidates are required to have lived in Togo continuously for 12 months immediately preceding an election. This of course eliminated Gilchrist Olympio, living in neighboring Ghana for his own safety. Street demonstrations against the new code ensued, undissuaded by contingents of antiriot police.

The March elections were once again postponed, and when Togolese voters went to the polls in late October 2002 there was little choice. Most opposition parties boycotted the election (and here the story gets drearily repetitive), calling it an "electoral farce." Unsurprisingly, President Eyadéma's Rally of the Togolese People (RPT) won 72 of 81 seats. In December the RPT used its majority to amend Togo's constitution, allowing President-General Eyadéma to yet again seek reelection.

That legal nicety dispatched, the engine of state proceeded along its usual paths to insure an Eyadéma victory. Opposition figures were intimidated, arrested and

President Faure Gnassingbé

tortured; marches and meetings were forbidden, and any expression of critical opinion was punished, all under the cover of law.

As presidential elections approached, the opposition, always prone to creating coalitions of unity, marched in disarray. Gilchrist Olympio's *Union des Forces du Changement* (UFC), Togo's main opposition party, withdrew from the umbrella group known as the *Coalition des Forces Démocratiques* (CFD) to nominate Olympio as their candidate for the presidency, only to have his candidacy banned for technical irregularities in his nomination papers. Unable to agree on a single nominee, the eight remaining CFD parties decided to present individual candidates.

The governing Togolese People's Rally (RPT) did the obvious and nominated President-General Eyadéma as its candidate, while the UFC nominated its deputy leader, the 75-year-old Emmanuel Bob-Akitani, a retired mining engineer who essentially ran as a proxy for Gilchrist Olympio. Four other opposition candidates managed to weave their way through the intricacies of the electoral code and find a place on the June 2003 ballot.

The electoral commission announced that Eyadéma won 57.22% of the votes cast. The UFC's Emmanuel Bob-Akitani came second with 34.14%, while the remaining votes were shared by the four other opposition candidates. Togo's ongoing political impasse appeared likely to continue for another five years, but President-General Eyadéma died suddenly in early February 2005, ending thirty-eight years of dictatorial rule.

The army quickly closed the borders, keeping the president's constitutional successor, the speaker of the Assembly, out of the country and installing a presidential son, Faure Gnassingbé, as president. The National Assembly, filled with ruling-party

placemen, gave political cover by amending the constitution to permit the succession. Togo's streets filled with protesters and the international community waxed indignant—as only it can when dealing with a small and insignificant country. The AU roused itself from somnolence to denounce the action and ECOWAS imposed sanctions; Faure Gnassingbé resigned, promising elections in 60 days.

The opposition actually managed some semblance of unity, nominating the UFC's elderly Emmanuel Bob Akitani, who everyone understood to be the stand-in for Gilchrist Olympio. With its skills at electoral fraud honed in past elections, and enormous financial resources, the Togolese People's Rally (RPT) generated a victory for its nominee: 60.15% of the vote to Faure Gnassingbé, with 38.25% for the opposition. Mass protests ensued; in the capital, gangs of opposition supporters erected burning barricades and pelted vehicles, but the army stepped in, bloodily, and crushed the insurrection. Between 400 and 500 people were killed, and thousands—at least 30,000—fled to Ghana or Benin.

Key to changing the country's political climate is the Intra-Togolese Dialogue—a national dialogue between government and opposition to resolve differences and establish a roadmap for ending stasis and stagnation. The dialogue was one of 22 commitments made by the Togolese government to the EU in April 2004—a set of conditions for rectifying Togo's "deficit of democracy" and restarting cooperation with the EU.

Among the pressing issues were those relating to free, fair and transparent elections: an independent electoral commission to organize and oversee elections, creation of a valid list of eligible voters (who would be issued counterfeit-proof identity cards), suppression of residence and citizenship restrictions on political candidacies, and equitable access to financing and media coverage during electoral campaigns. Another critical issue involved the need to keep army and security forces neutral in any political campaign. That of course raised two additional touchy issues: reforming the army to make it better reflect Togo's ethnic diversity, and an investigation of politically-inspired violence and the impunity thus far granted it.

By November 2004 the Eyadéma government had initiated dialogue with the core opposition parties, but the process was interrupted by the events surrounding death of Eyadéma in February 2005. They did not resume until April 2006. With the help and encouragement of facilitators from Burkina Faso and the Sant'-Egidio community in Rome, seven of the nine dialogue participants initialed a basic agreement in early July.

An Independent National Electoral Commission (CENI) consisting of 19 members—five from the presidential movement, two each from five opposition parties, and a further two representing civil society and two more representing the cabinet—was created to organize legislative elections in 2007. To coordinate and implement the various agreements, dialogue participants also agreed to form a national unity cabinet.

The agreement was not unanimous. Two major opposition parties refused to affix their signatures: Gilchrist Olympio's UFC—the least concessionary of all the parties—and the Democratic Convention of African Peoples (CDPA) of Leopold Gnivinvi. Dialogue participants agreed to use the good offices of President Compaoré of Burkina Faso to mediate differences. After nearly two weeks of intense negotiation, Compaoré got all to sign a Global Political Agreement (GPA) on August 20, 2006.

By mid-September President Gnassingbé had appointed a new prime minister to head the transitional government—Yawovi Agboyibo, a 63-year-old lawyer who had spent much of his life trying to end the dictatorship of president-general Eyadéma. His hopes of becoming prime minister dashed, Gilchrist Olympio rejected the new government. The UFC refused to join the unity cabinet, though its second vice president, Amah Gnassingbé, was permitted to enter the government as a minister of state on an individual basis.

In 2007, Togo held what may have been some of the freest elections in its history, though the ruling RPT clearly had a number of advantages in the run-up to voting. Unsurprisingly, Togo's dominant party won the legislative elections; more surprisingly, the elections were hailed internationally as relatively free and fair. The European Union soon afterwards reestablished international cooperation with Togo, a state that had been one of Africa's pariahs for many years.

In 2008, Gnassingbé appointed a new prime minister, Gilbert Houngbo. But perhaps more dramatic news came in April 2009 when Faure Gnassingbé's ambitious half-brother and erstwhile ally, Kpatcha Gnassingbé, was detained by Togolese security forces as he attempted to flee into the U.S. Embassy for sanctuary (in a scene somewhat reminiscent of the Sylvanus Olympio assassination). Kpatcha Gnassingbé claimed he was the victim of assassination attempts, while Faure Gnassingbé suspects Kpatcha's participation in coup plotting. Later that same month, Togolese news sources reported that another half-brother Essolizam Edem Gnassingbé, had also been detained along with others allegedly involved in a coup plot. While details are sketchy, the conflict within the Gnassingbé clan may suggest some wider rift among powerbrokers in a country where power has seemed indivisible for decades.

The Present: Contemporary Issues

The Togolese economy is mainly dependent on subsistence agriculture, which accounts for nearly 42% of the GDP and 75% of jobs. Combined exports of commercial crops like cotton, cocoa, and coffee, account for nearly 40% of total export earnings. Cotton is Togo's most important commercial crop. More than 230,000 Togolese earn their living from cotton, but their livelihoods are always subject to fluctuating weather and world prices.

The mining sector accounts for more than one-third of export earnings; phosphate mining is the most significant element of the sector, contributing 26% to 28% of export earnings—vying with cotton for primacy of place. Togo is the world's fifth largest exporter of calcium phosphate and possesses large reserves, estimated at over 150 million tons of high-grade ore.

Togo generates only 30% of its own electricity needs. For the rest it depends on electricity supplied by Ghana's Akosombo Dam. In 1998 water levels at the dam fell precipitously, and electricity rationing had to be introduced. To rectify its power insufficiencies, Togo is participating in the West African Pipeline Project to distribute Nigerian natural gas to Benin, Togo, and Ghana for the generation of electricity. The pipe, measuring 18 inches in diameter with a daily capacity of 400 million cubic feet, will stretch some 382 miles along the Gulf of Guinea coast, running mostly underwater. Deliveries were not expected to begin before the end of 2006, but even that deadline has passed because militants in the Niger Delta have repeatedly vandalized the pipeline.

Togo continues to suffer economic malaise, largely caused by its long term political crisis. Dependent on foreign aid for economic development, Togo has been largely cut off from international investment since death and violence marred its transition to democracy in 1991. As the economy shrank, an informal—and increasingly criminalized—economy developed. Illegal weapons and drugs, money laundering, human trafficking, and smuggling of all types came to dominate the country's trade. Togo is now considered one of the world's drug trafficking hubs.

Lomé has the deepest water of West Africa's ports and has picked up business with shippers frustrated by delays at container ports in Abidjan and Lagos. As a consequence, a new $100 million container handling facility is planned. The facility would be capable of unloading 200 to 250 containers an hour, much faster than existing facilities at the region's other ports.

The Future

Faure Gnassingbé seems to have settled into power with the confidence of the RPT and the military after a tumultuous beginning of his presidency, and his detention of his half-brothers in 2009 is likely to further cement his control. While the 2007 legislative elections were generally lauded by international observers, both party and army seem likely to retain their power and privilege. The country remains a long way from full democracy, a fact made more striking by the relative consolidation of democratic practice over the last two decades in neighboring Ghana and Benin. The RPT regime remains in control, and the ever-fractious opposition shows few signs of being able to overcome the dominance of the party and the military-state apparatus.

Economically, Togo seems likely to continue underperforming the continental average; at only 2.5% growth in 2007, Togo's economic expansion is barely sufficient to keep pace with population growth. With few natural resources and a still-lagging reputation among international donors, the prospects for major investment are scant. With domestic resource mobilization too limited to accelerate growth, Togo will likely find itself envying its West African neighbors in the short- to medium-term.

CENTRAL AFRICA

LIBYA

Tibesti Mtns

• Faya

CHAD

NIGER

Abéché •

SUDAN

Lake Chad

⊛ N'Djamena

Mandara Mtns

Shari R.

• Sarh

NIGERIA

Gotel Mtns • Ngaoundéré

CENTRAL AFRICAN REPUBLIC

• Bouar

CAMEROON

Ubangi R.

Bangassou •

Nkongsamba •
Mt. Cameroon

Bangui ⊛
Zongo •
Gbadolite •

⊛ Yaoundé

Malabo ⊛
Bioko Island

Douala •
Kribi •

Ubangi R.

Congo R. • Bumba

Lake Albert

UGANDA

EQUATORIAL GUINEA

Kisangani •

Bata •
Mbini •

RIO MUNI

CONGO
(Brazzaville)

Mbandaka •

Lake Edward

Libreville ⊛

GABON

Goma •

Port Gentil •

Ogooué R.

Lake Kivu

⊛ Kigali

Lambaréné •
Franceville •

CONGO
(Kinshasa)

Bukavu •

RWANDA

Lualaba R.

BURUNDI
Bujumbura ⊛

Brazzaville ⊛

Kasai R.

Sankuru R.

TANZANIA

Pointe Noire •

⊛ Kinshasa

Kikwit •

Lake Tanganyika

CABINDA
(Angola)

Matadi •

Kananga •

Cuango R.

Mbuji-Mayi •
Kabinda •

Kasai R.

Kamina •

Lake Mweru
Pweto •

Kolwezi •

Likasi •
Lubumbashi •

0   100   200   300 mi

0 100 200 300 400 500 km

ANGOLA

ZAMBIA

N

The Republic of Burundi

Aerial view of Bujumbura and the northernmost extent of Lake Tanganyika

Basic Facts

Area: 28,490 sq. km. = 11,000 sq. mi. (slightly larger than Maryland)

Population: 8,500,000 (UN 2007 est.)

Capital City: Bujumbura

Climate: Temperate, with an alternating wet season (October–April) and dry season (May–December).

Neighboring Countries: Rwanda (north); Tanzania (east): Congo-Kinshasa (west).

Official Languages: French, KiRundi

Other Principal Language: KiSwahili

Ethnic Groups: Hutu 85%, Tutsi 14%, Twa (Pygmy) 1%, Europeans 3,000, and South Asians 2,000

Principal Religions: Christian 67% (Roman Catholic 62%, Protestant 5%), indigenous beliefs 32%, and Muslim 1%.

Chief Commercial Products: Coffee, tea, sugar, cotton and hides

GNI Per Capita: $114 (World Bank 2008 est.)

Currency: Burundi franc

Former Colonial Status: Part of German East Africa (1899–1917); occupied by Belgian troops (1916), Belgian trust territory under League of Nations and United Nations (1923–1962).

Independence Date: July 1, 1962

Chief of State: Pierre Nkurunziza, President (since August 2005)

National Flag: Divided by a white diagonal cross into red panels (top and bottom) and green panels (hoist side and outer side) with a white disk superimposed at the center bearing three red six-pointed stars outlined in green arranged in a triangular design (one star above, two stars below).

Land and People

A cool, pleasant land of mountains and plateaus, the Republic of Burundi was known as Urundi before its independence; it was the southern portion of Ruanda-Urundi. Burundi is situated in the highlands of central Africa, and though only two degrees below the Equator, the climate is tempered by altitude. The legendary Lake Tanganyika, the longest fresh water lake in the world, separates Burundi and the Democratic Republic of the Congo. This amazing body of water is more than 2,500 feet above sea level on the surface, yet its floor reaches a depth of about 2,000 feet below sea level. The lake is rich in fish, hippopotamuses, crocodiles and other native species.

Eons ago a great strip of land between parallel faults in the earth sank to great

depths, forming the basin of the Red Sea and continuing into the land mass of Eastern and Central Africa. This unique land feature is known as the Great Rift Valley, an area of grassy, upland plains. The wet season has characteristic daily downpours with intermittent clear, sunny weather. Almost no rain falls during the five-month dry season.

Burundi's Twa people, less than 1% of the population, are almost politically invisible. None occupies an important post in the Burundi government. The highest position occupied by a Twa is that of Member of Parliament, and until the new constitution, there was only one. In local administration there are no Twa zone heads, no commune administrators or provincial governor. The only administrative position held by a Twa is that of a *nyum-bakumi*—leader of a set of ten households—for other Twa people.

Burundi, as many other African nations, has a long and deeply rooted musical heritage. Music is played at family gatherings and other special social events. The men sing kwishongora songs, with shouts and thrills, while women often sign bilito music. "Whispered singing" is a type of Burundian music that is performed at a low pitch, so that the music instruments can be heard properly.

The Past: Political and Economic History

For early history, see *Historical Background, The Colonial Period: The Germans* and *King Leopold and the Belgians.*

In the great wave of decolonization that began in the 1960s, Urundi was separated from Ruanda-Urundi and became a con-

147

Burundi

Former President Pierre Buyoya

stitutional monarchy in 1962. The Kingdom of Burundi was given independence as a monarchy under Mwami (King) Mwambutsa IV, but even at birth, the country was characterized by instability. In the lead-up to independence, legislative elections had resulted in a victory for the Union for National Progress (UPRONA), whose leader was Prince Rwagasore, the eldest son of Mwami Mwambutsa. UPRONA was a Tutsi-Hutu coalition party, but was dominated by Tutsi nobles of the *Ganwa* clan. Prince Rwagasore's assassination in October 1961 ushered in a period of political instability that characterizes Burundi to this day.

In 1963 ethnic violence forced thousands of Hutus to flee into Tanzania. Political violence erupted again in January 1965 when a Tutsi gunman killed the Hutu prime minister, Pierre Ngendandumwe. Following legislative elections in May of that year, in which Hutu had won 23 out of 33 seats in the National Assembly, Mwami Mwambutsa refused to appoint a Hutu prime minister, preferring to appoint his private secretary, Léopold Biha, and keep power centered in the crown. This prompted a coup attempt by Hutu policemen. Prime Minister Biha was seriously wounded by gunfire, Mwambutsa departed for Switzerland, 76 Hutu leaders were executed and the defense minister, Michel Micombero, was given absolute power.

Mwambutsa made a halfhearted effort to return to his kingdom, but was ousted by his son, Ntare, in July 1966. A few months later when the youthful king was out of the country, Micombero proclaimed

himself president of the first Republic of Burundi in November. He had the support of the Bahima clan of the Tutsi, traditionally jealous of Ganwa power.

Restless Hutus living in exile in Tanzania plotted revolution with the aid of the local government in mid-1972. Emboldened by drugs and assurances of invincibility from local folk priests, they mounted a swift campaign. The plot involved Mwami Ntare, but after being put under house arrest, he was later killed "while escaping." About 2,000 Tutsis were mercilessly slaughtered; they responded with a genocidal blood bath that took the lives of more than 200,000 Hutus within six weeks—about 5% of the population. Worst of all, the April-May killings were directed against educated Hutus. A second wave of Hutus poured over the Tanzanian border in May 1973.

The 1972 events generated the distrust and hatred in both Tutsi and Hutu communities, which lie at the heart of Burundi's problems today. They also became a source of tension within the Tutsi minority. Ultimately this led to the 1976 overthrow of Micombero in a military coup led by Col. Jean-Baptiste Bagaza, who initiated the Second Republic.

In 1980, Bagaza commenced a series of anti-Catholic Church measures; by 1987 more than 450 foreign priests had been expelled as he sought to bring the Church more thoroughly under the control of the state. He viewed the Church as an instrument of potential Hutu rebellion. Belgian Catholic priests were frequently Flemish, with their own sense of ethnic and linguistic identity. Flemish priests had a strong sense of identity with and sympathy for oppressed Hutu, because they themselves had suffered oppression by French speaking Walloons in Belgium.

The crisis in Church-state relations provoked yet again another military coup. Bagaza was ousted by a fellow clansman, Pierre Buyoya, in September 1987, and the Third Republic was declared. The new leader quickly welcomed back the expelled Catholics despite the suspicions of right-wing Tutsis. Buyoya introduced several progressive measures to deal with ethnic resentment. Efforts were made to achieve ethnic parity within the government, and a national commission was created to seek ways of strengthening national unity. Ideas developed in the capital, however, did not always translate well in the provinces. There, Tutsi civil servants continued to discriminate against Hutu citizens.

Another outburst of ethnic hatred was not long in coming. The local officials provoked it, and the Rwanda-based exiles encouraged it, Hutus in the northern provinces killed some 500 Tutsis in August 1988. In the backlash some 20,000

people were killed, most of them Hutu. Thousands more fled to Rwanda.

President Buyoya secured ratification of a new multiparty constitution in March 1992. It explicitly prohibited political organizations that advocated "tribalism, divisionism, or violence" and stipulated that all political parties must include both Hutu and Tutsi representatives. In the June 1993 elections that followed—the country's first free, democratic elections—Melchiore Ndadye, a Hutu, defeated Pierre Buyoya to be elected president. He ruled only briefly. In October, paratroopers loyal to former president Bagaza assassinated Ndadye. This set off another round of recriminatory ethnic slaughter. For more than a decade afterwards, Burundi was gripped by a cycle of terror and counter-terror referred to as *la crise*—the crisis.

Amid the violence Burundi's parliament finally chose Cyprien Ntaryamira, a moderate Hutu, as president. Ntaryamira took office in February 1994, but just a few months later President Ntaryamira was killed in the same plane crash that killed Rwanda's president and set off the genocide of that year. Amid general agreement that the security situation did not permit another round of elections, parliament eventually appointed another moderate Hutu, Sylvestre Ntibantunganya to the presidency.

General tensions were not eased. Rogue elements of the army, controlled by Tutsis, and extremist Hutu militias engaged in nearly daily atrocities against civilians. In November 1995 Burundi and its neighbors agreed to a regional peace initiative. Former Tanzanian President, Julius Nyerere, was designated as mediator between the various factions.

Mediation only seemed to intensify hostilities. Fearful and frustrated, the army intervened in July 1996. President Ntibantunganya went into hiding and Major Pierre Buyoya seized power, for a second time. In order to force a restoration of democracy, Burundi's neighbors united to impose economic sanctions. As with many such efforts, the goal was not achieved and the consequences were disastrous. The economy further deteriorated, malnutrition rates soared, and atrocities continued; sanctions could not stop the flow of arms into Burundi.

In June 1998 the government signed a Transitional Constitutional Act (TCA) designed to pave the way for the Tutsi-led government to share power with the mainly Hutu opposition. The TCA enlarged parliament by 57 new seats to make it more representative. The government appointed 27 members from Burundi's civil society; small parties not heretofore represented appointed nine of the new members, and the Hutu opposi-

Burundi

tion party, *Front pour la démocratie au Burundi* (FRODEBU), designated the remaining 21 seats.

With these power-sharing reforms as background, 17 delegations gathered in Arusha, Tanzania, to begin peace discussions. The most militant of the Hutu rebel groups, the Forces for the Defense of Democracy (FDD) and the hard-line *Party for the Liberation of the Hutu People-National Liberation Forces* (PALIPEHUTU-FNL) were excluded from the talks. Progress, which was sluggish at best, was brought to a halt by the death of the mediator, Julius Nyerere, in October 1999.

Facing the death of Nyerere, Africa's most distinguished ex-president, Nelson Mandela, was prevailed upon to take on the role of mediator and assumed his duties in February 2000. His presence brought great publicity to previously obscure discussions. His moral stature allowed him publicly to chastise all parties. His international prestige and contacts allowed him to proffer the carrot of aid to reconstruct a devastated country.

Nineteen parties signed the Arusha Peace and Reconciliation Agreement in August 2000, but key issues—including the leadership of the transitional period and agreement for a cease-fire—remained unresolved until July 2001. It was agreed then that President Buyoya would lead the first half of the three-year transition, with Domitien Ndayizeye of the main Hutu opposition party, FRODEBU, as vice president. In the second half of the transition, Burundi would have a Hutu president and a Tutsi vice president. Both the FDD and the FNL, excluded from the discussions, increased military activity against President Buyoya's government.

Negotiation with the rebel movements was always difficult, given their tendency to separate into factions and wings (more by personality than policy), but by late 2002 it began to look as though the long negotiations were at last fruitful: two smaller FLN and FDD factions signed a cease-fire in October. In December, President Buyoya and Pierre Nkurunziza, head of the principal FDD faction, signed a historic cease-fire (the first since 1993) in Arusha. Only the hard-line PALIPEHUTU-FNL rebels refused any cease-fire discussions.

As scheduled, President Buyoya relinquished office in April 2003, and was succeeded by his Hutu vice president, Domitien Ndayizeye, the FRODEBU leader. The whole structure of the transitional government remained fragile. Agathon Rwasa's PALIPEHUTU-FNL refused to join the peace process, rejected the transitional government entirely, and showed its strength by periodically assaulting the outskirts of Bujumbura. Mistrust and low-level intermittent fighting between government

Former President Domitien Ndayizeye
Photo by AFP/Peter Busomoke

and rebels continued, leaving the country in ruins—exsanguinated, indebted, and fearful.

Regional leaders kept the pressure up for Burundians to work out their differences through the new power-sharing institutions. The most sensitive issue was the reconstruction of the army. The old army was to be dismantled and a new army was to be created, made up of 50% government forces and 50% Hutu rebels. For Tutsis, the army is the bulwark of their security. For Hutus, it is the instrument of their oppression. Reconciling the two has been a task fraught with hazards and stumbling blocks, but for the first time in Burundi's history, the army's senior officer corps is open to members of the Hutu majority.

President Ndayizeye scheduled a referendum on a new constitution for the country in late February 2005. The text affirmed power sharing by ethnic quota: In the National Assembly 60% of the seats went to Hutus and 40% to Tutsis, with three seats reserved for Twa representation. Allocation of government positions followed with same distribution pattern: 60% for Hutu and 40% for Tutsi, while Senate membership was equally distributed between the two ethnicities with three seats reserved for Twa. Some 91.2% of the country's three million registered voters approved the text.

Legislative elections held in July 2005 affirmed the political dominance of the FDD, which won nearly 70% of the vote. President Ndayizeye's FRODEBU came second followed by UPRONA. Pierre Nkurunziza, the FDD leader, was nominated to be president and was overwhelmingly elected to office in August, during a joint meeting of the two houses of parliament.

The FNL initially refused to recognize the legitimacy of the power-sharing government and President Nkurunziza's elec-

tion, but by October 2005 it had split into rival factions. One, headed by Agathon Rwasa's former top lieutenant, Jean Bosco Sindayigaya, favored peace talks with Bujumbura. Rwasa remained hostile. His faction was the only one of Burundi's seven Hutu groups outside the peace process until March 2006, when he agreed to unconditional negotiations held in Tanzania (long supportive of the FNL) and mediated by South Africa.

These discussions concluded in early September 2006, when Agathon Rwasa, the FNL leader, and President Nkurunziza signed a ceasefire agreement. The peace talks had gone on for more than a decade following the assassination of the country's first Hutu president, Melchior Ndadaye, in 1993. During that time around 1.2 million people had been internally displaced; more than 300,000 people had been killed and about 15% of Burundi's children had been orphaned. If all goes as scheduled and the guns fall silent at long last, the ceasefire will be followed by integration of FNL troops into the armed forces and transformation of the FNL into a political party.

Pierre Nkurunziza, Burundi's president, belongs to the younger generation of Hutu leaders, radicalized by the assassination of President Melchior Ndadaye. He was born in 1963, the son of a former governor killed during anti-Hutu massacres in 1972. He studied physical education at the University of Burundi and was an assistant lecturer at the university before joining the rebellion.

The government received a particularly stinging rebuke in September 2006 when one of President Nkurunziza's two vice presidents, Alice Nzomukunda, resigned. A Hutu and member of the ruling CNDD-FDD party, Vice President Nzomukunda summarized her frustrations with the government and party: the country was on the path to overcome its problems, she said, "but corruption and economic embezzlement are undermining it." She specifically laid out a blistering attack on party chairman Hussein Radjabu, accusing him of constant interference in the government's work, not respecting the country's institutions, obstructing efforts to create a functional peacetime government, and misleading the population: "The government's hands," she told a press conference, "are tied by Hussein Radjabu."

Adding tinder to the fires she lit, Nzomukunda also questioned the coup plot the government had allegedly uncovered. The events surrounding the alleged coup went back to March 2006 when President Nkurunziza himself accused unnamed politicians of conspiring with officers of the national defense and police forces to overthrow his government. In

149

Burundi

August the government arrested former President Domitien Ndayizeye, head of the principal opposition party, as part of the conspiracy. Observers began to fear the regime's tolerance for dissent and opposition had ended, and a new, more authoritarian Pierre Nkurunziza had begun to emerge. In resigning from the government, Vice President Nzomukunda indicated she was unaware of any evidence of the plot.

In January 2007 Burundi's Supreme Court agreed. At the end of a trial that had begun in November, and in which the prosecutor had asked for death sentences, former-President Ndayizeye and four of his co-accused were cleared of all charges.

The one man who was toppled in this affair was CNDD-FDD's chairman, Hussein Radjabu, who had been linked to the now-failed prosecution of former-President Ndayizeye and blamed for the deteriorating human rights situation in Burundi. At a party meeting in February 2007, members vote to oust Radjabu from his chairmanship. The former chairman will not go gently into unemployment; he has protested the legality of his ouster and promises to take the issue to court.

The scourge of AIDS has reached tiny Burundi thanks to war, dislocation and poverty. There are probably over 250,000 HIV-positive people in the country, and some 25,000 Burundians die of AIDS annually. The most affected group is people aged between 15 and 49 years, the most productive section of society. Rural and urban areas have different HIV prevalence rates, with 20% and 7.5%, respectively.

The Present: Contemporary Issues

Agriculture is the mainstay of Burundi's economy, representing about 50% of GDP. Most cultivated land is devoted to subsistence crops—mainly cassava, bananas, and sweet potatoes, but widespread violence has driven many farmers from their fields. Cattle rearing is also an important source of food, as was fishing on Lake Tanganyika until it was banned by the government as a security measure to prevent rebel infiltration.

President Pierre Nkurunziza
©IRIN

The main cash crop is coffee, more than 90% of which is higher quality *arabica*. Coffee exports have accounted at times for over 95% of Burundi's foreign exchange revenues. With such heavy reliance on a single crop, the economy is seesawed by fluctuations in world coffee prices and periodically ravaged by natural calamity. The IMF long refused to give money to Burundi, claiming that it was only used to purchase arms, but a national teachers strike led some Western governments (primarily France and Belgium) to urge support during the transitional period, lest the peace process be jeopardized. In January 2004, the IMF approved a $104 million arrangement to support the country's economic reform program over the next three years.

In January 2009 Burundi completed the HIPC initiative, which means that its future debt cancelation will total approximately 1.6 billion dollars. This means that Burundi saves 75 million dollars a year in debt cancellation, some of which has already been used in eliminating primary

school fees and building over 1,100 new schools.

With less than half its population literate, the government has made primary-school education free, creating new demands on infrastructure (classrooms) and supplies (books and desks). Belgium, which for historical reasons has a significant commitment to Burundi, granted it $12.5 million for education, road construction and rural water supply. Of that total, $5.6 million is dedicated to book purchases for students and teachers and manufacture of 50,000 desks for primary schools.

The government has announced plans to move the capital from Bujumbura, at the western edge of the country, to Gitega, its most central city. The move promises to set off a building boom there, helping economic growth and providing much needed employment. In June 2009 the World Bank approved a 45 million grant to support sustained reconstruction in Burundi; some of this money, which is to be reimbursed over a 5 year period, will be spent to provide better infrastructure and services that contribute to the government's goal of decentralization.

The Future

The challenges facing Burundi are gigantic, and the greatest among them are ethnic reconciliation and economic and social reconstruction. Success in these tasks will depend, in considerable measure, on the goodwill and generosity of the international community, which is the basis for many of the specific reconstruction plans forwarded by the Nkurunziza government.

Surprisingly, perhaps, the country seemed to have stabilized a bit after 2005. In early 2008, sporadic clashes in the capital Bujumbura briefly suggested that the FNL had not succeeded in convincing all its factions to end the struggle. However in June 2009 the FNL laid down its weapons and established itself as a political party. At present, the future of stability and reconciliation depends on the FNL commitment to peace.

Conflict has devastated the economy. Burundi is one of the poorest countries in the world, ranking 172 out of 179 countries on the UN's *Human Development Index* for 2008. Its economy is estimated to have contracted by 25% during the war years. By some measures, GDP per capita fell from $180 in 1993 to as low as $90 in 2004, and it was only marginally improved—at $114—in 2007(this according to World Bank estimates in 2008 at international prices). About 68% of the population survives on less than one dollar a day, with many relying on subsistence agriculture. Even years of positive performance will not fully reverse the tragedies of recent decades.

The Republic of Cameroon

Basic Facts

Area: 475,400 sq. km. = 183,552 sq. mi. (size of California plus one-fourth of Oregon)

Population: 18,500,000 (UN 2007 est.)

Capital City: Yaoundé; pronounced Yah-oon-*deh*)

Climate: Hot and humid in the south, progressively becoming drier to the inland north; arid in the Lake Chad area.

Neighboring Countries: Nigeria (northwest); Chad (northeast); Central African Republic (east); Congo, Gabon, Equatorial Guinea (south)

Official Languages: French (East Cameroon) and English (West Cameroon)

Other Principal Languages: There are 24 major African language groups, involving more than 275 separate languages. Prominent are Akoose, Bafia, Bafut, Bakoko, Bakundu, Bamileke, Bamun, Basaa, Beti, Bulu, Duala, Eton, Fang, Fe'fe', Fufulde, Gbaya, Kanuri, Kenyang, Kom, Lamnso', Limbum, Mafa, Makaa, Masana, Mbo, Medumba, Mungaka, Musugu, Ngiemboon, Ngembe, Tupuri, Yemba. Cameroon Pidgin, an English-based Creole language, is spoken primarily in the southwest and northern provinces and has become a widespread lingua franca in Cameroon, spoken as a second language by more than half the population.

Ethnic Groups: Cameroon Highlanders (Bamilike, Bamoun) 31%, Equatorial Bantu (Beti) 19%, Kirdi 11%, Fulani 10%, Northwestern Bantu 8%, Eastern Nigritic 7%, other African 13%, non-African less than 1%

Principal Religions: Christianity (about 53%), traditional beliefs (about 25%), Islam (about 22%)

Chief Commercial Products: Crude oil and petroleum products, lumber, cocoa beans, aluminum, coffee, and cotton

GNI Per Capita: $1290 (World Bank 2008 est.)

Currency: CFA franc

Former Colonial Status: German Colony (1884–1916), British Colony in West Cameroon (1916–1961); French Colony is East Cameroon (1916–1960)

Independence Date: January 1, 1960 (East Cameroon); October 1, 1961 (West Cameroon independence and federation with East Cameroon)

Chief of State: Paul Biya, President (since 1982)

National Flag: Three vertical stripes of green, red and yellow with a yellow star in the red stripe.

Land and People

Cameroon is a land of contrasts, containing almost every species of flora and fauna of tropical Africa and numerous varieties of wild game, stretches north from the Atlantic in a "hinge" position between West and Central Africa. From the Polynesian-like beaches, washed by the waters of the Bight of Biafra, there rise towering mountains which proceed directly north into West Cameroon. Mount Cameroon, the tallest peak in western Africa, towering almost 14,000 feet high, is an active volcano located close to the seacoast. The southern part of Cameroon, extending eastward in a horizontal line, is characterized by a low coastal basin with

Cameroon

equatorial forests. In the more north-central part of the country there is a series of grassy plateaus whose heights reach 4,500 feet, but in the extreme northern Lake Chad region, the dry climate supports only seasonal grazing and nomadic herding, culminating in a marshland.

Cameroonians have a long history of dances and craft. Many tribal groups produce pottery, textiles, and sculptures that are very elaborate and are used in everyday practices. The Bamiléké and Bamoun are particularly notable for their displays of blue and white clothing, and beaded calabashes. The Bamoun are also knows for their lost-wax bronze sculptures.

The Past: Political and Economic History

For early history, see *Historical Background and Colonial Period: the Germans* and *Colonial Period: The French*.

Cameroon resulted from a merger of (French) East Cameroon and (British) West Cameroon, which gained independence respectively on January 1, 1960 and on October 1, 1961. Under the leadership of Ahmadou Ahidjo, the *Union nationale camerounaise* (UNC), the country adopted a federal constitution that enshrined a single-party system. President Ahidjo (from East Cameroon) and Vice President John Foncha (from West Cameroon) received 97.5% of the vote in 1970 elections. Constitutional reforms in 1972 eliminated the state government of the two regions, but guaranteed continuation of the French language in the East and English in the West.

The legislative and presidential elections, held in 1978 and 1980 respectively, confirmed the dominance of Ahidjo and the UNC. Ahidjo was elected to a fifth five-year term, and all candidates for parliament were from the UNC. During his long rule, power was centralized in the capital, and in Ahidjo's hands. The regime was authoritarian and repressive and justified its suppression of civil and human rights by a need to contain ethnic division.

President Ahidjo suddenly resigned on November 6, 1982, handing over power to his prime minister, Paul Biya, who completed Ahidjo's term of office. The former president was said to be exhausted, but he retained his leadership of the UNC, the country's sole political party. Biya soon ousted Ahidjo from party leadership and sent him into exile. In January 1984 elections, President Biya, a Christian from the south, was elected in his own right to a five-year term of office by a margin of 99.98%. With this mandate, Biya set about consolidating his own power.

To eliminate potential competition, Biya convinced the parliament to amend the constitution to remove the office of prime minister. To emphasize the unitary nature

President Paul Biya

of the state, most of whose powers he held personally, Biya had the country's name changed from the "United Republic of Cameroon" to simply the "Republic of Cameroon."

In early April 1984, Biya's Republican Guard mutinied. Fierce fighting erupted in Yaoundé—members of the Republican Guard, composed mostly of Islamic northerners, waged a pitched battle with regular army units. After the rebellion was contained, Biya announced that Ahidjo had organized it from. The official number of deaths was "about 70," but the actual number was probably close to 1,500. Within weeks, 35 insurrectionists were tried and summarily executed. Ahidjo was tried in absentia and condemned to death for complicity in the plot.

A year later, to demonstrate his "New Deal" policies, President Biya renamed the country's sole legal party the Cameroon People's Democratic Movement (RDPC). To add democratic content to the newly renamed party, 324 candidates were approved to contest 180 seats in the legislative elections of April 1988. Given a choice, voters sent a number of aging political lions into retirement. The result was a National Assembly with younger members. The president was reelected with a 98.75% majority. With his renewed mandate, Biya announced wide-ranging programs to deal with Cameroon's economic crisis.

Biya needed to implement structural adjustments and budget cuts in order to receive international aid. He agreed to downsize the bureaucracy and cut government expenditures. Belt-tightening hurt and resentments rose. To accommodate demands for greater democracy, product of political changes in Eastern Europe and stronger western emphasis on democracy as a precondition for aid, Biya approved a multiparty system in 1990.

Opposition parties proliferated. Some 48 contested the legislative elections in March 1992, but fractured, the opposition stood little chance against the RDCP. The ruling

party won 88 of 180 seats in the National Assembly. The principal opposition party was the National Union for Democracy and Progress (UNDP), which elected 68 members to parliament. Sixteen opposition parties boycotted the election, including that of popular English-speaker John Fru Ndi—the Social Democratic Front.

The presidential election was advanced from the spring of 1993 to October 1992 to catch the divided opposition unprepared, and when finally conducted it was marred by massive fraud, irregularities, and unfairness. The state-owned television, for example, gave two-and-a-half hours of time to Biya, but only 16 minutes to the opposition.

The same pattern prevailed in the 1997 legislative elections, with the RDCP increasing its legislative majority to 109 of 180 seats. John Fru Ndi's Social Democratic Front captured 43 seats to become the principal opposition party. As usual, widespread intimidation and fraud were reported.

October 1997 presidential elections were virtually meaningless. President Biya refused to allow an independent electoral commission to organize them, and the main opposition parties refused to participate. Most citizens treated it as a non-event, but the government reported that 60% of registered voters participated and gave 80% of their votes to Biya.

Political power in Cameroon is concentrated in the office of president. The president appoints the cabinet, which serves at his pleasure. He names judges, generals and governors, district administrators and the heads of state corporations. Parliament, dominated by President Biya's Cameroon People's Democratic Movement (RDPC), consistently defers to the legislative program chosen by the executive.

Unsurprisingly, Biya's control has been used to increase presidential powers. Constitutional amendments in 1996, for example, increased the presidential term to seven years. In general, presidential power is maintained through active repression of the political opposition, especially in election years.

The government closely controls the electoral process, which is organized through the Ministry of Territorial Administration. Members of oppositional ethnic groups and those living in areas dominated by the opposition are effectively prevented from registering to vote. The government operates almost all broadcast media (a small private Catholic station rebroadcasts programs from Vatican Radio), and coverage of opposition activity is underwhelming. Print media, of small circulation and limited to urban distribution, are subject to considerable government restrictions and libel laws.

Tensions continue in the Anglophone areas of Cameroon, which feel marginalized by the Francophone majority. Separatist demonstrations in the western regions are regular occurrences. So is their repression by state security forces. Northern resentments, going back to the events of 1984, persist. Many feeldiscriminated against and excluded from a fair share of national riches.

Legislative elections were held in June 2002, and in advance President Biya effected a major revitalization of the RDPC. Biya banned tribal chiefs from standing for party posts, and urged party activists not to be swayed by candidates willing to buy themselves into power. In a March 2002 party voting, some 70% of grassroots RDPC leaders were replaced. Party barons lost to young men and women, suggesting the party was reinvigorating itself with a bit of new blood.

The June elections resulted in a crushing victory for the RDPC, which took 149 of the 180 seats. John Fru Ndi's Social Democratic Front (SDF), driven by internal conflicts, won only 22, but remained the principal opposition party. The loss, in percentage terms, was even greater for the *Union nationale pour la Démocratie et le Progrès* (UNDP), which went from four seats to one.

The RDPC victory, worthy of a single-party state, may have been achieved by means typically associated with those regimes. A Roman Catholic NGO monitoring the election reported numerous irregularities, including phony polling places, and Douala's Cardinal, Christian Tumi, called them "obviously and intentionally" mismanaged.

In assembling his cabinet, President Biya seemed to have an eye on the 2004 presidential elections, enlarging it to nearly 50 to include every relevant region and ethnicity. In this cabinet of national union, even the UNDP, which had been reduced to a single parliamentary seat, was given two cabinet portfolios.

In order to balance Cameroon's delicate ethnic and regional differences, prime ministers are traditionally English-speakers, and Biya reappointed his Anglophone premier, Mafany Musonge, who holds an engineering degree from Stanford University. (Cameroon's third most important office, the speakership of the National Assembly, is traditionally held by a northerner.)

Premier Musonge acted as Biya's campaign manager in the October 2004 presidential elections. After 22 years in power, President Biya had little opposition and the voters had little enthusiasm. John Fru Ndi of the SDF and Adamou Ndam Njoya, representing a coalition of opposition parties, provided minimum challenge. The Interior Ministry announced a landslide for

Biya—75% of the vote with 80% of those eligible voting. The government figures were scarcely believable. Symptomatically, only 4.6 million of an estimated eight million people over the age of 20 who were qualified to vote actually got their names on electoral registers.

Cardinal Tumi expressed the sentiment of many: people had lost confidence in the government's ability to hold a fair and impartial election. All of them since independence, he forcefully declared, had been "surrounded by fraud." A Commonwealth observer group said many young people had failed to vote because they felt alienated from the political process.

To suggest change, President Biya appointed a new prime minister, Ephraïm Inoni. Like his predecessor, the new prime minister is an English speaker from the southwest, with degrees from the National School of Administration and an American MBA.

Legislative and municipal elections took place June 2007, and one could expect what is standard Cameroonian experience: heightened manipulation and diminished participation. The opposition, particularly John Fru Ndi's SDF, was more divided than usual.

Border Issues

Cameroon faces border tension with several neighbors. With Nigeria, there have been disputes over the Lake Chad basin area and tensions over the Bakassi peninsula, a 400-square mile swamp-infested area of southwest Cameroon thought to hold significant oil reserves. Both countries submitted their Bakassi claims to the International Court of Justice (ICJ) and in October 2002, the court decided in favor of

Cameroon. It took a bit longer for the two states to agree on implementory procedures, but in mid-June 2006 Presidents Biya and Obasnajo—accompanied by UN Secretary-General Kofi Annan and witnessed by representatives of France, the U.S., the United Kingdom and Germany—signed an agreement ending nearly a half-century of dispute. In August 2008, Nigeria withdrew its troops and formally handed over the peninsula to Cameroon. The southern section of the peninsula will be administered by Nigeria for another two years, giving residents an opportunity to decide if they wish to chose Cameroonian sovereignty or emigrate to Nigeria. Full administrative control of the area by Cameroon will not occur until 2011.

Actual border demarcation of Bakassi began in late 2005 and is the largest—1700 kilometers—and most expensive demarcation process currently being undertaken by the UN. By early 2007 only 500 kilometers had been mapped and marked, leaving another 1,000 kilometers that cross remote rain forests and a 3,000-meter high mountain range.

In the parched northern region, Cameroon's plans for irrigated agriculture brought it into conflict with both Nigeria and Chad. Nigeria has threatened to bring the country back to the ICJ over disputes involving development projects on the Benue River. Chad has threatened similar action over irrigation and rice production projects on the Logone River. Even the border with the Central African Republic has seen several incidents of incursion.

The Present: Contemporary Issues

For two years in a row in the late 1990s Cameroon topped Transparency Interna-

Traditional fishing

Photo by E. Dounais
Courtesy of APFT-ULB

Cameroon

tional's list of countries perceived as being corrupt. Stung by its classification as the world's most corrupt state and with its consequent investor mistrust and diplomatic chastening, President Biya's government lumbered into an anticorruption campaign. Progress was slow; by 2006, Cameroon was still only five steps above the most corrupt country in the world—bottom-ranked Haiti.

So commonplace are corrupt acts that Cameroonians, like the proverbial Eskimo describing snow, have elaborated a rich vocabulary to describe them. *Magouiller* means "to scheme," *pistonner le dossier* "to pull strings;" *bien parler* is to "do what you have to," while *engraisser la patte* is to "grease someone's palm."

Prime Minister Inoni has become the terror of the bureaucratic classes. Unannounced visits to ministries have resulted in those absent being sacked. Ministry doors are locked to ensure promptness; those who dally risk being fired. The names of 73 top civil servants accused of embezzling public funds were published in early 2005 to highlight the anticorruption campaign, and in March, 500 more were accused of either awarding themselves extra money or claiming salaries for "nonexistent" workers. The government estimated the scam cost it one million dollars a month.

In July 2006, President Biya declared a zero-tolerance policy on corruption and this time around appeared to give meaning to words. By October, Cameroonians were treated to the relatively rare experience of seeing former ministers (Finance, Energy and Water) and high-level civil servants indicted for a variety of financial scams and embezzlement.

Cameroon's economy was traditionally based on agriculture until the discovery of oil in the 1970s, but oil production peaked in 1985 at 158,000 barrels a day (bbl/d) and has been in steady decline ever since. After dropping to a drought of 60,000 bbl/d in 2005, production rose in 2006 to 90,000 bbl/d.

If no major oil fields are discovered, current major oil fields will be depleted by 2010. In 2002 the government revised its petroleum laws to provide greater investment incentives and subsequently there has been new exploration in all three of its major petroleum basins.

Cameroon briefly benefited from the construction of the oil export pipeline from neighboring Chad. The World Bank, despite stiff opposition from environmentalists, supplied 3% of the financing for the $3.5 billion pipeline project, and a consortium of major oil companies—Exxon-Mobil, Petronas (the Malaysian National Oil Company) and Chevron undertook the project. The pipeline was the largest

single investment project in sub-Saharan Africa and was completed in July 2003, one year ahead of schedule. Pipeline construction supported GDP growth in Cameroon, but once ended, economic growth slowed to a mere 2.6% in 2005.

In March 2007 Cameroon's National Radio announced that the United States planned to invest nearly $3 billion in the country's eastern province to mine cobalt. According to the American Ambassador, Niels Marquardt, the investment would be made, despite the delays in establishing the institutions necessary to fight corruption.

Aside from oil, the country's main revenue earners are timber, cotton, cocoa and aluminum (mostly produced from bauxite imported from Guinea). Together, they account for 78% of export receipts. Cameroon is the world's fifth largest cocoa producer, and cocoa provides about 40% of its exports. Still, declining world market prices have resulted in reduced production. In several areas, parts of cocoa plantations have been destroyed to pave way for food crops such as tomato, vegetables and plantain.

About 40% of Cameroon's land is forested, but the forests are disappearing rapidly because of irresponsible logging activity. Logging concessions are awarded by a bidding system. The winner is traditionally not the highest bidder, but the company prepared to offer the highest financial inducements to officials.

Concession holders are often unrestrained by law or morality. In 2003 Greenpeace documented the work of three Dutch companies logging Cameroon's forest. They all operated illegally, said the re-

port, causing severe ecological and economic damage. Logging operations destroyed local villagers' subsistence and cash crops. The illegal logging also robbed the government of vital taxes, since none were paid on the illegal cuttings.

Friends of the Earth-Cameroon has estimated that half the timber logged in the country is illegally cut, costing the state around $2.7 million a year in lost revenues. Some suggestion of the illegal trade comes from comparing declared exports to European countries with declared imports. In 1998, for example, Cameroon declared 57,038 cubic meters of timber destined for Portugal, while Portuguese figures for the same year indicated imports of 91,111 cubic meters.

Cameroon qualified for debt relief under the Highly Indebted Poor Countries (HIPC) program in late 2000, but was cut off from program benefits in August 2003 after an IMF mission found "considerable deterioration in Cameroonian public finances in 2003–2004." After his reelection in 2004 President Biya became more cognizant of his country's disastrous economic condition and more actively pursued policies to complete the HIPC program. Thus, the "zero-tolerance" corruption program.

Despite some skepticism, the IMF and World Bank indicated Cameroon had completed its obligations under the HIPC initiative in May 2006. It will now receive more than $1 billion in bilateral relief and multilateral aid. External debt will be reduced by 50%.

There is a significant and growing Chinese presence in Cameroon. From as early as 1983, with the Lagdo hydroelectric dam

Rainforest logs reach the sea

Photo by G. Philippart de Foy
Courtesy APFT-ULB

154

Cameroon

on the Benue River, China has made major infrastructure contributions. Following President Biya's 2003 trip to China, the China International Water & Electrical Corporation offered to build several dams to supply the National Electricity Company. Most recently a Chinese consortium, China Road and Bridge Corporation, won the contract to repair the dilapidated roads in and around Douala, the business capital.

Chinese President Hu Jintao began his 2007 eight-nation tour of Africa—his third since taking office—with a stop in Cameroon. He left after approving more than $54 million in grants and preferential loans and signing a series of health and education accords. China will build a pediatric hospital in Douala and supply medical equipment to a Yaoundé hospital; at least two rural schools were also promised.

The Future

Slow economic growth and the repressive nature of the political system leave Cameroon as one of Africa's great disappointments. The immense potential benefits of oil wealth have been squandered in one of the world's most corrupt systems, and investment in human capital has lagged (though the country maintains a relatively high literacy rate). Recent riots in major cities over the rising prices of staple commodities are an indicator of the public's dissatisfaction with the government.

Politically, the regime's electoral manipulations have increasingly alienated voters, especially the young. While some other countries have slowly developed somewhat improved democratic credentials, Cameroon seems to be stuck in time under Paul Biya's regime. Elections up through 2007 were dominated by the governing party. With Biya consolidating power, there are few prospects for democratic openings.

There are some positive notes as well. In March 2009, Pope Benedict XVII visited Cameroon and congratulated the country for the relatively peaceful coexistence between the Muslim and the Christian population. The country has prospects for continued peace and further economic investment from China and the western world, but the likelihood of improved governance under Biya is low.

155

The Central African Republic

The important, but costly, transportation of timber products

Basic Facts

Area: 626,780 sq. km. = 242,000 sq. mi. (slightly smaller than Texas)

Population: 4,300,000 (UN 2007 est.)

Capital City: Bangui (pronounced Ban-*ghee*)

Climate: Temperate, with a rainy season (June to October) and a dry season (November to May).

Neighboring Countries: Republic of Congo and Democratic Republic of Congo (south); Cameroon (west); Chad (northwest); Sudan (northeast and east)

Official Language: French

Other Principal Languages: Sangho (lingua franca and national language), Arabic, Hausa, Swahili

Ethnic Groups: Baya 34%, Banda 27%, Sara 10%, Mandjia 21%, Mboum 4%, M'Baka 4%, Europeans 6,500 (including 3,600 French)

Principal Religions: Indigenous beliefs 24%, Protestant 25%, Roman Catholic 25%, Muslim 15%, and other 11%. Note: animistic beliefs and practices strongly influence the Christian majority.

Chief Commercial Products: Diamonds, timber, cotton, coffee, tobacco

GNI Per Capita: $479 (World Bank 2008 est.)

Currency: CFA franc

Former Colonial Status: French Colony (1894–1960)

Independence Date: August 11, 1960.

Chief of State: General François Bozizé (by military action, March 15, 2003)

National Flag: Four horizontal stripes (from top to bottom) of blue, white, green and yellow, divided by a red stripe down the middle, with a yellow star on the left hand side of the blue stripe.

Land and People

Located in almost the exact center of Africa, the Central African Republic is a vast, rolling plateau rising 2,000 to 2,500 feet above sea level. Lying more than 300 miles from the sea, this sun-drenched land of agricultural and forest products found its original wealth in ivory from its once large herds of massive elephants. Prolific groups of wild animals roam the land today, making it one of the most zoologically interesting areas of Africa.

There is a small area of forest in the southwest, which is rapidly succeeded by the rolling plateaus of the plains, rising gently to the mountains of the northeast. Heavy rainstorms occur almost daily during the wet season from June to October, seldom permitting the ground to become dry. November is the start of the dry season when the leaves of the trees turn to brilliant hues because of lack of moisture. In the following weeks the leaves fall, and the grass, having grown to the height of more than five feet, turns tinder dry. Fire becomes a great danger as the drought continues.

The Ubangi River flows along a good portion of the southern border, then plunges south to join the waters of the mighty Congo.

The conga drum is the primary instrument used in the CAR. It is made out of wet leather, stretched over a hollowed-out length drum. They come in every size and shape and can be over a yard tall and can be heard several miles away, these drums were often used as speaking drums transmitting messages from one village to another in the absence of faster means of communication. Xylophones are also very popular musical instruments, made with wood and gourds.

The Past: Political and Economic History

For early history, see *Historical Background* and *The Colonial Period: the French.*

The Central African Republic's independence is intimately associated with the work of a Catholic priest, Barthélémy Boganda. The first African Catholic priest in Ubangui-Chari, as the colony was then known, Boganda represented the territory in the French National Assembly in 1946. His nationalist sentiments developed rapidly, and he left the priesthood and formed his own political party, the *Mouvement pour l'Évolution Sociale de l'Afrique Noire* (MESAN) in 1949. Responsible for the country's name (*la République Centrafricain*), its flag, national anthem and motto, Boganda profoundly influenced CAR's early history. Immensely popular, he was reelected deputy in 1951 and 1956.

Boganda was among those African nationalists who opposed the balkanization of the former French Federations into independent states, but when his federal notions received little support, he returned to Ubangui-Chari to work for its eventual independence. Boganda did not see the fruit of his labors. He died in a plane crash in March 1959.

Independence came on August 11, 1960, and the territory took the name Central African Republic. David Dacko became CAR's first president. Dacko soon created a single-party state and established close relations with the communist Chinese. The influx of Chinese technical and diplomatic personnel aroused the resentment of the military, which ousted Dacko on the night of December 31–January 1, 1966. General Jean-Bédel Bokassa assumed power, abolished the constitution, dissolved the legislature and centralized the administration in his appointed cabinet. Power seemed to be infectious for Bokassa, who later declared himself Emperor.

In late 1976 a new constitution created the Central African Empire. In late 1977 in sweltering Bangui, a crowd of over 3,000 guests witnessed Jean-Bédel Bokassa place a 2,000-diamond-encrusted crown on his head and proclaim himself Emperor Bokassa I. The spectacle was said to have cost well over $22 million in this landlocked country where the average per capita annual income was $120.

Opposition to Bokassa hardened at home and abroad. While visiting Libya in September 1979, he was overthrown by his cousin and advisor, former President David Dacko. With the support of French armed forces, Dacko reestablished the Republic, but the CAR continued to be

plagued by corrupt, inept government. Elections held in 1981 were clouded by charges of fraud, four months later when Army Chief of Staff General André Kolingba demanded President Dacko's resignation he quickly received it.

General Kolingba operated a virtual military dictatorship for the next decade. The new constitution of 1986 provided him a single-party state and a six-year term as president. He organized a new political party, the *Rassemblement démocratique centrafricain* (RDC), and in parliamentary elections, held in 1987, all candidates for the National Assembly had to belong to the presidential party. There was little to restrain Kolingba's exercise of power.

The presidential elections of 1986 took place shortly after the unexpected return of CAR's former emperor, Jean-Bédel Bokassa, who had fled virtual house arrest in France. Bokassa was put on trial, charged with murder and a variety of other crimes, the lurid details of which prompted international news coverage. After several months of intermittent action, the trial concluded in 1988 with Bokassa's guilt and death sentence. President Kolingba softened the sentence to life in prison and later shortened even this. The former emperor died of natural causes in 1996.

By the early 1990s, the citizens of the CAR had little to show for a decade of President Kolingba's authoritarian rule. Civil rights were severely restricted, human rights were systematically abused, the economy had deteriorated, and the treasury was empty.

Strikes and work stoppages by government employees, unpaid for months, culminated in riots. In April 1991, Kolingba, under heavy pressure, promised to allow political opposition. The newly responsive National Assembly revised the constitution to transform the country into a

multiparty democracy in July. President-General Kolingba, fearing he had lost control of things, proposed a "Grand National Debate" (GND) to discuss democratic transformation.

The opposition would have none of it, and when the GND was about to open, in August 1992, members of the United Democratic Forces—a coalition of 14 opposition parties—protested, demanding a genuine national conference to bring democracy to the country. President-General Kolingba sent in the troops. Soldiers attacked the marchers with tear gas, then plowed into the crowd swinging their rifle butts. One opposition leader was savagely beaten and later died of his wounds.

The situation continued to deteriorate. Elections were scheduled and then postponed. The opposition split. In May 1993 Kolingba's presidential guard mutinied, demanding its back wages. It was the first time the armed forces had rebelled against the regime, but it would not be the last.

In the late 1993 elections, Kolingba came in dead last. Ange-Félix Patassé of the *Movement for the Liberation of the Centrafrican People* (MLPC) beat out David Dacko to become president. Twelve years of military rule were ended, but President Patassé faced an empty treasury, a disgruntled civil service, an unpaid army, and a deeply divided country.

Years of military dictatorship had elevated army power and prestige. Soldiers were little prepared to see these cut back, as President Patassé had to do. In April 1996, when the government could not find sufficient funds to pay them, the troops mutinied. French troops crushed the mutiny and Patassé came up with money and promised amnesty, but soldiers mutinied a second time in May, after accusing Patassé of violating the amnesty by arresting some of the April mutineers. In November troops mutinied yet again, escalating their demands to include the President's resignation.

The demand highlighted the regional and ethnic conflicts that inundated the country. The mutineers were southerners, mostly members of the Yakoma tribe of ex-President Kolingba. Patassé is a northerner, a member the Baya tribe.

Mali's highly respected former military ruler, Amadou Toumani Touré, was invited to mediate. The Bangui Accords he brokered involved amnesties for mutineers, a government of national unity, and the deployment of African peacekeepers to replace French troops. Both parties signed the Accords in January 1997, but could not restore peace.

The Inter-African Surveillance Mission for the Bangui Accords (MISAB) was barely in place before it faced another mutiny in June. French and Chadian

troops responded with a "muscular offensive" against the mutineers, whacking them soundly into another cease-fire in early July 1997. French troops withdrew in mid-April 1998 and were replaced by the UN Mission in the Central African Republic (MINURCA).

Legislative elections in November and December 1998 did little to build a climate of trust. In the first round, President Patassé's MLPC had a slight lead, winning 26 seats to the opposition's 17. For the second round, 14 opposition parties signed an electoral pact to support the best-placed candidate against those of the MLPC. The results were inconclusive. The MLPC and its allies held 51 seats; the opposition, were it to be united, held 53. Seven independents were elected, making them the focal point of everyone's attention. "Discussions" with the independents went on, and, suddenly, there were defections to President Patassé's coalition. The defector was "bought," said the opposition spokesman. "We have a majority," said the president as he proceeded to appoint a prime minister.

This was the political climate that preceded the September 1999 presidential elections. The opposition could not agree on a single candidate to confront President Patassé, so ten names appeared on the presidential ballot. The most prominent candidates were former presidents David Dacko and André Kolingba. The opposition found much to complain about and rejected the results even before the election was held.

Hopes that Patassé would be forced into a runoff election were dashed. Some 56% of registered voters went to the polls and the president won by a razor slim majority: 51.6%. General Kolingba received 19.3% of the votes and David Dacko came in third with 11.1%. Observers declared the election free and fair. Any irregulari-

General Kolingba

Central African Republic

"Rebels" in north-central Central African Republic

©Nicholas Reader/IRIN

ties, they said, were not of a kind to affect the overall result.

The election brought no stability. Desperately poor, the Central African Republic teetered on the brink of implosion. Unable to pay civil servants their salaries, students their stipends, or retirees their pensions, the government faced an ongoing series of protests and demonstrations. A near-permanent strike of government workers began in November 2000 when demonstrators set up barricades and burned tires in the capital before being dispersed by security forces. They demanded nearly 30 months of back wages.

CAR represents a worst-case scenario for the abjectly poor state: economic crisis exacerbates political tensions and facilitates social disintegration. Crime in the capital and banditry in the countryside increased. The state had little capacity to project its authority beyond the Bangui city limits, and armed banditry reached insurrectional proportions, threatening the state's authority in the provinces. Bandits raped, robbed, and murdered at will, disrupting trade between nearby Chad and the Cameroonian port of Douala, the CAR's main outlet to the sea.

In May 2001 the troublesome General Kolingba instigated a *coup d'état* against the Patassé government, but the attempt was repressed by the intervention of Libyan troops and several hundred *Mouvement de libération du Congo* (MLC) troops of Jean-Pierre Bemba, who crossed the Ubangui River from their northern Congolese bases.

The regime turned increasingly paranoid. Patassé fired his defense, interior, security, and disarmament ministers in August, and army chief of staff General François Bozizé in October. Bozizé fled to neighboring Chad in November after an attempt to arrest him led to five days of fighting between his supporters and troops loyal to the government.

As the country deteriorated socially and economically, only foreign arms kept President Patassé in power. Forces loyal to General Bozizé invaded Bangui's northern suburbs in October 2002. After ten days of destructive fighting, they were driven out with the help of Libyan and Congolese forces. For Bangui's suffering citizenry, salvation was nearly as bad as rebel assault: undisciplined, Bemba's MLC troops raped and robbed the very people they were supposed to defend, further alienating them from President Patassé. It was the fifth coup attempt the CAR president had survived. He would not survive the sixth.

Soldiers loyal to General Bozizé, aided by Chadian mercenaries, left their Chadian sanctuary in March 2003 and completed the work they had begun the previous October. Bangui fell to the rebels in a day. There was almost no one left willing to defend the Patassé regime.

General Bozizé returned from Paris and was greeted as a liberator by Bangui crowds. Reportedly a thoughtful and deeply religious man, the general showed himself tough, generous, and moral in his initial pronouncements. "Thieves and other looters," he said, "will henceforth be considered military targets." The violence and looting in Bangui, particularly against figures of the former regime, ended quickly. Beginning the process of national reconciliation, Bozizé amnestied all those who had plotted the overthrow of President Patassé in May 2001. To head a transitional government of national unity, he called upon the Mr. Clean of CAR politics, Abel Goumba.

Nearly 77 years old, Goumba was a companion from the early days of Barthélémy Boganda, the republic's founder. A man of principle, Goumba had opposed each of the republic's four presidents (Dacko, Bokassa, Kolingba and Patassé). At the time of his appointment he was the leader of the Patriotic Front for Progress (FPP) party and head of a 12-member coalition of opposition parties.

The new regime's most pressing problem was the restoration of security. Achieving this in the capital was the easier task. Once done, Bangui's citizens felt free to "walk anywhere, even late at night, without worrying about getting shot or robbed," as one local put it. Outside the capital, however, the government still works to reassert its authority. In January 2004, after receiving vehicles and equipment from China, France, Morocco, and Sudan, the army sent 1,000 troops into the southwestern region—where most of the country's mines are located—to restore order. It also dispatched specially trained forces to fight banditry in the northern provinces.

In many cases it was difficult to determine who the "bandits" were. Some were Chadian mercenaries, hired to support Bozizé's invasion, who had not yet been sufficiently paid for their services. Others were unemployed soldiers loyal to former President Patassé or his defense minister, Jean-Jacques Demafouth, while still others were simply opportunistic highway robbers who set up roadblocks, plundered travelers, and held the more prosperous for ransom. In late April 2004, President Bozizé agreed to pay the Chadian fighters the local equivalent of $1,000 to encourage their return home.

Some of the money may have come from a $2 million interest-free loan given by China to help chronically cash-short Bangui deal with unpaid civil servants. The IMF and World Bank also offered emergency post-conflict aid, the first time the institutions had provided funding since October 2002. The financing helped

General François Bozizé, President

the regime push forward with its other central task, the restoration of democracy.

Voter registration began in September 2004, and voters overwhelmingly approved a new constitution in December. The transitional constitutional court approved only five of fifteen individuals who submitted their candidacy papers to run for president. Among the approved were François Bozizé, who declared himself an independent candidate, his vice president Abel Goumba, former President André Kolingba, and two others. The court disqualified all candidates from the MLPC, the country's former ruling party. After considerable public outcry, President-General Bozizé allowed three of them—Jean-Paul Ngoupandé, Martin Ziguélé, and Charles Massi—to seek the presidency.

When the ballots from the March 2005 election were counted, Bozizé topped the poll. With only 42.97% of the vote, he was forced into a runoff with the MLPC candidate, former Prime Minister Martin Ziguélé, who received 23.53%. In runoff elections 64.23% of the electorate opted to continue the president-general in office.

The election assured neither security nor stability. Initially aided by Chadian "irregulars" in his efforts to topple the Patassé regime, President Bozizé saw his country increasingly threatened by the spillover effects of civil conflict in Darfur and Chad. In early April 2006, Bozizé closed the border with Sudan after a column of some 20 pickup trucks loaded with Chadian rebels took a shortcut through CAR on their way to overthrow President Déby.

Birao, situated in the three-frontier-zone where the borders of CAR, Chad and Sudan meet, became a high priority target for Sudan-supported troublemakers. On October 30, 2006 rebels identifying themselves as men of the *Union des forces démocratiques pour le rassemblement* (UFDR: Union of Democratic Forces Coalition) captured the town; they were, it was reliably reported, a mixture of Central Africans and remnants of the Chadian mercenaries who once had fought for General Bozizé. Their arms and logistical support were Sudanese.

Defense agreements with France were invoked, and French firepower quickly destroyed rebel mortars and heavy machine guns. Their threatened advance on Bangui stopped, rebels fled back to their Sudanese sanctuary. This scenario was virtually replayed in March 2007, this time with French paratroopers and Mirage-fighter-jet support, as France acted robustly to contain the spillover effects of conflict in Darfur.

The March attack on Birao came less than a month after President Bozizé had signed a peace deal, brokered by Moamer Qadhafi, with one major rebel group, Abdoulaye Miskine's *Front démocratique de libération du peuple centrafricain* (FDPC). It was part of a national reconciliation process. By mid-April, even the UFDR military commander was saying that "the time has come to make peace and work together for the reconstruction of our country" as he too signed a peace accord with President Bozizé.

The rebels agreed to sequester their men in an army cantonment from where they will eventually be integrated into the national army. In return, the government accepted the UFDR as a political party and committed itself to introducing a law extending amnesty to former UFDR fighters. The inhabitants of Birao may not have heard of these developments. In March, following the French bombardment to oust the rebels, the UN reported that 90% of the city's population had fled. Out of a population of 14,000, only 600 people remained; 70% of the city's houses had been burned or partially destroyed, and neither schools nor hospital remained.

The Present: Contemporary Issues

CAR's economic situation remains precarious. President Bozizé inherited an economy in shambles. Mismanagement since Bokassa and continuing civil strife have led to general economic deterioration and deepening poverty for most citizens. At only $379 per capita, average annual incomes still have not returned to 1990 levels. Symptomatic of the country's abject poverty, life expectancy in 2005 was a mere 39.4 years. In early 2006 the UN's Office for the Coordination of Humanitarian Affairs (OCHA) estimated that life expectancy was falling at a rate of six months every year. On the UN's *Human Development Index* for 2006, CAR is ranked 171 out of 179—essentially the eighth poorest country in the world. According to one UN report, more than two-thirds of the population lives on less than a dollar a day.

Civil conflict has devastated the country, and regional banditry continues to disrupt the economy and displace people. Adding to local misery, the northern regions have also experienced an influx of refugees fleeing civil conflict in Sudan and Chad. UN sources estimated there were more than a million vulnerable people in the area, and the UN High Commissioner for Refugees called the area "the world's most neglected crisis." In February 2006 the UN's Office for the Coordination of Humanitarian Affairs (OCHA) convened a donors conference asking for $46 million to deal with the deteriorating situation.

Salary arrears and work stoppages to protest nonpayment of wages are regular features of life in the country. China helped bail the government out of difficult circumstances with a $2 million interest-free loan in March 2004. The money went to pay civil servants, but the effect was short lived. In October 2005 civil servants again went on strike for several weeks, demanding salary arrears going back some 45 months. France contributed over $2 million in budgetary aid in 2006 to keep the government more up-to-date in paying its employees.

Agriculture and forestry are the mainstays of economy, accounting for 56% of GNP and employing 66% of the workforce. Subsistence farming dominates, with farmers growing cassavas, yams, bananas, sorghum, millet, and rice. Cotton and coffee are cash crops, grown for export, but prices for both commodities have declined on world markets. Getting export crops to market in CAR's prevailing insecurity is risky at best.

The country has significant forestry potential, with over 60 commercially viable trees. Development of the sector is hampered by high transportation costs and delivery problems that can add 60% to production costs. Because it is landlocked, CAR must send its logs downriver via Brazzaville to Pointe-Noire, or by road to Douala in Cameroon—a costly proposition given the dilapidated conditions of Cameroonian roads. Neighboring countries that are not land-locked also appear to have an advantage in industrialization.

Diamonds have traditionally contributed half of CAR's foreign earnings, but production is affected by political instability. An estimated 80,000 small-scale miners recover about 500,000 carats each year, over half of which are of gem quality. Diamond exports account for about 54% of the nation's export earnings. From export taxes, the government earns between three and four million dollars annually, but smug-

Central African Republic

gling remains a significant problem. It is estimated that the 500,000 carats officially exported represent only one-half of the country's diamonds sold abroad.

With a resource-hungry economy China is keenly interested in CAR. When President Bozizé met with Chinese President Hu Jintao in August 2004, the Chinese leader said China was interested in exploring cooperation in the oil, diamond, iron ore, and timber sectors. With its plans to build new nuclear power plants, China is also interested in CAR's uranium deposits in the Bakouma basin. In 2006 President Bozizé opened the country's first major uranium mining operation in the Bakouma, run by the South African firm UraMin. There is considerable evidence that the oil basin currently being pumped in southern Chad extends across the border into the Central African Republic. China's national oil company, Sinopec, is reportedly seeking concessions in the area.

HIV/AIDS is rampant in the Central African Republic. In July 2006 President Bo-

zizé named it the "principal cause of death" for the country's most dynamic elements; by official figures, 15% of the population is affected by the disease. In reality, the percentage is probably higher. A disturbing phenomenon in the CAR's AIDS epidemic is the presence of elevated HIV/AIDS rates among the best-educated sectors of the population. AIDS was the principal cause of death among teachers, for example, between 1996 and 1998. "It's a profession," said one researcher, "where one is more exposed to easy sexual relations."

The current peace talks with rebel groups have been slowed but continue to hold. The parliament passed legislation grating an ammesty to the UFDR and another major rebel group. In December 2008 it also pledged to establish a new form of unity government. In January the new structure of the government was unveiled, including François Naouyama of the APRD and Djomo Didou of the UFDR, but the opposition says the changes to the cabinet are utterly insufficient.

The Future

The Central African Republic has long been one of Africa's weakest states. The legacy of the Bokassa years lingers: poor administration and weak governance have characterized C.A.R. ever since. There is little to suggest substantial improvement is in the cards, though the immediate conflicts seem to have subsided for the time. Conflicts with several rebel groups place the Bozizé government under considerable pressure, which the government in turn has often turned into excessive repression. Attempts at democratization, while occasionally uplifting, are ultimately fitful and unconvincing.

Even the prospects of increased mineral wealth do not suggest a brighter future; in the presence of instability, corruption, and political strife, subsoil resources often exacerbate social tensions more than they resolve them. The economy and politics alike suggest that the country will continue on a difficult trajectory.

The Republic of Chad

Tibesti Region, Northern Chad

Basic Facts

Area: 1,284,640 sq. km. = 496,000 sq. mi. (the size of Texas, New Mexico and Arizona)

Population: 10,800,000 (UN 2007 est.)

Capital City: N'Djaména

Climate: Dry desert in the north varies from 10° to 122°F.; the central and southern areas are warm with increasing rainfall and humidity in the South, where there is a six-month dry season.

Neighboring Countries: Cameroon (southwest); Niger and Nigeria (west); Libya (north); The Sudan (east); Central African Republic (southeast and south)

Official Languages: French and Arabic

Other Principal Languages: Over 100, including Gulay, Kanuri, Karanda, Maba, Marba, Marfa, Masana, Mundang, Musey, Ngambay, Sango (a Creole trade language), and Sar

Ethnic Groups: Muslims: (Arabs, Toubou, Hadjerai, Fulbe, Kotoko, Kanembou, Baguirmi, Boulala, Zaghawa, and Maba). Non-Muslims: (Sara, Ngambaye, Mbaye, Goulaye, Moundang, Moussei, Massa). Nonindigenous: 150,000 (of whom an estimated 1,000 are French)

Principal Religions: Muslim 51%, Christian 35%, animist 7%, other 7%

Chief Commercial Products: Cotton, cattle, and textiles

GNI Per Capita: $936 (World Bank 2008 est.)

Currency: CFA franc

Former Colonial Status: French Colony (1910–1960)

Independence Date: August 11, 1960

Chief of State: Idriss Déby Itno, President (since December 1990)

National Flag: Three vertical stripes of blue, gold and red.

Land and People

Landlocked Chad, more than 1,500 miles from any seaport, lies almost in the center of Africa and is one of the transitional nations between the desert to the north and the fertile southern area of the continent. For centuries it has been the crossroads of traders going back and forth between the Sahara-Mediterranean Sea region and the tropical areas of West Africa. Contact with Muslim traders may explain the conversion of some populations living in the Sahel region to Islam as early as the 9th century, before the arrival of nomadic Arab tribes.

Although Chad resembles a shallow basin in which Lake Chad, a former inland sea, occupies the "drain" position to the west, topographically it has three distinct regions. The Chadian Sahara in the North is a land of dry desert sand dunes that rise up to a height of 12,000 feet above sea level in the Tibesti Mountains. Only 1.2% of the population of Chad, mostly tribal nomads, inhabits this area. The endless expanse of desert, scorching by day, sinks to below freezing levels at night.

The central portion is a semiarid land of treeless plains; this section traditionally has received just enough rainfall to support cattle raising, but experiences periodic devastating droughts. The green southern area, with more ample rainfall, supports 45% of the country's population, who mainly engage in cotton cultivation.

Five countries share the Lake Chad Basin; which is fed by the Shari and Logone Rivers in the southwest corner of the nation. Lake Chad, once one of Africa's largest lakes, has been drying up and is now a mere fraction of its former size.

In July 2002 the French paleoanthropologist Michel Brunet presented a skull, unearthed in the Chadian north, which could be as old as seven million years old. Named "Toumai," the skull reveals both ape and human features. The skull could be the oldest example of a pre-human ancestor that walked upright. Scientists suspect Toumai is the closet specimen yet to the evolutionary split between humans and apes. Justifiably excited by the discovery, older than any such fossil remain found in the Rift Valley, Brunet told a Chadian audience that "the cradle of humanity is in Chad. Toumai is your ancestor."

The Past: Political and Economic History

For early history, see *Historical Background* and *The Colonial Period: The French.*

Under provisions of the constitution of the French Fifth Republic, Chad became an autonomous republic within the French Community in November 1958. At independence in August 1960, Chad was deeply divided between the black and often Christian populations of the more fertile and economically developed southwest, and the Arabized Muslim populations of the north. The south was more receptive to colonial rule; French language and culture were introduced. Christian missionaries made numerous converts in the south, increased educational opportunities, and improved healthcare. Conversely, the north rejected any education that did not include the teaching of Arabic and the Koran. In the south, the French introduced cotton cultivation and the area became economically successful, or as the French colonizers called it, "useful." Content to look back-

Chad

ward, the north experienced stagnation; its economy evolved little and the French came to think of it as "useless."

At independence, François (later Ngarta) Tombalbaye, a southerner, because the country's first president. He was a teacher and trade union leader. In 1963, Tombalbaye dissolved all political parties except his own *Parti progressiste tchadien* (PPT) and increasingly repressed both his fellow southerners and northerners. Northern Muslims coalesced behind the Chadian National Liberation Front (Frolinat) and rebelled against the central government. What started as reaction against the banning of political parties in 1963 turned into civil war by 1966.

Frolinat operated primarily in the north with the support of Libya, where it maintained bases. It advocated closer ties with the Arab states of North Africa and a reduction of French influence in Chad. French military forces stationed in Chad were brought in to suppress the revolt in 1973, but Frolinat continued its guerrilla operations with the help of Libyan weapons.

Tombalbaye accused the French of trying to unseat him in July 1973, and, in reaction, pursued an "Africanization" program. The single party was renamed National Movement for Cultural and Social Revolution; the use of Christian forenames was abolished (the president dropped "François" for Ngarta), as was the use of French names

for streets and places—except for Avenue Charles de Gaulle in the capital Fort Lamy (renamed N'Djaména). Economic conditions worsened and dissatisfaction increased, especially among the military.

In 1975 southern officers killed President Tombalbaye and replaced him with another southerner, Colonel Félix Malloum. By this time Frolinat had split (a continuing tradition among northern groups) into two factions, one willing to accept support from Libya under Goukouni Oueddeï, (pronounced Weh-day), and an anti-Libyan faction headed by Hissène Habré (pronounced Ah-bray). To unify a divided country, Col. Malloum agreed to share power with Habré, but the coalition was short-lived.

Malloum and Habré soon split, and, after losing a violent power struggle, Malloum was forced to flee N'Djaména in 1979. Northern faction leaders formed a coalition government headed by Goukouni Oueddeï, with Hissène Habré as prime minister. From this point Chad's civil conflict became less between north and south than a struggle among northern warlords.

French forces were asked to leave the country in May 1980; most Europeans went with them, and the U.S. Embassy was closed. The streets of N'Djaména became a no-man's land as the armies of Oueddeï and Habré struggled for supremacy. Libya

offered military help to Oueddeï's beleaguered forces, and from December 1980 to November 1981 Libya occupied most of the country. Habré's rebels, unable to compete with well-equipped Libyans, faded into eastern Chad to await a better opportunity to seize power.

Oueddeï asked Libyan forces to leave in late 1981, and when they had gone, Habré saw his chance. Within days his troops had seized a large part of the country, and he was on his way to an easy victory over Oueddeï. OAU peacekeeping forces moved into Chad and checked the rebel advance, driving Habré back to eastern Chad.

Life in N'Djaména temporarily returned to a semblance of order, but in mid-1982 Habré swept out of eastern Chad and, amid bitter fighting, seized the capital. The OAU troops remained neutral, Oueddeï escaped to Cameroon, and Hissène Habré declared himself president. The OAU recognized Habré's government, and its troops withdrew by the end of June. Brought to power by violence, Habré would rule with cruelty and terror. Neither brought stability.

With Libyan help, Oueddeï continued to resist the N'Djaména government, while France and Zaïre supported Habré. With destructive forces evenly balanced, fighting became sporadic after early 1984. However, diplomatic mediation remained fruitless given Chad's endemic factionalism.

Cattle herding

©Photographie Michel Hasson

When Libyan forces began building an airfield at Ouadi (Wadi) Doum in the northern desert, the French responded. The airfield was hit, and a Libyan plane bombed N'Djaména the next day. Then came the surprise: Oueddeï announced his resignation as head of the rebels, and declared his solidarity with Hissène Habré. Libya promptly placed him under arrest in Tripoli. This left Col. Qadhafi the sponsor of a revolution without a leader. Ouaddeï's rebels simply deserted the cause. With French assistance, the Chadian army struck Libyan units in northern Chad with devastating effect. By 1987 Libya had been forced out of the entire northern region, apart from the Aouzou strip and parts of Tibesti. (The International Court of Justice finally awarded the Aouzou Strip to Chad in 1994 and all Libyan forces withdrew from the territory a few months later.) About $1 billion in Soviet armaments was abandoned by the fleeing army. Habré regained control of N'Djaména in November 1988, but proved unable to master the country's divisive factionalism.

In April 1989, Idriss Déby, one of Habré's leading generals, defected and fled to Sudan, from where he invaded the country in November 1990. On December 2, his troops entered war-exhausted N'Djaména without battle, President Habré and the forces loyal to him having fled. A national charter was approved by Déby's Patriotic Salvation Movement (MPS) in February 1991, and Déby became the latest Chadian president. Since then President Déby has maintained a fragile, always intermittent, peace. Armed rebels have been offered amnesty and integration into the national armed forces; opposition political parties have been co-opted and their leaders given ministerial appointments. But as soon as one group reconciles with the government, a discontented faction hives off, or another group seems to spring up.

One could see the absence of Chadian unity in terms of a north/south division. Northerners are Arabized pastoralists with a long warrior tradition. Southerners are sedentary and Christianized, long subject to slaving raids by their northern neighbors. In reality, Chad's conflicts have as much to do with a vision of power and the nature of the state. Once lodged in N'Djaména, the group in power imposes a centralized view of the state and its authority, snuffing out resistance and denying individuality. In a situation where there are over 200 different ethnic groups to be satisfied, a more reasonable course might involve greater decentralization and localized autonomy. But the central government has usually rejected federalism, seeing it as a loss of power and control over the meager resources available.

The country's first free, multiparty presidential elections were held in June 1996. Idriss Déby won nearly 70% of the vote in a runoff election in July. The election was vigorously protested by the 14 other candidates who had run against him. In the 1997 legislative elections, Déby's MPS fell short of an outright majority, winning only 55 of 125 seats. The Union for Renewal and Democracy (URD)—the party of his southern presidential rival General Wadal Abdelkader Kamougué—won 31. Kamougué rallied to the government and was elected speaker of the National Assembly. As part of the calculus of coalition, Déby also appointed a southerner as prime minister.

The south remained restive, and by 1997 there was a resurgence of factional resistance. The revolt was triggered by discussions over the development of a major oil field, and, once again, the question of who controls resources and how they will be used. To highlight demands for greater participation in making those decisions, groups resorted to kidnapping Europeans.

Once President Déby had resolved things with southerners, there was an upsurge of kidnappings in the north. By October 1998, it was apparent that the government had to deal with yet another northern rebel movement. Led by a former defense minister, Youssouf Togoïmi, the *Mouvement pour la démocratie et la justice au Tchad* (MDJT) was centered in the sparsely populated Tibesti region—a mountainous, semi-desert area ideal for guerrilla warfare. The area, as a product of the war with Libya, is also one of the most heavily mined areas in the world, with thousands of antitank and antipersonnel mines.

The war continued through 2001 at considerable cost to the government. Libya offered mediation and ultimately got the two sides to sign a peace deal that ended three years of conflict. The accord provided for an immediate ceasefire, release of prisoners, rebel integration into the national army, and "government jobs" for MDJT leaders.

Tactically, the accord gave the MDJT, reportedly suffering from major resupply difficulties, badly needed breathing space. The government, in need of political stability to assure financing of the Doba oil project and smooth spring parliamentary elections, fulfilled its obligations. Parliament voted an amnesty bill for the rebels in February and political prisoners were released. It seemed the country was heading for its spring parliamentary elections in an atmosphere of uncharacteristic calm.

However, discussions broke down over the specifics of those "government jobs." Youssouf Togoïmi demanded nothing less

President Idriss Déby Itno

than the premiership, a position discarded by the government as "unconstitutional." The rebels themselves were divided; the intransigents supported Togoïmi in rejecting the agreement, but his deputy, Adoum Togoi, a former ambassador to Libya and reputedly close to the Libyans, argued for it. For his troubles, Togoi was briefly jailed.

In September 2002, Togoïmi died in a Libyan hospital after having been badly wounded in a landmine explosion. With its leader dead, the MDJT remains divided, split between a military high command hostile to President Déby and a political branch in exile more willing to negotiate. Each in turn has vexed the government.

The MDJT military wing reaffirmed its awkward presence in the spring of 2004 when it announced it had captured fleeing members of an Algerian terrorist group. Known in French as *Groupe salafiste pour la prédication et le combat* (GSPC), the terrorists were part of an Algerian Islamist organization wanted in connection with the kidnapping of several European tourists the year before.

As part of a State Department-sponsored program called the Pan-Sahel Initiative, the U.S. military was working with local security forces in Algeria, Chad, Mali, Niger, and Mauritania to capture or kill members of the Salafist group. GSPC members were detected at the Niger-Chad border; the Chadian army attacked and killed several. Those who survived fled to rugged mountains of Tibesti where they were captured by MDJT soldiers.

The capture posed delicate diplomatic and logistical problems for the governments wanting the Salafists: to deal directly with the MDJT would insult Chadian authorities, who had identified them as terrorists; to accept them from the MDJT, without government approval, would violate international law. Diplomats did not

Chad

Darfur children in a Chadian refugee camp ©IRIN

want to enter the area anyway, given safety concerns. When asked to bring their captives to the Niger border, the MDJT admitted the territory was so dangerous even they could not provide security. A resolution came when Libya successfully negotiated with the MDJT to hand over Ammari Saifi (aka Abderezak El Para) the Salafist leader. He was extradited to Algeria in October 2004.

The MDJT conflict is one example of Chad's highly fragmented political culture and the inability of N'Djaména to project its authority throughout the country. These problems were background to two important elections. In May 2001 presidential balloting, Déby won a controversial first round victory over six opponents. Chad's Constitutional Council verified the final results: Déby, 67.17% of the votes. His nearest competitor, longtime critic and opponent Ngarlejy Yorongar, only polled 16.35%.

EU observers regretted the "numerous defects and irregularities" that were observed. The government had restricted campaigning, used force to prevent demonstrations, and violently (but briefly) arrested opposition candidates. Threat, intimidation, and violence also characterized the April 2002 legislative elections, with similar success. President Déby's ruling Patriotic Salvation Movement (MPS) took 112 of the 155 seats, assuring him of a solid legislative majority, which allowed him to amend Chad's constitution.

The elections suggested President Déby was a man firmly in power, but power is often an illusion in Chad. When civil conflict broke out in the Darfur region of neighboring Sudan, it destabilized all of eastern Chad and nearly ended the Déby regime. Sudanese efforts to suppress a rebellion by ethnic cleansing produced a large exodus of refugees into eastern Chad. Among those most affected were numer-

ous Zaghawa people, ethnic kin of President Déby and his inner circle.

Déby sought to mediate the crisis, but Zaghawa people in his army and security forces thought direct support for persecuted ethnic kin a more appropriate response. Déby's opponents supplied arms clandestinely to Sudanese Zaghawa and organized a mutiny against the president. The attempted coup began the evening of May 16, 2004, led by officers of some of Chad's elite forces: the Republican Guard, the Nomadic National Guard, and the Presidential Security Guard. Loyalist forces stopped the mutineers and rapidly reasserted order in the capital with no loss of life on either side, but the incident showed the fragility of Déby's power.

President Déby's efforts to extend his presidential tenure further eroded his support among those closest to him (and most desirous of succeeding him). In parliament, Déby's MPS pushed through a controversial constitutional amendment removing a two-term limit on Chadian presidents. Approved by voters in June 2005, it allowed Déby to run for a third term in 2006, but solidified opposition against him.

The president became increasingly isolated as friends, family, and members of the presidential guard—the last line of defense—deserted him. By October 2005 the guard defections were so serious that Déby simple dissolved it. Several hundred military deserters fled to hideouts in Eastern Chad and announced creation of the *Socle* (Platform) *pour le changement, l'unité nationale et la démocracie,* with its rather ballistic acronym: SCUD. As defections from N'Djaména grew, new rebel groupings proliferated. In eastern Chad the new dissenters met the old opposition.

One such group was the *Rassemblement pour la démocracie et la liberté* (RDL), com-

posed primarily of Chadian "Arabs" and led by a former officer in the Chadian army, Mahamat Nour Abdelkerim. Nour had defected in 1994 and remained an intransigent resistant, dedicated to overthrowing the "tyrant" Déby. He and his men reportedly found support and employment from the regime in Khartoum as it battled to repress rebellion in Darfur. They rode, it is alleged, with the *janjaweed* in their terror raids against Darfur villagers.

By December 2005 at least eight rebel formations had publicized their existence in eastern Chad. Mahamat Nour Abdelkerim created the United Front for Change (*Front uni pour le changement*: FUC), but it was unclear how if differed, if at all, from the RDL. (Names and identities are very fluid in Chad.) With the RDL as its core, FUC was probably the largest and best organized of the rebel formations, and, with its Sudanese-supplied equipment, the best armed. To demonstrate its aptitude, FUC launched a major attack against the Chadian border city of Adré on December 18, easily crossing the border in a convoy of lightly armed, brand-new Toyota trucks. Chadian troops loyal to President Déby, some of them recently trained in counterterrorism by American forces, beat them and chased them back into Sudan. There were reports that Sudanese rebel forces had also participated in the defense of Adré. At least 300 died in the incident.

The attack on Adré was the most serious threat to the regime to this point. The president declared a "state of belligerence" and accused Sudan of being "the common enemy of the nation" as he sought to mobilize regional and international opinion to the support of his government. Regime survival required desperate measures.

In early January 2006 the government's relations with the World Bank turned hostile when Déby backed a law to reduce the amount of oil money to be set aside for development—the money was needed, said the government, to defend the country. The bank suspended loans and ordered the account that collected oil revenues to be frozen; the president responded by threatening to cut off oil deliveries before a compromise was reached.

Sensing opportunity, the president's opponents continued their efforts to overthrow the regime. The government announced it had thwarted an attempted military coup in March, and less than a month later, FUC re-launched military action from the east, this time aiming directly at N'Djaména, the capital. Another column of Sudanese-supported rebels, driving the inevitable Toyotas, entered Chad in the south, after having passed through the Central African Republic. With the danger of regime collapse apparent, France, with some 1,200 soldiers stationed in Chad, acted to prevent the inevitable chaos that would occur if the capital fell. French intelligence and logistical assistance helped the government fight off the attacking rebels and protect The city of N'Djaména. Following its military defeat, FUC's coalition fragmented along ethnic lines. A triumphal Déby proceeded to carry out presidential elections in May.

For the first time since multiparty politics returned to Chad, the main opposition refused to put up a candidate and was unanimous in calling on citizens to boycott the election. Déby faced four relatively unknown opponents, none of whom gathered more than 10% of the vote. Chad's Constitutional Council officially reported the president received nearly 65% of the ballots. Skeptical Chadians were also told 53% of registered voters had participated. It wasn't pretty, but you had to admire the president's guts in pushing through with the election given the chaos on the ground.

In December 2006 Déby negotiated and agreement with the FUC leader, Mahamat Nour Abdelkerim. Nour entered the government as minister of defense and two of his commanders were also given ministerial positions. Thousands of FUC combatants were to be integrated into the Chadian army, bringing considerable knowledge of the hills and caves of eastern Chad where rebels so often seek refuge. However, this did not end the civil strife in the country, which continues unabated to the present.

The Present: Contemporary Issues

Chad is one of the poorest countries in the world, ranking 170 out of 179 on the UN's 2008 *Human Development Index*. Its social statistics are grim: Out of every 1,000 children born, 99 will die at birth life expectancy is less than 50 years (2008); furthermore, only a quarter of the population over 15 years of age is literate.

Cotton and livestock have traditionally been the country's principal moneymakers, but economic development has been irregular and inconsistent, characterized by alternations of growth and decline brought on by drought, civil war, and continuing political instability. Cotton is the main export crop and, until 2002, Chad's most lucrative source of income. Cotton fields cover 10% of Chad's cultivated land. Annual production varies between 150,000 and 200,000 tons, but the value of cotton exports has declined significantly. In 1999 cotton represented 43% of exports, but dropped to 28% in 2002. In 2007, world cotton prices, had reached their lowest level since the Great Depression of the 1930s. Livestock overtook cotton as the country's major source of income in

2002. There are some 14 million head of livestock in Chad, including six million cattle, more than seven million sheep and goats, and over a million camels. Nearly 40% of the population is engaged in the livestock sector, which contributes about 20% of Chad's GDP. Cross-border smugglers, it is estimated, deprive the Chadian economy of close to two-thirds of its potential livestock taxes.

Economic development and poverty alleviation in Chad rest on oil production from southern oil fields at Doba. As of January 2008, reserves are estimated at 1.5 billion barrels, though Esso-Chad, the U.S.-Malaysian consortium, has announced another productive field near Timbré in southern Chad. Before that field comes on line, in a couple of years, peak production has been projected to be around 225,000 to 250,000 barrels per day. In 2008, Chad was pumping about 156,000 bbl/d. The crude oil from some 315 wells is transported through a 650-mile pipeline to an offshore marine terminal near Kribi, Cameroon.

Fearing oil income would be siphoned off by corruption or diverted from poverty alleviation projects, the World Bank, as the price of its participation, forced strict revenue controls. The revenue law, passed in January 1999, mandated that 85% of the oil earnings be dedicated to national health, education, agricultural and infrastructure projects; 5% is to go to the producing region of Doba, and another 10% is reserved for "future generations," deposited directly in a blocked account at Citibank in London, under control of the World Bank.

Given the pressing financial need of the regime to buy arms to defend itself, Déby laid claim to Chad's future, demanding the World Bank release funds deposited in the London account after parliament changed the basic oil revenue distribution law. The row went on for months, and in April, just as rebel forces were nearing his capital, Déby issued an ultimatum: release the funds or the pipeline would be closed down. (What he never mentioned was that the normal royalties and dividends from oil operations—amounting to some $766 million annually—continued to be paid, unimpeded by Bank action.)

In the compromise hammered out in late April 2006, the bank agreed to resume some loan disbursements for education, health, community development, HIV/AIDs, agriculture, electricity, water, and infrastructure.

China's penetration of the Chadian oil industry illustrates the flexibility of ideology and subtlety of practice that guides its resource-acquisition policy. In contrast to neighboring Sudan, where Chinese state corporations have explored and devel-

oped oil fields, built a pipeline, and constructed refineries, in Chad, one of the few countries that maintained diplomatic relations with Taiwan, Beijing quietly bought shares of private companies that already possessed exploration and development rights there. In 2003, for example, China National Petroleum Corp. (CNPC) and a subsidiary of China International Trust and Investment Corporation, Citic Resources Holdings, bought 50% of Swiss-based Cliveden Petroleum. Cliveden held a 50% share of an exploration concession covering 108 million acres in all of Chad's potential oil basins.

In August 2006 the Chadian government pragmatically decided to sever ties with Taiwan and reestablished diplomatic links with Beijing. Chinese Foreign Minister Li Zhaoxing was the first major leader to visit the country in January 2007, and before he left, he had cancelled much of Chad's debt to China and signed off on a "preferential loan" of some $26 million, plus a variety of other economic and development agreements.

Chad had the world's fastest growing economy in 2004, registering a one-time bump in GDP growth of 31%. Unfortunately, nearly all that growth occurred in the oil sector; in 2004 growth in the non-oil sector, which involves the vast bulk of Chadians, reached no more than 2%, leaving poverty untouched where the annual population growth is 3%. Moreover, by 2007 (after the uptick in investment), Chad had one of Africa's worst-performing economies (see "The Future" below). Chadians can justifiably ask where the benefits of oil production have gone when 80% of the population still has no access to drinking water, and when 37% of all children below the age of five are malnourished. One possible explanation is corruption: since oil revenues began to flow in 2004, Chad has dropped 15 places on Transparency International's corruption perceptions index. On the 2005 index, Chad was ranked at the very bottom, tied with Bangladesh as the world's most corrupt country.

Of all Chad's contemporary issues, the most pressing concern at present is the heightening of conflict with Sudan and the lingering question of the rebellion. The Darfur conflict of Western Sudan and the rebellion in Chad continue to reinforce one another, as the Chadian and Sudanese governments each accuse one another of destabilizing the region. In the absence of an end to the rebellion and the reestablishment of order along the Sudanese border, the country will not be able to move forward.

In early 2008, new groups of rebels emerged to attack the capital N'Djamena, in an attempt to overthrow Déby. After coming within just miles of the presiden-

Chad

tial palace (and after being repulsed in part by shows of support for Déby by French troops), the rebellion seemed to falter, leaving about 1,000 injured and probably over 100 dead. While it ultimately failed to overthrow Déby, this surge of violence resulted in a worsening humanitarian crisis, as thousands of Chadians fled across the southern border into Cameroon. To further complicate matters, the Justice and Equality Movement of Sudanese rebels (who fight the Sudanese government and its allies across the border in Darfur) dispatched reinforcements from their sanctuary in eastern Chad to support Déby. This clarified the common interests between Déby and the Sudanese rebels, and between the Sudanese government and the Chadian rebels

After a brief lull in the fighting that followed the signing of a peace accord between the two neighboring countries in early 2008, Chadian and Sudanese fighters have again fought as recently as May 2008. Diplomatic and economic relations between the two countries are cut off, and the border is militarized. That as many as 30,000 Chadians have recently fled *into* the war-torn region of Darfur (Sudan) is a suggestion of the degree of social displacement occurring in the country.

The Future

Chad's future is bleak; the country is moving towards increased violence and instability, in direct counterpoint to the violence and instability in Sudan. The country's stability in many ways is a reflection of the stability in its neighborto the east. In May 2009, two months after the ICC issued an arrest warrant against the Sudanese president, Omar al-Bashir, for crimes against humanities in Darfur, the governments of Chad and Sudan agreed to a cessation of all hostilities. It is unclear whether the countries will stick to the agreement. In June 2009, members of the Chadian army crossed over the border to Sudan in pursuit of Chadian rebels. The government in Khartoum has thus far tolerated these actions. In Chad's conflict-ridden environment, the promise of wealth from natural resources—including gas pipelines—looks like a proverbial Saharan mirage. The Déby government is beset by a range of difficulties that are likely only to worsen its repressive record. Neither the economic future nor the political future looks promising, though investment in natural resources may offer sporadic boosts to the economy. While many other African exporters of minerals and resources are witnessing massive investment and income booms, Chad is believed to have had the second-worst economic performance in Africa in 2007 (with a shrinking of the economy by over 1%), beating out only Zimbabwe.

The Republic of Congo

The hazards of the highway

Photo by G. Philippart de Foy
Courtesy APFT-ULB

Basic Facts
Area: 349,650 sq. km. = 135,000 sq. mi. (twice the size of Missouri)
Population: 3,800,000 (UN 2007 est.)
Capital City: Brazzaville
Climate: Tropically hot and humid
Neighboring Countries: Gabon (west); Cameroon (northwest); Central African Republic (north); Democratic Republic of the Congo (east, south)
Official Language: French
Other Principal Languages: Lingala and Munoukutuba (a Kikongo-based creole); both are lingua franca trade languages. Many local languages and dialects (of which Kikongo has the most users).
Ethnic Groups: Kongo 48%, Sangha 20%, M'Bochi 12%, Teke 17%, Europeans NA%; note—Europeans estimated at 8,500, mostly French, before the 1997 civil war; maybe half of that in 1998, following the widespread destruction of foreign businesses in 1997.
Principal Religions: Christian 50%, animist 48%, Muslim 2%
Chief Commercial Products: Oil, wood products and timber, potash, palm oil, cocoa, bananas, peanuts
GNI Per Capita: 3658 (World Bank 2008 est.)
Currency: CFA franc (no longer tied to the French franc)
Former Colonial Status: French Congo (1883–1910); one of the four territories of French Equatorial Africa (1910–1960)
Independence Date: August 15, 1960
Chief of State: Denis Sassou-Nguesso, President (since October 1997; re-elected July 2009, sworn in for new term August 14, 2009 as this book went to press)

National Flag: Diagonal green, yellow, and red stripes; the yellow is narrower dividing the two fields.

Land and People
This fertile, green land of ancient tradition lies immediately to the north of the great Congo River. Formerly a part of French Equatorial Africa, the country has the same general geographical features as Congo (Kinshasa) to the south. A low-lying, treeless plain extends 30 miles from the coast to the interior, succeeded by a mountainous region parallel to the coastline known as the Mayombe Escarpment. This is a region of sharply rising mountain ridges covered with jungle and dense growth. Further to the east extends the Niari River Valley, an important agricultural area, and to the north lies The Pool,

a region of treeless hills and a succession of grassy plains, covers some 50,000 square miles. Part of the Congo River Basin lies in the extreme northeast, a region of dense jungle and all but impassable plains. The climate is uniform and equatorial—hot and humid all year.

Tribal patterns dominate the social life of the Republic of Congo. Although discrimination is legally prohibited, tens of thousands of indigenous Pygmy people, living largely in the northern forest regions, have the social status of modern day slaves; many have Bantu masters to whom they are obligated from birth.

The Congo's most important human rights organization, the *Observatoire congolais des droits de l'homme* (OCDH), has criticized the government for failing to issue the indigenous pygmies identity cards or register their births. (Symptomatically, the legislature passed a law in August 2006 affirming the right of pygmies to vote.) OCDH has also documented significant numbers of indigenous pygmy women who have been victims of rape by Bantu men. According to the *Observatoire* spokesman, there were also cases of gang rapes, and "even of rapes perpetrated in police offices by the very people charged with protecting the population."

As in most of Sub-saharan Africa, storytelling is the common way of recapitulating history in Congo. Additionally, Congolese people are famous for their singing. Songs are common during the most common duties, like performing chores. Other forms of music include the Congolese rumba.

The Past: Political and Economic History
For early history, see *Historical Background* and *The Colonial Period: The French.*

Under the leadership of Félix Éboué, a black colonial administrator, French Equatorial Africa rallied to General Charles de Gaulle during World War II. A grateful de Gaulle made Éboué governor-general of FEA, and honored the federation's capital by gathering colonial administrators for the Brazzaville Conference of 1944 to discuss postwar colonial reforms.

Following World War II Congo was given a territorial assembly and representation in the French parliament, which increased both political awareness and activity in the colony. With General de Gaulle's Fifth French Republic, Congo became an autonomous republic within the Franco-African Community in 1958 and opted for full independence in 1960.

The Abbé Fulbert Youlou, a Catholic priest instrumental in charting the course toward independence, was installed as president in 1960. His party, *Union Démocratique pour la Défense des Intérêts Africains*

Congo (Brazzaville)

(UDDIA) drew its strength from southern peoples who had benefited most from colonial education and opportunity. The party advocated private ownership and close ties with France, but corruption, incompetence, massive labor unrest, and lack of French support led to a coup and Youlou's ouster in 1963. In typically French fashion, the three-day revolution was referred to as the "Trois Glorieuses"—mimicking the Parisian events of 1830.

His successor, Alphonse Massamba-Débat, took inspiration from French Marxism, and created the National Revolutionary Movement (MNR) as the country's single party. Congo became a "people's republic" with a red flag and the *Internationale* as its anthem. Socialist-inspired economic policies ensued for the next 25 years, with disastrous results. Continuing north-south regional tension and administrative incapacity led the military to replace Massamba-Débat with Major Marien Ngouabi in 1968.

Ngouabi maintained the socialist line, insisting that Marxism was a "universal science." He renamed the country the People's Republic of the Congo and replaced the MRN with the Congolese Labor Party (PCT) as the country's sole political party. With Ngouabi, a northerner, power shifted away from traditional power centers in the south. In highly politicized Brazzaville and other southern cities, opposition soon developed among both student and labor groups.

President Ngouabi was assassinated in March 1977; a military tribunal was hastily convened, which quickly accused and convicted Massambat-Débat of being behind the killing. He was executed and an 11-man military committee took control. Ngouabi's military successor, Col. Joachim Yhombi-Opango, lasted two years before he was at odds with the PCT. In 1979 he handed over the presidency to the PCT, which selected Col. Denis Sassou-Nguesso as his successor.

More politically attuned than his predecessors, Sassou-Nguesso maintained a delicate political balance among the leading political groups—the army, the trade unions, and Marxist intellectuals. Despite being the representative of the PCT's more militant wing, Sassou-Nguesso moderated the regime's Marxist rhetoric and established better relations with Western countries. With the fall of the Berlin Wall, Sassou-Nguesso began the task of dismantling Congolese Marxism.

The government dropped the party membership requirement for government Officials in 1990, and drafted a new constitution establishing a multiparty system. The country became "The Republic of Congo." In the March 1992 referendum the new constitution was adopted, which provided for new multiparty elections. Ultimately, 14 political parties participated. The *Union Panafricaine pour la Démocratie Sociale* (UPADS), led by Pascal Lissouba (Massamba-Débat's prime minister), won 39 of the 125 assembly seats. In August Lissouba was elected president, defeating Sassou-Nguesso.

Former President Sassou-Nguesso was granted amnesty for any acts committed during his years in office. Sassou-Nguesso, however, accepted neither graceful defeat nor political retreat.

The legislative elections of 1992 had been inconclusive, and the coalition government that resulted lasted only until late 1992. New elections, highly disputed, were held. President Lissouba's party won a razor-thin majority of 65 out of 125 seats in the National Assembly. A period of shaky parliamentary government ensued.

Political opponents organized private militias to oppose the government and President Lissouba created his own personal militia, to avoid any reliance on the national army. Each of the militias had its own distinctive, colorful, and threatening name. Bernard Kolélas, the charismatic mayor of Brazzaville, had the "Ninjas." Sassou-Nguesso's were "Cobras," and President Lissouba's, trained by Israelis, were "Zulus." In 1997 conflict broke out in Brazzaville as the government moved to eliminate Sassou-Nguesso's militia.

To combat his foes, President Lissouba recruited Israeli mercenaries to train his militiamen, but as the "Cobras" gained strength, he ordered more than $60 million in arms. Desperate for cash, Lissouba began discussions with an American oil company, and promptly lost the support of the French who refused to aid him against the forces of ex-President Sassou-Nguesso. Lissouba later charged that Sassou-Nguesso was supported by money coming from France's state oil giant Elf. Sassou-Nguesso also received interventionist support of Angolan forces. (Under Lissouba, Congo had become a launching pad for Cabindan rebels and a place through which Jonas Savimbi could sell the diamonds used to finance UNITA's war against the Angolan government.)

In the battle of the warlords Brazzaville was bombed and targeted by mortars, laid waste by internecine strife. Lissouba lost and fled into bitter exile. Elf returned to its damaged skyscraper office building and offered to contribute significantly to the rebuilding of Brazzaville. Angolan forces seemed to be a permanent presence in the Congo.

Denis Sassou-Nguesso's bloody conquest of Brazzaville did not end Congo's civil conflict. The civil war continued in the south throughout most of 1999. Pointe-Noire, Congo's economic capital, was virtually cut off from the rest of the country. Water and electricity supplies were disrupted by rebel activity. Some 800,000 people in the south were dislocated, many fleeing to the forest to escape the depredations of the rebels, the government, and its allies. Supported by Angolan troops and helicopter gunships, as well as by remnants of the Hutu *Interahamwe* and a few Chadian and DR Congo fighters, government troops turned the tide of battle against the rebels by mid-year—not without compiling a horrific human rights record.

By the end of 1999, offers of amnesty and integration into government security forces in exchange for disarmament had secured cease-fire agreements with major militia commanders. Soon after, President Sassou-Nguesso managed a "national dialogue" that brought together representatives of the government, the internal and external opposition, plus other political groups and civic organizations.

President Omar Bongo of Gabon, Sassou-Nguesso's son-in-law, mediated the process, and delegates focused on producing a draft constitution and preparing follow-up elections. There was little, if any, opportunity to address the causes that led to the Congolese conflict in the first place. Although billed as "all-inclusive," the national convention carefully excluded former President Pascal Lissouba and his last prime minister, Bernard Kolélas. Having been sentenced to death (*in absentia*) by Congolese judicial authorities, the two men were, said the government, ineligible to take part in the deliberations.

The draft constitution that emerged—tailored to the style and personality of Denis Sassou-Nguesso—featured a strong presidential regime. The president of the republic, elected for a seven-year term—with one renewable mandate—would wield exclusive executive power extensively. He would, for example, appoint the prime minister and could not be im-

President Sassou-Nguesso

peached by parliament; he could also reject its legislation and rule by decree.

In January 2002 the new constitution was approved by referendum—84% of those voting, according to government figures. Despite the calls by opposition parties to boycott the vote, the government announced that 78% of all registered voters participated in the balloting. (Sassou-Nguesso needed massive support to legitimize his assumption of power through force of arms.)

With Lissouba and Kolélas excluded, and the principal remaining opposition candidate withdrawing at the last minute, the presidential election was held in March 2002. To no one's surprise, Denis Sassou-Nguesso was the victor—garnering 89.4% of the vote. None of the six other candidates won as much as 3%. Reports of low voter-turnout notwithstanding, the interior minister released hardly-credible figures indicating 74.7% of the electorate had participated in the poll.

With a resurgence of militia violence in the south—remnants of the Kolélas' Ninjas, now operating under the leadership of Rev. Frédéric Bitsangou, better known as Pasteur Ntoumi—legislative elections scheduled for April 2002 were postponed to May. When the National Assembly races were over, the president's PCT had won 53 seats and the *Forces démocratiques unies* (FDU: United Democratic Forces)—a coalition of parties supporting him—30, a clear majority in the 153-member house.

The elections brought neither stability nor security. Pasteur Ntoumi's Ninjas continued their depredations in the Pool area and even managed to attack the vital rail link between Brazzaville and Pointe-Noire and bring commercial traffic to a standstill. In conducting its campaign against the rebels, the Congolese army seemed oblivious to both professionalism and human rights.

In March 2003 the government and Ninja rebels signed an agreement to end the crisis in the Pool region. Pasteur Ntoumi agreed to end hostilities, disarm his fighters, and help the state to reestablish its authority in the area. In return, the government agreed to extend amnesty to the Ninjas and reintegrate some of their members into the national army.

That the government's commitment to the peace accord was hypocritical seemed obvious when it asked Pasteur Ntoumi for a list of 250 rebels to be integrated into the armed forces. The rebel leader rejected the proposal, calling the government's quota "a drop in the ocean." In reaction, he indicated he would only disarm his militiamen when the government opened up political space, forming a government of national unity in which his *Conseil national de la résistance* (CNR) could take part.

The disarmament, demobilization and reintegration program (DDR)—administered by the UN Development Program and financed by the EU—made minimal progress. From 2001 to 2004 the government only demobilized some 9,000 ex-combatants.

In January 2006 the World Bank and IMF granted the government $17 million to disarm, demobilize and reintegrate 30,000 former combatants into the country's social fabric. Five years after signing a peace agreement, however, thousands of Ninjas still await integration into the military or assistance returning to civilian life. The pool area remains rife with weapons—between 37,000 and 40,000 according to one Swiss NGO. Incentives to surrender weapons have failed because the Ninjas have been required to turn them in Brazzaville and fear reprisal if seen with their weapons. Left in the hands of the unemployed, the weapons pose a continuing security threat, and easy resort to occasional banditry.

AIDS has made its appearance in Congo, traveling in the wake of civil disturbance and disruption. Nationally, government figures indicate 4.2% of the population is HIV positive. Infection rates are higher in the southern provinces (Pointe-Noire has a rate of 5%, while Brazzaville's is 3.3%) and among women (4.7%, as opposed to 3.8% for men). According to armed forces health officials, AIDS is the number one cause of death in the Congolese armed forces, a toll partially attributable to soldiers' frequenting of sex workers. Fourteen percent of Congolese servicemen have tested HIV-positive.

Unlike some of its neighbors, Congo has a relatively strong tradition of urbanization. One-sixth of the population has traditionally lived in the two principal cities, Brazzaville and Pointe-Noire. As a consequence, the country has one of the highest literacy rates in Black Africa, estimated at nearly 83%, though female literacy is generally lower—about 77%. Also related to this urban tradition is the relatively high percentage of Christians in the population—mostly Roman Catholic—and the early development of labor unions.

The Present: Contemporary Issues

The object of armed struggle in Congo is the state's oil revenue, about 70% of state income and 94% of all its export earnings. (Timber exports produce the remaining export income.) From 65,000 bbl/d in 1980, oil production peaked in 2000 at 280,000 bbl/d. It has since dropped to 227,000 bbl/d (2005) as oil fields matured. In 2005 the country was sub-Saharan Africa's sixth largest producer—after Nigeria, Angola, Sudan, Equatorial Guinea and Gabon. Mostly conducted offshore, the oil sector was virtually untouched by the events of the civil war. The rest of the economy was severely damaged by those events.

At least 20,000 people were killed in the various phases of the war, and 800,000 people were displaced. Half of Congo's agricultural output was destroyed, particularly in the south where the richest agricultural land is located. Some 75% of the country's livestock was also destroyed. Congo's highly urbanized population, especially in Brazzaville, has felt the impact deeply. Since 1997, the percentage of the urban population below the poverty line has increased from 30% to 70% (2004). Half the population is unemployed, and life expectancy is only 54.5 years (2009).

Reduced conflict has allowed the government to reopen railroad service between Brazzaville and Pointe-Noire and dredge the port of Pointe-Noire, the only deepwater port on Africa's western coastline south of Dakar. Since 1987, when it was last thoroughly dredged, the port had silted up and lost some six feet of depth. The government has invested some $30 million in repairing the Congo-Ocean railroad linking Brazzaville and Pointe-Noire.

Reopening the Congo River, the railroad, and the port, all significantly benefit the timber industry—after oil, Congo's most important source of income. There are two main areas of commercially exploitable forests in Congo. In the south forests cover more than 11 million acres, and by 1995, nearly 10 million acres were held as logging concessions. In the more isolated north there are some 22 million acres of commercially useful forests, but exploitation here was much slower given transport difficulties.

During the war when river and rail traffic was curtailed, loggers in the north had to ship their timber by road via Cameroon to Douala, adding considerably to their costs. Normally they would have floated logs downriver to the main river port of Brazzaville and then on to Pointe-Noire by train. In October 2003 local officials in the southwest accused Chinese and Malaysian companies of violating state regulations and over-logging their concessions. The Chinese firm Man Faï Taï issued a categorical denial, asserting that though logging was "highly industrialized," the firm was "far from maximal production in the Congo." Hardly a reassuring comment.

In August 2006 President Sassou-Nguesso announced the continuing expansion of logging operations in Congo: from 1 million cubic meters in 2005, production increased to 1.5 million cubic meters in 2006.

The reality of Congo's diamond resources is totally uncertain, especially after the country was suspended in mid-2004 from participation in the Kimberley Process Certification Scheme, designed to keep

Congo (Brazzaville)

illicit diamonds from the market. At best around 50,000 carats are produced annually, almost exclusively by individual miners. When the country's annual exportation figures of three million to five million carats could not be explained to a visiting Kimberley mission, Congo's participation was suspended, and the mission concluded that its entire production was illicit.

Given the terrible damage inflicted by years of civil war, investors are hesitant about placing money in the Congo. The country's biggest problem is finding the resources to repair infrastructure and productive capacity—estimated at nearly $2 billion. China has managed to penetrate Congo's oil sector, long a French preserve, by granting loans through its Export-Import Bank that are paid back in oil. In 2003, for example, it advanced $238 million—85% of total estimated costs—to build a hydroelectric dam at Imboulou, some 133 miles north of Brazzaville, where the Congo and Kasai rivers meet. The capital has long suffered chronic power shortages; Imboulou will generate 120 MW, more than doubling the country's installed capacity and reducing Brazzaville's dependency on electricity supplied by its neighbor, the Democratic Republic of the Congo (DRC).

Built by a consortium of two Chinese firms, Imboulou is estimated to be completed in 2009. The government expects the project to create 900 permanent jobs and 2,000 temporary ones. A paved construction road is expected to produce additional economic benefits from improved access to the region.

Government deficits over the years have created a huge total debt of $8.57 billion as of mid-2005—one of the world's highest per capita debt burdens. In 2007

London Club cancelled some 80% of Congo foreing debt. Currently debt service is about 1.2% of export earnings.

Agreement with the IMF has been difficult given what it sees as a lack of transparency in the operations of the *Société nationale des pétroles du Congo* (SNPC), Congo's national oil company, and continuing budgetary deficits. The government did not help its image for financial restraint when the president hired 3,450 new civil servants in 2004, adding to an already-bloated 70,000 government employees. Nevertheless, following publication of audits of both SNPC and the government's oil revenues, the IMF expressed "guarded optimism" about Congo's economic and political situation and cautiously extended some $84 million in December 2004.

Whether or not additional funding will be forthcoming is questionable. The Publish What You Pay coalition says that some $300 million of Congo's $1-billion oil revenues in 2004 simply evaporated, and independent auditors trying to make sense of the books were refused SNPC records. Global Witness, another close observer of the industry, has long argued that people close to President Sassou-Nguesso have profited from corrupt practices within the industry. On Transparency International's 2006 *Corruption Perceptions Index* Congo is ranked only four steps above Haiti, the world's most corrupt country.

It did not help when the president ousted his finance minister, Roger Andely, in a January, 2005 cabinet reshuffle. Andely had almost single-handedly been responsible for the transparency in oil accounts that led to IMF funding the month before. One year later, in January 2006, Prime Minister Isidore Myouba admitted the obvious: Congo did indeed conceal part of its oil

revenues, sometimes using "unorthodox methods." They were justified, he argued, to protect Congo from "vulture creditors."

The Future

Oil output will rise over the next few years as new fields come onstream. The French oil giant, Total, has already indicated its Moho-Bilondo field begins production at 90,000 bbl/d starting from 2008. Increased oil revenues will not make the government any more democratic or its oil operations more transparent. Local human rights campaigners and transparency advocates will continue to have risky careers.

Economically, Congo has potential, but the political system remains shaky. The invitation extended by Denis Sassou-Nguesso to former adversary Pascal Lissouba to return to Congo may have signaled a shift in the political winds towards some reconciliation, but Lissouba had not yet returned to Congo as of mid-2008. Elections for the presidency are scheduled for July 12, 2009, but the legislative elections in 2007 were not a promising warm-up. The U.S. State Department declared that the elections "were widely viewed as disorganized and marred by irregularities, with low voter turnout." The Constitutional Court ruled out a leading contender, former prime minister Ange Edouard Poungui of the UPADS party (Lissouba's former party), on the grounds that he had not resided continuously in the country for the last two years. This leave Matthias Dzon of the ARD (*Alliance pour la République et la Démocratie*) as the leading opposition candidate. Some political parties have already boycotted the elections, and the result is likely to be another display of Sassou-Nguesso's control over Congo's fragile political system.

A marginalized minority, the indigenous Pygmy people of Congo's forest areas. Here a group of Baka/Batwa children in an Ibamba village.   ©Andrew Itoua/IRIN

The Democratic Republic of the Congo

The casualness of death. Kinois view the body of a policeman killed in faction fighting, August 2006.

Note: This country has been known as Belgian Congo, Congo (Leopoldville), the Democratic Republic of the Congo, Zaïre, and most recently, Democratic Republic of the Congo.

Basic Facts

Area: 2,345,410 sq. km. = 905,562.8 sq. mi. (slightly less than one-fourth the size of the U.S.)

Population: 62,600,000 (UN 2007 est.)

Capital City: Kinshasa

Climate: Warm and humid tropical weather in the western and central areas, temperate in the eastern highlands

Neighboring Countries: Congo (north, west); Central African Republic, Sudan (north); Uganda, Rwanda, Burundi and Tanzania (east); Zambia and Angola (south)

Official Language: French

Other Principal Languages: Over 200 African languages are spoken. Most prominent are the Alur, Bembe, Chokwe, Fuliiru, Hunde, Kituba (a creole based on the KiKongo dialect spoken in Manianga area of the lower Congo River), Kinyarwanda, KiKongo, Lega, Lingala (a lingua franca trade language), Luba, Lugbara, Mangbetu, Mongo, Nandi, Ndo, Ngbaka, Phende, Sanga, Shi, Songe, Swahili, Tetela, and Zande.

Ethnic Groups: Over 200 African ethnic groups of which the majority are Bantu; the four largest peoples—Mongo, Luba, Kongo and the Mangbetu-Azande make up about 45% of the population.

Principal Religions: Roman Catholic 50%, Protestant 20%, Kimbanguist 10%, Muslim 10%, other sects and traditional beliefs 10%

Chief Commercial Products: Diamonds, copper, coffee, cobalt, and crude oil

GNI Per Capita: $206 (World Bank 2008 est.)

Currency: Congolese franc (CF)

Former Colonial Status: Personal possession of King Leopold II of Belgium (1885–1907); Belgian Colony (1907–1960)

Independence Date: June 30, 1960

Chief of State: Joseph Kabila, President (appointed January 25, 2001; elected October 2006)

National Flag: A sky blue field, divided diagonally from lower left by a red stripe bordered by two narrow yellow stripes. A yellow, five-pointed star appears in the upper left corner.

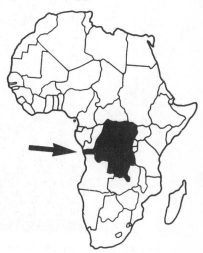

Congo (Kinshasa)

Land and People

The deep green region of the Congo has intrigued explorers, adventurers and writers for centuries, becoming one of the popular stereotypes of Africa in the Western mind. Dark rain forests abounding in game adjoin huge mining developments and vast plantations, some of which have been broken down into smaller farms. The very size of the Congo—as large as Western Europe—is one of its most distinctive features. Even more interesting, this huge nation has only a 25-mile-long coastline which allows it to "breathe" on the South Atlantic Ocean.

There are three distinctive features of this land mass: the immense river basin of the Congo and its tributaries, tropically hot and humid; the rich mining areas are located in the eastern sector and the upland plains in the northeast and southeast with tall, rippling grasses and snow-capped mountains rising to almost 17,000 feet in the east near the Equator. The eastern lake region, which includes Lake Kivu and the western shores of lakes Tanganyika, Mweru, Albert and Edward, is unsurpassed in scenic beauty and abounds in wildlife.

Tributaries of the great Congo River flow from these lakes into the Lualaba River, which in turn becomes the Congo after it reaches 4° south latitude. From this point, the Congo surges in a wide, island-dotted course through the tropical forests, joined by its other tributaries. Three hundred miles inland from the Atlantic, at Malebo Pool (near bustling Kinshasa), the river widens into a lake, continuing on to the sea with a width of up to ten miles. The river is navigable for the most part and widely used in commerce, interrupted only by cataracts at Malebo Falls (formerly Stanley Falls) and below Kinshasa. Railway bypasses have been constructed at these cataracts to maintain the continuity of commerce.

Years of civil conflict have greatly affected the people of Congo, but the art industry has flourished in Kinshasa, and most particularly the music industry. Zairean/Congolese Soukous music, also known as Kwassa-Kwassa, originated in Kinshasa and became a popular musical sensation across Africa in the 1990s, leading many to consider Kinshasa Africa's music capital. Congolese music and dance remain popular on pan-African radio and on TV. Some foreign music has been adapted into the local rhythms to create new fusions of Congolese jazz, soukous, hiphop, and electronica. The Congotronics releases have become a worldwide sensation in recent years.

The Past: Political and Economic History

For early history, see *Historical Background* and *The Colonial Period: King Leopold and the Belgians.*

Belgian rule in Africa was characterized by control through compulsion. Though little effort was made prior to independence to prepare the Congo for self—rule, local government reforms in 1957 presented an opportunity for political participation, and Congolese *évolués*—the colony's miniscule educated elite—responded quickly. Bakongo *évolués* formed the *Alliance des Bakongo* (ABAKO) based in Léopoldville (now Kinshasa). Though ethnically based, ABAKO first articulated the demand for Congolese independence, and became a forceful voice of anticolonial protest, under the leadership of Joseph Kasavubu.

Once started, nationalist sentiments gathered enthusiastic followings. The most important multiethnic grouping dedicated to the Congo's national unity was the Congolese National Movement (MNC). With Patrice Lumumba at its head, the MNC became the most militant advocate of the colony's independence. When French Congo, across the river, was offered independence by President Charles de Gaulle in 1958, there was increased pressure on Belgium to grant independence to its colony. An impending threat of independence, coupled with tumbling world copper prices, led to a withdrawal of foreign capital from the country in the late 1950s, weakening the economy and creating widespread unemployment.

In January 1959 the Belgian administration's decision to cancel an ABAKO meeting in Léopoldville led to violent urban protests. Virtually the entire African population of the city took to the streets, and protest soon turned into looting. When finally suppressed, the Léopoldville riots officially resulted in 47 Congolese dead; in reality, many more were probably killed. Shocked, the administration advanced the timetable for independence.

In this turbulent atmosphere, Belgium summoned African leaders to Brussels in early 1960 and announced that independence would become effective on June 30. A multitude of new parties sprang up, almost overnight. The intense political activity served as a forewarning to thousands of Europeans, who began to leave the Congo in droves. In parliamentary elections Lumumba's MNC won the greatest number of seats, but not enough to govern without coalition partners. After ten days of bargaining behind closed doors, Lumumba announced a 37-member cabinet, containing officials from no fewer than 16 parties. When independence was formally declared, Patrice Lumumba became prime minister and Joseph Kasavubu president of the renamed Democratic Republic of the Congo.

The country quickly deteriorated into lawlessness, rebellion, anarchy, revolt, and secession. Disintegration began when the *Force Publique*, Congo's army, mutinied on July 5, immediately followed by the intervention of Belgian paratroopers sent to protect the lives of Belgian citizens. Hundreds of whites were mercilessly slaughtered and others beaten and tortured. The Congolese government was incapable of action, incapacitated by a lethal power struggle between Lumumba and Kasavubu, each of whom dismissed the other. Almost simultaneously Katanga, Congo's richest province, declared itself independent on July 11 under the leadership of Moïse Tshombe. On July 12 Tshombe and Kasavuvu jointly appealed to the UN for assistance in restoring order.

The arrival of the UN peacekeeping force only increased the friction between President Kasavubu and Prime Minister Lumumba. Lumumba demanded that UN forces suppress the Katangese secession, by force if necessary, and Kasavubu categorically refused the idea. In September

President Kasavubu (center) and Premier Lumumba confer with Belgian army chief, 1960

172

Congo (Kinshasa)

The high way to travel   Photo by Maaike Göbel

power as an African chief. Katanga became Shaba and the Congo River became the Zaïre River. Zaïriois, the citizens of the newly renamed country, were required to adopt African names.

The constitution was revised in 1974 to contain "Mobutuism," which embodied the president's thoughts and teachings. It became the required curriculum even in Zaïre's Catholic schools. Most plantations and farms owned by foreigners were nationalized, and all mineral ores had to be refined within Zaïre, even though there were insufficient facilities to perform the task.

Infrastructure deteriorated rapidly as the MPR state and its ideology of Mobutism proved inadequate to the tasks of national integration and governance. Increasingly the state was held together by little more than a web of client-patron relations sustained by state resources. The regime gave rise to the term "kleptocracy"—rule by thieves.

Relative peace and stability prevailed until 1977 and 1978 when Katangan rebels, based in Angola, launched a series of invasions into Shaba (ex-Katanga). The rebels had to be driven out with the aid of foreign troops—French, Belgian and Moroccan. Elections in 1977 resulted in another victory for Mobutu and his party. The legislature, however, became meaningless as Mobutu increasingly ruled by decree. Despite this, foreign aid continued to pour in on the theory that Zaïre was a bastion against communism. From 1965 to 1991 Zaïre received more than $1.5 billion in U.S. economic and military aid. While he was still favored by the U.S., Jonas Savimbi and UNITA, the Angolan anti-Marxist movement, received much of their assistance through Zaïre.

Realizing that his personal security and future were clouded, Mobutu summoned Israeli military personnel to train a presidential guard in 1982. They performed well, and the elite guard slowly became the only coherent and capable force in Zaïre. The remaining armed forces were expected to make their way by theft and corruption. Government workers were unpaid and were expected to survive the same way. Bribery and corruption became coping mechanisms for government workers. While workers scrambled to keep alive, President Mobutu became one of the richest men in the world. In 1992, according to the World Bank, 64.7% of Zaïre's budget was reserved for Mobutu's "discretionary spending." According to Transparency International, Mobutu embezzled $5 billion from his country.

With the collapse of the Eastern European socialist model, Zaïre was no longer seen as a necessary bastion against communism. Development programs were

Lumumba turned to the Soviet Union for assistance in sending Congolese troops to Katanga, introducing cold-war politics into the Congo crisis. Amid further provincial secessions and increased violence, Army Chief of Staff Col. Joseph Mobutu announced on September 14 that the army would henceforth govern in association with a caretaker government headed by President Kasavubu.

Kasavubu decided to eliminate his rival, Lumumba, once and for all. The army captured the charismatic leader in December, and Kasavubu turned him over to the self-proclaimed President of Katanga, Moïse Tshombe. Lumumba was shortly thereafter killed, with Belgian complicity and probably American foreknowledge.

Even though Kasavubu's sacrifice of Lumumba to the Katanga secessionists was intended to facilitate the breakaway province's return to a united Congo, the Katangan secession continued until early 1963 when Tshombe gave in to the central government. UN troops withdrew in midyear, and unrest and rebellion in the provinces continued as the central government was unable to assert its authority. From January to August 1964 rural insurgency engulfed five of Congo's 21 provinces, and in desperation President

Kasavubu appointed Moïse Tshombe as premier. Ironically, the defeated secessionist used foreign mercenaries and Belgian paratroopers to put down secession and assert the central government's authority over a unified state. President Kasavubu, frightened and envious of Tshombe's growing popularity, fired him as premier, whereupon Colonel Joseph Désiré Mobutu took center stage and ousted the president in late 1965.

Mobutu in Power

Conditions remained unstable in the eastern Congo even after former Prime Minister Tshombe's exile and house arrest in Algeria. But General Mobutu maintained the loyalty of the army and skillfully played ethnic and political factions against each other to consolidate his control. Pressured by the U.S. and other foreign powers to hold elections, he created the *Mouvement Populaire de la Révolution* (Popular Movement for the Revolution; MPR) and was elected unopposed as president in 1970.

In 1971 Mobutu elaborated a campaign of cultural nationalism or "authenticity." He renamed the country Zaïre and himself Mobutu Sese Seko, donning a leopard skin cap as the symbol of his status and

173

Congo (Kinshasa)

suddenly engulfed Zaïre. Hutu militia forces (the *Interahamwe* driven from Rwanda in 1994) had attacked Rwanda from their Zaïre refugee camps. Despite repeated requests, the Mobutu government had done nothing to curb their violence, which quickly turned even more hostile when Hutu forces linked up with remnants of the Zaïrian armed forces (FAZ) to attack local Tutsi, the Banyamulenge, in eastern Zaïre. To prevent another genocide, Rwanda and its allies, particularly Uganda, invaded Zaïre.

Laurent Kabila

Plucked from obscurity to provide a non-Tutsi face to the insurgency was the semiretired roly-poly professional revolutionary Laurent Kabila. A Luba from Katanga, he had been long engaged in the anti-Mobutu struggle, but always in secondary roles.

When Che Guevara, the charismatic Cuban revolutionary who was looking for further fertile fields to ply his trade, arrived in eastern Zaïre he ran across Kabila and provided a contemptuous critique of his revolutionary potential. Despite being "the best of the Congolese leaders," Kabila was seen as "too addicted to drink and women," but he was available when the call to leadership came.

Once the insurgency began, there was little effective resistance. The Zaïrian army fled in terror before the offensive; they had little loyalty except to themselves. The only thing that impeded Kabila's *Alliance des Forces Démocratiques pour la Libération du Congo-Zaïre* (AFDL) was the fact that there were no roads or bridges, just rutted, frequently flooded, and muddy areas that allowed trucks to pass irregularly. Because of these conditions, it took until May 1997 for the insurgent army to reach Kinshasa.

Laurent Kabila proclaimed himself president and took the oath of office on May 31, 1997. He promised democracy, but said elections could not be held for two years because of the need to bring order to the country. To fit with its new aspirations, the country was once again renamed. Mobutu's Zaïre became, again, the Democratic Republic of the Congo (DRC). Laurent Kabila spent most of 1997–1998 consolidating his power.

By August 1998, it had become apparent that Kabila was little more than a mini-Mobutu. The security demands of Rwanda and Uganda were still unmet, Hutu rebels still posed threats from bases in the Congo, and enemies of the Museveni regime scampered back and forth across the border, doing damage to Ugandan citizens. Inside the Congo Banyamulenge Tutsi had little sense they would be incorporated into any national dialogue,

cancelled and the economy deteriorated even further. Pressure mounted to open up the political system.

In April 1990 President Mobutu agreed to end the ban on opposition parties and appointed a transitional government. Liberalization of the regime was, of course, illusory. May student protests at the University of Lumumbashi (ex-Elizabethville) were brutally suppressed. Anywhere from 50 to 150 students were killed, according to Amnesty International.

When soldiers threatened to rebel over unpaid wages, the government resorted to printing more money—in higher denominations as inflation mounted—or gave them free reign to pillage and loot. In September 1991 they rioted and devastated Kinshasa. Some 2,000 French and Belgian troops had to be ferried in to evacuate 20,000 foreign nationals from the city. The president increasingly absented himself from his capital, seeking refuge in the sumptuous comfort of a fortress-palace at Gbadolite in northwest Zaïre. Conditions in the country continued to deteriorate.

Finally, after many promises and even more avoidance, Mobutu capitulated to the holding of a Sovereign National Conference in 1992. Over 2,000 representatives from various political parties and civil

society attended. The conference took its "sovereign" power seriously and elected Étienne Tshisekedi, leader of the *Union pour la Démocratie et le Progrès Social* (UDPS) as prime minister.

By the end of the year Mobutu had created a rival government with its own prime minister. Rival pro- and anti-Mobutu governments created a stalemate that was only broken when a compromise merged the two governments in 1994. A High Council of the Republic-Parliament of Transition (HCR-PT) was created with the resilient Mobutu as head of state. The HCR-PT repeatedly scheduled presidential and legislative elections over the next two years, but they never took place.

By now, Zaïre's economy was barely functional. So much of the state's resources had been diverted away into Mobutu's patronage network that capital investment was impossible. Several copper mines of Shaba, for example, had been flooded and idle for years. The Mobutu regime had become the mirror image of Leopold II's—personal, arbitrary, and venal.

In 1996 Mobutu traveled to Switzerland for extensive treatment of prostate cancer. While there, a Rwandan-backed rebel force captured much of eastern Zaïre as ethnic tensions in neighboring Rwanda

Congo (Kinshasa)

Mobutu Sese Seko

and it became evident that Kabila was moving to place relatives and members of his own ethnic group in the most important positions of power. Nepotism was accompanied by its partner vice, corruption.

When Kabila sacked his Rwandan military advisors and sent them packing—the very people responsible for elevating him to presidential status—the crisis of confidence came to a head. A second rebellion arose in the east no sooner than the plane bearing the exiled advisors landed. A brilliant tactical flight to the west brought rebel forces close to the doors of Kinshasa and for a moment it looked as though the regime was doomed. A fearful Kabila called upon his fellow authoritarians in Angola and Zimbabwe. Both presidents, Dos Santos and Mugabe, responded with interventionist forces. The western threat was ended and military action focused on the eastern front.

The Second Rebellion developed into Africa's first continental war. Besides Angola and Zimbabwe, Namibia, Chad, Sudan and Libya came to the support of the Kabila government. Rwanda and Uganda supported local Congolese rebel factions. By mid-1999 the Democratic Republic of the Congo had been, *de facto*, partitioned. The rebel coalition controlled the eastern third of the country. Laurent Kabila remained in office by virtue of foreign arms.

Having enjoyed initial military success, the rebel forces opposing him soon fell to internal strife. The principal rebel group, the *Rassemblement Congolais pour la Démocratie* (RCD) split in two. Rwanda and Uganda, themselves divided on the best way to fight the war, supported different rebel factions. Yet a third rebel faction emerged under the leadership of Jean-Pierre Bemba, the leader of the *Mouvement pour la Libération Congolaise* (MLC). Backed by Uganda, Bemba took charge of the rebellion's northern front. Rwanda and Uganda themselves engaged in heated fighting around Kisangani on at least two occasions.

The Lusaka Agreement

War and peace continued, intermittently bringing hope and despair to everyday Congolese. Peace prospects seemed hopeful in the summer of 1999 as warring states gathered in Zambia's capital, Lusaka. Conditions for ending the war were defined and a precise timetable was set, a sign of the terminal optimism of conference participants.

Within 24 hours of the signing, hostilities were to cease. To ensure compliance, an international force would collect weapons from civilians and supervise the withdrawal of all foreign troops. The agreement also envisioned tracking down and disarming armed groups, screening for mass killers and war criminals, and ultimately the handing over of suspected *génocidaires* to the International Criminal Tribunal for Rwanda (ICTR) in Arusha, Tanzania. (The "armed groups" were fundamentally the rebel oppositions destabilizing Rwanda, Uganda, and Burundi, along with Angola's principal *bête noire*: Jonas Savimbi's UNITA.)

Forty-five days after signing the Lusaka agreement, the DRC government, the *Rassemblement Congolais pour la Démocratie* (RCD), the *Mouvement de Libération Congolais* (MLC), unarmed opposition groups and Congolese civil society were to begin open political negotiations amongst themselves—an Inter-Congolese Dialogue—leading to the creation of a new political dispensation for the Congo.

On paper the plan looked wonderful, but political reality and diplomatic brilliance are hardly the same. President Kabila signed the Lusaka cease-fire to avoid losing the war. Quibble, protest, rejection, and delay provided time to rebuild his forces, but additional Chinese arms and North Korean training were of little avail.

In February 2000 the Security Council approved a worthless Congo peacekeeping force of some 500, backed by about 1,000 soldiers. The 500 could hardly monitor a cease-fire only reluctantly and intermittently observed in a country the size of Western Europe. The year 2000, unsurprisingly, was punctuated by regular violations of the cease-fire and dramatic successes of the rebel alliance.

Kabila's Military Failures

In August 2000 President Laurent Kabila announced his government would no longer observe the Lusaka accord because Congo was occupied by Uganda and Rwanda. In October the Congolese army (FAC) and its allies attacked Rwandan and rebel forces on the southern Katangan Front. The attack was intended to open a corridor for Burundian Hutu rebels—members of the *Forces de la Défense de la Démocratie* (FDD)—to infiltrate Burundi.

Burundi was always considered the weakest link in the anti-Kabila alliance. If it could be destabilized, the government would have to withdraw its troops from the Congo.

The government coalition was initially successful, but its lines were overextended. Roads were in such miserable shape that the Zimbabwean heavy artillery could not be resupplied. When the Rwandan Patriotic Army (RPA) and its allies counterattacked, Kabila's troops retreated precipitously. The government's military failure was completed in early December when Rwandan troops and their RCD-Goma allies captured the strategic southeastern city of Pweto, a critical gateway to the riches of Katanga province, Kabila's homeland.

At least 200 of Pweto's defenders—Rwandan Hutu *Interahamwe*, Burundian Hutu rebels, and members of FAC—were killed. Those not killed, up to 10,000 including a full battalion of Zimbabwean soldiers, fled across the border into Zambia.

The rout of Kabila's forces prompted a debate within the Rwandan government. Some thought the victory should be exploited to destroy the Interahamwe in Katanga completely, and some even argued for tracking them down in Zambia. The diplomatically attuned successfully argued the backlash against such a move would simply be too costly. Indeed, Pweto was the high-water mark of Rwandan arms in the Congo; other events were soon to tip the balance towards more peaceful solutions.

Laurent Kabila Assassinated

Many in Kinshasa had the feeling the Kabila regime had entered its final stages by September 2000. In his regular search for plots, conspiracies, and opposition, President Kabila ultimately turned on his initial supporters.

One of those was Anselme Masasu, a founding leader of the AFDL. Masasu had commanded the army of child soldiers (*kadogos*) from Eastern Congo that swept into Kinshasa in the wake of Kabila's victory. In October 2000 he was reported to have made subversive comments at a meeting of some 1,200 *kadogos* and was subsequently arrested and tortured, along with many others of eastern origin. Some 47 were executed in the presence of President Kabila, who allegedly killed several himself. Anselme Masasu and eight of his companions were reportedly sent to Katanga where they were murdered on November 27. Masasu's murder resonated strongly among the *kadogos*, and its rumor was a factor in their massive desertion at the battle of Pweto. Others plotted more direct action to avenge the murder of their commander—the assassination of Laurent Kabila.

175

Congo (Kinshasa)

Former President Laurent Kabila

Kabila was assassinated on January 16, 2001, 40 years to the day, after the murder of Patrice Lumumba. According to the official version, he was shot by one of his own *kadogo* bodyguards, Rachidi Kasereka, who was, in turn, shot to death by Kabila's aide-de-camp, Col. Eddy Kapend.

Col. Kapend and around 80 others were accused of plotting Kabila's death and were sent before a special military tribunal. Lawyers had little or no contact with them and little capacity to prepare their defenses. In January 2003, Kapend, and 29 others were convicted of plotting and killing Kabila and sentenced to death.

The consequences of Kabila's death were significant for the Congo. Laurent's son, Joseph Kabila, elevated to the presidency by his father's inner circle and their Angolan and Zimbabwean backers, reached out for international understanding and support. With that in hand, he quickly reversed many of his father's decisions blocking implementation of the Lusaka agreement.

Joseph Kabila

Joseph Kabila had long enjoyed the confidence of his father, alternating military assignments with more confidential missions on his father's behalf. Quiet, direct and frank, Joseph is stylistically very different from his father. He rejected the "Marble Palace," built by Mobutu and favored by his father, and worked from the OAU's Kinshasa headquarters. Educated in Tanzania and Uganda, Kabila reportedly feels more comfortable speaking English than French. When elevated to the presidency he was serving as the army chief of staff. He was 29 years old—Africa's youngest president.

With the guidance of Sir Ketumile Masire, the OAU facilitator, participants in the Inter-Congolese Dialogue reached an agreement in the South African resort of Sun City in Spring 2002. Nearly 400 delegates, representing the government, rebel factions, opposition parties, and civil society, met to thrash out plans to end conflict and begin Congo's reconstruction.

Follow-up meetings led to the withdrawal of Rwandan and most Ugandan and Zimbabwean troops by early November, and in December 2002, dialogue participants signed an agreement in Pretoria to share power in a transitional government. By March 2003 a transitional constitution had been hammered out, and on April 2 delegates signed the last agreements to organize the transition—under Joseph Kabila and a power-sharing government—leading to the first democratic elections since independence. The agreement was fundamentally an accord among belligerents to maintain themselves at the center of the state in the post-belligerence period. The spoils of office and impunity from crimes committed were powerful inducements to participate in transitional arrangements. The transition period was to be two years, but ultimately, that would have to be extended for another year.

Under the transitional agreements, President Kabila shared power with four vice presidents—one each from his government, the two main rebel groups, and the unarmed opposition. The vice presidents included Jean-Pierre Bemba, the leader of the *Mouvement de libération du Congo*; Abdoulaye Yerodia Ndombasi, a longtime Kabila ally; Arthur Z'Ahidi Ngoma, a longtime opposition politician who represented the unarmed political opposition, and RCD-Goma's secretary-general, Azarias Ruberwa.

The transitional National Assembly and Senate agreed on the text of a new constitution. In it, presidential powers are limited, and a president can serve a maximum of two five-year terms. The minimum age for presidential candidates was lowered to 30 from 35, allowing Joseph Kabila, then 33, to run for office. Strikingly, and perhaps the most hopeful sign, the new constitution recognizes as citizens all ethnic groups present at independence in 1960. That grants citizenship to the thousands of Rwandans, Hutu and Tutsi, whose presence has long been so contentious. In a national referendum held December 18, 2005, 84% of Congolese voters approved the new governing instrument.

Definitive adoption of the constitution permitted a vote on an electoral law and establishment of an electoral calendar that would end the transitional period. Presidential elections, which took place the end of July 2006, were the culmination of Congo's long and difficult transition. Despite a variety of problems, real and po-

President Joseph Kabila

tential, more than 70 individuals signed up to contest the presidency, a number that, if anything, testifies to the ego-strength of Congolese politicians. Thirty-three made the electoral commission's final list of candidates. Besides Joseph Kabila, Vice Presidents Bemba, Ruberwa, and Z'Ahidi campaigned, along with several individuals associated with the former Mobuto regime, and Antoine Gizenga, once a colleague of Patrice Lumumba. (Rather than pay the nonrefundable $50,000 registration fee, Gizenga chose the alternative, offering 50,000 voters' signatures and photocopies of their indentity cards. "I don't come," he said. "with a financial guarantee, but a republican one.")

In many ways, the election was Joseph Kabila's to lose. The People's Party for Reconstruction and Democracy (PPRD), founded by his supporters in 2002, was the only party to have established offices throughout the country, and it aggressively campaigned on the president's behalf. The absence of the other "national" party, Etienne Tshisekedi's UDPS, which opted to boycott the election, also benefited the president. Kabila campaigned as an independent, above the political fray, but the state-controlled media very politically skewed their coverage to benefit the president.

The best Kabila's opponents could hope for was a runoff election, a not unlikely outcome given the large number of candidates. In the first round, Kabila received 44.8% of all votes cast, not quite enough to avoid a runoff. The second-place finisher was Jean-Pierre Bemba with 20%. In the crucial third-place spot was the grand old man of Congolese politics, the octogenarian Antoine Gizenga; leading the *Parti Lumumbiste Unifié* (PALU), Gizenga gained the support of 13% of Congo's voters. The poll revealed a powerful regional divide in the country. President Kabila obtained a landslide victory in the East (including, improbably, 97% of the vote in the town of Bukavu); Jean-Pierra Bemba ran strongest in the West, and actually won a majority of votes in Kinshasa, where Kabila managed only a paltry 17%.

Not surprisingly, fighting broke out between troops loyal to President Kabila and those loyal to Vice President Bemba almost as soon as the results were announced on August 20. (Each had a personal guard during the transitional period. The president's praetorians numbered between 10,000 and 15,000, Bemba's motlier crew was probably less than 500. Neither had been forced to disarm during the transition.) Bemba properties bore the brunt of a frontal attack with tanks and troops: two television stations belonging to Bemba and accused of broadcasting programs critical of Kabila, personal residences, and his personal helicopter. Heavy fighting left at least 23 civilians and soldiers dead. Under intense diplomatic pressure, Kabila and Bemba called upon their troops to withdraw and the fighting ceased.

Once the guns were silenced it was time for political deal making before the presidential runoff. Antoine Gizenga signed an agreement with President Kabila promising support in exchange for the post of prime minister. Gizenga's backing gave Kabila vital support in the west, and in Kinshasa, where he was weakest. The old oppositionist played his cards well. Kabila won the runoff, 58% to Bemba's 42%. True to his word, Kabila asked Gizenga to become the new republic's first prime minister. In the National Assembly, Prime Minister Gizenga has an easy working majority. Parties supporting President Kabila dominate the legislature, taking over 220 out of 500 seats, while Gizenga's PALU won an additional 35. Jean-Pierre Bemba's *Mouvement pour la Libération Congolaise* (MLC) won 64 seats.

It is unlikely former Vice President Bemba, or the MLC for that matter, will ever function as meaningful opposition to an increasingly authoritarian Joseph Kabila. In March 2007 his personal guard refused a government ultimatum to disband and be integrated into the national army; Bemba's security would be assured, said the government, by 12 policeman. Overwhelming force was used to repress resistance: army, police, presidential guards and even Angolan troops, an Agence France Presse reporter verified. The latter was, of course, denied by a government spokesman, but the whole affair reeked of the Savimbi strategy: in essence, the only good rebel is a dead rebel. The former vice president escaped with his life, finding asylum in the South African embassy. Others were not so lucky. The German ambassador estimated that somewhere between 200 and 500 had died in the violence.

Étienne Tshisekedi, UDPS leader

The government issued a warrant to arrest Bemba, accusing him of treason "in using the armed forces for his own ends," and the DRC's chief prosecutor was quick to add that parliament would be asked to lift the immunity he held as a senator. In the new Democratic Republic of the Congo, the leader of the opposition would be hounded into exile (Portugal, for "medical" reasons). The MLC's party headquarters were pretty much destroyed, as were its television stations. Without a leader, the parliamentary opposition was in disarray. Elsewhere, party members reported police harassment and arrests. Fear was rife.

Thus did Joseph Kabila begin his term as Congo's first president elected in multiparty competitive elections in some forty years. Little seemed to have changed.

The Present: Contemporary Issues

To this day the government accuses Rwanda of taking military action in Eastern DRC against the Hutu rebels. In January 2009 both governments started a joint venture against the rebels and the Tutsi rebel leader Laurent Nkunda was arrested in after attempting to cross over to Rwanda. Kinshasa, Congo's capital, remains a testament to the Congolese capacity to suffer and endure. A hugely swollen population escaping the devastation of war, estimated now to be near seven million, survived cut off from the city's traditional sources of food. Half of Kinshasa's food supply was lost when rebels captured fertile Equateur province and controlled the river that once carried food to the capital. Virtually every available parcel of ground in the city was planted with foodstuffs to supplement the meager food supply.

The majority of *Kinois* (the city's inhabitants) had to content themselves with a single, frugal, daily meal, usually eaten at night so they can go to sleep with a full stomach. Parents fasted for two or three days to provide food for their children, but malnutrition grew and with it, an increase in childhood disease and death.

At the time of independence, Congo was one of the potentially richest nations in the world, with vast deposits of natural resources. The Congo contains 80% of the world's cobalt (essential in hi-tech and defense production), 10% of its copper, and one-third of its diamonds. There are also considerable reserves of gold, uranium, and manganese. But government corruption, mismanagement, and extravagance destroyed Congo's economy. War only furthered the collapse.

A statistical description of the Congo today is appalling. The country, after benefiting from the HIPC initiative is istil 7 billion dollars indebted. More than 70% of the population lives in absolute poverty and 85% is unemployed. Industry operates at a mere 25% of capacity, and there is a tax base of less than one million people in a country of more than 60 million. Its GDP rose by a modest 5.6% in 2003, having fallen by 2% in 2001, and 11.3% in 2000. Growth of 6.5% in 2005 suggests increasing investor confidence following the power-sharing agreements of 2003. The social impact of economic collapse can be seen in two additional statistics: life expectancy is only 54 years, and infant mortality is very high: 81 per thousand. The world average is 54 (2008).

Production in all key sectors declined dramatically under President Mobuto, and suffered worse during the 1997–2002 civil war. The mining sector imploded. *La Général des Carrières et des Mines* (Gécamines), once the crown jewel of the Congo mining industry, reached near-terminal decline. State-owned Gécamines' production fell drastically from the late 1980s, when copper output was consistently 400,000 to 500,000 tons a year (t/y)— about 7% to 8% of global production. By 2005 its production was about 17,000 t/y. The World Bank has worked to restructure and revitalize the company, getting Paul Fortin, a Canadian, appointed as Gécamines' managing director. Copper production has improved, from 22, 481 tons in 2006 to 33, 655 tons in 2007.

The difficulties of genuine reform in the mining sector are illustrated by one of Fortin's most delicate tasks—review of three mining contracts that account for 75% of Gecamines' mineral assest base. Approved in 2005 by the transitional government of Joseph Kabila, the contracts were signed without benefit of thorough analysis and evaluation. The World Bank's principal mining specialist described the assets transferred to the three companies involved as exceeding the "norms for ra-

Congo (Kinshasa)

Bridge repair in the eastern province.

©Paul Carlson Foundation

The Future

The Democratic Republic of the Congo seems to be emerging slowly from the horrific civil wars that ravaged the country between the mid-1990s and 2003. In 2007 and 2008, Joseph Kabila's government signed pacts with a range of actors, including the government of Rwanda and a variety of armed groups in eastern D.R.C. These are intended to subdue the *interahamwe* militias of Rwandan origin, among other actors, and to provide buffer zones between lingering groups of rebels and the central government. In theory, this will facilitate respect of human rights on the part of the government. However, given the difficulty facing D.R. Congo in enforcing the rule of law across the vast territory, there is reason for skepticism.

The country's economic problems remain enormous. There is little infrastructure to link the regions to Kinshasa, so the new constitution's creation of 25 semi-autonomous provinces (up from 11) was a concession to political reality. Each of the provinces will have its own legislature, which will provide ample employment opportunities for the political class. Each will also be allowed to keep 40% of the revenues it earns, which provides ample opportunities for corruption. On Transparency International's 2006 *Corruption Perceptions Index*, the country was ranked equally corrupt as Chad and Sudan, just two places above bottom-ranked Haiti.

tional and highest use of the mineral assets." The possibility of any contract revision is slight. The mining province of Katanga is Kabila's political stronghold and he has installed his allies on the Gécamines board of directors. Any recommendation by Managing Director Fortin can be vetoed by the board.

Chinese companies have rapidly moved into Katanga's copper belt since President Joseph Kabila visited Beijing in March 2005. Beijing-based Colec is in discussions to rehabilitate the Kamatanda mines and three copper and cobalt plants—with a planned cost of $27.5 million. Chinese businessmen in Katanga are also at the heart of a boom in ore-processing plants. Feza Mining, expected to produce 4,000 tons of copper alloy and 1,000 tons of cobalt annually, is joint Chinese-Congolese development. As a consequence of increased investment, sector analysts expect copper output to rise to 100,000 to 120,000 t/y in the next five years.

Whether this will relieve poverty and suffering in Katanga is dubious. Global Witness succinctly described Congolese reality in its 2006 report, *Digging in Corruption*: "The mining sector in Katanga is characterized by widespread corruption and fraud at all levels. . . . Government officials are actively colluding with trading companies in circumventing control procedures and the payment of taxes. The profits are serving to line the pockets of a small but powerful elite—politicians and businessmen who are exploiting the local population and subverting natural riches for their private ends."

Market transport in the eastern region: the Tsjugoudu, a hand-crafted bicycle made almost entirely of wood and capable of carrying up to 400 pounds of produce to market.

Photo by Theodore Trefon

178

The Republic of Equatorial Guinea

Selling yoghurt

Photo by Cayuela Serrano
Courtesy: APFT-ULB

Land and People

On the protected shoreline of mainland Equatorial Guinea, hot and humid Rio Muni, the narrow white sandy beach quickly gives way to thick growth of interior rain forest, where immense ebony, mahogany and oak trees crowd each other to bask in the sun. It is uniformly hot and oppressive. Few roads penetrate into the interior, but the land is thick with streams that are the home of giant frogs. As long as one foot and weighing up to eight pounds, they perch majestically on the spray-drenched rocks, their tongues darting out to catch unwary insects.

The scenic island of Bioko is large and was productive until the 1970s, being the source of one of the best varieties of cocoa in the world. Production was on large plantations; contract labor from Nigeria was imported, but almost all fled during the brutalities of the Macías Nguema regime. Ships from many nations called at the port, and the international airport was the base from which relief supplies were flown into strife-torn Nigeria in the early 1970s.

The use of marijuana is widespread and traditional. Referred to as the "sacred weed of the people" and once used only in traditional ceremonies, marijuana has found its way into every level of Equatorial Guinean society. The drug provides, for the poor, escape from worsening poverty amid the riches of an oil boom. One of Malabo's poor said he and his companions "take refuge in marijuana. At least it helps us to take a less aggressive view of life."

The Past: Political and Economic History

For early history, see *Historical Background* and *The Colonial Period: The Spanish.*

The provinces known as Spanish Guinea were made internally self-governing in 1963, and their name was changed to

Basic Facts

Area: 28,051 sq. km. = 10,830 sq. mi. (slightly larger than Vermont)

Population: 633,000 (CIA World Fact Book 2009 est.)

Capital City: Malabo

Climate: Tropically hot and humid

Neighboring Countries: Cameroon (north); Gabon (east and south). The island portion of the country lies some twenty miles off the west coast of Cameroon.

Official Languages: Spanish and French

Other Principal Languages: Fang, Bubi, Ibo, and Pidgin English

Ethnic Groups: Bioko (primarily Bubi, some Fernandinos), Rio Muni (primarily Fang), Europeans less than 1,000, mostly Spanish

Principal Religions: Most people are nominally Roman Catholic; traditional tribal beliefs are intermingled with their Christian faith.

Chief Commercial Products: Petroleum, timber, and cocoa

GNI Per Capita: $12,860 (World Bank 2008 est.)

Currency: CFA franc

Former Colonial Status: Spanish Colony (island 1778–1968, mainland 1885–1968)

Independence Date: October 12, 1968

Chief of State: Brig. Gen. Teodoro Obiang Nguema Mbasogo, President (pronounced Tay-oh-dor-oh Oh-be-ang N-gway-mah M-bah-so-go)

National Flag: Three horizontal stripes of green, white and red, with a blue aquamarine isosceles triangle next to the staff. Centered in the white stripe is the coat of arms: six yellow six-pointed stars (representing the mainland and five offshore islands) above a gray shield bearing a silk-cotton tree and below which is a scroll with the motto UNIDAD, PAZ, JUSTICIA (Unity, Peace, Justice)

Note: Between 1974 and the present, geographic place names have been changed from Spanish to African and then to *other* African designations and back to Spanish. The island, first known as Fernando Po, was renamed by the late president in his own honor. It then was designated *Bioko* after an early king of the region. The mainland, formerly Rio Muni, became Mbini, but it is now again generally called Rio Muni.

Equatorial Guinea

Equatorial Guinea. Spain granted independence to Equatorial Guinea in 1968. In UN-supervised elections mainland Fang outnumbered the more educated Bubi of Fernando Po, and their candidate, Francisco Macías Nguema, became the country's first president.

Macías Nguema's paranoid style quickly became apparent. Prominent political figures were arrested and executed on grounds they were plotting his overthrow. Family members were installed in key government posts, but they remained under close surveillance. Cocoa plantations were nationalized, and the economy spiraled downward. In 1972 Macías Nguema's hand-picked National Assembly named him "President for Life." He assumed absolute personal power in 1973 and had the island of Fernando Po renamed in his honor. Titles were collected: in addition to "President for Life," Macías Nguema was also "Grand Master of Education, Science and Culture."

As his paranoia increased, life became more and more grim for the citizenry. Death squads formed by the "Macias Youth" roamed the countryside, raping, looting and killing. Mass executions were held while loudspeakers blared a recording of "Those Were the Days, My Friend." Others were buried up to their necks—to be eaten alive by insects. Educated Guineans, mostly Bubi, were specially targeted for slaughter.

A militant atheist, Macías Nguema was especially venomous towards Christians. He ordered his picture to hang beside the altar of every church in the country and compelled priests and pastors to recite the slogan "All for Macias" at every service. The World Council of Churches branded him a "modern Caligula." One island visitor called the country "the concentration camp of Africa—a cottage-industry Dachau."

By 1979, when he was overthrown, Macías Nguema is believed to have murdered 50,000 Guineans. Another 100,000, one-third of the country's population, had been driven into exile. Among the dead were two-thirds of the last elected national assembly and 10 of the 12 original cabinet ministers. Guinea's small educated class had been virtually eliminated through death or flight.

In the summer of 1979 Macías Nguema was overthrown by his nephew, and deputy defense minister, Lt. Col. Teodoro Obiang Nguema Mbasogo. Any joy at Macías Nguema's fall was restrained. Lt. Colonel Obiang Nguema had been one of the principal architects of the Macías reign of terror, and human rights groups had long accused him of personal involvement in a number of killings.

His governance of the country has been repressive and dictatorial. Until 1993 he operated through a single party, the Democratic Party of Equatorial Guinea (PDGE), and concentrated political power in his own hands. Economic power was concentrated in the hands of the Nguema clan.

Although multiparty elections were introduced in 1993, nothing approaching democracy exists in Equatorial Guinea. President Obiang was elected to a seven-year term in 1996 in a contest dominated by fraud and intimidation. The government and 14 opposition groups signed a national pact in April 1997 agreeing to the basic conditions for future legislative elections. One month later, however, the government announced that a plot to overthrow the president had been uncovered. This set off another wave of political repression. Relations with Spain deteriorated when Spain granted asylum to Severo Moto, leader of the *Partido del Progreso de Guinea Ecuatorial* (PPGE) and alleged leader of the so-called coup.

In pique, Obiang made French the official language of this former Spanish colony. In May 1997 Severo Moto, along with 11 others, was tried *in absentia* for treason, found guilty and sentenced to 101 years imprisonment. The PPGE was banned in June, indicating just how quickly the opposition can be dispatched in Equatorial Guinea.

A new separatist group emerged in January 1998, attacking three police posts and killing several people. It identified itself as the Movement for Self-determination for the Island of Bioko (MAIB) and demanded independence for the island's indigenous population of Bubi peoples, marginalized and excluded from the country's political and economic life by the mainland Fang. Mass arrests followed. Fifteen Bubi were condemned to death by a military court. The sentence was reduced in September, by presidential grace, to life imprisonment after an outpouring of international protest.

March 1999 legislative elections could be called farcical were it not for the thuggish brutality of the Obiang Nguema regime. Opposition candidates were threatened, arbitrarily arrested, and prevented from campaigning. For the election itself, additional polling places were set up in schools, barracks and state-owned enterprises, close to the governing party's adherents. Alliances between parties were prohibited. On election day armed soldiers or other security agents stood inside polling areas. Voters were often forced to cast their ballots publicly. Unsurprisingly the PDGE won 75 of 80 parliamentary seats. Appeals to the National Electoral Commission would be unavailing. Its chairman was also the minister of the interior.

The European Union and most other bodies who had been requested to send observers refused to sanction any of this by their presence. Little wonder Freedom House lists Equatorial Guinea among "the worst of the worst," in its 2005 report on the world's most repressive societies.

The government strictly controls freedom of speech and press. Press laws authorize government censorship of all publications, and the Ministry of Information can require prepublication approval of article content. Self-censorship is the better part of valor. All electronic media are censured. The ruling party controls the country's main publications, radio and television. It owns and operates Radio Malabo, the most widely heard station. Only in 1998 did the government allow the country's first private domestic radio station, Radio Ansonga, but that is owned by Minister of Waters and Forests, Fishing and Environment Teodoro ("Teodorino") Obiang Nguema, the president's eldest son.

State and family are closely conjoined in Equatorial Guinea. The president's second son, Gabriel Mbegha Obiang Lima, is state secretary for oil, while his brother-in-law, Teodoro Biyogo Nsue, once Equatorial Guinea's ambassador to the UN, now manages family/country interests in the U.S., including a $300 million to $500 million bank account. The state security apparatus is dominated by his closest relatives, for this is a task, says the president, that cannot be confided in strangers: "I must be able to count on loyal people." (For his personal protection, Obiang relies on a contingent of Moroccan troops.)

His brother Armengol Ondo Nguema is director general of national security and one of the most feared men in the country. Another brother, Antonio Mba Nguema, is also part of the security service, as is his son-in-law, Julian Ondo Nkumu.

It is the state security apparatus that is most responsible for Equatorial Guinea's appalling human rights record. The U.S. State Department's *Human Rights Practices Report* (2005) said the government's hu-

President Obiang Nguema Mbasogo

Equatorial Guinea

man rights record remained poor and it continued to commit or condone serious abuses, including torture and beating of prisoners and detainees, life-threatening prison conditions, arbitrary arrest and incommunicado detention.

Because of Guinea's sleazy human rights record the U.S. kept President Obiang at arms length until April 2006 when he met with Secretary of State Condoleezza Rice. The meeting came shortly before the visit of Chinese President Hu Jintao to Washington. China's national oil company had already signed an oil exploration agreement with Equatorial Guinea, and one could not help thinking geopolitical considerations weighed heavily in the decision. Certainly it should not have been as a reward for what Secretary Rice's own department called "small, haphazard steps toward the development of [a] participatory political system" made under President Obiang.

In the lead-up to presidential elections in late 2002 regime critics were subjected to the usual harassment, repression and torture; the country's four main opposition parties withdrew, saying the balloting was so rigged there was no way there could be a fair election. With well over 90% of the votes, Teodoro Obiang Nguema Mbasogo was reelected to another seven-year term as president. The constitution places no limits on the number of terms a president may serve.

In early 2004 rumors of an impending coup circulated in Malabo, but they were given substance in early March when 15 mercenaries were arrested in the country and another 64, allegedly on their way, were taken off a plane in Zimbabwe. The government hastily pointed fingers at its *bête noire*, Severo Moto, head of the opposition Progress Party, funded by what the minister of information called "enemies and multinational companies." The *Economist* magazine claimed to have documents linking Armengol Ondo Nguema, the president's brother and secret service chief, and the mercenary leader, Nick du Toit.

Indeed, dissention within the clan Nguema is very real. Reportedly seriously ill with prostate cancer, President Obiang has sought to assure the presidential succession by his eldest son, "Teodorino" Obiang Nguema, a young man whose flamboyant lifestyle has captivated the Western press, but whose trenchant criticisms of his uncles, the generals, has fostered bitter enmity in them and cordial dislike within the army. The younger Obiang has accused them of control and expropriation of both the economy and the apparatus of the state and deliberately absented himself from the country in protest. In a deeply patriarchal society questions of age are important, and the

generals detest the thought of taking orders from one junior to them. Equatorial Guinea's opposition thought the whole brouhaha was just another attempt by the regime to divert attention from forthcoming elections, and certainly it did.

Parliamentary seats had been increased in September 2003—to 100 from 80—to allow the "democratic opposition" to be represented in the legislature, but almost all the candidates of the two main opposition parties were rejected on technical grounds.

The PDGE and its electoral coalition took 98 out of 100 seats in parliament and 237 municipal councillors out of 244. The main opposition Convergence for Social Democracy (CPSD) got two seats in parliament and only seven on local municipal councils.

Criticized that the country's oil wealth had made little improvement in the lives of ordinary citizens, President Obiang launched a blistering attack on civil servants and his own cabinet as the parties responsible. In late June 2006 he was reported to have raged: "If it's necessary to change the government, the entire government will go. If it's necessary to replace every civil servant, they will all be replaced." Mincing no words, he went on to say that "corruption," "ignorance," "irregularities," and "badly taken decisions," had undermined the effectiveness of both cabinet and bureaucracy and produced the miserable conditions (or as the president phrased it, "difficult situation") in which the bulk of Equatorial Guinea's citizens lived.

Dutifully obedient to his president's wishes, Prime Minister Abia Biteo Borico

submitted his cabinet's resignation in August, allowing the president to give the country "a new spirit and dynamism with a new governmental team." Ricardo Mangué Obama Nfubea (no relation to the U.S. president) was named prime minister. Mangué Obama Nfubea, like the President, is ethnically a Fang. While the Fang—about 80% of the population—are the country's majority people, the prime minister's office has traditionally been reserved for a Bubi, the original inhabitants of Bioko Island. He served as prime minister for two years before falling out of favor with Obiang in 2008.

The past year has seen further upheaval in Equatorial Guinea's politics. In August 2008, President Obiang dismissed his entire cabinet, replacing Mangué Obama Nfubea with Ignácio Milam Tang, also of the Fang ethnic group. The reshuffle was supposedly to root out corruption in the Mangué Obama Nfubea government, but also served to scramble any ambitious politicians who sought an independent power base.

In February 2009, gunfire erupted around the presidential palace. The government blamed 15 Nigerian rebels for the assault. While the attack failed, it showed the lingering divisiveness of politics in Equatorial Guinea, and suggests that Obiang continues to face occasional challenges to his total grip on power.

The Present: Contemporary Issues

The export of cocoa and coffee has been the traditional backbone of the nation's economy, but under Macías Nguema the plantations were nationalized and destroyed. In the 1960s nearly 98,000 acres

President Teodoro Obiang Nguema and Secretary of State Condoleezza Rice, April 2006

Photo Courtesy State Department

181

Equatorial Guinea

were devoted to cocoa production, mostly on Bioko Island; by the 1980s, only 7,400 acres remained in production. Annual yields fell from 38,000 metric tons to a low of 4,500 tons. Coffee production similarly collapsed. About 8,500 metric tons, most of it grown by African farmers on small plots in Rio Muni, were produced in 1968. By the late 1980s production had fallen to 1,000 tons.

There were few incentives for farmers to continue cocoa cultivation until 2006, when the government was sloshing around in oil profits. In 2005 Equatorial Guinea exported only 2,227 tons of cacao, worth about $1.25 million. To provide additional incentives for the 2005–2006 agricultural campaign, the government pledged to subsidize the price offered farmers, nearly doubling what they would get on the open market. It also agreed to liquidate the debts farmers had built up with exporters during the 2004–2005 season.

Equatorial Guinea's reversal of economic fortune began in the 1990s with the discovery of oil in the Gulf of Guinea. By 2005 oil production averaged 356,000 barrels per day (bbl/d). Equatorial Guinea has overtaken Gabon to become sub-Saharan Africa's third biggest oil producer (after Nigeria and Angola). Oil, with proven reserves of 1.77 billion barrels, accounts for 97% of the country's exports, and 80% of GDP, a gigantic share.

The oil economy means the people of Rio Muni no longer live in rural solitude. Four-wheel-drive vehicles driving along the faded elegance of Spanish colonial boulevards suggest the ruling elite has begun to enjoy the economic fruits of political power. Symptomatically, as of April 2006, only Mercedes Benz vehicles are permitted as taxis. By contrast, the dispossessed suffer daily water and power cutoffs and drinking water regularly polluted by drainage water, mainly because of broken pipes.

There are also reserves of some 1.3 trillion cubic feet of gas. Marathon Oil Company has started site work to construct a liquefied natural gas (LNG) facility on Bioko Island; supply contracts have been signed with Nigeria, but those with Cameroon have been delayed because of disputed claims over areas of the Gulf of Guinea. As a consequence, Marathon's hope of supplying 3.4 million tons of LNG by late 2007 was delayed.

Gazprom, the Russian natural gas behemoth has entered the Guinean market. In September 2006 it concluded an agreement with the *Société nationale de gaz* (Sonagaz) for joint production of LNG.

With its oil bonanza, the country's economy has grown with enormous rapidity. In 2004, Equatorial Guinea was the fastest growing economy in the world; in 2005, the country's real gross domestic product (GDP) grew 15.4%. The average over roughly the last decade has been somewhere over 15%/year, though figures are far from transparent.

The average citizen, however, has yet to experience a higher standard of living from the oil revenues. The World Bank has been uncharacteristically blunt, saying that oil revenue has had "no impact on Equatorial Guinea's dismal social indicators." Health-care spending for example, has *declined* from 6% to just over 1% of the budget. Malabo, the capital, suffers from chronic water shortages.

How much money has come in, where it is deposited, and how it is being spent are all unclear. President Obiang has told the IMF these statistics are state secrets. In January 2003 the *Los Angeles Times* lifted one small corner of the veil that conceals state patrimonialism. According to its investigations Equatorial Guinea kept an account with Riggs Bank in Washington DC where international oil companies directly deposited at least $300 million. The account was controlled exclusively by President Obiang. As he told a reporter for the *New Statesman*, "I am the one who arranges things in this country because in Africa there are a lot of problems of corruption . . . I'm 100 per cent sure of all the oil revenue because the one who signs is me."

The U.S. has attached great importance to developing Equatorial Guinea's oil sector to lessen its dependence on Middle Eastern suppliers. Washington's new enthusiasm for the country can be seen in the State Department's approval for Military Professional Resources Inc. (MPRI)—a private firm run by Pentagon retirees out of Alexandria, Va.—to help the government develop a coast guard to protect its offshore oil fields. Those are being operated by American firms like ExxonMobil, ChevronTexaco, and Amerada Hess. In January 2007 the government signed a five-year deal with MPRI to train army units and the presidential guard.

Given increased American presence in the country, the U.S. reopened its embassy in Malabo in October 2003. Business was conducted by a chargé d'affaires rather than a full ambassador until November 2006, when the first American ambassador in eleven years arrived in Malabo.

China is poised to participate in Equatorial Guinea's oil bonanza. In February 2006 the China National Offshore Oil Company Africa Limited, a subsidiary of China's largest offshore oil producer (CNOOC), signed a product share contract with the country's national oil company giving it explorations rights over the next five years in an area of some 2,287 square kilometers.

In January 2007 Foreign Minister Li Zhaoxing made Equatorial Guinea the second stop on his seven-nation tour of Africa. The fruits of his discussions were announced in April: China Road and Bridge Corporation won a port construction deal valued at $425 million.

Oil revenues have allowed the Obiang regime to enrich and further entrench itself. As it had controlled jobs in the bureaucracy, awarding them to its faithful supporters, the clan Nguema controls access to the new, high-paying jobs of the oil industry. The best jobs are reserved for the PDGE faithful.

Developments in the petroleum sector have overshadowed the other important resource for the country's ruling clan: timber. Initially small scale, logging operations exploded around 1994 when huge Asian transnationals moved in. By the mid-1990s there were more than 20 logging companies exploiting the rain forest on concessions reportedly owned by President Obiang. Forestry became the second most important economic sector after oil, but aggressive logging threatens the approximately 3.2 million acres of forestland in mainland Equatorial Guinea with over-harvesting.

The Future

The attack on the presidential palace in Equatorial Guinea in February 2009 demonstrates the unsettled nature of the country's politics, but the Nguema clan seems largely secure in power, and there is no prospect for democracy here. The best the opposition can hope for from the new oil wealth is that the presence of hundreds of foreigners might restrain regime repression. Tensions within the clan, particularly focused on President Obiang Nguema's eldest son, could still explode in violence, as the abortive March 2004 coup suggests.

Equatorial Guinea has been, by some accounts, the fastest growing economy in the world in recent years. This does not, however, mean significant economic and social change for most citizens. Entirely an artifact of oil investment, the growth has failed to "trickle down" to the average person. The future remains bleak for those who are not directly benefiting from oil revenues, state patronage, or both.

Given the sudden strategic importance of Equatorial Guinea (due to its location and its oil resources), there is a reasonable expectation that the country will receive considerably greater attention from the American government and international investors. Still, it is uncertain what this will mean for democracy or for improving the standard of living for most living in the country.

The Republic of Gabon (pronounced Gah-bonh)

Gabonese school children chasing soap bubbles

Photo by Marian Zeldin

Basic Facts

Area: 264,180 sq. km. = 102,000 sq. mi. (about the size of Colorado)

Population: 1,300,000 (UN 2007 est.)

Capital City: Libreville

Climate: Hot and humid. Although there is almost no rain from June to September, the humidity remains quite high. Rainfall in the remaining months totals more than 100 inches per year.

Neighboring Countries: Equatorial Guinea (northwest); Cameroon (north); Congo (east, south)

Official Language: French

Other Principal Languages: Around 40. Prominently: Mbere, Myene, Fang (a widely used *lingua franca*), Njebi, Punu, Sira, and Teke

Principal Religions: Christian 55%–75%, Muslim less than 1%, and animist

Ethnic Groups: Prominently: Fang, Eshira, Bapounou, Bateke; about 6,000 French

Chief Commercial Products: Crude oil, timber, and manganese

GDP Per Capita: $10,941 (World Bank 2008 est.)

GNI Per Capita: $5,941 (World Bank 2006 est.; GNI/capita is much lower than GDP/capita due largely to earnings of foreign multinational corporations in oil industry).

Currency: CFA franc

Former Colonial Status: French Colony (1903–1960)

Independence Date: August 17, 1960

Chief of State: Rose Francine Rogombe, Interim President (since June 2009)

National Flag: A tricolor, with horizontal stripes of green (top), golden yellow and royal blue.

Land and People

Lying astride the Equator on the west coast of Africa, Gabon is a land of hot and humid rain forest with heavy rainfall. The coastal lowlands from 20 to 120 miles in depth receive up to 150 inches of rain per year. A series of densely forested plateaus rise farther inland, spreading from the northeast to the southeast of the country with altitudes from 1,000 to 2,000 feet. The remainder of the land is covered by gentle, round mountains extending to heights of 5,200 feet.

A common manifestation of culture in Gabon is through the use of masks, The Fang—a bantu-speaking group—is characterized by organized clarity and distinct lines and shapes. Masks are worn in ceremonies and for hunting. The faces are painted white with black features. Also some tribes center their art around the rituals for death. Because of the lack of systematic tourism, and western influence art is seldom commercialized.

Gabon

The Past: Political and Economic History

For early history, see *Historical Background* and *The Colonial Period: The French.*

Under the constitution of France's Fifth Republic, Gabon achieved self-government in 1958 and full independence in 1960 under President Léon Mba. At independence there were two major political parties—Mba's Gabon Democratic Bloc (BDG) and the Social Democratic Union of Gabon, led by J.H. Aubame. Efforts by President Mba to eliminate his rival and institute a single-party state led to a rebellion of young military officers in February 1964. They deposed the president, but French troops intervened the next day and reinstated Mba. When Mba died in 1967, he was succeeded by Vice President Albert Bongo, who took over the one-party state.

In 1973 Bongo was reelected president. He announced that he was renouncing Roman Catholicism and adopting Islam, changing his name from Albert-Bernard to El-Hadj Omar. Bongo's single-party regime was authoritarian, quick to suppress the slightest sign of opposition, completely deaf to appeals for multiparty democracy, and utterly corrupt.

Declining oil prices in the 1980s brought on an economic downturn and increased political unrest. In 1990 budgetary belt-tightening—a consequence of austerities imposed by structural adjustment programs—set off street demonstrations by students and workers.

Shaken, Bongo at first rejected the notion of multiparty democracy, but quickly reversed his position. Opposition parties were legalized, but in parliamentary elections held in September and October the government demonstrated its reluctance

Former President Omar Bongo

to have its fate determined by voters. In what would become a recurring scenario, the election was manipulated and the opposition decried its fraudulence.

In December 1993 Bongo was reelected president by a modest 51% majority. His principal opponent was Father Paul Mba Abessole of the National Rally of Woodcutters (*Rassemblement National des Bûcherons*; RNB), but ten other candidates effectively diluted opposition voting. Complaints about electoral irregularities continued months afterwards.

The same scenario was repeated in the presidential election of December 1998. President Bongo was again opposed by Libreville's mayor, Paul Mba Abessole, leading the RNB, and Pierre Mamboundou of the High Resistance Council (*Haut conseil de la résistance*; HCR). The Ministry of the Interior announced final results: Bongo

66.55% and elected on the first ballot; Mamboundou, said the ministry, won 16.54% and Abessole collected 13.41%.

Observers noted the ministry had managed to add another 30,000 voters to the electoral lists a mere 48 hours before the election. Voters in precincts known to favor the opposition discovered that their polling place had been transferred to another site, usually at some distance. The regime even managed to hire its own election observers—longtime friends of President Bongo in French legal circles. They dutifully reported that all was well.

Washington, Paris, and Geneva investigations have revealed the nature and extent of President Bongo's personal enrichment from Gabon's oil production. A U.S. Senate investigation has named him as one of a "rogues' gallery" of foreign leaders who have funneled millions through American banks. In Switzerland an investigative judge developed testimony on the practice of offering "bonuses" to leaders of oil-producing states to secure exploration permits. Money—a minimum of $100 million—went into at least three accounts belonging to Bongo, but held in another name. In October 2000, the Gabonese parliament offered protection to the president by amending the constitution to give former heads of state immunity from legal prosecution for any act committed in the performance of their official duties.

Legislative elections in December 2001 were yet another disaster. Opposition parties threatened to boycott when the electoral commission announced that the electoral rolls contained 778,000 eligible voters—nearly 75% of the country's population. Cleanup reduced the number to a little less than 600,000, but 80% of those preferred to stay home rather than go to the polls on election day.

The courts invalidated 10% of the elections, including one in which the winning candidate carried ballots from polling place to counting center. This scarcely affected the result. Bongo's ruling Gabonese Democratic Party (PDG) went into the election holding 90 of 120 seats and emerged with almost the same number. Some 24 parties put up candidates, but only eight could be considered oppositional. Even President Bongo's traditional rival, Paul Mba Abessole, broke with opposition calls to boycott the election.

Since becoming mayor of Libreville, Abessole had become an apostle of "convivial opposition," and the RNB participated in December's legislative elections with a clear eye to the future. Their reward came in January 2002 when Bongo called for an "opening" of the government. Four members of the opposition were included in the new cabinet. Abessole was given the portfolio charged with human

Oil storage at Port Gentil

rights; all the more powerful ministries were tightly controlled by the Bongo clique.

Control of state resources allowed President Bongo to fund and co-opt the opposition for years, and the regular migration from opposition to presidential supporter eroded public confidence in both the political system and individual politicians. Massive absenteeism has characterized recent elections. The turnout in the December 2002 local elections was so dismal that the opposition called for their annulment. One election official put it quite simply: "I don't know if the Gabonese have lost their sense of patriotism," he said, "but it's clear that they don't believe in elections any more."

Parliament amended the constitution in July 2003 to repeal a two-term limit for the head of state. Taking nothing for granted, parliament also amended the constitution to reduce the electoral process to a single round of voting: the candidate with the most votes on the first ballot, regardless of how few, will be declared the victor. The provisions guarantee lifetime tenure for President Bongo.

Already in power for 37 years, President Bongo ran again in the November 2005 presidential elections. His opponents were four, but none had much chance against the well oiled electoral machinery of the PDG. President Bongo swept the field with 79% of the vote. Pierre Mamboundou, now leading the Union of Gabonese People (UPG), was expected to pose the greatest challenge, but received a paltry 13% of the vote, slightly down from his 16% showing in 1998. Zacharie Myboto, a former PDG heavyweight who had resigned from the party to run against the president, came in third with nearly 7%. The usual charges of electoral rigging were dismissed by Gabon's constitutional court, which declared Bongo officially re-elected in January 2006.

The December 2006 legislative elections delivered a similar crushing defeat to the opposition. The governing PDG won 82 of 120 seats in the National Assembly outright; 13 more deputies were elected from parties allied to it. The four "independents" were assumed to be favorable to the PDG. Pierre Mamboundou, runner up in the last presidential race, became the leader of the opposition when his UPG won eight parliamentary seats; the opposition Gabonese Union for Democracy and Development, led by the other defeated presidential candidate, Zacharie Myboto, won four seats. Given opposition thinness in the assembly, it poses little challenge to President Bongo.

The Present: Contemporary Issues

On June 8th, 2009 President Omar Bongo died in a Spanish Clinic at age 73. He had been Africa's longest-standing president, with an incredible 47 years in power. He left his country with no vice-president and a power vacuum. Senate speaker Rose Rogombe was sworn in as interim president on June 10th. Her mandate includes calling for elections within 45 days. Activists are claiming that no member of the current government should stand for re-election, but the Gabonese Democratic Party will likely hand-pick who is going to be the winner of the next democratic elections. The likeliest designate is Bongo's 50 year old son, Ali.

Gabon is the richest of sub-Saharan Africa's tropical states because of oil, timber and mineral extraction. It is the region's sixth largest oil producer, and crude oil exports are the backbone of the economy. Oil contributes 43% of GDP and represents 81% of total export revenues. Sixty-five percent of government revenue comes from the oil sector, and budgets are seriously affected by price fluctuations in the world market. With a per capita income figure over $5,000, Gabon's wealth seems confirmed, but the reality is much different. An estimated 40% of the population is unemployed, and 60% to 70% of Gabonese live below the poverty line—less than one dollar a day.

Oil is a nonrenewable resource, and in Gabon production is slowing as fields age and become exhausted. No major discoveries have been made in recent years, and oil production has not grown since the mid-1990s. At the moment, much hope rests on ultra-deepwater drilling. From a peak of 371,000 bbl/d in 1997, daily production declined to 237,000 bbl/d in 2006.

Until the recent spike in oil revenues, Gabon's budgets usually ran deficits, leading to a regular state of financial crisis. One critical aspect of the crisis is Gabon's huge accumulated debt—over $3.8 billion (2004). Debt servicing gobbles up nearly 50% of the budget. Civil service salaries constitute another 19% of the budget, leaving nothing for investment and little for social services.

The government is desperate to renegotiate its debt and to this end has sought assistance from the IMF. The country is hardly a model of good governance and financial accountability. Lavish public spending regularly exceeds budgetary limits and needs to be significantly curtailed, but the prime minister was hardly a model of belt-tightening when he appointed a cabinet of 50 members in early 2007.

As Gabon has seen its oil production (which is onshore) decline, it has eyed offshore possibilities. In February 2003, Gabon asserted sovereignty over the island of Mbanié in Equatorial Guinea's Bay of Corisco. The islet had been a point of contention since 1972, but took on strategic

Maize cropping in the rainforest

Photo by A. Binot
Courtesy of APFT–ULB

importance with the discovery of vast oil reserves in Equatorial Guinea's waters. In July 2004 the two governments announced an agreement to establish a Joint Oil Zone around the island, but its maritime boundaries were unresolved. In February 2006 UN Secretary-General Kofi Annan announced the two presidents had agreed to begin meetings on border demarcation; he expected the issue would be resolved "definitely before the end of the year." It was not.

Gabon's forestry sector is the country's second largest industry and, after the civil service, the country's second largest employer. Thick forests cover 76% of the country, and exports of timber have risen in recent years. In 1957, less than 10% of Gabon's forests were allocated as logging concessions; today more than half have been designated for logging. There is concern that, like oil, this resource may be rapidly exhausted. The government's new forestry code envisions a network of national parks, and President Bongo indicated the government planned to devote 10% of the national territory to the development of protected forest areas.

Having banned the cutting of its own old-growth trees in 1998, China became dependent on imported wood from places like Malaysia, Burma, Indonesia, or Gabon. It buys, for example, some 65% of Gabon's annual 2.5 million cubic meters of mahogany exports. It also imports 1.5 million cubic meters of *Okoumé*, a softwood used in making plywood. That in turn is used to manufacture cheap bedroom furniture exported everywhere.

Gabon has become increasingly dependent on Chinese markets, and Chinese aid and cooperation loom large in Gabon's economic development. President Bongo has traveled to China nine times, and over

Gabon

the decades has met with Mao Tse-tung, Chou En-lai, and Deng Xiaoping. When China's present leader, Hu Jintao, visited the African continent in February 2004, Gabon was his only sub-Saharan stop, after Algeria and Egypt—two other oil-producing states.

As oil revenues decline, the Bongo government has pressed China and other investors to commit to development of its minerals sector. Gabon is the world's number two producer of manganese (after South Africa), and China is already the metal's principal importer. Huge reserves of iron, estimated at one billion tons, are located in the far north at Belinga, but the absence of adequate infrastructure to mine and move the ore has prevented development of the deposits. Given its voracious need for raw materials and its state corporations unhindered by the need to make a profit, China's seemingly uneconomic commitment to Belinga may be understood. Development of Belinga will require construction of a hydroelectric dam on the Ivindo River to provide energy to operate mining equipment, two additional rail connections to the Transgabon Railroad, and construction of a deepwater port at Santa Clara to transport the ore.

China has already executed several high-profile projects in Gabon including hospitals in Franceville and Libreville and both the National Assembly and Senate buildings. One Chinese project became high profile when it fudged the boundaries of conservation and resource exploitation. China Petroleum & Chemical Corporation, more simply known as Sinopec, secured a concession to explore for oil in Gabon's Loango National Park, a small preserve of three climate zones—seashore,

savanna, and forest—and photogenic wildlife—elephants, gorillas, and chimpanzees. (Tourist brochures referred to it as "Africa's Last Paradise.") Sinopec's environmental impact study was rejected by the Gabonese environment and national parks ministry, which demanded the company cease its operations. This Sinopec refused to do, claiming authorization from the ministry of mines, and blissfully went about establishing the infrastructure of exploration.

Roads were cut into the forest, trees massively cleared away, and a village for 450 workers constructed. Dynamite, in theory forbidden in a national park, facilitated destruction. Environmentalists were furious; the Gabonese government, which had lofted its eco-credentials by classifying one tenth of its territory a natural reserve, was embarrassed. Donors, including the EU, U.S., France, and the World Bank, which had set aside $10 million for Gabon's nature reserves, wrote letters of angry outrage. Ultimately the national parks council ordered Sinopec to halt its exploration activities. The company packed up men, machines and dynamite sticks and departed paradise in October 2006.

Politics and economy are very much family affairs in Gabon. The president's eldest son, Christian, is a former deputy director-general of the National Timber Company (SNBG), which holds a monopoly on the commercialization of the two most valuable timber species—*Okoumé* and *Ozigo*. A deputy director-general of the *Union Gabonaise de Banques*, Christian Bongo is also president of the Transgabon railroad's administrative council; the principal stockholders of the railroad are timber companies.

Another presidential son, Ali, in addition to being Gabon's defense minister, is also chairman of the board of OPRAG, the country's port authority through which Gabon's principal natural resources—oil and timber—are shipped. It is not surprising that in Gabon the richest 20% of the population receives over 90% of the income, while somewhere between 60% and 70% of all Gabonese live in poverty.

Situated on a strategically located peninsula, Libreville has experienced rapid growth. With a population of nearly 600,000, the city is dependent on imported food and is usually ranked among the most expensive cities in the world to live in. The poor of Libreville, seeking food and firewood in the surrounding area, contribute to enormous environmental pressures building up on the peninsula.

Over 60% of the population is literate. Two institutions of higher learning, Omar Bongo University (OBU) in Libreville and the Masuku University of Science and Technology at Franceville in the east, together enroll some 11,000 students in somewhat difficult circumstances. Built in the prosperous 1970s, OBU was designed to accommodate 3,000 students, but currently enrolls 9,000. There are no current subscriptions for scientific journals, the most recent of which go back to the 1980s, and there are reportedly only 20 or so computers available.

The Future

After so many decades in power, Bongo had become the singular nexus through which power flowed; he was able to manipulate the levers of power with relative ease. The biggest challenge facing Gabon in the months to come relates to filling Bongo's empty seat. Whether or not the power vacuum will lead to a power struggle depends on the ability of the country's ruling party and elites to assemble a new, inclusive government. The forthcoming elections, assuming these are held, will be a key juncture that determines the course of future events.

Economically, the country continues to rely heavily on oil resources. These have made Gabon wealthier than most other countries in Africa, but the oil revenues have been widely distributed. As highlighted by the figures at the top of this chapter, there is a dramatic and depressing difference between the Gross Domestic Product (which counts the economic activity occurring in Gabonese territory) and the Gross National Income (which counts the income that Gabonese people themselves receive). The oil price increases in recent years may seem to be a bonanza for oil exporters, but there is little sign that Gabon is leveraging this opportunity into successful, longer-term investments.

The lagoon area near Port Gentil

The Republic of Rwanda (pronounced Roo-*wahn*-dah)

The Murambi Genocide Memorial

Photo by Ruth Evans

Basic Facts

Area: 28,900 sq. km. = 11,158 sq. mi. (slightly larger than Maryland)

Population: 9,998,000 (UN 2008 est.)

Capital City: Kigali

Climate: Temperate, with dry seasons (January–February, June–September) and wet seasons (March–May, October–December)

Neighboring Countries: Congo-Kinshasa (west); Uganda (northeast); Tanzania (east); Burundi (south)

Official Languages: English, French, and KiNyarwanda

Other Principal Languages: KiSwahili

Ethnic Groups: Hutu 84%, Tutsi 15%, Twa (Pygmy) 1%. These are rough estimates; it is impossible to establish Rwanda's ethnic makeup accurately because the government has forbidden ethnic monitoring and has removed ethnicity from Rwandans' identity documents.

Principal Religions: Roman Catholic 65%, Protestant 9%, Muslim 1%, indigenous beliefs and other 25%

Chief Commercial Products: Coffee, tea, hides, and tin ore.

GNP Per Capita: $420 (World Bank 2007 est.)

Currency: Rwanda franc

Former Colonial Status: Part of German East Africa (1899–1916); occupied by Belgian troops (1916); Belgian trust territory under the League of Nations and the United Nations (1923–1962).

Independence Date: July 1, 1962

Chief of State: Paul Kagame, President

National Flag: Three horizontal stripes. On top sky blue, with a full sun of 24 yellow rays in the top right-hand corner. In the middle, a yellow stripe and on the bottom a green stripe, each half the width of the upper blue stripe.

Land and People

Rwanda, once called the "African Switzerland," is a land lying in the eastern lake region of Africa, composed for the most part of a gently rolling hilly plateau land. Sharp volcanic peaks rise to towering heights in the west on the border of Lake Kivu. Another mountain range lies to the northwest, topped by Mt. Karisimbi, at a height of 13,520 feet. Rwanda has a mild and temperate climate—the temperature seldom rises above 80°F during the daytime and the nights are always cool, with frost in the highlands and the mountains.

Centuries ago the Virunga volcanoes, some of which are still active, dammed up a section of the Great Western Rift Valley, creating Lake Kivu. This lake drains into Lake Tanganyika to the south through the waters of the Ruzizi River. Volcanic activity thus diverted water that previously flowed northward to the Nile River, forcing it to flow westward to the Atlantic through the immense Congo River.

Music and dance are an important part of the lives of Rwandans, being the Intore Dance the biggest exponent of this tradition. The Intore—"the chosen ones," also called Rwandan Ballet—is a musical tradition that celebrates heroism and victory through a mix of choreography and raw aggression. The traditional dance, once

Rwanda

exclusive to the courts of the kings, can now be seen among the villages or at the National Museum of Butare.

The Past: Political and Economic History

For early history, see *Historical Background, The Colonial Period: The Germans* and *The Colonial Period: King Leopold and the Belgians.*

In 1957, at the close of the colonial period, restless Hutu, weary of their serfdom, began to organize and articulate a political program. They demanded a voice equal to their numbers and rose in revolt in 1959.

The 1959 revolution produced a civil war between Hutu and Tutsi. Mwami Kigeri V was forced into exile, along with thousands of other Tutsi. Hundreds of Tutsi were killed. With the success of the "Hutu Revolution," the monarchy was abolished and communal elections were scheduled for 1960. Conducted under Belgian supervision, they resulted in a triumph for the *Parti du Mouvement de l'Émancipation du Peuple Hutu* (PARMEHUTU). Rwanda was declared a republic in January 1961 and became independent the next year under the leadership of Grégoire Kayibanda, Rwanda's first president. Ethnic clashes erupted again in 1963, driving more Tutsi into exile.

Under Kayibanda, opposition parties were gradually eliminated, and PARMEHUTU was the only party to present candidates for the elections of 1965. The party was routinely returned to office in 1969.

Renewed strife between the Hutus and the Tutsi minority occurred in March 1973 following ethnic violence in neighboring Burundi. Kayibanda was criticized for being too lenient with the Tutsi, whose ethnic confreres were slaughtering thousands of Hutus in Burundi. At the same time regional tensions between northern and southern Hutus intensified. Suspecting Defense Minister Juvenal Habyarimana—the lone northerner in the Cabinet—of disloyalty, Kayibanda ordered him arrested. This resulted in a military coup by General Habyarimana on July 5, 1973, and a reordering of Rwandan politics. Power was shifted from civilians to *militaries,* and from Hutu of central Rwanda to those from the northern provinces.

In 1975 President-General Habyarimana founded his own party, the *Mouvement Révolutionaire National pour le Développement* (MRND), assumed the party chairmanship, and so melded state and party hierarchies that one was indistinguishable from the other, down to the lowest level of administration. The regime increasingly discriminated against both Tutsi and Hutu not from the northwest. Within this privileged group there emerged an inner circle of friends and relatives of the president-general and his wife; the fruits of association with the presidential circle were great economic and political power. The *akazu,* or "little house," as this group was known, shared a Hutu supremacist ideology.

By 1990 Habyarimana and MRND were facing increasing opposition from other Hutu factions. On October 1st of that year the Rwanda Patriotic Front (RPF) attacked the country from Uganda. The RPF was originally founded by the children of Tutsi refugees who had fled the country during the earlier Hutu revolution. President Habyarimana used the invasion as an excuse to arrest thousands of his opponents, both Tutsi and Hutu.

Under pressure from internal opponents, the international community, and the RPF invasion, Habyarimana finally agreed to a new constitution and multi-party elections in June 1991. The MRND was given a superficial facelift—renamed the *Mouvement Républicain National pour la Démocratie et le Développement* (MRND). In April 1992 a transitional government, which included the opposition, was formed. For the first time the MRND became a minority party in the government, holding only 9 of 19 ministerial portfolios. Crucially, however, it maintained its control over local administration.

The new government opened negotiations with the RPF. The result, known as the Arusha Accords, provided for the sharing of military and civilian power between the RPF, opposition parties, and the MRND. If implemented, this would have meant demobilization for many in Habyarimana's army and a significant loss of power, privilege, and profit for the Habyarimana inner circle.

To prevent such a loss, hardliners resorted to the last defense of the fearful: ethnic division and incitement to violence. Tutsi were collectively stigmatized as accomplices of the RPF, as were Hutu opponents, especially if they did not hail from the northwest provinces. Hutu opposition parties were successfully divided, each hiving off a wing that supported the government. Hutu party youth wings, the most notorious of which was the MRND's *Interahamwe,* were organized and given military training. Lists of persons to be eliminated were prepared, and arms were distributed to Hutu civilians by local administrations, controlled by the MRND. The regime would need only a spark to ignite the whole machine of destruction.

Fighting in Burundi following the assassination of its democratically elected Hutu president was a major factor in igniting the Rwandan genocide of April 1994. Tutsis from Burundi poured into Rwanda by the tens of thousands. Clandestine and government radio stations in both nations fueled the flames of hatred ("You [Tutsis] are cockroaches! We will kill you!").

The Rwandan genocide started in early April 1994 when a plane carrying President Habyarimana and the Hutu president of Burundi was shot down while landing at Kigali airport. The enraged presidential guard embarked on barbaric slaughter of anyone considered the president's enemy—all Tutsi and any Hutu moderate. There is as yet no definitive forensic investigation of the crash. It is most probable that disgruntled Hutu military personnel were the perpetrators.

Upon Habyarimana's death, members of his inner circle took control of the state and turned it into an instrument of genocide to maintain their power. The holocaust unleashed was horrifying in its dimensions. Conducted through the armed forces and the *Interahamwe* militia, the slaughter took upwards of 937,000 people over a 13-week period. Seventy-five percent of the country's Tutsi population was killed, most of them in the first five weeks.

Former President Bizimungu

President Paul Kagame

At the slaughter's peak, five people per minute were being killed.

Once the slaughter began, Western countries acted timidly and ineffectively, allowing the regime to consolidate its position and continue the genocide. The magisterial Human Rights Watch report, *Leave None to Tell the Story*, is devastating in its condemnation of Western governments: "The Americans were interested in saving money, the Belgians were interested in saving face, and the French were interested in saving their ally, the genocidal government." "All of that took priority over saving lives." In 2008 the Rwandan government accused France of complicity.

The Rwanda Patriotic Front (RPF) army, made up of diaspora Tutsi who had lived in Uganda and had been an important part of Yoweri Museveni's efforts to topple the government there, took the capital of Kigali in July. Protected by a French "humanitarian" intervention, the Rwandan army and militias (trained and armed by the French) fled to Zaïre, along with thousands of Hutu who now feared for their lives. Hutu militants took over the refugee camps and turned them into training grounds for yet another round of ethnic confrontation. The Tutsi search for security in this situation dominated every action of the RPF coalition government established by General Paul Kagame.

When President Mobutu proved incapable or unwilling to control Hutu extremists in Zaïre, the RPF intervened and supported a successful rebellion against Mobutu. Laurent Kabila was installed in his place in 1997, and a year later, when Kabila himself had failed in his commitments to Rwandan security, a second intervention was undertaken, this time in support of Congolese Tutsi, called Banyamulenge, and other groups disenchanted with Kabila. Rwandan military activity in the Congo was not without criticism, including charges of smuggling, corruption, and human rights abuses.

In April 2000 parliament elected Vice President and Minister of Defense Paul Kagame Rwanda's first Tutsi president. In his inaugural address, Kagame called upon diaspora Rwandans to return home to rebuild the country. He also justified the presence of Rwandan troops in the Congo as central to Rwanda's security concerns: Hutu *génocidaires* were sheltering in the Congo where they had been given arms and were allowed to carry out military training. Their only goal was to kill Rwandan citizens and destroy what had been reconstructed.

Following those guidelines, Rwandan military action focused on *Interahamwe* elements armed and employed by the Kabila government. Fighting in Katanga resulted in a crushing defeat for the DRC government and its allies defending Pweto in early December 2000. Congo's then army chief of staff, Joseph Kabila, had to beat a humiliating retreat, abandoning his helicopter to escape the rout by ferryboat.

Pweto marked a high water mark for Rwandan arms and suggested the difficulty of its position before the international community. Hundreds of *Interahamwe* escaped across the border into Zambia, but the army held back from pursuing and destroying them, fearful of international reaction.

The Clinton administration, perhaps driven by the guilt of inaction during Rwanda's genocide in 1994, was lavish in praise and generous in support of the RPF government. Emergency military aid amounting to $75 million had been dispatched soon after the RPF had installed itself in Kigali. The Bush administration, in contrast, seemed more concerned about Rwandan militarism and its penetration deep into the Congo.

The government's priority is thus the arrest and trial of those Hutu strategists who conspired to create and implement the plan to destroy the Tutsi people. One example is Félicien Kabuga, described as "a mastermind behind the genocide." He was Rwanda's richest man, possessed of tea estates, transport companies and a variety of shops and factories. Part of the *akazu*—the Hutu elite that controlled wealth and power in Rwanda under President Habyarimana—Kabuga used his wealth to create *Radio Télévision Libre des Mille Collines* (RTLM), the most vile of the anti-Tutsi propaganda machines. He also used his wealth to import vast numbers of machetes to arm the *génocidaires*.

Kabuga remains at large, after at least one failed attempt (January 2003) to capture him in Kenya, where his money apparently bought safety from prosecution for the most heinous of crimes. Thousands of unrepentant Hutu extremists still shelter in the Congo; to Rwandans, they remain an omnipresent threat. In April 2005 the government signed cooperation agreements with police agencies in ten East Africa countries. Besides cooperation in eradicating illegal drugs and crime, the agreements will facilitate the transfer of criminals who flee to other countries to escape justice. The Rwandan government hopes the accords will help apprehend genocide perpetrators like Kabuga.

The relation between Rwanda and Congo is delicate. The Rwandan interventions in eastern Congo, with the formal objective of preventing another genocide, have killed thousands. Rwanda is known for supporting the Tutsi militia National Congress for the Defence of the People (CNDP) in Congo.

In January of 2009, an agreement between the two countries led to the arrest of the general Laurent Nkunda, leader of the CNDP. The agreement establishes that Rwanda break up the CNDP and hand over Mr Nkunda. Congo is meant to integrate the former CNDP's soldiers into the army and let Rwandan troops cross the border to fight against the Hutu militia, the Democratic Front for the Liberation of Rwanda (FDLR), composed of former génocidaires.

The International Criminal Tribunal for Rwanda (ICTR), which was created to try the genocide masterminds, has faced a variety of difficulties that have slowed its actions. In ten years only 32 cases have been completed, with 28 people convicted and five acquitted. By mid-2007, 11 trials were in progress involving 27 accused. Eighteen indicted individuals are still at large, largely due to the unwillingness of nations to track down and extradite the accused. Since 1995 the court has spent a billion dollars in its efforts.

Domestically, President Kagame's principal goal is national reconciliation, without which there can be no peace, development, stability or progress. The previous mandatory national identity card, which bore the owner's ethnic identification, has been abolished. "Solidarity camps" reeducate both Hutu fighters returning from the Congo to seek reintegration into the Rwandan army and young Hutus who were arrested and imprisoned as child participants in the 1994 genocide.

New national symbols—anthem, flag and coat-of-arms—were created in 2001. The new flag has a golden sun with 24 rays on a field of green, yellow and blue. President Kagame said the colors stood

Rwanda

Ankole cattle grazing on the hills of Rwanda

for prosperity, wealth, peace and happiness. Where the old national anthem lauded the supremacy of Rwanda's Hutu majority, the new one praises Rwanda's natural beauty and refers to its people simply as Rwandans. It was composed by a group of jailed Hutus awaiting trial on charges of genocide.

More than 120,000 prisoners were jailed for crimes arising from the 1994 genocide and kept in appalling conditions of incarceration. To break the judicial logjam, the government passed two pieces of legislation. One defined four categories of criminality, and the other created a system of grassroots justice—traditional village courts called *gacaca*.

Under the new judicial legislation, only category one criminals—masterminds of the genocide—would be tried in the regular court system. All others would be brought before *gacaca* courts—ten villagers elected to hear and pass judgment.

Suspects would have to confront relatives, their own and those of their victims, a process that might, it is hoped, provide catharsis and reconciliation. Those who had participated in the genocidal events of 1994 as children and have passed through a solidarity camp were expected to bear witness against those who had ordered and directed their murderous activities.

Truth-telling is at the heart of the child-participant's reeducation, and truth, perhaps more than justice, is the goal of the *gacaca* system. Rwanda's minister of justice has described the system succinctly: "We've already seen in group trials that when people are brought together in a commune they do tell the truth. We take them to where the crime was committed, everyone comes, including witnesses, and they are charged there. The suspect fears to lie because everyone knows what happened."

The *gacaca* system has its flaws, but its roots are in traditional processes of reconciliation and may represent the best solution for a practical problem. The *gacaca* trials began in February 2005, but already several have been marred by a resurgence of violence. When a woman and her husband who were due to testify in one trial outside Kigali were hacked to death by unidentified people, most other witnesses refused to testify. Elsewhere genocide survivors have been murdered and others intimidated into fearful withdrawal of their witness; at least one *gacaca* judge has been murdered—by a relative—for not quashing an indictment.

In post-genocide Rwanda political life has been circumscribed. Given the experience of ethnic parties that fulminated group hatred, parties are prohibited from mentioning any ethnic affiliation. In local elections there is no party campaigning: candidates stand as individuals, not representatives of parties. On the other hand, women have, by design and by requirement, played a prominent role in Rwandan politics since 1994, such that the participation of women in parliament attains levels seen only in a handful of Scandinavian countries.

Forming a political party in these circumstances is a risky business. Former President Bizimungu, a Hutu who was the symbol of national reconciliation in the early post-genocide years, spent nearly one and a half years in jail after attempting to form his own political party—the Democratic Renewal Party (PDR). In his trial, which concluded in June 2004, Bizimungu was sentenced to 15 years in jail for embezzlement, inciting violence, and "associating the criminals." In April 2007, three years into his sentence, Bizimungu received a presidential pardon and was released from prison.

By taking on such a high-profile individual, the government made abundantly clear its policies of reconciliation and unity would tolerate nothing that even hinted at "divisionism"—political language and appeal based on ethnic identity. Indeed, where language can be lethal, hate speech receives no tolerance. Rwandan police used all the high-tech capacity at their disposal to track down one hate monger who told genocide survivors, on live call-in radio, "we will kill you again." The punishment for such genocide revisionism is ten to 20 years in jail. The president's attempt to mitigate ethnic identity has been criticized by human rights groups, who allege that outlawing ethnicity violates basic freedoms of expression. In 2007–08, around 1,300 cases involving genocide ideology were initiated in Rwandan courts. Some foreign critics, including journalists, are banned from the country.

The Rwandan parliament adopted a new constitution on April 23, 2003. The constitution creates a semi-presidential regime, with a president elected by universal suffrage for a seven-year term (once renewable) and a bicameral parliament. Only 53 deputies of the 80-member National Assembly are elected by universal suffrage; the rest are designated in the name of their social category: 24 women, two youths, and one handicapped person.

The 26-member Senate is chosen indirectly. Local officials in each of Rwanda's 12 provinces select a senator and the president of the republic nominates eight; political parties appoint four, while colleges and universities elect the remaining two. Senators serve for a nonrenewable eight-year period.

One interesting (but potentially awkward) constitutional innovation attests to a desire to diffuse political power and emphasize unity in governance: the president, prime minister, and president of the National Assembly must all belong to a different political party. To prevent the dangerous hate mongering that facilitated genocide, political parties are strictly limited; they are not permitted to hold public meetings outside of electoral periods, and are strictly forbidden to make any reference, in any manner, to ethnic, religious, regional or clan differences. Several parties were forced to change their statutes and names: the *Parti démocrate islamique*, for example, became the *Parti démocrate idéal*, while the *Parti démocrate chrétien* (Christian) became the *Parti démocrate centriste*.

Eight political parties were registered to participate in the presidential and legislative elections that followed approval of the constitution. As the candidate of the Rwanda Patriotic Front, Paul Kagame won an overwhelming victory in August 2003 elections: 95% of the electorate supported the man who had ended Rwanda's genocidal regime and restored significant security to the country.

His nearest opponent was Faustin Twagiramungu, a moderate Hutu. Twagiramungu had opposed President Habyarimana and helped revive the Republican Democratic Movement (MDR) of Grégoire Kayibanda, Rwanda's first president. He barely escaped assassination when the genocide began, and became prime minister in the transitional government of July 1994. He received only 3.6% of the votes cast.

In September of 2008, the parliamentary election guaranteed 42 of the 53 seats for the Rwandan Patriotic Front coalition. The Social Democratic Party won 7 seats. The Liberal Party got 4 seats. No opposition party participated—the coalition of about a dozen opposite parties called United Democratic Forces have been on exile since the end of the genocide.

Rwanda's politics have achieved a unique distinction since 2008. For probably the first time in world history, women make up the majority of a democratically-elected Parliament, with 56% of the seats. The Constitution of Rwanda provides for a 30-percent minimum quota for women in Parliament The balance between sexes aims to guarantee laws against rape and protecting sexual abuse victims.

In April 2004, the tenth anniversary of the genocide, President Kagame inaugurated a national genocide museum on one of Kigali's many hills; it stands atop five concrete tombs containing hundreds of coffins filled with the remains of an estimated 250,000 people killed in and around Kigali.

In the presence of presidents Thabo Mbeki of South Africa, Yoweri Museveni of Uganda and Mwai Kibaki of Kenya, as well as the Belgian prime minister, Guy Verhofstadt, Kagame spoke movingly of the events a decade before: "It was deliberate, calculated, cold blooded; and the architects were keen to kill, rape, rob, ravage and inflict pain and agony. This was a result of distorted ideology that preached death and hatred."

"We are prepared," he added, "that what happened here should never happen again not only in Rwanda but anywhere in the world." (Rwanda was the first to send a peacekeeping contingent to Darfur as its genocide began to unfold.)

The ceremonies of remembrance also displayed Rwanda's profound contempt for the shameful role of France in the decade-old events. In biting and undiplomatic language, President Kagame detailed French activities in Rwanda: "Their role is self-evident," he said, going on to accuse them of arming and training government soldiers and militias and of being aware the extremists intended to commit genocide.

France also provided an escape route to Zaïre for Hutu extremists as the RPF neared Kigali. It evacuated 394 regime officials by air—including President Habyarimana's widow—who were deeply implicated in planning the genocide. Unlike Belgium, France has yet to apologize for its actions in Rwanda.

President Kagame's outrage seemed a response to an investigative report by a French judge looking into the downing of the Habyarimana plane in 1994. His conclusion, leaked to the Parisian daily *Le Monde* shortly before the tenth anniversary ceremonies, relied on regime dissidents and Kagame opponents who had long repeated the story that Kagame himself had given direct orders for the rocket attack on the plane.

In December 2006, the judge recommended President Kagame be brought before the ICTR for "presumed participation" in the downing of Habyarimana's plane; arrest warrants on the same charges were also issued for eight of Kagame's close collaborators. Little judicial action is likely: in April 2007 the ICTR rejected a request from defendants before the court to prosecute Kagame for complicity in his predecessor's death.

President Kagame ended all diplomatic relations with France; French schools and cultural centers are shuttered, and Belgium looks after its interests. In August 2008 he charged that Paris had provided diplomatic, military and logistical support to Hutus. In February 2007 he also announced that Rwanda would seek admission to the Commonwealth.

Though it might prefer historical amnesia, France will not easily escape reflection on Rwanda. Patrick de Saint-Exupéry, a leading journalist with the French daily *Le Figaro*, has published a searing indictment of French actions in Rwanda: *l'Inavouable, la France au Rwanda*, Paris: Editions Les Arènes, 2004. (In English, the same ground is covered by Andrew Wallis in *Silent Accomplice: The Untold Story of France's Role in the Rwandan Genocide*, London: I. B. Tauris, 2006.) In February 2005 French lawyers lodged six formal complaints with a military tribunal on behalf of genocide victims.

The complaints allege complicity in the genocide on the part of French soldiers and have resulted in tense jurisdictional disputes in the judicial system. One courageous investigating judge, Bridgitte Raynaud, pursued her inquiry by traveling to Rwanda to conduct interviews, a move vigorously opposed by both the French Foreign and Defense ministries. Shortly after she had compiled her preliminary report, the dossier was taken from her and handed over to another investigator. Military authorities appealed the validity of her investigation. Under pressure from her successor, Judge Florence Michon, the French government has announced the declassification of 105 military secret service documents relating to events in Rwanda.

About 90% of the people of Rwanda live on homesteads scattered on Rwanda's densely crowded hills. Houses are set within enclosures surrounded by cultivated fields. In addition to growing crops, most farmers also raise small livestock—goats, chickens and rabbits. Only wealthy individuals have one or more cows. This pattern of family enclosures provides Rwandans with much valued privacy. Living close to their fields also allows farmers to better protect their crops from theft. Although most Rwandans are Christian, particularly among the Hutus, almost half retain traditional beliefs. Relations between the Rwandan government and the Catholic Church remain strained given the participation of clergy in genocide activities. Two priests have already been sentenced to death for participation in the genocide. Many Rwandans lost faith in their church, and though it is still a predominantly Catholic country, Rwanda's fastest growing religion is Islam.

HIV/AIDS has become a major crisis. The virus was already working its way into Rwandan society by 1990, but the genocide contributed to its explosive growth. The mass rape of Tutsi women was an integral part of the planned genocide. Radio propaganda taunted Hutus with a mythology of Tutsi women: they were taller, more beautiful, arrogant and threateningly dangerous because of their sexual wiles. They had to be "tasted" and humiliated before being killed. According to the UN, at least 250,000 women were raped in Rwanda in 1994; more than two-thirds of the rape survivors are HIV-positive.

In July 2001 Rwanda's National Commission for the Struggle Against AIDS indicated that one HIV-infected baby is born every six hours. Twenty to thirty percent of pregnant women have been found HIV-positive, and 40,000 to 50,000 babies are born HIV-infected every year. At least 10% of the Rwandan population is believed to be HIV-positive.

There are several vectors through which Rwanda's silent death is spread. One consequence of the 1994 genocide was that with so many men killed, female survivors were prepared to share husbands in order to have a family. The practice of sharing men, known as "*kwinjira,*" is widespread in rural areas. Health officials say that it represents the greatest challenge to their efforts to combat the spread of AIDS.

Rwanda

Kigale's street children, most of them AIDS orphans, were found to be sexually active at very early ages in a recent Johns Hopkins survey. Thirty-five percent of the young children aged 6–10 were already sexually active. Between 11 and 14 years of age 47.4% were active, while 81% at 15 and above fell into the sexually active category. The survey concluded that its interviewees were a "high risk population characterized by early sexual experimentation, multiple sex partners, unprotected sex, drug use and poor nutrition."

Malaria is another disease that strikes Rwanda. However, the country is an example of a successful policy against the disease through a strategy that combines the distribution of nets impregnated with long-lasting insecticides, indoor spraying and medicines. In a short period of time, cases and deaths from malaria have dropped by two-thirds.

The Present: Contemporary Issues

Often described as the land of a thousand hills, Rwanda is a country whose economy is largely based on subsistence agriculture. For the past several years, it has been engaged in a process of economic reconstruction following the genocide of 1994 which effectively cut Rwanda's GDP in half. Roads, bridges, and whole sectors of the economy were destroyed. Thanks to several years of relative stability, the GDP has grown annually, showing a healthy 5% growth rate in 2005. Growth is fueled by a booming construction industry (buildings seem to be popping up on every corner in Kigale) and increasing agricultural production.

Agriculture employs more than 90% of the population and contributes about 42.2% of GDP (2005). Rwanda's most important exports are coffee and tea, which bring about 80% to 90% of export revenues. Tea production is strategically important to the country's economic development. Over the past 30 years it has grown consistently and now occupies 27,000 farmers and 30,000 workers. It is also the country's second most important export, representing 36% of total export earnings. In addition to coffee and tea, Rwanda also exports over 54 tons of flowers to European countries annually, making them the third largest export commodity.

The government's biggest economic problem, apart from security costs, remains the integration of more than two million refugees returning home. Housing, jobs, and land are of critical importance. Some have been living as refugees since 1959. So many returnees did not speak French that the government was compelled to make English an official language. There are political as well as economic tensions between those who returned and those who stayed and survived the genocide. Survivors complain that returnees, with considerably more capital, are favored and privileged.

In Rwanda the victims have largely accepted integrating the former génocidaires into the society. The former FDLR soldiers are being promised new lives in Rwanda, after a process of indoctrination. Several challenges rise when a country tries to peacefully accommodate victims and murderers.

Rwanda, the land of a thousand hills, needs to accommodate a population of nine million and steadily increasing demographic pressure. Population growth in 2005 was only 1.7%, but by official estimates, a three percent annual population growth translates into a 93% increase in poverty. As a consequence the government is drafting a law that may set a limit of three children per family.

Rwanda is a heavily indebted poor country (HIPC) with a total debt of $1.4 billion as of 2004; its budget remains heavily dependent on foreign aid. At the July 2005 summit of the world's richest countries, known as the G-8, leaders pledged to cancel the debt of the world's most indebted countries, including Rwanda. The country would be eligible for a 100% cancellation once it completes the requirements of the HIPC program.

China has long been a significant investor in infrastructure projects, helping to build critical roads in a country without railways or navigable rivers. In May 2000, Chinese authorities agreed to fund a feasibility study for a rail link between Kigali and Northern Tanzania. China has also offered economic cooperation in agriculture (rice plantations and irrigation projects), energy (training in solar energy technology), and education. It has helped reestablish the Rwandan cement industry, while Chinese firms have rehabilitated the National Stadium and built the Kigali Conference Center. President Kagame last visited China in 2001 to celebrate 30 years of diplomatic relations.

The Future

Though vastly improved, the question of security in Rwanda is not resolved. After the agreement with Congo, the Hutu militia FDLR was reduced to fragments hidden into the forest. The fear is that the FDLR—after losing their mineral revenues—will emerge from the jungle more desperate and dangerous. Also, other tensions might emerge from bringing the former Tutsi CNDP into Congo's army. With the question of security lingering, the legacy of the 1994 genocide remains present, as the country attempts to move through a painful reconciliation process.

Already one of the most densely populated countries on the continent, Rwanda faces increased demographic pressure with a growing population. Land use and allocation issues loom large. The economy grew at about 6% per year in 2007 and 2008, which is above the rate of population growth. This might contribute to social harmony if that rhythm can be maintained, but the economic setback of 2009 complicates these prospects.

Rwanda has achieved a miraculous degree of social reconciliation in the decade and a half since the genocide. The gacaca courts, the International Criminal Tribunal for Rwanda, the documentation efforts of international and domestic activists, and the actions of the RPF government itself have each contributed in part to the efforts at justice. While the country faces many of Africa's most significant problems—poverty, HIV/AIDS, unemployed youth, and lingering ethnic tension—Rwanda also exhibits some prospects of social development for the future.

Rwandan peacekeepers, the first to be volunteered for service in Darfur, return home after a six-month stint in the genocidal region supporting the African Union mission. Logistical assistance for the homeward journey was provided by the U.S. Air Force.
Photo by Master Sgt. David D. Underwood, Jr., courtesy U.S. Air Force

The Democratic Republic of São Tomé and Príncipe

(pronounced Sow Toe-*may* and *Preen-see*-pay)

São Tomé's volcanic shoreline

Photo by Fabien Violas

Basic Facts

Land: 1001 sq. km.= 385 sq. mi. São Tomé is 275 miles off the coast of The Gabon; Príncipe is 125 miles off mainland Equatorial Guinea. Both lie just north of the Equator. (About one-third the size of Rhode Island.)

Population: 158,000 (UN 2007 est.)

Capital City: São Tomé

Climate: Tropical; hot, humid; one rainy season (October to May)

Official Language: Portuguese

Other Principal Language: Crioulo

Ethnic Groups: Mestico, Angolares (descendants of Angolan slaves), Forros (descendants of freed slaves), *Serviçais* (contract laborers from Angola, Mozambique, and Cape Verde), Tongas (children of *Serviçais* born on the islands), and Europeans (primarily Portuguese)

Principal Religions: Roman Catholic, Evangelical Protestant, and Seventh-day Adventist

Chief Commercial Products: Cocoa, copra, coffee, palm, and oil

GNI Per Capita: $390 (World Bank 2006 est.)

Currency: dobra (Db)

Independence Date: July 12, 1975 (from Portugal)

Chief of State: Fradique Melo Bandiera de Menezes, President (since July 2001)

National Flag: Three horizontal bands of green (top), yellow (double width), and green with two black five-pointed stars placed side by side in the center of the yellow band and a red isosceles triangle based on the hoist side; uses the popular pan-African colors of Ethiopia.

Land and People

São Tomé and Príncipe form an archipelago of two main islands and several associated islets lying just north of the Equator. Of volcanic origins, the islands have fertile central highlands from which numerous fast flowing streams carry soil to the ocean. Tropical rain forests cover 75% of the land area and shelter flora and fauna similar to that found on mainland Equatorial Guinea.

Wilder than Cape Verde and closer to Europe than the Caribbean, São Tomé and Príncipe represent a relatively unspoiled paradise for tourists. Clean beaches, the stunning Blue Lagoon, rain forest and mountains with the Obo Natural Park are all available to the intrepid. These would appear to be few: over the last decade the number of visitors to the islands has averaged around 6,000 a year. The climate is equatorial, with the driest and coolest months being from June to September. Roads are few, and any serious tourism requires four-wheel-drive vehicles. São Tomé, the capital, has a wealth of down-at-the-heels colonial architecture. The city's atmosphere is unrushed and unhurried. Blackouts are frequent, adding to the somnambulant mood. For many the best cup of coffee in the world comes from local beans.

The Past: Political and Economic History

For early history, see *Historical Background* and *The Colonial Period: The Portuguese.*

A Committee for the Liberation of São Tomé and Príncipe was created in exile in 1960. It changed its name to the Move-

São Tomé and Príncipe

ment for the Liberation of São Tomé and Príncipe (MLSTP) in 1972. Unlike its counterpart in Guinea-Bissau, the MLSTP never mounted a guerrilla campaign against the Portuguese.

Following the overthrow of the Salazar dictatorship in 1974, African troops in São Tomé mutinied, and the new government agreed to hand over power to the MLSTP in 1975. Independence was granted on July 12, 1975. Most Portuguese had already departed, taking skills and capital with them. At independence, the Portuguese legacy was a 90% illiteracy rate, few skilled workers, and abandoned plantations.

The MLSTP became the nation's sole political party and ruled with little tolerance for opposition for 15 years. Its leader, Manuel Pinto da Costa, assumed the new nation's presidency, and Miguel Trovoada, another founder of the MLSTP, was elected prime minister.

To cope with the country's disastrous economic inheritance, President Pinto da Costa turned to Marxist-Leninist models of political and economic organization. Most plantations were nationalized, and no one was allowed to own more than 247 acres. The single ruling party largely absorbed the country's organizational life. Social control and surveillance were organized through a series of people's militias set up in workplaces and villages.

When cocoa prices collapsed in the mid-1980s, the economy was severely damaged. Popular dissatisfaction led to a process of liberalization, and multiparty democracy was introduced in 1990. Constitutional reforms included the direct election of the president, and Miguel Trovoada, whom Pinto da Costa had accused of complicity in a coup plot and had jailed from 1979 to 1981, returned from exile to battle his old comrade-in-arms for the presidency. Running as an independent, Trovoada won. He survived a coup attempt in 1995 and went on to win reelection to a second five-year term in 1996 against his old foe, Manuel Pinto da Costa. The country's political and economic crisis continued.

In November 1998 legislative elections the MLSTP, in alliance with the Social Democratic Party (PSD), won an absolute majority 31 of 55 seats in the National Assembly. President Trovoada's Independent Democratic Action (ADI: *Accao Democratica Independente*) became the official opposition. São Tomé's politics remained bitter, personal and contentious.

The government continued to face serious social agitation in the late 1990s. Workers saw their own conditions deteriorating while rumors of a huge oil bonanza were rife. Civil servants, including doctors and teachers, regularly struck to protest their salaries and working conditions. In July 1999, president Trovoada

admitted that salaries and pensions were inadequate.

More darkly, he sent a warning to the government: "São Tomé's oil cannot be a matter for political colleagues, friends and relatives. Its revenue should benefit citizens and the population as a whole." With remarkable candor Trovoada accused "a number of citizens and political leaders of eagerly getting themselves into positions to reap fabulous personal benefits." The battle lines were sharply drawn for the next presidential election.

The July 2001 election results came as a surprise to many. The best known name—former President Manuel Pinto da Costa—went down to a humiliating defeat, unable to get enough votes to force a runoff election. Fradique de Menezes, a wealthy businessman, was elected president with 56.31% of the vote. Pinto da Costa received only 38.73%, with the remaining ballots distributed among three minor candidates.

For most São Toméans, Pinto da Costa resurrected memories of authoritarian single-party rule and disastrous Marxist-Leninist economic policies under the MLSTP. Fradique de Menezes interjected an entrepreneurial dynamism into the campaign. Where da Costa spoke of a fair

distribution of oil and gas revenues, de Menezes said he would encourage their investment in agriculture, the mainstay of the country's economy.

In addition to wanting abandoned agricultural concerns to be rehabilitated, de Menezes presented a thoughtful analysis of the country's problems and prospects. The bloated bureaucracy created by the MLSTP would have to be reduced and good managers for the public sector found. "We have made lots of mistakes in our 26 years of independence," he said. "We have destroyed what little we inherited from the colonial era. Does it make any sense that there should be only one hospital in the entire country?"

Stalemate between the new president and the MLSTP majority in parliament made cohabitation impossible. The National Assembly was dissolved and legislative elections held in March 2002. The political kaleidoscope shifted slightly, but in the end things remained pretty much the same. The ADI went through an internal crisis, divided between supporters of ex-President Trovoada's son Patrice, and the party's secretary-general, Carlos Neves. President de Menezes backed the formation of the Democratic Movement of Forces for Change (MDFM), which attracted a number of ADI dissidents and joined with the only other party to hold seats in the National Assembly—the *Partido da Convergencia Democratica* (PCD). Patrice Trovoada, wealthy and ambitious, linked up five parties to create an opposition alliance, Ue-Kedadji (Light of Day).

Since party platforms were largely similar, voters could make few sharp distinctions; the election resulted in a virtual tie, the MLSTP winning 24 seats and the MDFM/PCD 23. Ue-Kedadji took the remaining eight seats. President de Menezes, who had hoped for a parliamentary majority, was forced to accept a coalition national unity government.

São Tomé has a semi-presidential political system that combines aspects of both presidential and parliamentary systems. It is the president who nominates the prime minister, who must be approved by the National Assembly. It is a recipe for institutional conflict, with both executive and legislature vying for primacy. Tensions between president and Assembly are regular, persistent and potentially destabilizing. They spiked in early 2003 as President de Menezes dealt with the sensitive issues surrounding São Tomé's oil future and its relationship with the colossus to the north, Nigeria.

Finding three oil contracts signed by the Trovoada government grossly unfair, de Menezes decided to reject them and demand renegotiation. The president was also engaged in delicate negotiations with

Nigeria over disputed boundaries, critical because of potentially vast oil resources located in the disputed territories. Since the negotiations were being handled by the president and his natural resources minister, Rafael Branco, almost exclusively, the institutional jealousy of the Assembly was roused. (Once the boundary dispute was settled valuable exploration rights would be sold off, a honey pot to which legislative factions did not want to be denied access.)

Legislation was introduced to amend the constitution and reduce the power of the presidency. Among other things, the president's ability to negotiate international treaties would be limited. Terming the proposed reforms a "palace coup," President de Menezes vetoed the amendment package and dissolved the Assembly. Mediators managed to soothe ruffled feathers. The dissolution was withdrawn and the Assembly agreed to a package of constitutional amendments to reduce the power of the presidency, but also reduce the possibility of hostile cohabitation between presidents and prime ministers.

Relations with Nigeria pit a São Toméan David against the Nigerian Goliath. The resources are utterly asymmetrical, with Nigeria having 800 times the population. To resolve the boundary dispute, President de Menezes deftly lined up a number of backers. Membership in the community of Lusophone (Portuguese-speaking) states gave access to the experience of East Timor, renegotiating its oil contracts with Australia. More importantly, it brought the weight of countervailing influence from West Africa's other petroleum giant, Angola. Finally, he mobilized support in the United States, stressing São Tomé's democratic credentials, (relative) stability, and strategic location in an oil-producing area that could easily replace a hostile, dangerous, and unstable Middle East. It worked.

The Americans pressured Nigeria to give up efforts to station a force of two hundred soldiers in São Tomé. Three questionable oil contracts were successfully renegotiated, and, once those impediments had been cleared away, the boundary settlement was finalized.

Despite successful conclusion of the boundary and contract issues, political tensions between the president and his critics persisted, fanning social discontent as the bulk of the population saw no improvement in its life circumstances. On July 16, 2003, soldiers staged a *coup d'état*, seizing key sites and arresting government ministers. (President de Menezes himself was in Nigeria at the time.) The coup was mounted by local soldiers (grievances about living conditions, salary arrears, obsolete equipment, and government corruption) and members of a small,

President Fradique de Menezes
Photo by AFP/Andre Kosters

shadowy, and marginal political party, the *Frente Democrata Cristã* (FDC: Christian Democratic Front).

Universally condemned, the coup ended within a week. President de Menezes was reinstated, but agreed to greater transparency in oil negotiations and greater respect for the separation of powers between the presidency and parliament. Parliament unanimously approved a general amnesty for the putschists, while Nigeria, South Africa and the United States agreed to take on the role of guarantors of the country's stability.

By March 2004 political tensions between president and parliament reached crisis proportions over the development of São Tomé's oil resources. Prime Minister Maria das Neves (MLSTP) demanded the resignations of her ministers of natural resources and foreign affairs, both of whom she accused of negotiating petroleum agreements without her knowledge. Both ministers were members of the president's Democratic Movement of Forces for Change (MDFM) party, and when the two other MDFM ministers resigned in solidarity, the prime minister's three-party coalition government was reduced to two parties and the slimmest of majorities in parliament.

After months of rivalry, Menezes dismissed das Neves in September 2004 when her name was raised in a corruption scandal. Damião Vaz d'Almeida, a former labor minister, was asked to form a government and managed to cobble together a coalition of MLSTP and ADI ministers. His tenure was brief. In June 2005 he resigned following controversial and disadvanta-

geous oil exploration awards imposed by Nigeria as part of its Joint Development Zone agreement with São Tomé. As his replacement President Menezes appointed another MLSTP figure, Maria do Carmo Silveira, the former governor of the Central Bank. Testimony to the persistent tensions between president and government, Silveira was the sixth prime minister Menezes had appointed since his election in 2001.

Parliamentary elections in March 2006 provided no clear political mandate to São Tomé's contending factions and offered little prospect of future political stability for the country. The MDFM, which had previously been in opposition, took 23 of 55 legislative seats. Its main rival, the MLSTP, returned with slightly fewer seats—20. The big winner was Patrice Trovoada's Independent Democratic Action (ADI), which increased its representation to 11 from its previous four. The remaining seat was won by the small *Novo Rumo* (New Direction) party.

To unseat President Menezes the MLSTP unprecedentedly agreed not to run its own candidate in the July 2006 presidential elections; instead, it backed the ADI's Patrice Trovoada. The ploy was to no avail. Menezes won 58.85% of the votes cast, a decisive victory over Trovoada's 37.73%.

In his concession speech, Trovoada wished his opponent "good luck," and continued, with oracular obscurity, by saying he would be "attentive to every measure taken by Fradique de Menezes as president of the republic, notably the way in which he exercises power." He would, said the loser, "defend the stability of São Tomé et Principe."

For virtually the entire first term, President Menezes was confronted by hostile governments and parliaments. Constitutional amendments approved in early 2003, which took effect in September 2006 at the beginning of his second term of office, clarified the respective authority of both president and prime minister. In the new dispensation the president can appoint prime ministers, dissolve parliament and call elections.

The clarification of authority in a formal-legal sense has done little to sort out the political scene, however. Following Maria do Carmo Silveira, in April 2008, Tomé Vera Cruz took the prime ministerial post at the head of the winning coalition. This lasted for a year, until Menezes appointed his rival Patrice Trovoada as prime minister. Trovoada's government lasted even less time, being defeated in a no confidence vote within months. Joaquim Rafael Branco of the MLSTP/PSD became the prime minister, and remains in the post to the present.

São Tomé and Príncipe

The Present: Contemporary Issues

The country has been traditionally dependent on the export of cocoa. In 1975 Portuguese plantation farmers held 90% of all cultivated land on the islands. After independence, with a regime in the thrall of Stalinist economic thinking, the cocoa plantations were collectivized. Production collapsed and the plantations deteriorated. From exports of 11,400 tons of cocoa in 1900, production plummeted to 4,000 in 1996.

São Tomé's dependence on cocoa has been virtually total, and it suffers greatly from the fluctuation of cocoa prices on world markets. Any fall in prices is especially disastrous for small producers, many of whom are forced into debt. The islands have consequently faced vertiginous inflation and high unemployment.

The most important potential for São Tomé lies in its oil prospects. President de Menezes successfully renegotiated several onerous industry contracts, the worst of which goes back to 1997 when one of the minnows of the industry, Louisiana-based Environmental Remediation Holding Corporation (ERHC), secured a contract which gave it enormous control over the country's oil development. After a new contract with the company modifying overly generous provisions was initialed in 2003, São Tomé and Nigeria signed a settlement of their boundary dispute.

The settlement creates a Joint Development Zone (JDZ) out of the area of overlapping claims. The two states will jointly develop the JDZ and share the resources on a split of 60% for Nigeria and 40% for São Tomé. (Reserves in the JDZ could potentially amount to 14 billion barrels.) In February 2005 the two signed the first agreement for exploration in the JDZ with a consortium headed by ChevronTexaco and ExxonMobil. The signature bonus was nearly $125 million.

A second round of bidding for exploration rights in additional JDZ blocks in December 2005 proved highly controversial when many of the winners turned out to be obscure Nigerian firms with little experience and less capital, but with solid political connections in both Nigeria and São Tomé. The islands' attorney general found serious flaws with the whole process, much to his country's financial detriment. The entire bidding round was subject, he said, to "serious procedural deficiencies and political manipulation, including the award of interests to many unqualified firms or firms with inferior qualifications, technically and financially."

One of those companies was the already notorious Environmental Remediation Holding Corporation (ERHC). The firm, now called ERHC Energy and controlled by a Nigerian capitalist, had no experience with deepwater drilling and reportedly only one paid employee, its president. What it did have were preferential rights to equity in São Tomé's oil acreage and valuable fee waivers earned by providing technical and financial services in the 1990s. It exercised them in the December bidding round. According to Attorney General Adelino Pereira, ERHC's participation discouraged more qualified companies from bidding because of "reputational, financial and technical concerns." Because the company had no obligation to pay the requisite signature bonus, São Tomé lost approximately $60 million.

Actual oil production is many years off. While São Tomé awaits discovery and production from the JDZ, Nigeria is to provide it with 10,000 barrels of crude oil daily, thus providing an oil dividend income before actual production begins.

Until oil investment and production revenues begin to flow, São Tomé will remain largely dependent on foreign aid. Foreign aid, mostly supplied by Taiwan, France, and Portugal, accounts for about 80% of GDP and covers 95% of public investment. That represents one of the highest per capita aid rates in the world— $239.4 per person (2003).

The World Bank and IMF have agreed to help reduce the country's debt obligations through the Highly Indebted Poor Countries Initiative. In March 2007 São Tomé reached a completion point in the program; its debt reduction will amount to some $263.46 million.

São Tomé is central to the U.S. strategy for ensuring security of oil supplies from the Gulf of Guinea. In early 2004 it agreed to finance an $800,000 viability study for expanding São Tomé and Príncipe's international airport and building a deepwater port. The islands are an ideal location for monitoring satellite observations of the Gulf of Guinea.

The Future

São Tomé and Príncipe is one of the African continent's more democratic polities, though politics on the islands is tumultuous. President de Menezes has gone through a number of prime ministers and governments in recent years. The political situation gives rise to frequent interpersonal and partisan tensions, but these do not appear to be going beyond what is to be expected in a democratic polity. Paradoxically, the trials and tribulations of the country's politics may be impressive: crises of particular governments in São Tomé and Príncipe have not become crises of the constitutional regime.

Somewhat more worryingly, concerns about a coup plot surfaced in February 2009, with the authorities turning back a small boat replete with armed men and detaining a number of people for questioning. While de Menezes claimed he was entertaining the notion of leaving power if he was the cause of conflict and discord, he also hastened to announce to the international and domestic press in February that "the armed forces and paramilitary" had told him "We are with you."

The question of political progress in the country is made all the more pressing with the prospects for economic change in the islands. With control of oil revenues at stake, political tensions in São Tomé are more important than ever. Foreign investment, combined with American naval interest in the oil-rich waters along this stretch of the Atlantic, make São Tomé and Príncipe a country to watch in the near future.

São Tomé's rain forest

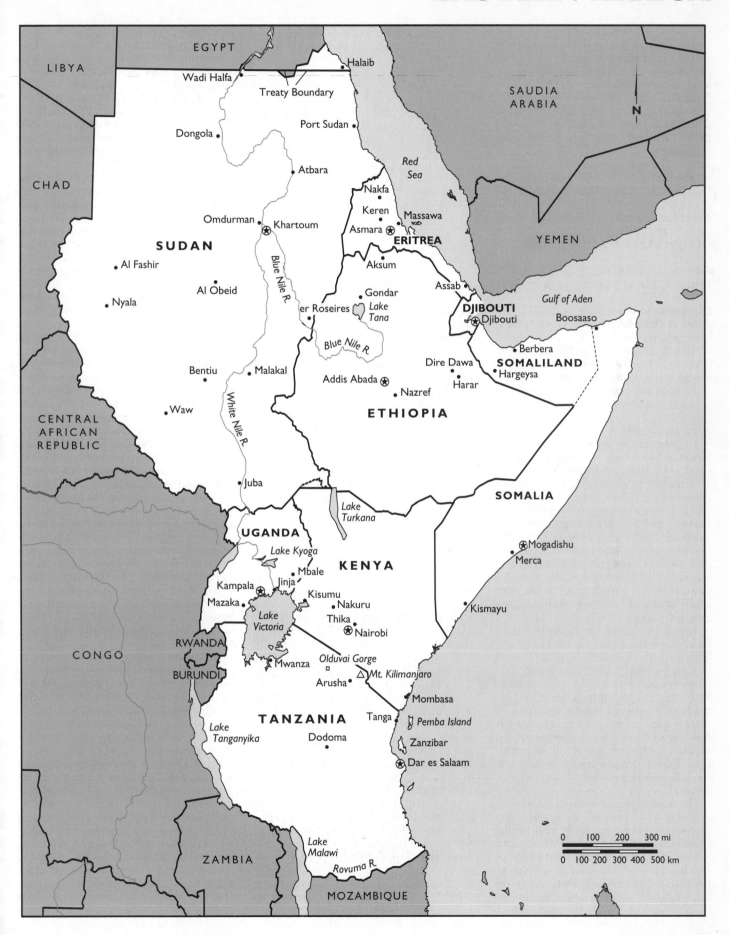

EASTERN AFRICA

LIBYA

EGYPT

Halaib

Wadi Halfa

Treaty Boundary

Port Sudan

CHAD

Dongola

Atbara

Red Sea

Nakfa

Keren

Massawa

Omdurman

Khartoum

Asmara

ERITREA

SUDAN

Al Fashir

Aksum

Al Obeid

er Roseires

Gondar

Lake Tana

Assab

DJIBOUTI

Gulf of Aden

Boosaaso

Nyala

Blue Nile R.

Blue Nile R.

Djibouti

Berbera

SOMALILAND

Bentiu

Malakal

Addis Abada

Dire Dawa

Hargeysa

CENTRAL AFRICAN REPUBLIC

Waw

White Nile R.

Nazref

Harar

ETHIOPIA

Juba

Lake Turkana

SOMALIA

UGANDA

Lake Kyoga

Mbale

KENYA

Mogadishu

Merca

Kampala

Jinja

Kisumu

Mazaka

Lake Victoria

Nakuru

Thika

Nairobi

Kismayu

CONGO

RWANDA

Mwanza

Olduvai Gorge

BURUNDI

△ *Mt. Kilimanjaro*

Arusha

Mombasa

Pemba Island

Tanga

TANZANIA

Zanzibar

Lake Tanganyika

Dodoma

Dar es Salaam

ZAMBIA

Lake Malawi

Rovuma R.

MOZAMBIQUE

SAUDIA ARABIA

N

YEMEN

| 0 | 100 | 200 | 300 mi |
| 0 | 100 200 300 400 | 500 km |

197

The Republic of Djibouti (pronounced Gee-booty)

Basic Facts
Area: 23,000 sq. km. = 9,000 sq. mi. (slightly larger than Massachusetts)
Population: 833,000 (UN 2007 est.)
Capital City: Djibouti
Neighboring Countries: Ethiopia (north, west, south); Somali Republic (southeast)
Official Language: Arabic, French
Other Principal Languages: Somali, Afar (Danakil)
Ethnic Groups: Somali 60%, Afar 35%, French, Arab, Ethiopian, and Italian 5%
Principal Religions: Muslim 94%, Christian 6%
Chief Commercial Products: Hides and skins, and coffee (in transit)
GDP Per Capita: $1,240 (World Bank 2008 est.)
Currency: Djibouti franc
Former Colonial Status: French Territory (1896–1977)
Independence Date: June 27, 1977
Chief of State: Ismail Omar Guelleh, President (since April 1999)
National Flag: Two equal horizontal bands of light blue (top) and light green with a white isosceles triangle based on the hoist side bearing a red five-pointed star in the center.

Land and People
The Republic of Djibouti is a tiny, sun-blistered pocket of land strategically located at the entrance to the Red Sea. The only reason for its separate existence as a colony was the deep, natural harbor at the city of Djibouti, through which Ethiopian exports and imports traveled overland since the beginning of the century. The desert country of the interior is parched and bleak, an irregular landscape seen infrequently by other than the nomadic herdsmen who pass through. It has been said that this area is even too hot for the devil.

The city of Djibouti is distinctly French in atmosphere; about 24,000 Europeans live in the capital, including the French military—actually foreign legionnaires—who wander through the town in tight khaki shorts and white "kepi" hats. Soldiers with shaved heads and tattoos nightly pack the bars and restaurants the police once tried to close down as offensive to "good morals in a Muslim country." The French are joined by some of the 1,000 German soldiers now on duty in Djibouti.

The price of pleasure is high in Djibouti. A beer in town costs $6, a pizza $17. The prices, and cultural sensitivity, have helped keep U.S. servicemen off the streets and largely confined to a camp that brings in its own supplies and contributes almost nothing to the economy. When they do come to town, Americans tend to come in the afternoon and wear civilian clothes.

A widespread practice is the use of *khat* (or *qat*), a stimulant common throughout the Horn of Africa. Much of Djibouti's business activity grinds to a halt at midday, partly because of the heat and partly because this is when the daily plane from Ethiopia arrives bringing about 12 tons of the drug. It is a social drug that is never swallowed, only chewed as the user moves from stimulation to contemplative stupor. Women are discouraged from chewing *khat*, and if they do it, it must be done in seclusion.

The Past: Political and Economic History
For early history, see *Historical Background* and *The Colonial Period: the French*.

France, after granting all of its remaining African colonies independence in 1960 did not concern itself with this remaining African territory until 1966. De Gaulle's August 1966 visit was marked by two days of public demonstrations by Somalis demanding independence. France conducted a referendum in March 1967 in which 60% chose to remain associated with France. In July of that year, the name French Somaliland formally changed to the French Territory of Afars and Issas to avoid any encouragement to expansionist ambitions in Somalia.

Hassan Gouled Aptidon, an Issa, easily won the ensuing presidential elections and an interethnic government was formed with an Afar, Ahmed Dini, serving as prime minister. Successive elections in 1981 and 1986 returned the unopposed president with majorities of over 90% and affirmed Issa domination of Djibouti politics.

In November 1991 a devastating civil war erupted between the Issa-led government and a predominantly Afar rebel group, which termed itself the Front for the Restoration of Unity and Democracy (FRUD). Responding to criticisms of its monopoly of political power, President

Aptidon's government decided to permit multiparty politics and allowed the registration of four political parties in 1992. Only two, Aptidon's People's Rally for Progress (RPP)—the only legal party in Djibouti from 1981 to 1992—and the Party for Democratic Renewal (PRD) contested the National Assembly election. The PRD withdrew its candidates after claiming there were too many opportunities for electoral fraud. The RPP won all 65 Assembly seats with a turnout of only 50%.

In 1994 a moderate faction of the FRUD signed a peace agreement with the government, ending three years of civil war. In this accord the government agreed to recognize FRUD as a legitimate political party and named two FRUD leaders, Afars, to cabinet positions in 1995. In December 1997 elections the ruling RPP-FRUD coalition won all 65 legislative seats.

At the age of 83, elderly and frail, President Aptidon announced that he would not stand for reelection in 1999. In April Djibouti conducted its second multiparty presidential elections and the overwhelming victory went to Aptidon's nephew, *Chef de Cabinet*, and longtime director of security services, Ismail Omar Guelleh. His campaign was slick and well-financed. Colored posters covered the walls of Djibouti; thousands of green T-shirts and hats bearing his name were distributed to Djibouti's numerous unemployed. His opponent was the seasoned politician Moussa Ahmed Idriss, a leader in the campaign for independence who served in the French parliament from 1962 until 1967. The Idriss campaign had substantially fewer resources, yet Idriss received about a quarter of the votes cast. It was an election in which both wings of FRUD participated rather than boycotted. Those who had reconciled themselves to the government supported Ismail Omar Guelleh; those who remained in armed opposition urged support of Idriss.

The usual severity of the regime to its critics continues under President Guelleh, who seems little tolerant of criticism. The government, which owns the principal newspaper, *La Nation*, has particularly little patience with the opposition press. Charges of "distributing false information" can land an editor in jail and earn the newspaper a lengthy banning. The government also owns the radio and television stations. Neither is a source of critical judgment against the government.

In February 2000 Ahmed Dini's wing of FRUD signed an agreement on "reform and civil harmony" with the Djibouti government, seeming to bring closure to the Afar rebellion. The agreement called for rehabilitation of zones devastated by the civil war, compensation of victims of the conflict, and "real devolution, granting a

Djibouti

wide degree of autonomy to the regions concerned."

A section of the agreement on democratization suggested FRUD's sense of exclusion from Djibouti politics. It referred to the need for "equitable representation" and an administration within which "the various national communities are equally represented." The reality of political power in Djibouti is that the Issa, the dominant Somali clan, control the ruling party and are disproportionately represented in bureaucratic and military ranks. Among the Issa, the president's subclan, the Mamassan, predominates.

Negotiations between the government and representatives of FRUD's armed faction on the specifics of the agreement began in April 2000. They ultimately concluded with a peace accord signed in May 2001, and the demobilization of FRUD fighters went smoothly. Of 1,074 disbanded troops, some 300 were integrated into the government's forces and 700 returned to their villages.

The peace agreement allowed the FRUD-Armé to be authorized as a political party when a multiparty system was approved in September 2002; as a legal party it is known as the *Alliance Républicaine pour le Développement* (ARD). Legislative elections scheduled for late 2002 were postponed to allow the numerous parties registered to organize and campaign effectively. They were ultimately held in January 2003.

In Djibouti's first multiparty elections, two coalitions competed for seats in the country's 65-seat legislature. On the government side, the *Union pour la majorité présidentielle's* (UMP) list was dominated by nominees of President Guelleh's RPP (two-thirds) and FRUD-legal (one-third). Two smaller parties were allocated two positions each on the list. The opposition rallied under the banner of the *Union pour l'alternance démocratique* (UAD: Union for

Democratic Change) which was dominated by candidates of Ahmed Dini's ARD.

With a winner-take-all district system, election results distorted opposition strength. UMP parties supporting President Guelleh won 62.2% of the votes, against 36.9% for the opposition, but took every legislative seat. For the first time, six women are represented in parliament. Ahmed Dini, who led the Union for a Democratic Alternative, said, not without justification, the poll had been rigged and claimed his group had won at least 22 seats.

Even the government was willing to admit the voter lists were hopelessly out of date. In an interview, the interior minister said they went back to the colonial period. "There are many dead people on the lists because our citizens do not normally report deaths," he said. "We have people who are 120 years old or more on the lists."

After the terrorist attacks of September 11, 2001, Djibouti became the hub of Western antiterrorist activity. In addition to having France's largest military contingent, Djibouti has allowed U.S. and European forces (notably German, but also Spanish, British and Italian) to use its airport facilities. For Americans the main goal is to put American forces in position to strike cells of Al Qaeda in Yemen or East Africa. Indeed, it was CIA operatives in Djibouti who directed the launch of a Hellfire missile that struck a car carrying Qaed Salim Sinan al-Harethi, a close ally of Osama bin Laden, and the mastermind of the attack on the USS Cole in Yemen's port of Aden—an attack that killed 17 U.S. Navy sailors.

Djibouti's April 2005 presidential election went off without a hitch (by local standards) and without an opposition candidate. Longtime opponent Ahmed Dini Ahmed had died the preceding September, at age 72, and the only other candidate, Mohamed Daoud Chehem, withdrew in March citing difficulties in raising campaign funds. Opposition parties called a boycott and the police had to use tear gas to disperse hundreds of protesters who blocked the streets with burning tires, but President Guelleh was reelected to a second six-year term.

Since then President Guellah has been preoccupied with events in neighboring Somalia. The Ethiopian intervention to support the Transitional Federal Government was not helpful, he thought, and the use of American planes (from their Djibouti base) against Islamists fleeing Mogadishu in early 2007 was a cause for considerable embarrassment.

In June 2008 Eritrean and Dijiboutian troops collided in the Ras Doumeira border area. Dijibouti's government claimed Eritrea was responsible for the deaths of

nine soldiers, but Eritrea denies launching the attack.

The Present: Contemporary Issues

The 1991–94 civil war expanded the army from 3,000 men to 18,000, devastated infrastructure and bankrupted the state. The national debt is estimated to be around $429 million (2005). To pay for the war, public utilities were raided and payments were delayed to creditors and state employees. When the government proposed reducing public salaries, which account for nearly 80% of the budget, a general strike was declared, and the government had to suspend planned reforms. Salary arrears to government workers continue to plague the government, and it remains dependent on the generosity of friends to make up budgetary shortfalls.

With less than 1% of its soil arable and with virtually no industry, Djibouti has had problems of food security following the increasing prices on imported food. Aside from livestock, its one traditional resource was salt, mined from a "lake" of salt deposits over 1,800 feet deep. From time immemorial, Afar nomads have brought their camels to Assal, loaded them with salt and led them to Ethiopia, where their cargo is exchanged for cereal and other goods. Large-scale exploitation of Assal's salt began in 1998 and increasingly trucks have replaced the traditional miner and his camel.

Today Djibouti is dependent on its strategic location on one of the busiest sea-lanes of the world. Modernized to receive container cargoes, port facilities are the heart of the Djibouti economy. Border conflict between neighboring Ethiopia and Eritrea significantly increased activities at Djibouti port as Ethiopia diverted its trade from the Eritrean ports of Assab and Massawa. Eighty percent of all goods handled by the port are now destined for landlocked Ethiopia. As a consequence of significantly increased usage, the port has become so congested the government sought funding for a new and much larger facility at Doraleh, about five miles east of the current port.

The new facilities are being built in two phases—first an oil terminal and then a container area and free trade zone. The government hopes the project will make Djibouti a transshipment hub for the countries of the Common Market for Eastern and Southern Africa (COMESA). Most of the work is being done by companies based in the Persian Gulf state of Dubai.

Dubai-based Horizon Terminals, Ltd. completed the new Doraleh oil terminal in February 2006. Another Dubai company, DP World, announced plans to build a $300 million container terminal at Doraleh. The port officially opened in Febru-

President Guelleh's campaign poster

Djibouti

Djibouti Nomads   ©IRIN

ary 2009, it is the most modern and largest port terminal in East Africa. In addition to Doraleh, Dubai companies run the old port of Djibouti and the Djbouti airport. The commercial director of Djibouti port had nothing but praise for Dubai's contribution to his country's economic development: "Dubai has done in five years what France did not do during 115 years of colonization. And Dubai is doing it without showing any arrogance."

Strenuous efforts have also been made to improve rail and road connections between the port and Ethiopia to speed the transfer of imports. The 500-mile Djibouti to Addis railroad, constructed by France in 1897, suffers from dilapidated equipment more than 50 years old. The EU has granted a $40 million loan to upgrade the line. This includes enlarging its rails to accommodate the most modern locomotives, reinforcing viaducts and metal bridges, and replacing its communication system. With improvements the line will have the capacity to carry one million metric tons of freight annually.

Significant income is derived from the presence of foreign troops in Djibouti. France maintains a force of 2,800 strong there, making it France's largest foreign military base. The United States has made Djibouti a center for its war on terrorism, and some 1,500 American soldiers are stationed there. The country also hosts an additional 800 German and 50 Spanish troops.

The U.S. government has committed an additional $2 million to renovate state-run Radio Djibouti, along with $100,000 in annual rent, in exchange for a strategic transmission station the U.S. is building. The targeted audience: Yemen and the southern regions of Saudi Arabia.

As with other African leaders, President Guellah is encouraging Chinese investment in his country. Chinese developers

are being encouraged to build hotels and resorts in northern Djibouti to take advantage of unparalleled scuba diving opportunities. The government is currently in discussion with a Chinese national salt company to exploit local resources, and hopes to interest other companies in its mining and thermal energy sectors.

Female Genital Cutting (FGC) is common in Djibouti. A 2002 survey of 1,000 women by Djibouti's Health Ministry concluded that 98% of them had been circumcised. Infibulation, one of the most brutal forms of FGC, is the most prevalent in Djibouti. The inner labia and clitoris are first cut away, and then the remaining lips are sewn together, leaving only a small hole for urination and menstruation. The practice is a major contributor to Djibouti's relatively high maternal mortality rate: 69 deaths for each 10,000 live births. Article 333 of Djibouti's *Penal Code* outlaws the practice of FGC, but few people have ever

been arrested. In February 2005 the government signed the African Union's Maputo Protocol on FGC that requires member states to ban the practice.

A severe drought affecting much of Eastern Africa in later 2005 had a major impact on the traditional culture of Somali pastoralists. More than 150,000 were threatened as water holes dried up and pasturelands were degraded. Some affected populations abandoned their traditional pastures and moved entire villages to the outskirts of the capital as food security worsened.

The Future

President Guelleh has few resources with which to confront Djibouti's poverty, so his openness to Western military forces is understandable. The country has few natural resources, apart from its strategic location, and its economic future will continue to be dominated by services provided to the shipping industry and to Western governments seeking to maintain a presence in the volatile Horn of Africa. Still, unemployment and poverty look to be significant problems for the foreseeable future. Given the moderate version of Islam in the country, the government is unlikely to suffer any severe consequences from the presence of these troops. The future of Djibouti—both economically and politically—will be inextricably linked to the presence of French and American troops in the region.

Politically, Djibouti continues to be dominated by the single party, and there are few prospects for a robust opposition. While the country's residents cannot expect rich political contestation, there is little sign of significant conflict or civil unrest. The civil wars of previous decades seem to be contained.

A West Virginia Air National Guard crew lands its 1st C-5 in Djibouti

Photo by Sgt. Lee Harshman, courtesy U.S. Air Force

The State of Eritrea

Downtown Asmara

Basic Facts

Area: 93,679 sq. km. = 40,800 sq. mi. (larger than Maine)

Population: 4,900,000 (UN 2007 est.)

Capital City: Asmara

Climate: Generally dry, moderate to chilly in the central highlands; hot and dry in the desert regions, hot and humid along the coastline.

Neighboring Countries: Sudan (north and east); Ethiopia (south); Djibouti (southeast)

Official Languages: None, though Arabic and English are often used on official letterheads.

Other Principal Languages: Afar, Amharic, Arabic, Tigre and Kunama, and Tigrinya

Ethnic Groups: Tigrinya 50%, Tigre and Kunama 40%, Afar 4%, Saho (Red Sea coast dwellers) 3%, other 3%

Principal Religions: Muslim, Coptic Christian, Roman Catholic, Protestant

Chief Commercial Products: Livestock, sorghum, textiles, food, and small manufactures

GNI Per Capita: $220 (World Bank 2006 est.)

Currency: Nakfa

Former Colonial Status: Italian colony (1890–1941); British trusteeship (1941–1952); absorbed by Ethiopia 1962–1991, (defeat of Ethiopian forces), referendum in April 1993 resulted in total independence.

Independence Date: May 24, 1991

Chief of State: Isaias Afwerki, President (since April 1993)

National Flag: A red triangle at the pole divides a green field at the top, from a blue one at the bottom. A gold wreath encircling a gold olive branch is centered on the pole side of the red triangle.

Land and People

Geological evidence indicates that Eritrea was a relatively flat plateau of green trees and grass prior to the arrival of modern mankind. At some unknown time, massive earthquakes caused the land to change into a terrain of sharp peaks accentuated by smoldering, active volcanoes which spewed their lava freely. Although the volcanoes are now dead, the peaks remain, often rising to more than 14,000 feet, with a craggy appearance caused by lava rock formations. Except for the coastal areas, the climate is moderate, with frost appearing above 11,000 feet. Variation in temperature from noon to midnight may be as much as 60 degrees.

Eritrea is semiarid at best, and rainfall is irregular. This, combined with the rugged terrain that dominates all but the coast along the Red Sea, makes the land somewhat inhospitable and generally incapable of producing field crops. Rainfall depends upon prevailing wind direction. If the currents aloft are from southwest to northeast, moisture capable of generating rainfall arrives from central Africa's vast rain forest area. But if the prevailing pattern is from the northwest to the southeast, the hot winds of the Sahara and sub-Sahara arrive and roast any crops that are planted.

Eritrea

Asmara, Eritrea's capital, is a delightful Italian-style city, sometimes called a "second Milan." Its main street is lined with palm trees, and many of its 400,000 inhabitants can often be found sipping espresso at sidewalk cafes. Its best restaurant is Italian and service there is provided by courtly and elderly Italian-speaking waiters. Eritrea's favorite drink is cappuccino, and like Italians, Eritreans share a national passion for cycle racing.

The Italian occupiers who built up Asmara in the 1930s left a legacy of experimentation in modern architectural styles. Among others, European Art Deco and Italian Futurism both found expression in colonial construction, and the city is known to architectural historians as one of the best concentrations of modernism in the world. To preserve this heritage, Asmara has established an historical district of one and a half square miles in the heart of the city; alterations to any significant buildings there are restricted.

Women are honored and possess an equality undreamed of elsewhere on the continent. During the war of liberation at least a third of the 100,000-strong rebel force was composed of women. After the war, new laws made women fully equal to men with rights to own land, to choose their own mates and even divorce them.

Much remains to do to change the status of women at home more completely. The National Union of Eritrean Women estimates that 90% of women are illiterate. They have thus far organized literacy classes for over 26,000 women.

The Past: Political and Economic History

For details of early history, see *Historical Background* and *The Colonial Period: the Italians.*

The Italian conquest of Eritrea and later of Ethiopia effectively created a separate identity for each. After the Italians were expelled in 1941, the British assumed control over the territory. Under pressure from the British and Ethiopia, the UN adopted a plan for federating Eritrea and Ethiopia in 1950. This was intended to protect Eritrean autonomy, but almost immediately after the federation went into effect, Eritrean rights were abridged or violated by the Ethiopian imperial government. Political parties were banned in 1955, followed by the banning of trade unions in 1958. In 1959 the name "Eritrean Government" was changed to "Eritrean Administration," and Ethiopian law was imposed. Resistance to this administrative subordination was manifested by the creation of the Eritrean Liberation Front (ELF) in 1958.

Increasing pressure on Eritreans from Addis Ababa to renounce their autonomy was ultimately successful in November 1962. A compliant Eritrean Assembly voted unanimously for the abolition of Eritrea's federal status, reducing Eritrea to a simple province of the Ethiopian empire. The liberation struggle began in earnest at the same time.

In 1974 the Ethiopian monarchy collapsed and power was seized by the military. Lt. Col. Mengistu Haile Mariam assumed power as head of state and chairman of the governing military council known as the Derg. The regime was totalitarian in style, financed by the Soviet Union and Eastern block, and assisted by Cuba in a massive militarization of the country. War against the Eritrean rebels continued through the late 1980s. When the Soviet Union, otherwise occupied in Afghanistan, announced that it would not renew its defense and cooperation agreement with Ethiopia, army morale plummeted. The Eritrean People's Liberation Front (EPLF) joined with internal opposition to the Derg, advanced on Ethiopian positions, and ultimately drove Mengistu into exile in 1991.

The EPLF established a provisional government in May 1991 with its leader Isaias Afwerki as its head. Independence was overwhelmingly ratified in a UN-monitored referendum in April 1993. Freely contested elections chose a National Assembly that in turn appointed Afwerki as president of the Provisional Government of Eritrea (PGE). The EPLF renamed itself the People's Front for Democracy and Justice (PFDJ) in early 1994 and became the country's only political party.

The new government faced enormous challenges. A constitution had to be written, a judiciary created, a school system reconstructed, refugees reintegrated and ex-guerrillas demobilized. Underlying all was the need to rehabilitate a badly damaged infrastructure and reform the collapsed institutions of a centrally planned economy. In March 1994 the National Assembly established a constitutional commission and members traveled throughout the country and to Eritrean communities abroad, holding meetings to explain constitutional options and solicit input. The new constitution that resulted from this broad consultative process was ratified by the constituent assembly on May 24, 1997. Elections to implement the constitution were postponed; they have yet to be held.

A full judiciary system has yet to be installed. Given the absence of legally trained personnel, the Justice Ministry has been unable to process a large volume of civilian corruption cases. These were handled by the Ministry of Defense and in 1997 some 2,314 civilians were tried by special military courts.

At its peak fighting strength the EPLF army grew to nearly 110,000 fighters—nearly 3% of the total population. Since a fragile peacetime economy could not support such numbers, the government began to demobilize 50% to 60% of the army in 1993. Those who had served longest and had the fewest civilian skills were given higher compensation, more intensive training and more psychological counseling. Special attention was given to women fighters who made up 30% of the EPLF's combat forces. By 1998 the army had shrunk to 47,000, but then the country went to war again with Ethiopia.

Eritrean law obliges every citizen between the ages of 18 and 40 to do national service, but national service in war took on a new meaning. Hostilities with Ethiopia broke out in May 1998. In April 1999 the government conducted evening raids across the country, rounding up young people who might have skipped out on national service. Unless they could identify themselves as a mother, pregnant or a veteran, young Eritreans were put on buses and taken off to a police station for questioning.

At issue in the conflict with Ethiopia was an obscure triangle of land, 155 square miles of rocky barrenness called the Badme Triangle. Unlocatable on most maps, the triangle became the focus of national pride on both sides of the border. Both presidents Afwerki and Meles found themselves in a situation from which it was difficult to retreat. Pride and personality, on both sides, generated a cultivated knack for stubbornness. Negotiations had, by May 2000, brought no resolution to the conflict. As soon as the last negotiators left, Ethiopia launched another massive attack. A surprise advance against a presumably impregnable pass brought crushing victory in 19 days, after which Ethiopia announced its war aims achieved.

President Isaias Afwerki

A cease-fire was announced in June 2000 and actually lasted through the conclusion of December peace negotiations conducted in Algiers. The Algiers Agreement called for a pullback of troops and creation of a demilitarized zone manned by several thousand UN peacekeepers. A five-member Eritrea-Ethiopia Boundary Commission (EEBC) was established to demarcate the disputed border. Overall, the war had mobilized 200,000 fighters into the army. It cost the lives of 19,000 Eritreans, displaced tens of thousands, and set back development plans for decades.

The Boundary Commission rendered its decision in April 2002. The language of the 125-page decision was sufficiently obscure to allow both countries to claim victory: Badme, for example, was not explicitly mentioned in the text. Both countries launched a propaganda campaign seeking to convince their citizens that the sacrifices of war had not been in vain.

Tensions between the two countries spiked as demarcation approached in spring 2003. In March the EEBC affirmed that Badme, the *casus belli* of recent conflict, was part of Eritrea. The Ethiopian prime minister rejected the decision, calling it "a blatant miscarriage of justice," as well as "illegal, unjust and irresponsible." Beating the drums and sounding the trumpets, he warned the decision could lead to "another round of war."

No one seemed to know what to do or had the will to do anything. The Eritrean government continued to insist the border ruling be implemented. Finally, faced with international immobility, Eritrea acted. In October 2006 it moved troops and tanks into the demilitarized buffer zone to do, it said, agricultural work, like harvesting. Prime Minister Meles caustically responded: "You don't need tanks to pick crops."

The UN-appointed demarcation panel began to visibly wash its hands of the whole affair by the end of November. It told both Eritrea and Ethiopia to resolve the six-year dispute or risk having the UN take the matter into its own hands. It was a threat that bore little likelihood of ending the enmity between Asmara and Addis Ababa. The United Nations' top peacekeeping official seemed to admit as much in early 2007 when described the peace process between the rivals as "failing." The 620-mile border remains undemarcated and a source of constant tension in the region.

As relations with Ethiopia worsened, the government mended fences in Sudan. It successfully mediated a settlement between Khartoum and the Eastern Front (EF), whose forces had been fighting a low-level insurgency for the past decade. The Asmara Peace Agreement was signed in October 2006. Its aims were similar to more familiar proposals for Southern and Darfur rebels: greater autonomy and control of natural resources. Under terms of the accord, the EF was to name an aide to President Bashir, get a junior minister's post and eight seats in parliament.

Eritrea's relations with Sudan were completely transformed, and with that transformation, the country began to be reevaluated as a major player in the conflict-filled region. From antagonism and support of hostile rebel movements, President Bashir praised the efforts of Eritrea to secure peace in Sudan. Even the EU, which had complained bitterly about a lack of transparency in Eritrea, and whose ambassador to the country had called it "a dictatorship under the presidency of President Isaias (Afwerki)," changed its tune. In May 2007, President Afwerki visited the EU Commission offices in Brussels to a warm reception and hopes for a "new kind of relations between the Commission and Eritrea." The EU development commissioner singled out for praise Eritrea's efforts in Somalia, though the country funneled arms through the country's Islamic Courts Union rulers to rebel groups in Ethiopia, namely the Ogaden National Liberation Front (ONLF) and the Oromo Liberation Front (OLF). Inside Somalia, Eritrea funded, armed, trained and advised insurgents, especially the al-Shabab militia, the most radical arm of the Islamic Courts Union.

President Afwerki has yet to work out a redemptive relationship with his domestic opposition. Forming a new political party is still illegal, and the government has closed the private press and arrested dissidents, journalists and prominent Eritreans whose only crime was to campaign for greater democracy.

Safe in cyberspace, the dissidents organized a new political party—the Eritrean People's Liberation Front Democratic Party, or EPLFDP, to challenge the "autocratic and incorrigible" EPLF regime. As the first opposition party to emerge from within the EPLF, the new Democratic Party has more credibility than external opposition groups backed by Ethiopia and Sudan.

Relations with neighbors deteriorated further in 2008 and 2009 as troops from Er-

Italian Art Deco architecture of Asmara

Eritrea

itrea and Djibouti clashed along the border between the two countries. Djibouti and the United States, among others, claimed Eritrea was the aggressor, though the government in Asmara denied any wrongdoing.

Conflict took on another troubling form in November 2008 when a group called the Red Sea Afar Democratic Organization (RSADO) attacked a military base, injuring and killing up to a hundred people. Asmara is now facing conflict within its territories as well as militarized territorial disputes along its western and southern boundaries.

The Present: Contemporary Issues

In the 1930s Eritrea was an exporting nation, and when World War II disrupted East African imports from Europe, Eritrea supplied the markets. Post-war demand shrank in the 1950s, and in the 1960s, as a province of Ethiopia, the economy was starved of investment and began to deteriorate. With the installation of the Mengistu regime in 1974, Ethiopia adopted a command economy and economic decisions were made by *apparatchiks* working in the capital. Most private assets were nationalized, drying up foreign investment. Recurrent drought, famine and nearly three decades of armed struggle intensified the destructive effects of centrally directed policies.

At its liberation in 1991, Eritrea inherited an economy neglected, isolated and virtually destroyed by war. When independence was achieved in 1993, the government, turning its back on its own Marxist background, began a remarkable effort to rebuild infrastructure, liberalize the economy and aggressively seek foreign investment.

Those efforts were effectively ended by the 1998–99 war with neighboring Ethiopia. By spring 1999, Eritrea was bearing the costs of at least 40,000 refugees, driven out of Ethiopia. It had also gone on an expensive shopping spree for armaments. Eritrea purchased top-of-the-line fighter planes (MiG-29s), but these proved too sophisticated for inexperienced Eritrean pilots, and Eastern European pilots had to fly them. Because of the war, the achievements of years were lost in months; reconstruction costs are estimated at $800 million.

Eritrea is no longer a shining model of development. The economy has slowed. GDP grew by only 1.8% in 2004, according to World Bank figures, while population continued to grow far too rapidly: 4.3%. In 2005, GDP growth barely registered—.05%—while population growth galloped ahead at 3.9%.

The consequences of war represent an enormous drag on the economy. Demobi-

lization and reintegration efforts are costly, and some 48,000 people who were internally displaced, either by war or drought, still remain in camps. Psychologically the country seems mobilized on a permanent-war basis. One in every 21 Eritreans serves in its armed forces—an estimated 202,000 out a total population of 4.7 million—the highest proportion of a nation's population in military service in the world. Police periodically raid nightclubs or other hangouts of the young looking for draft dodgers, and they continue the practice of detaining and arresting the parents of individuals who have evaded national service duties.

Much of the cost of war was financed by the Eritrean diaspora. At the height of the war crisis in May 2000, when it was uncertain if Ethiopia would march on Asmara, 3,000 Eritreans living abroad bought land in the capital where they could ultimately build homes. These sales brought in a total of $29 million to the treasury. Throughout the war the government sold bonds and raised some $200 million in contributions from Eritreans who had emigrated abroad.

Modernization of the port of Massawa, ongoing since 1999, has concluded. Around $35 million was spent on renovation and expansion of facilities, and the port now has the capacity of docking big ships. In December 2005 a Marsk cargo ship holding 1,722 containers was the first to land its cargo at the port. Previously such large ships had to unload at Jeddah, Saudi Arabia, and their containers transshipped in smaller vessels to Eritrea.

Plans for renovating the seaport of Assab are in abeyance. Ethiopia's president once promised to turn Assab into a watering hole for camels, and there is little likelihood Ethiopia will be using the port, having shifted its imports to the port of Djibouti.

One potential bright spot has been the announcement by a Canadian mining company that it discovered high grade gold at Bisha, less than 100 miles west of Asmara; exploratory drilling began in April 2005. The company noted the property has "excellent port facilities on the Red Sea."

There is still a stigma attached to HIV/AIDS in Eritrea. People do not talk about it openly, and figures on its penetration into the population are sketchy. The Health Ministry's AIDS control program estimates that there may be as many as 70,000 HIV-positive people in the country—about 2% of the population. More ominously, the ministry suggests the infection rate may be doubling every 18 months.

AIDS awareness programs have recently been taken to refugee camps. Between various entertainments, talks on the risks and dangers of the disease are given, the use of condoms demonstrated and prophylactics distributed. The World Bank has provided a $40 million credit to assist the government awareness programs.

Freedom of religious expression is limited in Eritrea. In 2002 all but four religions in the country—Islam, Eritrean Orthodox, Roman Catholic, and Evangelical Lutheran—were required to register with the government and cease all activities until their applications had been approved. Registration required a history of the group in the country, an explanation of its "uniqueness," and the benefits it offered over those already present. Reports indicate that those caught engaged in religious practices associated with unapproved churches are, shall we say, roughly treated.

The Future

Pressures on the Afwerki regime are enormous; the response has typically been repression. The government takes a bashing for its less than sterling human rights record. The European Parliament has said President Afwerki rules the country "with an iron grip" and expressed concern over the country's "authoritarian trend." The U.S. State Department asserts that the regime has harassed, arrested, and detained members of minority religious sects. The United States has reportedly even pondered placing Eritrea on the list of state sponsors of terrorism. Amnesty International calls torture, arbitrary detention, and political arrests "widespread."

The border demarcation with Ethiopia remains unsettled and volatile, with Ethiopia recently rejecting the latest attempt to secure a demarcation line. The year 2008 saw the neighboring nation of Djibouti also drawn into the conflict, as Eritrean troops clashed with Djiboutian troops over the demarcation line between those two countries. The international community is concerned that full-scale war between could erupt once again now that the UN has voted to remove peacekeepers from the region, and since Eritrea is accused of violating a UN ultimatum to remove troops from disputed territory along the border with Djibouti. Such tensions dominate Eritrean political life, and the uncertainty these tensions generate makes much-needed economic investment untenable. With militarization, economic resources are also diverted from other productive ends. The Eritrean economy thus looks unlikely to advance until a range of regional conflicts is resolved.

The Federal Democratic Republic of Ethiopia

Earning a living on Lake Awasa

Basic Facts

Area: 1,178,450 sq. km.= 455,000 sq. mi. (larger than Texas and New Mexico)

Population: 83,100,000 (UN 2007 est.)

Capital City: Addis Ababa

Climate: Hot in the lowlands, cool and invigorating in the plateau highland. There are normally two wet seasons (June–September and February–April).

Neighboring Countries: Kenya (southwest); The Sudan (west); Somali Republic, Djibouti (east, Southeast), Eritrea (northwest)

Official Languages: Amharic, English

Other Principal Languages: Tigrinya, Orominga, Guaraginga, Somali, and Arabic

Ethnic Groups: Amhara, Gurage, Oromo, Sidamo Shankella, Somali Afar, and Tigrean

Principal Religions: Muslim 45%–50%, Ethiopian Orthodox 35%–40%, animist 12%, other 3%–8%

Chief Commercial Products: Coffee, leather products, gold, oilseeds, beeswax and honey

GNI Per Capita: $160 (World Bank 2006 est.)

Currency: Birr

Former Colonial Status: Ethiopia has never been a colony in its history of almost 4,500 years. It was briefly occupied by the Italians (1936–1941).

National Holiday: National Revolution Day, September 12 (1974)

Chief of State: Girma Wolde-Giorgis, President (since October 2001)

Head of Government: Meles Zenawi, Prime Minister

National Flag: Three equal horizontal bands of green (top), yellow, and red with a yellow pentagram and single yellow rays emanating from the angles between the points on a light blue disk centered on the three bands. Ethiopia is the oldest independent country in Africa, and the colors of her flag were so often adopted by other African countries upon independence that they became known as the pan-African colors.

Land and People

Many centuries before the advent of modern mankind, Ethiopia was a relatively flat land of green grass and trees. Severe earthquakes occurred, causing fiery volcanoes to push skyward, spewing molten lava throughout the land.

Today, Ethiopia is a land of sharp mountains rising to more than 15,000 feet. Their

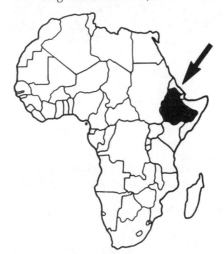

rough appearance is produced by volcanic rock formations. The Rift depression enters the country in the southeast, and the majestic peaks on either side of the gorge march in parallel formation towards the Red Sea. Slightly above Addis Ababa, the mountains separate and those on the left hand proceed north to the Red Sea at Asmara in Eritrea; the right hand peaks extend towards the Somali Republic.

The rugged terrain is one of the most isolated in the world. Surrounded by desert and arid land on all sides, the mountains rise so swiftly that they are almost impenetrable. The Blue Nile, originating from the cool waters of Lake Tana, flows through a gorge more magnificent than the Grand Canyon of Arizona. This river channel, more than a mile deep and 20 miles across in places, is bordered by slopes of deep green vegetation.

The climate of the highland plateaus and mountains is temperate and invigorating. Frost occurs regularly above 11,000 feet, where the daily range in temperature may span as much as 80° from noon to midnight.

The Ethiopian Orthodox Church is one of the world's oldest, Christianity having become the state religion around the same time the Emperor Constantine converted to Christianity. Tradition has it that the first Christian to be baptized was an Ethiopian noble who was on his way home from a pilgrimage to Jerusalem when he met the Apostle Philip. Baptism scenes are a recurring motif in Ethiopian art.

An extraordinary feature of the Ethiopian Church is its historic connection to the Old Testament and Jerusalem. Ethiopi-

Ethiopia

ans celebrated the Sabbath on Saturday for over a millennium. Most Ethiopian churches are consecrated with a symbolic Ark of the Covenant, and tradition has it that the original Ark was brought to Ethiopia by Menelik I, son of the Queen of Sheba, following a visit to his father, King Solomon. The story of Soloman and the Queen is a popular motif in Ethiopian religious art. The original Ark is claimed by some to be in the Church of St. Mary of Zion in Aksum.

The Ethiopian church calendar is more than seven years behind the rest of the world. In September 2007 Ethiopians will celebrate the 2,000th anniversary of the birth of Christ.

Lalibela, in a mountainous region some 400 miles north of Addis Ababa, was a "New Jerusalem" for Ethiopian Christians in the 13th century. Eleven medieval churches were carved out of solid rock there. They have been declared World Heritage sites by UNESCO and are principal tourist attractions for Ethiopian visitors.

The Past: Political and Economic History

For early history, see *Historical Background* and *The Colonial Period: The Italians.*

Haile Selassie became emperor in 1930 and within a year promulgated a constitution that provided for a two-chamber legislature. In reality, he retained absolute power over the affairs of Ethiopia. A short time later, the Italians invaded and conquered the country. Following the return of the emperor in 1941, increasing emphasis was placed on modernization of the country. The constitution was amended in 1955, providing for a Chamber of Deputies elected by universal suffrage to four-year terms, and a Senate, selected by the emperor from among distinguished Ethiopians to serve for six years. Another state institution was the Crown Council, a traditional institution, which included the crown prince and the archbishop of the Ethiopian Coptic Church, as well as other dignitaries drawn from the ruling class; it assisted in forming basic policy and was convened at the call of the monarch.

Eritrea was joined with Ethiopia in 1962, but the Eritrean Liberation Front, formed in 1958, organized an armed resistance that would ultimately achieve independence after three decades of struggle.

Ethiopia remained a deeply conservative nation ruled by an elite of wealthy landowners. The beginning of the end of this system began in the 1970s with a series of natural and man-made disasters. Drought gripped the nation in 1972; rising prices and unemployment brought hordes of refugees to the cities from the parched countryside. The military, reacting to high prices, demanded higher sal-

aries and started a limited military rebellion. Emperor Haile Selassie, aged and shaken, granted a partial increase. In the south, there were riots caused by an absence of land reform; peasants seized productive plantation land owned by absentee landlords.

Civil unrest led to the deposition of the aging Haile Selassie on September 12, 1974. A provisional administrative council of soldiers, known as the Derg ("committee"), seized power and installed a socialist military dictatorship. Beginning what would become standard practice, the Derg summarily executed 50 members of the royal family, ministers, generals and dignitaries of the imperial government. The emperor himself was strangled to death on August 22, 1975.

Lt. Col. Mengistu Haile Mariam assumed leadership of the Derg in February

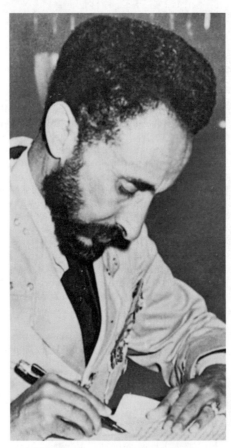

Former Emperor Haile Selassie

1977, after having his two predecessors killed. Mengistu turned Ethiopia into a totalitarian state and communist killing field. From 1977 through early 1978 thousands of suspected enemies of the Derg were tortured and killed in a purge known as the "red terror." Communism was officially adopted, a Soviet-style constitution promulgated, and the Workers Party of Ethiopia created, complete with a ham-

mer and sickle flag. Resistance, equally inspired by Marxist-Leninist thinking and practice, developed in all the major regions of the country.

To deprive the rebels of popular support, the government resorted to "resettlement" and "villagization." The first resettled people from the often-arid north to the rainier southern regions. Rejecting forced resettlement, peasants fled to Sudan and Somalia, creating huge refugee camps there. Many were shot—in the back—while fleeing. In the squalor of the refugee camps, thousands died. The second program was designed to control rural peoples so they would be unable to support rebel movements. It also was intended to make the collectivization of agriculture easier. The government did not hesitate to use foreign aid, including food, to lure people into these programs.

Sensing Ethiopia's weakened condition, the Somali Republic unleashed a band of rebels (and later regular army troops) to seize the Ogaden Desert region, where most of the people were ethnic Somalis. By mid-1977 they had penetrated as far as Dire Dawa. Mengistu's Soviet supporters sent massive quantities of arms and technical personnel to Ethiopia, placing the USSR in the embarrassing position of being patron and supporter of both sides of a war in which neither party had any interest in compromise. This was brief; the Somalis ejected the Soviets from their nation and turned to the United States for support.

The war was short. Soviet arms were followed by a wave of Cuban troops—flown from Angola—to support the fledgling communist regime. By early 1978 the Somalis had been routed, but the Ogaden remains unstable even today.

Incapable of dealing with drought and famine, the Derg's military dictatorship faced regional insurrections against its repression, particularly in the northern regions of Tigray and Eritrea. Officially created in February 1975, the Tigrayan Peoples Liberation Front (TPLF) announced its goal was "the establishment of an Independent Democratic Republic of Tigray." Allied with the Eritrean People's Liberation Front (EPLF), the TPLF waged incessant guerrilla warfare against the Derg. In 1989, the TPLF, representing a minority of only 7% of the Ethiopian population, merged with other ethnically based opposition groups to form the Ethiopian People's Revolutionary Democratic Front (EPRDF). By May 1991, EPRDF forces were advancing on Addis Ababa; Mengistu fled to Zimbabwe where he was granted asylum by President Mugabe. On May 27 EPRDF troops took control of the capital, and a transitional government under the leadership of the TPLF chairman, Meles Zenawi, was formed.

Ethiopia

Meles Zenawi was born Legesse Zenawi, the third and youngest child of a member of the lower Tigrayan nobility. He saw himself, as did other Tigrayan students, a victim of discrimination by the Amhara, who had dominated Ethiopian political life since the rule of Emperor Menelik. After two years as a premedical student, he dropped out of school to join the nationalist struggle in Tigray. It was at this point that he adopted his *nom de guerre* of Meles Zenawi, honoring Meles Tekle, a Tigrayan nationalist student killed in 1974. In 1985, Meles founded the Marxist-Leninist League of Tigray (MLLT) as a "vanguard party" within the TPLF. His intellectual model at the time was Envar Hoxha, the repressive ruler of Albania. Meles took over the leadership of the TPLF in 1989, linked with other opposition groups, and brought about the downfall of the Derg's military dictatorship.

One partner in the dictatorship's successful overthrow, the Eritrean People's Liberation Front, had already established—in May 1991—a separate regional government in the province; in April 1993, Eritreans voted for independence from Ethiopia.

In December 1994 the constituent assembly completed the new constitution of a Federal Democratic Republic of Ethiopia. It established a federal state and emphasized decentralized administration based on ten essentially ethnically defined regions. Regions are granted broad powers for social and economic development, the right to raise and spend their own revenues and, most remarkably, the right, in theory, to secede from the Ethiopian state. For the Tigrayan leadership at the core the EPRDF, the constitution was a means of redressing the grievances of Ethiopia's various "nationalities" against the Amhara. It is a revolutionary break with the highly centralized structures of the empire and its Marxist successor.

In reality, political power in Ethiopia is relatively centralized around Meles Zenawi, the TPLF, and its allies within the EPRDF. Elections for Ethiopia's first popularly chosen parliament and regional legislatures were held in May and June 1995. Most opposition parties boycotted the elections, resulting in a landslide for the EPRDF. As head of the dominant force within the EPRDF, Meles was appointed to a five-year term as prime minister.

With its ethnic and regional emphasis, the new system spawned a plethora of new political parties—65 in all are registered, but most were created by or are satellites of the EPRDF, itself dominated by the Tigrayan Peoples Liberation Front (TPLF). Meles Zenawi combines a variety of functions that emphasize his centrality: He is chairman of the TPLF, chairman of the EPRDF and prime minister.

Centrifugal forces, reflecting Ethiopia's origins as a conquest state, tear at the heart of the new Ethiopia. Members of the Oromo Liberation Front have resorted to urban terror and earned a repressive response from the government. Afar separatists shuttle back and forth across the border with Djibouti, and Islamist Somali separatists continue to convulse the Ogaden. The model for each is the province of Eritrea, which gained its independence constitutionally.

Despite the constitution's commitment to regional and ethnic rights, the government seems more willing to repress than share power. People unwilling to join the EPRDF are castigated as "narrow nationalists," harassed and imprisoned. In the

Lt. Col. Mengistu Haile Mariam

Oromia and Somali regions, human rights groups have documented hundreds of "disappearances." Ethiopia held elections for a federal parliament, and nine regional assemblies in May 2000. It was only the second time that nationwide elections had been held in the country. The opposition was given an unprecedented opportunity to air its grievances in a series of public debates. Largely attended, the debates were rebroadcast on state-run radio and television, but everywhere it was an uphill battle for the opposition.

Not a single opposition candidate managed to secure the 500 signatures necessary for nomination in the northern Tigray region. Elsewhere the EPRDF's satellite and creature parties dominated the electoral process. Prime Minister Meles' four-party coalition won overwhelmingly: 479 of the 547 parliamentary seats. When par-

liament convened in October, it reelected Meles to another five-year term.

War With Eritrea

Much to the surprise of the world community, minor hostilities occurred between Ethiopia and Eritrea in May 1998, escalating to major warfare in early June. At issue in the conflict was an obscure triangle of land, 155 square miles of rocky barrenness called the Badme Triangle. Unlocatable on most maps, the triangle became the focus of national pride on both sides of the border. Both Prime Minister Meles and President Afwerki found themselves in a situation from which it was difficult to retreat. The internal pressures on Meles were particularly intense. Amhara imperialists had never accepted the loss of what they considered the Eritrean province, and the loss of the Red Sea ports rankled deeply, even among the Oromo majority. Galling too was the perception that the TPLF leadership had conceded too much by letting Eritrea secede and assume no share of the national debt.

Pride and personality generated stubbornness, on both sides. Negotiations had, by early May 2000, brought no resolution to the conflict. As soon as the last negotiators left, Ethiopia launched another massive attack. A surprise advance against a presumably impregnable pass brought crushing victory in 19 days, after which Ethiopia announced its war aims achieved.

A cease-fire was announced in June 2000 and actually lasted through the conclusion of December peace negotiations conducted in Algiers. The Algiers Agreement called for a pullback of troops and creation of a demilitarized zone manned by several thousand UN peacekeepers. A five-member Eritrea-Ethiopia Boundary Commission (EEBC) was established to demarcate the disputed border. Overall, the war had cost the government $397 million and increased its military expenditures by 8.2% per year during the war. Damages were calculated in the billions of dollars.

The Boundary Commission rendered its decision in April 2002. The language of the 125-page decision was sufficiently obscure to allow both countries to claim victory: Badme, for example, was not explicitly mentioned in the text. Both countries launched a propaganda campaign seeking to convince its citizens that the sacrifices of war had not been in vain.

Tensions between the two countries spiked as demarcation approached in spring 2003. In March the EEBC affirmed that Badme, the *causa belli* of recent conflict, was part of Eritrea. The Ethiopian prime minister rejected the decision, calling it "a blatant miscarriage of justice," as well as "illegal, unjust and irresponsible."

Ethiopia

Beating the drums and sounding the trumpets, he warned the decision could lead to "another round of war."

No one seemed to know what to do or had the will to do anything. The Eritrean government continued to insist the border ruling be implemented. Finally, faced with international immobility, Eritrea acted. In October 2006 it moved troops and tanks into the demilitarized buffer zone to do, it said, agricultural work, like harvesting. Prime Minister Meles caustically responded: "You don't need tanks to pick crops."

The UN-appointed demarcation panel began to visibly wash its hands of the whole affair by the end of November. It told both Eritrea and Ethiopia to resolve the six-year dispute or risk having the UN take the matter into its own hands. It was a threat that bore little likelihood of ending the enmity between Asmara and Addis Ababa. The United Nations' top peace-keeping official seemed to admit as much in early 2007 when described the peace process between the rivals as "failing."

The 620-mile border remains undemarcated and a source of constant tension in the region.

Postwar Dissidence

The war and its resolution provoked dissent and impacted the leadership in both Ethiopia and Eritrea. In March 2001, 12 members of the TPLF central committee openly opposed Meles. The dissidents were narrowly defeated, removed from their party positions, and subjected to corruption charges that would keep them busy in the courts. Their supporters were also purged from their positions. Ethiopia's president, Negasso Gidada, spoke out in favor of the dissidents, and described Meles as ruthless as the former dictator Mengistu Haile Mariam. He soon

Prime Minister Meles Zenawi

found himself forced to resign, and parliament quickly elected a new president, Girma Wolde-Giorgis, in October 2001.

In general, the regime neither understands nor appreciates dissent of any kind. A peaceful demonstration by Addis Ababa University students in April 2001 was violently broken up by the police. Two days of rioting ensued, resulting in the deaths of at least 31 people and injuries to hundreds of others. Thousands were interned without charges, and prominent human rights defenders were arrested as "instigators" of the riots.

Antigovernment dissent by Oromo students at both high school and university levels was robustly repressed by Oromiya state police, which regularly employ violence to disperse peaceful marches protesting regional governmental policies. Oromiya, the largest and most populous Ethiopian state, is dominated by Oromos, Ethiopia's largest ethnic group. Federal and regional governments tend to view all forms of protest as instigated by the rebel Oromo Liberation Front (OLF), which has led a decade-long armed struggle for regional autonomy for Oromiya.

Parliamentary elections were held in May 2005 against this background of ethnic tension and political repression. The EPRDF faced two new electoral coalitions. One, the Coalition for Unity and Democracy (CUD) was made up of four parties and had at its core the All Amhara People's Organization. It called for liberalization of the economy and private ownership of land. It gave voice to the Amhara imperial vision of Ethiopia by opposing the constitution's emphasis on ethnic federalism. Instead, it called for more power for the central government and greater emphasis on being "Ethiopian" rather than being from a particular ethnic group. The second coalition, the United Ethiopian Democratic Forces (UEDF), linked 14 parties (five inside Ethiopia and nine based abroad) with the Oromo National Congress as its dominant core. In contrast to CUD, the UEDF demanded greater regional autonomy.

When provisional election results were announced in late May it was clear the government would have a majority in parliament, but the opposition had cut deeply into its preponderance. The final returns, greatly delayed, gave the ruling EPRDF 296 seats, enough to form a government. The opposition took 174 seats, up from 12 in the previous legislature. CUD won a landslide victory in the capital, defeating the city's mayor and several ministers and taking all 23 seats representing the city.

The electoral results were bitterly, and lethally, contested at every stage. In June, CUD sought to prevent release of provisional results, claiming massive vote rigging. Three days of violent protests against the alleged fraud resulted in many deaths in Addis Ababa. As the protests spread from the capital, thousands were arrested and Human Rights Watch reported that security forces killed "dozens of protesters and arbitrarily detained thousands of people across the country. One year later, the commission of inquiry examining the events reported that 193 civilians—nearly four times the number originally claimed by the government—and six members of the security forces were killed; 763 civilians and 71 member of the security forces were injured, many seriously.

CUD rejected the official election results announced in August, and announced plans for massive antigovernment demonstrations for early October 2005. Their impact was blunted by large-scale arrests of opposition supporters beforehand, and when parliament met on October 10, the EPRDF majority elected Meles Zenawi prime minister. Its session was boycotted by 100 CUD deputies; those from the UEDF opposition faction rejected the boycott and took up their seats.

Rock-carved Church of St. George, Lalibela

Photo by Judi Iranyi

The Annunciation   Photo by Judi Iranyi

As tensions between CUD and EPRDF increased, it was clear that CUD chairman Hailu Shawel was thinking in terms of the types of street demonstrations and popular actions that had toppled repressive regimes in Eastern Europe. Amid a variety of protests, CUD called for strikes and boycotts of government-run breweries and state media. "The ruling party runs construction firms and printing companies, which will be targeted," the CUD spokesman added. He also asked drivers to honk their horns for three days and stay at home for five in mid-November.

Both sides reverted to form. Violent demonstrations rocked Addis Ababa for several days; thousands of opposition supporters were detained; at least 46 died. In mid-December government prosecutors cast their nets broadly and heavily: 129 opposition leaders, reporters, and aid workers were charged with crimes ranging from treason to genocide. The trial of 111 defendants opened in May 2006. It is the country's biggest court case since the genocide trial against the former Marxist dictator, Haile Meriam Mengistu, 14 years earlier. It remains ongoing.

Having dealt with the threat of domestic insurrection, the Meles government was soon faced with an even greater security threat to Ethiopia: the expansion of Islamist control in neighboring Somalia. From June to July 2006 the Islamic Courts Union (ICU) routed the war-lords, im-

posed order on Mogadishu, and threatened the hopelessly weak Transitional Federal Government. To consolidate power, Islamist leaders fanned the flames of Somali nationalism against the traditional enemy—Ethiopia. After Ethiopia sent military forces to support the interim government, the ICU leader, Sheikh Hassan Dahir Aweys, went into rhetorical overdrive, ordering a "holy war" to drive the Ethiopians from Somalia.

By October Prime Minister Meles bluntly said his country was "technically" at war with Somali Islamists. They were "spoiling for a fight," he told a Reuters reporter, "declaring jihad against Ethiopia almost every other week." ICU extremists also revived Pan-Somali irredentist claims to the territories of neighboring states (Djibouti, Ethiopia and Kenya) occupied by Somalis. This, combined with the Islamists' reliance on Eritrea and their military support of Ethiopian rebel groups (the Ogaden National Liberation Front and the Oromo Liberation Front) drew the Addis Ababa government into war with the Mogadishu militants.

Ethiopia began military action against the Islamist regime in December 2006, with covert American support and intelligence. Ethiopian tanks, artillery batteries and military jets made quick work of the ill-equipped Islamist militia. The Ethiopian government announced it had detained 41 terrorism suspects from 17 coun-

tries who had been fighting for Somalia's Islamist movement. In June 2008, an agreement between the ICU and Somalia's transitional government included a provision for the removal of Ethiopian troops from the country. The Ethiopian withdrawal from Somalia was completed in early 2009.

The Present: Contemporary Issues

Despite its Marxist origins, the government has embarked on a program of economic reform, including privatization of state enterprises. Progress is slow: most of the manufacturing sector remains under state control.

Liberalization of the economy is seen as essential for attracting foreign investment, and the project is not without its success: the economy grew a striking 12.4% in 1996. That was, of course, before the war with Eritrea. The economy shrank by 1.9% in 1998 after the war began, and has been erratic since then, as Ethiopia experiences the effects of periodic drought and famine. Real GDP growth in 2003 was minus 3.9% but soared by 13.1% in 2004. In 2005 the economy managed a healthy 8.7% growth despite political instability.

At modest and irregular levels, however, economic growth has had little impact because of the country's fast-growing population. Ethiopia produces about two million people every year; the population has essentially doubled in 20 years.

Industrial development has been agriculture-driven. Small-scale agriculture involves 85% of the population, generates 80% of Ethiopian exports and contributed 47.7% to the GDP (2005). Only 10.9% of Ethiopia's total land surface is under intense agricultural cultivation. There has been much criticism of the government's agriculture-based industrial development policies. Seeking greater liberalization, critics have called for private land ownership, which, they believe, would help farmers secure bank loans and adopt modern agricultural techniques. Prime Minister Zenawi has quashed any move in this direction: Land would remain, he has said, state property.

A strong argument can be made that land tenure is the central issue in Ethiopian development. Peasants have no right to own land; they have no security of land tenure and little incentive to produce above mere subsistence levels. The consequence is the persistence of famine, whether under Imperial, Derg, or EPRDF governments. Under the emperor, peasants were deprived of their production by a feudal system; under the Derg and EPRDF, state ownership was substituted, continuing the disincentive to produce. (The government argues that if land were privatized before industrial growth has

Ethiopia

occurred, peasants would sell their holdings and move to the cities where they would be unable to find employment.)

Ethiopian economic development focuses on the necessity of increasing agricultural production. More than a million people died of starvation between 1984 and 1990. Since 1992 the government has established a series of grain storehouses to be better prepared when drought and famine occur. Without this advanced planning, the death toll from reoccurring drought and famine would be significantly greater. Though most Ethiopians usually produce enough food to support themselves, distributing and commercializing any excess faces difficulties. Most farmers live at least a half a day from a usable road.

Transportation inefficiencies, storage, and handling costs make product delivery in state-controlled agriculture slow and costly. It takes, for example, 20 to 30 days for a sack of grain to go from producer to consumer, instead of the two to three days it takes to cover the distance.

As part of a food security program, the government has plans for major infrastructure developments of both transportation and dams. The World Bank is providing financing and at least 12 international construction firms, many of them Chinese, have bid on the projects that will focus on farm-to-market or feeder roads.

The government also has ambitious plans to develop irrigation agriculture. Since water management and increased electricity are essential for both agricultural and industrial development, the government plans to complete seven hydroelectric dams on the Blue Nile in the next five years. The dams would increase the present 340 megawatts electric-generating capacity of the country to 713 megawatts. Such proposals are viewed by Egypt, well downstream, but utterly dependent on the flow of Nile waters from the Ethiopian highlands, with the greatest concern.

The birthplace of coffee, Ethiopia is Africa's leading coffee exporter. The crop once accounted for 65% of the country's foreign exchange earnings. (Nearly one million families are dependent on coffee for their income. Another 15 million households benefit indirectly from coffee sales.) The international coffee market is glutted as a consequence of new entrants into the market, however, and prices have plummeted.

Starbucks and the government settled a trademark dispute in May 2007; Ethiopia will secure rights to three coffee names—Harar, Sidamo, and Yirgacheffe—through the U.S. Patent and Trademark Office. Oxfam International, the British NGO, estimated the agreement might worth as much as $100 million a year to Ethiopia.

Coffee farmers disappointed by diminishing world prices have turned to growing *khat*, a shrub whose leaves have a psychotropic effect when chewed. Already a valuable traditional export to neighboring Djibouti and Somalia, the rewards of *khat* production are lucrative. Income from *khat* is often five times higher than coffee, and it can be harvested twice a year. Oxfam has warned that within ten years Ethiopia's coffee growing areas may be fully converted to fields of *khat* to meet the massive demand for the drug in East Africa and the Middle East.

Ethiopia is estimated to have 75 million head of livestock, the largest concentration in Africa. Its pastoralists face multiple afflictions. Regional diseases, like Rift Valley fever, can completely shut down a market when traditional buyers, like Saudi Arabia and the Gulf states, prohibit import of East African livestock. Persistent cycles of drought decimate herds, while those animals that survive bring less than optimal prices. Hides and skins remain important export items for Ethiopia, second only to coffee.

Despite drought, famine, and border warfare, about 200,000 tourists still come to Ethiopia every year, so attractive are its landscape and cultural treasures. The country has seven UNESCO World Heritage sites, and its paleontological remains are probably the most famous in the world. China has made Ethiopia one of eight African countries "approved" as a destination for Chinese tourists—little surprising since the country is one of its principal points of penetration into the continent.

Since 1998, when an agreement to foster investment relations between the two countries was signed, the government has been unrelenting in its efforts to attract Chinese investment. More than 70 companies have been granted operating licenses. Manufacturers are producing goods ranging from pharmaceuticals to construction materials like iron and cement. Chinese businesses are involved in textiles, electricity, and mining, as well as major infrastructure projects from roads to hydroelectric dams and their associated irrigation projects. In March 2006 the Chinese company, Zhongyuan Petroleum Exploration Bureau, began its first oil exploration well in the Gambella basin of western Ethiopia. Zhongyuan employees working an oil field in the Ogaden region were attacked in May 2007 by unidentified gunmen; 74 people were killed, nine of them Chinese. The government blamed the ONLF.

Government efforts to deal with the AIDS pandemic have proved ineffective. In April 2000 President Negaso Gidada publicly admitted that the AIDS pandemic had spread to rural areas. Official figures are ominous. About three million people

are living with HIV/AIDS, and the Health Ministry estimates that another 1,000 people are infected daily. The infection kills at least 600 every day and has already orphaned five million children. Caring for orphans costs $115 million a month in a country with an annual health budget of only $140 million.

AIDS is greater threat than the periodic famines which receive much greater international attention. Ethiopia has the third largest population of people living with HIV/AIDS in the world. The HIV infection rate has reached the critical level of 10% of the sexually active population—those between the ages of 15 and 49. At that point economic growth begins to be impacted. The disease has already contributed to lowering life expectancy in Ethiopia—from 45 years in 1990 to 42.7 years in 2005.

Following years of drought and rural famine, Ethiopia is facing an explosion of urban growth as rural families migrate to cities. Urban expansion is increasing at around 6% a year and Addis Ababa, the capital, now has a population of some four million, making it one of the largest cities in sub-Saharan Africa.

The Future

The Meles Zenawi regime has not found adequate ways to accommodate dissent, and dissenters themselves seem intolerant of dialogue. Future growth prospects are limited by weak infrastructure and other structural difficulties, including the continuing possibility of drought and food shortages.

Some of Ethiopia's greatest contemporary challenges are in international relations. Conflict with Eritrea is an omnipresent concern, with 2008 seeming to bring the two countries back once again to the brink of war. Such conflict, should it recur, would inevitably divert scarce economic resources to the military action. Similarly, the Ethiopian presence in Somalia has been eliminated, though the country must remain wary of events in the sadly failed state to its south and east.

Ethiopia is not fully democratic, but there have been signs in recent years that the regime is allowing for some limited degree of political autonomy. The ethno-federal arrangement in Ethiopia enables regions of the country to act with some autonomy from the central government. This has generated the pressures from secessionist movements that threaten to compromise the territorial integrity of the country. The combination of economic challenges and political uncertainty present Ethiopia with a range of major social problems. The hope is that an eventual demilitarization of political life will make some degree of economic investment possible.

The Republic of Kenya

Modern Nairobi   Photo by Bev Klein

Basic Facts

Area: 582,750 sq. km. = 225,000 sq. mi. (larger than twice the size of Nevada)

Population: 34,300,000 (UN 2007 est.)

Capital City: Nairobi

Climate: Hot and dry in the area from the Tana River to the north and northeast; hot and dry, but with a short rainy season in the southeast area below the Tana River; temperate and usually moist in the central highlands and southwestern grassy plains, with two wet seasons.

Neighboring Countries: Tanzania (south, southwest); Uganda (west); Sudan (northwest); Ethiopia (north); Somali Republic (northeast)

Official Languages: KiSwahili, English

Other Principal Languages: More than 60 languages are spoken. Prominently: Borana, Digo, Duruma, Embu, Gikuyu, Giryama, Gusii, Kalenjin, Kamba, Logooli, Luo, Luyia, Maasai, Meru, Pökoot, Saamia, Taita, Teso, and Turkana

Ethnic Groups: Kikuyu 22%, Luhya 14%, Luo 13%, Kalenjin 12%, Kamba 11%, Kisii 6%, Meru 6%, and other African 15%. Non-African (Asian, European, and Arab) 1%

Principal Religions: Protestant 45%, Roman Catholic 33%, indigenous beliefs 10%, Muslim 10%, other 2%

Chief Commercial Products: Tea, flowers, coffee, and refined petroleum products

GNI Per Capita: $530 (World Bank 2006 est.)

Currency: Kenya shilling

Former Colonial Status: British Protectorate (1895–1963).

Independence Date: December 12, 1963.

Chief of State: Mwai Kibaki, President (since December 2002)

National Flag: Three horizontal stripes of black, red and green separated by narrow white stripes; a shield with two crossed spears is in the center.

Land and People

Lying immediately below the heart of Africa on the east coast, Kenya extends from the Indian Ocean to the lake region of East Africa. North of the winding Tana River, there is an arid countryside that slowly rises to the southern mountains of Ethiopia. About 75% of the country is arid or semiarid, similar to the type of land found in the Somali Republic. Nomadic pastoralists, like the Pokot, tend their herds in the eastern regions and make frequent cross-border raids into Uganda.

South of the Tana River, the coastline is hot and oppressively humid; this is the only part of Kenya that is truly tropical. This gives way immediately to thorn bush country of gently rising land extending about 175 miles from the coast.

The south-central portion of Kenya is a beautiful land of high plateaus stretching between the mountains. Mount Kenya, in this area, reaches a height of 17,040 feet 80 miles north of Nairobi. The Gregory Rift, extending in an almost straight line to the south from Lake Rudolf, is an immense trench almost 3,000 feet lower than the mountains that enclose it.

From the western side of these rift formations, the land slowly descends to the shores of Lake Victoria. The cool climate of the southeastern and south-central areas is invigorating—though the Equator divides these regions from northern Kenya, the climate is temperate because of the altitude. These are normally fertile lands; it

is frequently possible in many sections to harvest two crops each year. Intermittent droughts, however, affect both productivity and hydroelectric potential. Given the limited availability of arable land, those droughts have also caused significant migration from the countryside to urban centers.

Kenyans felt enormous pride in October 2004 when the Norwegian parliament awarded the Nobel Peace Prize to environmentalist and human rights campaigner Wangari Maathai. She became the first African woman to win the prize since it was initiated in 1901, and only one of seven persons from the continent to be so honored (Albert Schweitzer: 1952; Albert Lutuli: 1960; Anwar Sadat: 1978; Desmond Tutu: 1984; Nelson Mandela and Fredrik de Klerk: 1993, preceded her).

From the late 1970s she led the "Green Belt Movement," which mobilized poor women throughout the continent to replant millions of trees to slow deforestation and desertification. In Kenya, she was long a political activist who challenged the regime of Daniel arap Moi when its policies, often saturated with corrupt practices, threatened Kenya's natural resources of parks and animals and forests. For her labors she was frequently beaten and jailed.

The Past: Political and Economic History

For early history, see *Historical Background* and *The Colonial Period: The British*.

The years leading up to Kenyan independence saw Kenya became the first East African colony to include an African on its legislative council in 1944. At almost the same time the Kenyan African Union (KAU) was created to campaign for better lands and independence for Africans. In 1947 the group chose as its leader Jomo Kenyatta, a prominent Kikuyu activist who had recently returned from a long

211

Kenya

residence in Europe. As noted in the chapter on colonial history, a Kikuyu-led secret society, the Mau Mau, launched a guerrilla campaign against white farmers in 1952. The revolt had its origins in the land issue and was specifically directed against European land ownership. When Kenya became a British crown colony, Africans were dispossessed from their lands, leaseholds were restricted to white settlers, and a "White-Highlands" policy herded the Kikuyu onto overcrowded reserves. The Mau Mau insurgency terrorized Kenya for nearly five years. During the "emergency" declared by the government, defense forces killed over 13,500 Africans, mostly Kikuyu; the Mau Mau killed some 100 Europeans.

Suspected of directing the Mau Mau, Jomo Kenyatta and nearly 100 other Africans were arrested immediately after the proclamation of the state of emergency. KAU was banned and its leaders charged with causing disorder or inciting other persons to cause disorder. In April 1953 Kenyatta was sentenced to a seven-year imprisonment for "managing the Mau Mau terrorist organization."

Following suppression of the Mau Mau insurgency in 1956, the British government gradually steered the country toward African majority rule. African membership on the legislative council was increased, and Africans were offered ministerial posts. In 1960 the principle of one man, one vote was conceded, and KAU, which had done so much to move Kenya to independence, split along largely ethnic lines. Tom Mboya and Oginga Odinga formed the Kenya African National Union (KANU) with a strong Kikuyu and Luo membership. In opposition to the Kikuyu/Luo grouping, Kenya African Democratic Union (KADU) was created to represent smaller tribes—Luhya and others—who feared domination by larger ones. Ethnic division would be a continuing characteristic of Kenyan politics.

KANU elected Kenyatta (still detained even after having completed his sentence) its president *in absentia*. He was finally released in August 1961 and negotiated the arrangements that led to Kenya's independence in 1963. May 1963 elections resulted in an overwhelming victory for Kenyatta and KANU. As part of Kenyatta's ethnic balancing, Oginga Odinga, a Luo, became vice president. A year later, following intense political lobbying and negotiation, KANU and KADU merged.

Odinga, very much to the political left, became increasingly disillusioned with the KANU government, which, he felt, had abandoned the socialist principles that had brought it to power. He advocated a ceiling on the amount of land that could be owned by any one individual—500 acres, but this unsettled white farmers and KANU elites who had begun to accumulate property. The party closed ranks to divest itself of a troublesome critic. The assault was organized by a fellow Luo and founder of KANU, Tom Mboya. Odinga resigned the vice presidency, talking darkly of "international forces concerned with the ideological colonization of the country." The government's guiding star, he asserted, had become "personal gain."

The ideological rift led to Odinga's expulsion from KANU and his formation of a left-wing opposition party, the Kenya Peoples' Union (KPU). Elections in 1966 gave an overwhelming majority to KANU; Odinga's Kenya People's Union won only a handful of seats. The KANU government nevertheless did all in its power to suppress KPU. Its opportunity came in 1969 when the most prominent Luo in the government, Tom Mboya, was assassinated on the verge of presidential and parliamentary elections.

While touring the Luo heartland, President Kenyatta encountered crowds of anti-government demonstrators. When his bodyguards fired on hostile, but scarcely violent, Luo demonstrators, several were killed and many wounded. Odinga was blamed, his KPU party banned, and he himself placed under house arrest.

With Odinga out of the picture, there was no one to oppose Kenyatta. He was reelected unopposed. The 1969 general election also gave birth to the single-chamber legislature in which KANU held overwhelming dominance. Kenya had become a *de facto* single-party state.

Kenyatta was reelected again in 1974 and died in office in 1978, when he was succeeded by his vice president, Daniel arap Moi (pronounced moy). President Moi won his own term of office in the 1979 elections, and KANU officially made Kenya a single-party state in 1982. An attempted air force coup in August the same year was quickly suppressed, but strong Luo involvement further marginalized Odinga and his Luo supporters. Odinga's son, Raila, was detained for alleged involvement in the plot. President Moi disbanded the air force and closed the University in Nairobi where student supporters of the coup were numerous.

Early elections were called by KANU and held in September 1983. Unopposed, Moi was reelected president. He proceeded to govern an ethnically divided Kenya with authoritarian firmness. Urban Kikuyus of Nairobi charged him with cronyism as he appointed fellow Kalenjin tribesmen to lucrative government positions. The secret ballot was abolished in favor of a "queuing" system where people have to publicly line up according to their political preferences. This led to intimidation and widespread election fraud. Voter participation plummeted; in some districts there was only a 20% turnout, down from the former 90%.

The International Monetary Fund indicated that Kenyans owned $2.62 billion in overseas bank accounts, a mere hint of Kenya's massive corruption. Corruption charges resulted not in reform, but rather in a crackdown on dissent. Many government critics fled the country. In 1990 six opposition leaders, including an aging Oginga Odinga, formed the Forum for the Restoration of Democracy (FORD) to lobby for democratic change. FORD

Maasai woman seated before a traditional plastered structure

Photo by Lance Fuchs

Kenya

Kenyan mother and children

Photo by Mary Ellen Grabski

brought together Luo, Kikuyu and Luhya in common opposition to KANU's single-party monopoly. A massive demonstration in Nairobi in late 1991, punctuated with cries of "peace" and "democracy" was met with tear gas and riot batons. The government dismissed the participants as agitators and anarchists.

Further protest came from international aid agencies—the International Monetary Fund, the World Bank and several creditor nations—all of which cut off money destined for Kenya. This was more than the Moi regime could stand; quietly, provisions for multiparty elections in 1992 were made. Parliament repealed the one-party section of the constitution, several new parties were allowed to form, and multiparty elections were scheduled for December 1992.

To protect KANU, and his own tenure, Moi immediately embarked on a course intended to divide (and conquer). The opposition cooperatively split among themselves; this included division within the ranks of FORD, which had initially transcended traditional tribal rivalries. In August 1992 it split into two factions: FORD-Asili, led by a Kikuyu, Kenneth Matiba, and FORD-Kenya, led by Odinga, a Luo.

The election period was characterized by widespread ethnic tension and violence, deliberately manipulated by politicians. It was particularly virulent in the Rift Valley province. Hundreds were killed and thousands of potential voters were disenfranchised when forced to flee their homes. Young Kalenjin and Maasai were recruited into gangs to terrorize sus-

pected supporters of the opposition—primarily members of the Kikuyu, Luhya and Kamba tribes. Their property was looted, their homes set afire, and if they did not flee, their lives were forfeited. Their lands were subsequently occupied by government supporters—the wages of violence.

For added insurance, KANU legislators pushed through a constitutional amendment providing that a presidential candidate, to be elected, must win at least 25% of the vote in five of Kenya's seven districts. Since he and his Kalenjin tribesmen controlled the western mountain district and other areas through political patronage, this virtually assured that none of his three principal opponents stood a chance. When the votes were tallied, Moi won a mere 36% of the vote, but earned another five-year term.

In the legislature, things were more realistic. KANU elected 95 delegates to 88 for the opposition. Riots broke out on opening day in 1993; Moi simply dissolved the legislature rather than face such vocal opposition, the first in a decade. The International Monetary Fund, infuriated by the printing of special shillings to finance KANU's effort in the election, imposed more rigid conditions on future loans.

The regime's severest critic, Oginga Odinga, died in 1994. His son, Raila, lost the struggle for leadership of FORD-Kenya, left the party and formed the National Democratic Party (NDP), which became a principal voice for the opposition.

The December 1997 elections reproduced the whole dreary cycle of violence,

conflict, repression, and lost opportunities. Candidates and human rights workers were harassed and intimidated. Members of the thuggish KANU youth wing and security forces blocked meetings and rallies. Once again opposition parties failed to unite behind a single candidate—another continuing feature of Kenyan politics; their appeals were tribal rather than national. Moi was reelected by winning a mere 40% of the popular vote and the required 25% of the votes cast in five of the now eight provinces. His majority in parliament was razor thin. KANU emerged with only 109 out of 222 seats.

The 1997 elections were held in an environment of uncertainty. In July the International Monetary Fund (IMF) refused to lend any longer to Kenya, largely because corruption was so blatant it was constricting economic growth. Confirming the IMF's concern, the Commissioner-General of Kenya's Revenue Authority stunned the nation by disclosing that the country annually lost $1.68 billion through corruption.

President Moi responded by declaring war on corruption and creating the Kenya Anti-Corruption Authority (KACA). Corrupt bureaucrats were reportedly gripped by panic, but remained calm enough to bring legal action against KACA. In December 2000 a three-judge constitutional court ruled the Authority illegal, setting off alarm bells within the donor community, which already knew the judiciary to be one of the most corrupt of Kenya's numerous corrupt institutions.

As part of a calculated set of responses to impress the IMF, Moi also appointed Richard Leakey, a well-known critic of Kenyan politics, to head its civil service. Leakey, part of the world-famous paleontology family, was a long-time friend of World Bank President James Wolfensohn, and his appointment achieved its desired goal. The IMF resumed lending to Kenya in July 2000, but with the strictest of conditions.

These required enactment of anticorruption and economic crimes bills, and ethics legislation requiring public officials to declare their wealth and liabilities. Another condition required weekly IMF inspections of the Central Bank of Kenya accounts. The conditions were humiliating, but, given the pervasive depth of corruption in Kenya, essential.

Leakey's tenure as head of Kenya's civil service was brief—less than two years—but long enough to ruffle lots of feathers. He resigned in March 2001, and almost simultaneously the IMF stopped its lending to Kenya, citing "serious setbacks" to the fight against corruption.

President Moi announced that he would step down at the end of his term in 2002

Kenya

President Mwai Kibaki

and made a number of changes to prepare KANU for the next set of elections. Speaking of the need for "new blood," he appointed the opposition leader Raila Odinga (Oginga Odinga's son) to his cabinet, forming Kenya's first coalition government in June 2001. (Odinga had been imprisoned without trial by Moi for eight years following the attempted coup in 1982.) In October, the president appointed Jomo Kenyatta's son, Uhuru Kenyatta to parliament; this was rapidly followed by a cabinet post for Kenyatta.

KANU voted to absorb Odinga's smaller National Democratic Party (NDP) in March 2002, revolutionizing Kenyan politics by co-opting the opposition. The NDP leader, Raila Odinga, was unanimously chosen the new party's general-secretary. Four so-called Young Turks were chosen as vice presidents. The most prominent was Uhuru Kenyatta, clearly President Moi's favorite. President Moi was named chairman of KANU, with extraordinary powers that made him a virtual one-man party.

The president then forced the selection of his chosen successor: Uhuru Kenyatta, a young and politically inexperienced businessman, but a Kikuyu and bearer of a name worth its weight in political gold. Kenyatta's selection was an olive branch to Kenya's largest tribe, largely marginalized over the past 24 years. Whatever electoral advantage might have come of this, however, was offset by the divisions the decision created in KANU.

Party barons and stalwarts defected in droves and marched into opposition. Led by Raila Odinga, they formed the "Rainbow Coalition" to incorporate all shades and hues of opposition. In October Rainbow merged with the Liberal Democratic Party (LDP), while 13 other opposition parties, representing a variety of regions

and all Kenya's major tribes, coalesced to form the National Alliance Party of Kenya (NAK). In short order NAK merged with LDP to form a super alliance known as the National Rainbow Coalition (NARC). United, they agreed on a single candidate to oppose KANU's Kenyatta: Mwai Kibaki, also a Kikuyu.

At 71, Kibaki had already had a long political career. A founder of KANU, he had spent the last decade trying to drive it from office. An economist, he served as finance minister for both Jomo Kenyatta and Daniel Moi (1969–1982), and then as Moi's vice president, until removed in 1988. Three years later he formed his own party and unsuccessfully ran for president in the shamefully violent and rigged elections of 1992 and 1997. The third time would prove the charm.

In December 2002 KANU faced a virtually united opposition. (There were three other minor candidates.) Voters gave Mwai Kibaki a convincing victory: 62.2% of the vote to Kenyatta's 31.3%. If anything sustained coalitions and motivated voters, it was a common hostility to Daniel arap Moi and his family and friends, many of whom had richly profited from his long tenure in office. Candidate Kibaki had made corruption and economic revitalization principal planks in his campaign.

Kibaki's National Rainbow Coalition (NARC) won 125 of the 210 elected seats in parliament against KANU's 64. The new government moved quickly to deal with corruption. President Kibaki appointed an anticorruption czar, John Githongo, a young journalist who had long campaigned against corruption as a newspaper colum-

nist. A number of anticorruption commissions were organized, with quick results. By the end of 2003 half of Kenya's most senior judges—23 in all—had been suspended after an anticorruption commission had gathered evidence against them. Results were less apparent on a new constitution.

Wrangling over a new constitution has been going on for over five years. President Kibaki promised a document within 100 days of his election, but that was not to be. At stake were interests that focused on efforts to curtail presidential powers and create the office of prime minister. Kibaki loyalists, among them a cabal of fellow Kikuyus, wanted the presidency to retain its enormous powers. Supporters of Raila Odinga were furious that the president and his minions reneged on an alleged pre-campaign pact that promised the premiership to Odinga.

The issue split the NARC coalition, with Kibaki's National Alliance Party (NAP) and Odinga's Liberal Democratic Party (LDP) pulling in different directions. The cabinet was permanently divided; Kenyans took to the streets to protest delay with such vehemence that riot police have had to intervene with tear gas and batons to control (and create) violence.

When the courts ruled the new constitution could not be simply adopted by parliament, but required a referendum, the two sides coalesced. Those supporting the government's 200-page draft constitution chose the banana as their symbol (to aid illiterate voters). Their opponents chose the orange, and Kenya's fruit bowl was off and running. MPs slugged it out with each other; at least 24 people were

Nairobi slums, overrun with plastic bags

214

killed in protests, and the cabinet was so badly divided it barely met.

Orange campaigners effectively argued the draft created a stronger presidency and was designed to secure the political dominance of Kikuyu elites. When Kenyans went to the polls in November 2005, they handed top banana Mwai Kibaki a humiliating defeat. The constitutional draft was rejected by 57% of the voters.

There has not been as decisive a resolution of the issue of corruption. In July 2004 the British high commissioner to Kenya, the United Kingdom's highest ranking diplomat, used blunt language to articulate concern and contempt for the slow pace of Kenya's anticorruption campaign. Speaking to a group of British businessmen, Ambassador Edward Clay said that corruption had cost Kenya some $188 million just since President Kibaki took office in December 2002. Corrupt ministers, he went on, were "eating like gluttons" and "vomiting on the shoes of donors." Overall, he noted, corruption accounted for about 8% of Kenya's total GDP.

It was not as though President Kibaki was unaware. His anticorruption czar, John Githongo, had opened several dossiers dealing with fraudulent contracts signed by the Moi government and honored by Kibaki's. Representing an alliance of business and party interests, the contracts were typically signed with shell companies that provided nonexistent services to the government. Monies paid on the contracts were channeled back into party treasuries to grease the machinery of electoral campaigning. The president was duly briefed on his findings, but seemed to do little. Githongo's investigations named names and stepped on toes. After receiving death threats, he fled to England in February 2005.

Living in exile, he sent a 36-page summary of his findings to both the president and the Kenya Anti-Corruption Commission (KACC) in November. Hearing from neither, he sent a copy to one of Kenya's most prominent newspapers, the *Daily Nation*, and the whole sordid mess unfolded in public print. "Grand Larceny Routine Since 1963," the paper headlined in early February 2006, pretty well summarizing Kenya's massive corruption.

The two most outrageous scandals are the Goldenberg and the Anglo Leasing affairs. The Goldenberg scandal, which took place in the early 1990s during the presidency of Daniel arap Moi, involved fictitious gold and diamond exports; losses amounted to some $600 million. Top officials were implicated, including Moi and several of his ministers, but none have been prosecuted. (The Kenyan businessman who is alleged to be the plot's mastermind and four others, including President Moi's chief of intelligence, have been charged with a variety of offenses linked to the alleged theft of about $100 million.)

In 2003 President Kibaki's government announced it had contracted with Kroll Associates, international forensic accountants, to find money plundered by members of the former regime. Less than a year later Kroll reported that it had traced almost a billion dollars to banks in Switzerland, Luxembourg, Austria, the Netherlands, Italy, the United Kingdom, and the Gulf States. A more recent study by the Kenya branch of Transparency International asserts that the country loses $1.2 billion annually to graft.

The problem that President Kibaki has utterly failed to deal with was articulated by John Githongo: the networks of corrupt officials and business people that thrived under Daniel Arap Moi continued to operate. The Anglo Leasing scandal illustrates the case. A fictitious company, Anglo Leasing and Finance Limited was awarded contracts to supply a system for producing passports that could not be forged. Millions of dollars were paid to the firm before the scam was detected in 2004. It was, however, one among many such fake companies, and certainly not the first, but has now lent its name to describe the fraud generically. The "Anglo Leasing" investigations have covered contracts signed by both KANU and NARC governments.

In October 2006 the Kenya Anti-Corruption Commission (KACC) recommended prosecution of four former cabinet ministers in connection with $300 million worth of faulty Anglo Leasing contracts. The four investigative reports were forwarded to Attorney General Amos Wako for prosecution, but he found them wanting, sent them back to the KACC, and effectively postponed any prosecution until after elections in 2007.

Kibaki announced his intention to run for a second term in 2007. NARC, the political coalition that brought him electoral success long ago fragmented, but reformulated as NARC-Kenya and clearly supportive of the president, the party has been successful in recent by-elections. Despite his abject failure to deal with the corruption problem, Kibaki seemed better positioned for the election than any of his potential rivals in mid-2007. He could justifiably claim some economic success and wins plaudits for eliminating fees for primary school children. (Parents still have to bear the cost of books, transportation and school supplies.) Kibaki also benefited from division within the opposition, but reelection was far from secure.

Potential opponents to Kibaki briefly coalesced in the Orange Democratic Movement, which included opposition leaders Uhuru Kenyatta (of KANU), Raila Odinga (formerly of the LDP), and another rival, Kalonzo Musyoka. By mid-2007, the Odinga and Musyoka factions had split the ODM into two pieces (the ODM under Odinga and the ODM-Kenya under Musyoka). Kenyatta split away from the ODM coalition and decided to back the incumbent Kibaki, as did former president and erstwhile Kibaki opponent Daniel arap Moi.

The split in the opposition seemed to advantage Kibaki and his coalition Party of National Unity (PNU) as the December elections approached, but the polling between the sitting president and Raila

A class in Nairobi

Kenya

Wangari Maathai, Noble Peace Prize winner

Odinga proved quite close, and through much of the fall of 2007 Odinga held a lead. After the elections, Kibaki claimed victory and was backed in his claim by the Electoral Commission, but there were widespread allegations of electoral improprieties that lit a fuse under Kenya's volatile political system.

Violent clashes broke out across the country in the wake of the election results. Thousands were displaced and well over 1,000 killed in the ensuing months. Ominously for the future, the clash took on clear ethnic overtones (with Kibaki having drawn support from Kenya's traditionally dominant Kikuyu, while Odinga's support came from the Luo, as well as the Kalenjin and other smaller ethnic groups).

As the situation threatened to deteriorate into something approaching civil war, Kibaki and Odinga narrowly managed to pull it back from the brink with an unlikely power-sharing agreement: Kibaki would retain the presidency, but Odinga would be placed in the reinstated position of prime minister, a position abolished back in 1964 under founding father Jomo Kenyatta.

President Kibaki and Odinga presided over a 40-member grand coalition cabinet that included Vice President Kalonzo Musyoka, and Uhuru Kenyatta and Musalia Mudavadi as new deputy prime ministers. While the composition of the cabinet has held, the tenuous nature of the power-sharing agreement came to light in 2009 when Odinga accused Kibaki of sidelining the ODM. Odinga threatened to boycott future cabinet meetings, thereby generating a crisis of government. The resolution of the dispute is still unclear as this edition goes to press.

The Present: Contemporary Issues

Alongside the political system, the AIDS pandemic is one of Kenya's greatest di-lemmas. Cultural patterns and behaviors long facilitated its progress, but new political leadership has been key to reducing the secrecy and stigma that once surrounded the disease. In November 1999 President Moi declared the disease a "national disaster," but three years later so little had been done UNICEF called it a "national crisis" and made desperate appeals to politicians to make AIDS part of the election agenda.

The Kibaki government has adopted a more public and activist stance. The president himself has described AIDS as the "greatest threat" to the country and urged all Kenyans to be tested for the HIV virus. His government has made AIDS education compulsory, even at primary school level; a shift in attitude and practice seems to have occurred. In December 2004 the government optimistically announced that the HIV/AIDs infection rate had dropped from 14% to about 7%, and that public awareness of the disease had increased to an estimated 90% nationwide.

From one of the world's highest HIV/AIDS infection rates, then, notable declines have begun to be seen. In part, of course, this is attributable to the deaths of many living with HIV/AIDS, but it also suggests a slowing of the rates of infection. There were about 2.5 million people living with the disease in 2000; four years later it was 1.4 million. The death toll, once staggering, has begun to slow. (Government policy receives little support from Luci Kibaki, Kenya's first lady, who has told students that young people had "no business" using condoms.)

Well over 1.5 million Kenyans had already died of AIDS by the end of 2004. Their deaths have left roughly 1.8 million AIDS orphans. Gender disparities in the infection's distribution are enormous: twice as many women as men suffer the disease. To make matters worse, in the 15 to 24-year-old category, the number of infected women is four times that of men. The rapid spread of AIDS among Kenya's women reflects fundamental economic and cultural realities. Rural poverty has driven young girls, children really, to the cities where the best job they can find is child care. Their salary is $10 to $15 a month. Since this is insufficient to provide for family needs at home, many turn to prostitution.

It is encouraging to note that several Nairobi pharmaceutical companies are now producing high quality generic AIDS drugs, and the Health Ministry has begun to place orders. Pregnant women, rape victims, and hospital inpatients have first priority.

Although officially outlawed in 2001, Female Genital Cutting (FGC) remains deeply embedded in traditional cultures, including the Maasai. According to a 1998 survey, 38% of women between the ages of 15 and 49 were estimated to have undergone FGC. In the most basic form of the practice, the covering of the clitoris is removed; among the Maasai, the practice involves cutting away the entire clitoris, together with the labia majora and labia minora. A Maasai girl traditionally undergoes FGC upon before she is married, which can be quite young. A rite of passage marking the transition from childhood to adult status, the operation is expected to be endured in silence. To cry would be a sign of childish weakness.

Having meager mineral resources, the economy of Kenya has traditionally rested on agriculture and tourism. Prior to 1979 Kenya was relatively prosperous—at least for the clique of politicians and businessmen who controlled the nation's wealth. A series of economic shocks—a spike in oil prices, drought, crop failure, and famine—increased borrowing and aid dependency. Government corruption siphoned off far too much of what was received, and the economy declined for years.

International donors insistently pressured President Moi to introduce economic liberalization, end corruption, and begin greater transparency in government. In July 1997, when the government refused to meet reform commitments made earlier, the IMF refused any further loans. The IMF suspension sent the mismanaged economy into steep decline, from which it made little improvement. Growth was minimal until 2005 when one began to see the consequences of changed policy, and Kenya reported GDP growth of 5.8%. Growth in 2006 was 6.1%, the highest growth rate in three decades. Much of this has been attributed to the revival of agriculture and the growth of related sectors like agribusiness.

Despite a seemingly robust economy, growth does not necessarily or immediately translate into improved life situations for ordinary Kenyans. Social statistics all indicate that Kenyans are worse off today than they were at independence. Infant mortality for under-five-year-olds rose from 74 per thousand in 1992 to 120 in 2005; life expectancy is only 49 years. The UN's *Human Development Index* ranked Kenya 152 out of 177 countries in 2006; at the end of the 1980s, it placed 90th. Almost 23% of Kenya's population lives on less than one dollar a day, and 58% on less than two dollars a day. Experts estimate that it would take an annual growth rate of 10% for a decade before ordinary people can begin to feel the impact.

Kenya remains fundamentally an agricultural country. It is the major source of income for the bulk of the population, employing well over 80% of rural inhabitants. Despite its scale, agriculture contributes only 27.4% of GDP (2005). An acute shortage of arable land, and uneven distribution of that which is, has meant that most farmers work plots of less than five acres.

Tea has been one focus of the government's attention; fortunately for the industry, that attention has provided support without interference. It's one of the economy's success stories. Kenya is now the world's second largest exporter of black tea. Liberalization of the market and favorable climatic conditions have pro-

duced bumper crops. The tea sector employs over two million people across the country, but the industry is threatened by the expansion of Chinese tea growing.

Kenya's coffee industry has been similarly impacted by expanded coffee production in Asia, but the industry is much more highly regulated than tea and has suffered more. Small producers are forced to be members of "cooperative societies" in order to be able to sell the produce and these have suffered chronic mismanagement and corruption. The result has been that farmers have often not been paid for their produce.

Flower growing is the fastest growing part of Kenya's agricultural sector, in part because it has less government regulation and interference. Since the early 1990s flower exports have increased around 20% per year. Kenya is now the EU's biggest source of cut flower imports—principally roses (74%) and carnations. Flower growing now surpasses coffee and probably tourism as a source of foreign exchange, and is only second to tea as an income producer. Most flower farms are located in rural areas and thus have considerable impact on both the local population and environment. Cultivation is relatively labor intensive, requiring about 200 workers for 15 acres. The workers, mostly women, earn about $1.50 per day, and the industry indirectly supports an estimated

500,000 people. There is increasing concern about the environmental and health impact of fertilizers and agricultural chemicals used by growers. Doctors report growing cases of bronchitis and breathing problems, severe headaches, loss of hair, and chest pains attributed to industry chemicals.

With beautiful beaches, abundant wildlife and a well-organized system of national parks, Kenya has long been a favorite tourist destination. Contributing about 12% of the economy, spending by tourists has been one of Kenya's most important foreign exchange earners. The industry directly employs a reported 300,000 people, while another 200,000 work in sectors that benefit from it. Since 1998, however, the industry has been undermined by Islamist terrorism.

In 1998 the U.S. embassies in both Kenya and Tanzania were simultaneously bombed in al-Qaeda attacks, killing 224 people. On November 28, 2002, an Israeli-owned hotel near the port city of Mombasa was bombed by a group of suicide attackers, only a few minutes after an Israeli airliner escaped two missiles fired as it was taking off from Mombasa airport. In each case Kenya's hotels and resorts subsequently experienced huge cancellations of reservations. In Mombasa, a leading Imam, Sheikh Ali Shee, explicitly warned American and Israeli tourists to

High above the plain

Photo by Bev Klein

217

Kenya

stay away. "There is an undeclared war between their countries and the Muslim world," he said. "It is not good for them to come until the [Palestinian] problem is solved." It will be some time before the industry achieves its goal of bringing two million tourists a year to Kenya.

As western tourists look elsewhere, some slack is being taken up by Chinese tourists. China granted Kenya "Preferred Destination Status" in 2004 and since then Chinese arrivals have more than doubled. China has also allocated Kenya Airways landing rights in several Chinese cities; direct flights between the two countries are expected to increase the number of Chinese visitors.

Chinese President Hu Jintao visited Kenya in late April 2006, and at the conclusion of his tour several commercial agreements were signed. Potentially the most important was an oil-exploration deal that allowed China National Offshore Oil Corporation to explore off Kenya's Indian Ocean coast. The total area open to exploration is 44,534 square miles; access to the area is reportedly free, with payment to be made only if reserves are discovered.

Kenya is also betting on being a regional leader in information technology. The initial public offering of shares in Safaricom, a mobile phone service provider, generated a frenzy in Kenya in 2008, with reports of many citizens making their first ever equity investments by grabbing up single shares of the fashionable stock. Safaricom is a world leader in extending banking services to the poor in rural areas using transfers via mobile phone, an innovation that has the potential to alleviate poverty and spur economic growth. While it is unwise to be overly optimistic about the applications of technology and their consequences for African societies, Kenya does offer some insight into the reasons for the enthusiasm. Broadband is also being extended into Kenya, making it a possible hub for much of East and Central Africa.

The Future

Kenya seems to have recovered partially from the deadly clashes between supporters of Mwai Kibaki and supporters of Raila Odinga in early 2008. In a country with a political system long seen as dysfunctional, social instability and spasms of inter-ethnic violence took many

Kenyans and outsiders by surprise. The creative power-sharing agreement between Mwai Kibaki and Raila Odinga is holding, but in tenuous fashion. Power-sharing arrangements are rare (and even more rarely successful) in sub-Saharan African politics, and the difficulties in this arrangement are illustrated by Odinga's recent decision to boycott cabinet meetings. It is unlikely that Kenya's ethnic rivalries and unrest are over.

Economically, the country will inevitably suffer some consequences from the shock to its stability, as well as from the global financial crisis. This is unfortunate under any circumstances, but it seems particularly ill-timed after 2007, when Kenya's growth was estimated at comfortably over 6%, a figure that placed it above the continental average and above the population growth rate. Even with the unrest, there are positive signs, however. These include the recent public offering by Safaricom and the expansion of broadband access through submarine cables under the Indian Ocean, a project that came to fruition in 2009. If political stability can hold, domestic and international capital may increasingly be mobilized in the ways needed to promote development.

Market day in Kenya

The Somali Democratic Republic

Life amid the ruins: soccer in Mogadishu

©Jose Cendo, AFP/Getty Images

Basic Facts

Area: 637,140 sq. km. = 246,000 sq. mi. (slightly larger than Texas)

Population: 9,800,000 of which an estimated 3 million live in Somaliland. (CIA World Fact Book 2009 est.)

Capital City: Mogadishu

Climate: Hot, with scarce and irregular rainfall and frequent droughts.

Neighboring Countries: Djibouti (northwest); Ethiopia (west); Kenya (southwest).

Official Languages: Somali, Arabic

Other Principal Languages: Italian, English

Ethnic Groups: Darod (north-northeast); Hawiya (central area); Rahanwein (South); Ishaak (north central area); all of the foregoing are collectively referred to as Somali (85%); Bantu and other non-Somali 15% (including 30,000 Arabs)

Principal Religion: Sunni Muslim

Chief Commercial Products: Livestock, bananas, hides, and fish

GDP Per Capita: 264$ (CIA World Fact Book, 2008 est.)

Currency: 1 Somali shilling = 100 cents

Former Colonial Status: The north was a British protectorate (1897–1960); the South was an Italian colony (1892–1941); British administration (1941–1949); Italian trust territory (1949–1960).

Independence Date: July 1, 1960

Chief of State: Sheikh Sharif Sheikh Ahmed, (since January 29th), who serves as Transitional Federal President.

National Flag: A five-pointed white star on an azure blue background.

Land and People

The Somali Republic, the easternmost nation of Africa, covers an area often referred to as the *Horn of Africa*; it has a 1,700-mile coastline on the tropical waters of the Gulf of Aden and the Indian Ocean. Although the northern part of the country is hilly, reaching altitudes of 4,000 feet, the larger portion to the south is a flat, semi-arid land, which is uniformly hot. During the "dry season" there is almost no vegetation, and both man and beast wait for the cool of the evening to travel and hunt.

Acacia trees, with their roots reaching far into the land to obtain precious water, spread their umbrella-like foliage, providing what little shade there is in the vacant countryside. Goats and antelope must stand on their hind legs to reach their precious food from these trees.

Like men in Kenya and Ethiopia, Somalis and Somalilanders enjoy the stimulation that comes from chewing *khat*, a shrub whose leaves have a psychotropic effect when chewed. The leaves are imported from Kenya and can cost the user up to five dollars a day, well beyond the average wage in the country. For importers, the profits of the *khat* trade are lucrative, and a number of the luxurious homes going up in Hargeisa, the capital, belong to *khat* traders.

In many ways the supreme cultural achievement of Somalia can be found in its poetry. Oral verse is central to the Somali way of life. It is a means of mass communication, preserving history and shaping contemporary events, expressing personal and public sentiment and experience. Travelers invariably comment on the Somali love of harmonious sound, elaborate image, and alliterative arabesque." Distinguished poets were heard by huge audiences of national radio and showcased by the BBC's Africa Service. Their allusive and metaphoric language confounded the foreign censor and stimulated the nationalist cause. The Somali poetic tradition remains today, not entirely muted by conflict, not entirely destroyed by political repression. So embedded in Somali consciousness is poetry that it is part of the texture and discourse of clan reconciliation meetings, the bedrock of Somali politics. Somalia's first female pop star, Maryam Mursal continues to evoke the Somali poetic tradition with her music.

The Past: Political and Economic History

For early history, see *Historical Background, The Colonial Period: The Italians; The British.*

Modern Somalia is the result of the merger of former British Somaliland and *Somalia Italiana* in 1960. Each came with a different colonial history and experience and those differences are at the heart of modern Somalia's present situation. British Somaliland became independent on June 26, 1960; five days later, on July 1, it joined Italian Somalia to form the Somali Republic. At independence there was no common administrative language. English was spoken in the former British protectorate, Italian in the larger *Somalia Italiana*. Somali, though spoken by all, did not exist as a written language until the 1970s.

The British interest in Somaliland was purely strategic: control of the entrance to the Red Sea and cheap provisions for

Somalia

Aden, its garrison at the tip of the Arabian Peninsula. As a consequence, indirect rule was administratively appropriate. Northern Somalis were left to follow their own customs; traditional procedures for resolving conflicts among nomadic clan groups remained in place. Italy's treatment of Somalia was much different. Southern Somalis were forced to adopt Italian law, and nomad customs, especially traditional mechanisms for conflict resolution between clans, were abolished. Resistance was intense and military confrontation continued to the late 1920s.

From British Somaliland emerged a well-educated elite, while Italy introduced mass education in the south, but at a relatively low level, creating a mass of very nationalistic semi-intellectuals. At unification, then, there was little in common between the two partners save a vague sense of "Somali" identity. To preserve the union, which gave expression to that identity, northerners gave up much. The capital was located in the southern city of Mogadishu. Most of the technical positions in the new government were filled by better-trained northerners, but the bulk of political appointments went to southerners. Political parties proliferated, reflecting the fragmentary nature of Somali clan politics, and at one point Somalia had more parties per capita than any democratic state aside from Israel. (In the last multi-party elections held, March 1969, more than 60 parties competed.)

This multitude of parties also expressed substantial differences in political style and orientation. With a dominant position in parliament, southern nationalists, pro-Arab and militantly pan-Somali, pushed the idea of a "greater Somalia"—a claim on Somali-inhabited areas of neighboring Kenya and Ethiopia. "Modernists," mostly northerners, stressed economic and social development and urged improved relations with other African states. Out of this welter of conflicting tendencies, the Somali Youth League gradually assumed a dominant position, successfully cutting across regional and clan loyalties. And under the leadership of Prime Minister Mohamed Ibrahim Egal (1967–69), a northerner educated at English public schools from Exeter to London, Somalia significantly improved its relations with Kenya and Ethiopia, but its fledgling constitutional democracy was brought to an end in October 1969, when the army and police, led by Maj. General Mohamed Siyad Barré, seized power in a bloodless coup. Prime Minister Egal was thrown in jail where he remained for 12 years.

Siyad Barré was born in the Ogaden area of Ethiopia, an area once part of Italian East Africa but returned by the British to Ethiopia in 1948. Nicknamed

"Afweyne" or "Mighty Mouth" by his fellow herdboys, Siyad later traveled to Mogadishu for what formal education he had and ultimately became a member of the *Polizia Africana Italiana*. He rose within police ranks to become the first Somali commissioned as a full police officer, and by 1960, when Somalia became independent, Siyad won accelerated promotion to the rank of brigadier-general of police. With the formation of the Somali National Army in April 1960, Siyad transferred from police to army as one of its deputy commanders and he was promoted to commander in chief in 1965.

After the coup, Siyad moved quickly to eliminate the institutions and personnel of Somalia's democracy. Important political figures like Prime Minster Egal were detained, the constitution suspended, the National Assembly closed, all parties banned, and the Supreme Court was abolished. The coup-makers designated themselves the Supreme Revolutionary Council (SRC) and assumed full executive and legislative power, concentrated in the hands of Siyad Barré himself. Major-General Mohamed Siyad Barré became head of state and chairman of the SRC, its politburo, the cabinet, and the committees for defense, security, and judicial matters. His models were Nasser and Kim Il Sung, and as with them, a cult of personality soon emerged. "Afweyne" would ultimately be touted as "The Father of Wisdom." When in power, the SRC renamed the country the Somali Democratic Republic.

Sweeping changes were introduced into Somali life. Clan and kinship ties were officially banned and the new regime promised to root out all references to clanship. To replace traditional Somali private justice—blood vengeance or blood money

**Transitional Federal President
Abdullahi Yusuf Ahmed**

payments between groups—the government introduced the death sentence for those convicted of homicide. In what is probably its most enduring achievement, the regime introduced a Latin script to make Somali a written language and aggressively pursued literacy in the new script.

In 1974, Siyad signed a treaty of cooperation with the Soviet Union and the institutional functions of a Marxist dictatorship were gradually set in place. The regime opted for "scientific socialism" and in a few years most sectors of the economy were brought under state control. Banks, insurance companies, electrical power production, petroleum distribution, sugar estates and refineries, were all nationalized. One exception to this nationalization program was the large banana plantations, which represented significant foreign investment. State-run enterprises were created and given absolute monopolies as the foundation of an economy run on heavy government intervention. Private traders were prohibited from importing, storing, purchasing or distributing food items.

The usual apparatus of state repression also emerged: The National Security Service (NNS), answerable to Siyad Barré himself, began to create its own interrogation and detention centers, courts, and prisons. Barré also built a vast propaganda machine (obviously helped by literacy in the new script) that generated posters, poems, songs and speeches to praise the "father of the revolution."

Resources were lavished on an expansion of Somali military forces much to the consternation of neighboring countries, especially those with significant Somali minorities. For years Somalia had secretly assisted Somali, Oromo, Eritrean and other nationalities opposed to the central governments of Kenya and Ethiopia, but in June 1977, when the Ethiopian regime seemed both weakened by drought and politically vulnerable, the policy of clandestine support ended. The Somali army was instead authorized to intervene directly in Ethiopia to assist the Western Somali Liberation Front fighting for the return of the Ogaden to Greater Somalia. The Somali army entered the Ogaden in July and overran it.

Expansionist excess was severely punished, however. The Soviet Union, with alliances with both Ethiopia and Somalia, turned against the unorthodox Siyad Barré. War materiel was airlifted to Ethiopia, and a Russian-directed Ethiopian army, with Cuban regiments in support, defeated Somali forces and sent their remnants scurrying back across the border. The army was humiliated and lost its legitimacy as the guardian of pan-Somali

The Somali eagle   Photo by Ahmed in Burco

nationalism. The country was stunned, and soon overwhelmed by an influx of refugees fleeing the reimposition of Ethiopian authority in the Ogaden. By 1979 there were officially 1.3 million refugees in the country, more than half of whom were located in the north. The regime's limited resources and even more limited capacity to deliver services increased tensions between the government and the northern clans.

Clan-based opposition grew, but was brutally repressed. Siyad Barré became increasingly dependent on his own clan and family, to whom he distributed the majority of government appointments and, with them, opportunities for corruption. Alliances shifted, with the regime signing on with the Americans after the debacle of the Ogaden war. "Scientific socialism" was abandoned and U.S. forces gained access to Somali military facilities, many of which were upgraded. Somali officers were given training in U.S. military schools, and America came to the country's aid when invaded by Ethiopia in 1982.

Regime incapacity, economic mismanagement and human rights abuses moved Somalis from disillusionment to anger andopposition increased. A few senior officers who escaped a bungled coup attempt in 1978 fled to Ethiopia and created the first opposition movement: the Somali Salvation Democratic Front (SSDF). In 1981 a second opposition movement, the Somali National Movement (SNM) was created in London by disgruntled businessmen, religious leaders, intellectuals and army officers, mostly from the north-

ern Isaaq clan. SNM organized guerrilla operations out of Ethiopia against the regime, and by 1988 an all-out civil war developed. Siyad Barré focused his wrath, and American-supported military might, against his northern opposition.

Hargeisa, Somalia's second largest city and the former capital of British Somaliland, was bombed, strafed and rocketed. Some 50,000 people are believed to have lost their lives there as a result of summary executions, aerial bombardments and ground attacks. Streams of refugees fleeing the devastation were not spared by government planes and the term "genocide" came to be used more and more frequently by human rights observers.

The northern economy was assaulted. Market centers throughout the northwest were destroyed; transport routes were mined and rendered unusable. Wells, on which nomadic pastoralists are dependent, were poisoned. Trade closed down and the northern economy collapsed with the closure of Berbera port from 1989 to 1991. Economic stress strained traditional kinship obligations of support to the maximum. Social stress was intensified when a major drought hit the area in 1991–92 at the height of the civil war and famine killed between 300,000 and 500,000 and affected millions more.

Civil strife gradually expanded throughout Somalia, leading to the formation of other opposition movements. The United Somali Congress (USC) was formed in 1987 by largely Hawiye-clan exiles in Italy. The USC quickly divided into two rival factions based on different subclans. One faction, led by General Aideed, allied with

the Somali National Movement, which provided arms. An Ogadeni-led Somali Patriotic Movement (SPM) was formed in 1989 when the highest ranking Ogadeni in the government, the minister of defense, was arrested.

Siyad Barré was increasingly isolated, defended only by his heavily armed presidential guard, drawn exclusively from his Marehan clan. As 1990 drew to a close, rebel forces entered Mogadishu, and early the next year Siyad Barré and his loyalists fled the city. By then, little was left of Somalia as a country.

The army fractured into factions focused on rival clan leaders who became warlords intent on control of territory and whatever resources remained that would sustain their power.

The war in the south produced major population dislocations. A third of the population became internal refugees, and at least a quarter of a million migrated to Mogadishu. When fighting in the capital intensified, there was a similar outflow of people.

The humanitarian disaster brought about Operation Restore Hope, launched in 1992 under UN auspices. The Somalia project was well-intended, but vague and shifting in direction. It started out to protect the delivery of humanitarian aid, but then refocused on creating a secure environment, which logically entailed demobilization of warlord factions. These, of course, had little interest in losing the source of their power and resisted. When General Aideed was identified as the chief troublemaker, the project again refocused on his capture. When the wily general's forces shot down an American helicopter (the infamous "Black Hawk Down" incident) and killed several American troops, the U.S. withdrew. The project yet again refocused, now seeking negotiation with General Aideed. TV images of a dead American soldier dragged triumphantly through the streets of Mogadishu shocked the American public and left policymakers horrified at the prospect of committing American ground troops anywhere in the world.

The international humanitarian effort in Somalia was budgeted at 1.5 billion dollars a year. It was the most expensive humanitarian effort ever undertaken, and in virtually every way it was a failure. By early 2000, four warlords still contended over divided Mogadishu. General Aideed, who was killed in a gun battle with rivals in 1996, was replaced as faction leader by his son, a young man who somewhat ironically held American citizenship and once served in the U.S. Marine Corps. Various negotiations between southern faction leaders conducted in Egypt, Kenya, Ethiopia and Libya achieved nothing.

Somalia

Djibouti's president, Ismail Omar Guelleh, convened the 13th Somali national reconciliation conference in May 2000. The conference brought together clan elders, religious leaders, academics, businessmen and, for the first time, a group of women. Over 2,000 Somalis met for over three months at Arta, Djibouti, to thrash out new institutions for the Somali state. A Transitional National Assembly was selected, which then proceeded to elect a transitional head of state. Abdulkassim Salat Hassan, a former interior minister of the Siyad Barré regime, won out over some 20 rivals for the new office of transitional president. His term of office was set at three years, during which time the Transition National Government (TNG) he headed was to establish the procedures for creating permanent institutions for the renovated state.

The leadership of Somaliland and Puntland rejected the Arta results, complaining particularly about the predominance of individuals prominent in the Siyad Barré regime, a government that did so much to destroy the north. The warlords simply treated Arta as another faction, and suggested that the transitional president would have to negotiate with them to bring lasting peace to Somalia.

An overly optimistic international community awarded the Arta TNG Somalia's seats at the United Nations, the Organization of African Unity and the Arab League. None of these designations improved the TNG's capacity to govern, or its acceptance by those it sought to govern. By the time its mandate ran out in 2003 it was little more than another Mogadishu faction.

Front and back of the Somali Shilling

Ethiopia did much to undermine the TNG. In early 2001 it gathered the major warlords in Addis Ababa in what was nothing more than an anti-Arta conference. In March they announced creation of a Somali Reconciliation and Restoration Council (SRRC). Given post-9/11 concerns about Somalia as a refuge for terrorists, the U.S. encouraged President Moi of Kenya to use his good offices to reconcile the SRRC and the TNG.

In May 2002 Kenya, Ethiopia and Djibouti were designated by the principal regional organization—the Inter-Governmental Authority for Development (IGAD)—to persuade Somalia's faction leaders, clan leaders, and members of civil society to attend yet another peace conference. After more than two years of lengthy discussion, the conference made a breakthrough in August 2004. A 275-person transitional federal parliament was selected. By early October they had agreed on an interim president, Colonel Abdullahi Yusuf Ahmed, Puntland's warlord chief, and in December President Yusuf appointed Ali Mohammed Gedi as prime minister. Gedi is a member of the Hawiye clan that dominates Mogadishu and much of southern Somalia; his cabinet, consisting of some 79 individuals, reflected the delicacy of distributing employment possibilities among the various Somali clans

spawning hope that the government might have success in its dealings.

However, whatever hope the transitional federal institutions had engendered seemed to dissipate once they returned to Somalia. The president, the prime minister and their supporters have established themselves 56 miles north of Mogadishu in relatively peaceful Jowhar, a city over which they exercised no authority. In protest, the speaker of the transitional parliament, and about 100 MPs chose to return to Mogadishu.

For the Transitional Federal Government (TFG), the capital was insecure and unwelcoming. Mogadishu remained a violent, divided city. Militia members, estimated to total some 50,000, manned roadblocks (an important source of funding) and patrolled sections of the city to assert the power of their patrons—warlords or the Islamic Courts Union (ICU). The first Islamic Court was set up in 1994 to provide law and order for the anarchic capital. Their effectiveness extended their dominion, and brought them into competition with the city's warlords.

Encouraged by American funding, the Mogadishu warlords created an Alliance for the Restoration of Peace and Counter-Terrorism (ARPCT) in February 2006. The coalition's founders charged that Islamic radicals were behind a wave of assassina-

Prime Minister Gedi

Somalia

**Somaliland President
Dahir Riyale Kahin**

tions of intellectuals, military officials, and prominent civil society figures, all supporters of the Transitional Federal Government. A spokesman for the Courts denied all and noted that "Somali society is 100 percent Muslim and it is not possible for a Muslim to kill his own brother." One month later, Issa Osman Issa blew himself up while assembling a bomb in a Mogadishu apartment. According to the police, Mr. Issa was a member of *Al-Ittihad Al-Islamiya*, a terrorist group with links to al-Qaeda; his bomb was to be used in an attack on Prime Minister Gedi.

Factional fighting in Mogadishu during the first half of 2006 was the worst in years and had all the aspects of an end-game scenario: either warlords or Islamists would triumph. By early June the victor was clear: the militias of the Islamic Courts Union (ICU) had driven the warlords out of the city and asserted their control. The city was reunited, weapons removed from the streets, port and airport reopened. By December, the ICU controlled most of southern Somalia, from the Kenyan border to autonomous Puntland. The TFG's diminished political space was no more than Baidoa, where its military security was assured by Ethiopian troops. Fatally hubristic, the radical Islamists at the heart of the UIC declared jihad against the Ethiopian "invaders," threatened Baidoa, and hastened the collapse of their movement.

At the heart of the ICU was *Al-Ittihad Al-Islamiya*, a terrorist group with links to al-Qaeda. Its operatives had worked with al-Qaeda since 1993 in various attacks on American interests, including the Black Hawk Down incident in Mogadishu and the bombing of the American embassy in Nairobi, Kenya. *Al-Ittihad Al-Islamiya's* chief, Sheikh Hassan Dahir Aweys, emerged

as one of the most radical ICU leaders. The Sheikh featured prominently on both American and United Nations terrorist watch lists. In 2001 he was identified by the United Nations as an associate of Osama bin Laden, and member states were asked to freeze his assets. By the Americans he was believed to be one of the "Black Hawk Down" masterminds.

Once in control, the Islamic Courts imposed strict *sharia* law. Live music was banned; movie theaters shuttered, and video rental shops closed. Fear became a useful administrative tool. Punishments for *sharia* violation became public ritual and spectacle: Marijuana smokers were lashed and murderers executed. Religious obligations were enforced: all trade and public transportation were banned during prayer times. Indeed, prayer was mandatory. "Everybody must leave his business and go for prayer when the muezzin is heard," said a deputy security chief. "Anybody who does not obey will face painful punishment."

To consolidate power, Islamist leaders fanned the flames of Somali nationalism against the traditional enemy—Ethiopia. After Ethiopia sent military forces to support the TFG in its Baidoa redoubt, Sheikh Aweys ordered a "holy war" to drive the Ethiopians from Somalia.

By October Prime Minister Meles of Ethiopia bluntly said his country was "technically" at war with Somali Islamists. They were "spoiling for a fight," he told a Reuters reporter, "declaring Jihad against Ethiopia almost every other week." A UIC attack on Biadoa in December brought quick riposte. Ethiopian tanks, artillery batteries, and military jets, using the best American satellite intelligence, made quick work of the ill-equipped Islamist militia. The authority of the Islamic Courts simply dissolved; its leaders fled and Mogadishu abandoned.

In January 2007 combined military action, involving U.S., Ethiopian and Kenyan forces, pursued and tracked down the most wanted terrorists sheltered and employed by the UIC although only with limited success. Some hint as to the richly fertile ground Somalia provided for international terrorism came in April 2007: the Ethiopian government announced it had detained 41 terrorism suspects from 17 countries who had been fighting for Somalia's Islamist movement.

The Present: Contemporary Issues

Livestock has been among Somalia's most profitable sectors of the economy, but veterinary health facilities are weak and consequently, Somali herds are sub-

Islamic Court Militia in Mogadishu ©Abdimalik Yusuf/IRIN

Somalia

ject to periodic outbreaks of disease. In the south the most important commercial crop comes from banana plantations. The plantations, controlled by two major firms, one Italian and the other American (Dole), represent the only examples of modern agricultural techniques in the country—irrigation systems and modern farm machinery.

Coastal waters off northern Somalia contain rich fishing grounds, but the absence of any governmental control of its waters has encouraged illegal plundering by a variety of fishing fleets. Using the newest and most destructive of techniques—drift nets and dynamiting to break up coral reefs where lobsters and other highly prized catch live—these mechanized fishermen destroy livelihoods of local fishermen, not to mention the destruction of one of the world most biodiverse habitats.

Traditionally, Somali fishermen used nets only between September and April. In the hot season between May and August, indigenous fishermen use only hooks to catch their prey. To industrialized fishing operations that know no such limitations, the profits are enormous. Within 75 days of fishing, each ship gets up to 420 tons of fish out of Somali waters. The catch is worth $6.3 million.

To stop illegal fishing, locals armed themselves and their boats and kept watch on the coast. When they captured a foreign fishing vessel, its occupants were forced to pay a cash fine for the illegal practice. What started out as self-protection by So-

mali fishermen has evolved into full-scale piracy. Several pirate groups now operate along Somalia's 1,880-mile coastline, Africa's longest, and Somali waters are the world's most dangerous, according to the UN and NATO.

Despite allowing US vessels to patrol the Somali waters, the government has been unable to control the issue of piracy. In 2008 alone, 111 pirate attacks were recorded, of which 42 were successful at capturing a vessel and in the first three months of 2009, 68 attacks were recorded. In response to the increased piracy of one of the world's most important trade routes, the US, the EU, NATO and several Asian countries, sent part of their naval fleets to help control the problem, which could have severe economic consequences. As much as 30% of the world's oil passes through the Gulf of Aden, and the insecurity in delivering oil could contribute to the already volatile oil prices. Amongst merchant ships, fishing boats and other commercial ships, an oil tanker, the Sirius Star, was captured, and more than $25m demanded in ransom. Though few of the ships have had the same value as the Sirius Star, ransoms typically range between one and three million dollars, making piracy a very lucrative business. The owners of the Sirius Star eventually paid $3 million in ransom, before the tanker could continue with its $100 million worth of crude oil, after almost two months in captivity.

As the industry of piracy has grown, so has the sophistication of its perpetrators. For many pirates, spending weeks at sea

with no success is common. As the foreign navies step up their presence in the area, it will be even more costly to embark on the sometimes 500 miles long sail to intercept the commercial ships. The ships, weapons, gas and food the pirates need for their missions are huge expenses upfront, so a network of investors and suppliers has been created on Somalia's coast, who take percentages of the ransom money when a mission has been a success. In fact, at present, the City of Eyl, a safe-haven for pirates, thrives almost solely off the contributions made by piracy.

Much of the money generated by piracy however, lands in the hands of a militant group called Al-Shabab, now the strongest opposition to the transitory government. The group has denied discussing a truce if any foreign troops remain in the country. In early January 2009, Ethiopian troops who had been present since 2006 left Somalia. Ethiopia argued they withdrew in victory, while in fact, Ethiopia's presence in Somalia seems to have reunited radical Islamists, in the form of Al-Shabab, and only a few thousand international troops from Kenya and Burundi remain in Somalia, barely protecting elements of the government. The UN has refused sending peace-keeping forces, because "there is not peace to keep." The AU has pledged forces, but two years after the commitment, only two of the seven countries that promised troops have fulfilled the promise.

As a consequence, Al-Shabab is thriving more than ever. Within hours after Ethiopia left their strongholds in Somalia, including important trade routes, which are the source of funding for the weak transitional government, Al-Shabab took over. Almost entirely in control of the coast line, Al-Shabab has a substantial income generated by privacy, as Al-Shabab many times acts as an investor in the industry. With the revenues, Al-Shabab is able to provide its soldiers and supporters with a monthly salary—for many, around 100 dollars—a very substantial amount considering the average income of less than 250 dollars a year. There have been speculations that the overwhelming upsurge in radical Islamist support is due to the earnings opportunities, rather than an ideological affiliating with Al-Shabab's destructive cause.

In December 2008, a row broke out in the transitional government about how to deal with Al-Shabab. The president, Abdullahi Yusuf Ahmed, tried to force through a vote of no confidence in his own prime minister, who, Yusuf felt, was not willing to confront the issue of the Islamists. Yusuf did so after weeks of unrest in the government, but he failed to convince parliament and as a consequence, Yusuf stepped down the 29th of December, leaving the speaker of

At the Burco, Somaliland market even satellite dishes are available

Photo by Ahmed in Burco

224

parliament in the presidential role till a new government could be elected. On January 31st, Sheikh Sharif Sheikh Ahmed was elected the new president of the Transitional Federal Government.

———— • ————

Republic of Somaliland:
Area: 68.000 sq. miles—About the size of Georgia
Population: 3,500,000 (est. 2009)
Capital City: Hargeysa
Currency: Somaliland Shilling
Independence Date: May 18, 1991
Chief of State: Dahir Riyale Kahin
National Flag: three horizontal, parallel, stripes and equal sections (green, white, red from top), with top section inscribed in white Arabic characters "There is no God but Allah and Mohammad was his prophet" and a five-pointed black star centered in the middle section.

In northwest Somalia, where British indirect rule did not destroy traditional Somali systems of conflict resolution, leaders opted for reconciliation rather than rivalry. Somali-style peace conferences, large-scale regional gatherings lasting anywhere from two to six months, managed to stabilize clan relationships. At a grand *shir*, or council, which concluded in February 1991, Isaaq clans representing 80% of the population of former British Somaliland reached an agreement with other clans. Independence was declared in the same year with the rallying cry "No More Mogadishu."

There have been at least three of these grand councils, called "national conferences," to work out the form and structure of the state. Two elected assemblies exist. One is essentially a small lower parliamentary house. The other is a council of elders, larger than the first and consisting of clan representatives. This chamber of elders cannot be dissolved by the president, and those who replace members who have died, been recalled or incapacitated must come from the same clan or subclan. The system was ratified in a constitution approved by two-thirds of the representatives in February 1997. Submitted to a referendum, the constitution received overwhelming approval from Somalilanders in May 2001.

In 1993 elders and citizens chose Muhammed Ibrahim Egal, the last prime minister of democratic Somalia, as president of the "Republic of Somaliland." He was reelected to a five-year term as president in 1997, died in May 2002 and was immediately succeeded by Somaliland's vice president, Dahir Riyale Kahin who remains president.

Denied recognition as a sovereign state by an international community fixated on recreating a unitary state for Somalia, Somaliland has made remarkable progress on its own. Heavy weapons were surrendered voluntarily and often stored unguarded. State controls on the economy were virtually eliminated, and trade and commerce began to thrive. Even more remarkable has been the emergence of a stable and democratic political system operating under the rule of law. A constitution provides Somaliland's legal framework, and under its provisions for presidential succession the country made a smooth transition following the death of President Egal.

President Kahin presided over the next stage of Somaliland's political development—the preparation for presidential and parliamentary elections. Political parties were legalized and participated in municipal elections of December 2002. Of six parties participating, three emerged with sufficient support to be allowed to run candidates in the April 2003 presidential elections: the United People's Democratic Party (UDUB), the governing party founded by President Egal; Kulmiye or United Party, led by Ahmed Muhammad Silanyo, a former planning minister; and the Justice and Welfare Party (UCID), founded by Faisal Ali Warabe, a civil engineer who emphasized the notion of good governance in his campaign.

In an important decision seen to limit the role of clan identity, the Supreme Court disallowed independent candidacies in the presidential elections. Each of the three candidates were forced to seek support among a broad range of clans and subclans.

When the results were tabulated, the election turned out to be a real squeaker. By a mere 80 votes, President Dahir Riyale Kahin defeated his closest rival, Ahmed Mohamed Silanyo. Clan elders headed off a potentially volatile situation by convincing Silanyo to accept the results. That he did, and that Somaliland avoided the post-electoral violence so common elsewhere in Africa, attests to the political maturity of a young democracy.

Somaliland's third experience with multiparty democratic elections came in September 2005, when voters elected members of parliament for the first time. The three parties put up 246 candidates, including seven women, for the legislature's 82 seats. International observers called the election generally free and fair and each of the parties will send a sizable delegation to parliament. UDUB won 33 seats, while Kulmiye and UCID took 28 and 21 respectively. Two of the new parliamentarians are women.

Somaliland has many of the attributes of a fully functioning state. It has its own flag and currency, and its citizens drive with national license plates. It has a constitution, which allowed it to weather a succession crisis after President Egal suddenly died, and, perhaps most remarkably, in a deeply traditional society it has effectively moved from clan voting to individual voting in a multiparty democracy. It has, for the most part, seen peace and prosperity, having chosen politics over violence. None of this, however, has brought international recognition of its statehood.

Somaliland's appeals for recognition were severely tested by a series of murders targeting foreign aid workers. The series began in October 2003 with the shooting death of an Italian doctor, Annalena Tonelli, who was killed outside the hospital she had founded in Borama. This was followed by the murder of two British teachers the same month, unsettling aid workers and expatriates. When two German aid workers were ambushed and killed in March 2004, NGOs and international aid agencies decided to withdraw their personnel from Somaliland for security reasons.

Eight men, all Islamic radicals, were sentenced to death for three of the murders in November 2005. Shouting "Allah Akbar" (God is great) when the sentence was announced, they defiantly told the judge "We should not be killed for assassinating infidels." The judge rejected their claim. "The religion is clear," he said. "It does not encourage the assassination of innocent Muslims or non-Muslims."

The Somaliland government has an annual budget of around $18 million. Employing something like 26,000 people, it spends 70% of its revenues on salaries. Revenues are mostly derived from port duties at Berbera where activity has recently increased. UN agencies have used it for transporting food relief to Ethiopia, and the Ethiopian government has turned to it in a search for alternatives to the Eritrean port of Asab.

Ethiopian Airlines has begun twice-weekly flights to Hargeysa, Somaliland's capital. International flights from the Gulf states, East Africa and Europe already land at Hargeysa and Berbera airports, generating about $1.5 million in revenues for the government. As of 2001, Somaliland businessmen began to pay income and profit taxes, which increased government revenues.

Wealth and profits are largely based on livestock trade, meat and hide exports. Some 1.5 million head of sheep and livestock were exported in 2000, while in 1999 about 2 million head had been exported. A new skin and hide factory has been opened to produce export-quality leather.

In 2000, Somaliland would normally have expected to export 2 million to 2.5 million head of sheep to Saudi Arabia, as

Somalia

well as 100,000 head of cattle to Yemen, but the states imposed a livestock ban in October after an outbreak of Rift Valley Fever (RVF). UN agencies have since found no traces of the disease in Somaliland cattle, but Saudi officials have kept the ban in place, despite lifting it for Ethiopian livestock. In normal years the country expects to earn from $150 million to $200 million in foreign exchange from the livestock trade. This would normally earn the government some $8 million–$9 million in taxes, over 30% of its total budget. Cutoff of the trade has meant a budgetary downsizing for the government.

While the livestock ban is in effect, Somaliland is largely dependent on remittances by overseas Somalis, estimated at $500 million a year. Given the absence of international assistance, contributions by the Somaliland diaspora have been crucial in the country's development. Somaliland now has two universities and several vocational colleges whose construction was greatly aided by diaspora remittances.

The entrepreneurial spirit abounds in Somaliland. Businessmen there have created one of the cheapest telephone systems in Africa: International calls are $1.50 a minute in the day and only 80 cents at night. Traders are working to export frankincense and myrrh, and exploration has

begun for oil and gemstones. A recently discovered reef of high-quality emeralds—several miles long—holds much promise as an alternative source of income.

———— • ————

The Future

Somalia's future depends on both internal and external consensus, and the prospects of constructing a true Somali state are poor. Internal actors, be they clan elders, fundamentalist Islamist clerics, or the recalcitrant mini-states of Somaliland and Puntland, cannot agree on the minimum amount of authority to be granted any central government. Meanwhile, the anarchic state of affairs invites external intervention; the United States has conducted air strikes against extremists in the country throughout 2008 and 2009, targeting terror-suspects who take refuge in Somalia.

Until recently the best Somaliland could hope for in its campaign for international recognition was observer status at the UN and a similar status at the AU. Things may be changing. A February 2006 AU mission report argued that Somaliland's case should not be "linked to the notion of 'opening a Pandora's box.'" It went on to note that the "lack of recognition ties the hands of the authorities and people of So-

maliland" as they pursue their reconstruction and development goals. In May 2007 Somaliland sent a formal request to the African Union (AU) asking to be recognized as an independent African government.

Somalia as a whole faces one of the most dire human situations in the world. As of June 2009, more than 2 million of the countries nine, are displaced, on the run or homeless. An even greater number, fast approaching 40% of the country's population, relies on foreign aid to survive. Many have pleaded with the UN and the AU to intervene in the Somali affairs to avoid the looming crisis, but both have shown little interest. In light of the food crisis which continues to shake the African continent, more than 50% of the population will be malnourished by 2015, if the crisis cannot be avoided.

There is sporadic hope, however, that the exit of Ethiopian forces in December 2008 will encourage moderate Islamists to join the transitional government, rather than the militant groups haunting both the cities and the countryside of Somalia. If the country can avoid the looming standoff between government forces and radical Islamists, it is likely the international community will be more willing to intervene to facilitate peace, but as of now, there is little substance to these hopes.

A Somali nomad and his camels

Photo by Ahmed in Burco

The Republic of the Sudan

Death in Darfur: A Janjaweed militiaman.

AFP/Getty Images

Basic Facts

Area: 2,504,530 sq. km. = 967,000 sq. mi. (an area as large as the U.S. east of the Mississippi joined by Louisiana, Arkansas and Missouri)

Population: 38,600,000 (UN 2007 est.)

Capital City: Khartoum

Climate: The northern half is arid desert, the middle and southern areas are temperate and semiarid; the southwest is hot with a six month rainy season.

Neighboring Countries: Congo-Kinshasa and Central African Republic (southwest); Chad (west); Libya (northwest); Kenya and Uganda (southeast)

Official Language: Arabic

Other Principal Languages: Acholi, Bari, Bedawi, Dinka, Fulfulde, Fur, Hausa, Kanuri, Kenuzi-Dongola, Masalit, Nobiin, Nuer, Otuho, Shilluk, Toposa

Ethnic Groups: Black 52% (prominently including Acholi, Dinka, Nuer, Shilluk), Arab 39%, Beja 6%, foreigners 2%, other 1%

Principal Religions: Sunni Muslim 70% (in north), indigenous beliefs 25%, Christian 5% (mostly in south and Khartoum)

Chief Commercial Products: Oil, cotton, sesame, livestock/meat, and gum Arabic

GNI Per Capita: $640 (World Bank 2006 est.)

Currency: 1 Sudanese pound (£Sd) = 100 piastres

Former Colonial Status: Egyptian (1821–1885); British–Egyptian (1899–1956)

Independence Date: January 1, 1956

Chief of State: Omar Hassan Ahmed al-Bashir, President (appointed by Sudan's

RCC, October 1993; before that, Chairman, Revolutionary Command Council for National Salvation (RCC) from June 1989

National Flag: Three horizontal stripes of red, white and black with a green isosceles triangle at the pole.

Land and People

Sudan is the largest nation in Africa, covering an area of almost one million square miles. The vast Sahara Desert lies in the northern sector and is succeeded by a semiarid plains country in the region near Khartoum, the capital city. This gently rolling territory is succeeded in the south by tropical plains land with more abundant rainfall; in the extreme south, the land becomes choked by dense jungle growth. The historic Nile River, the longest in the world, virtually divides the country and is the main route of north-south communication and travel between the Mediterranean Sea and the lower part of the African continent. The river has two points of origin—the waters of Lake Victoria flow into a portion known as the Victoria Nile. After a short distance, the river becomes lost in the Sudd swamp region of southern Sudan, which covers an immense area of land. The stream emerges again to flow northward through central Sudan. The Blue Nile originates to the east near Lake Tana in the mountains of Ethiopia. The two rivers join at Khartoum to form the main Nile, which, as it proceeds through northern Sudan, has a slight downward slope, interrupted periodically

by rough cataracts. As it nears Wadi Halfa on the Egyptian border, the Nile shapes itself into an almost perfect "S" curve. Were it not for the predominantly muddy waters of this river, much of Sudan and Egypt would be empty and desolate. High mountains rise in the extreme east of Sudan, close to the Ethiopian border and along the Red Sea coast. Other mountains are found to the west on the Chad border, and in the south.

UNESCO designated Gebel Barkel and four other Nubian locations as World Heritage sites in 2003. The sites contain tombs, temples, pyramids, living complexes, and palaces that testify to the importance of the ancient cultures of Napata, Meroë, and

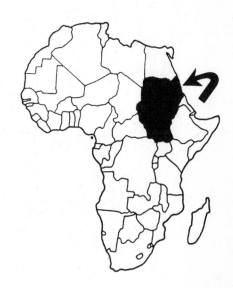

227

Sudan

Kush. The 8th-century rulers of Kush conquered and ruled Egypt as the 25th dynasty. Non-recognition of Nubia's pharaonic heritage is one of the complaints this northern people lodges against Khartoum's Islamist regime.

The Past: Political and Economic History

For early history, see *Historical Background* and *The Colonial Period: The British.*

Sudan has been riven by internal conflict for most of its history. That conflict has usually been referred to as one between a Muslim North and a Christian South, but that description is highly misleading. Conflict in Sudan is neither exclusively regional nor exclusively religious given the country's enormous complexity. Indeed, Sudanese themselves refer to the country as *laham ras* (literally "head-meat"), a term that refers to the highly divergent taste, texture and appearance of parts of cooked sheep's head, a popular Sudanese dish.

In this culturally complex situation, a central problem facing the state is defining its identity. Contemporary conflict is fueled by vastly divergent historical identities. For Sudan there is no unifying identity; diversity is division. Northern Sudan was conquered and unified by the Egyptian viceroy of the Ottoman sultan in 1821. Egyptian rulers claimed southern Sudan, but were unable to establish effective control over its fragmented animist populations. Access to the South was not possible until after 1839, and from that point both the Ottoman rulers and their Arab Sudanese subjects saw the South only as a source of manpower. Slavers from both groups aggressively raided southern peoples.

Not until the 1880s was a sense of Sudanese identity articulated in opposition to the Egyptian conquerors. In 1881 a religious leader proclaimed himself the Mahdi or "expected one" and began to unify peoples in western and central Sudan. Drawing upon discontent with Ottoman-Egyptian exploitation, the Mahdi led a nationalist revolt culminating in the fall of Khartoum in 1885. The Mahdi died shortly afterwards, but his state survived until destroyed by an Anglo-Egyptian

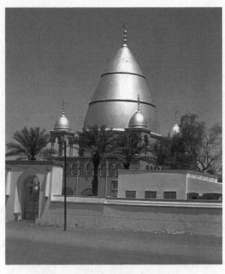

Tomb of the Mahdi, Khartoum

army under Lord Kitchener in 1889. Sudan was proclaimed a condominium in 1899, and governed by a joint British-Egyptian administration until 1956. Northern Arab Muslims were privileged by the condominium administration and in turn, looked down on the black African animists of the south. For black Africans of southern Sudan, the memory of slave raids meant that any pale-skinned person was a potential slaver.

Though one speaks of northern Muslim populations and southern animists, neither of these populations is in any way monolithic. Sudanese Muslims are divided by affiliation with rival religious brotherhoods. The Mahdi's followers called themselves *ansars*, and the Ansar sect today is the largest of the Sudanese Muslim brotherhoods. During the period of Ottoman-Egyptian rule, Turkish-Egyptians developed close relations with another Muslin brotherhood, known as the Khatmiyya. The second most important brotherhood today, the Khatmiyya retains its original pro-Egyptian, anti-Mahdist identity. Each of these two rival brotherhoods is associated with a separate political party. Mahdists are the core of the Umma Party, while the Khatmiyya forms the core of the Democratic Unionist Party (DUP). The leader of the Umma Party, Dr. Sadiq al-Mahdi, is a descendent of the first Mahdi. Smaller than either the Ansar or Khatmiyya is the more militant and fundamentalist Muslim Brotherhood led by Hassan al-Turabi and very much the core of the National Islamic Front (NIF). These sectarian groupings also have their secular opponents in the North, Muslims and non-Muslims whose vision of Sudanese identity is not based on political Islam.

Southern black African animists (and today a small number of Christians) are even more divided. Symptomatically, over

Sudan States

228

Sudan

a hundred languages are spoken in Sudan, most of them in the south. The two major southern ethnic groups, the Dinka and Nuer, are segmentary societies with no traditions of overarching leadership and governance. Both are cattle raising people. Both were traditional rivals for pasturage and objects of mutual cattle raids. Khartoum governments, dominated by northerners, have traditionally exploited such rivalries. Within each group segments vie with each other for scarce resources and produce intra-ethnic rivalries that can be exploited by the Khartoum government. Similarly, historical antagonisms between cattle pastoralists like the Nuer or Dinka and settled farming peoples create fissures that work against southern political unity.

These cultural diversities help explain Sudan's continuing history of political instability and conflict. At independence in 1956, a civilian regime, deeply divided between its Muslim partners, was incapacitated by internal division and overthrown by a military coup in 1958. The military in turn, reneging on its promises to restore civilian government, was driven from office and succeeded by another coalition government. Power sharing between Umma and Unionist parties could not overcome problems of factionalism, economic stagnation and ethnic dissidence in the south. Espousing pan-Arab-Nationalism and professing pro-Soviet sentiments, General Jaafar Nimeri took advantage of dissatisfaction with this civilian regime and overthrew it in 1969. Soviet arms poured into Sudan. But only two years later disputes between Marxist and non-Marxist elements within the ruling military coalition resulted in an abortive communist coup. Anti-Marxist elements quickly restored Nimeri, who, seeing the light, did a political about face and sought aid from the United States.

In 1972 the government reached a peace agreement with southern rebels. Signed at Addis Ababa, the accord made the south a self-governing region, but ultimately offered only a brief respite to Sudan's endemic conflict. After Emperor Haile Selassie was overthrown in neighboring Ethiopia by a Marxist military coup in 1974, Sudan was seen as a bulwark against communism in the region. American arms poured into the country, and Sudan became another pawn on the chessboard of cold war politics.

Secure with American arms and support, General Nimeri began an Islamization campaign in 1983. Traditional Islamic punishments drawn from the *sharia* were incorporated into the penal code. Amputations for theft and public lashings for alcohol possession became common. When religious leaders like Sadiq al-Mahdi questioned the general's credentials for creating an Islamic state, they were thrown in jail. Civil liberties were suspended and a state of emergency declared. Rights granted southerners for a degree of autonomy were curtailed and two army battalions mutinied under the leadership of a southern Dinka, Colonel John Garang, in 1984. This began Sudan's present ongoing civil war. General Nimeri himself fell in a bloodless coup a year later and was ultimately replaced by a civilian coalition again headed by Sadiq al-Mahdi.

The Southern People's Liberation Army (SPLA), founded by Garang, found a ready supply of arms from Marxist Ethiopia and by 1987, Soviet tanks and artillery supplied to the SPLA allowed it to fight positional battles and capture population

Dr. Sadiq al-Mahdi

centers. Subject to government bombardment and raids by its militias, massive numbers of southerners were displaced from their homes or fled to neighboring countries. The civilian government in Khartoum remained faction-ridden and indecisive, incapable of winning the war. At the very moment negotiations with the rebels seemed on the verge of success, the regime was overthrown by General Omar Hassan al-Bashir in 1989.

The new military regime came to power with the backing of the militant National Islamic Front (NIF) party headed by Hassan al-Turabi. It quickly abolished the constitution, all political parties (except the NIF), and trade unions. Press freedoms were curtailed, and strict dress and behavior codes imposed on women. More than 78,000 people were purged from the army, police and civil administration to make way for those of more militant Muslim

faith. Support for the new regime came from Iran, enabling the government to make massive purchases of arms from China and the former Soviet republics. These were used to step up the war against the south. In addition to an ideology of militant Islam, the discovery of huge southern oil reserves in the 1970s also fueled the desire of Khartoum to control its southern provinces. Emptying the oil producing regions of their black African animist populations became a deliberate government goal, even at the price of massive destruction and loss of life.

The overthrow in 1991 of Ethiopia's Marxist regime and questions about continued arms supply led to a factional breakup of the SPLA. Under the leadership of Riek Machar, a Nuer faction broke off and proclaimed its goal of independence from Sudan. John Garang remained head of the now, largely Dinka, SPLA and claimed his goal a unified, secular Sudan. The clash of these three visions of Sudanese identity—an Arab-Muslim Sudan, a Sudan divided into two separate states, or a unified secular Sudan—continues to the present. Fluid loyalties and deliberately divisive strategies by the Khartoum regime have led to a bewildering and complex set of shifting alliances and coalitions, few of which can be identified with much more than a desire to overthrow the present regime.

By 1995 northern and southern opponents of the regime had joined forces in the National Democratic Alliance (NDA), and by January 1997 the NDA could mount an offensive on three fronts in eastern Sudan. Troops involved came from all the members of the Alliance. The main spearhead came from the Sudan People's Liberation Army commanded by colonel John Garang, but also included elements from the Beja Congress and northern groups such as Sadiq al-Mahdi's Umma and Mohamed Osman al-Mirghani's Democratic Unionist Party (DUP).

In response, Khartoum rallied southern dissidents and signed a peace agreement with Riek Machar and other breakaway SPLA faction leaders in April 1997. Pro-government southerners were linked together under the name of the United Democratic Salvation Front (UDSF) headed by Machar; about 25 of their militias came together in the South Sudan Defense Force (SSDF) generously supported by Khartoum.

In February and March 1999 a seemingly successful series of reconciliation meetings between Dinka and Nuer leaders were held. The resulting Wunlit Covenant demonstrated the vitality of traditional conflict resolution procedures. Agreements were reached through consensus. Rituals surrounding the agreement stamped it with

229

Sudan

the mark of tradition. The slaughter of a large white bull by traditional spiritual leaders of both communities symbolized peace and an end to the conflict.

President Bashir had to face not only the growing unity of his southern enemies, but also a growing threat to his authority from within the National Congress Party (NCP), the renamed National Islamic Front. His approach was twofold. A peace agreement was signed with Sadiq al-Mahdi, driving a wedge in the NDA and rallying a leading Muslim cleric to his side in preparation for his struggle with Hassan al-Turabi. Turabi, speaker of parliament and also al-Mahdi's brother-in-law, seemed to be on the verge of reducing the president's position in both party and state. Al-Bashir's response amounted to an internal coup. In late 1999 he acted decisively to curtail al-Turabi. Parliament was dissolved and a state of emergency declared, allowing the president to rule by decree.

In May 2000 al-Turabi was suspended as secretary-general of the National Congress Party and accused of plotting against the government. Formally expelled from the party in June, he announced creation of a new political party, the Popular National Congress (PNC), better known now as simply the Popular Congress (PC).

With the principal spokesman for political Islam sidetracked, President al-Bashir wooed, and won, the return of some of the northern political elite, including former president Numeiry and Sadiq al-Mahdi, who returned to lead his popular Umma Party. Ahmad al-Mirghani, a senior leader of the Democratic Unionist Party (DUP), has also returned, after 12 years of exile.

Relations with formerly hostile neighbors were improved. Al-Bashir allowed Ugan-

dan army troops to pursue members of Joseph Kony's Lord's Resistence Army to their Sudanese hideouts. Internally, however, he continued to terrorize civilians living around the disputed Bentiu oil fields. Fugitives from the offensive reported that troops—backed by tanks, helicopter gunships and aerial bombardments—were torturing, slaughtering and burning men, women and children in a drive to evict all non-Arabs from oil-producing areas.

When al-Bashir called presidential and legislative elections for December 2000, few were interested and few participated. No elections could be held in the south for security reasons, and where they were held in the north, they were actively boycotted by the major opposition parties. Official reports indicated 63% of eligible voters went to the polls, a figure that produced hoots of derision from the opposition who claimed not more than 7% had participated. Bashir and the NCP won, overwhelmingly.

In February 2001, Hassan al-Turabi was arrested and jailed after his PNC had signed a memorandum of understanding with Sudan People's Liberation Army (SPLA). The linkage between Turabi and his arch foe, John Garang, was unexpected, unprecedented, and to many of his followers, inexplicable, unless, that is, one accepts the infinite mutability of Sudanese politicians. Hassan al-Turabi remained under house arrest, a prisoner of the state he helped to create, until freed in October 2003 while the Bashir government was negotiating a peace settlement with its southern opponents.

Sudan and its civil war rose high on Washington's list of priorities after the September 11 attacks. This was, after all, where Osama bin Laden had lived from

1991 until he was expelled in 1996. Even before those events, however, the House of Representatives had already passed the Sudan Peace Act in June 2001 by 422 to 2. The act would "punish those who trade in blood oil," said its sponsors, by imposing capital market sanctions on companies investing in Sudan. It would also provide $10 million to Sudanese opposition forces.

To push the Sudanese peace process forward, President Bush appointed former Senator John Danforth, an Episcopal minister, as Special Envoy for Peace in the Sudan. U.S. reengagement in the Sudanese peace process galvanized regional efforts. With Kenyan leadership, IGAD (the InterGovernmental Authority on Development consisting of Kenya, Eritrea, Ethiopia, Djibouti, Sudan, Somalia and Uganda) brought the government of Sudan and the SPLA together at Machakos, Kenya and, to the surprise of many, produced a framework for peace in July 2002. Both sides made concessions. The government agreed to a referendum on self-determination for southern Sudan—after six and a half years—and the SPLA accepted the application of *sharia* law in the North.

The Machakos Protocol provided the framework and momentum for negotiation on several important issues: wealth-sharing, power-sharing, application of *sharia* in Khartoum, and defining the border between North and South.

Wealth-sharing agreements came first, aided by experts from the World Bank and IMF who brought ideas and experience from other similar situations. Oil revenues will be split 50-50, after deducting 2% to go to oil-producing areas.

A power-sharing agreement creates a separate Government of Southern Sudan, which will receive a "significant devolution of powers" from the national government. President Bashir will remain in office until national elections can be held, and Sudan will have two vice presidents (appointed by the president). John Garang would be first vice president of the national government and president of the southern government.

The parties agreed to a bicameral national legislature. The majority of the National Assembly's seats will be apportioned to the National Congress Party (52%), while the SPLM will be allocated 28%. Other northern political forces will receive 14%, with the remaining 6% going to additional southern forces. The upper house, or Council of States, will have two representatives from each of Sudan's states. A census will be held by the second year of the interim period and general elections by the end of the third year.

On the application of *sharia* law in Khartoum, it was agreed that non-Muslims would not be subject to its provisions in

John Garang shakes hands with President Omar Hassan al-Bashir as President Kibaki of Kenya looks on.

President Omar Hassan al-Bashir

the capital. The rights of non-Muslims are to be protected by a special commission appointed by the president.

From these discussions emerged the Comprehensive Peace Agreement (CPA), which was officially signed in January 2005, ending 20 years of civil conflict between north and south. It took the lives of 1.5 million people to arrive at this point. Calling it a "new path" for Sudan, President Bashir signed a power-sharing constitution to implement the CPA in early July. Former prime minister and opposition leader Sadiq al-Mahdi broke the general mood of relief and optimism by condemning it. The constitution was, for him, a mere bilateral deal between John Garang's SPLM and the ruling party that would lead to "dyarchy"—a country ruled by two people.

John Garang was accorded a tumultuous welcome when he arrived in Khartoum to be sworn in as national vice president in July; simultaneously he became the head of the autonomous administration of southern Sudan for the next six years. Before the month was out, however, Garang died in a helicopter crash. The SPLM moved quickly to fill the void. Its deputy chairman, Salva Kiir Miyardeit, was named his successor and assumed his offices as national vice president and head of the government of southern Sudan.

Kiir struggles to create an administration to implement provisions of the CPA. The challenges he faces are many, from the fundamental undercapacity of Southern Sudan in terms of educated and trained manpower, to the reluctance of Khartoum to fulfill its CPA obligations, to the existence of spoiler forces whose arms and ambitions could yet unsettle the agreement and disatabilize the south.

Even as the government made peace with southerners, however, President Bashir faced resistance, rebellion, and insurgency elsewhere. Some northern peoples, like the Beja and the Nubians, felt as marginalized as Garang's southerners and resentful at the exclusivity of the CPA. More ominously, new groups emerged in Darfur to press their demands during the Kenyan negotiations, and the government's response created a humanitarian disaster.

Darfur

The Sudan Liberation Army (SLA) took up arms against the government in February 2003, accusing it of ignoring the Darfur region and demanding a place at the negotiating table. Shortly afterwards a second armed group—the Justice and Equality Movement (JEM)—emerged to make the same claims. Both rebel groups recruited from the region's African (and largely Muslim) populations—notably Fur, Zaghawa and Massaleit peoples—all of whom had historical conflicts with Arab pastoralists over water and grazing rights. In the 1980s these traditional tensions had been intensified by the central government, which took to arming Arab militia groups to disrupt and destabilize black African communities that might be sympathetic to John Garang's SPLA.

With the emergence of the SLA and JEM, Khartoum saw the hands of its enemies everywhere and resorted to the same tactics. Arab militias were armed and given a free hand to target civilian populations suspected of supporting the rebellion. The most notorious of the militias were the *janjaweed*. Supplied with AK-47s and riding on horseback or cameback, the *janjaweed* attacked villages across Darfur, burning and looting entire settlements, raping, and pillaging. The *janjaweed* destroyed fields, orchards, and granaries, and branded those they raped on their hands to make them permanent outcasts. Attacks were frequently supported by government shelling, often from helicopter gunship, followed by the use of regular government troops.

More than 2.5 million people have been displaced; some 1.9 million live in camps in Darfur and approximately 250,000 have fled to Chad, where they live in equally wretched circumstances. More than 400,000 have died of disease, malnutrition and violence. Four million people in Darfur, two-thirds of the population, are dependent on humanitarian aid for survival, but food is everywhere in limited supply as humanitarian agencies are frequently prohibited from entering the area, or simply withdraw because it is too unsafe. Little wonder the UN has identified Darfur as the world's greatest humanitarian cri-

sis. Bringing those responsible to the bar of justice may prove elusive.

UN Secretary-General Annan identified the International Criminal Court (ICC) in The Hague as "the most logical place" to try suspects in the Darfur atrocities, and a special UN inquiry turned over a list of 51 names of potential suspects to the court in March 2005. The ICC handed down its first Sudanese war crimes indictments in February 2007. Charged were Ali Muhammad al Abd-al-Rahman ("Ali Kushayb"), the alleged Janjaweed commander, and Ahmad Muhammad Harun, the former head of the government's Darfur task force and now, ironically, Sudan's minister of humanitairan affairs. The pair bore what the court calls "criminal responsibility" for war crimes and crimes against humanity, including torture, murder and rape. In August 2008 President Bashir was indicted.

Eyewitnesses reported Harun telling a gathering of 1,000 *janjaweed*—assembled to receive their share of looted cattle—that their mission was "to burn all the region down." Kushayb then ordered his men to "get rid of every Fur" and turn their territory into Dar al-Arab, or Land of the Arab. To emphasize the command, he axed three prisoners to death while his men shook their fists and shouted "Janjaweed, Janjaweed." Harun, his boss, sat under a nearby tree and cheered.

The Security Council has voted to refer Darfur war crimes suspects to the ICC, but the practical utility of the resolution is dubious: the Sudanese government has made clear its refusal to permit any of its citizens to appear before the court. It even tried a bit of legal legerdemain, creating Special Criminal Tribunals (SCT) in Darfur to bring the guilty to justice. It's an interesting conception of justice: those who complain and identify their attackers are often intimidated by police to withdraw their identifications and charges. Impunity remains the order of the day in Darfur.

One major sticking point at the UN Security Council is that China, a permanent member, will veto any action that would jeopardize its oil investments in Sudan. Additionally, both China and Russia are major arms suppliers to the Khartoum regime, a lucrative trade neither wishes to end. Qatar, the Gulf emirate, held a temporary seat on the Council into 2007 as the representative of the Arab bloc, and it proved to be one of Sudan's strongest allies, repeatedly stalling efforts to implement targeted sanctions against Sudanese responsible for the devastation of Darfur.

Khartoum has managed to dissemble and delay, postponing every effort by the international community to end atrocity and genocide in Darfur. Accordingly, in 2007 the West moved (slowly) towards

Sudan

stronger words and deeds. On April 18, 2007, during a speech at Washington's Holocaust Museum, President George W. Bush warned Sudan's president that he had one "last chance" to end the violence in Darfur before the United States imposed strict economic sanctions and considered "even sterner" measures. The Bashir regime verbally accepted the notion of a large UN force of peacekeepers, but at the same time it was resupplying its forces in the region with military arms and equipment in planes repainted to resemble UN or African Union planes.

On May 28, President George W. Bush announced heightened unilateral financial sanctions against 31 Sudanese firms, mostly in the oil business, and three individuals, one of whom was the Sudanese minister of humaniarian affairs, Ahmad Muhammad Harun. China, which absorbs some two-thirds of Sudan's oil production, objected. In Beijing, China's special envoy for Darfur (whose appointment was a Chinese concession to pressure to become more active in ending conflict in Darfur) coldly noted that more pressure would not resolve the problem and indeed would complicate the search for solutions.

China itself had increasingly become the focus of attention as an international constituency of concern moved Darfur from being a dusty, desert backwater to a foreign policy concern equivalent to Afghanistan, Iran, Iraq and North Korea. Hollywood glitterati and French presidential candidates spoke of Darfur and equally asserted the road to Khartoum lay through Beijing.

Mia Farrow, who had visited Darfur twice as a goodwill ambassador for UNICEF, wrote in the *Wall Street Journal* that "Beijing is uniquely positioned to put a stop to the slaughter, yet they have so far been unabashed in their refusal to do so." Her ire was partially directed at Steven Spielberg, who was helping stage China's Olympic ceremonies. Farrow asked acidly "[does Mr. Spielberg really want to go down in history as the Leni Riefenstahl of the Beijing games?" Farrow noted that the official slogan of the Beijing games was quickly being replaced by another: rather than 'One World, One Dream,' people were beginning to speak of the 'Genocide Games.'

Chinese spokesmen could do little more than deplore attempts to politicize the games, but calls to boycott the 2008 Olympic games were a genuine threat to China's post-Tiananmen Square coming out party. In early May 2007 China announced that it had named a senior diplomat as its first ever special envoy to Africa, with Darfur his special focus.

As 2007 progressed, the crises in Sudan seemed to multiply with the return of north-south conflict and outright clashes with the neighboring nation of Chad. While Darfur continued to occupy the headlines, the conflict between north and south recurred as the SPLM briefly removed itself from government in protest over a perceived unwillingness by the government to enforce the 2005 peace accord. Arab militias later clashed with SPLM forces over oil-producing Abyei, and this threatened to unravel any progress made on the north-south question in recent years. Al-Bashir and the southern leader Salva Kiir reached an accord in August 2008 on managing Abyei.

In the meantime, Sudan briefly reached an accord with the Chadian government, under which both countries would stop harboring rebels that attack the other. Yet this accord, reached in early 2008, has also proved fragile. Just weeks after raids by rebels into the Chadian capital of N'Djamena, rebels from Darfur conducted their own raids into the outskirts of Khartoum. The Chadian and Sudanese governments each accused the other of complicity with the respective rebel groups, and of destabilizing tactics; the two countries cut off diplomatic relations and seemed poised on the brink of outright war.

Against this backdrop, the Darfur conflict carries on, albeit now with a small international peacekeeping presence. The United Nations authorized a joint force with the African Union (UNAMID; United Nations African Union Mission in Darfur) for up to approximately 28,000 men. While promising, the present force is woefully undermanned and undersupported, at around 8,000 personnel. While the African Union and the UN both support the premise of African Union leadership, there is a sense that the mission is too resource-poor to stop the conflict and requires greater logistical support from international actors beyond the continent.

Following the 2008 indictment of Omar al-Bashir, events accelerated into 2009. Hassan al-Turabi suggested that al-Bashir might turn himself into the Hague to face prosecution, which earned al-Turabi an arrest in January 2009. In March, the International Criminal Court in the Hague issued an arrest warrant against Sudan's head of state, making him a fugitive from international justice.

In the meantime, militarization and violence heightened in the central Sudanese state of South Kordofan. The Sudanese army increased its presence in the state in late 2008 (ostensibly in anticipation of an attack from Darfur's rebel groups), and clashes in 2009 over land rights resulted in several hundred dead. This threatened to add another locus to Sudan's crisis of internal strife.

Perhaps the original geographic conflict was between south Sudan and the north, and this conflict too showed a possibility of resurfacing. Salva Kiir announced in 2009 that his southern Sudanese administration (Government of Southern Sudan, or GOSS) was rearming to prevent any reinvasion from the north. It is doing so in

Darfur refugees, victimized by Janjaweed and government forces. ©IRIN

apparent preparation for an eventual plebiscite in south Sudan in 2011 which is expected to result in a majority vote for independence; according to Kiir, the GOSS must be ready with legitimate armed forces when the referendum comes. However, conflict between ethnic groups is also breaking out within southern Sudan, and the GOSS and its military seems to have little capacity to stop it. The sheer number of conflicts (Darfur, South Kordofan, the north-south conflict, and ethnic conflict within the south) complicates the resolution of any one of Sudan's crises.

The Present: Contemporary Issues

The issue of slavery in the Sudan highlights the age-old relationship between expansive Arab nomads in the North and sedentary animist or Christian farmers in the South. In January 1999 Christian Solidarity International (CSI), a Swiss-based human rights group, announced its redemption of 1,050 slaves in the Sudan, the largest number ever liberated at one time. The group accused Sudanese armed forces of capturing and using Christian and animist black Africans as slaves and war booty. It was, the group said, "one of the most potent instruments of its declared jihad (holy war) against communities that resist its totalitarian policies of forced Islamization and Arabization."

Sudan has the highest prevalence of female genital cutting (FGC) in the world.

Almost 90% of the female population in the North endure the removal of the clitoris, in many cases in its most extreme form, infibulation. The labia are stitched together to cover the urethra and most of the vagina. Only a small opening, tiny as a matchstick or large as a small fingertip, is left to pass urine and menstrual blood. In September 2003 the minister of health expressed his government's commitment to eradicate FGC.

War long sapped Sudan's capacity for growth, development, or improved life for its citizens. It cost the government half of its budget annually, President Omar al-Bashir once admitted. Oil from Sudan's southern oil fields has helped reduce budgetary deficits, but not arms purchases. Sudan produced an average of 414,000 barrels per day (bbl/d) in 2006, up from 363,000 bbl/d in 2005.

Proven oil reserves stand at five billion barrels as of January 2007. Oil sales bring in more than $8 billion annually, allowing the government to expand and improve homegrown weapons production, and purchase modern weapons systems from suppliers like China and Russia. The armaments bill is hefty: over the years Sudan external debt has risen to $19 billion.

Sudan's crude oil exports began in August 1999 when a 1,000-mile pipeline from southern Sudan to the Red Sea was opened. The pipeline was built by the Greater Nile Petroleum Operating Company (GNPOC),

a consortium dominated by the state oil firms of China, Malaysia, and Sudan. China's assistance in the pipeline construction is being paid off in oil, and Khartoum is the biggest supplier of African crude to China's energy-hungry economy; Sudan accounts for 10% of Chinese oil imports.

China's huge investment in Sudan's petroleum industry is at the heart of advocacy groups' divestment project. Individuals (like Warren Buffet and his Berkshire Hathaway company), mutual fund operators (like Fidelity), and state pension funds (like CalPERS) have been targeted by activists demanding they sell off the stocks of companies morally tainted by their association with and support of the government of Sudan. Buffet brushed the advocates aside, saying there was no evidence that PetroChina, listed on both the New York and Hong Kong stock exchanges, had any operations in Sudan. Its parent company, China National Petroleum Company (CNPC), he admitted, did work in Sudan, but as a subsidiary, PetroChina had no influence on CNPC's policies. The argument was entirely disingenuous, as the two share an intimate, opaque, and symbiotic relationship. Managements of the two companies completely overlap; asset transfers, at subsidized rates, frequently take place between them, and ultimately, as the Sudan Divestment Task Force notes, CNPC is completely reliant on PetroChina for its financial health.

Control over Sudan's oil reserves were at the heart of the struggle between the SPLA and Khartoum's Islamist regime. Two-fifths of the country's known reserves are located in rebel-controlled territory, which provided stimulus to producing the Comprehensive Peace Agreement (CPA) signed in early 2005. The CPA calls for a 50-50 sharing of oil revenues. Ambiguities and uncertainties remain about whether or not the autonomous government of the South will be able to issue exploration permits.

High crude oil prices and increased production have meant impressive economic growth, at about 8% in 2005, 11% in 2006, and nearly 13% in 2007. This has also meant a significant spike in net foreign investment—from $392.2 million in 2000, to $2.3 billion in 2005. One immediate consequence of all this money sloshing about is inflation, which rose from an annual rate of 5.6% in December 2005 to 15.7% in December 2006. Another consequence is a building boom which is transforming and modernizing once-sleepy Khartoum; bridges and office towers are rising, most notably in the glamorous al-Mogran project situated at the confluence of the Blue Nile and the White Nile. In the suddenly stylish city, the new petro-elite has access to the latest modern luxuries, from plasma TVs to $165,000 BMWs.

Photomontage imagery designed to highlight China's support of Sudan's genocidal regime while it also sought international acceptance through the 2008 Olympic Games. A full-page advertisement in major American newspapers in June 2007 asked: "How many more will die in Darfur before China acts to end the genocide?"

Photomontage by SaveDarfur.org

Sudan

Before the oil boom, Sudan's economy was traditionally dependent on agriculture and pastoral activity. About 65% of the population makes its living through crop growing or animal grazing. Principal food crops consist of millet, sorghum, rice, cassava, wheat, peanuts, beans and bananas. Exports are primarily cotton, livestock and gum Arabic.

In the South, agricultural activity is mainly pastoral, with the main domestic livestock being cattle. Sheep, goats, camels and chickens are also reared. Sudan is an important supplier of sheep meat to the Arab world and is building new slaughterhouses in order to service this huge market.

At the Giad industrial complex, some 30 miles south of Khartoum, Sudan has a significant arms manufacturing capacity. Rocket-propelled grenades, machine guns and mortars are already produced there and the government looks to an expansion of arms manufacture. It has signed an oil-for-manufactures agreement with the Russian republic of Tartarstan, bartering oil for KamAZ trucks and various high-tech products, and would like the Tartars to set up an assembly line at Giad to produce the trucks locally. On a visit to the Tartar capital, Kazan, the Sudanese delegation was particularly interested in Tu-214 aircraft, Mi-17 helicopters and military optical sighting devices. Three Giad firms were placed on the list of companies subject to increased U.S. financial sanctions in May 2007.

Rehabilitation of war-ravaged southern Sudan will be a gargantuan task, physically and financially. The CPA's six-year transition period will allow the regional government to construct and rehabilitate basic infrastructure. The size of Kenya and Uganda put together, southern Sudan has never had an inch of tarmac roads. The Southern government plans to tarmac twelve key roads to integrate the region with northern Sudan, the Greater Horn of Africa, and Great Lakes areas, creating a market space of some 300 million people. Two railroad linkages, one from Juba—the South's regional capital—to Mombasa and the other to Kisangani in the Democratic Republic of the Congo, are also envisioned. Another key element of the regional government's development plans is a hydroelectric dam at Fulla or Bedden Falls south of Juba.

The Future

Internationally, Sudan is viewed mainly through the lens of the tragedy and the horror in Darfur, though the regime also causes problems elsewhere. The people of Darfur will not be fully protected by the small number of African Union and UN troops available as peacekeepers. While much of the killing is now years past, the crisis continues to rage and to enrage. On Darfur, one of the underappreciated facets of the crisis has been the role of China, though recognition of the Chinese role is increasing. The ideological tenets of the Chinese government—which include "non-interference," or "respect of sovereignty" of other nations—in practice mean a willingness to tolerate genocidal regimes. Amid the massive suffering in the country, Sudan grew at approximately 13% in 2007. This is largely for precisely the reasons noted above: investment—especially from the Chinese—in the country's oil production. Meanwhile, divestment from Sudan is increasingly taking root in Western countries. The arrest warrant from the International Criminal Court for the head of state Omar al-Bashir presents an intriguing test case for international justice. Yet the African Union and Arab League expressed support for him, and he himself rejects the charges.

Yet conflict in Sudan extends well beyond Darfur. It was a positive signal in August 2008 that foes from the northern and southern parts of the country reached an agreement on administering the disputed oil-rich region of Abyei. But any enthusiasm from the agreement must be short-lived as conflicts emerge within the south and between the south and north, as well as in South Kordofan state.

It is often said that the problem in Africa is misunderstood as governments having too much power, when in fact they have too *little*. It may seem curious to suggest this in the case of Sudan, and surely outside observers elsewhere would not wish the genocidal regime of Omar al-Bashir to be stronger. Yet the fundamental problem of Sudan is surely the structural inability of the government in Khartoum (over the years) to develop a meaningful set of interactions between the state and people in Sudanese society. The conflict and unrest that plague the country are ultimately attributable to a persistent inability to govern and enforce the rule of law over Sudan's vast territory. African dictatorships emerge where governments cannot draw upon rich social and political networks, whereas developed polities thrive on rich relationships between government and governed. Given Sudan's geography, demography, economy, and environment, there is little reason to expect betterment in the coming years, oil investment notwithstanding.

Child warrior in Sudan

The United Republic of Tanzania

Basic Facts

Area: 939,652 sq. km. = 362,800 sq. mi. (includes the islands of Zanzibar and Pemba; as large as Texas and most of New Mexico).

Population: 40,400,000 (UN 2007 est.)

Capital City: Dar es Salaam. Some government offices have been moved to Dodoma, which is to be the new capital at an undetermined time.

Climate: Tropically hot and humid in the coastal area, hot and dry in the central plateau and semi-temperate in the highlands where cooler weather prevails as the altitude increases.

Neighboring Countries: Mozambique (southeast); Malawi, Zambia (southwest); Congo (Kinshasa), Burundi, Rwanda (west); Uganda (northwest); Kenya (northeast)

Official Languages: KiSwahili, English

Other Principal Languages: Arabic (widely spoken in Zanzibar). Kiswahili (Swahili) is the mother tongue of the Bantu people living in Zanzibar and nearby coastal Tanzania; although Kiswahili is Bantu in structure and origin, its vocabulary draws on a variety of sources, including Arabic and English, and it has become the lingua franca of central and eastern Africa; the first language of most people is one of the local languages. Prominent among these are Bena, Chagga, Gogo, Ha, Haya, Maasai, Makonde, Nilamba, Nyakyusa, Nyamwezi, Nyaturu, Ruguru, Shambala, Sukuma, and Yao.

Ethnic Groups: Mainland—native African 99% (of which 95% are Bantu consisting of more than 130 tribes), other 1% (consisting of Asian, European, and Arab); Zanzibar—Arab, native African, mixed Arab and native African

Principal Religions: Mainland—Christian 30%, Muslim 35%, indigenous beliefs 35%; Zanzibar—more than 99% Muslim

Chief Commercial Products: Gold, coffee, manufactured goods, cotton, cashew nuts, minerals, tobacco, and sisal

GNI Per Capita: $340 (World Bank 2006 est.)

Currency: Tanzania shilling

Former Colonial Status: German Colony (1885–1917); British Mandate under the League of Nations and Trustee-ship under the United Nations (1919–1961)

Independence Date: April 26, 1964. Tanganyika became independent 9 December 1961 (from UK-administered UN trusteeship); Zanzibar became independent December 10, 1963 (from UK); Tanganyika united with Zanzibar April 26, 1964 to form the United Republic of Tanganyika and Zanzibar; renamed United Republic of Tanzania October 29, 1964.

Chief of State: Jakaya Mrisho Kikwete, President, since December 2005

National Flag: A triangle of green in the upper left corner; a triangle of blue in the lower right-hand corner with a broad band of black between the two. These three colors are separated by narrow yellow bands.

Land and People

Tanzania is a large, picturesque country lying just south of the Equator, extending between the great lakes of Central Africa and the Indian Ocean, with a 500-mile coastline. A fertile plain of up to 40 miles in width stretches along the coastline; the land slowly rises in the interior to a large central plateau averaging 4,000 feet in altitude. A mountain range of moderate height in the middle of Tanzania extends from north to south. At the north end of these peaks, Mount Kilimanjaro rises in majestic splendor to the height of 19,340 feet—the tallest peak in Africa, which, though only three degrees south of the Equator, is capped by snow and icy glaciers year around, though the famed snows

Tanzania

are melting due to climate change. Farther to the northwest, immense, freshwater Lake Victoria spreads its sparkling breadth across the semiarid plain.

A chain of towering mountains extends along the length of the entire western border, sharply descending to Lake Tanganyika, which is 2,534 feet deep. This long, narrow body of water was created centuries ago when an immense fault of land descended sharply, creating an earthquake of immeasurable proportions, and forming what is now called the Great Western Rift Valley. The large East African lakes contribute an area of 20,000 square miles of inland water to the area of Tanzania. Abundant rainfall supports dense vegetation in the coastal area, but the central plateau, hot and dry, has an average of 25 inches of rainfall per year. In the higher elevations, cooler weather prevails and there is more abundant rainfall, produced by the rush of warm air up the high slopes of the mountains.

The Past: Political and Economic History

For early history, see *Historical Background, The Colonial Period: The Germans* and *The Colonial Period: The British.*

As a result of pre-independence elections in 1960, the Tanganyika African National Union (TANU), energetically led by its founder, Julius Nyerere, was installed in power. Nyerere, the son of a minor chief of the small Zanaki tribe, had been sent to a Catholic mission school as a boy. He later trained as a teacher at Makerere University College in Uganda and, with Catholic assistance, went on to Edinburgh University, where he received a master's degree in 1949. When he returned home in 1953, he was one of only two Tanganyikans trained in foreign universities, and a year later he formed TANU to agitate against British rule. Under Nyerere's leadership, TANU effectively mobilized African sentiment and led the country to independence. Granted independence by Great Britain on December 9, 1961, Tanganyika was a de facto single-party state. Nyerere became the country's first president.

In 1964 Nyerere proceeded to institutionalize the one-party system. Following Eastern European models, TANU would be the sole means of organizing political expression in the country. Meanwhile, the neighboring island nation of Zanzibar, independent in 1963, experienced a destabilizing revolution that would ultimately link it to Tanganyika.

Zanzibar

Before the 1964 revolution, Zanzibar—a collective noun which refers to both Zanzibar (or Unguja) and Pemba islands and their volcanic neighbors—was a highly

Former President Nyerere

stratified society. A majority of the population, 76%, was African; Arabs made up 16%, but monopolized political power and controlled the economy of clove plantations. Trade was dominated by a smaller Indian population. After World War II, the racial structure of Zanzibar society was increasingly challenged by the majority African population. They experienced economic and social discrimination and limited opportunities.

Political parties were first organized in the 1950s and reflected Zanzibar's racial divide. The Zanzibar Nationalist Party (ZNP) was largely Arab and Arabized Africans; the supporters of the Afro-Shirazi Party (ASP) were Africans, often descendants of a long mixture of Arab, Persian and African heritage. In June 1963 Zanzibar gained internal self-government. A ZNP-led coalition emerged victorious in July elections, with Sultan Jamsid ibn Abdullah becoming head of state and Prime Minister Hamadi, an Arab, becoming government leader. Zanzibar was declared independent on December 10, 1963, but a month later on January 13, 1964, the Arab-dominated government was overthrown in a bloody revolution. Thousands of Arabs and Indians were massacred, the sultan deposed, and a republic declared, under the control of a 32-man Zanzibar Revolutionary Council led by Abeid Karume of the ASP.

Marxist-Leninist thinking was used to legitimize a tropical tyranny. The ASP monopolized political power as Zanzibar's sole legal party, and used its control of state machinery to punish its enemies, usually ZNP supporters. All land was nationalized, political opponents thrown in jail and murdered, and a massive exodus of Arabs and Asians began amid continuing disorder. Karume appealed to neighboring Tanganyika for aid in maintaining law and order. Nyerere's government, fearing the consequences of continuing in-

President Jakaya Mrisho Kikwete

stability, dispatched Tanganyikan police forces, and in April 1964 Zanzibar and Tanganyika formed a union, later formally designated the United Republic of Tanzania. The governing parties of each partner shared a similar outlook and had long cooperated with each other. Though Nyerere's socialism was more moderate than Karume's, the union strengthened left-radical pressures on TANU.

Tanzania

In 1964 TANU also faced instability on the mainland. Economic discontent had been fomented by trade unions and the army had mutinied in various parts of the country as soldiers protested low pay and the slow pace of Africanization of the lower officer grades. Nervous about a professional army, the government disbanded it and replaced it by a highly politicized Tanzanian People's Defense Force (TPDF). The emulation of "popular democracies" was intensified following Nyerere's visit to China in 1965.

The Chinese told him that farmers were the most conservative members of society and must be uprooted from the land if socialism were to be built. Nyerere had used the KiSwahili term *ujamaa,* meaning "familyhood," to describe the ideal of communal cooperation he sought to develop, but this was given a more conventional socialist definition in TANU's Arusha Declaration of 1967. The government was asked to nationalize all means of production and to prepare development plans that did not rely on foreign assistance. Planned villages, as in China, resulted. Peasants were forcibly transferred to new villages without consultation and without compensation for the loss of their houses and farms. Unremarkably, production declined.

In 1977 Tanzania adopted a new constitution, which explicitly subordinated all organs of state to the party. At the same time, TANU and the Afro-Shirazi Party

Tanzania

merged to form a single party known as the Chama Cha Mapinduzi—the Revolutionary Party, or CCM for short. Within the union, Zanzibar has considerable autonomy—its own president, who serves as Tanzanian vice president, and chief minister, responsible for most affairs aside from defense and international relations. Under the constitution, Tanzania's lawmaking body, the National Assembly, consists of 228 members, of whom 118 are elected from mainland constituencies and 50 from Zanzibar. Additional members are appointed by government and various "mass organizations." Given the leading role of the CCM and its monopoly of power, however, the legislature was relatively meaningless.

To reinvigorate a complacent party, an interesting variant on the one-party theme was introduced in the mid-1980s: CCM would approve two candidates for most constituencies, providing some illusion of democratic choice. Indeed, some government ministers were defeated in this manner.

President Nyerere was confirmed in office by plebiscites (it can hardly be called an election when only one candidate is running) held in 1965, 1970, 1975 and 1985. In that year he retired from the presidency, but retained the post of CCM chairman. His chosen successor was Ali Hassan Mwinyi, the former president of Zanzibar. It was during Mwinyi's two terms in office that the socialist chickens came home to roost.

The economy was bankrupt and its intellectual model proved equally bankrupt with the collapse of the Soviet Union. Plans were made to privatize some state companies and open the economic door a crack. Courageously, the government introduced the notion of competitive democracy and the constitution was amended to make Tanzania a multiparty state in 1992. Ben Mkapa was elected president in Tanzania's first competitive election, held in 1995.

The elections, characterized by administrative ineptitude, were chaotic. The situation in the capital was so bad—election officials absent, ballots lost, polls opening late, if at all—that the whole thing had to be redone after being declared null and void. Opposition parties claimed it was all a CCM plot and withdrew, but when the dust settled, on the mainland at least, 30 years of single-party rule had given way to actual party competition. Chama Cha Mapinduzi continued to control parliament, winning 186 of 232 elective seats; as CCM's candidate, Mkapa beat three opponents, winning a total of 61.8% of ballots cast.

The 2000 elections in many ways seemed a repeat of those held in 1995. President

Cloth market, Zanzibar   Photo by Beverly Ingram

Mkapa overwhelmed his opposition with nearly 75% of the vote, and CCM continued its dominance in parliament, holding 244 of 274 seats.

Turmoil reigned in Zanzibar however. The CCM organization there—always more authoritarian than its mainland counterpart—made life much tougher for its Civic United Front (CUF) opponents. Government security forces and CCM toughs harassed and intimidated CUF candidates and supporters on both Pemba and Unguja. On election day, ballots and registration lists conveniently failed to arrive on time in opposition strongholds.

The situation on Pemba was such a disaster the Zanzibar Electoral Commission (ZEC) nullified the results and reran the elections. CUF boycotted the reruns, with the expected result: The ZEC announced that CCM's Amani Abeid Karume won the Zanzibar presidency with 67%, beating the CUF's Seif Shariff Hamad, who took 33%.

The European Union, the OAU, and the United States all criticized the conduct of the election, but Amani Karume, the former minister of communication and transport and eldest son of Zanzibar's first president, Abeid Karume, seemed little inclined to make concessions to the opposition. CUF protests would continue to the elections of 2005.

In preparation for presidential and parliamentary elections scheduled for October 2005, Chama Cha Mapinduzi's national congress chose Foreign Affairs Minister Jakaya Mrisho Kikwete as its standard bearer in May. Zanzibar's CCM branch acted with authoritarian dispatch to eliminate the candidacy of Dr. Mohammed Gharib Bilal against the incumbent, President Amani Abeid Karume.

The 2005 election results were a landslide victory for CCM and raise questions about just how meaningful "multiparty" elections are in Tanzania. Presented a choice of candidates put up by ten political parties, Tanzanians chose the CCM's Jakaya Mrisho Kikwete overwhelmingly. He received 80.24% of all votes cast; his nearest rival, if that term could be used, was the CUF's Ibrahim Lipumba, who received 11.7% of the vote.

The CCM's electoral tsunami also swept its representatives massively into parliament. The party won 206 out of 232 elected seats; a distant second-place finisher was the CUF with 19 seats. Three minor parties shared the seven remaining seats.

In Zanzibar, CCM pulled out all the traditional devices and ploys to limit its contentious CUF rival, leaving itself open to ongoing criticism for electoral manipulations. A month before elections, the head of the Zanzibar Electoral Commission reported that 700 people had registered to vote more than once and he expected that more names would be found. Indeed, a week before the election he announced the Commission had found 2,000 "bogus" names had been added to the electoral register. CUF claimed its supporters were intimidated by what it called "Janjawid"—thuggish young men hired by the government to harass the opposition. Public demonstrations and protests were suppressed with violence. CCM candidates carried 30 of the 49 legislative seats while CUF won the rest. In the presidential race, the CCM's Amani Abeid Karume won 53.2% of the vote; Seif Sharif Hamad, the CUF standardbearer, took 46.1%.

One explanation for CCM's domination of Tanazanian political space is the party's

237

Tanzania

control of enormous financial resources that are lavishly spread about to assure electoral success. Indeed, electoral corruption is constitutionally enshrined by what is known as the "takrima," or African hospitality, clause. The clause allows individuals, groups or political parties to give gifts as a "show of African hospitality." No limits are placed on the amount, time, place or purpose of such gifts. Former Prime Minister Joseph Warioba, probably Tanzania's foremost anticorruption figure, observed that in his country "democracy is on auction and only available to the highest bidder."

The Present: Contemporary Issues

One of President Nyerere's greatest achievements was improving education and literacy in Tanzania. Primary education was made universally accessible with a primary school in every village. When challenged with his policy failures by World Bank officials, the president is reported to have responded that "The British Empire left us a country with 85% illiterates, two engineers and twelve doctors. When I left office, we had 9% illiterates and thousands of engineers and doctors."

Since those ebullient days investment in education went into decline, and literacy fell to 63% by 1990. Concentrated international assistance and effort have begun to effect a change: literacy was up to 69.4% in 2006. A quarter of Tanzanian adults still have no education, and women are twice as likely as men to miss out.

The government introduced free primary education in 2001 and school registrations shot up from four million to eight million children by 2007. In the initial period many classrooms lacked teachers and were sorely dilapidated. Overcrowding was a serious problem in places like Dar es Salaam where classes averaged 145 children per classroom. A UNICEF report highlighted the key problems in Tanzania's educational system; these included a serious shortage of books and teachers who are poorly trained and unmotivated. The report also criticized teaching methods, and characterized the overall school environment as one of fear and boredom rather than interaction and real learning. Secondary education languished. While primary education was universalized, there was no concomitant expansion of public education at the secondary level, where fees have to be paid. As a consequence Tanzania had the lowest rate of public secondary education in the world—just under 7%. The situation has begun to turn around. With the government helping communities across the country build secondary schools, more children are being encouraged to contin-

ued their schooling. The Education Ministry has set the target of a 50% net enrollment rate by 2010.

Retention of teaching staff remains a critical problem because the government has done little to improve the living standards of teachers. Given the opportunity, they are likely to quit their jobs and try other options. One Oxfam researcher described it succinctly: "The majority of them feel that teaching is not a respected profession any more. The low status of teaching in society has to do with the deteriorating incomes and poor living conditions of teachers, which have cost them the respect of even the pupil."

The present capital, Dar es Salaam (Haven of Peace), has become a densely congested city, suffering the consequences of urban growth. To "open up" the interior regions of the country and escape the congestion of the capital, centrally located Dodoma has been selected as the new capital city. Actual relocation of government functions will probably stretch over a period of ten years because of limited funds.

Nyerere's socialist program damaged the productive economy, though it did emphasize public services. Tanzanian policies emphasized government control over all aspects of the nation's economic life, with heavy spending on education and health. Inspired by the Chinese experience, the government resettled peasant farmers in planned villages. This facilitated the distribution of services, but had disastrous effects on agricultural production, which plummeted. Government-owned industries and businesses were costly failures and a drain on national resources. As agricultural production diminished and the expenses of nationalized companies rose, national income fell, foreign debt increased and Tanzania became increasingly dependent on the generosity of international donors.

In 1986 the government finally launched a comprehensive economic reform and

President Mkapa has continued his predecessor's efforts to liberalize the economy. Agricultural marketing was liberalized to allow some play of market forces. Privatization of state-owned enterprises has been undertaken, exchange rates have been freed, and red tape reduced. Stubborn resistance and ingrained practices have slowed transformation.

Corruption is pandemic in Tanzania ("In my country," said former Prime Minister Joseph Warioba, the chairman of President Mkapa's anticorruption commission, "you have to pay a bribe for everything.") The very public anticorruption campaign, which followed the Warioba Report, resulted in hundreds of state bureaucrats being fired, but there have been few prosecutions, and none have yet been completed. Corruption remains.

Most farmers are small-scale (with about four acres of land) and remain at virtually subsistence level. In Tanzania more than 90% of agricultural workers are women, many of them single mothers. They often work not only their own piece of land, but supplement their income by working on commercial farms, where they tend to be underpaid.

Agricultural practice and inputs need improvement, but land legislation—rewritten in 1999—still makes it difficult for farmers to mortgage their land and find credit to develop their productivity. The Kikwete administration recognizes the importance of the sector and has initiated a nine-year development program to transform rural agriculture.

Local roads also need to be improved to provide access to markets, but even where there is access, liberalization has not raised the prices paid to farmers. Certainly commodity prices have fallen generally, but in Tanzania, buyers have formed cartels that function to keep prices down even more.

Government taxes and license fees are extensive. There are, for example, 26 different taxes, levies and licenses imposed

Tea harvest

Photo by Beverly Ingram

238

on the coffee industry, Tanzania's third biggest foreign exchange earner. A recent study found Tanzania's taxes to be the highest of five peer coffee-producing countries (Uganda, Ethiopia, Costa Rica, Guatemala and Tanzania).

The heavy hand of taxes and regulation has impacted small-scale coffee farmers, who account for 95% of the country's total output. They have the lowest yields in the region. Tanzanian coffee farmers average an estimated 152 pounds an acre, while Kenya's turn out 625 per acre, for example. Coffee production continues to decline, but in May 2007 Starbucks, the world's largest coffee retailer, signed an agreement with the Association of Kilimanjaro Speciality Coffee Growers that may lead to increased production.

The island of Pemba, part of Zanzibar, produces 80% of the country's clove crop. Always a bit of a socialist laggard, the Zanzibar government has been slow to liberalize the island's agricultural policy. There is only a single buyer for cloves—the Zanzibar State Trading Corporation (ZSTC). The company has traditionally offered such low prices to producers that they have usually preferred to smuggle their crops to neighboring Kenya.

Tourism, which had replaced cloves as Zanzibar's principal source of foreign exchange, has plummeted with the rise of Islamist terrorism in the region. When Western nations warned their citizens of possible terrorist attacks in the islands in 2003, hotels almost immediately suffered 50% cancellation rates.

An upsurge of Islamist moralism on Zanzibar could threaten the tourist industry even more. During the 2003 Ramadan season, young Islamic toughs beat up a number of Muslim women whom they considered inappropriately dressed. In March 2004, police had to use tear gas to disperse hundreds of demonstrators from the Islamic Awareness Society agitating for government adoption of Islamic (*Sharia*) law.

While tourism has become sensitive to international politics, mining has become the fastest growing sector of Tanzania's economy, led by rising gold sales. As the sector opened to private investment, mineral sales rose from $15 million in 1996 to over $400 million in 2002. Sector growth has been continual: 15.4% in 2004 and 15.7% in 2005. It now contributes 3.5% of GDP.

Gold accounts for the biggest portion of sector revenues. More than 48 tons were exported in 2004, making Tanzania the third largest African gold producer (after South Africa and Ghana). Despite industry growth, its impact on poverty reduction and job creation has been slim, and the entire mining sector has come under

intense scrutiny. Pressure is building for the government to reexamine existing mining contracts to assure local communities a fair share of company profits.

Tanzania also possesses considerable deposits of gemstones—green tourmaline, sapphires, garnets, diamonds, rubies and emeralds. Smuggling remains a problem as the example of tanzanite indicates. Tanzanite is a precious blue stone found only in Tanzania southwest of Mount Kilimanjaro. Strangely, Kenya became the world's largest exporter of Tanzanite. In December 2002 the American Gem Trade Association named tanzanite an additional birthstone for the month of December. This was the first time a birthstone has been added to the existing list since 1912.

For any type of mining venture in Tanzania, infrastructure is a problem. Roads are inadequate and in disrepair. Availability of water and electricity is often problematic. During the drought conditions of 2006 there were power shortages throughout the country. Most hydroelectric stations had to produce well below capacity in the absence of sufficient water. Needless to say, individuals were inconvenienced and the manufacturing and service sectors impacted. Upon his arrival in Beijing for the Sino-African Summit of 2006, President Kikwete received an energy-assistance pledge from Chinese President Hu Jin Tao. Using coal mined in Tanzania's southern region, Chinese generators would help boost national electricity production.

At 18.5 million head, the national cattle herd is the third largest in Africa—after Ethiopia and Sudan—but conditions are so rudimentary the export of cattle, beef, and related products earned only about $4 million. Processing plants can barely handle local demand. Transportation to the port of Dar es Salaam is handicapped by hopelessly inadequate roads made impassable by seasonal rains. Bovine diseases cannot be controlled where 80% of the country's 1,998 cattle dips are malfunctioning and veterinary drugs are either too expensive or unavailable. To curb the spread of Rift Valley Fever (RVF) in March 2007, for example, the government had to order 1.8 million doses of RVF vaccines. The estimated cost was $12 million.

The greatest drag on the Tanzanian economy was its international debt, but this has been mitigated in recent years. As of 2005, debt totaled $6.2 billion. Given its impoverished nature, Tanzania was admitted to the World Bank's Heavily Indebted Poor Country (HIPC) program in 2001. Further debt relief came in 2005 when the G-8, the world's richest nations, agreed to cancel the multilateral debt of 19 of the world's poorest countries, Tanzania among them.

The Future

Tanzania has become a relatively stable polity in recent years, though it has not attained the level of full democracy. Most indicators are respectable and improving, with elections being passable, if not flawless, and civil liberties being protected, albeit imperfectly. The country was singled out for praise from President Barack Obama for a variety of achievements in advance of Obama's visit to Africa. There is little indication that the country will suffer from the major strife seen in its neighbor Kenya; rather, it is likely the country will continue on its relatively unspectacular trajectory. The biggest challenge is probably that political and religious tensions persist on Zanzibar where the opposition continues to be treated with force and violence. The question of greater autonomy for the island, indeed, whether it should become a separate state, will become more salient.

Economic growth picked up between 2005 and 2008, though it (like other countries in Africa and worldwide) will almost certainly see a decline from robust growth this year. Agriculture accounts for 44.5% of GDP (2005), but occupies 80% of the work force. Tanzania is buffeted by extremes of drought and flooding. Prices for most of its main agricultural products—coffee, sisal, cotton, tobacco, cashew nuts and tea—have tended to decline, though the country's terms of trade may have reversed in 2007 and 2008. In this challenging environment, the much vaunted liberalization of agriculture has not produce the benefits many had hoped. The country will long remain one of the poorest on earth, even if it does move slowly in the right direction.

Mass production of sculpture for the tourist trade   Photo by Jude Barnes

The Republic of Uganda

Uganda's tropical rain forest

Photo by Pat Crowell

Basic Facts

Area: 235,690 sq. km. = 91,080 sq. mi.

Population: 30,900,000 (UN 2007 est.)

Capital City: Kampala

Climate: Temperate, though equatorial, because of altitudes averaging 4,500 feet with ample rainfall in most years (except in the semiarid northwest) interrupted by two short dry seasons.

Neighboring Countries: Rwanda, Tanzania (southwest); Congo-Kinshasa (west); The Sudan (north); Kenya (northeast).

Official Language: English is taught in grade schools, used in courts of law and by most newspapers and some radio broadcasts. Ganda (or Luganda) is preferred for native-language publications in the capital.

Other Principal Languages: Over forty. Prominently: Acholi, Alur, Chiga, Ganda, Karamojong, Kenyi, Lango, Masaba, Nyankore Nyoro, Rwanda, Sogo, Teso, Tooro

Ethnic Groups: Baganda, Karamojong, Basogo, Iteso, Langi, Rwanda, Bagisu, Acholi, Lugbara, Bunyoro, Batobo, non-African (European, Asian, Arab)

Principal Religions: Roman Catholic 33%, Protestant 33%, Muslim 16%, indigenous beliefs 18%

Chief Commercial Products: Coffee, fish and fish products, flowers, tobacco, electricity, cotton, and tea

GNI Per Capita: $280 (World Bank 2006 est.)

Currency: Uganda shilling

Former Colonial Status: British Protectorate (1894–1962)

Independence Date: October 9, 1962

Chief of State: Yoweri Museveni, President

National Flag: Six bands of black, yellow and red (repeated) with a silver circle in the center enclosing a crested crane.

Land and People

This fertile expanse of highland bestrides the Equator in central East Africa between the Eastern and Western Rift formations. Uganda, dotted with lakes, and with immense Lake Victoria in the south, lies at an altitude of between 3,000 and 6,000 feet. If this country were at a lower altitude, its climate would be hot, moist and oppressive, but it is quite pleasantly temperate with ample rainfall to support intense cultivation. In the extreme northeast, the climate is dry and prone to drought.

Approximately 15% of the country is covered by fresh water. The Ruwenzori Mountains to the west divide Uganda from the Democratic Republic of the Congo, having altitudes of almost 17,000 feet. In the southwest, close to Rwanda, the Virunga range of active volcanoes reaches skyward. In the east, Mount Elgon rises to a height of 14,000 feet, prominent among its neighbors of the Eastern Rift Mountains.

The Victoria Nile originates from the banks of Lake Victoria, heavily populated with hippopotamuses and crocodiles, and flows to Lake Kyoga, an irregularly shaped body of water with large swamps. From there the Nile flows north and west through immense mountains to empty into Lake Albert. The Albert Nile flows northward, leaving Uganda at the Sudanese border to continue its journey of more than 4,000 miles to the Mediterranean Sea.

Living in Uganda's northeast corner are the Karamojong, a pastoralist minority of some 100,000 people. The Karamojong are Nilotic, while the bulk of Ugandans are Bantus. Among them the cow is supreme. Milk and blood (drawn during the dry season when the animal produces no milk) provide the principal sources of Karamojong protein. Wealth, power and status are all based on cattle ownership.

The Karamojong illustrate all the problems of Uganda's underdeveloped and wretchedly poor north. Persistent drought has diminished their livestock and impoverished them further. Poverty, and the easy availability of arms, has increased banditry and insecurity. Unemployment is high. Literacy is a mere 6% (compared with a national average of 70%), diseases and child mortality are the highest in the country, and only 1% of them has ever used a telephone.

The Past: Political and Economic History

For early history, see *Historical Background* and *The Colonial Period: The British*.

The United Kingdom of Uganda was granted internal autonomy on March 1, 1962, becoming fully independent on October 9 of that year. The government initially consisted of a federation of the kingdoms of Buganda, Busoga, Butoro and Bunyoro, which retained local autonomy, while the rest of the country was governed by the central government. Sir Ed-

ward Frederick Mutesa II, Kabaka of Buganda, became the first president and Sir William W. Nadiope, king of Bunyoro, was the first vice president. Prime Minister Milton Obote wielded considerable power within the central government. The cabinet was selected by a coalition of Obote's People's Congress Party and the Buganda KabakaYekka Party; the formerly dominant Democratic Party was in the minority.

The post independence era was dominated by two figures who reduced Uganda to a grisly shambles, replete with starvation and widespread deaths. Milton Obote was the first (1963–1971, 1980–1985) and the second was a military figure, Idi Amin (1971–1979).

Charging Kabaka Mutesa with making personal profits from the supply of arms in connection with a rebellion in neighboring Zaïre, Obote dismissed him and seized the government. The hereditary king barely escaped when the army stormed the presidential palace; he lived in exiled poverty until his death in 1969. (His remains were ceremoniously returned to Uganda in 1971.)

Obote abolished the old constitution and the traditional kingdoms; his PCP became the sole party, and he steered Uganda sharply to a socialist economy. As he appointed more and more of his fellow tribesmen to public offices, tensions mounted and political instability increased. Finally the army revolted, uniting behind Idi Amin in January 1971.

General Amin, who had once been the Ugandan heavyweight boxing champion, was initially popular, but he wasted no time alienating just about everyone. Some 70,000 Asians, mainly Indians and Pakistanis, were expelled in 1972 with little thought of their importance to the economy as merchants and traders. The expul-

sion won Amin immense support from those to whom he gave property and merchandise seized from Asian merchants. Controversial and damaging though the expulsion was, the ultimate consequence was that Uganda today has one of the biggest black middle classes in Africa.

Initial admiration of Field Marshall Amin quickly turned to fear. Educated Ugandans began to leave the country to escape his whims. Brutality became the order of the day by 1974. Secret executions, massacres and torture were among his favorite methods, and he personally participated in some of these grisly acts.

Military efforts to oust him failed, and perpetrators were executed on the spot. The economy all but disappeared by 1978, and the country seethed with unrest. Amin tried to distract attention from his failures by claiming that Tanzania had invaded Uganda; he "responded" by having his troops invade Tanzania. They captured about 710 square miles before withdrawing.

President Julius Nyerere of Tanzania used the invasion as an excuse to get rid of Amin. Tanzanian troops, augmented by Ugandan exiles, mounted a swift invasion. Amin's forces, demoralized by his behavior, crumbled after fierce fighting had claimed the lives of many.

The conquering army entered Kampala in April 1979 and was greeted jubilantly. In the confusion, Amin escaped. Yusufu Lule was installed as president, but he was quickly replaced by Godfrey Binaisa, whose term of office was equally short-lived. Obote supporters plotted Binaisa's overthrow, and Obote returned to Uganda in May 1980.

December 1980 elections were outrageously stolen by Obote, driving his political rivals into rebellion. One of those was Yoweri Museveni, who had contributed significantly to the military overthrow of Amin. Refusing to accept the fraudulent election results, he formed a guerrilla group and "went to the bush with only 26 guns and organized the National Resistance Army (NRA) to oppose the tyranny that Obote's regime had unleashed upon the population," as his website describes it. Five years of strife followed; an estimated one million fled and 300,000 lost their lives.

In January 1986 Museveni's rebel band, which now called itself the National Resistance Army (NRA), shot its way into Kampala and seized control of the country. In victory the NRA became the first guerrilla army to oust an incumbent African regime. Museveni became president as the head of the National Resistance Movement (NRM) and began the difficult task of rebuilding Uganda. He was determined to break the cycle of violence that

Idi Amin

had destroyed Uganda, restore democracy and foster economic development. Those goals required an entire rethinking of the institutions and practices that had bedeviled and destroyed the country.

Chief among the objects of his criticism were the traditional political parties, which he castigated as "sectarian and divisive," responsible for the country's political and economic ills. Political parties were prohibited, and political participation was organized within the framework of the broad-based National Revolutionary Movement (NRM). All would belong, and candidates would stand for office on personal merit rather than party platform. This was the beginning of what would come to be known as the nonparty movement system.

Since the regime had come to power by force of arms promising to restore democracy and individual liberties, one of its first projects was a constitutional commission that could develop the framework which restored the rule of law. Once in existence, the commission toured the entire country and consulted broadly.

The whole process demonstrated a remarkable shift from the tradition of constitutions created on high and presented to the people. Here, people actually participated in developing the document that would shape their lives and futures.

The transition from anarchy to constitutionalism was lengthy; the constitutional commission's draft was debated and ratified by a popularly elected constituent assembly on July 12, 1995, and promulgated by President Museveni on October 8. The constitution that emerged from this process was equally lengthy. In its final form, the constitution weighed in with 287 articles and seven addenda, making the Uganda Constitution ten times longer than that of the United States.

Milton Obote

Uganda

The constitution outlaws traditional political party activities, including sponsoring candidates for election. For Museveni, a country like Uganda, divided along ethnic and religious fault lines, simply could not afford the divisiveness of party competition. Parliament was constitutionally prohibited, however, from establishing a single-party state. After five years experience with the movement system, the constitution promised voters an opportunity to assess the system in a referendum.

President Museveni's personal rule was legitimized by May 1996 elections held in accordance with the new constitution. His election slogan was "No Change," and he campaigned on his record: He had ended Uganda's cycle of blood and dictatorship, boosted security through the army, and built economic success that saw the gross domestic product grow by 10% in 1994. He won handily, beating two opposition candidates. It was the first free and open presidential vote in 30 years.

Parliamentary elections followed in July 1996. There are 214 directly elected members and a number of indirectly elected seats for representatives of women (39), youth (5), workers (3), the disabled (5) and the army (10).

Northern Uganda, site of LRA activity

President Yoweri Museveni

Museveni had inherited a wasteland of human devastation in 1986. Piles of skulls remained at crossroads, remainders of the grisly days since independence. The economy was stagnant. Transportation and communication systems had been destroyed by war, production disrupted. The state was bankrupt; revenue from taxation was virtually nonexistent. To change course, agreements were made with the IMF. The economy was liberalized to include producer incentives, loans were secured to rehabilitate infrastructure, and the economy (starting from virtually nothing) responded with eye-catching growth rates.

Rebels and Regional Conflicts

Although economic vibrancy returned to Uganda, not all its citizens shared in its changed conditions. In border areas to the west and north, the Uganda Peoples Defense Force (UPDF) faced ongoing resistance and rebellion from those marginalized economically and politically. In the north, the Lord's Resistance Army (LRA), supported by Khartoum's meddlesome anti-Museveni regime, has waged war for years. Led by a former Roman Catholic altar boy, Joseph Kony, the LRA recruits its soldiers by kidnapping children (30,839 between 1986 and 2001 according to UNICEF), male and female, and sending them off to Sudanese camps for military training or sexual service. Those who flee or disobey are maimed or murdered as punishment. Kony's stated goal is to overthrow Museveni and rule Uganda in accordance with the Ten Commandments.

The rebels—Museveni calls them terrorists—have killed thousands, destroyed homes and property, and prevented the distribution of social services or development projects in an already dirt-poor region. More than 1.4 million people have been forced to leave their homes. At least 300,000 of them live in "protected villages" organized by the army to prevent the enemy from getting food and assistance from fellow Acholi tribesmen. Virtually the whole of northern Uganda became a humanitarian disaster area.

Sudan long offered support for LRA forces and other destabilizing elements as a tit-for-tat response. President Museveni shared with his colleagues in Eritrea and Ethiopia a common hostility to Sudan's Islamist regime and supported John Garang's SPLA in its resistance to the government in Khartoum.

A successful guerrilla commander, Museveni has shown sympathy for more than Sudanese rebels. Uganda was the training ground for members of the Tutsi-led Rwandan Patriotic Front which invaded and defeated the genocidal regime installed in Kigali. Museveni was also a central figure in organizing the forces that overthrew the Mobutu regime in Zaïre. It all represented an enormously self-confident foreign policy, distinctly at odds with the OAU traditions of nonintervention and respect for borders.

Uganda's support of the anti-Kabila rebels raised fundamental questions about how a country as poor as Uganda could afford the increased defense expenditures necessary to conduct these operations. In part, the answer is simple: the war was self-financed through exploitation of Congo's rich resources. The war effort was early dominated by the question of resource extraction. Congo's wealth would corrupt all who came near and tarnish the

Uganda

reputations of the Ugandan army and its officers.

Corruption permeated the entire army operation. Timber prices in Uganda fell sharply because Ugandan troops in the Congo had flooded the market with cheap wood smuggled from the war zone. The tentacles of corruption spread throughout the region as ports in Kenya and Tanzania served as points of transshipment for timber, coffee and minerals headed for Asian markets.

Corruption, already notable in Uganda, became all pervasive and inched closer to President Museveni himself. His half-brother, Major-General Salim Saleh, who seemed to shuttle back and forth between the private and public sectors, was everywhere touched by the taint of corruption.

Uganda's joint support with Rwanda of the anti-Kabila coalition unraveled in 1999. In 2000 each country massed troops on its respective borders and seemed near war. Charges of supporting and training hostile forces were made by both parties, but diplomacy prevailed. Confidence-building measures—like exchanging military inspection teams—were created in 2002, but tensions remain.

The terrorist attacks on New York and Washington in September 2001 helped to transform Uganda's relations with Sudan. The UN placed the LRA on a list of terrorist organizations and, eager to be counted amongst the antiterrorists, Sudan gave permission for the Ugandan army to pursue Joseph Kony's forces into Sudanese territory.

Using heavy artillery, the Uganda People's Democratic Army (UPDA) launched operation "Iron Fist," against the LRA's Sudanese bases in March 2002. No prisoners were taken and UN humanitarian organizations lamented that any hostage children had probably died under the bombs of the Ugandan army. The rebels responded by multiplying their attacks against Ugandan civilians in the north in ways that were, if possible, even more violent, vicious and destructive than previous efforts. Hostages were taken, children kidnapped to replace fallen rebels, women raped and men castrated and left to bleed to death. The effort seemed two-fold. One goal was to terrify local inhabitants and keep them from providing valuable intelligence on rebel locations and movements to the army. The other was to delegitimize the Museveni regime by proving the army's incapacity to protect local inhabitants.

Despite army press releases, the UPDA could not defeat the LRA. The rebels seem able to move with ease across borders, entering Sudan or the Demoratic Republic of Congo at will. Little seemed to diminish their destructive ravaging. In June 2005,

President Museveni promised to forgive Kony if he surrendered, and got no response. In October, the International Criminal Court issued arrest warrants for Kony and five senior aides, but none has yet been served on the illusive enemy; local leaders worried the warrants would derail ongoing efforts to end the conflict.

Conditions in Northern Uganda, probably the least developed area of the country, spiraled downward. To resident Acholi, driven to refugee camps by LRA depredations and government policy, the army seems more predator than protector. The rains failed for several years in a row, and the land became dry, dusty and cropless. Schools were deserted and market stalls emptied and abandoned. Granaries were empty and underfed cattle, the pride of northern pastoralists, no longer provided the milk and blood of traditional sustenance. The word "akoro," meaning "hunger," was heard everywhere: In some areas people were living on one bowl of boiled leaves a day. UN officials called it the world's worst forgotten humanitarian crisis.

Those displaced by LRA violence became dependent on food handouts, because it was simply too dangerous to live in villages and farm the land—even if the rains came. Insecurity also created the phenomenon of "night commuters"; every night as many as 20,000 children walk miles from their villages to the relative safety of cities where they spend the night in public buildings or on the streets.

The most sustained peace efforts in 20 years of seemingly interminable conflict was initiated by Salva Kiir's government

of Southern Sudan in 2006. The proposal was different from all other attempts to negotiate an end to the conflict. For the first time, negotiations would take place outside Uganda—in the Southern Sudanese capital of Juba—and would be structured and presided over by a third-party mediator, Riek Machar, Slava Kiir's vice president.

For both the LRA and Uganda, the proposal's timing may have been critical. Annual costs of the war to Uganda are estimated at $85 million, totaling a staggering $1.7 billion over its course. Donors, who fund some 40% of the Ugandan budget, had become increasingly critical of defense expenses. The LRA also faced an increasingly hostile regional and international environment. The ICC had issued warrants for the group's top leadership, and the UN Security Council had called for coordinated military action against it. With the signing of the Comprehensive Peace Agreement (CPA) between Khartoum and Juba, it had also lost, at least ostensibly, its principal supplier of arms and money.

As talks progressed, Joseph Kony declared a unilateral ceasefire on August 4, 2006. The offer was matched on August 19, when Salva Kiir and President Museveni jointly announced the UPDF would halt operations against the LRA, if the rebels agreed to assemble at two designated assembly points. These ad hoc initiatives were formally confirmed when a Cessation of Hostilities Agreement (CHA) was signed on August 26.

Confidence-building measures were implemented between the two antagonists.

Fighting corruption with billboards

Photo by Pat Crowell

243

Uganda

Kony was permitted to visit his mother in Uganda for the first time in 20 years, for example, and he and President Museveni spoke several times by telephone. A renewed presidential offer of amnesty and efforts to suspend the ICC warrants seemed not to speed negotiations. The rebel delegation, which was being paid a *per diem* of $70, found reason to complain about the Sudanese mediator and seemed to be shopping for a more favorable venue. Tired of delay, President al-Bashir of Sudan announced in early January that he was prepared to create a joint military force to eliminate the LRA: "We do not want them. If we cannot find a peaceful solution to the LRA conflict, then we must pursue a military solution."

Shortly afterwards the LRA announced their disengagement from the peace process, citing security concerns and demanding the talks' relocation to a neutral country and mediator. Discussions resumed, at Juba, near the end of April 2008, and seemed to lead to the prospects for a peace settlement. Joseph Kony, however, failed to turn up to sign a peace agreement in late 2008. This prompted a new offensive from Ugandan, Congolese, and south Sudanese forces, which in turn prompted Kony to re-seek a ceasefire. Nonetheless, the LRA continues its activities. The conflict is ongoing and unresolved in 2009, though the Ugandan government may be gaining the upper hand in a long-stalemated conflict.

The Movement and Multipartyism

In June 2000 Ugandans were asked to voice their opinions on the "movement system." A referendum asked if the movement system should be maintained, or if the country should adopt a multiparty system of democracy. The campaign became personalized—a referendum for or against Yoweri Museveni. Sensing the mood of a country relatively satisfied with Museveni's tenure, the opposition decided to boycott the vote. More than 90% of those who voted chose to retain the movement system.

There was little interest in Uganda's presidential election, scheduled for March 2001, until Kizza Besigye entered the race. Dr. Besigye was no ordinary challenger. He was one of the original NRA fighters and Museveni's personal physician during the long bush war; he had also served as a minister in Museveni's NRM government, but had become disillusioned.

He criticized regime corruption and nepotism, as well as Uganda's involvement in the Congo war. He accused the president of becoming increasingly autocratic and of turning the ruling movement into a party intolerant of competition. The president and his supporters experienced a sense of betrayal, and the campaign became unnecessarily violent and ramified regionally.

Tensions with Rwanda were magnified. Kigali was accused of contributing large sums to the Besigye campaign. Dr. Besigye's wife, a member of parliament, added to heightened suspicion between the two countries by accusing the Museveni government of aiding the *Interahamwe*, one of Rwanda's greatest bêtes noires.

When all the votes were counted, President Museveni won by a huge margin, receiving 69.3% of the vote. Dr. Besigye, who ran second with 27.8% of the vote, refused to accept the results, charging fraud and intimidation. The victory may have been sweet for President Museveni, but the campaign damaged his reputation.

Equally damaging was the April 2001 report of a panel of experts to the UN Security Council on "Illegal Exploitation of Natural Resources and Other Forms of Wealth in the Democratic Republic of the Congo." Names were named, and they came very near the president himself. The panel specifically singled out the president's half brother, Major-General Salim Saleh and his wife Jovia Akandwanaho, as being "at the core of the illegal exploitation of natural resources in areas controlled by Uganda." President Museveni, it said, had "put himself in the position of accomplice" by choosing not to act when information on corrupt practices was brought to his attention. Denials were, of course, issued, but the accumulation of wealth by the president's family is a major factor in a growing opposition to Museveni.

Parliamentary elections in June 2001 provided some small hint of discontent. Since there are no parties, candidates were either for or against the government, and President Museveni was faced with the defeat of 12 cabinet ministers. Only two, it should be said, were replaced by individuals who actually opposed the government.

With the approach of presidential elections in 2006, there were pressures to return Uganda to multipartyism. President Museveni seized the opportunity to polish his image by becoming a born-again democrat. In late February 2003, Ugandans learned their president, long the advocate of "no-party democracy," had decided to allow parties after all.

By the end of March, the ruling NRM announced concurrence, and just to make things legal, Uganda's constitutional court announced its decision on the challenge to the *Political Parties and Organisations Act*. Siding with the opposition, it declared unconstitutional those parts of the law which forbade political parties from carrying out their activities. The decision liberated parties and transformed Uganda's political space. By early 2004, 50 political parties had applied for registration in preparation for the 2006 elections. The first to apply for the new designation was the NRM, rechristened the National Resistance Movement—Organisation (NRMO).

Against a background of increasing insecurity in the northern provinces and increasing political tension in the run-up to the 2006 general elections, President Museveni made the politically hazardous decision to seek repeal of constitutional provisions limiting a president to two five-year terms. The amendment needed only a two-thirds majority vote in parliament, which was obligingly offered by the NRM-dominated legislature in July 2005.

As a sop to democratic sensitivities, the government scheduled a referendum shortly afterwards to return Uganda to multiparty politics. Voters were presented with the simple question: "Do you agree to open up political space to allow those who wish to join different organisations/parties to do so to compete for political power?" President Museveni traversed the country campaigning for a "Yes" vote, but six opposition parties denounced it as a democratic smokescreen and called for a boycott. They claimed Museveni had only accepted the referendum to distract people from the constitutional amendment designed, as they put it, to make him "president for life." The boycott was successful, or the issue seemed not to grip the electorate. Less than 30% of eligible voters participated, but 92.5% of those agreed to return the country to multiparty competitive elections in 2006. In them, it was clear, President Museveni would be a candidate to succeed himself.

Donors, and here it should be noted that 40% of Uganda's budget is financed by international aid, became increasingly skeptical of the regime's democratic intentions. The United Kingdom cancelled millions in aid to Uganda, saying the country had not done enough to establish fair multiparty politics. Other European donors—Netherlands, Sweden, and Norway—also withheld or cut back their contributions. U.S. President George Bush reportedly urged Museveni to give up third-term plans, but he was not dissuaded.

In October, Kizza Besigye returned to Uganda after four years of self-imposed exile to be the presidential candidate of the Forum for Democratic Change (FDC). In less than a month he was charged with treason, terrorism and rape, arrested, denied bail, and jailed. Antigovernment riots convulsed the capital, and donors cut off more funding. Uganda's attorney-general urged the electoral commission to deny Besigye's presidential candidacy, arguing his nomination would be "tainted."

In early January 2006, however, Uganda's High Court released Besigye on bail

Uganda

and allowed him to campaign. With the collapse of efforts to exclude his most threatening opponent, President Museveni faced four challengers in the presidential race: Dr. Besigye of the FDC; Kampala's mayor John Ssebaana, representing the Democratic Party (DP); Miria Kalule Obote, widow of former dictator Milton Obote, representing the UPC; and a veterinary doctor, Abed Bwanika, running as an independent.

The campaign was not, shall we say, a model of democratic deportment. Human Rights Watch, always a bit hypercritical, described it as "marred by intimidation of the opposition, military interference in the courts and bias in campaign funding and media coverage." EU observers criticized the "lack of a level playing field," but Uganda's Supreme Court threw out Dr. Besigye's petition to nullify election results because of massive malpractice.

When the late February 2006 ballots were tabulated, Yoweri Museveni was once again Uganda's president. He took 59% of the vote. Despite five candidates, it was really a two-man race. Kizza Besigye, his main rival, took 37%. The three also-rans received just over 3% of the tally; voter turnout was 65%. President Museveni's total vote was 10% lower than his 2001 performance; not unexpectedly, he did poorly in the northern regions and was soundly defeated in Kampala.

In legislative elections the voters did a bit of housecleaning. At least 80 MPs were defeated, including 17 who held ministerial portfolios. The NRM will continue to dominate the legislature, with 190 seats in the 304-member body; the delegation from Dr. Besigye's Forum for Democratic Change is in distant second place with 35 seats. The UPC won 13 seats and the DP nine; two smaller parties elected a single representative each and 37 members of the new parliament were elected as independents. One new face in the legislature: First Lady Janet Museveni.

Though losing the presidential race, candidate Besigye's woes are partially mitigated. In March a judge declared him innocent of the rape charge, calling the prosecution case "crude and amateurish."

The Present: Contemporary Issues

Uganda's HIV/AIDS program has come to be viewed as a model for states affected by the pandemic. A decade ago, more than 18% of Ugandan adults were living with HIV/AIDS. The death of a young and productive breadwinner left many families in poverty. AIDS orphans epitomized the problem. Innocent, they suffered. Most had no access to education, labor skills, and employment. They became street kids, an urban poor; alienated and unemployed, they became a potential threat to

Murchison Falls
Photo by Virginia Grady

social stability. The problem was recognized early and a commitment was made to deal with it.

In many ways the program's success reflects the political culture of President Museveni's regime. Museveni has been as inclusive as possible, encouraging different actors to contribute in whatever way they could. He appointed a bishop for example, as one of the leaders of the Uganda AIDS Commission, but all the major sectarian communities participated. For its part, the Islamic Medical Association of Uganda worked with Imams to incorporate HIV/AIDS prevention information into their spiritual teachings.

Openness of discussion and commitment to education, characteristics of Museveni's rebel insurgency from the beginning, have also characterized the country's approach to AIDS. In 1988 Uganda's most famous popular singer, Philly Lutaaya, returned from Sweden after four years of political exile. In April 1989 he shocked his fans and fellow Ugandans by announcing he had AIDS. For the next eight months he led a personal crusade against AIDS. Then, at the age of 38, he died. The admission and death of so public a figure elevated HIV/AIDS to public discussion from the dark recesses of shame. Once there, action was possible.

The Uganda AIDS program is reputed to be one of the most aggressive. It fea-

tures education and testing, counseling and condoms. By far the most striking feature of Uganda's success is the drastic reduction in multiple partnering by Ugandan adults. Among women aged 15 and above, the number reporting multiple sexual partners fell from 18.4% in 1989 to 2.5% in 2000. The program is open to trials of new drugs, and indeed, nevirapine studies in Uganda showed the transmission of HIV from mother to child was reduced to about 13%.

Overall the HIV/AIDS prevalence rate in adults has declined significantly, from 18.5% in the early 1990s to 4.1% (at the low end of the average range) in 2003. Despite the good news, the problem remains enormous. At least 900,000 people have died of HIV/AIDS since the onset of the pandemic in the 1980s. UNAIDS estimates that 78,000 died of it in 2003. An estimated 1.9 million Ugandans carry the HIV virus, and according to government figures released in early 2002, Uganda has an estimated 1.7 million orphans, the highest number in the world. The number is expected to rise to 3.5 million by 2010. The average life expectancy for Ugandans—just 48.9 years—is expected to decline in the next ten years.

The government committed itself to offering free antiretroviral (ARV) treatment to those in urgent need as of January 2004. It intended to have 60,000 people on the life-extending drugs by the end of 2005 but achieved that goal by mid-year. By July over 65,000 Ugandans were receiving treatment.

Ongoing civil conflict in northern Uganda may reverse the gains made so far. As rape has increasingly become an instrument of war, high HIV infection rates among rebels and government soldiers have been found. UNICEF and government officials have reported 90% of children rescued from Lord's Resistance Army rebels are HIV positive. According to the NGO World Vision International, AIDS is killing three times more people than the ongoing war against the LRA. The Ugandan Health Ministry released a report in August 2005 indicating that among those displaced by the LRA terror campaign, at least 1,000 a week die of disease. The principal culprits are malaria and HIV/AIDS.

By the time President Museveni assumed power in 1986, Uganda had become one of the poorest countries in the world. Socialist planning meant state intervention in nearly all sectors of the economy. Social services had collapsed and infrastructure had crumbled. Under President Museveni Uganda liberalized its economy and became the poster child of international lending agencies: Real GDP growth has averaged 6.7% since 1995.

245

Uganda

Uganda's economic picture is not, however, entirely rosy. Twenty years of warfare in the north is estimated to have cost the country 3% of its GDP. Economic growth is also being eroded by the effects of population growth, estimated at 3.5% a year in 2005. With government efforts to diversify the economy, GDP growth has shown slow improvement: 4.7% in 2003, 5.7% in 2004, and 6.6% in 2005.

Uganda's economy is agriculture-based. The sector employs over 80% of the work force, and contributes about 32.7% of GDP (2005). Coffee has traditionally been the country's biggest export earner. In 1996 Uganda exported 4.15 million bags of coffee, which accounted for 65% of its export income. The expansion of coffee plantations in Asia over the past few years, however, has produced a glut of coffee on international markets and severely reduced prices. Coffee now accounts for less than 30% of export earnings, a decline hastened by crop disease, aging trees, poor crop management, poor soil fertility, and poor post-harvest handling practices. Some 60% of coffee farmers have abandoned coffee production for crops with better returns.

Significant efforts have been made to diversify the economy, once almost totally reliant on coffee exports. Tea remains important, though struggling to regain its former status. In 1972, Uganda produced 23,000 metric tons of tea, but by 1991, after years of neglect by the Idi Amin regime, only 8,800 tons were produced. Since then strenuous efforts have been made to reclaim some 42,000 acres that had returned to bush. Tea is now Uganda's third leading export, after coffee and fish.

The government is seeking to further boost tea production, but marketing conditions are extremely difficult and the high cost of Ugandan electricity puts tea growers at a competitive disadvantage; its erratic supply also discourages investors from opening new areas for tea production. Transportation costs are also high. In March 2003 the Uganda Tea Association reported that most producers received less than they spent on production and transportation—on average about 23% less.

Fishing and fish processing have increasing importance among Uganda's exports, especially since the EU lifted its ban (because of sanitation and pesticide concerns) on imports in 2000. In 2001 Uganda exported 28,627 tons of fish, earning about $80 million. With demand increasing among consumers trying to avoid the health risks of red meat, the country earned more in 2002—$87.5 million—from less tonnage—25,159 tons.

The fishing industry still faces many challenges. Pesticide poisoning of lakes is related to a longer-range but potentially even more damaging problem: the water hyacinth. Probably brought in by Belgians as an ornamental plant, the hyacinth has no known natural predators and, like a cancer, grows with amazing rapidity. The whole of Lake Victoria, the world's second largest freshwater lake, is threatened. Once colonized, the plant impedes fishing boats and can ultimately kill off the entire fish stock.

Already, 70,000 tons of hyacinth press against the outer walls of Uganda's Owen Falls hydroelectric dam, 80 km east of Kampala, which supplies electricity to Kenya and Tanzania. Engineers wonder how much weight it can take. Thus far spraying aquatic herbicides directly onto the plants has been the most effective method of reducing weed infestation quickly.

Construction of the hydroelectric dam and 250 MW power station at Bujagali Falls, near the source of the Nile River, was scheduled to begin in mid-2006, but the project, mired in corruption and controversy from its inception, was delayed. Environmentalists argued mightily against the dam, arguing the site supports the growing whitewater tourism industry and long term is a serious "hydrological risk," given the potential for serious drought due to global climate change. Supporters of the project argued that energy shortages constrained social and economic growth. The International Finance Corporation, for example, estimated that energy shortages and blackouts cut GDP growth by 1% in the 2005–2006 financial year. By increasing energy output, Bujagali would contribute to industrialization and economic growth. Finally, in April 2007 the World Bank approved a package of $360 million in loans and guarantees for the project.

One area of potential growth should be mentioned: oil. In early April 2003, the Canadian firm, Heritage Oil, announced that its explorations suggested Uganda had a potential oil reserve of "several billion barrels." Two wells were drilled and oil was encountered. In early March 2007 the company it had a cumulative flow rate of 13,893 barrels of oil per day (bbl/d) from one of its wells in Western Uganda. Heritage followed this with another announcement of another major find in January 2009.

The Future

Uganda's economic development is still dependent on external aid. An estimated growth rate of 6% in 2007 probably overstated the dynamism in the economy, and the economy surely suffered from the global meltdown in 2008 and 2009. Nonetheless, Uganda remains on track for relatively greater political stability than in previous decades, which should facilitate investment in productive enterprise and in human capital over the long term. Conscientious investment in HIV/AIDS reduction also sets Uganda apart from many other African countries.

Diminishing civil strife and containing regional conflict are high-priority issues in the political arena. The Juba peace process offered hope for a negotiated settlement of the conflict that has devastated northern Uganda for so long, but the LRA's recalcitrance has prevented any resolution of the insurrection. Uganda is still not a full-fledged democracy, and will not be so for the immediate future, but the slow move to multiparty governance seems to suggest some releasing of political tensions.

Coffee berries

INDIAN OCEAN ISLAND NATIONS

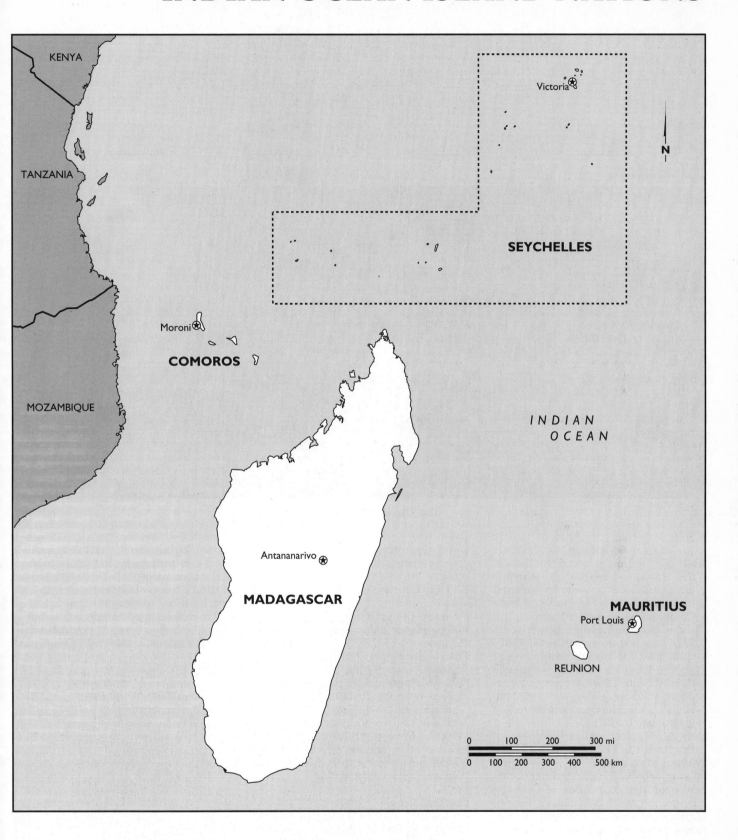

The Union of the Comoros

The Grande Mosque, Moroni   ©IRIN

Basic Facts

Area: 2,170 sq. km. = 838 sq. mi. The Comoro group consists of three mountainous islands lying between Tanzania and the northern coast of Madagascar: Grand Comore (also known as Njazidja), Anjouan (Nzwani), and Mohéli (Mwali). Mayotte a possible fourth island with a substantial Christian minority, opposed joining the other three and, although claimed by the Union, remains a dependency of France, and in March 2009 referendum voted to be a French overseas department by 2011.

Climate: Tropical marine; rainy season (November to May); cyclones possible during rainy season.

Population: 839,000 (UN 2007 est.) An estimated 150,000 persons of Comoran origin also reside in France.

Capital City: Moroni (on Grande Comore)

Ethnic Groups: Antalote, Cafre, Makoa, Oimatsaha, Sakalava

Principal Religions: Sunni Muslim 98%, Roman Catholic 2%

Official Languages: Arabic, French

Other Principal Languages: Comoran (a blend of Swahili and Arabic).

Chief Commercial Products: Vanilla, ylang-ylang, cloves, perfume oil, and copra

GNI Per Capita: $855 (World Bank 2008 est.)

Currency: Comoran franc

Independence Date: July 6, 1975 (from France)

Chief of State: Ahmed Abdallah Mohamed Sambi, President (since May 2006)

National Flag: From the pole as its base, a green triangle, containing a crescent pointing right with four stars (one for each of the islands, plus one for Mayotte), arranged vertically, between the crescent tips. This lies on a field of four equal horizontal stripes, from the top: yellow, white, red, and blue.

Land and People

The people of the Comoros are a blend of Arab, African and Indian Ocean heritage. They speak Cormoran, closely related to the Swahili of East Africa, which is written in Arabic script. The language is enriched with borrowings from the many cultures that have made contact with the islands. Indian, Persian, Arabic, Portu-

guese, English, and French words have all been added to the basic African vocabulary. Given island isolation, there are four distinct dialects of Comoran spoken, each specific to one of the four islands.

The dominant religion in the islands is Islam, and islanders are predominantly Sunni Muslims. Traditional Islam tended

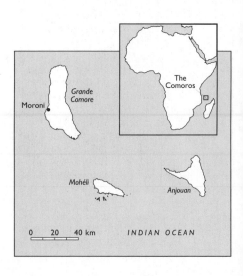

248

Comoros

**President Ahmed Abdallah
Mohamed Sambi**

to incorporate local African belief and customs, like a belief in malevolent djinns and the importance of lavish weddings to secure social status. Surviving African traditions can also be detected in the property rights Comoran women enjoy. Islamic law tends to recognize only male ownership and inheritance of land, but in the Comoros, certain property, called *magnahouli*, is controlled by women and inherited through the female line, suggesting a surviving African matriarchal tradition.

A Comoran marriage, especially among social elites, is often a prearranged union between an older man and a younger woman and is celebrated by a grand wedding, especially if it is a first marriage. Before the marriage the groom is expected to provide a fulsome dowry for his bride, including expensive clothing, gold and jewelry, which she is entitled to keep if they divorce. As further proof of his status within the community, the groom must also pay for a party of several days to which the entire village and friends and relatives from around the country are invited. Food, drink, and accommodation are all at his expense.

The festivities of the grand marriage extend over several days, but as compensation, the groom is allowed to wear a special sash signifying his status as a grand noble. Among those who can afford it, marriage tends to be polygynous and matrilocal—the husband moves into the home of his wife. The practice reflects the survival of African matrilineal traditions, as well as the practice of merchant traders who established families in more than one community.

In a deeply conservative Muslim society, women dress modestly, favoring colorful saris, but do not cover their faces. Against the fierce Comoran sun women protect

themselves with a yellowish facial cream, called *m'sidzanou*. Made of ground sandalwood and perfumed oils like ylang-ylang or jasmine, it is applied to the face as either a full mask or in a dappled pattern.

The Past: Political and Economic History

For early history, see *Historical Background* and *The Colonial Period: The French.*

Grand Comore and its capital, Moroni, are dominated by the Karthala, one of the world's largest active volcanoes that irrupted as recently as April 2005. Referred to by the French as Anjouan, and by early English visitors as Johanna, Nzwani has been called the "pearl" of the Indian Ocean. With forested hillsides and rivers tumbling to the sea it is a beautiful island. It is essentially a triangle with approximately 31 miles on each side and a total area of 164 square miles.

Anjouan is the most densely populated island in the Comoro archipelago (over 1,280 persons per square mile). Most live in small communities found throughout the island. The major towns are Mutsamudu on the western side, the present capital, and Domoni on the eastern side, an ancient capital and seaport.

Its volcanic peak, Mount Ntingi, 1,575 meters high, is covered with vegetation, including large ferns, tropical mahoganies, and wild orchids, in contrast with the three points of the triangle, which are less luxuriant due to centuries of cultivation. Anjouan is the premiere producer of essential oils including ylang-ylang, jasmine, cassis, basilic, palmarosa, and orange flower.

In 1975, Anjouan was one of the three islands to make up the newly formed independent republic of the Comoro Islands. The first president of the independent country, Ahmed Abdallah, was from there and his shrine is in his hometown of Domoni. The third president, Said Mohamed Djohar, was also a resident of Domoni and a schoolmate of Ahmed Abdallah.

After WWII the islands became Overseas French Territories and were represented in the French National Assembly. Agreement was reached in 1973 to grant independence in 1978, but on July 6, 1975, the Comoran parliament declared unilateral independence. Deputies from Mayotte abstained from this vote, and as a result the Comoran government had effective control over only Grand Comore, Anjouan, and Mohéli. Mayotte remains under French jurisdiction to this day.

The government of President Mohamed Taki Abdoulkarim, a deeply religious Sunni Muslim, was elected in 1996 following a mercenary-led coup that deposed President Djohar Said Mohamed.

(Mercenaries, especially the Frenchman Bob Denard, played a prominent role in several coups and coup attempts on the Comoros islands.) He went on to establish Islam as the basis of law: the death penalty, restrictions on the consumption of alcohol, and censuring women who wore mini-skirts were all announced. In October 1996, Taki amended the constitution, strengthening the powers of the presidency and sharply eroding the powers of individual islands—the source of much future disturbance.

Taki's government directed little development money to Anjouan and Mohéli; unemployment there rose to 90%. Islanders also thought themselves unfairly taxed in indirect ways. They had, for example, to make an expensive trip across the 50-mile straits to the capital to obtain any official documents. And always there was the nearby example of Mayotte. By remaining with France, the citizens of Mayotte enjoyed free education, health benefits and a minimum wage. Rejected by France when reunion with the former colonial power was proposed, Anjouan and Mohéli declared unilateral independence in August 1997.

A February 1998 referendum adopted a new independence constitution, but economic reality argued against the case for independence. Both Anjouan and Mohéli are volcanic islands with few exports, poor economies, and a population problem; there was little likelihood they could do it alone.

President Taki died suddenly of natural causes in November 1998. His death left the Islamic federation leaderless while facing the political impasse of secession. Tadjiddine Ben Said Massounde, the elderly president of the Comoros high court, was persuaded to accept an interim

Ex-President Azali Assoumani

249

Comoros

presidency. The opposition leader Abbas Djoussouf was appointed prime minister in an effort to create a government of national unity. International pressure was exercised, and ultimately representatives of the three islands agreed to attend a reconciliation conference on the island of Madagascar in April 1999.

The Madagascar conference produced agreement on the tentative outlines of a new Comoran state. The islands would have greater autonomy. Each would have its local executive and parliament after a one-year transition. To the central government would be reserved defense, foreign affairs, the issuance of currency, higher education and research. The federal presidency, elected by the National Assembly, would be rotated between the three islands every three years.

On Grand Comore, anti-Anjouan riots broke out when the details of the agreement were announced. The government accused opposition politicians of fomenting the troubles and sent in heavily armed troops to restore order. Since the best order to a military mind is martial order, the Comoran army effected the nation's 18th *coup d'état*, avoiding what seemed to be a slide into chaos and anarchy.

The army commander, Colonel Azali Assoumani, told his countrymen that the army had acted to insure "the survival of our nation and state." The army, he said, would remain in power for a year. That year came and went in April 2000, and little had changed. There was no return to civilian government, and no one had been able to put Comoros together again. Anjouan continued its separatist ways under Lt. Col. Said Abeid, who organized a series of farcical "elections" to legitimize Anjouan independence.

Colonels Azali and Abeid met in August 2000, and finally, after months of tortuous negotiations, a Comoran national reconciliation forum met at Fomboni, Mohéli's capital, in February 2001. Details of the new institutional arrangements were painfully produced, and a new constitution, under which the islands would each elect their own president and be governed as "autonomous entities freely managing their own affairs," was approved by referendum in December 2001. Under the new arrangements the Federal Islamic Republic of the Comoros would be replaced with a new Comoran Union whose mandate would be limited to affairs of religion and nationality, currency, foreign, and defense policy. The Union presidency, elected every four years, would progressively rotate among the three islands.

Elections in March and April 2002 began to implement the new dispensation. This being the Comoros, the elections were not without complaint and criticism.

Opposition was expressed by Islamic parties, upset that the Islamic nature of the state had not been affirmed. Voters on the main island, Grande Comore, rejected their new constitution in a March referendum, forcing revision and delay of presidential elections there.

Colonel Azali himself won the Union presidency, and, after ratifying a revised constitution, Grande Comore chose a former opposition MP, Abdou Soule Elbak, as its president. Tensions and mutual recriminations between the two presidents—island and federal—pushed Grande Comore near the brink of chaos.

Exploiting constitutional ambiguities Elbak called for equal control over Grande Comore's financial sector, pitting his government against the Union government and putting the business community in an administrative quandary. In early 2003 businesses received separate mailings from the two governments' finance ministries. Both presented themselves as the appropriate authority for the collection of fees, taxes, and licenses. Many businesses refused to become an arbiter between contending regimes and pronounced a plague on both their houses: they announced a freeze on tax payments until the conflict was resolved.

Diplomatic efforts by South Africa and the African Union produced an agreement on control of security forces and tax collection in August 2003. Island presidents would administer the police forces (the gendarmerie) stationed on their islands, while the Union president would control the country's army. A further reconciliation accord was signed in December 2003, defining the formula for sharing customs revenues. Twenty-eight percent would go to the Union; 32.5% to Grand Comore; 30.5% for Anjouan, and 9% for Moheli. This paved the way for legislative elections in early 2004.

Elections for local assemblies on each of the country's three islands in March 2004 were a smashing victory for the supporters of island autonomy; they similarly won April elections to the federal assembly, taking 12 of 18 elected seats.

With some degree of institutional stability, no matter how tenuous, established, President Azali focused on the Union's desperate economic situation, seeking to gain access to credit from the IMF, World Bank, and disillusioned donors, headed by France. Given Comoran claims on Mayotte, relations between the islands and France remained chilly at best. A Franco-Comoran joint commission last met in 1992, and President Azali was the only leader of a French-speaking country that has not been received by a French president.

A thaw occurred in January 2005 when French President Jacques Chirac received Azali Assoumani on an official state visit. It was, of course, increasingly in France's

Ylang-Ylang flower

Photo by Powell Harrison

250

interest to restore aid and kick-start development plans: well-off Mayotte was experiencing significantly increased illegal migration from the impoverished Comoros. At a regional donors conference held at Port Louis, Mauritius in December 2005, France contributed 40% of the total $280 million pledged to assist Comoran development. Disbursement of the monies would be largely dependent on the success of the Union's elections to the rotating presidency in 2006.

Following the 2001 agreement, it was Anjouan's turn to nominate candidates for the Union presidency in 2006. April preliminaries on the island reduced a field of 13 candidates to three. Ahmed Abdallah Mohamed Sambi, a Sunni cleric and founding member of the Islamic National Front for Justice party, won 24% of the votes cast; Mohamed Djanffari, the current vice president of the federal National Assembly and a former member of the French air force arrived in second place with 13% of the votes; and Abderemane Ibrahim Halidi, a former prime minister supported by President Azali, polled more than 10% of first round votes.

Comoran voters opted for the islands' leading Islamist, Ahmed Abdallah Sambi, to lead them for the next four years. Educated in Saudi Arabia and Iran, Sambi had long been known as "The Ayatollah." A familiar figure on the islands, Sambi had actively participated in public demonstrations against Israel, the war in Bosnia, and any reduction of taxes on alcohol. During his campaign, he repeatedly told audiences he intended to show "the true face" of Islam. His campaign was reportedly financed with Iranian money, and at least one of his opponents, Halidi, called him "the representative of Iran in the Comoros." At age 48, and a shrewd businessman (heading at least three businesses), Sambi seems to be a realist. In an *Agence France Presse* interview he said he believed in an Islamic regime, but the Comoran economic situation did not permit it "for the moment."

Federalism in the Union seems to create tensions and potential for violence. In 2007, the island of Anjouan selected Mohamed Bacar as its president. Bacar then held local elections in defiance of the central government. In an attempt to slow the move towards autonomy in Anjouan, the center demanded Bacar step down, and blockaded the island. In 2008, the central government, backed by African Union troops, ultimately invaded the island, sending Bacar fleeing.

The traditionally open and tolerant version of Comoran Islam is under intense pressure with the rise of Islamic fundamentalism in the islands. The radical strain of Islam has been introduced with missionary zeal by young Comorans who have studied abroad. Lacking funds or blocked by immigration laws from studying in France, many seeking higher education were easily recruited by Islamic centers in Sudan and Saudi Arabia where Wahhabite fundamentalism prevailed. Comoros' chronic poverty and instability proved fertile recruiting grounds for the fundamentalists.

One recruit was Fazul Abdullah Mohammed, described by the FBI as a computer whiz fluent in several languages, including French, Arabic and English. Born in the Comoros, he is said to have trained with Osama bin Laden in Afghanistan and spent time in Somalia. He is charged by the U.S. in the 1998 terror attack on its embassy in Nairobi, Kenya, and is on the FBI's list of 22 most wanted terrorists. Investigators have since named him the mastermind behind the November 28, 2002, suicide attack on the Paradise Hotel in Mombasa, Kenya.

The Present: Contemporary Issues

In many ways, the islands are caught in a poverty spiral. GDP grew by an unimpressive 1.9% in 2004, woefully inadequate to improve the life circumstances of a population that was growing rapidly—about 2.4% annually. Things were worse in 2006; GDP growth had dropped to just 1.2% as the economy was slammed by increased costs for imported oil and decreased prices for exported vanilla.

Endemic political instability is exacerbated by the government's regular revenue shortfall. Foreign investors have shied away; international lenders have remained hesitant, and donors, many involved in continuing mediation between conflicting actors in the Comoran political theater, show demonstrable fatigue. External debt remains high—estimated at $280 million (2007)—about 70% of the country's total GDP.

Since early 2005, the Union has been under a surveillance program signed with the IMF as a prerequisite for assistance in reducing its external debt. Conditions involve infinitely greater control of budget deficits, particularly establishing precise objectives for a ceiling on the public payroll. Political support at every level has traditionally been secured by distributing government jobs.

Further efforts to liberalize the economy are also needed: privatizations of government businesses, an end to the government monopoly on rice imports, and greater competition in the banking sector. Once these goals have been achieved the islands can be considered for admission to debt reduction programs.

The Comoran export economy is based on vanilla, cloves, and ylang-ylang, an essence popular in perfume making. Traditionally, Comoros has generated about 200 tons of processed vanilla per year, but production has been declining. The decline has been attributed to aging vines, bad weather, and farmers discouraged by previous poor sales. In 2006 only 75 tons of vanilla were produced. Prices paid vanilla farmers rise and fall according to international conditions. From $300/kg in 2003, vanilla prices dropped to less than $50/kg in 2005. In 2006 the value of vanilla exports fell by half, driving even more producers out of the market.

With world market prices and demand for cloves remaining high, Comoran clove farmers reported the only increase in volume and value among the economy's three basic export commodities. Clove production in 2006 was about 3,500 tons, well up from 2005 (1,500 tons). As a consequence, the spice accounted for 66% of Comoros exports in 2006. The Comoros have long been the world's leading producer of the essence of ylang-ylang. Production is localized on Anjouan Island. Indeed, it was the island's feeling that it was not being given its fair share of ylang-ylang revenues that led to its secession efforts.

The Future

Political tensions between the Union and its member islands, arising from basic disagreement over the distribution of powers between the two, came to a head in March 2008 when Comoran and African Union troops reinvaded Anjouan to quell a rebellion led by Anjouan separatist Mohamed Bacar. Bacar had run fraudulent elections on the island and had refused the central government's demands that he re-run the elections or cede power. While the success of the mission to stop Bacar seemed to herald possible stability, the underlying conflict is not resolved.

The status of the island of Mayotte is also the source of some tension. In a March 2009 referendum, the island voted to become a French overseas department by 2011. The Comoran government maintained that the result was "null and void," though the result is likely to go into full effect.

Comoros has a troubled political history, with much instability and many coups (as highlighted by the role of the French mercenary Bob Denard). There is some limited degree of political liberty on the islands now, but the conflict between the islands themselves is the dominant story for the foreseeable future. Meanwhile, 80% of the population is involved in the agricultural sector, yet the islands must import a significant portion of their foodstuffs—a difficult combination for the economic future.

The Republic of Madagascar

Basic Facts

Area: 595,000 sq. km. = 229,730 sq. mi. (somewhat smaller than Texas)

Population: 19,700,000 (UN 2007 est.)

Capital City: Antananarivo; pronounced Tah-nah-nah-reev

Climate: Interior-warm and rainy (November–April); cool and dry (May–October); the southern portion of the island is semiarid. The coastal areas are uniformly hotter than the inland altitudes. The east coast has a heavy, almost year-round rainfall brought by Indian Ocean trade winds and monsoons.

Neighboring Countries: The closest neighbor of this island republic is Mozambique, 300 miles west on the African mainland.

Official Language: Malagasy, French, and English

Other Principal Languages: Malagasy is universally understood and spoken by the people although there are several dialects, particularly in the coastal areas.

Ethnic Groups: Malayo-Indonesian (Merina and related Betsileo), Cotiers (mixed African, Malayo-Indonesian, and Arab ancestry—Betsimisaraka, Tsimihety, Antaisaka, Sakalava), French, Indian, Creole, Comoran

Principal Religions: Indigenous beliefs 52%, Christian 41% (the Roman Catholic Church is the largest denomination, followed by the Reformed Protestant Church of Jesus Christ in Madagascar: FJKM), Muslim 7%

Chief Commercial Products: Prawns, coffee, vanilla, cotton, sugar and cloves and petroleum products

GNI Per Capita: $290 (World Bank 2006 est.)

Currency: Ariary, made up of five subdivisions called iraimbilanja. The ariary, introduced in mid-2003, is worth five of the former Malagasy francs, which remained legal tender until the end of November, 2003 and exchangeable until the end of 2009.

Former Colonial Status: French Protectorate (1894–1960)

Independence Date: June 26, 1960.

Chief of State: Andry Rajoelina, President (since military-backed take-over in March 2009)

National Flag: A vertical stripe of white closest to the pole with two horizontal stripes of red and green.

Land and People

The Republic of Madagascar, the fourth-largest island of the world and larger than France, Netherlands, Belgium and Luxembourg combined, is situated in the Indian Ocean off the southeastern part of Africa. It split from the African continent 165 million years ago and has been isolated from all other land by deep water for some 88 million years. As a consequence some 100 unique terrestrial mammal species are found on the island.

The west coast, facing the Mozambique Channel, is a low, tropically wet and dry region, particularly in the extreme south. A series of broad plateaus rise from the coast to increasing heights of 2,300 to 4,500 feet. More abundant rainfall occurs here, and the altitude tempers the otherwise hot climate. Almost daily rains fall during the summer; the weather from May to October is cooler when temperatures in the higher altitudes drop as low as the freezing point. Several mountain ranges rise above this tableland—Mount Tsaratanana majestically looms to a height of 9,450 feet.

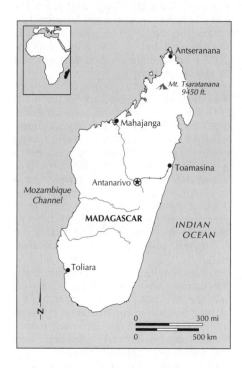

The eastern shore is a narrow strip between the sea and the steep sides of the mountains. Washed by the warm waters of the Indian Ocean, and visited by the trade winds and monsoons, this coastal strip is almost uniformly hot and humid, with an annual rainfall exceeding 110 inches.

The diversity in the heritage of the people of this great island is modified by the fact that all speak or understand the highly developed language called Malagasy, which—like the Malagasy themselves—is a synthesis of Indonesian, Polynesian, African, Arab and European influences. As in most preliterate cultures, traditional Malagasy oratory is replete with the unhurried telling of ancestral proverbs, metaphors, and riddles, often in a participatory dialogue of call and response. It is communication that is neither fast nor direct, and, for its proponents, it is fiercely threatened by modern cell phones, whose costly charges induce brevity, speed and avoidance of ancestral wisdom.

Although about 41% of the people are Christian, most have joined traditional beliefs with ancestor worship of Hindu origin—a religious combination of East and West. During the *Famadihana* ceremony, for example, the dead are exhumed and feted as guests just returned from an extended absence. They are entertained, danced with, regaled with stories of recent family events, turned to for advice, and then reburied with fine new shrouds and presents. It placates the ancestors, who can bless or curse the activities of the living.

The capital of Antananarivo is located on the site of the old capital city of the Merina Kingdom in the high plateau region. Its population of nearly two million consists largely of Merina people. Of Indonesian origins, the Merina are physically distinct from the more African coastal peoples, having lighter features and straighter hair.

The Past: Political and Economic History

For early history, see *Historical Background* and *The Colonial Period: The French.*

Philibert Tsiranana (*Feel*-eh-bear Tsear-ah-*nah*; the last vowel in Malagasy names is not pronounced), a moderate, was the first president after independence in 1960. His health gradually failed, and he was unable to deal effectively with a Maoist uprising in the South in 1971. All power was given to the military in 1972, eventually headed by Lt. Commander Didier Ratsiraka (*Deed*-yay Rot-see-rakh) as President of the Supreme Council of the Revolution.

Known as the Red Admiral, even issuing his own little red book of thoughts in emulation of Chairman Mao, Ratsiraka was the instigator of the Malagasy socialist revolution of 1975. The Malagasy Republic was replaced by the Democratic Republic of Madagascar. Government control of the economy under Ratsiraka rose dramatically. Just as dramatically, the economy declined. Backed by the military, Ratsiraka was reelected to successive seven-year terms in 1982 and 1989. Violence marked the regime in the early 1990s, when Ratsiraka used the military to resist a pro-democracy movement. The blackest day was August 10, 1991 when he ordered troops to fire on a huge crowd of protesters surging around the presidential palace. Fourteen people were killed and hundreds wounded. IMF economic support was suspended.

In 1991, a High Authority for State Transition, presided over by Albert Zafy, was instituted following large-scale protests. A new constitution creating a parliamen-

Former President Marc Ravalomana

tary democracy was adopted in 1992, and in 1993, Zafy won the presidential election after a long battle for multiparty democracy. It soon became apparent that constitutional democracy did not guarantee governmental stability. In less than five years following its adoption, there would be six changes of government, three changes of prime ministers, two motions of censure and a presidential impeachment. Recognizing the weakness of executive authority confronted with a boisterously fragmented parliament, legislators revised the constitution to reinforce presidential powers. In 1996, after a long-running battle with parliament, President Zafy was impeached and ultimately deposed when the High Constitutional Court confirmed his impeachment by the National Assembly.

Presidential elections in December 1997 resulted in the return of the Red Admiral, Didier Ratsiraka, from political desert to presidential palace. A reformed Marxist, Ratsiraka spoke now of decentralization and economic liberalism. He quickly called a referendum to decentralize governmental authority to six semiautonomous provinces in March 1998. These would be run by provincial councils elected by universal suffrage. In turn, provincial councils would elect a provincial governor and exercise control over economic and social programs.

Additional constitutional provisions included in the referendum significantly enhanced presidential authority. He would have the power to nominate the prime minister with no obligation to choose him from the political majority in parliament. The president would also have the power to dissolve parliament and nominate the most important magistrates of an "independent judiciary." Presidential impeachment would be more difficult. The goal of these provisions, said proponents, was to end the permanent political instability created by the 1992 constitution.

Voters were confronted with a single, not particularly informative question: "Do you accept the project to amend the constitution to give greater dimension to the development of all regions and to rein-

force national unity?" In a country where only 50% of the population is literate, only 50,000 copies of the revised constitutional text were distributed, and those in French, not Malagasy. The opposition called for a boycott of the election, saying it would be a return to a totalitarian regime. When final results were tabulated, only 34% of registered voters managed to bring themselves to the polls, and the referendum passed by the thinnest of margins: 50.62%.

The new regional assemblies marked a slight shift of thinking on the part of the government. Previous regimes had emphasized national unity by concentrating authority at the center. Antananarivo, the capital, was privileged politically and economically, to the detriment of distant regions. The new assemblies were to be granted limited taxing abilities to fund regional programs. Money would still flow from the center for obvious reasons: Antananarivo accounts for three-fifths of the state's tax collection.

Demonstrating high political skepticism, 60% to 70% of registered voters boycotted the December 2000 regional elections. When the final results were in, President Ratsiraka's AREMA (*L'Avant-Garde du Renouveau de Madagascar*) party, or "independents" associated with it, captured most of the 336 regional assembly seats. Only in the capital were President Ratsiraka's supporters beaten.

Senate elections of February 2001 produced similar results: AREMA easily grabbed a majority of senatorships—49 out of 60. With AREMA dominating Madagascan political space, President Ratsiraka seemed well positioned to call the shots in Madagascar's presidential election.

Held in December 2001, the election pitted President Ratsiraka, one of Africa's political dinosaurs—aged, ill, and tainted with corruption—against a self-made millionaire businessman, Marc Ravalomanana, the youthful, dynamic, and popular mayor of Antananarivo. The election set capital against provinces, newly empowered by decentralization, with devastating consequences for the country. Official results—later annulled—gave Ravalomanana a clear lead, but not the absolute majority needed to win the election outright—46.49% of the vote to Ratsiraka's 40.64%.

The incumbent president called for a second-round runoff, but Ravalomanana, accusing his opponent of fraud and vote rigging, claimed outright victory. He accused election officials of falsifying results and insisted that tally sheets drawn up by his own agents showed he won 52% of the vote, rather than the 46% claimed by the Interior Ministry. Ravalomanana supporters organized a general strike in January 2002, and tens of thousands of strikers closed the capital down; daily protests

continued for weeks, with no concession from Ratsiraka. Representatives of the OAU attempted mediation, but were unsuccessful.

In February 2002 Ravalomanana declared himself president, staged an inauguration surrounded by judges and officers of the Ratsiraka regime, and appointed a prime minister. Ratsiraka loyalists withdrew to the coastal city of Toamasina and made it an alternative capital. After Ravalomanana announced his own cabinet, the island essentially had two governments, with every post duplicated, including the governor of the central bank.

Ratsiraka decreed martial law in Antananarivo, but the army, deeply divided, remained neutral. His supporters resorted to direct action. The pro-Ratsiraka governor of Toamasina installed roadblocks on the main route to the capital, preventing movement of food or fuel to the capital. At least six bridges linking the inland capital to coastal ports were destroyed in an effort to strangle the city economically.

Amid increasing violence, Madagascar's Supreme Court annulled first-round election results in April and ordered a recount by the High Constitutional Court (HCC). After the recount, the HCC reported Ravalomanana had won an overall majority—51% to 36% for his rival. On May 6, he formally assumed the presidency and stepped up military action against Ratsiraka forces. Judicial success brought recognition by the United States at the end of June, quickly followed by France. The OAU, unsuccessful at diplomacy, saw its unity dissolve when Senegal endorsed President Ravalomanana on July 4. Fearing the precedent of self-proclaimed presidents, it persisted in obtuseness, declaring Ravalomanana's win had not been "legally constituted." (Indeed, Madagascar would not regain its seat until July 2003, when the African Union, the OAU's successor, finally recognized the

Oxen transport   Photo by Char Glacy

Madagascar

Ravalomanana government.) Three days later, on July 7, 2002, ex-President Ratsiraka flew to France and exile.

To give proof of President Ravalomanana's support and legitimacy, Western donors pressured the new government to hold early parliamentary elections. The "carrot" as they say in such cases, was the early release of the first portion of $2.3 billion they had pledged to help reconstruct the country over the next four years.

The elections were held in December, and though 40 parties vied for 160 National Assembly seats, President Ravalomanana's *Tiako i Madagasikara* (TiM: I Love Madagascar party) won an overwhelming victory: an absolute majority of 102 seats. With National Solidarity, the wider coalition of parties supporting the president, pro-Ravalomanana forces controlled 132 legislative seats.

The new government has rejected efforts by the AREMA-dominated Senate to pass an amnesty bill for all those involved in the 2002 events. For his role in the crisis former President Ratsiraka was sentenced, *in absentia*, to five years in prison, as was his daughter Sophie, found guilty of blowing up a bridge during the civil conflict.

Local elections in November 2003 suggest one reason why the political establishment opposes a general amnesty. Though the president's *Tiako I Magasikara* party was generally successful, winning 29 out of the 45 cities that have municipal governments, it clearly dominated the north and the region of the capital, but appeared much weaker in other outlying areas. Madagascar's second city, the port of Toamasina, remained, for example, in AREMA control. Given this center-periphery disconnect, it is easy to see why some might fear a general amnesty might lead to the return of political exiles who could destabilize the regime.

Some degree of stability seemed to be assured with the December 2006 presidential elections. Despite a field of 14 candidates, President Ravalomanana soundly thumped the opposition, winning a first ballot reelection with 55% of all votes cast. With nearly 12% of the vote, his nearest rival was the former speaker of parliament, Jean Lahiniriko, sacked by his TIM colleagues in the National Assembly after praising Iran's nuclear program. The third-place finisher was Roland Ratsiraka, the mayor of Madagascar's second city, Toamasina, and nephew of former-President Didier Ratsiraka. He received a little over 10% of the ballots in an election that saw some 65% of registered voters participating.

With such popular backing, President Ravalomanana introduced a series of controversial constitutional reforms in early 2007. To facilitate local economic development Madagascar's six autonomous regions, described as "too vast," would be phased out, replaced by the current 22 regions as arenas of decision-making. To encourage greater foreign investment and closer ties with the anglophone world, English would become a national language. Most controversially, presidential powers would be increased: the president will have authority to make laws directly if he declares a state of emergency. When submitted to the electorate in April, more than 75% approved the changes.

Political bitterness lingered within a restive army. From November 2006 to April 2007 Madagascan security forces foiled at least three attempted assassinations of the president. At least 25 army officers were summoned for questioning. But military discontent with Ravalomanana would only become clear with a take-over of power in 2009 that seemed a cross between a "people power" social revolution and a military coup.

Ravalomanana's downfall began in earnest in January 2009, when the government closed down TV stations and radio stations run by the opposition. Protests turned violent, and dozens of Malagasys were killed, some by the authorities. In response, the mayor of the capital city Antananarivo, Andry Rajoelina, spearheaded a demonstrative opposition movement and called upon the president to resign. To heighten the stakes, the young, charismatic, and ambitious Rajoelina also declared himself the rightful leader of Madagascar.

Ravalomanana dismissed Rajoelina, but popular sentiment seemed to swing towards the mayor as more citizens were killed in clashes. Finally, in March, several top military brass declared allegiance to Rajoelina's shadow government, leading Ravalomanana to tender an ambiguous resignation and flee into exile in South Africa. International observers condemned the takeover, and Ravalomanana periodically asserted his legitimate claim to power from abroad, but Rajoelina seems to have consolidated power (at least temporarily) at this time.

The Present: Contemporary Issues

Rural poverty has generated a migration to the cities, especially Antananarivo. Now surrounded by shantytowns, the city is a microcosm of the island's problems: malnutrition, unhealthy living conditions, street children, traffic congestion, contaminated water, pollution, underemployment and insecurity. Life expectancy is just 55.8 years.

Recognizing the importance of education for development, the government abolished school fees in 2002. Since then there has been a campaign to build new classrooms, recruit teachers and distribute supplies as basic as pens, pencils, and paper. Given the magnitude of need, there remains much to be done before one can speak of universal free education in Madagascar.

The economic balance sheet of the initial Ratsiraka years was an unmitigated disaster. Sixteen years of socialism, from 1974 to 1991, produced unprecedented decline. Key sectors of the economy were nationalized. Banks and insurance companies, export-import businesses, oil companies,

Scenic coastline near Fort Dauphine

Photo by Ruth Evans

and the principal firms in energy, mines, construction and navel repairs all became state agencies. Expatriate businessmen left the country, usually without indemnification, and there was nothing to attract new investors. By 1985 only 10% of total investments were private.

Under the socialist regime industry represented only 15% of the GDP and employed a mere 1% of active workers. Factories operated at only 30% to 40% of their capacity and a massive state investment program produced only white elephants—huge factories built at enormous cost that were never able to function.

In agriculture, farmers soon lost confidence in the regime's cooperatives, returning to subsistence agriculture. With the deterioration of roads, provisioning cities with food became a problem and Madagascar, once a food exporting country, began to import foodstuffs, especially rice. By 1989 the annual average income fell below $210.

When he returned to power in 1997, President Ratsiraka was forced to make a 180-degree turn—to put in place, under the guidance of the World Bank and IMF, a market economy. Action to disengage the state through privatization of its large companies was slow, hesitant, and often indecisive. By the time he left office in 2002, definitively but reluctantly, there had been some improvement: Average annual income rose to $250—where it had been ten years before—and economic growth was around 6%. Most benefits from economic liberalization went to a minority of urban dwellers employed in the textile industry, the country's largest export earner.

The political crisis following the December 2001 elections vitiated much of the country's economic improvement. Particularly hard hit were textile companies operating in economic development zones around Antananarivo. Unable to import fabric, factories had to close and send their workers home.

Overall, industrial output fell between 70% and 90%, and tourism virtually ceased, with revenues falling 95%. Commercial properties lost 50% to 60% of their tenants, and the World Bank estimated the dispute cost the country $12 million to $14 million a day. Economic growth for 2002 was a negative 12%.

In response, the Ravalomanana government instituted business-friendly economic and financial policies and opened the economy to foreign investment. The president likes to boast, frequently, that he runs the country like a business nowadays. For the first time since 1960, foreigners are permitted to buy real estate—no more than 7.9 acres and only if they have at least $500,000 backup. With stability

and liberalization, Madagascar's economy has achieved consistent growth. GDP rose by 5.3% in 2004 and 4.6% in 2005. To mark a symbolic break with its socialist past, the government replaced the Malagasy franc with a precolonial currency, the ariary.

Key to the government's development plans is the country's deteriorated road system. At independence it had 21,700 miles of useable roads, but these had dwindled to just 9,300 miles by 2001, making transport difficult—hazardous, expensive, and time-consuming. The National Fund for Road Maintenance, funded with fuel taxes and road tolls, being inadequate to the task, the EU has offered the biggest assistance for road construction and maintenance. Nearly $400 million have been spent on upgrading the system and some 3,700 miles of new roads constructed.

One of the government's highest priorities is the agricultural sector. It dominates the Madagascan economy, employing some 85% of the working population and contributing 27.9% of GDP (2005). The sector is dominated by small-scale farms that produce both export and food crops. To improve production, various taxes and duties on fertilizers and machinery have been reduced. The government's repair and development of road infrastructure is a key to improving distribution and commercialization of the farmers' produce. Rice is Madagascar's main food crop, with production averaging around 2.5 million tons annually. This is not enough to satisfy internal consumption needs and the country must import additional quantities. In October 2003 thirty Vietnamese experts and technicians arrived to provide advice on increasing rice production. (In 20 years Vietnamese rice production increased 300%; in the same period Malagasy production rose by only 25%.)

Maize, bananas, sweet potatoes, groundnuts, pineapples, coconuts, and sugar are also grown for local consumption. The economy's dependence on agriculture makes it subject to the caprice of a frequently hostile Mother Nature. Drought, locusts, and cyclones visit Madagascar nearly every year.

Vanilla used to be the number one export crop, but natural calamities, governmental inefficiencies in marketing, and high local taxes reduced production at the same time Mexico and Indonesia were increasing theirs. Madagascar produces nearly 60% to 65% of the world's vanilla supply. Some 70,000 vanilla farmers produce between 4,500 and 5,500 tons of green vanilla in a good year. After drying and processing, some 1,500 tons are available for export and can bring in $200 million or more to the economy.

Madagascar is rich in mineral resources, including a variety of precious and semi-

precious gemstones such as garnets, emeralds, rubies and sapphires. Development of large nickel deposits at Ambatovy, 80 miles east of the capital, is in progress. Estimates indicate the mine holds 125 million tons of nickel and could produce 60,000 tons annually. If achieved, that would be the third-largest production output in the world.

President Ravalomanana has aggressively sought out foreign investment, and Madagascar's offshore waters have attracted the interest of international oil companies. In December 2004 Exxon Mobil paid $25 million for exploration rights in 36,000 square kilometers of coastal waters. The company sank its first exploration well in early 2007. China has long maintained a presence in the country, sending some 14 medical teams since 1975 to treat millions of Malagasy. President Ravalomanana visited China in 2004 and produced agreements from his hosts to construct an international conference center and a cement factory, as well as investments in the country's mineral resources.

The World Bank and IMF have recognized Madagascar's extreme poverty and qualified the country for debt relief of $1.9 billion under the Highly Indebted Poor Countries (HIPC) initiative. To reward good governance and sound economic policies, the world's richest countries also voted to cancel the debt owed to multilateral institutions (IMF, World Bank, African Development Bank) by HIPC countries at their July 2005 summit. Reduction of debt service payments has allowed the government to redirect debt service spending to poverty reduction programs.

The Future

The ouster of Ravalomanana and his replacement with Rajoelina has thrown Madagascar into turmoil. The military seems to back the young president, but Ravalomanana remains an important figure in his exile. Politically, Madagascar's fledgling democracy has taken a beating to its reputation. Political reforms, including attempts at decentralizing power, seemed to suggest that the government was more willing to share and distribute authority than those in many other African states, but the Rajoelina government is inscrutable thus far.

As a very low-income country, Madagascar needs substantial investment to accelerate economic advancement. Yet development initiatives are immensely controversial, not least due to the likelihood of ecological consequences. Madagascar's miraculous ecosystems may be seen as one of mankind's greatest "natural heritage sites," making rapid development a difficult proposition.

The Republic of Mauritius

President Anerood Jugnauth

Basic Facts

Area: 1,856 sq. km. = 717 sq. mi. (about the size of Rhode Island)

Dependencies: Rodrigues Island, the Agalega Islands and Cargados Carajos Shoals; Mauritius also claims sovereignty over the Chagos Archipelago, part of the British Indian Ocean Territory, where U.S. Naval Base Diego Garcia is located.

Population: 1,300,000 (UN 2007 est.)

Capital City: Port Louis

Climate: Tropically hot and humid, with slightly cooler temperatures in the highlands of Mauritius which rise as high as 2,500 feet.

Neighboring Countries: Mauritius is located 550 miles east of Madagascar; Rodrigues is 350 miles northeast of Mauritius.

Official Language: English

Other Principal Languages: Creole (spoken by 70% of the population), Bojpoori (from Bihar, India), French, Hindi, Urdu, and Hakka

Ethnic Groups: Indo-Mauritian 68%, Creole 27%, Sino-Mauritian 3%, Franco-Mauritian 2%

Principal Religions: Hindu 52%, Christian 28.3% (Roman Catholic 26%, Protestant 2.3%), Muslim 16.6%, and other 3.1%

Principal Commercial Products: Clothing and textiles, sugar

GNI Per Capita: $5,260 (World Bank 2006 est.)

Currency: Mauritius Rupee

Former Colonial Status: French possession (1715–1810); British possession (1810–1968)

Independence Date: March 12, 1968

Chief of State: Anerood Jugnauth, President (since October 2003)

Head of Government: Navin Ramgoolam, Prime Minister (since July 2005)

National Flag: Red, blue, gold and green horizontal stripes.

Land and People

The landmass that is now the island of Mauritius is the result of volcanic activity that occurred thousands of years ago. The craggy, hardened lava, covered with fine ash and silt was in turn covered with a carpet of green vegetation, growing swiftly in the tropical sun. The island is a series of plateaus and interesting variations caused by small streams, waterfalls, crevices and coastal indentations. The island of Rodrigues is a dependency of Mauritius.

The population of Mauritius is culturally diverse, reflecting the island's colonial history. Europeans brought in both Indians and Africans to work the sugar plantations. Today, about 63% of the population is Indian and overwhelmingly Hindu (52%). Thirty percent of the population is African-Creole, 5% Chinese and 2% European. The various ethnic groups tend to have limited interaction with each other. The government has managed to increase literacy from 60% to 100% largely by making education free. University education remains elitist, restricted to a select few. Only 3% of Mauritians obtain university degrees. This impacts the government's efforts to attract high-tech companies.

The Past: Political and Economic History

For early history, see *Historical Background, The Colonial Period: The French,* and *The Colonial Period: The British.*

Following World War II, the worldwide surge of nationalism gradually entered Mauritius, particularly among those of Indian descent who had become a majority of the population. When Great Britain announced the withdrawal "east of the

MAURITIUS

Poudre D'Or
Port Louis
Beau Bassin
Quatre Bornes
Curepipe
INDIAN OCEAN
Souillac

0   30 km
0   30 mi

Suez" in 1966, Mauritius was intended to be a part of this plan. Ethnic diversity was the biggest problem—the Indian majority favored independence, but the Creoles were opposed.

To placate the Creoles, a complicated plan was devised to apportion the seats of the legislature among the ethnic groups, and elections were held. Hindu Indians were able to win a parliamentary majority; Creoles became the minority. Muslim Indians were unable to elect a single representative.

For about 41 years until 1982, Sir Seewoosagur Ramgoolam and his Labor Party dominated the political scene. The party was challenged in the June 1982 elections by a French Mauritian, Paul Bérenger. The vote was so split along party and ethnic lines that a coalition government emerged, headed by Anerood Jugnauth with Bérenger as finance minister. A second collapse in the government in mid-1983 led to a second election. To compete more effectively, Jugnauth organized the Mauritian Socialist Movement (MSM), which defeated Bérenger's Mauritian Militant Movement (MMM). Jugnauth continued in power until late 1995 when he erred politically, proposing a constitutional amendment to incorporate vernacular languages (Hindi, Urdu, Tamil, Marathi, Telegu, Mandarin and Arabic) into primary education. His principal associates in the coalition resigned, and the amendment failed. The Assembly had to be dissolved and new elections called.

An opposition alliance won all 60 seats in the 20 island districts. Navin Ramgoolam, son of Sir Seewoosagur, became the new prime minister, but no basic changes in government economic development policies resulted.

The language issue highlights the multiracial, multilingual and multireligious nature of Mauritian society. Unlike many former British colonies, Mauritius retained the Westminster model, but without winner-take-all provisions. Each communal group constituting the Mauritian nation obtains representation in the National Assembly, but communal tensions can and do arise. In early 1998, Prime Minister Ramgoolam ordered a holiday to celebrate the Hindu festival, which drew the criticism of opposition leaders fearful of the economic consequences of too many sectarian holidays.

Class differences are sharp on Mauritius. Seventeen white Franco-Mauritian families own over half the island's cultivated land. They control not only agriculture but industry too. At the other end of the socioeconomic scale are the Creoles who often have no school certificates or vocational training. They frequently end up working as laborers, disaffected from

Prime Minister Navin Ramgoolam

a system in which they share so little—an urban poor, dangerous and volatile.

For the fall 2000 elections Bérenger and Jugnauth formed an electoral alliance. In a preelection pact the two agreed that if they won, MSM chief Sir Anerood Jugnauth, a Hindu, would serve as prime minister for the first three years; after that MMM leader Paul Bérenger, a Franco-Mauritian, would rule for the next three, becoming the nation's first non-Hindu leader since independence from Britain in 1968.

Discontent with the state of the economy and dissatisfaction with the handling of communal tensions lay at the heart of the campaign. Despite 43 parties fielding candidates, the election was a straightforward fight between the alliance and former Prime Minister Ramgoolam's Labor Party-led coalition. When the final tallies were in, the alliance won a smashing victory: 54 out of 62 seats in assembly.

Since then the government has made an effort to make parliament more representative of minority interests. It announced a proposal in March 2002 to increase the size of the National Assembly, from 62 to 92 members. The additional 30 members would be proportionally chosen from parties that received more than 10% of the vote, but the constitutional amendment needed was never passed. Instead Mauritius uses a two-tier election process. Sixty-two members are elected from 21 constituencies by popular vote. An additional eight members are chosen from a list of "best losers" to assure ethnic minority representation.

The power-sharing agreement between Jugnauth and Bérenger was implemented in September 2003. President Offmann resigned and was replaced by Prime Minister Jugnauth who left his position, making way for Paul Bérenger to become prime minister.

Bitterness from Britain's 1968 removal of the Chagos archipelago from the administrative control of Mauritius still lingers. The archipelago, which includes the island of Diego Garcia, was cleared of nearly 5,000 inhabitants and leased to the United States for use as a military and nuclear base. In return the British reportedly were able to obtain Trident submarines on favorable terms. The military base, originally intended to counter the Soviet threat, has proved its utility both in the 1991 Gulf War and the 2003 Iraqi campaign when allied bombing missions took off from its 12,000-foot runway. The lease expires in 2016.

In the July 2005 parliamentary elections opposition leader Navin Ramgoolam successfully exploited a declining economy. Leading the Social Alliance (SA), Ramgoolam criticized the Bérenger government for failing to prepare the island for the end of textile quotas and the elimination of EU sugar subsidies. The SA won 38 of 62 contested parliamentary seats and Ramgoolam was designated the island's new prime minister. Ramgoolam, 57, a doctor and lawyer who is the son of the first postindependence prime minister, returned to the job he held between 1995 and 2000. The job hasn't gotten any easier.

Having to respond to problems of the domestic economy and the impact of globalization has put the Social Alliance, a coalition of the Mauritius Labor Party and the Mauritian Social Democratic Party, on the defensive as it introduces change. Efforts to eliminate rice and flour subsidies and reform the pension system by extending the retirement age to 65 brought charges from the opposition that basic consumer items would now be unaffordable for many and that the budget was "pro-capitalist"—fighting words in socially-oriented Mauritius.

A frustrated finance minister responded, bitingly, that the problem "is that there is no doctor or economist on the other side of the House." Righteously indignant, as only politicians can be, the opposition walked out, protesting the minister's "arrogance." It was the first time the opposition, the MMM and the MSM, had acted in accord in a long time.

The Mauritian Socialist Movement (MSM), headed by Pravind Jugnauth, the son of former-Prime Minister (and now President) Anerood Jugnauth was having internal problems even before the legislative elections of 2005. Pravind himself could not retain a seat in his own constituency and thus does not sit in the National Assembly, a fact that does not enhance his ambition to someday become prime minister. The MSM was given another body blow when Ashok Jugnauth, uncle of Pravind and brother of

Anerood—politics in Mauritius is quite familial—tendered his resignation from the party. When Paul Bérenger, erstwhile ally of Pravind Jugnauth, began to speak of Ashok as the next prime minister, what minimal unity the MMM-MSM coalition had enjoyed quickly dissolved.

The Present: Contemporary Issues

Mauritius has transformed its economy since independence when it was essentially dependent on the export of sugar to Great Britain. In the 1960s sugar accounted for nearly 80% of agricultural production and 86% of export earnings. Sugar is still king, but in the nearly 40 years since independence, Mauritius has diversified its economy to create supports in light manufacturing, particularly textiles, tourism and, more recently, information technology.

The sugar industry is facing difficult times. In 2005 the European Union agreed to end quotas and price subsidies given former colonial states; sugar prices will be reduced just over a third over the next four years: 5% in 2007; 17% in 2008, and 11% in 2009. The 18 sugar-producing countries affected, including Mauritius, will lose significant export revenues as a consequence. To mitigate losses, the EU has proposed a special fund to help such countries diversify and restructure their economies. To access this fund the government has begun a major reform of the sugar industry.

To increase productivity small-scale holdings will be consolidated. De-rocking will be undertaken to make them amenable to mechanized harvesting. Since sugar is the only agriculture crop that has been successful on the island—("What alternative crops?" asked the agricultural minister when queried about diversifying crops. "Do you want us to turn out like Afghanistan?")—more cane fields will be planted. Sugar production will expand from 50% to 81% of total land cultivated. Concentration and consolidation will also be effected in sugar processing: seven of eleven sugar factories will be closed. A voluntary retirement scheme is available to support those factory workers who will lose their jobs.

To extract full value from the sugar cane, more power plants burning "bagasse" (a residue from cane) to produce electricity will be commissioned. Since 2002 the industry has been producing about 40% of the island's electricity using bagasse and import charcoal. A second bagasse-electricity station is scheduled to open in 2007. When fully operational, some 60% to 70% of Mauritian electricity will be generated from renewable fuel.

Similarly, molasses created during the sugar-refining process is being used to

Mauritius

produce ethanol used in a blended fuel for vehicles. The Alcodis distillery has increased its ethanol production from a few million liters for domestic consumption to 30 million liters for the export market.

Light manufacturing, dominated by textiles, accounted for 21.4% of GDP in 2004. At one time there were more than 500 textile factories concentrated in Mauritius' Economic Processing Zone. They employed close to 90,000 workers, and they made Mauritius the world's second-largest exporter of woolen knits. Since the late 1990s, however, thousands of Mauritians have been cast out of the textile factories as they closed or downsized. Following September 11, exports to the U.S. fell by 15%. The economy faced even greater challenges with the ending of textile quotas beginning in 2005; cheap Chinese goods are poised to drive everything else from the marketplace. Textile firms have left in droves for Asian nations like China and India, where costs are lower and which can now export unlimited amounts of clothing to Western nations. Job losses in textile manufacturing contribute significantly to the country's growing unemployment rate.

Tourism is the country's second-largest source of export revenues after textiles and represents one of the greatest potential growth areas. Mauritius has always marketed itself as an upscale vacation site, but faced with declines in sugar and textiles, the government hopes to expand the industry—achieving two million arrivals a year by 2015. Some 860,000 visitors came in 2007.

Information and communication technology are slated to become a fourth pillar of the economy. The plan involves creating "cyber cities" that will provide a world-class telecommunications network via satellite and fiber-optic cable. (There is a fiber-optic cable that runs by the island on its way from Europe to southern India's high-tech corridor.)

The project will require skilled workers, and in these, Mauritius is deficient. Despite doubling the size of the computer engineering department at the University of Mauritius, the country still only produces 500 to 600 qualified information technology specialists a year. In collaboration with the Massachusetts Institute of Technology, the university has set up a virtual learning center that gives Mauritian students access to course materials used at MIT.

The government is investing heavily in education to produce the manpower needed for its future cyber-cities. The island's educational system has been entirely overhauled. School hours will be extended 45 minutes, and nine compulsory subjects—including languages, mathematics, science, and information technology—have been inserted into the curriculum.

The government's diversification and development plans face practical difficulties. Budgetary deficits over the past few years have accumulated; public sector debt now amounts to two-thirds of GDP. The government now spends more on debt servicing than on education and health. A fast growth rate could help reduce this deficit, but growth has faltered; it was 4.2% in 2004 and only marginally better at 4.6% in 2005. Unemployment remains a serious issue: in 2004 it stood at 8.5%, but rose to 9.5% in 2005. In human terms, that represents a little over 50,000 jobless.

The Future

Economic reform is often initially painful, with benefits unrolling only over the long term. Rising inflation and unemployment have fuelled discontent among the poor. Continued political stability in Mauritius will depend upon the government's ability to ease social suffering during the transitional period of its reform efforts without stripping itself of the revenues to continue development investment.

Politically, Mauritius is one of Africa's great success stories. With a solid economy and some geographic separation from many of the continent's problems, Mauritius has retained a solid democratic foundation for years. Stability in the island nation is a model for many other African countries, though the conditions on the island are unique and not replicable elsewhere.

A 2,000 rupee note with a traditional ox cart moving the island's important sugar crop

The Republic of the Seychelles (*Say*-shells)

Presidential Palace

Photo by Powell Harrison

Basic Facts

Area: 100 sq. mi., about 1,000 miles off the east coast of Kenya in the Indian Ocean, consisting of some 115 islands, half of which are mountainous and very scenic. The others are little more than coral atolls.

Population: 87,000 (UN 2007 est.)

Capital City: Victoria (on Mahé, pronounced Mah-*hay*)

Climate: tropical marine; humid; cooler season during southeast monsoon (late May to September); warmer season during northwest monsoon (March to May).

Official Languages: English, French

Other Principal Languages: Seselwa, a French-based Creole

Ethnic Groups: Seychellois (mixture of Asians, Africans, and Europeans)

Religions: Roman Catholic 86.6%, Anglican 6.8%, other Christian 2.5%, other 4.1%

Chief Commercial Products: Processed fish (tuna), prawns, cinnamon bark, copra, tea and vanilla

GNI Per Capita: $8,290 (World Bank 2006 est.)

Independence Date: June 29, 1976 (from UK)

Chief of State: James Alix Michel, President (since April 2004)

National Flag: Five oblique bands of blue (hoist side), yellow, red, white, and green (bottom) radiating from the bottom of the hoist side.

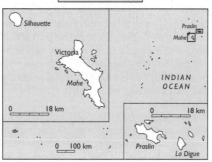

Land and People

Located in the western Indian Ocean, 1,000 miles off the coast of East Africa, the Seychelles comprises 115 islands, spread over 154,000 square miles of the Indian Ocean. Lying just below the Equator, the islands have been dubbed a "Garden of Eden" because of the lushness and diversity of their scenery. The main archipelago consists of 42 granitic islands—thrown up by volcanic action to heights of a half mile above sea level—and some 73 coral atolls, low, flat and only a few feet above the sea. Mahé, with its lush hills and luxurious beaches, is the largest and most populated of the islands, with almost 90% of the nation's total population of 80,000. Praslin and La Digue are the other major islands. Others, like Denis Island, a coral atoll, Sainte Anne, Bird Island, and Cousine, the smallest of the granite islands, are privately owned nature reserves usually associated with an upscale resort. Fregate, only one square mile in size, was named after a bird and is now the home of tens of thousands of them.

The population of the Seychelles is relatively homogenous, the result of frequent

259

Seychelles

President James Michel of The Seychelles

intermarriage between the island's original French settlers and Africans who settled after the islands were ceded to Britain in the early 1800s. Small Indian and Chinese minorities also exist. Most of the population is Roman Catholic, and almost everyone speaks Creole.

Upon assuming leadership in 1977, President René invited his fellow citizens to "create the new man, with his roots." The "root" of this new Seychellois identity would be its "créolité"—its "creoleness." Since then government policy has affirmed and cultivated a common culture based on Creole roots. The language has become the first spoken and written language of everyone (English and French are the second and third languages), and the world's only Creole Institute can be found on Mahé. Each October Victoria hosts the world's largest Creole festival, featuring artists and writers from the diverse Creole world—Mauritius, Reunion, the French Caribbean islands, Guyana, etc.

In April 2002 the SPPF government celebrated 25 years of rule since the coup (or "liberation" as party stalwarts prefer to call it) that brought it to power. The government describes itself as "paternalistic"—a fusion of socialism and capitalism, and in many ways its achievements are striking. Gone are the days when 30 families—the *grands blancs*—controlled wealth and property on the islands. Free access to education and health, a right to housing, and guaranteed employment have created a costly social security system unequaled on the African continent. Seychellois have the highest per capita income of all the African states.

The islands boast two UNESCO World Heritage Sites. The first, Aldabra, is the world's largest raised atoll, and hosts the world's largest colony of giant tortoises (150,000 of them) along with the last remaining flightless birds in the Indian Ocean. The second is the Vallée de Mai on Praslin, the only place on earth where one finds the black parrot and the rare palm trees that bear the giant Coco de Mer or sea coconut, the world's largest and heaviest

seed, perhaps better known for a voluptuous shape that reminds the erotically susceptible of portions of the female anatomy.

The Past: Political and Economic History

For early history, see *Historical Background* and *The Colonial Period: The French* and *The Colonial Period: The British*

The British colony was granted self-government in 1975 and independence in 1976. James R. Mancham, the islands' first president, was overthrown in 1977 by a leftist *coup d'état* led by his prime minister, France Albert René. In 1979 René revised the constitution and created a one-party socialist state controlled by his Seychelles People's Progressive Front (SPPF).

In good Leninist fashion, a multiparty political system was not permitted until 1991, and Seychelles' first democratic multiparty elections were held in 1993. René triumphed over former President James Mancham, and the SPPF retained control of the National Assembly.

In March 1997 elections, President René was returned to power with 66.65% of the votes. James Mancham, leader of the opposition Democratic Party (DP), was the big loser, receiving only 14% of the vote, down from the 35% he had won in 1993. Reverend Wavel Ramkalawan, leader of the United Opposition (UO), drew 20% of presidential ballots, and his party replaced the DP as official opposition by winning 26% of the votes cast in legislative elections. Still, in Seychelles' mixed system of single member districts and proportional representation, that only earned the party three seats in the National Assembly. Once again, the SPPF swept the legislative elections, winning 30 seats. Mancham's DP saw its parliamentary representation drop from five seats to one.

Snap presidential elections were called in September 2001, well before the expiration of the president's term of office in 2003 and well before the country's increasingly difficult economic circumstances really began to hurt. With a bit of vote-buying, charged the opposition, René secured 54% of the vote, beating off a vigorous challenge from the Seychelles National Party's Wavel Ramkalawan, who won 45% of the votes.

Seychelles' opposition leader, Reverend Ramkalawan, has proved much less conciliatory than his predecessor and much more formidable. As such he became the object of a smear campaign by the SPPF-controlled press before the legislative election of 2002. (Despite its total dominance, the SPPF made few concessions to its opposition.)

Seychelles' one daily newspaper and single radio and television service are government controlled. Coverage of the political opposition is highly restricted.

Regar, an independent weekly that supports the SNP, has been consistently targeted by President René and other government officials with costly defamation lawsuits. The courts, whose judges had all been appointed by René, inevitably found the paper guilty and fined it heavily. This was part of René's policy of crushing any voice of opposition, even if it only has a print run of 3,000.

In December 2005 *Regar*'s offices were burned, damaging its printing press. The attack took place after the paper had exposed an alleged corrupt property deal implicating a senior member of the SPPF; as of mid-2007 no suspects had yet been charged. *Regar*'s management suspended publication in October 2006 to protest its legal harassment. The decision to cease publication came after an unprecedented fine of 350,000 rupees—over $57,000—for publishing a photo of the Seychelles Tourism Board president fishing in restricted waters. The photo had already appeared in the *Seychelles Nation*, the government's daily newspaper.

President René called early parliamentary elections in December 2002, well before the normal expiration of the Assembly's mandate, and presumably before the impact of a declining economy would be felt by too many voters. Once again René did all he could to prevent an opposition victory. Typically, opposition SNP candidates and supporters were intimidated: Police were generally in attendance at all its meetings, but looked away when gangs of SPPF partisans menaced the opposition. To divide the opposition, James Mancham's Democratic Party, moribund since its disastrous defeat in 1998, seemed to have been given financing by the government. Tacitly admitting the country's economic slowdown, the SPPF made "Things Can Only Get Better" its campaign slogan.

René's SPPF won handily, but saw its massive majority eroded, down from 30 to 24. Reverend Ramkalawan's SNP took the remaining 11 seats in the National Assembly. The Democratic Party failed to achieve the minimum 10% required to earn a seat by proportional representation.

Having secured his last hurrah, President René retired from office in April 2004; he was succeeded by Vice President James Michel, but maintained his position as head of the Seychelles People's Progressive Front. President Michel was elected president in his own right in July 2006, winning 54% of the votes to Reverend Ramkalawan's 46%. For the Seychelles, this was a close race.

When the government proposed legislation to ban political parties and religious groups from owning a radio station in late 2006, the opposition simply walked out. The boycott lasted five months. Fed up with stalemate, President Michel called a snap election for May 2007 hoping to secure an even larger SPPF majority. The voters—and some 85% participated—returned both parties to parliament with exactly the same representation as before: 23 members of the SPPF, 11 for the SNP.

The Present: Contemporary Issues

Isolated in the vast Indian Ocean, the Seychelles promote themselves as an idyllic tourist location. Some 130,000 people visit the islands annually and account for 70% of their hard currency. It's upscale tourism only, and until recently charter flights were not permitted. The fear was that budget passengers would lower the tone of the island and not spend enough money. The number of visitors is limited to 150,000 a year, and no more than 4,500 are permitted at any one time. The government also controls the quantity and quality of hotels and does not permit camping. Accommodations are correspondingly pricey. Comrade workers will find no rest and recreation in this socialist Garden of Eden.

In the latter part of 2002 the government permitted charter flights to revivify a softening industry. As a consequence, Seychelles has experienced record visitation rates. More than 140,000 visitors reached the islands in 2006, a 9% increase over 2005; in 2007 the government expects 150,000 arrivals. With 6,000 hotel beds currently available, and projects on the drawing boards that would increase that number to 10,000 in 2010, the government has begun to contemplate the need to cap sector development.

Seychelles has one of the highest living standards in Africa with a remarkable per capita Gross National Income (GNI) of more than $8,100, but the economy is only recently coming out of a major contraction. World Bank figures show GDP declined by over 10% during 2001–05. It was a rough period for the country: Seychelles' net international reserves were depleted and government debt grew alarmingly.

The foreign currency shortage resulted in empty shelves in the shops, inflation, and a black market where a dollar cost ten rupees compared to the official rate of five. By mid-2001 the government was forcing foreign tourists to pay all their bills in foreign currency rather than local rupees. Passengers at the island's international airport were reportedly searched for travelers' checks.

Because of its cash crunch, the government defaulted on its bonds, taking its place with other financial deadbeats like Liberia and Zimbabwe—all of whom are barred from borrowing from multilateral lenders. Its accumulated debt rose from $265 million in 2001 to $615 million in 2005.

The IMF blamed the crisis on excessive government involvement in the economy, including price controls, foreign exchange allocation, restrictive import licensing, and many government-owned monopolies in manufacturing and distribution. According to a recent EU study, government expenditures account for some 62% of GDP. The economy is dominated by the Seychelles Marketing Board (SMB), the islands' largest employer. SMB possesses a variety of import and export monopolies and has a share of almost every enterprise.

The IMF and EU offer a simple prescription for Seychelles' welfare-state woes: privatize government monopolies, eliminate price controls, devalue the rupee, permit foreign investment and drop controls on foreign exchange. Locally, Reverend Ramkalawan argues that the only way to regain investors' confidence and revitalize the economy is to liberalize it. If nothing changes, he says, "we will go under."

Though few structural changes have been made in the economy under President Michel, Seychelles has begun to emerge from its economic doldrums. Driven by record increases in tourist arrivals and a booming construction sector, the economy began a turnaround in the latter half of 2005. Real GDP grew by 4.5% in 2006.

Seychelles takes advantage of its greatest natural resource, fishing. Its exclusive economic zone gives it control of more than 386,000 square miles of Indian Ocean, abundant in rich fishing grounds. A fleet of patrol boats enforces the exclusion zone, and all fishing vessels must stop in Victoria port, register their catch, and pay the appropriate fees. Increasingly, however, high operating costs have put Seychelles at a disadvantage. The ports of Mombassa, Kenya, and Dar es Salaam, Tanzania, offer more services at lower cost.

Fishing licenses and fees bring in about $7 million annually, but the government decided that added value could be better achieved by processing the catch locally. In 1995, it joined with Heinz to build a new cannery on reclaimed land in Victoria harbor. President Michel announced in March 2006 that Lehman Brothers Merchant Banking had bought out the Heinz interest in the cannery (60%) and envisioned increasing annual production by 30%, from 85,000 tons a year to 110,000 tons over the next three years.

The Future

The obdurate former President René was unwilling to liberalize the Seychelles economy despite the recommendations of the IMF, the World Bank, the European Union and the local private sector. His successor, James Michel, faces the consequences, but given the dominance of the SPPF, and the patronage possibilities of government-controlled businesses with which to continue that control, there would appear to be little incentive for rapid change. On the other hand, Michel has spent the last year going hat-in-hand to the international community for foreign aid, and the government may have to make considerable concessions. Given the downturn in global tourism, the Seychelles are seeking debt reduction to accompany a major IMF aid package from late 2008. It is to be expected that international support will come with some form of economic conditionality.

On the political front, there is reason to be hopeful that the Seychelles is moving in the direction of increased political liberalism, as many middle-income economies do. Only the relative dominance of the local media by the state seems to prevent the small island nation from being considered a full democracy; political rights seem on the rise, and many civil liberties are protected. In this, the archipelago seems to be ahead of the curve on the African continent.

Unloading a rich cargo of tuna in Victoria harbor   ©IRIN

SOUTHERN AFRICA

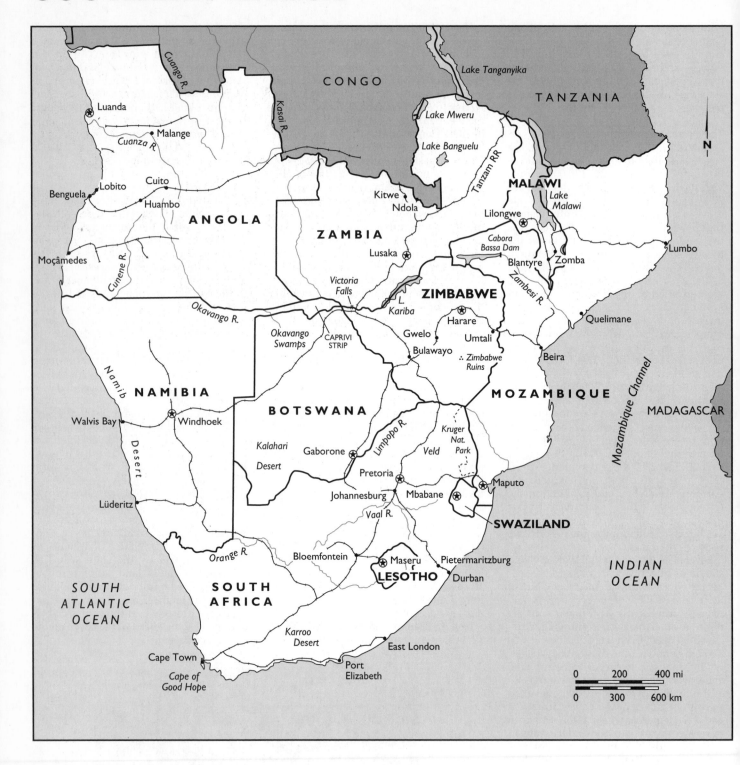

CONGO

TANZANIA

Lake Tanganyika

Cuango R.

Luanda

Malange

Cuanza R.

Lake Mweru

Lake Banguelu

Kasai R.

Cuito

Lobito

Benguela

Huambo

ANGOLA

Kitwe

Ndola

ZAMBIA

Lusaka

Tanzam RR

MALAWI

Lilongwe

Lake Malawi

Lumbo

Moçâmedes

Cunene R.

Cabora Bassa Dam

Blantyre

Zomba

Zambesi R.

Victoria Falls

Okavango R.

L. Kariba

ZIMBABWE

Quelimane

Okavango Swamps

CAPRIVI STRIP

Harare

Gwelo

Umtali

Bulawayo

∴ Zimbabwe Ruins

Beira

N a m i b

NAMIBIA

Walvis Bay

Windhoek

BOTSWANA

MOZAMBIQUE

Mozambique Channel

MADAGASCAR

Kalahari Desert

Gaborone

Limpopo R.

Veld

Kruger Nat. Park

Maputo

Lüderitz

Desert

Pretoria

Johannesburg

Mbabane

SWAZILAND

Vaal R.

Orange R.

Bloemfontein

Maseru

Pietermaritzburg

LESOTHO

Durban

INDIAN OCEAN

SOUTH ATLANTIC OCEAN

SOUTH AFRICA

Karroo Desert

East London

Cape Town

Port Elizabeth

Cape of Good Hope

| 0 | 200 | 400 mi |
| 0 | 300 | 600 km |

N

The Republic of Angola

Basic Facts

Area: 1,245,790 sq. km. = 481,000 sq. mi. (about four times the size of New Mexico)

Population: 17,500,000 (UN 2008 est.)

Capital City: Luanda

Climate: Moist and warm in the north, dryer and hot in the large, central plateau area; arid, semidesert in the south.

Neighboring Countries: Congo-Kinshasa (north); Namibia (south); Zambia (southeast)

Official Language: Portuguese

Other Principal Languages: Over forty African languages, including Tchokwe, Kikongo, Kwanyama, Mbundu, Nyaneka, and Umbundu

Ethnic Groups: Ovimbundu 37%, Kimbundu 25%, Bakongo 13%, Mestico (mixed European and African) 2%, European 1%, and other 22%

Principal Religions: Indigenous beliefs 47%, Roman Catholic 38%, Protestant 15% (1998 est.)

Chief Commercial Products: Crude oil 90%, diamonds, refined petroleum products, gas, coffee, sisal, fish and fish products, timber, cotton

GNP Per Capita: $5,709 (World Bank 2007 est.)

Currency: kwanza

Former Colonial Status: Portuguese Colony until November 11, 1975; actual control passed in early 1975.

Independence Date: November 11, 1975

Chief of State: José Eduardo dos Santos, President (since 1979, with disputed elections in September 1992).

National Flag: Two horizontal stripes of equal width, red and black, upon which is centered a 5-pointed yellow star, halfway surrounded by a wheel and crossed by a machete.

Land and People

For most of its sprawling area, Angola is a high, grassy plateau ranging from

The consequences of civil war: massive destruction of infrastructure

©IRIN

3,000 to 4,000 feet above sea level, dotted by occasional trees and brush—barely enough to withstand the scorching heat of the day. The coastal belt, home to about 20% of the population, is from 15 to 60 miles wide, stretching from the tropical mouth of the mighty Congo River, down to the palm-lined central beaches, and then on to the reddish sands of the Namib Desert in the extreme south. Lofty mountains drive eastward, splitting the country in half until the terrain gradually levels out, dipping first northeast into the hot, steaming rain forest of Congo's river basin and then southeast to isolated, semiarid land.

Angola's mountains are the source of numerous rivers, which fan out in all directions. The Cuanza River, Angola's largest, twists north for 600 miles in a wavering half-circle and then drains into the Atlantic below cosmopolitan Luanda. The Cunene's cold waters gush southward down the mountains, slow as they pass through the plains, become sluggish in the silent desert, then lazily turn westward and are caught by the huge Cunene Dam, which regulates its flow as it forms the 175-mile border with Namibia to the ocean. Another river, in the northeast, offers unique drama. Meandering aimlessly across the sun-parched grasslands, the Lucala unexpectedly reaches a wide, curved rock shelf where the placid waters suddenly plunge into a 350-foot gorge, sending up a heavy spray-mist, which transforms the immediate area into a lush oasis, rich with dark mosses and tropical

foliage—the Duque de Bragança Falls—a truly spectacular sight. Again docile, the river moves across the flat land and joins the waters of the larger Cuanza.

Until 1974 there were two cultures in Angola—the approximately 300,000 Europeans, mostly Portuguese, who were the businessmen and farmers, and that of the original inhabitants of the land. The latter lived a marginal existence in the cities and in the hinterland, working as laborers in the factories and fields of Angola. A small group of these lived as *assimilados*—they adopted European customs and the Portuguese language. They now are the leadership of the Popular Movement for the Liberation of Angola (MPLA, or Movimento Popular de Libertação de Angola), Angola's governing party.

In 2010, Angola will be hosting the African Nations Cup, a soccer competition that involves the continent's 16 top teams. A 50,000-seat stadium is being built in Camama. Soccer is a big passion for Angolans, inherited from Portugal. The event is seen as an opportunity to create jobs, build infrastructure, attract foreign investors and boost the economy

The Past: Political and Economic History

For early history, see *Historical Background* and *The Colonial Period: The Portuguese.*

Portugal's abusive colonial policies in Africa generated increasing resistance and resentment in the 1950s. While assimilation had produced a small group of educated Angolans, mostly *mestiços*, even

Angola

these recognized there was no equality of treatment for Africans. In the countryside, the settlement of white farmers and use of forced labor embittered the rural peasantry. Anticolonial, nationalist sentiment first coalesced in Luanda, the capital, with the formation of the Popular Movement for the Liberation of Angola (MPLA) in 1956. The heart of the movement was a multiracial core of leftist urban intellectuals. Its ethnic core resided in the Mbundu people of Luanda and the surrounding area. As of 1962, the group was headed by Agostinho Neto, an assimilated Mbundu physician.

The MPLA's greatest rival in the early years was the National Front for the Liberation of Angola (FNLA). Led by Holden Roberto, FNLA began as a spokesman for ethnic interests of Angola's northern Bakongo peoples, but by 1958 it expanded its goals to independence for all Angola. A national liberation army was created, and young Angolans were sent to North Africa to train with Algerian forces engaged in their own nationalist struggle. A Revolutionary Government of Angola in Exile (GRAE), headquartered in Leopoldville, was also created and claimed sole representation of the interests of the Angolan people.

A falling-out between Holden Roberto and his foreign minister in the GRAE, Jonas Savimbi, led to the creation of the National Union for the Total Independence of Angola (UNITA) in 1964. The group's membership was rooted in Angola's largest ethnic group, the Ovimbundu, peasant farmers who dominated the fertile central highlands. In 1965 Savimbi (who had earned a doctorate in political science from the University of Lausanne, Switzerland) and several of his followers went to China where they received military training and became disciples of Maoism. Like its rivals, UNITA claimed to be the sole representative of the Angolan people.

Angola's march to independence centered on these three military-political groups. They had one common enemy, Portugal, but differing nationalist visions. Each was specifically rooted in the geographical and ethnic reality of Angola and drew on different sources of external support that intensified rivalries, both personal and ideological. At a time of intense ideological competition internationally, each of the groups ultimately became an extension of Cold War rivalries between East and West.

With its Marxist-Leninist orientation, the MPLA attracted the support of the international left. Its military cadres received training in Eastern Europe and Cuba. Recently independent African states with similar left-leaning inclinations pro-

vided sympathetic support. Soviet arms transited through Tanzania and Zambia to supply its forces.

The nationalist struggles in its African colonies drained Portugal's will and resources. Some 11,000 Portuguese soldiers had been killed by 1974, and on April 25 of that year disgruntled military officers overthrew the Portuguese government and began the process leading to decolonization. Angola's transition to independence was difficult. A transitional government involving all three nationalist groups was created, but Portuguese settlers resisted and rioted. Rivalries between the three nationalist groups intensified. External aid and intervention increased.

The United States supported the pro-Western FNLA when it seemed the strongest of the groups, but it later shifted its support to UNITA. The Soviet Union responded with increased arms deliveries to the MPLA, and Cuba sent military instructors and combat troops. OAU negotiators brought Neto, Roberto, and Savimbi together in June 1975 to produce a draft constitution for independent Angola, but soon afterwards the transitional government collapsed. The FNLA and UNITA withdrew, and, recognizing their military weakness individually against the MPLA army, united and declared war against the MPLA. Group rivalry turned into civil war.

In support of the FNLA-UNITA alliance, South Africa, which had already worked with Portugal fighting nationalist guerrillas in Angola, sent in an invasion force to protect hydroelectric facilities on the Cunene River in August 1975. A larger

Jonas Savimbi, former leader of UNITA

South African-led force invaded Angola in October. Six provincial capitals were occupied, and the invaders came within 62 miles of Luanda.

To combat this threat, the MPLA received a massive increase in Soviet military aid, while Cuba poured thousands of troops into the country; the military balance tipped in its favor. South African support of the FNLA and UNITA tainted both groups. Portugal granted independence amid the chaos of civil war on November 11, 1975, marking the end of 400 years of Portuguese colonial rule.

The MPLA, in control of the capital, proclaimed the People's Republic of Angola. A rival "Democratic People's Republic of Angola" was proclaimed by the FNLA-UNITA alliance, but it was clear the MPLA, backed by some 10,000 to 12,000 Cuban troops, had emerged on top. International recognition followed, and the MPLA moved to create a Marxist-Leninist single-party state. Agostinho Neto served as both MPLA secretary-general and president of Angola. With Cuban assistance the FNLA was defeated militarily, leaving only one rival to dispute the MPLA government's legitimacy, Jonas Savimbi's UNITA.

President Neto died following an operation on September 10, 1979 and was succeeded by his foreign minister, José Eduardo dos Santos. Angola faced continuing instability from internal and external elements. UNITA continued armed resistance to the MPLA government. South Africa also undertook incursions into Angola to root out guerrilla bases supporting the SWAPO (Southwest Africa People's Organization), the rebel group attempting to create an independent state in present-day Namibia; this resulted in clashes between Cuban and South African troops.

The linked external problems were resolved in a grand diplomatic solution of 1988. South Africa agreed to the independence of South West Africa, while Cuba and South Africa jointly agreed to withdraw their troops from Angola. The only irksome presence that remained was Jonas Savimbi and UNITA.

Political negotiations between MPLA and UNITA resulted in a June 1991 ceasefire, but the lull in fighting was short-lived. Angola's single party constitution was amended to permit multiparty elections, and these were scheduled for September 1992. President dos Santos won a plurality of votes on the first ballot, but UNITA refused to accept the results, claiming widespread fraud. Within a few days UNITA resumed the civil war. UNITA supporters were chased from Luanda, and the second round of elections was never held. Full-scale fighting continued until a peace accord was signed in Lusaka, Zambia in November 1994. The

Lusaka Protocol called for demilitarization of UNITA and the creation of a national army integrating UNITA elements into the Angola Armed Forces, plus a government of national unity and the extension of state administration to areas formerly under UNITA control. Still, neither side was deeply committed to the peace accord, and the MPLA government continued to seek the total destruction of UNITA and the elimination of its leader, Jonas Savimbi.

The year 1995 was marked by a major UN effort to begin to implement the Lusaka provisions. By April 1998 virtually all the Lusaka provisions had been implemented. UNITA had turned over almost all of the territory under its control to government administration, disarmed most of its soldiers and shut down its propaganda radio. For its part, the Angolan government recognized UNITA as an unarmed political party with the right to organize and campaign throughout the country. Savimbi was officially recognized as the main opposition leader with rights to hold regular consultations with President dos Santos, access to government media and the right to visit Angolan embassies abroad. For his personal safety, Savimbi was permitted a bodyguard of 400 men, ultimately to be reduced to 150. UNITA's participation in a Government of National Reconciliation (GURN) was realized with the inclusion of 70 deputies in parliament and seven ministerial portfolios.

Again, however, the seeming resolution proved ephemeral. In September 1997 the MPLA government suspended UNITA's ministers, vice-ministers, and parliamentarians, threatening GURN's existence. The government mounted an effort to destroy UNITA as a political party by inducing a number of UNITA figures participating in GURN to break with Savimbi and form a new party. UNITA-Renovado, as it was called, deposed Savimbi as president was recognized by the government as the authentic "interlocutor for national reconciliation."

In the countryside, far from the probing eyes of reporters or UN monitoring teams, the Angola National Police (ANP) pursued another systematic approach to UNITA's destruction, violently targeting party leadership and grassroots structures. UNITA administrators, party officials and those simply accused of collaborating with UNITA were murdered.

After UNITA closed its radio station, the government filled the airwaves with what Western diplomats referred to as "fabricated news reports of UNITA atrocities." The UN and the United States issued statements denouncing the use of "false information" and "provocative rhetoric." The government's intent was clear: to create an

President José Eduardo dos Santos

atmosphere of fear and justify a renewal of hostilities against its foe.

Mobutu's Fall and Its Consequences

As the long-standing Mobutu regime in neighboring Zaïre (now Democratic Republic of the Congo) finally crumbled in the 1990s, the MPLA saw another opportunity to destroy UNITA. It intervened militarily in Zaïre and Congo-Brazzaville to destroy Savimbi's support and supply bases. Mobutu, who had long aided UNITA, was an obvious target; Angolan troops were sent to assist his opponent, Laurent Kabila. President Lissouba of Congo (Brazzaville) had also aided UNITA, so when civil war erupted between Lissouba and ex-president Sassou-Nguesso, Angolan planes bombed the capital and helped dispatch Lissouba to exile. Angolan Troops entered Congo-Brazzaville to ferret out UNITA bases from which Savimbi's forces had led attacks on the oil-rich enclave of Cabinda (see below).

The MPLA was willing to stir international conflict for domestic objectives, and made clear they would once again take up the fight against UNITA. At the MPLA party congress in December 1998 President dos Santos bluntly stated "the only way to achieve peace in Angola is through the political and military neutralization of UNITA and its president." By spring 1999 both the government and UNITA had restocked their weapons. With no peace to observe, the UN withdrew, its \$2.2-billion mission having expired in utter failure.

Having spent half a billion dollars on new armament and possessed of overwhelming superiority in weaponry, the Angolan forced Savimbi and UNITA to melt into the landscape and resort to traditional guerilla tactics. By 2001 the government had eliminated UNITA's capacity to conduct conventional warfare, but

has not destroyed the group. Savimbi's sphere of operations was limited to the province of Moxico, a vast underpopulated region bordering Zambia. The government adopted a scorched earth policy in the province, removing any civilians that might have aided the rebels. The army eventually captured a number of Savimbi's leading officers and penetrated his security network. After more than 30 years of guerilla war, Savimbi was at last pursued, cornered, and killed on February 22, 2002.

Savimbi's death dramatically transformed Angola's political landscape. Within six weeks of his death, UNITA's military commander signed a cease-fire. Parliament voted a blanket amnesty covering "all civilians and soldiers, Angolan or foreign, who committed crimes against the security of the Angolan state." The civil war, which had devastated Angola for some 27 years, left more than 500,000 dead, 100,000 maimed, 100,000 orphaned, and 3.1 million—roughly a quarter of the population—displaced by the fighting. In the last year of the war alone the government's scorched earth policies had forced 400,000 more people to flee their homes.

In parallel, the MPLA government found itself faced with growing demands for some negotiated settlement from civil society. Over the years Angola's civil society had grown larger, stronger, and bold enough to condemn the government's war that had destroyed the country but not the enemy. Increasingly vociferous church groups and humanitarian organizations lead the way. Military destruction remained the preferred option for the government, however, which continued to buy arms wherever it could.

With Savimbi gone, dos Santos announced in August 2001 that he would not contest the next presidential election, and would work on his legacy—the reconstruction of Angola, whose economy was left in shambles. GDP had fallen 48% over the previous 25 years. Infrastructure outside of Luanda, the capital, had been destroyed and the state's capacity to deliver services minimal. The state's vast oil wealth had contributed little to human development.

The government and UNITA are working towards creating a post-Savimbi Angola. The two have agreed (amongst themselves and without consulting others) to a new constitution. Under its provisions, considerable authority would be concentrated in the presidency. The president will name and can remove the prime minister. He will also appoint provincial governors, but appointments will be made from nominations of the party that receives the majority of votes in the province. The two parties also agreed on a single-chamber

Angola

Working to rebuild a bridge. ©IRIN

parliament, though a consultative body incorporating traditional leaders and local officials may yet emerge.

There is little to suggest the MPLA is interested in changing much in Angola. Its main goal is to maintain control and dominate the opposition. In February 2003, for example, the Catholic radio station, Radio Ecclesia, was attacked for practicing what the minister of information called "antenna terrorism." The party has also refused to disband its civilian militias, armed by the government during the civil war, and seems to turn a blind eye when militia thugs intimidate UNITA organizers in the provinces. UNITA's new leader, Isaïas Samakuva (chosen by a party congress in June 2003), has charged the MPLA is "set on returning to the time of a one-party state."

Given its Marxist origins and Stalinist orientation, the MPLA does find change a difficult prospect. At the party's fifth national congress in December 2003 José Eduardo dos Santos was unanimously reelected party president; there was no alternative candidate and voting was done publicly, by a show of hands.

Electoral laws approved in April 2005 suggest the MPLA's unwillingness to share power. A new National Electoral Commission (CNE) that will organize the elections has 11 members, nearly two-thirds of them will come from MPLA milieus.

In September 2008, Angola held its Legislative elections. The MPLA had the ma-jority of seats (81,6%), followed by UNITA (10,2%). This was also the country's first election with the new quota that establishes 30% of the candidates must be female. Although the opposition claimed fraud, the 2008 legislative election suggested some advances for democracy in the country. The main problem was the disorganization of the process, especially in the capital Luanda, where 29% of the voters live. Presidential balloting has been tentatively scheduled for later in 2009, but dos Santos has called for a new constitution before the elections can be held. The result is that the vote will be held only in 2010.

Between the MPLA and UNITA leadership lies the chasm of culture and history and race. UNITA emerged as a factor in the liberation struggle from the perception that the MPLA was dominated by mixed-race intellectuals from the coastal cities. Historically the Luandan elite had looked down on countryside folk as inept and inferior. Savimbi sought to exploit and mobilize those differences. UNITA is based on the highland Ovimbundu people. It has always claimed to represent "real Africans," "sons of the soil," "living in the bush" against a better-educated, wealthy, cosmopolitan urban elite. As almost living proof of the cultural division, dos Santos left Luanda to visit the rest of the country only once in seven years, during a brief campaign swing. Savimbi's populist nationalism, with potential appeal to the dis-possessed masses living in the squalor of squatter shacks on the outskirts of Luanda, was deeply threatening to the status and perks of the urban elite.

The MPLA's mechanisms of threat and intimidation remain operative, particularly in the countryside. It has refused to dissolve its former militia, the paramilitary Civil Defense Organization (*defesa civil*), which has been involved in several violent encounters. Police agents intimidate, rob, harass and kill citizens, particularly those who may not agree with the government it would appear.

Members of the *Partido de Apoio Democrático e Progresso de Angola* (PADEPA: Party for Democratic Support and Progress) have been the most gutsy (and persistent) in testing the regime's tolerance of dissent. Several were arrested in September 2006 for allegedly instigating disobedience and rebellion by protesting the planned closure of Luanda's largest informal market, the Roque Santerio. (The land on which the market operates, right on the seaside, is much desired by politically well-connected property developers.) In November, police denied the group permits to demonstrate in front of the French Embassy to protest official corruption and to demand a return of public funds allegedly deposited by the fraudsters in French banks. One hundred and ten protesters were arrested for disturbing the peace as they approached the embassy. Police detained 27 who identified themselves as members of PADEPA; tried and found guilty, they were sentenced to a month in prison, later converted to a $2000 fine.

It is unlikely most Angolans heard the news. While private media, print and broadcast, are permitted in Angola, they are tightly controlled and restricted to Luanda only. The government has a monopoly of nationwide broadcasting, both of radio and TV. Opposition parties are often denied broadcast time, and are infrequently mentioned in the government daily newspaper, the *Jornal de Angola*.

UNITA, while remaining the principal opposition party, is weakened by internal division. In parliament, the MPLA, as it has done previously, has induced members to abandon the party and join the MPLA. The result of this could be twofold: the MPLA could obtain the supermajority needed to amend the constitution at will, and UNITA will lose considerable public election funding for having a smaller parliamentary delegation. UNITA will hold its second general congress since Jonas Savimbi's murder in June 2007, and President Isaias Samakuvu is likely to encounter stiff competition for the job from the younger and more charismatic Abel Civikuvuku.

Cabinda

With an area of just a bit more than 2,800 square miles, the Cabinda enclave is completely separated from Angola by a narrow stretch of land on either side of the Congo River. It exists as a consequence of colonial power politics. Leopold II, the brash and entrepreneurial Belgian king, wanted access to the sea for the Congo Free State, his personal fief in the heart of Africa. The Portuguese government, possessed of little capacity to protest, was pressured into making the concession.

The enclave contains around 250,000 Cabindans, most of whom would probably prefer independence if given a chance. Cabinda produces nearly 70% of Angola's oil from its offshore wells. Like the people of the Niger Delta, Cabindans feel exploited, abused, and short-changed. Cabinda reportedly receives 10% of the taxes paid by the oil companies—Chevron is the dominant player on the Cabinda fields—but FLEC (*Frente de Libertação do Enclava de Cabinda*, or the Liberation Front for the Cabinda Enclave) has long argued this is insufficient. The argument finds little sympathy in Luanda.

In April 2001 the former president of Portugal, Mario Soares, commented on the continuing struggle for self-determination in Cabinda. The nearly 30-year liberation struggle was, said Soares, "no internal Angolan affair." "Anyone who supports self-determination," he added, "cannot deny the right of a population to discuss the issue, and when this reaches the pitch it has in Cabinda, it moves out of the realm of domestic politics." The speech was occasioned by kidnappings of Portuguese workers by various elements of the FLEC. Abducted to focus international attention on FLEC's demands for self-determination, some of the captured workers had been held for nearly a year when Soares spoke.

Cabindan separatism stems from several sources beyond the obvious economic incentives. Ethnically and linguistically, Cabindans are more closely akin to peoples of southwestern Congo. Historically, the enclave was administered separately by the Portuguese until 1956, and this provided a clear sense of distinctness from Angola. "In our souls, we don't feel we are Angolans, we are Cabindans," said one FLEC leader. There is also a sense of historical exclusion. Cabindan interests were not represented in discussions between mainstream nationalist groups and Portugal that resulted in independence. The feeling then, and now, was that the enclave was simply arbitrarily annexed to Angola at independence. Even the recent Lusaka agreement was restricted to the MPLA government and UNITA and ignored FLEC demands.

Chinese Premier Wen Jiabao welcomed by President dos Santos, June 2006.

For years the dos Santos regime failed to eliminate the various FLEC factions. (One reason for Angola's military advance into the two Congos was to eliminate the support and refuge both UNITA *and* FLEC groups found there.) With Jonas Savimbi's death, however, the Angolan army launched a massive offensive against FLEC forces. There were no official figures, but journalists and NGOs estimated the number of troops involved at anywhere from 10,000 to 35,000 soldiers (a number all the more striking when compared to Cabinda's small total population.)

To deal with the separatists, the army adopted a scorched-earth policy, where destroyed villages, summary executions, rape, and torture featured prominently. It managed to capture the secessionists' forest strongholds and control the area through force and violence. In December 2004, Human Rights Watch reported that the army had "arbitrarily detained and tortured civilians with impunity."

Only 10,000 Cabindans have wage-paying jobs. Unemployment is estimated as high as 90%. There is only one hospital for the entire province—220 beds—and Cabindans, inhabitants to Angola's richest oil province, have to queue up for gasoline. (Angola's only refinery is at Luanda, and gasoline, in insufficient quantities, is shipped by boat to Cabinda.) Most consumer goods have to be imported from Congo-Brazzaville, at exorbitant prices.

Given the savagery of repression and its resultant insecurity, there were signs Cabindans might be willing to set aside their demands for independence temporarily. Father Jorge Kongo, an outspo-

ken priest and human rights campaigner, noted that independence was no longer peoples' principal concern. Now, he said, they were more concerned with personal safety and survival. In February 2005 tens of thousands rallied in Cabinda city to support self-rule for the province.

With its usual dilatory pace and obfuscatory tactics, the government forwarded discussion proposals "about a special status for Cabinda" to the Cabinda Forum for Dialogue (FCD) in February 2006. FCD, an umbrella group that includes representatives of FLEC and the Cabindan church among others, had been recognized as the representative body for the enclave's secessionist movements. Negotiations continued for several months, and in August 2006 the government announced that it had signed a peace agreement with General Antonio Bento Bembe, FLEC's secretary-general. The accord recognized Cabinda's unique history and provided "special designation," but not autonomy, for the enclave. Amnesty for those who turned in their weapons was voted by parliament, and some demobilized fighters will be trained and integrated into the Angolan army or police. When interviewed for his reaction, FLEC's president, N'Zita Henrique Tiago, living in Parisian exile, said he was unaware of the agreement. A FLEC spokesman charged that Bembe had no power to speak for the group and was in reality on the government payroll. Symptomatically, General Geraldo Nunda, speaking in February 2007, expressed satisfaction at the completion of military matters in "northern" Cabinda. Elsewhere in the enclave low-level violence reportedly continued.

Angola

The Present: Contemporary Issues

Angola ranked 161 out of 177 states on the UN Development Program's *Human Development Index* in 2006. Some 60% to 70% of the population lives below the poverty line, and access to health services is abysmal, with only about eight physicians per 100,000 people. Infant mortality is extraordinarily high and life expectancy low. Together, war and corruption have led to this sorry state of affairs.

The devastation produced by more than 30 years of continuous conflict is almost beyond description: bridges, streets and roads, communications systems, airstrips, hospitals, and schools all need reconstruction. Hundreds of thousands of people live in shantytowns of utmost squalor and misery on the outskirts of the capital. The war has also left a legacy of antipersonnel land mines—12 million to 15 million of them, more than one for every man, woman and child in the country; an estimated 70,000 to 200,000 people have lost limbs to them.

Luanda now has four million inhabitants, but only about 20,000 of them have running water or modern toilets. Whole sections—always the poorer—of its capital are a vision of hell, "ringed by mountains of garbage" and "soaked by rivulets of human waste." As far back as 1994 it was estimated that it would require 22,000 dump trucks to remove Luanda's accumulated refuse, and that was when the city was just half its current population of 4.5 million. In the absence of such potable tap water, millions of Luanda's poor pay up to 10,000 times more for drinking water—transported by expensive private delivery trucks—than the elite who are connected to water systems. These conditions have generated one of the continent's worst cholera epidemics in decades. Between February and June 2006, 43,000 Angolans were stricken by the disease; more than 1,600 of them died in this country that accumulated a budgetary surplus of $2 billion in 2005.

With the bulk of government resources devoted to defeating its armed opponents (military spending was 21.2% of GDP in 2000) or corruptly siphoned off to private coffers, Angola's health system collapsed. In an unusually frank report, *Medecins Sans Frontières* (MSF: Doctors without Borders) reported in 2000 that Angolan authorities displayed "a striking lack of interest in the health of their population." Between 1997 and 2001, the government allocated an average of only 3.3% of its expenditures to health care—less than half the average budgeted (7.2%) by members of the Southern African Development Community. In 2007, after five years of peace, the national budget only allocated 3.69% to health expenditures. Angola is thus a paradox: a country of great wealth and dramatic misery.. Fueled by high oil prices and greater control of its diamond producing areas, Angola has turned in eye-popping growth statistics. In 2006 GDP grew by 17.6%. In 2008, Angola became Africa's biggest oil producer, overcoming Nigeria. The government is some of the oil revenues to build infrastructure, such as roads and sewage system.

Angola produced an average 2 million barrels per day (bbl/d) in 2008. Those production figures may be reduced by quota restrictions decreed by OPEC, which Angola joined as the group's 12th member in January 2007. Oil income accounts for some 90% of the state's revenues and over 40% of its GDP.

In addition to its oil resources, Angola is the world's fourth largest diamond producer, accounting for 12% of world production. In 2005 it produced $892.7 million in diamond revenues—about 6% of the country's total export income. Diamond reserves are enormous: estimated at 40 million carats in alluvial diamonds and another 50 million carats in kimberlite form. The World Bank predicts that in 20 years Angola could become the world's largest diamond producer.

These expectations are based on the government's increasing control of diamond-producing areas since the end of the civil war. It has also, somewhat brutally, dealt with a massive influx of foreigners who sought to take advantage of the country's diamond resources. To control illegal mining activities, the government conducted a series of raids from December 2003 through April 2004. Police and soldiers destroyed miners huts, seized firearms, generators, sieves, scales and satellite phones. Amid stories of rampant torture and abuse, the government admitted it had expelled 11,000 people, largely Congolese, to end "exploitation of economic resources."

Despite the abundance of natural-resource wealth, Angola usually runs huge budgetary deficits, and the country is a major debtor, having accumulated an estimated $9.7 billion in debts (2003). With oil-bonanza revenues spilling out of its coffers, Angola has begun to pay down its debt and reduced its dependence on multilateral lenders. The dos Santos government has long claimed its long civil war was the principal cause of its huge external debt. Equally contributory is an Olympian corruption that provides a comfortable life for President dos Santos, his family and supporters. (The president's eldest daughter, Isabel, is widely reported to have extensive holdings in both oil and mining operations. Many of the Angolan generals own or have shares in the numerous security firms that are essential to business, especially the diamond business.) They have enriched themselves through their government connections while three quarters of the country's population lives on less than $1 a day. Symptomatically, Transparency International's 2006 *Corruption Perceptions Index* ranks Angola very near the bottom—only four steps above bottom-ranked Haiti.

The books of the national oil company, Sonangol, are virtual state secrets. A Swiss judge elicited from the former president of Elf-Gabon the revelation that oil companies had paid hidden commissions—"bonuses" in "petrospeak"—of more than a billion dollars to secure Angolan exploration permits in 1998. Much of it disappears off the books. An IMF report gave a five-year total (1997–2001) for money unaccounted for in state finances of $4.36 billion. Another IMF report indicated that more than $900 million had gone missing in 2003 alone.

With the IMF refusing to sanction loans until some degree of transparency and accountability has been achieved, Angola has largely turned to Chinese loans to fund reconstruction and rehabilitation projects. The lines of credit or loans are large (two billion dollars in March 2004 alone), generous (interest-free), and repaid in oil, desperately needed by China's burgeoning economy. In an official visit in February 2005 by Chinese Vice Premier Zeng Peiyan, the two governments announced plans to develop a joint oil exploration project in Angola's offshore fields, an agreement for "the long-term supply of oil" to China, and development of a new refinery. In addition, Chinese

Children receiving food aid at San'Antonia school, Benguela   ©IRIN

companies are building a new finance ministry, a new justice ministry, and rehabilitating the Benguela railroad. The new Chinese-built Luanda General Hospital opened in March 2006, and in the same month, the first stone was laid in a project to build 5,000 apartments in Cabinda. Construction of the 44 buildings, each 15-stories tall, will involve 5,000 workers, 20% of them Chinese, and take 30 months.

The Future

With an oil boom attracting attention from the United States and China, there are reasons to believe that Angola will continue its recent run of rapid economic growth. On the back of skyrocketing oil prices, Angola's economy grew in 2007 at a clip of over 12%, which was a rate faster than China. But this is not to say Angolans can look forward to rapid improvements in their standards of living. The MPLA and UNITA have largely ended the traumatic

period of arbitrary murder and pillage under the civil war, yet governance remains poor. Angola may have shifted from being a conflict zone to a post-conflict zone, with elections that, despite far from being free and fair, offer some limited hope for democratization in the country. The MPLA can be expected to continue its dominance, whether presidential elections are held in 2009 (as originally scheduled) or 2010 (after a new constitutional convention, as dos Santos has proposed).

Both the economy and the political reality are quite contradictory. State coffers are witnessing massive inflows, making improvements in public services and investment a real possibility. Still, this has translated into few gains for the majority of Angolans. Much government income is squandered in corruption, wasteful spending and inefficient services. Improving the capacity of the state to serve a broader population is a prerequi-

site for alleviating poverty. The government claims to be investing in agriculture, in an attempt to diversify the economy. The oil and diamond industries, in addition to being based on limited resources, do not create enough jobs for the population. The 2008 economic crisis strongly hit the Angolan economy by affecting the prices of both diamonds and oil. In January 2009 the government cancelled the World Diamond Summit, an indication that the industry is entering a crisis.

In sum, Angola offers some of the starkest contrasts in Africa: burgeoning investment and major prospects for international investors in a commodity boom, coupled with rampant poverty, corruption, and a lack of state commitment to human capacity and welfare. Angola's most violent days may be behind it, but it is not clear that its best days are visible anywhere on the horizon.

The Republic of Botswana

Basic Facts

Area: 569,800 sq. km. = 220,000 sq. mi. (slightly larger than France)

Population: 1,900,000 (UN 2007 est.)

Capital City: Gaborone (pronounced Ha-bo-ro-neh)

Climate: Subtropical, with temperatures as high as 100°F. in the summer (November–April) and as low as 20°F. in winter (May–October). Rainfall varies from 25 inches per year in the north to 9 inches or less in the southern Kalahari Desert.

Neighboring Countries: Namibia (west and north); Zambia (north); Zimbabwe (northeast); South Africa (south).

Official Languages: English, seTswana

Other Principal Languages: Afrikaans, Herero, Kalanga, Kgalagadi, Kung and other Bushman languages, Mbukushu, Subia, Tswana, Yeye

Ethnic Groups: Tswana (or Setswana) 79%, Kalanga 11%, Basarwa 3%, other, including Kgalagadi and white 7%

Principal Religions: Indigenous beliefs 50%, Christian 50%

Chief Commercial Products: Diamonds, copper, nickel, coal and meat processing

GNI Per Capita: $5,180 (World Bank 2006 est.)

Currency: 1 pula = 100 thebe

Former Colonial Status: British Protectorate (1885–1966)

Independence Date: September 30, 1966

Chief of State: Seretse Khama Ian Khama, President (since April 2008)

National Flag: Five horizontal stripes of blue, white, black, white and blue.

Land and People

Botswana is a large, landlocked country that lies in the transition zone between the dry deserts of South Africa and the forests of Angola. In the South, a vast area is covered by the shifting red sands of the Kalahari Desert, occasionally interrupted by limestone rock formations and clumps of grass and scrub brush at the few places where water is close to the land surface.

The change from desert to grassland is so gradual that it is hard to see where the first ceases and the latter begins. The growth becomes increasingly thicker and there are frequent patches of trees. Annual rainfall slowly increases until it reaches a level required to support farmland where the food and cattle of the nation are produced in non-drought years.

Vegetation becomes dense in the north, and the land turns into the marshland of the Okavango Swamp, fed by the Okavango River flowing from the low mountains of Angola. There is no exit to the ocean for these waters. The country's elevation, averaging 3,300 feet, modifies its subtropical climate.

One of the highest concentrations of rock art in the world is located at Tsodilo. There are over 4,500 paintings in less than four square miles. The site, classified by UNESCO as a World Heritage site, is frequently referred to as the "Louvre of the Desert."

The government's heavy-handed development plans for the San people of the Kalahari have drawn international attention. Most of Botswana's 50,000 San population have already been relocated into 63 resettlement villages, where, the government says, water, health and education services can be better provided. The resettlement villages, miles from the traditional hunting grounds of the San, have been likened to American Indian reservations.

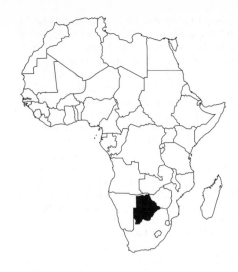

The Past: Political and Economic History

For early history, see *Historical Background* and *The Colonial Period: The British.*

After gaining independence on September 30, 1966, the pre-independence government continued in office. Elections since then have resulted in substantial majorities in the Legislative Assembly for the Botswana Democratic Party (BDP). There are three other small political parties which actively compete in the free elections, but they have yet to dislodge the BDP from its political primacy.

The chiefs of the eight largest tribes are permanent members of the House of Chiefs and are joined by seven other subchiefs. The National Assembly consists of 57 directly elected representatives (four additional seats are nominated by the president), but it cannot act upon matters concerning internal tribal affairs without first submitting a draft to the House of Chiefs.

Elections in October 1979 resulted in a resounding victory for President Sir Seretse Khama (who had been reelected chief executive since independence), with almost 60% of the voters turning out at the polls. He was to have served for another five years, but suddenly died in June 1980; Vice President Quett K.J. Masire was installed to fill out his term and was reelected in September 1984. Khama's eldest son, Seretse Khama Ian Khama, was installed in May 1979 as Paramount Chief of the Bamangwato, the largest of the Twsana-speaking tribes; he also served as commander of the Botswana Defense Force until 1998.

For 18 years President Masire maintained the multiparty traditions of democratic Botswana and exercised a conservative fiscal restraint on the use of the country's riches, producing 16 years of budget surpluses and large foreign reserves. After his initial election as presi-dent in 1984, he led his BDP to successive electoral victories in 1989 and 1994.

With a broadly diverse constituency—civil servants, trade unionists, business people, cattle ranchers, and rural traditionalists—the BDP is subject to internal factionalism. As two party factions vied for party control before the 1999 elections, President Masire decided to retire to avoid an open split in the party. He secured passage of legislation providing for the automatic succession of Botswana's vice president and in November 1997 announced his retirement, effective in six months. On April 1, 1998, he was succeeded by his vice president and finance minister, Festus Mogae.

Almost simultaneously, Lieutenant-General Seretse Khama Ian Khama resigned as chief of the Botswana Defense Force. Having consulted with traditional Bamangwato leaders, he was given temporary release from his chieftaincy to pursue a career in politics. Moving swiftly to fill the vacant vice presidency, Mogae nominated General Khama to the position. With the popular Khama on his side, Mogae effectively closed off internal opposition to his leadership of the BDP. An Oxford University graduate, Mogae was seen as a pragmatic, no-nonsense leader, capable of uniting and energizing a fractured and complacent BDP. In the fall 1999 parliamentary elections, Mogae's political wisdom in appointing Khama became manifest. The dashing young general campaigned vigorously, often flying about the country in military helicopters to galvanize party and electorate.

The BDP's victory was abetted by a serious split in the opposition. In 1998, Botswana National Front (BNF) dissidents withdrew and formed the Botswana Congress Party (BCP). Separated, the two parties, along with the smaller Botswana Alliance Movement (BAM), contested the October 1999 parliamentary elections. Divided, the opposition was decimated. The BDP swept 33 of 40 elected seats, even winning four of eight urban seats traditionally occupied by the opposition.

In the October 2004 elections, little changed. The BDP, supported by its traditional rural base, took 44 of 57 directly elected seats in the National Assembly. Victory was again facilitated by opposition division: in most districts the BNF and the BCP put up rival candidates, allowing the Botswana Democratic Party to win several districts with a plurality of votes. The BNF won 12 seats and the BCP one. Despite its dominance in the legislature, the BDP won only 52% of the vote nationwide.

Botswana's president is chosen by the National Assembly following legislative elections, and the BDP majority reelected President Mogae to his second five-year term. The October elections also confirmed the political strength of Vice-President Seretse Khama Ian Khama. Most of the BDP deputies were Khama loyalists, and several of the new cabinet members had served in the Botswana Defense Force, which Khama once commanded. Mogae indicated he would step down in 2008 to make way for Khama to succeed him, thus giving Khama 18 months as head of state before the next legislative elections in October 2009.

As promised, Mogae turned the reins over to Khama as president. Despite his lineage as the eldest son of Botswana's founding father, Khama has failed to quell differences within the BDP. In April 2007 four main opposition parties—Botswana Alliance Movement (BAM), Botswana National Front (BNF), Botswana Congress Party (BCP) and Botswana People's Party (BPP)—were in talks to form a united front to challenge the BDP and prevent the presidency from becoming "a dynasty."

With political and economic chaos in neighboring Zimbabwe, Botswana has had to confront an influx of refugees. Border communities are particularly affected and resentments are high. Xenophobia is rising with complaints about immigrants taking jobs from citizens and rising petty crime rates attributed to the refugees. Thousands of illegal immigrants are deported annually. Shortly after an outbreak of foot and mouth disease in the Zimbabwe border area, the government decided to build a 13-foot electric fence along the entire 310-mile border to keep out diseased cattle. The solar-powered fence, capable of delivering a 220-volt shock (nasty but not fatal), will be patrolled 24 hours a day by security forces.

The Present: Contemporary Issues

Botswana has one of the highest HIV/AIDS infection rates in Africa. Nearly 40%

The Okavango Delta   Photo by Judi Iranyi

of sexually active adults are infected. These grim figures emerge even after an extensive government education campaign. Billboards, posters and bumper stickers in cities and villages throughout the country warn of the dangers of unprotected sex, with messages like "Don't let casual sex kill Botswana's future" and "Be wise, condomise." The government provides free distribution of condoms in all public institutions.

Festus Mogae went to extraordinary lengths to publicize the public health crisis, and early indications are that Khama will do the same. A refreshing contrast with his South African counterpart Thabo Mbeki, Mogae mentioned HIV/AIDS in

A young Botswanan woman
Photo by Joann Sandlin

nearly every speech, and in March 2001 he chillingly warned his countrymen that Botswana faced extinction if it failed to slow the spread of the deadly virus within the next five years. He has tried to break the culture of silence and shame surrounding AIDS by personally revealing the results of his own HIV test (negative) and encouraging his ministers to do the same. As of January 1, 2004 HIV tests became automatic at government hospitals and clinics unless patients specifically decline them.

Botswana now has one of the most significant anti-HIV/AIDS campaigns in the world. It is funded by Microsoft's Bill Gates, while the international drug company, Merck, has pledged $50 million and provides an unlimited supply of antiretroviral (ARV) medicines. In 2006 the government distributed ARVs to some 68,000 individuals. It hopes to increase the number to 150,000 by 2009.

Despite these efforts, the virus continues to spread, with an estimated five new infections per hour and 75 deaths a day. (If there were a similar AIDS death rate in the U.S., 15,000 Americans a day would die.) There are more than 65,000 AIDS orphans, and that figure is projected to double or triple by 2010. Life expectancy has dropped from over 65 to 35.5 (2004), while Botswanans spend their weekends at funerals.

Since independence Botswana's economy has shown impressive growth, averaging 10% per year from 1976 through 1991. More recently it has shown signs of slowing down, with GDP growth not more than 4.9% in 2004 and 3.8% in 2005.

Botswana's economy is diamonds. The country is the world's largest diamond

271

Botswana

producer, having 25% of the world diamond market in terms of value. Diamonds account for 70% of its export earnings, 30% of its gross domestic product and more than half of all government revenues. All of this is generated by Debswana, a company equally owned by the government and De Beers of South Africa. In the 2006 production year Debswana set a new record—18.6 million carats.

Faced with significant unemployment—as high as 40%—Botswana has pressured its mining partner, De Beers, to help it enter the lucrative diamond-processing industry. Globally, rough diamond production worth $12 billion hugely increases in value—to around $65 billion—by the time it is sold in jewelry shops. Botswana had particularly strong leverage when it came time for De Beers to renew its diamond mining licenses: its high quality stone account for about two-thirds of the De Beers output. As a consequence, De Beers agreed to transfer its diamond-mixing operations—mixing them into assortments to be purchased by those licensed to buy in bulk—from London to Gaboronne by 2009.

An additional possibility of improving diamond revenues is to add value by cutting and polishing the gems locally. Internationally, the trade is dominated by low-wage India, which controls 95% of the market. Because of wage differentials De Beers was reluctant to pursue local diamond transformation, but after the Leviev Group, owned by the Israeli billionaire Lev Leviev showed interest in establishing a polishing plant in Botswana, De Beers reversed track. In May 2006 it signed an agreement with Botswana to set up facilities to cut, polish and market the stones. By the end of 2006 there were four diamond cutting factories in Botswana; eleven others have been licensed and are due to open in the next two years.

Despite the economic dominance of diamonds, the bulk of Botswana's workforce is employed in agriculture, though the primary sector contributes only 2.6% of GDP. The national cattle herd is almost three million head and represents an important source of food, income and employment, either directly or indirectly, through related industries (processing and canning meat products, hide tanning, shoes and other leather products).

The state-run Botswana Meat Commission (BMC) coordinates and processes meat production and has a statutory monopoly on the export of beef. Botswana has a quota 18,900 tons of beef for entry into the European Union, but because of erratic supply, it has never been able to meet the quota. European sales account for 90% of total exports. BMC efforts to revitalize the industry have been hindered by drought and periodic outbreaks of foot and mouth disease. The latest, in May 2006, was caused by infected cattle from Zimbabwe, where government and farmers are too poor to vaccinate cattle. Thousands of head of cattle had to be destroyed to control the disease; the country's two abattoirs were closed, jobs and revenues lost.

The driving imperative of Botswana's government is diversification of the economy. Mining jobs account for only 3.6% of the country's workforce, and attempts to diversify into manufacturing have barely dented an unemployment rate estimated at 21%. Young, jobless voters have been the principal support of opposition parties, and the government has been unable to generate sufficient new jobs to absorb the 27,000 school leavers who enter the employment market each year.

The government welcomes diversification investment from any source, and China, which has already built hospitals, schools, and roads in the country, is a major potential investor. China has granted several African countries, including Botswana, "approved" status as a destination for its outbound tourists, and President Mogae has singled out tourism as a potential area for Chinese investment.

There is, however, growing resentment from the grass roots about the country's increasing Chinese presence. "They do not contribute anything to Botswana," said one critic. "They do not even rent our houses. They would rather plant shacks on the site. It is even difficult for them to attract and keep local talent because they underpay us and subject us to insults and racist slurs."

Botswana AIDS poster   Photo by Judi Iranyi

Botswana's era of annual budgetary surpluses is over. Economists estimate Botswana's GDP growth rate will drop by 1.5%; within 25 years the country's economy will be 31% smaller than it would have been without the pandemic.

Tensions with neighboring Namibia have diminished. Their border dispute over an island in the Okavango River was settled in Botswana's favor by the International Court of Justice in December 1999, and the two countries have agreed on a border demarcation. Unresolved are tensions created by Namibian desires to pump water from the Okavango River to its parched capital, Windhoek. The river goes nowhere, but in good years it floods the vast Okavango delta in northern Botswana, attracting millions of birds and animals which are the country's principal tourist attraction. Namibia's plans would threaten the delta, which accounts for 75% of Botswana's earnings from tourism, contributes 6% to its gross national product, and employs thousands.

The Future

While Botswana is an African leader in many categories, including its historical record of democracy and economic growth, it is difficult to prognosticate about the medium-term in Botswana because the country's future depends largely upon whether HIV/AIDS can be contained and reversed. Effective progress in combating the disease in Africa has the potential to benefit Botswana more than any other country, given its relatively robust institutions and the stability that underpins the country's potential. Conversely, if the crisis continues unabated, then Festus Mogae's prediction of social collapse is a real possibility.

Seemingly well-off, Botswana presents a paradox: despite rapid economic growth, its human development statistics have declined. Development has been uneven. Pockets of severe poverty persist in rural areas, the consequence of a contracting agricultural sector that was starved of investment and development while the mining sector was expanded. The perils of this approach were made clearest when Botswana announced in early 2009 that it would be forced to half its diamond production given plummeting international demand for the stones.

Politically, Botswana remains stable and retains a good record of civil liberties, human rights, and political opportunities. Seretse Khama Ian Khama's first years in the presidency as successor to Mogae have again illustrated the peaceful transitions that mark the country's record. However, only if HIV/AIDS can be halted will Botswana regain its mantle as sub-Saharan Africa's greatest success story.

The Kingdom of Lesotho (pronounced (Leh-*su*-tu)

Catholic Church, National University of Roma, Lesotho   Photo by Joe Joyner

Basic Facts

Area: 30,303 sq. km. = 11,700 sq. mi. (somewhat larger than Maryland)

Population: 2,000,000 (UN 2007 est.)

Capital City: Maseru

Climate: Temperate. Summers hot, winters cool to cold; humidity generally low and evenings cool year round. Rainy season in summer, winters dry. Southern hemisphere seasons are reversed.

Neighboring Countries: Lesotho is completely surrounded by the Republic of South Africa.

Official Languages: Sesotho, English

Other Principal Languages: Zulu, Xhosa

Ethnic Groups: Sotho 99.7%, Europeans Asians, and others, 0.3%

Principal Religions: Christian 80%; the rest indigenous beliefs

Chief Commercial Products: Manufactures 65% (clothing, footwear, road vehicles), wool and mohair 7%, food and live animals 7%

GNI Per Capita: $960 (World Bank 2006 est.)

Currency: 1 loti = 100 lisenti (at par with South African rand)

Former Colonial Status: British Protectorate (1868–1966)

Chief of State: King Letsie III

Head of Government: Pakalitha Mosisili, Prime Minister

Independence Date: October 4, 1966

National Flag: Three horizontal stripes of blue (top), white, and green. The colors represent rain, peace, and prosperity respectively; centered in the white stripe is a black cone-shaped hat worn by indigenous Basotho; the flag was unfurled in October 2006 to celebrate 40 years of independence.

Land and People

Lying deep within the lofty peaks of the Drakensburg Mountains, Lesotho is completely surrounded by South Africa. One-fourth of the land is relatively low—from 5,000 to 6,000 feet above sea level. The warm sun of Africa raises the temperatures in this agricultural region during the summer. The rest of the nation is made up of scenic highlands from 6,000 to 9,000 feet, with some peaks rising as high as 11,000 feet above sea level.

The snow-capped Drakensburg Mountains form a natural boundary between Lesotho and KwaZulu-Natal Province of the Republic of South Africa; they also provide water for the neighboring country. The mountain snows melt, and, augmented by gentle and usually uniform rainfall, the water flows into the small streams, that unite to form the Orange and Tugela rivers, which flow into an otherwise somewhat dry South Africa.

In times immemorial the Bushmen established a thinly populated society high in the mountains of Lesotho. The waves of Bantu migration from east and central

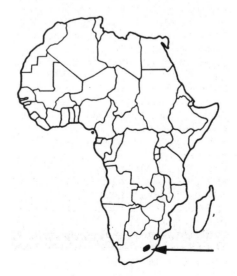

Africa of the 17th century reached the country and settled among the Bushmen. The two ethnic groups intermarried during succeeding generations, and their descendants are known as Basutos, or Basothos.

The Past: Political and Economic History

For early history, see *Historical Background, The Colonial Period: The British.*

An independence agreement was reached in 1966 whereby the colony, called Basutoland, would become independent under Chief Leabua Jonathan. The Union Jack was finally lowered at Maseru on October 4, 1966.

When friction developed between Leabua Jonathan and King Moshoeshoe (pronounced Mo-*shway*-shway), the hereditary monarch, Jonathan had the king placed under house arrest. Elections held in early 1970 pitted Chief Jonathan's Basotho National Party against the leftist Basotho Congress Party, led by Ntsu Mokhele. When Jonathan realized he was being defeated, he announced a state of emergency, arrested the opposition and took steps that led to the exile of the king. (After agreeing to stay out of politics, the king returned the following year.)

In late 1973, Jonathan announced plans to make Lesotho a one-party state. Mokhele and his followers attempted a coup in early 1974, which failed. Reprisals were taken not only against the leadership (some of whom escaped to South Africa and Botswana) and members of the BCP, but also villages suspected of harboring BCP followers were destroyed. A single-party state is rarely benevolent towards its opponents.

South Africa's apartheid regime raided Maseru and other parts of the country in 1982–1983 in pursuit of ANC activists. Chief Jonathan denounced the actions, denied granting sanctuary to members of the ANC and closed the borders. He further alienated South Africa by visiting communist China, North Korea, Yugoslavia, Romania and Bulgaria in mid-1983. This also infuriated the Catholic clergy, who had strongly supported the government (Jonathan was Roman Catholic).

Elections were not held after 1970, and there was no indication when they would be held until the BNP Congress in November 1984. In July 1985, Chief Jonathan announced that balloting would take place in September, but when no opposition candidates registered to run by the August 14 deadline, he declared there was no need for an election. The move was denounced as a farce. Increasingly leftist, Jonathan continued to develop the institutions of a single-party state. He formed a "Youth League of Chief Jonathan's Basotho Na-

273

Lesotho

tional Party" and imported North Korean "advisers." This set the conservative element within the military on edge.

Finally, on January 20, 1986 the Lesotho military acted, ousting Chief Jonathan. A Military Council was installed, headed by Major General Metsing Lekhanya; the border with South Africa was reopened. Pretoria (wink, wink) denied having anything to do with the coup.

The military government amnestied all imprisoned opposition leaders, including Ntsu Mokhele. The king, however, decreed that all political activity would cease for two years and set himself at opposition to the military. From 1987 increasing powers were wielded by the king—too many for the comfort of General Lekhanya, who sent him into exile in the spring of 1990.

To legitimize itself, the military installed the eldest son of the king, Crown Prince Mohato Sereng Seeisa (King Letsie III) as monarch in late 1990. Military control was tenuous, and under pressure, parliamentary elections were held in 1993. The result gave the BCP all 65 seats in the National Assembly, and Ntsu Mokhele, now a centrist, became prime minister. Moshoeshoe II was restored to the throne in January 1995, but died under mysterious circumstances in an auto accident in early 1996. He was succeeded by the crown prince.

In early 1997, factional efforts to oust Mokhele from BCP leadership failed. Mokhele responded in July by leaving the BCP, taking a majority of 40 members of parliament with him and creating the Lesotho Congress for Democracy (LCD). The new formation then declared itself the government and took over the BCP's black, green and red colors. King Letsie dissolved the squabbling parliament in February 1998 to prepare for May elections.

When the election results were announced, the LCD had won 79 out of 80 parliamentary seats. Ntsu Mokhele having been sidelined from active politics by age and health, Pakalitha Mosisili was chosen prime minister. The opposition, stung by the magnitude of its defeat, could only imagine it the consequence of fraud. Protests were mounted and became virtually round-the-clock affairs. When the king's palace was blockaded by protesters, electoral experts from Botswana, South Africa and Zimbabwe, guarantors of Lesotho's democracy since 1994, were called in to examine the election.

The probe was completed in two weeks, but its publication was delayed, which only added fuel to the protesters' indignation. When finally released, the commission's report evinced "serious concerns" about the general election, but its overall conclusion, expressed in tortured

His Majesty King Letsie III

prose and double negatives, was that "We cannot postulate that the result does not reflect the will of the Lesotho electorate."

Demonstrators closed down government offices in the capital, Maseru, locked the gates of parliament, and shut down the Lesotho Bank. In the midst of the demonstrations junior army officers mutinied, took their seniors prisoner and forced their resignation. Sensing a coup very much in the air, the government requested assistance from the Southern African Development Community (SADC).

South Africa and Botswana agreed to intervene to restore order. South Africa sent in an initial force of 600 soldiers on September 22, 1998, but was unprepared for stiff resistance from the Lesotho army. Botswana's forces, responsible for securing Maseru, were delayed, which had disastrous consequences for the city. Young Lesotho nationalists vented their rage at South Africa by looting, burning, and destroying businesses owned by South Africans. The flames spread and much of the capital was reduced to ruins. Some 60 people died in the events.

Negotiations produced an Interim Political Authority (IPA) that would steer the country to new elections. The IPA consisted of two members from each of Lesotho's 12 political parties, and was supposed to conclude its work in 18 months. It eventually took four years to produce a plan to which all parties agreed: 80 Assembly seats would remain single-member districts while an additional 40 would be distributed by proportional representation.

The results of the election, held in May 2002, proved the disputed 1998 elections had been no fluke. Once again the LCD won a sweeping victory, taking 77 of the 120 seats for an absolute majority in par-

liament. The Lesotho People's Congress (LPC) secured 21 seats, and other opposition parties took the rest. Observers were unanimous in declaring it free, fair, and transparent, undercutting the complaints of fraud issued by discontented losers.

Comfortable electoral majorities conduce to complacency, and aging leaders who do not retire when expected prompt factionalism. Few were surprised when Lesotho's charismatic ex-foreign minister, Tom Thabane, took 17 other LCD across the parliamentary aisle and joined the opposition to Prime Minister Mosisili in October 2006. Thabane's new party, the All Basotho Convention (ABC), was an open enticement for further LCD defections, something the government could not afford. His majority reduced to a dangerously thin two votes, Mosisili called upon the king to dissolve parliament. Elections were scheduled for February 2007.

Far better organized than its opponents, the LCD once again triumphed, taking 61 of the 80 contested constituencies. Its principal rival, ABC, came in second with 17 seats. Of the 40 seats distributed proportionally, the LCD's alliance partner, the National Independence Party, won 21; the ABC's ally, the Lesotho Worker Party, took ten. Prime Minister Mosisili began his new term with an enviably comfortable majority. Observers assessed the election as "credible, free and fair," but the opposition claimed collusion between the electoral commission and the LDC in the distribution of the proportional seats. The Southern African Development Community (SADC) has sent a delegation to Lesotho to assess the claims.

In 2009, the big news out of Lesotho was the government's report of an assassination attempt against the prime minister on April 22. Armed gunmen attacked the president's home in Maseru, and three were killed by the authorities. Mosisili survived unscathed, but the unsettling event generated condemnation from South Africa's interim president and the Southern African Development Community (SADC).

The Present: Contemporary Issues

The people of Lesotho have a very high rate of literacy—82.2%—in spite of the fact that they live, for the most part, in rural isolation: only 18% of the population is urbanized. Sheep and cattle raising occupy their daily lives among the scenic peaks and plateaus, but all is not idyllic. Deeply impoverished, Lesotho has few employment opportunities, and Basotho men regularly migrate to South Africa to find work. Mobility and prolonged residence away from families little conduce to chastity. The result has been an extremely high HIV/AIDS infection rate and consequent social and economic devastation.

United Nations Development Program statistics show that 31% of Lesotho's economically productive population (between the ages of 15 and 49) is infected. Women are the most vulnerable, and 52% of all pregnant women in urban areas have tested positive for HIV. According to government figures 75% of all new infections are found among girls. Life expectancy dropped to 35.6 years in 2004; it had been as high as 56 years for women in 2001, according to the Lesotho Bureau of Statistics.

More than 70 people a day die from AIDS-related illnesses. They leave behind a growing legacy of orphaned and vulnerable children. There are more than 73,000 AIDS orphans in the kingdom and indications that child prostitution is at an all time high in Maseru.

Prime Minister Mosisili started a campaign for universal voluntary HIV/AIDS testing, but cultural taboos on talking about sex have thwarted these efforts. The social stigma attached to HIV remains the greatest obstacle to dealing with the epidemic. In these conditions it's difficult to get the government's free antiretroviral drugs to the people who need them.

Lesotho celebrated 40 years of independence in October 2006 by unfurling a new national flag. It replaced one designed by the military government after the 1986 coup with its martial overtones: spears, club and shield on the same colors.

Lesotho is completely surrounded by South Africa and, possessing no significant natural resources, is economically dependent on its larger neighbor. The agricultural sector represents 17.4% of GDP (2004) and employs 24% of the labor force. Approximately 85% of rural households are dependent on agriculture for their livelihoods, but only 11% of the country is suitable for agriculture; the rest is hills. As a result, large numbers of Basotho men traditionally leave to work in the mines of South Africa. At one time 70% of rural household income came from remittances sent by migrant workers.

Crop yields and livestock numbers have fallen since the 1970s due to drought, hailstorms, tornados, excessive rains and other uncharitable acts of nature. Disease, theft, and mismanagement have also diminished agricultural production; AIDS has only exacerbated the problem by weakening and killing those most capable of bringing in the harvest.

Cattle are still employed to do the bulk of plowing, and stock theft has severely affected agricultural output. In its 2002–2003 budget the government allocated enough money to purchase a fleet of 50 tractors to increase agricultural output. As farmers are being resettled to make way for the Highlands Water Project, alternative crops like seed potatoes, giant garlic and paprika are being introduced to give them added income.

With the shrinking of mining jobs, many Basotho men were forced to return to Lesotho and face extended unemployment. From 1995 to 2001, the number of migrant mine workers employed in South Africa declined from 104,000 to an estimated 59,000. This steady decline in jobs has pushed Lesotho's unemployment rate to a staggering 40% to 45%. Remittances by emigrant workers, so critical to the Lesotho economy, have also plummeted. They once contributed about 67% of the country's GDP (1990), but declined to about 33% in 1996 and are much less today.

The kingdom's principal revenues are now customs receipts from the Southern African Customs Union (SACU), and annual royalties from South Africa—payments made for water produced by the Lesotho Highlands Water Project (LHWP)—Lesotho's "white gold." Water-derived income—about $30 million a year—is now the largest single source of foreign exchange in the kingdom and provides 75% of the state's budget.

With an elaborate series of dams, tunnels and canals, the LHWP diverts the waters of the Orange River, in the mountains of Lesotho, to drier industrial areas of South Africa. Estimated to cost around $4 billion, the project was one of Africa's biggest civil engineering undertakings. The completion of the project's first phase was officially celebrated in March 2004; extensive corruption investigations into construction contracts are ongoing.

The LHWP, it should be noted, represents one of the ironies of development projects. The Mohale Dam will inundate Lesotho's most fertile land area, the only region which produced a food surplus. In supporting the project, the World Bank argued that earnings from water sales to South Africa would far exceed the value of Mohale Valley crops.

The second irony of the LHWP is that while it supplies South Africa with millions of cubic meters of water per year, Maseru and other lowland districts of Lesotho suffer serious water shortages. Feasibility studies for a Lesotho Lowlands Water Supply Scheme (LLWSS) to supply water to Maseru and the surrounding area have been conducted. The project is estimated to cost nearly $200 million and no offers to bid it have yet been tendered.

The water supplied by the LLWSS is needed to support Maseru's developing industrial base, particularly its clothing manufactures. As a consequence of the U.S. African Growth Opportunities Act (AGOA), East Asian textile firms rushed in to take advantage of cheap labor and reduced duties on African manufactured goods entering the U.S. The number of textile factories in Maseru rose significantly, and clothing manufacture became a key growth factor for Lesotho's economy. The factories could import fabric and export manufactured clothing items, and with AGOA, they could avoid a 17% duty on cotton goods and a 33% duty on synthetics. Textile manufacturers invested more than $100 million in Lesotho and created thousands of new jobs; the industry grew to be Lesotho's largest employer, with over 50,000 workers. By 2003 the industry represented 10.5% of Lesotho's GDP and was the country's biggest foreign exchange earner.

All this changed beginning in January 2005 when the end of worldwide textile quotas went into effect. Over the December holiday period six foreign-owned textile factories closed their doors, leaving 6,650 workers jobless. Even worse, the owners—from China, Taiwan, Mauritius and Malaysia—departed without informing or paying their employees.

The action was typical of the new textile factories whose labor practices had long been criticized by trade unions. Working conditions were described as "appalling," with poor wages and unduly long working hours. Many employees were required to work seven days a week with additional overtime to meet production targets, and failure to do so resulted in wage cuts.

The Future

Lesotho is one of the world's lowest-income democracies. Unlike South Africa, the country has little industrial base to speak of, and relies on a variety of national survival techniques, including migrants' remittances and the exportation of its primary natural resource: water; the latter of these two was affected by a massive drought in 2007, which only serves to underline the precariousness of economic situations for the citizens of Lesotho. Massive poverty and unemployment—estimated at 45%—persist. Growth is estimated to have been about 4.8% in 2007, which is too slow to put a significant dent in these unemployment figures, and this figure has almost certainly worsened in the last year.

In the political arena, the country remains a volatile democracy, with fragmented institutions; the presence of about twenty registered political parties in a small country is indicative of the level of political activity. Prospects for future stability are called into question by internal struggles among and between leading political parties, as evidenced by the protests over the allocation of parliamentary seats following polling in 2007. The country's democracy seems relatively secure (despite the assassination attempt on the prime minister in April 2009), but not very efficacious.

The Republic of Malawi

Malawi's future

Photo by Sean Patrick

Basic Facts

Area: 95,053 sq. km. = 36,700 sq. mi. (the size of Indiana)

Population: 14,300,000 (UN 2007 est.)

Capital City: Lilongwe

Climate: Hot in the low-lying extreme South; cool and temperate in the highlands with heavy rains (November–April); the amount of rainfall is related to the altitude.

Neighboring Countries: Mozambique (south, southwest, southeast); Zambia (northwest); Tanzania (northeast)

Official Languages: English and Chichewa

Other Principal Languages: Lomwe, Ngoni, NyakYusa-Ngonde, Nyanja, Sena, Tonga, Tumbuka, and Yao

Ethnic Groups: Chewa, Nyanja, Tumbuko, Yao, Lomwe, Sena, Tonga, Ngoni, Ngonde, Asian, and European

Principal Religions: Protestant 55%, Roman Catholic 20%, Muslim 20%, traditional indigenous beliefs

Chief Commercial Products: tobacco, tea, cotton, coffee, and sugar

GNI Per Capita: $250 (World Bank 2007 est.)

Currency: 1 kwacha = 100 tambala

Former Colonial Status: British Colony (1883–1964)

Independence Date: July 6, 1964

Chief of State: Dr. Bingu wa Mutharika, President (since May 2004, re-elected in 2009)

National Flag: Three equal horizontal bands of black (top), red, and green with a radiant, rising, red sun centered in the black band.

Land and People

Malawi, formerly known as Nyasaland, is a country of high mountains covered with lush, green foliage, interspersed with large, sparkling lakes and fertile plateaus. Situated on the western edge of the Rift Valley, Lake Nyasa (also known as Lake Malawi) spreads its long, deep waters over three-fourths of the eastern boundary of Malawi. The surface of this body of water is 1,500 feet above sea level; the water extends to a depth of 2,300 feet, thus the floor of Lake Nyasa is over 700 feet below sea level. The lake pours into the River Shire, which flows southward to join the Zambesi River 250 miles away.

The countryside of Malawi has characteristic plateaus in the middle and on the top of steep mountains. For the most part, these are 3,000 to 4,000 feet above sea level, but rise as high as 8,000 feet in the north. Immediately south of Lake Nyasa are the Shire Highlands, gently rolling plateau country which is 3,000 feet high. From this green, almost level land, the mountain peaks of Zomba and Mlanje tower to heights of 7,000 and 10,000 feet, respectively.

The altitude modifies an otherwise equatorial climate. From November to April it is pleasantly warm with equatorial rains and sudden thunderstorms. Towards the end of March, the storms reach their peak, after which the rainfall rapidly diminishes. From May to September wet mists float down from the highlands, invading the cool and dry reaches of the

plateaus. There is almost no rainfall during these months.

For strikingly beautiful scenery, Malawi is almost unexcelled by any other nation on the African continent.

Malawi is one of the most densely populated countries in Africa, with an average population of 117 per square kilometer. The shape of the country has tended to emphasize regional concentration of its various ethnic groups. This concentration has provided the basis of political support for the country's three main political parties. The UDF draws its strength from the south; the MCP is centrally based, and AFORD is strongest in the north.

The Past: Political and Economic History

For early history, see *Historical Background* and *The Colonial Period: The British*.

The Nyasaland African Congress (NAC) was formed in 1944 to give expression to African political aspirations, long subordinated to the interests of European settlers. In 1953 Britain yielded to settler pressures to create a larger economic space, yoking Nyasaland with Northern and Southern Rhodesia in what was called the Central African Federation. The move prompted bitter opposition from Africans, and the NAC gained popular support by mobilizing nationalist sentiment to oppose the federation. One longtime opponent of British federation plans was Dr. Hastings Kamuzu Banda, an Edinburgh-trained medical practitioner. Even though working in Ghana, Banda was active in the nationalist cause, and was finally persuaded to return to Nyasaland to lead the NAC. He did so in 1958.

As president of the Nyasaland African Congress, he toured the colony and effectively mobilized nationalist sentiment. Universal suffrage was demanded and disturbances ensued. Colonial authorities declared a state of emergency in 1959 and jailed the troublesome Dr. Banda. As pressures built, Banda was released (1960), only to be invited, a few months later, to

276

participate in discussions leading to a new constitution for Nyasaland. Under the new arrangements, Africans were granted a majority in the colony's Legislative Council. Elections in 1961 gave Banda's Malawi Congress Party (MCP) 22 out of 28 seats, and Banda served as minister of natural resources and local government until becoming prime minister in 1963. In that year the federation was dissolved and a year later, on July 6, 1964, Nyasaland became independent as Malawi.

A new constitution made Malawi a single-party state under the MCP in 1966, and Banda established himself as President-for-Life in 1970. He ruled with autocratic firmness for 30 years, consistently (some would say ruthlessly) suppressing any opposition. During the 1980s, elections involved only MCP candidates, selected by Banda. Opposition figures died under very suspicious circumstances, and President Banda became increasingly authoritarian. Human rights violations, particularly those involving the MCP's Malawi Young Pioneers, which emerged as a paramilitary organization, became common and a cult of personality flourished around Banda.

Under external and internal pressures for political liberalization, the life president grudgingly agreed to a referendum, which was held in 1993. He was stunned when 67% voted for multiparty democracy. Illness overtook the president in late 1993, forcing him to go to Johannesburg for brain surgery. During his absence a presidential council was formed and the life presidency was abolished; the MCP's grip was ended; its youth group was officially disbanded, and a new constitution was adopted.

Malawi held multiparty elections in 1994 for the first time in three decades. The United Democratic Front (UDF), a new party whose political base lay in the densely populated south, emerged victorious. The UDF's candidate for president, Bakili Muluzi, received 47% of the vote to Banda's 34%. Muluzi's UDF also won an 83-seat plurality in the National Assembly, where it joined with independents and disaffected opposition members to create a working majority. The elections demonstrated a marked regional division within the country. The UDF dominated the south, while Banda's Malawi Congress Party took the center and the Alliance for Democracy (AFORD) the north.

In 1995 the new government tried Banda and his supporters for the 1983 murders of opposition leaders. Well into his 90s, Banda was totally deaf, senile, and too ill to attend the sessions. A seven-member court (controversially) acquitted all defendants in December. In early 1996 Banda addressed the nation on radio and apologized for any and all wrongs that might have occurred

Dr. Bingu wa Mutharika, President

during his 30-year tenure. He died in November 1996, remembered for his leadership of the nationalist struggle that gave Malawi independence; a surprising sentiment towards a leader who used an iron fist in the country for decades.

For the presidential elections of May 1999, the MCP and AFORD formed an electoral coalition to oust President Muluzi. The MCP leader, Gwanda Chakuamba, was designated the alliance's presidential candidate, and AFORD leader Chakufwa Chihana was chosen for the vice-presidential slot, much to the annoyance of the MCP deputy leader, John Tembo. Once President Banda's right-hand man, Tembo was perhaps the MCP's longest-serving politician and had long been ambitious for the presidency.

President Muluzi was reelected with 52.4% of the vote to Gwanda Chakuamba's 45.2%, and his United Democratic Front won 93 seats in the National Assembly—less than a majority in the 192-seat house. The MCP won 66 seats and its AFORD ally picked up 29 seats. The opposition vigorously protested election irregularities and took their case to the courts, but found no support there. Efforts to boycott parliament failed to find unanimity within the opposition, and rancorous division soon dominated Malawi's politics.

The Malawi Congress Party was split by a sulfurous clash between Chakuamba and John Tembo, still smarting from being pushed aside as a vice-presidential candidate in the 1999 elections. The party suddenly had two leaders and two factions, with Tembo's faction opportunistically siding with the UDF in many parliamentary votes.

The ruling UDF fared little better. President Muluzi's interest in seeking a third

term (which would require a constitutional amendment) angered some party leaders who split off to oppose it. Critics of the president were ruthlessly dealt with.

The third-term issue dominated political life for the next two years, dividing both the ruling party and opposition and rousing a storm of indignation in the country—led by the powerful religious lobby. Two attempts were made to amend the constitution to permit Muluzi to run for a third five-year term, but each failed. The president conceded defeat in March 2003, announcing he would not seek an additional term in office.

Punishment to those who had not supported third-term efforts was soon meted out. In early April Muluzi sacked his entire cabinet, getting rid of anyone who had not supported the constitutional amendment and anyone who might have shown an interest in running for the presidency. Leaving nothing to democratic uncertainty, Muluzi also designated his potential successor—a 68-year-old economist, Bingu wa Mutharika. Dr. Mutharika had been deputy governor of the Reserve Bank of Malawi before being appointed economics minister in Muluzi's new "national unity" cabinet. To provide sectarian balance for his UDF ticket, President Muluzi chose a fellow Muslim, Cassim Chilumpha, for the vice-presidential slot.

Muluzi's authoritarian style and thwarted ambitions polarized Malawi, divided the UDF, and prompted a host of party defections. Two former UDF leaders—Muluzi's vice president, Justin Malewezi and ex-Foreign Minister Brown Mpinganjira—both ran for the presidency in the May 2004 elections.

A deeply divided electorate produced a minority victory for Mutharika, the UDF/AFORD nominee, who won only 35% of the vote. His nearest rivals were John Tembo (MPC) with 27%, and Gwanda Chakuamba, who received 26% representing an opposition coalition of seven parties known as *Mgwirizano* (Unity). The election was not without its problems; observers stopped short of calling it both free and fair, and the opposition lodged a court challenge to the results. The new president also faced a parliament with an opposition majority.

Assumed to be little more than a Muluzi tool, President Mutharika soon proved to be his own man. Where the previous administration had handled the country's monumental corruption problem with kid gloves, Mutharika declared "zero tolerance." Comfortably feathered nests were rudely jolted. At least five senior UDF figures faced criminal charges, and in February 2006 a former education minister was given a five-year prison term for corruption.

The president's relations with the UDF deteriorated completely. In February 2005

Malawi

Mutharika resigned from the party, accusing Muluzi of frustrating his anticorruption campaign and of plotting to assassinate him. He then launched his own Democratic Progressive Party (DPP), which drew support from independents and disgruntled members of the UDF. Since then Malawi's political scene has been bitter, personal, and utterly dysfunctional. The parliamentary opposition has attempted to impeach the president and tried to force those who defected to the DPP from their seats in the legislature. Thus far, Malawi's voters seem to be saying "good riddance" to the old parties; the DPP won six by-elections held by May 2006.

For President Mutharika work with a vice president chosen by former President Muluzi rather than himself proved impossible. The president accused his deputy, Vice President Cassim Chilumpha, of insubordination, running a parallel government, and failing to perform his duties. After corruption charges against Chilumpha were dismissed by the courts, and an outright presidential firing of Chilumpha declared illegal, the vice president was arrested for treason in April 2006, charged with hiring South African assassins to murder President Mutharika. His trial began in 2007, but a sentence has yet to be issued.

In 2009, the president was re-elected for second term. Mutharika had undoubtedly gained some popularity for his anti-corruption campaigns, but the elections were also imperfect. European Union observers (as well as reputable African observers such as John Kufuor of Ghana) noted in particular the pro-incumbent bias in the state-owned media. Opposition leader John Tembo of the Malawi Congress Party claimed the elections were fraudulent after receiving less than one-third of the reported vote, and former president Muluzi objected to the election on the grounds that he should have been able to run again. The Constitutional Court rejected his claim only days before the election, on the grounds that he had previously served two terms.

The Present: Contemporary Issues

Malawi has one of the highest HIV/AIDS infection rates in the world. Government figures indicate an estimated one million Malawians are HIV-positive and at least 70,000 people die of AIDS every year. Around 250 people are newly infected each day, and HIV/AIDS patients occupy at least 70% of Malawi's hospital beds. The disease has cut Malawi's life expectancy to just 40.5 years.

The plight of the country's estimated one million AIDS orphans has been highlighted by the American pop singer Madonna. Her charity, Raising Malawi, plans an orphanage for up to 4,000 children. More controversially, she was granted temporary custody of a Malawian baby boy whom she sought to adopt. She eventually was given the permission, and as of this date, is trying her case in the Malawi supreme court, to obtain permission for another child.

Malawi is desperately poor. With little in the way of mineral resources, its economy is agriculture-dependent; the sector supports nine out of ten Malawians, most of whom work as smallholders rather than on large plantations. Few smallholder farmers have access to productive land, a situation particularly difficult in the southern region where agriculture is dominated by large estates growing cash crops like tea and tobacco. Government policy under President Mutharika seeks to better support small-scale farmers, but he got no support from a hostile parliament.

Landlocked, Malawi faces high transport bills—estimated as high as 40% of total import costs. The shortest and cheapest route to the sea for Malawi is the 48-mile rail link to Mozambique's port of Nacala. The track had fallen into disrepair during Mozambique's civil war (which ended in 1992) and Western donors helped rehabilitate it. Tobacco, which alone accounts for about 70% of export revenue, demonstrates many of the problems of economic development in Malawi. World prices have declined, and farmers barely earn enough to repay loans taken out for current crops.

Cannabis, known in the southern African region as "Malawi Gold," remains a big business despite police crackdowns. "It's so bad," said one police spokesman, "that we refuse to release figures indicating how much marijuana Malawi grows annually, in case the figures encourage even more people to grow the weed."

The economic impact of Malawi's HIV/AIDS epidemic is significant. An estimated 5.8% of Malawi's farm labor force has died of AIDS. The government spends nearly $123,500 (outside its operating budget) to finance the funeral expenses of civil servants who die. HIV/AIDS is predicted to lower Malawi's GDP at least 10% by 2010.

Concerned with Malawi's endemic corruption and fiscal management the IMF stopped aid disbursements to the country in December 2000. (About a third of the country's annual budget was expected to disappear into the pockets of leading politicians and their clients.) The impact was critical: up to 80% of Malawi's development budget was funded by donors, and once the IMF had made its decision, most donors followed suit.

Under President Mutharika, the government has put its financial house in better order. An IMF mission in late 2004 was "encouraged by recent signs that Malawi's economy is strengthening," and in August 2005 a new poverty reduction program was approved. It provides gradual reduction in domestic debt and debt servicing for the first time since the late 1990s.

Malnutrition is chronic and some 49% of all children are stunted. The country is currently experiencing one of the worst hunger emergencies in Africa, but political instability and impasse inhibit action.

The Future

Malawi is one of the poorest countries on earth: per capita income is extremely low and the country comes in at 166 out of 177 on the UN's *Human Development Index* for 2006. Sixty-five percent of the population lives below the poverty line—less than one dollar per day. Economic growth is sluggish at best—under 3% in recent years—and is limited further by an annual population growth averaging over 2%. Malawi's four major export crops—tobacco, tea, sugar and coffee—account for more than 90% of the country's export revenue.

With the re-election of the president, there is some opportunity for for improvements in the government's impact. However, the difficult relationship between opposition parties and the president mean trust is in short supply. Observers of Malawi can anticipate much of the opposition's energy will be spent fighting presidential initiatives, though opposition parties typically have minor impacts on African political outcomes.

While not the most repressive country on the continent, Malawi's democratic credentials remain suspect. Continued foreign aid may support the government budget to a large degree, and the economy to an extent, but Malawi does not look like a candidate to become one of Africa's economic or political leaders in the early 21st century.

In Malawi the coffin maker is open 24 hours a day   Photo by Ruth Evans

The Republic of Mozambique (pronounced Moe-zam-*beek*)

Electoral Remains ©IRIN

Basic Facts

Area: 786,762 sq. km. = 303,769 sq. mi. (twice the size of California)

Population: 21,400,000 (UN 2007 est.)

Capital City: Maputo

Climate: Tropically hot and humid, modified somewhat in the mountain areas close to Lake Nyasa, the uplands bordering Zimbabwe and in coastline, cooled by ocean breezes.

Neighboring Countries: Tanzania (north); Malawi, Zambia (northwest); Zimbabwe (west); South Africa, Swaziland (southwest); Madagascar lies 300 to 600 miles off the coast.

Official Language: Portuguese

Other Principal Languages: Over 30, including Chopi, Chwabo, Lomwe, Makhuwa, Makonde, Marendje, Nyanja, Ronga, Sena, Shona, Tsonga, and Tswa

Ethnic Groups: Indigenous tribal groups 99.66% (Shangaan, Chokwe, Manyika, Sena, Makua, and others), Europeans 0.06% Euro-Africans 0.2%, Indians 0.08%

Principal Religions: Indigenous beliefs 50%, Christian 30%, and Muslim 20%

Chief Commercial Products: Aluminum, prawns and other fish, cotton, cashew nuts, timber, sugar and copra

GNI Per Capita: $310 (World Bank 2006 est.)

Currency: 1 metical (Mt) = 100 centavos

Former Colonial Status: Portugal claimed that Mozambique was an integral part of Portugal until September 7, 1974; a provisional government was decreed to wield power until formal independence.

Independence Date: June 25, 1975

Chief of State: Armando Emilio Guebuza, President

National Flag: Three equal horizontal bands of green (top), black, and yellow with a red isosceles triangle based on the pole side; the black band is edged in white; centered in the triangle is a yellow five-pointed star bearing a crossed rifle and hoe in black superimposed on an open white book.

Land and People

The flat terrain of the coastline of Mozambique, filled with dense, tropical jungle in areas which are not cleared, gives way gradually to a series of plateaus and highlands, which gently rise toward high mountains in the part closest to the western borders. Towering green peaks are located in the Lake Nyasa area, and the temperature is moderated by the altitude. Most of the intense agricultural production takes place in the coastal lowlands and surrounding plateaus.

The Past: Political and Economic History

For early history, see *Historical Background* and *The Colonial Period: The Portuguese.*

Nationalist resistance to Portugal's colonialism was organized in 1962 by left-wing Mozambique exiles living in neighboring Tanzania. Under the leadership of Eduardo Mondlane they formed the Mozambique Liberation Front (*Frente de Libertação de Moçambique*: Frelimo) and began a guerrilla war against the Portuguese in 1964. Mondlane was assassinated in 1969, but the war effort was continued and expanded by his successor, Samora Machel.

Portugal poured some 70,000 troops into the colony to suppress the insurrection, but by the early 1970s it could do little more than defend the cities. Frelimo controlled most of the countryside and drained Portuguese manpower, resources,

Mozambique

and will. Disgruntled army officers overthrew the Portuguese government in April 1974, and the new government granted Mozambique its independence a year later. Frelimo created a single-party state organized on Marxist-Leninist principles with Machel as president.

The Portuguese colonial legacy was appallingly meager. After more than 400 years of Portuguese presence, more than 90% of Mozambique's population was illiterate. For the entire country there were only 80 doctors and 100 high school teachers. The new government imposed socialist organization and planning, including large-scale nationalization, leading to a massive exodus of Portuguese colonists.

Over 100,000 left, taking with them the bulk of the country's administrative and managerial skills. What they could not take, they destroyed. Some drove tractors into the sea; others ripped plumbing out of buildings. Factories were destroyed; government files and business records were burned.

Some 4,000 commercial farms were abandoned, resulting in disastrous declines in export-crop production. Following Stalinist precedent, the Frelimo government collectivized agriculture. State farms were created; agricultural cooperatives and communal villages were organized. Major portions of export earnings were devoted to the purchase of farm equipment, but there weren't enough skilled mechanics to maintain them, nor enough income to buy spare parts. Costly farm machinery lay idle as Soviet theories of mechanized agriculture proved inadequate to African reality.

Created, for the most part, by Lusophone urban elites, the Frelimo government, like its colonial predecessor, based itself on the cities, especially the capital—renamed Maputo. It increasingly grew out of touch with the countryside. The government appointed village "presidents" loyal to Frelimo and discarded traditional chiefs. Government-set prices for food crops were kept low to placate Frelimo's urban constituency, but they offered peasant farmers no incentive to produce. Not unexpectedly, farmers returned to subsistence production.

By 1983 even the most starry-eyed Marxists had to admit that socialism as practiced was a miserable failure. Eighty percent of state resources had gone to state farms, but they represented only 10% of the country's agricultural sector and had proved costly failures. Given a shortage of trained manpower, basic record keeping and production reports were virtually impossible. One major state farm operated 42,000 acres with one bookkeeper and a novice economist. State farms and enterprises sent false reports to the government because they had no facts to report. When the government made it a crime to submit false reports, it got none at all.

Overt opposition to Frelimo's policies coalesced with the aid of the white government of neighboring Rhodesia in 1976. Fearful of Mozambican aid to Robert Mugabe's rebel forces fighting to dislodge it, the Rhodesian government organized Mozambican dissidents into an opposition army that called itself the Mozambican National Resistance (*Resistência Nacional Moçambicana:* Renamo). When Mugabe's forces triumphed in Rhodesia, support of Renamo fell to the apartheid government of South Africa, equally terrified of black radicalism on its borders supporting its own black opposition, the African National Congress (ANC).

Rural, conservative, traditional, and speaking the indigenous languages of the illiterate populations of central and northern Mozambique—everything, in short, that Frelimo was not—Renamo was implacably opposed to the Leviathan state Frelimo sought to create. For some 16 years it engaged the Frelimo government in bloody civil war, the objects of its wrath anything and everything that symbolized the Frelimo state. Roads and rails, utility lines, schools, clinics and stores, farms and factories were all destroyed. The economy was brought to a standstill. Well over 100,000 were killed; more than a million were displaced.

Faced with civil war and a collapsed economy, Frelimo's Fourth Party Congress, held in 1983, began to shift the state away from inept centralized planning and forced social organization. President Machel, who once thundered to his audience that "Our country will be the grave of capitalism and exploitation," began to solicit western investors.

By 1984, the government sought to cut off its Renamo opponent by severing its ties with South Africa. A mutual agreement was reached at the border town of Nkomati: Mozambique would end sanctuary and support for ANC forces and, in exchange, South Africa would end its military support for Renamo. Despite the Nkomati Accord, the South African army continued to aid and supply Renamo forces, and they, in turn, continued their depredations in Mozambique.

In October 1986 President Machel was killed when his plane, Russian built and piloted, crashed under mysterious circumstances shortly before landing in Maputo; suspicions of South African involvement have yet to be allayed. Frelimo's central committee met and elected Mozambique's foreign minister, Joachim Chissano, party chairman. As such, he automatically became president.

President Chissano, regarded as a moderate and the man who had convinced Samora Machel to make overtures to western capital, expanded Machel's tentative opening to the West. The end of the Cold War forced change on Mozambique's Marxists. With Chissano as party leader, Frelimo's Fifth Congress dramatically ended the party's official Marxist-Leninist orientation in 1989. Chissano learned the language of Western democracy and economic liberalism. Multiparty

At the Mozambique Zimbabwe border   Photo by David Johns

Mozambique

elections became possible, and dutiful acquiescence to IMF economic reform policies was offered.

In October 1992, President Chissano and Afonso Dhlakama, Renamo's chief, signed a peace accord. Deep mutual suspicion, 16 years of devastating civil war and diametrically opposed ideological visions separated the two. Frelimo has never accepted Renamo as a legitimate representative of those rejected and marginalized by its policies. To this day it still refers to Renamo as "bandits," but Mozambique has now seen two multiparty presidential and parliamentary elections.

The first electoral competition between the two antagonists came in 1994. Opposition to President Chissano came from Renamo and Dhlakama and ten other presidential candidates. The elections graphically showed the regional cleavage of Mozambique. Frelimo was popular in southern, more populated areas and swept the capital of Maputo. Chissano won slightly more than half the votes cast for president. Dhlakama ran strongly in the north—a thousand miles from Maputo—and central areas, winning 34% of presidential votes. Renamo ran ahead of its leader in parliamentary races, winning 112 of 250 seats in the Assembly of the Republic to Frelimo's 129.

Municipal elections in June 1998 were meant to implement Frelimo's decentralization policies. Instead, they displayed Frelimo's fundamental resistance to surrendering control over local authorities. Frelimo proposed to devolve authority to only 33 larger cities already organized and dominated by executive councils appointed by, and totally integrated into, the structure of the Frelimo state.

Renamo, encouraging the power of traditional rural authorities, demanded official recognition of their role in local communities. This the government rejected, and Renamo declared an election boycott. So successful was the call nationally that 85% of registered voters absented themselves from the polls. In 19 of the 33 constituencies allowed to elect municipal assemblies, Frelimo was the only party competing. In the northern cities of Nampula and Beira, abstention rates were 92% and 90%.

Nationally, parliamentary majorities allowed the Frelimo government to liberalize a state-dominated economy and become the darling of donors and international lending agencies. Development money poured into Mozambique. Growth rates were eye-popping, but the process was not without its downside as criminal elements found expansion opportunities galore.

In the December 1999 presidential election figures, President Chissano won a

Mozambique Provinces

surprisingly close victory, collecting 52.3% of the vote to Afonso Dhlakama's 47.7%. In elections for the 250-seat Assembly of the Republic, all minor parties received less than 5% of the vote and were completely shut out. Frelimo took 133 seats, Renamo 117. There were serious questions about the results. Indeed, some diplomatic observers suspected Dhlakama actually won. Mozambique's Supreme Court ultimately rejected, by a split vote, the request by Renamo and a coalition of smaller parties to invalidate the results. Political tensions persisted.

The crisis peaked in November 2000 when national protests against rigged elections went tragically awry in the northern community of Montepuez. Demonstrators converged on the police station and began to liberate arms and prisoners. Seven policemen were beaten to death after they had fired on the crowd; at least 18 demonstrators were shot to death. Nationally, over 40 people were killed in the demonstrations, most of them by police bullets.

The next day security forces began a dragnet to arrest Renamo leaders and sympathizers throughout the northern region. Hundreds were arrested. Most were jailed in deplorable conditions of overcrowding. In Montepuez, 84 prisoners died in a single night from asphyxia. Record keeping was so bad the police had no idea of who had died. Their bodies were buried in a mass grave.

Almost before the bodies had been buried Mozambique received an additional shock: Carlos Cardoso, the country's most respected investigative journalist, was assassinated—gangland style. His exposés had revealed growing and pervasive corruption in the Frelimo state; his death highlighted the country's growing crime and criminality. Two years later, in November 2002, six individuals were tried for murder and complicity. The trial, broadcast live on radio and TV, was conducted in a high security prison in Maputo for safety reasons.

Testimony publicly confirmed the ramification of corruption through every level of the Frelimo state. At the heart of the conspiracy were two members of the rich, powerful, and politically well-connected Abdul Satar family. Cardoso was investigating how they defrauded a state-owned bank of $14 million, and the trial elicited allegations of international drug dealing, money laundering, and customs fraud, all of which was abetted by corruption in various state administrative structures.

One of the defendants—Aníbal António dos Santos Júnior ("Anibalzinho"), the man responsible for organizing the assassination and hiring the gunmen—was tried in absentia, having "escaped" a high security prison in September 2002, shortly before the trial began. It was a release that could have only been authorized at the highest level, and Attorney General Joaquim Madeira called it "a body blow to our judicial system." The minister of the interior (in whose jurisdiction the prison system falls) was so complacent about the whole affair, he could only respond to a parliamentary question by a question of his own: "In what part of the world do prisoners not escape from jails?"

Trial testimony brought the Cardoso murder very close to President Chissano himself. Three of the defendants testified that Nyimpine Chissano, the president's eldest son (and business partner of the Abdul Satars) had paid for the assassination. The lead investigator confirmed that one of the defendants had "confessed in a number of conversations" that President Chissano's eldest son had ordered the assassination. When called before the court, Nyimpine denied everything, but the trial judge, courageously persisting in the face of threats on his life, opened a dossier for further investigation of "others" who might have been involved in the murder.

At the end of January 2003, all six were found guilty of Cardoso's murder and sentenced to jail for 23 to 28 years. Anibalzinho, captured in South Africa the day before the sentence was rendered, received the longest sentence. In addition to jail time, the defendants had to pay restitution to the Cardoso family—four billion

281

Mozambique

Armando Guebuza, President

Meticais, about $175,000. The Mozambican press named the judge "personality of the year."

The case continued as soap opera: Anibalzinho once again escaped, in May 2004, this time to Canada. Captured and retried, he was yet again found guilty on nine different charges in January 2006, and handed even stiffer punishment: 30 years in jail and payment of 14 billion meticais ($560,000) to his victim's children. Having granted extraordinary privileges to such a dangerous inmate—like having his meals brought in by relatives—Mozambican police claimed to have frustrated yet another escape attempt in March 2006. A young niece allegedly brought dinner and escape tools: a screwdriver secreted in a radio, small tubes of super glue hidden in a packet of soap, and a tin of shoe polish. (It would appear to take little to escape Mozambican confinement.) Less than 48 hours later, his privileges revoked, Anibalzinho fashioned a noose from his own trousers and tried to hang himself from the bars of his prison cell, but was deterred by seemingly now more vigilant guards.

Charges against Nyimpine Chissano for involvement in the Cardoso assassination remain in judicial limbo. In May 2006 Mozambique's state prosecutor charged the former president's son with "joint moral authorship" of the Cardoso murder. Appeals of all those convicted in the case were rejected by a three-judge panel of Mozambique's Supreme Court in February 2007. This may clear the way for Nyimpine Chissano to stand trial.

When President Chissano announced that he would not run for a third term, he set off a political scramble between the party traditionalists (socialist hardliners who think President Chissano had gone too far in economic liberalization) and modernists (who want to go even further). In June 2002, Frelimo's central committee overwhelmingly elected Armando Guebuza, head of Frelimo's parliamentary group, the party's secretary-general and thus its candidate in the next presidential election.

A militant of the earliest Frelimo days, Guebuza had the reputation of being a tough politician. At independence it was Guebuza who launched the "24/20" slogan that gave Portuguese settlers 24 hours to leave with only 20 pounds of baggage. He is also associated with the vaguely Stalinist forced removal program of 1983, where the urban unemployed were moved to sparsely populated northern rural areas.

With the fall of the Soviet Union Guebuza effected an ideological conversion, becoming a pro-Western, free-market liberal; in the process he became one of the country's richest men. He has extensive interests in a variety of sectors—banking, export-import, tourism, fishing, transport—and his business partners are frequently government colleagues or involved in state companies.

The revelations of the Cardoso trial badly damaged Frelimo's credibility and prestige. It also strengthened, in the words of one October 2006 governance-monitoring report, "the public's perception that organized criminal elements have connections with senior government officials." There is a very real concern that the state has been captured by criminal elements. As one Frelimo legislator put it: "clearly the state has been highly infiltrated by organized crime." In urging officials to act promptly against corruption, he articulated the central dilemma facing Mozambique: "If the state does not control the bandits, the bandits will control it." In January 2007 the interior minister admitted that criminals had infiltrated the police and promised to reform police recruitment.

Renamo has been incapable of capitalizing on crime and corruption in an electoral process controlled by the Frelimo state. December 2004 presidential and parliamentary elections pitted Afonso Dhlakama as Renamo's standard bearer against Frelimo's Armando Guebuza. Far better organized and financed, Frelimo won massively. Guebuza took 63.74% of the vote and Dhlakama 31.74%. Frelimo captured nine of eleven provinces, winning 160 seats in the Assembly of the Republic, Mozambique's unicameral legislature; Renamo took the remaining 90 seats. Smaller parties were completely shut out.

No one was willing to call the election both free and fair. Renamo justifiably lodged complaints: in at least 100 polling stations in central and northern Mozambique (Renamo's traditional stronghold) official figures put the turnout at between 92% and 101%, almost all of which went to Frelimo candidates. The announcement of official results was delayed for more than two weeks, giving more than ample time to manipulate electoral computers. The voters themselves could not have cared less: only 36% of those eligible actually took the time to vote, suggesting a general popular fatigue with the Frelimo state, the venality of its politicians, and its willingness to tolerate impunity for both the criminal and the corrupt.

Provincial elections are likely to occur before the end of the year, but it is unlikely Renamo will have any greater success against Frelimo than it has had in the past. The governing party neither understands nor appreciates any notion of regime change. As recently as April 2007, one former interior minister told a training class at the national police academy that Frelimo should be "in practice a sin-

View of the Cabora Bassa Dam   AP/Wide World Photo

gle party, though in a multiparty system." Other parties could continue to exist and stand in elections, he was reported saying, but "it was Frelimo that should govern the country on its own and at all levels."

The Present: Contemporary Issues

Since the end of the civil war, Mozambique has become an important transit area for illicit drugs. Cocaine, for example, is shipped from Columbia to Brazil and then into Mozambique for redistribution to other parts of the world. Heroine is transported from Pakistan to Dubai, then to Tanzania, from whence it is shipped into Mozambique for international distribution. In 2001 it was estimated that more than one ton of cocaine and heroin passed through the country each month. According to one observer of the Mozambique scene, the value of the illegal drug trade passing through the country represented more than all legal foreign trade combined.

Corruption from high to low facilitates the traffic. Customs officials are bribed to enable entry and removal of the drugs; immigration officers provide identity and residence papers to the traffickers; police are bribed to turn a blind eye to the trade, and judicial officers are put on the payroll in case the traffickers are ever (rarely) brought to trial.

Attorney General Joaquim Madeira was the first AG to speak openly about corruption and propose ways of dealing with it. His annual reports to parliament have detailed the processes by which the entire judicial system, including attorneys and judges has failed. The police too have been subject to his withering criticism. "It is not possible to combat crime with policemen who are allies of the underworld or who derive benefits from it," he told parliament in his 2001 report.

As the Cardoso case illustrated, criminal elements have so corrupted the police and judicial systems they can order the assassination of investigators and prosecutors with impunity. In his April 2007 report Attorney-General Madeira told how corruption investigators continued to be intimidated: their cars were photographed, their arrival and departure times checked.

Madeira also reported that many suspects were refusing to cooperate with Mozambique's Central Office for the Fight against Corruption (GCCC). "They think it is shameful and humiliating to appear before the GCCC," he remarked, "but they don't think the acts they committed, and the reason they are called to the Office, were shameful." Clearly indicting Mozambique's political elite, Madeira told parliamentarians they lived in "a country where the criminals wear suits and ties and dresses, where they eat with us, laugh with us and work with us." Nearly 200 civil servants were dismissed in 2006 for corruption, but the greatest worry is that the magnitude of corrupt practices may have escaped the ability of parliament to control and monitor the state.

It did not help President Guebuza's pledge to take a tough stand against corruption when the head of Mozambique's anticorruption unit, Isabel Rupia, was dismissed from office without explanation in September 2005. A victim of an attempted assassination herself, Rupia was the country's most vigorous graft fighter.

The international community has been determined to make Mozambique a showpiece of capitalist development. A darling of the donor community, 60% of Mozambique's budget is made up of foreign aid. What has the government done to warrant this support? Basically, it has created one of the most open economic regimes in Africa, aggressively pursued foreign investment, and actively dismantled the state-centered economy of its Marxist past. The consequence has been eye-popping economic growth figures (10% in 2006), suggesting Mozambique has one of the most dynamic economies in southern Africa.

All is not steadily progressive, however. Mozambique's economy is fundamentally agricultural, with farming employing 80% of the working population. Given the absence of transport and transportation links, most farmers produce only enough for their own subsistence needs. They toil with the most rudimentary of techniques: only 7% of farmers use traction (animal or mechanical) and only 2% use fertilizers or pesticides. The typical farmer is usually a woman (with a baby on her back) who turns the soil with nothing more than a hoe.

More than 54% of Mozambique's nearly 19 million people continue to live in absolute poverty, the vast majority in rural areas distant from the economic success story of Maputo, the capital. Industrial development has been privileged—to the detriment of agricultural development. From 34% of GDP in 1991, the agricultural sector has fallen to 25.2%; concomitantly, industry now represents 35.1% of GDP (2004).

Until the advent of its aluminum plant, Mozambique's biggest export earner had been prawns. Despite this eclipse, the fisheries industry remains important. In 2006, Mozambique exported 15,875 tons of fisheries produce, slightly down from 15,910 tons in 2005. The greatest portion of this—9,300 tons in 2006—consisted of prawns, largely exported to Europe. The sector generated around $128 million in 2005.

Cotton and cashews were once Mozambique's two largest cash crops and the nation's largest foreign currency earners. Production of both crops fell dramatically during the civil war, and both are subject to the less than tender mercies of fluctuating demand and prices in the world market.

Cotton, mostly grown in northern Mozambique, involves about 200,000 peasant families. Collapsing market prices have severely weakened production enthusiasm on the part of farmers, and the EU has granted economic assistance to help them shift to alternative crops. Despite hostile local and international conditions, Mozambique farmers produced 122,282 tons of cotton in the 2005–2006 campaign—the highest figure in 35 years.

Mozambique was once the world's largest producer of cashews, but the stock of trees has been destroyed by war, ravaged by disease, and reduced in production as a consequence of aging. An estimated one million trees die or go out of production each year because of age, disease or neglect. On average only 300,000 have been planted annually to replace them. Normal production had been around 50,000 tons a year, mostly grown in the northern province of Nampula, but in 2002–2003 the government's rejuvenation project began to pay off. Production increased to more than 65,000 tons. In the 2004–2005 harvest season 105,337 tons were produced, with 60,000 tons exported raw to India for processing. Drought reduced production to 62,821 tons the following year.

The cashew industry suffered greatly from trade liberalization imposed by the World Bank and the International Monetary Fund (IMF), which forced all the large mechanized processing plants to close. The bulk of Mozambique's cashews are sold to India, and the government is seeking to convince Indian companies to take advantage of cheap labor and save transportation costs by opening their own processing plants in Mozambique. In recent years there has been a processing revival, based on smaller factories using intensive manual or semi-manual shelling methods. Currently some 18 factories, employing nearly 6,000 workers, are operating. They have the capacity to process 32,000 tons of nuts, but only handled some 22,000 tons in the 2005–2006 season.

Mozambique's once thriving sugar industry is also being revived. Thanks to rehabilitation efforts, 2005 was the best year for sugar production in three decades. A total of 265,000 tons of refined sugar were produced, along with 81,000 tons of molasses. Unfavorable climatic conditions reduced production in 2006 to 242,000 tons. Somewhat optimistically, Prime Minister Luisa Diogo has predicted production could reach half a million tons by 2009.

One huge megaproject suggests the country's economic vitality, and poten-

Mozambique

tial—an aluminum smelter located at Maputo. A joint venture between British, Japanese and South African investors, Mozal represents an investment of $1.34 billion. The first aluminum was poured in July 2000, and Mozambique's first aluminum exports were shipped in August. Mozal completed an extension project, doubling its annual capacity to 551,000 tons of aluminum ingots in April 2003. On the drawing boards is a third phase, which will add another 250,000 tons of production capacity; any expansion, however, is dependent on availability of electricity.

Some sense of the scale of the Mozal project lies in its consumption of electricity. It uses four times Mozambique's average national consumption—excluding Mozal—of 250 MW. Another 520 MW will be required to raise capacity in phase three, and the government is actively seeking investments for new hydroelectric power stations to ease its energy crisis. The most important of these projects is the proposed Mepanda Uncua dam. To be built on the Zambezi River, some 43 miles from the existing dam at Cabora Bassa, Mepanda Uncua could generate 1,300 MW. The project is estimated to cost $2.3 billion, and the government signed a Memorandum of Understanding with China's Eximbank for funding in April 2006.

The South African energy company Sasol has won the rights to commercialize Mozambique's natural gas riches. The Pande and Temane gas fields give Sasol proven reserves of 2.8 trillion cubic feet—enough gas for 30 years. The company will construct a pipeline to carry the gas to Maputo and South Africa. Ownership of the pipeline will be shared: 50% by Sasol, with the governments of South Africa and Mozambique each holding a 25% share. In the future, natural gas could easily vie with aluminum as Mozambique's most valuable export. It will also assist in alleviating Mozambique's desperate need for additional electricity to power continued industrialization: a gas-fired power station in Inhambane province could produce 750 megawatts.

In northern Mozambique, Dublin-based Kenmare Resources has begun production of titanium from heavy mineral sands. Rich in titanium dioxide, the sands do not require smelting to be upgraded, and the project will reputedly become one of the world's lowest cost titanium producers. As with all major industrial projects in Mozambique, electricity is in short or nonexistent supply. Kenmare installed a 105-mile line to bring electricity generated by Cabora Bassa dam.

Cabora Bassa, built in 1974 by Portugal on the Zambezi River, has an output of 3,700 MW, but has long been in ruinous financial circumstances. Initially owned by Portugal (85%) and Mozambique (15%), the dam was to have been transferred to Mozambique relatively shortly after independence, when the Portuguese government's investment in the mammoth project had been paid off. That had to be postponed after Renamo blew up much of the transmission system's infrastructure.

The operating company has also been burdened with unprofitable energy contracts and deadbeat customers. Its largest client is the South African energy giant, Eskom, which pays a ridiculously low price for its electricity and has shown itself obstinate in renegotiating the purchase agreement. The Zimbabwe Electricity Supply Authority (ZESA) owes the company more than ten million dollars for electricity supplied.

After years of delay, the transfer of Cabora Bassa to Mozambican control was finally effected in October 2006. Ownership of the operating company, *Hidroeléctrica de Cahora Bassa* (HCB), has been restructured. Mozambique is to hold 85% of HCB shares and Portugal the remaining 15%.

The Future

Progress has been slow for the average Mozambican in the search for economic progress. Current adult illiteracy rates of just over 50% still disguise regional and gender differences: about two-thirds of adults living in rural areas are illiterate, and probably over four out of five rural women are similarly disadvantaged. Low school enrollment remains a challenge to development plans. Development is highly unbalanced, with most centering in the southern regions, especially around Maputo.

That said, Mozambique offers investment opportunities for the intrepid and well-financed capitalist. The Mozal aluminum smelter and hydroelectric power from the Cabora Bassa dam have been the motors of the industrial sector for several years, but Mozambique also appears to be a country where mining companies are prospecting for deposits ranging from coal to titanium to gold. Even in 2008, Mozambique's growth rate may have topped 6%.

Economic disequilibrium in the country, with poverty in the north, will continue to fuel political differences, but FRELIMO and RENAMO in recent years have reached a pattern of peaceful (if wary) coexistence. The combination of relative stability, economic recovery, and investment opportunities means Mozambique may be poised to move in the right direction as a more favorable destination for international capital and a locus of greater opportunity for the country's residents.

The port of Maputo

The Republic of Namibia

Christus Kirche (Lutheran), Windhoek
Photo by Judi Iranyi

A small minority—some 50,000 whites—have enjoyed the wealth of Namibia, and the vast majority have been living, for the most part, in poverty, engaging in herding livestock to support themselves. Namibia has 4,045 commercial farms—70% of them owned by whites. According to the United Nations Development Programme, Namibia has the highest level of income inequality in the world. With a Gini index of 74.3 (a higher score indicates higher income inequality, with 100 as the maximum), Namibia demonstrates the dichotomy of a nation home to both diamond magnates and subsistence farmers.

The Past: Political and Economic History

For early history, see *Historical Background* and *The Colonial Period: British* and *The Germans*.

South Africa controlled the area under a mandate from the League of Nations after occupying it in 1915. After the creation of the United Nations, all previously mandated dependent territories came under its supervision. In most cases, the mandates transformed into trusteeships, which required annual reports concerning the territory's development and progress towards eventual independence.

South Africa applied for "permission" to make South-West Africa part of that nation in 1946. The UN rejected the proposal, but offered South Africa a trusteeship. South Africa rejected the offer and moved to incorporate the land within its national boundaries despite UN protests. By 1949, certain South African laws extended to South-West Africa, and its white representatives sat in the South African parliament. The UN condemned South Africa for its failure to live up to the terms of the UN Charter, but this meant nothing in the absence of force.

Basic Facts

Area: 823,620 sq. km. = 318,000 sq. mi. (twice the size of California)

Population: 2,108,665 (CIA World Fact Book 2009 est.)

Capital City: Windhoek

Climate: Hot and dry except in the Caprivi Strip, which has more rainfall.

Neighboring Countries: Angola (north); South Africa (south); Botswana (east); Zambia (northeast)

Official Language: English

Other Principal Languages: Afrikaans common language of most of the population and about 60% of the white population, German 32%; indigenous languages: Oshivambo, Herero, Damara, Nama and Kavanga

Ethnic Groups: Black 87.5%, white 6%, mixed 6.5% About 50% of the population belong to the Ovambo people and 9% to the Kavangos people; other ethnic groups are: Herero 7%, Damara 7%, Nama 5%, Caprivian 4%, Bushmen 3%, Baster 2%, Tswana 0.5%

Principal Religions: Christian 80% to 90% (Lutheran 50% at least, other Christian denominations 30%), native religions 10% to 20%

Chief Commercial Products: Diamonds, copper, gold, zinc, lead, uranium; cattle, processed fish, and karakul skins

GNI Per Capita: $3,805 (World Bank 2008 est.)

Currency: Namibian dollar

Former Colonial Status: The Republic of South Africa asserted control of the territory (as South-West Africa), claiming a mandate under the League of Nations continued since the formation of the United Nations. The UN passed a resolution in 1966 declaring South-West Africa to be under direct UN control and designated the area *Namibia* in 1968.

Independence Date: March 21, 1990

Chief of State: Hifikepunye Pohamba, President

National Flag: Diagonal stripes of blue, red and green separated by thin white stripes. On the blue stripe, near the pole, is a golden sunburst.

Land and People

Just inland from the Atlantic Ocean, the narrow white beach of Namibia quickly disappears to reveal a 60-mile-wide stretch of red-colored Namib Desert that runs the entire length of the coastline. The barren Kalahari Desert stretches along the north and eastern borders of the territory, occasionally interrupted by harsh formations of gray rock and thin scrub vegetation. The only rain in this region comes from torrential storms that occasionally gather—the desert quickly swallows the rapid downpour without leaving a trace of moisture.

The central area of Namibia is a vast plateau suited to raising sheep and cattle. Here, there is somewhat more rain, which permits a thin forage to cover the soil. This region produces thousands of karakul sheep, the lambs of which are treasured for their shiny black, curly pelts used in fur coats.

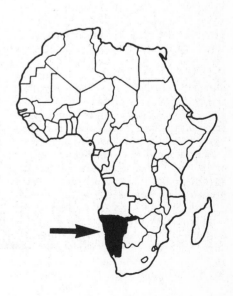

Namibia

During the 1960s, nationalist sentiment coalesced in the South-West African People's Organization, or SWAPO, which sought majority rule and independence for the territory. While its political leaders headquartered in Dar es Salaam, Tanzania, SWAPO's fighters roamed the territory, recruiting volunteers, terrorizing black and white farmers, sabotaging public utilities and ambushing army patrols. South Africa reacted quickly, rounding up and jailing hundreds of guerrillas, including the group's leader, Herman Toivo ja Toivo. The ruling white government sentenced Toivo to 20 years imprisonment on Robben Island, South Africa, after convicting him of "crimes against state security" in 1968. Backed by surrounding black-majority nations committed to the struggle against apartheid, SWAPO intensified its armed resistance.

By 1966, the UN decided to terminate the South African "mandate." It renamed the territory Namibia (derived from the name of the Namib Desert) and recognized SWAPO as the "representative" of the Namibian people. After considerable diplomatic pressure from the U.S., Canada, Britain, France and West Germany, South Africa agreed to peace discussions that would include SWAPO representatives.

The first talks in early 1978 ended in failure, and negotiations dragged on for quite a time. Angola's Marxist regime further complicated the situation by its support of SWAPO and providing of refuge for its guerilla fighters. South Africa, which was aiding UNITA rebels in their efforts to overthrow the Marxist regime in Luanda, invaded Angola in 1982–1984 to clean out SWAPO fighters. Clashes between South African forces and Cuban troops, present in the country since 1976, intensified the regional war.

In 1983, South Africa declared a "linkage" policy: South African troops in Angola would not withdraw until Cuban troops withdrew first. Angola and Cuba responded firmly: Cuban troops would only depart after South African withdrew its forces.

Inside Namibia, SWAPO increasingly resorted to terrorist tactics, and government forces engaged in widespread atrocities in retaliation. SWAPO sought to punish defectors, accusing over 2,000 Namibians, some of whom had merely sought more democracy within the movement, of spying for South Africa and flung into crude prisons located in Angola. Many "disappeared" with Stalinist efficiency.

By 1988, the external actors saw the Namibian situation as counterproductive to their own interests. The involved nations reached a grand diplomatic solution in December 1988. South Africa agreed to the independence of South-West Africa, while Cuba and South Africa jointly agreed to withdraw their troops from Angola. Namibia would hold free elections for a national assembly that would draft a constitution leading to independence in April 1990.

After a brief transition period, almost 98% of registered voters participated in elections for the constituent assembly. SWAPO took 57% of the vote, short of the two-thirds majority that would have given it free reign in writing a new constitution. The Democratic Turnhalle Alliance, a multiracial coalition of conservatives with white leadership, received 29% of the vote. In February 1990, the Constituent Assembly adopted a constitution, creating a multiparty system, limiting its executive president to two five-year terms, and enshrining a bill of rights. Distancing itself from its socialist background, SWAPO voted to include provisions that granted private ownership of property and affirmed a mixed economy where foreign investment would be encouraged. The collapse of the Soviet Union had diminished the allure of socialist utopias.

The Constituent Assembly converted itself into the National Assembly on February 16, 1990, and unanimously elected Sam Nujoma as Namibia's first president. The nation's first presidential election took place in December 1994, and Nujoma swept to triumphant victory, thrashing his DTA opponent, Mishake Muyongo, with nearly 70% of votes cast. SWAPO gained an overwhelming majority in parliament.

Nujoma's political dominance posed problems for SWAPO as it contemplated presidential elections in 1999. Despite the constitutional prohibition on more than two terms, Nujoma announced in April 1997, "I am still young and if the people of Namibia want me to continue making a contribution I will continue to do so." Dutiful and deferential to its leader, the 1997 SWAPO party congress recommended the amendment of the constitution to allow the president a third term.

SWAPO parliamentarians dutifully amended the constitution, but the move provoked a split in the party. Ben Ulenga, a former guerrilla, trade unionist and Namibian high commissioner (ambassador) in London, resigned from SWAPO and formed an opposition party—Congress of Democrats. He ran for president in the 1999 elections.

Ulenga had impressive credentials as a candidate. His liberation struggle experience was impeccable—wounded in combat and 15 years detention on Robben Island. His disillusionment with SWAPO began even before independence, when thousands of fighters disappeared without explanation in SWAPO detention camps. Nujoma's decision to seek a third term confirmed that disillusionment. Ulenga shocked the party with a scathing attack on Nujoma's autocratic rule, corruption, and the very idea of a third mandate for the president.

The Congress of Democrats was the first credible alternative to SWAPO to emerge, particularly in its traditional northern strongholds. Ulenga himself was also an Ovambo from the north, a center of SWAPO strength. The election was hard fought and not without the usual bullying

Weaver, Karakulia Center, Swakopmund

Photo by Connie Abell

The Namib Desert   Photo by Judi Iranyi

tactics by SWAPO and its supporters. Ulenga accused his old party of corruption, arrogant leadership, and mismanagement of an economy struggling with a 35% jobless rate.

When Mishake Muyongo, the longtime leader of the opposition DTA. Called for the secession of Caprivi, he damaged his party's reputation, providing little hope that the party could provide an effective challenge to SWAPO. The December election proved a smashing success for SWAPO; Nujoma obtained 76.8% of the vote, while Ulenga garnered only 10.5%. The DTA's Katuurike Kaura won 9.6%, and a fourth candidate trailed the field with a mere 3%.

In the National Assembly elections, SWAPO increased its electoral support, winning 76% of the vote. Because the seats in the 72-member house are proportional to election results, SWAPO won 55 seats, the Congress of Democrats and the DTA each collected seven seats, and the United Democratic Front (UDF) got two, while the small Monitor Action Group settled for one.

President Nujoma's authoritarian style did not change, affirmed by his single-handed commitment of Namibian armed forces in support of Laurent Kabila in the Congo. The actual number of troops committed, the number who died, or even the overall costs of the adventure remain shrouded in mystery. After his reelection, Nujoma also allowed Angolan troops to enter Namibian territory—without any reference to parliament—to search out and destroy bases and personnel of Jonas Savimbi's UNITA.

In late 1998, Nujoma faced secessionist agitation in the remote Caprivi. The Caprivi Strip, Namibia's panhandle, had long been a center of opposition. During the independence struggle South Africa stationed forces in Caprivi to fight SWAPO and received the collaboration of local peoples—a fact which hardly generated sympathy among SWAPO decision makers. As an opposition area, Caprivi regularly received less than its fair share in the distribution of development funds. SWAPO believes that friends are rewarded, enemies deprived.

In November 2001, at age 72, President Nujoma announced that he would not be a candidate for office in 2004, but he maintained absolute control over the selection of his successor. At SWAPO party meetings in August 2002, Nujoma made it abundantly clear that the party would consider no nominees other than his for top party jobs and successfully imposed his choices for party vice president, secretary-general, and deputy secretary-general on the membership.

Nor did he tolerate factionalism among those jockeying to become his successor. SWAPO appointed neither of the two principal figures earlier bruited as possible successors, Prime Minister Hage Geingob or Hidipo Hamutenya, then minister of trade and industry, to top party posts. Prime Minister Geingob's political career came to a humiliating end. SWAPO removed Geingob from the party's politburo and demoted him from the premiership to a secondary ministry, which he refused to accept. Geingob became the executive secretary of the Washington-based Global Coalition for Africa and resigned his parliamentary seat in February 2003.

In his waning years as Namibia's absolute ruler, President Nujoma resembled a lesser version of Zimbabwe's Robert Mu-

gabe. Poorly educated (he was a shepherd and office cleaner before beginning his guerilla career), Nujoma always admired the highly educated Mugabe and often followed his lead. Like Mugabe, Nujoma had his nation intervene in Congo and also raised awareness toward the land issue.

In Namibia, whites—mainly Afrikaners and descendents of German settlers—make up only 6% of the population, but they own half the land. The government opted for a voluntary system of land acquisition (willing buyer, willing seller), but has been frustrated with the pace of change. According to government figures, Namibia spends over 20 million Namibian dollars ($2.5 million) every year to buy farms for redistribution. By 2004, however, only some 124 farms had voluntarily changed hands, though redistribution to "landless peasants" may not fully describe the results. Government ministers, including Nujoma and his personally anointed nominee as SWAPO vice president, Hifikepunye Pohamba, have purchased some of these.

Choosing SWAPO's candidate for the state presidency was a bruising affair. President Nujoma vigorously supported his lands minister, Hifikepunye Pohamba, as the party's next presidential nominee. He had already secured Pohamba's election as SWAPO's vice president and simply destroyed others who might have sought the nomination. He peremptorily fired Hidipo Hamutenya, his foreign minister, undercutting Hamutenya's support before SWAPO's party congress in May 2004. Cowed before raw political power, most delegates dutifully voted for Pohamba. In the second round of balloting, he received 341 delegate votes—67%; Hamutenya received the support of a courageous 33%—167 ballots. (The party expelled the man who nominated Hamutenya, former Trade Minister Jesaya Nyamu, in December 2005, accused by President Nujoma of promoting division, violence, and factionalism.)

In the November 2004 elections, seven parties ran presidential candidates, but so overwhelming was the SWAPO juggernaut that even the most successful of Pohamba's opponents, Ben Ulenga representing the Congress of Democrats (CoD), could garner only a feeble 7.3%, less than he had received in 1999. Pohamba swept the polls with 76.4% of the vote, a testimony to SWAPO's control of the election machinery and its unwillingness to lose power. Outcry from protesters drew attention to possible corruption, and the High Court in Windhoek saw too many irregularities to approve the results. It ordered the Electoral Commission to recount the entire presidential election in ten days, but little changed. CoD, for example, earned precisely one additional vote.

Namibia

In parliamentary elections, SWAPO secured 75% of the vote, winning 55 out of 72 seats in the National Assembly. The CoD became the leading opposition party with a paltry five seats, with four going to the DTA and three to the United Democratic Front; five additional seats went to minor parties.

In his March 2005 inauguration address, President Pohamba pledged to address corruption "with a sledgehammer," and his first test on the issue came soon. By August, tales of government corruption unwound and swirled around the president. One of the biggest involved the disappearance of $5.2 billion siphoned off from the Social Security Commission (SSC)—whose income comes from monthly taxes levied on Namibian workers—and invested in Avid Investment Corporation; another $1.15 billion sunk into the Avid quicksand came from a SWAPO business arm, Kalahari Holdings. The principal facilitator of these transactions was an Avid director, Paulus Kapia, deputy minister for works, transport and communication, who used his position as secretary of the SWAPO Youth League to secure the investments in Avid—and lucrative kickbacks for himself. The whole affair made headlines when Avid filed for bankruptcy and could not repay the SSC.

By the end of August President Pohamba had forced Kapia to resign from the cabinet, but the SWAPO politburo failed to expel him from the party; instead, it merely suspended his membership and asked that he resign from parliament. A protégé and spokesman for former President Nujoma, Kapia seemed to enjoy protection at the highest party level, illustrating President Pohamba's greatest political problem: though his party enjoys unchallenged dominance in Namibia, the party presidency remains firmly in the grip of Sam Nujoma. It is a situation fraught with potentials for tension and conflict. Not controlling the party, Pohamba will find it difficult to initiate action against senior party officials who "are busy milking the system," as opposition leader Ben Ulenga remarked.

Paulus Kapia finally resigned from parliament in November. That he is the first government leader since independence in 1990 to be sacked for corruption suggests how deeply embedded corruption is, and how long it has been tolerated by SWAPO's leadership. When Namibia's Ombudsman, Bience Gawanas, resigned to accept a position with the African Union, she noted that her office received daily complaints of unethical behavior and corruption, and lamented that the government lost millions of dollars to corruption that could have been used for national development.

In 2007, SWAPO convened a party congress to select its officers, and reconfirmed President Pohamba as the party's candidate for the 2009 general election. The election is scheduled for November, and all indications are that Pohamba and SWAPO will continue to dominate the political scene. According to government statistics, about 75 million acres are owned by whites and only 5.4 million by black farmers. Absentee landlords own a further 7.1 million acres. (The state itself owns 5.6 million acres of land.) The consequence of this is obvious: The World Bank indicates that income distribution in Namibia "is one of the most unequal in the world." Indeed, the UN's *Human Development Report* for 2006 ranked Namibia as the country with the most unequal distribution of wealth in the world. (The figures are somewhat misleading since they include none of the oil-producing sheikdoms.)

Hifikepunye Pohamba, President

HIV/AIDS has become a critical problem for Namibia. According to UNAIDS, Namibia is among the top five countries most afflicted by the virus—right up there with Botswana, Zimbabwe, Swaziland and Lesotho. The disease has spread with extraordinary speed—from an infection rate of 4% in 1992 to present estimates ranging as high as 31.7% (2005).

The government has targeted Namibia's gay and lesbian community for special condemnation and harassment. The minister of home affairs has urged police to "eliminate gays and lesbians from the face of Namibia," and ex-President Nujoma once called gays and lesbians "unnatural," "ungodly," "un-African," and "idiots who should be condemned."

The Present: Contemporary Issues

Namibia's modern market sector produces most of its wealth; the traditional subsistence agricultural sector supports most of its labor force. Principal exports

are diamonds, and the Namibian economy depends greatly on Namdeb, its largest mining company. Namdeb, jointly owned by the Namibian government and De Beers of South Africa, accounts for 10% of the country's GDP and 30% of its exports; it is the biggest tax payer and, apart from the government, the country's biggest employer.

With at least a 40% unemployment rate, the government has cast about for any means of job creation in the diamond industry, where technology has increasingly replaced human labor. One possibility of adding value to diamonds is cutting and polishing. DeBeers opened a polishing factory in 1999 and young Namibians proved themselves the rivals of counterparts in traditional diamond-polishing centers like Tel Aviv, Antwerp and Johannesburg. While quality was high, cost-effectiveness was not, largely because of high labor costs reflecting strong Namibian labor unions. Polishing a diamond in Asia cost between $10 and $15; in Namibia, the cost was almost double. Given the economic disadvantages, DeBeers' interest in Namibia waned.

Labor unions did not stop the Leviev group, owned by the Israeli billionaire Lev Leviev, from opening Africa's largest diamond-cutting factory in Namibia. Opened in 2004, the factory employs more than 200 young Namibians; 430 more are being trained in different cutting and polishing methods by some 67 overseas trainers. About a thousand diamonds a day are polished at the factory.

Chinese demand for minerals has driven prices so high that interest in Namibian uranium has been revitalized. The Rössing uranium mine, the country's largest, produced 3,711 tons in 2005—the highest production level since independence—and has moved from survival mode to expansion. The uranium rush is on. Development of a second major mine, the Langer Heinrich, began in 2005 and the mine made its first product shipment in March 2007. Owners are hoping for annual production of 1,300 tons and an expected lifespan of 17 years. With Rössing and Langer Heinrich, Namibia will control about 15% of the world's uranium production.

Energy to run its nascent industries is a major concern for Namibia. About half the country's daily power consumption of 500 MW is imported from South Africa, and its supplier, Eskom, announced in 2004 that it would have to curtail future sales as the needs of South African industries increased. This has stimulated development of the Kudu gas field, located some 105 miles off the southern coast, with its proven reserves of 1.3 trillion cubic feet of natural gas. Long thought too expensive to be profitable, the project's finances have been reassessed in light of rising prices and increased demand and it has been given a go-ahead. The project is currently estimated to cost $1.16 billion; electricity production is expected to begin in 2009.

One of the Nujoma government's most grandiose proposals was for a hydroelectric project on the Cunene River, shared with Angola, at Epupa. Initial estimates set the cost at $540 million, but controversy surrounding the project was enormous: a dam would eliminate a major scenic wonder—the Epupa Falls, displace more than 1,000 local inhabitants, destroy 380 square kilometers of grazing land and inundate 160 Himba graves and 95 cultural sites. Angola, which shares the river border and whose cooperation is necessary, has alternative site plans for hydroelectric development on the river.

Feasibility studies are being conducted at the Baynes site, some 21 miles downstream from Epupa Falls. The site is more environmentally sensitive: situated in a narrow gorge, it has a smaller inundation area and consequently less evaporation. The studies could take until 2008 to be completed and if the project goes ahead, it would not be completed until 2017.

Budgetary profligacy within the party-state means there usually is not much capital available for major investments such as these. The principal cause is ever-increasing spending on the state bureaucracy and its creature comforts. The government is building a lavish new State House complex, described as a "high priority project," to accommodate the president and high state bureaucrats. Like Louis XIV escaping the din and danger of Paris for Versailles, President Nujoma planned a vast new presidential village on a mountainside south of Windhoek.

Inspired by a presidential visit to North Korea, the project includes a residence and office for the president, cabinet chambers, conference rooms, a banquet hall large enough to accommodate between 400 and 500 guests, and a guesthouse complex designed to accommodate six heads of state and their entourages. A security cordon around the complex would displace a number of area homeowners. North Korean-built, the project has received a nearly $10 million grant from China and is expected to cost around $83 million before completion. Namibia's National Society of Human Rights has criticized building such a lavish project while Namibians still face food shortages.

Namibia has a hugely bloated civil service—more than 77,000 workers in a country with a population of around two million people—which expands to accommodate the needs of the SWAPO faithful. Efforts to trim this fatty mass by funding early retirement schemes have yet to produce results.

The Future

Namibia is one of Africa's few democracies, according to Freedom House. Still, like his predecessor Nujoma, President Pohamba makes little distinction between state and party, appointing the SWAPO Secretary-General as a minister of state in his new cabinet, and sanctioning the use of state power to silence party critics. In early May 2007, the government moved to control call-in programs on national radio. Central to the decision were claims that some callers regularly displayed a lack of respect for former President Nujoma; the liberation movement that legitimized itself in the independence struggle continues to demand deference, even in the presence of relative political liberties. SWAPO is likely to continue its political domination in the elections scheduled for later in 2009.

Economically, the country is better off than many African countries in the region, but troubles remain. Corruption continues to swirl inside government. SWAPO membership has long been a means of personal advancement. For many, becoming a politician has been a way to get rich quickly. During the April 2006 budget discussions in parliament, the Deputy Minister of Labor and Social Welfare made the point explicitly, arguing vehemently for "jobs for comrades." The omnipresent specter of HIV/AIDS across southern Africa gives further worry; apart from the human tragedy, this has severe economic consequences going forward.

Herero women in their finery   Courtesy: CALTEX

The Republic of South Africa

Modern, sophisticated Johannesburg at night

Basic Facts

Area: 1,222,470 sq. km. = 472,000 sq. mi. (three times the size of California)

Population: 48,600,000 (UN 2007 est.)

Capital Cities: Pretoria/Tshwane (administrative); Cape Town (legislative); Bloemfontein (judicial).

Climate: Temperate and sunny. The eastern coastal belt is hot and humid; the western areas are dry and hot. Only high mountain peaks are covered with snow during winter.

Neighboring Countries: Namibia (northwest); Botswana, Zimbabwe (north); Mozambique, Swaziland (northeast); Lesotho is enclosed by South Africa.

Official Languages: 11 official languages, granted "parity of esteem" in the Constitution. They include Afrikaans, English, Ndebele, Pedi, Sotho, Swazi, Tsonga, Tswana, Venda, Xhosa, and Zulu.

Other Principal Languages: Fanagolo, a Zulu-based pidgin, widely used in towns and gold, diamond, coal, and copper mining areas. About 70% of the vocabulary comes from Zulu, 24% from English, 6% from Afrikaans. Also Tamil and Urdu, especially in KwaZulu-Natal.

Ethnic Groups: Estimated 76% black Africans—Nguni (Zulu, Xhosa, Swazi, Ndebele), Sotho-Tswana, Venda, Tsonga-Shangaan, Khoisan; 13% whites—Afrikaners, British, other Europeans; 8.5% colored, 2.5% Indian.

Principal Religions: Christian 68% (includes most whites and Coloreds, about 60% of blacks and about 40% of Indians), Muslim 2%, Hindu 1.5% (60% of Indians), traditional and animistic 28.5%.

Chief Commercial Products: Gold, other minerals and metals, food, chemicals.

GNI Per Capita: $6,170 (World Bank 2008 est.)

Currency: Rand

Former Colonial Status: Member of the British Commonwealth as the Union of South Africa (1910–1961). Previously, British authority in a colonial sense was sporadic in the Orange Free State and Transvaal.

Independence Date: May 31, 1910 (from UK).

Chief of State: Jacob Zuma (pronounced Zoo-ma), President (since May 2009)

National Flag: From the pole, a black triangle separated by a thin gold stripe from thick green stripes which join to extend horizontally across the flag; there is a white stripe on either side of it separating the green from a field of red at the top and one of blue at the bottom.

South Africa

Land and People

Washed on the west by the South Atlantic and on the east by the Indian Ocean, the Republic of South Africa occupies the southernmost part of the continent. This land of bright, sunny days and cool nights has a consistently uniform climate year around, with a mean annual temperature of slightly less than 60°F.

In the extreme southern Cape area, there is a period of rain between April and September, but December–May is warm and dry. The western coast is washed by the cool Benguela Current originating in Antarctica, which produces a climate that supports a large colony of penguins on the shoreline. Farther inland to the north, after the interruptions of the Cedarburg, Swartberg and Louga Mountains, the land stretches forth in a vast, semiarid region known as the Karroo Desert. This is not a true desert as encountered in the central Sahara, since the periodic light rainfall supports vegetation, which provides food for many species of wildlife. Occasional sharp projections of volcanic rock stand prominently in an otherwise flat land.

The eastern coast along the warm Indian Ocean is hot and humid, supporting almost every type of wild game known to southern Africa. In modern times, this climate has fostered the growth of high intensity agriculture similar to that found in southern California. Brilliant white sand beaches line the coast, adjacent to multicolored coral formations. The northwestern central territory, is a high plains land (veldt), stretching to the north from the scenic peaks of the Drakensburg Mountains. Receiving ample rainfall for the most part, its temperate climate supports rich farmland; the land also contains huge gold and diamond deposits.

The northeastern plains are lower than the high veldt to the south. Tourists from around the world travel to Kruger National Park. Here, all game lives in protected areas, and visitors cannot get out of their autos, which proceed slowly along the road to enable their occupants to see and photograph the many species.

Two-thirds of South Africa is desert, semidesert, marginal cropland or urban. Altogether, only 12% is ideally suited for intensive cultivation.

The Past: Political and Economic History

Before the arrival of Dutch East India Company employees in 1652, South Africa was thinly populated by Bushmen and a very few pygmies. Bartholomew Diaz had reached the southern Cape in 1486, six years before Columbus touched the West Indies. The rough, inhospitable appearance of the Cape region attracted only free Dutch burghers, sent to grow grain and make wine to supply ships bound to and from Dutch East India possessions.

Trekkers' Monument, Pretoria

Settlement

French Huguenot refugee settlers, fleeing religious persecution under Louis XIV at the close of the 17th century, joined the Dutch burghers in the Cape. The two peoples gradually melded into a single society and gradually expanded in a northeast direction; cattle-raising was their principal undertaking. Because of the need for farm labor, settlers brought slaves from West Africa and later from Asia. They added to modest numbers of Hottentots working under conditions of virtual slavery. Most pioneers had multiple children. The children born of the union of settlers and slaves became the ancestors of today's Cape Colored population of South Africa.

After much competition between Dutch and English merchant capitalists, British interests ultimately came to dominate the Cape. In 1795, the Dutch asserted formal control, acting under the authority of the exiled Dutch Prince of Orange. All pretenses were abandoned in 1806 when Britain seized Cape Colony as a strategic base protecting its developing trade with India. The British abolished the slave trade, creating labor shortages and setting the interests of Dutch farmers at odds with British colonial authority. British authority heralded the arrival of substantial numbers of British colonists, increasing competition for land.

The new settler farms and towns faced chronic shortages of labor since Britain abolished the slave trade in 1807. Increasingly, farmers enslaved native Africans to supply needed labor. When slavery in the region ultimately ended in 1834, about 35,000 people received emancipation.

The Dutch, or Boer, farmers chafed under British authority, and to escape it, many went northeastward into what were Orange Free State and Natal. At the same time, numerous Bantu tribes from the north were occupying the area. Conflicts with the settlers were inevitable as white settlers became more numerous. Their numbers grew substantially during the period of the Great Trek, which pushed north and east of the Orange River in 1835–42.

Anglo-Boer Disputes

The Boers, Dutch-descended people, having migrated to escape British authority, preferred to live in isolated communities where their independence could thrive. Inevitably, they would come in conflict with the British. Over a period of years, the British tried various forms of government, the success of which directly related to their ability to leave the Boers alone; the British implemented trial self-government in Natal, Transvaal and the Orange Free State. Discovery of immense sources of wealth in diamonds (1867) and gold (1886), however, brought in hordes

291

South Africa

In Kruger National Park

of fortune-seekers. The Boers actively disliked the new people, calling them outlanders, but the processes of transformation had begun. The Boers could no longer maintain their lifestyle of isolation.

Towns sprang up virtually overnight because of the new mineral wealth. Johannesburg, laid out in 1886, soon had a population of more than 100,000, about half of whom were black. The Boer republics (Orange Free State and Transvaal) grew increasingly linked to the world economy through their supply of precious minerals. Cecil Rhodes consolidated the diamond industry under a single producer—De Beers Consolidated Mines—in 1889, and became prime minister of Cape Colony in 1890.

President Paul Kruger, the Boer leader of Transvaal, correctly concluded that Rhodes was financing an anti-Boer movement among the outlanders. The first tangible act was the aborted raid (1895) led by Rhodes' lieutenant, Leander Starr Jameson, allegedly in support of an outlander uprising. In the fallout, Rhodes lost his position as prime minister, and relations between the British and the Boers soured even more.

A minor dispute over voting rights of immigrants was the pretext for the Boer War of 1899–1902, but the area had become too valuable—following the discovery of gold in the Transvaal Highveld—to escape the ambit of British imperial control. By the end of the conflict, British morale was at a low. They built concentration camps for Boer women and children, some 25,000 of whom died of disease and neglect. (14,000 Africans died in separate camps.) Some 500,000 British troops were required to defeat over about 87,000 Boers, who

knew the territory better and became effective guerrilla fighters. Although often thought of as a "white man's war," both sides employed Africans—at least 10,000 of them fought for the British. With both sides weary and weakened, Republican forces sued for peace. The signing of the Treaty of Vereeniging on May 31, 1902, recognized their military defeat: the Boers became British subjects. Left unresolved was the question of citizenship for Africans in post-conflict South Africa.

The Union of South Africa

Principally in response to the pleas of General Jan Christiaan Smuts (Boer commander-in-chief of the Republican forces in the Cape Colony during the final months of the war), the British established the Union of South Africa in 1910, thereby granting self-government in Transvaal and Orange Free State. The constitution bound together the two former Boer republics with the British Cape Colony and Natal. The government established an administrative capital at Pretoria (Transvaal), a legislative capital at Cape Town (Cape Colony) and a judicial seat at Bloemfontein (Orange Free State), an arrangement that still prevails.

At the same time, General Louis Botha and James Hertzog founded the South African Party. It was moderate, encompassing both English and Afrikaans speakers, stressing the equality of both, and pressing for independent status within the British Empire. Within a short time, however, Hertzog and the rural, conservative Boers split off to form the Nationalist Party (1914).

The Native Land Act (1913) limited the areas in which native Africans could own

or occupy. Along with the Land Act of 1936, over 87% of the land ended up under the control of South Africa's white minority. The Native Land Act also restricted the movement of Asians. Controversy over these restrictions led to the creation of the Native National Congress—the precursor of the African National Congress—and a civil rights campaign among the Indian population, then led by the young lawyer, Mohandas K. (Mahatma) Gandhi. The Native Land Act of 1913 was the beginning of legal separation of the races—Apartheid—which would be more fully enacted into law after World War II.

World Wars and the Interwar Period

South Africa joined in World War I, fighting the Germans in their African possessions (German South West Africa, German East Africa, now Namibia and Tanzania). Hertzog appeared at the Paris Peace Conference at the close of the conflict to demand independence for South Africa, but Britain ignored him. Because no other logical power was in the region, South Africa received a League of Nations mandate to control the former German colony of South West Africa in 1919. (This mandate continued without interruption until Namibia earned independence 1990.) The British ultimately recognized the Union of South Africa as an independent nation within the British Commonwealth in 1931.

Until 1934 the government was controlled by either or both the South African Party (Smuts) and the National Party (Hertzog). When the two merged, adopting the name United South African Nationalist Party, conservative members of Hertzog's National Party withdrew and maintained the old party name under the leadership of Daniel F. Malan. Since the turn of the century, anti-black sentiments had been slowly crystallizing. Malan's National Party ultimately exploited these feelings.

South Africa declared war on the Axis Powers of World War II, but its participation was minimal because of its distant location from the fighting. Further, a sizable Boer contingent in parliament had no use for liberal English speakers. During the opening years of World War II, this group expressed little regret at a possible defeat of England by Germany.

The end of the conflict was the end of the Hertzog-Smuts coalition, which had been in power since 1934. As 1948 elections approached, the National Party, then led by Daniel F. Malan, campaigned on an openly racist platform, advocating that white South Africans insure their moral and financial future by enacting into law Apartheid, the Dutch Boer word for "separate" (pronounced a-PAR-tate).

Apartheid

Prime Minister Malan and the National Party wasted no time in their efforts to deliver the promises made during the 1948 campaign. Four major acts created the basic structure of Apartheid. Within a year, citizenship and other important rights for black Africans ended.

Perhaps the most fundamental law calculated to transform the country was the Group Areas Act of 1950, which placed race classification at the center of South African policy. Combined with earlier land acts, the Group Areas Act strictly limited the areas in which a person could live based on race. Provisions of the act forced an estimated 3.5 million black people to leave their native lands.

The Group Areas Act essentially denied blacks any possibility of ownership based on their occupation of land. Thus, if a given tract was within a "white only" area, all that was necessary to oust a black person was proof that he was not white and therefore it was illegal for him to occupy the tract by living on it.

The Population Registration Act classified everyone living in South Africa by race at the time of his birth: black, white, Asiatic, Coloured, or other. This determination controlled almost every aspect of a person's future—where he lived, worked, went to school, wages, voting (if any), property ownership, etc., and became a foundation for the laws requiring that everyone have a passbook. In many cases, it was illegal for a person to be in a given area.

The Internal Security Act of 1982 granted virtual dictatorial powers to the government and abolished any semblance of civil rights that remained. It provided for the banning of organizations opposed to the state, made it illegal for individuals to belong to them, imposed involuntary censorship on the press, allowed detention without trial of persons suspected of terrorism, and imprisonment of anyone for ten days without any charges.

To enforce Apartheid laws, the police developed an intensive system of espionage—informants and control calculated to strike fear into the hearts of all. The use of informants was widespread, enabling police to arrest would-be criminals before they attempted any crime. Prison facilities intentionally further exacerbated the ends of justice under Apartheid. If the degree of proof of the guilt of an individual was dubious or flawed, he or she might well die in prison awaiting trial. "Slipped on the soap while taking a shower" . . . "fell downstairs" . . . "was assaulted" . . . "died while trying to escape" were all heard with frequency in South Africa if, indeed, anything was heard at all.

Before the days of compulsory censorship, newspapers followed the principles

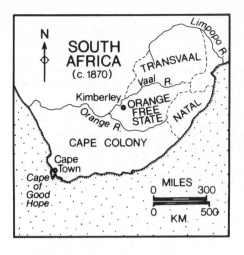

of "voluntary" censorship. At the most fundamental level, this simply meant that newspapers avoided publishing anything embarrassing to the state. If a newspaper violated this imperative too seriously or too often (elusive quantities), paper supplies, bank credit and often telephone service evaporated. Worst of all, no official at whom a finger could be pointed ever did anything illegal. Things just happened.

The Publication Bill unashamedly demanded censored reporting of black activities in the press. It demanded that the media exercise "due care and responsibility concerning matters which can have the effect of stirring up feelings of hostility between different racial, ethnic, religious or cultural groups" in South Africa. True to the form of Boer religious conservatism, it professed to "avoid the spirit of permissiveness and moral decay sweeping the world and communications media in the country."

The African National Congress

The African National Congress initially formed in response to the Land Act of 1913. Passage of the act resulted in the expulsion of some people without adequate compensation from lands they and their ancestors had occupied for generations. The organization had little mass appeal prior to 1948 because of limited political awareness and limited economic strength. The group's leadership was generally conservative, hoping to deal with the white-dominated government in seeking redress for land seizures. After 1948, with the advent of Apartheid, it became a militant force, openly sympathetic with communist thinking, and determined to oust the white minority from power and seize the economic wealth of the nation in the name of black power.

In the immediate postwar period, communist rhetoric and action terrified South Africa's government. It outlawed the South African Communist Party (SACP)

in 1950 and ANC, under the leadership of Nelson Mandela, responded with a campaign of civil disobedience. Repression intensified, and at Sharpeville in 1960, the government killed nearly 70 black demonstrators and wounded another 180, many of whom purportedly the police shot in the back as they were running away. The ANC was promptly banned; in response, its military wing, Umkhonto we Sizwe (Spear of the Nation: MK), launched a sabotage campaign in 1961. The government issued warrants for the fugitive leadership of both the SACP and ANC in 1962.

After a year and a half as fugitive, Nelson Mandela was tried in 1964 (the Rivonia trial) and found guilty. The sentence was life imprisonment without possibility of parole. The government sent Mandela to Robben Island Prison, noted for its harsh conditions. The leadership not arrested remained underground, taking refuge in neighboring and nearby nations such as Zambia (the location of its headquarters), Mozambique, Tanzania and Botswana. From these exile posts, they directed the affairs of the ANC.

During the 25 years after Mandela's trial, the ANC grew steadily as the rigid racial separation and denial became far more onerous. (During the 1970s, the Apartheid government forcibly resettled more than three million people in black "homelands.") Ironically, the ANC helped to found the Inkatha Freedom Party of the Zulus in 1974, feeling that the anti-Apartheid movement ought to have some lawful presence in South Africa.

The ANC successfully mobilized international public opinion against Apartheid.

General Jan Christiaan Smuts

South Africa

In the United States, it enlisted the aid of the Congressional Black Caucus. Many governments worldwide embargoed trade and aggressively pursued other economic sanctions against South Africa.

Urban Overcrowding and Resulting Unrest

During the 1960s and onward, there was a continual influx into black townships, which were located on the edge of every major and smaller city of South Africa; a reason for this was the starkly primitive conditions prevailing in rural areas and the influx of immigrants from surrounding African nations. South Africa tried to limit expansion of these urban slums by adopting an identity card (pass book) system intended to protect employed workers around the cities from competition by illegal immigrants. (The government did not repeal these "pass laws" until 1986.)

To take the population pressure off black townships, the government established African Bantustans (or "homelands") with the Promotion of Bantu Self-Government Act in 1959. The act originally created eight (later ten) separate black tribal and geographical units. (The Bantu Administration and Development Department, known by its acronym, BAD, ran Bantustan affairs from Pretoria.) The Bantustan lands were overcrowded and overgrazed. Industry and employment were next to nonexistent; healthcare and education lacked resources. The Bantustans did not reduce the government's burden to provide decent housing and services to its black "citizens" and neu-tralize black political power, as was the white government's initial intention for giving them power. Technically, all township residents were required to vote in the homeland from which they or their ancestors had come, or in which the government assigned them to vote.

Soweto

In 1953 the government had ordered that instruction in all high schools be 50% in Afrikaans and 50% in English, but not in the native language of the pupils—used during the first six years of a young person's schooling. This was to become a flashpoint between the Apartheid regime and black students in Soweto in 1976.

Soweto, outside of the large city of Johannesburg, was one of the early black townships. It had a great many four-room houses built by the government, and on the surface appeared reasonably presentable. In reality, only about 15% of them had inside running water and toilet facilities. The great majority of the homes had six to eight people crowded in very limited space with no heat.

As early as 1960, black citizens of Sharpeville demonstrated a capability and willingness to use firearms against the police, both black and white. The disturbance that is most widely remembered occurred in Soweto in mid-1976, and arose out of the 1953 language agreement.

That agreement had established a 50-50 use of English and Afrikaans in secondary school instruction, but many schools ignored this in favor of English only. This was eminently sensible—Afrikaans was and is a parochial language compared to English. This was, however, unacceptable to Boer nationalists. Boer members of the parliament, led by the archconservative, Dr. Andries Treurnicht, insisted on 50% Afrikaans in high school classrooms.

Soweto teachers spread the word of the new policy enforcement. Protests began on June 16 and within hours, a disturbance turned into a riot that lasted until the 24th; before the riot was over, 174 blacks and two whites died. There were 1,222 black casualties, contrasting sharply with six whites wounded. The government suppressed the riot with excessive force, and President Pieter Botha retracted the demand that schools use Afrikaans as a language of instruction.

The reaction of most students to the Soweto riot was to boycott schools as a way for the powerless to express their anger. (The long term consequences of boycotting the schools would later be evident in the lack of formal education among many of the black leaders post-1994.) The slogan "liberation before education" became a watchword, but it proved to be costly. As black majority rule approached in 1994, it became evident that 18 years of school boycotts had left South Africa a generation of young illiterates.

Black Homelands

President Vorster adopted a "solution" to racial problems for the government in the form of a Bantu Homelands Citizenship Act (1970). The Act made every black South African, irrespective of actual residence, a citizen of one of ten homelands,

Port of Durban

each designated for specific ethnic groups. As such, the government classified blacks as "foreigners" and excluded from the South African body politic. Between 1960 and 1985, the government forcibly evicted some 3.5 million blacks from their land under the homeland system.

The government granted each homeland internal self-government and when a homeland requested independence, it was to be granted. Transkei, in the southeast, with about 3 million inhabitants, was the first (1976). The next occurred the following year when the government granted self-rule to Bophuthatswana ("homeland of the Tswanas"), a nation in six separated areas with 2.1 million people. Most of its parts lay to the north, bordering Botswana. Venda, with almost half a million, became independent in 1979 and Ciskei in 1981. No nation in the world recognized these creations as "independent."

The "Black Homelands" solution addressed only a portion of South Africa's social and economic impasse. More than 14 million black people lived in townships adjacent to the largest cities and industrial areas of South Africa; even the government classified them as "detribalized." However, to express themselves politically, they were required to vote in the homeland to which the government assigned to them (which had no role or vote in the white government of South Africa) whether or not they had ever been physically present. The system of identity cards intentionally served to determine who could live outside his or her "homeland."

Attempted Reforms

President Pieter W. Botha, as early as 1980, saw the need for additional reform and embarked on a wide-ranging series of measures that would have revolutionized the system of Apartheid. He proposed elimination of the Group Areas Act, the Slums Act and the Community Development Act; the names sounded innocent, but the laws were essential tools of Apartheid. Conservatives in the National Party, led by the intractable Andries Treurnicht, resisted any reform whatsoever. They persuaded the president to embark on a "new" approach that ultimately led to violence and change in South Africa.

The plan was an attempt to placate both international opinion and internal resistance by blacks to white rule. It was supposed to be the answer to the exclusion of blacks from any participation in government. In the mid-1970s, the government concocted a new constitutional scheme.

A Three-House National Assembly . . . (With No Blacks)

To appear to be as democratic as possible, the new constitution created a three-

A spice market in Durban, where the city's Indian heritage is everywhere apparent.
Photo by Nancy Sprotte

house National Assembly, with a large body restricted to white membership, and two smaller units to represent Coloureds and Indians, but no blacks. For blacks, control of the townships in which they were a majority was their only political representation.

In this way, the government felt black leadership could contain increasing unrest in the townships and, at the same time, satisfy the hunger for self-rule. The Boer leadership stood firm in the belief that they had given something of value to the blacks of South Africa. The ANC correctly saw it as no more than just another chapter in the book of Apartheid.

The new National Assembly had a 185-seat white parliament, a 92-seat one for Coloureds and a third for Asians (46 seats). The smaller houses had no powers except with respect to matters of concern to the minority they represented. The larger white parliament could veto any act of the other two. This three-tiered system of parliament, coupled with black "home rule" proved to be white South Africa's most costly and serious mistake, for it was instrumental in the downfall of white-controlled government.

The plan itself was unworkable, and quickly gave way to a government by oligarchy: the Presidential Council of about 60 members proposed all laws and the parliament became a rubber stamp. Across the nation, blacks negatively reacted to this system, and protested by making South Africa ungovernable.

The ANC devised a two-pronged agenda to accomplish its aim of seizing control of

South Africa (it did not envision doing its will through the ballot box until the early 1990s). First, using violence as a tool against non-Zulu black South Africans, the ANC made an effort to coerce all persons, particularly within the townships, to become members of the party or sympathizers with the cause. The ANC accomplished their goal by making it dangerous not to fall within one of the two categories. Second, the ANC leadership recognized that Inkatha, led by Mangosuthu Gatsha Buthelezi, was a potential rival that had to be eliminated or at least controlled in the struggle for power that was to come. Both of these programs unleashed terrible violence, but the police were virtually helpless to deal with it because of its sheer magnitude.

The ANC ordered a boycott of all township elections. Those who participated, and assumed office in township governments, were received threats and ridicule. The ANC regarded those in township governments as subservient Uncle Toms for cooperating with the despised white-controlled government. They, and anyone cooperating with them, became acceptable targets of ANC and MK violence. The most grisly of deaths was from "necklacing"—having a tire filled with gasoline placed around one's neck and lit with a match. After violence rose to the level hoped for, the ANC and its sympathizers began to use the turmoil as justification for disinvestment and sanction programs against South Africa by foreign businesses.

In the decade 1984–1994, over 20,000 blacks lost their lives fighting for the end

South Africa

of Apartheid in South Africa. About half of them (11,000) died after 1990 when the government released Nelson Mandela from prison. The South African Defense Forces murdered about 1,500 of those killed. Ninety-four percent of the horrific township violence was murder of blacks by blacks. The commission that developed those figures also concluded that of the black on black homicides, those killed were about 85% ANC members or supporters, or lived in ANC-controlled areas.

Inkatha Freedom Party and Chief Buthelezi

By the early 1970s, the white government had almost completely dismantled the ANC, having imprisoned the majority of the party's important leaders and demoralizing most followers. The system of spies and informants developed by the South African Defense Forces made it dangerous to belong to the underground organization or to be a communist comrade-in-arms. In order to try to maintain some form of legal pressure against Apartheid, the ANC leadership recognized the need to have a Zulu-based organization to bring pressure on the white government.

The Zulus had a history of bad relations with the Xhosas, the second largest tribal group in South Africa, but the core of the ANC. Thus, although they had no particular affinity for potential rivals, it was a matter of practicality for the ANC to encourage and assist the founding of the Inkatha Freedom Party (IFP) in 1974. Its leader was and is Chief Mangosuthu Gatsha Buthelezi (Man-go-soo-too Gat-sha Boo-teh-lay-zee), known for his ability to communicate with the white leadership, despite Inkatha's staunch opposition to Apartheid.

Buthelezi believed that change in South Africa was possible, but he also believed that if changes occurred in such a manner as to impoverish the country, they would be worthless. His attitudes largely reflected the lifestyles of most of the members of Inkatha, as well as most Zulu non-members.

Xhosas and Sothos tended to cluster with their families in shantytowns around large industrial and mining centers of South Africa, which led to children growing up in poverty and hardship. The Zulus, on the other hand, were the chief clientele of hostels—shelters for male workers with a minimum of comfort and convenience—where they lived for usually 27 out of 30 days. On days off, they went back home (where they had been sending their wages after expenses) to their wives and children. Living in this manner, their needs were minimal, their wages were comparatively high, and family tensions and quarrels were usually low level—since they

didn't have time to escalate. Of equal importance, wives and children lacked the exposure to the crime, violence, and deprivations of the townships.

In reaction to ANC efforts to destabilize South Africa with violence, National Party leadership established an informal alliance with Inkatha to help combat rising violence. Members of the South African Defense Force armed and trained the Zulus. As this became evident to the MK leadership, they redoubled efforts against Zulus.

Among Zulu customs, the carrying of traditional weapons is important. They are uniquely associated with the passage from boyhood to manhood. Though not carried at all times, their presence certainly marks the bearer as a Zulu. For reasons that are not clear, a South African judge in 1989 ruled that they were dangerous weapons in the eyes of the law, and therefore called for a law making them illegal to carry in public. The government agreed, and told the Zulus they could not carry spears and axes as they had in the past. When resorting to violence, which Zulus considered to be for defensive purposes, they used modern weaponry.

Chief Buthelezi and his followers were shocked at the decision. He and Goodwill Zwelithini, king of the Zulus, denounced the measure directly. Together with conservative white South Africans, the chief began to speak with regularity of a black state seceding from South Africa under his leadership. A system of strong federalism was favored, creating the equivalent of states' rights. This attracted favorable interest among many white conservatives, who wanted to establish a "white homeland" in the event of a black-dominated government in South Africa.

President F.W. de Klerk

With the townships in revolt and South Africa in a state of emergency, Nelson Mandela wrote to then President Pieter W. Botha in 1988, urgently stating the two should confer about matters vital to the future of the nation. Under a shroud of secrecy, the conservative president Botha met with Mandela.

President Botha suffered a stroke in January 1989, but after a brief recuperation, he announced in March that he would resume his duties as president. There was immediate opposition from the party leadership, which nominated Frederik W. de Klerk to run in September elections. Three weeks before the elections, an angry and frustrated Botha made a television broadcast denouncing de Klerk, the ANC and anyone else he thought to be hostile, and resigned his presidency.

Nelson Mandela

Nelson Mandela was born in Umtata (later within the homeland of Transkei) in 1918. When the Apartheid government banned the ANC in 1962, Mandela went underground. The government apprehended Mandela and charged him under the anticommunist and antiterrorism laws, sentencing him to life imprisonment without hope of parole. While in prison, he kept abreast of current matters in South Africa, including the turn to violence and terrorism that characterized the period of 1984–1989.

When F.W. de Klerk became president in 1989, the government sought out more extensive contacts with Mandela. This ultimately led to his release from prison, along with Walter Sisulu and other ANC activists. President de Klerk had correctly concluded that continued detention of

Part of a large photomontage celebrating the development of freedom in South Africa

Photo by Cezar Ornatowski

South African Vineyards

Photo by Christine Farrington

Mandela would be counterproductive—and that his chances for meaningful negotiations had greater probability if he conducted them with the older generation of ANC leaders. These negotiations would start a reform program to dismantle Apartheid.

In February 1990, de Klerk ordered Mandela's release, whose name by that time had become high profile symbol of the anti-Apartheid cause. The ANC next signed a peace accord that lifted the state of emergency. Almost immediately, the ANC made Mandela its deputy president, effectively making him the face and power head of the organization. He walked a tight wire astutely, keeping his base of followers mobilized, while negotiating with President de Klerk, traveling abroad in search of desperately needed funding, and acknowledging that the anti-Apartheid rival, Inkatha, deserved some sort of recognition. A year later, in 1991, the international community lifted many of the sanctions against South Africa, as the Apartheid government repealed most of its laws.

Mandela's conduct, which the more radical members of the ANC viewed as too concessionary, infuriated the proponents of black power, confrontation, and seizure of the state by bloody revolution. Some of his early statements played to that audience, but shocked white South Africans: "We have waited too long for our freedom. We can no longer wait. Now is the time to intensify the struggle on all fronts. To relax our efforts now would be a mistake which generations to come will not be able to forgive."

In the same speech, as if to confirm the worst fears of white South Africans, he insisted upon nationalization of South African industries, in particular, the immense Anglo-American Mining Company—a multinational consortium with worldwide interests as well as its diamond and gold mines in South Africa. In 1992, when he concluded that his advocacy of sanctions and disinvestment was the wrong policy, Mandela found that trying to turn away from these policies in order to attract investment to South Africa was far harder than he had imagined. His earlier position had generated suspicion and distrust regarding ANC economic policy.

Many had expected Mandela to be a dedicated, violent revolutionary, gripped by the misjudgments of an uninformed old age. He instead showed an unwavering commitment to racial reconciliation, having understood the difference between a revolutionary movement and a political party charged with governing a country. Development of the country and improvement in the lives of its citizens would require, above all, the political stability that would give confidence and assurance to investors on whom that development largely depended.

The pressures on Mandela were tremendous, as he risked the disfavor of the militant wing of the ANC, conditioned by years of a struggle mentality and ideologically shaped by economic thinking that exalted the role of a highly centralized state. The tensions between Mandela's moderation, and the militants' more radical claims were constant. In the case of his wife, Winnie Madikizela-Mandela, they were even personal. After many months, they finally opted to part ways. Mandela thus separated himself from a figure romanticized by some of the most youth-

South Africa

ful and radical elements of the party as "Mother of the Nation."

Winnie Mandela

As an ANC activist, Winnie Mandela lived in internal exile for years. Violating her exile in 1986, she worked her way to Soweto, a black township outside of Johannesburg. A luxurious home, complete with swimming pool, had been built for her amid the two-room tarpaper and tin shanties of the town. There was a minor uproar of protest, so she did not immediately move in.

When she did, she formed "The Winnie Mandela Soccer Team," a gang of young thugs that proceeded to terrorize Soweto and other nearby black townships. Trials of real and imagined offenders took place in her home, where she often "presided." She issued out sentences of beating and death. The most notable incident occurred in 1988 when the "team" kidnapped a 13-year-old boy from a Soweto Methodist Church shelter and took him to Mandela's house. They accused the boy of being a police informer and beat him severely, with Winnie Mandela herself reportedly taking part. Taken to a nearby field by the "team," he was murdered.

Acting through his lawyer from prison, Nelson Mandela ordered her to release three other kidnapped youths and to disband the "team." The ANC ousted Winnie Mandela. During her trial, interruptions came from radical members of the ANC who threatened and actually kidnapped co-defendants and state witnesses, removing them from the country. After listening to her testimony, the judge (there was no jury trial in South Africa) called her a "calm, composed, deliberate and unblushing liar." The judge sentenced Winnie to six years in jail; an appeals court sustained the conviction in early June 1993 but, in a political decision, vacated the prison sentence.

Though Winnie Mandela's trial occurred after Nelson Mandela's release from prison, neither Mr. Mandela nor the ANC leadership rallied to Winnie's defense. An effort of radicals sought to rejoin Winnie to the ANC leadership by becoming president of the Women's Auxiliary. While her husband was trying to engage in meaningful negotiations with the white government, Winnie appealed to the militant sector of the ANC; they remembered her for her famous 1987 statement: "With our matchboxes and our necklaces, we shall liberate!"

Under pressure from senior ANC officials, Mandela divorced his wife in early 1996. One reason was that if Winnie were in any position of power, foreign investors would be hesitant to support the new South Africa. Ex-President Mandela has since remarried with Graça Machel, the widow of President Samora Machel of Mozambique.

By April 2003, a South African court found Winnie Madikizela-Mandela guilty of 43 charges of fraud and 25 of bank theft and sentence her to jail. "The state's evidence is overwhelming," said the judge as he found her guilty of obtaining bank loans worth more than $120,000 in the name of bogus employees of the ANC Women's League, of which she was president. The courts sentenced her to five years in jail, where she was to serve a minimum of eight months, with the rest of the time spent doing community service. Madikizela-Mandela resigned her parliamentary seat and positions in the ANC. The party did not place her on its list of candidates for the 2004 elections.

The Repeal of Apartheid

President de Klerk and the Natinoal Party repealed the major Apartheid laws in 1990–91, after over 40 years. Among other changes, this allowed Black Africans the freedom to move about their own country.

One claim among white South Africans—even those liberals who supported the repeal—was that the end of the militarized state generated an upsurge of crime. At night, the streets of the formerly bustling city of Johannesburg went vacant. Luxury hotels closed and fences and walls around homes in white suburbs grew higher. Prison bars at the windows, together with elaborate security systems became the order of the day. Purse snatching and petty thievery were common in cities, rural areas, and small towns.

Constitutional Negotiations

In 1991 the various competing elements in South Africa began meeting informally and later in conferences of CODESA—Congress for a Democratic South Africa. Prior to negotiations, several Apartheid laws had been repealed and political exiles (often common criminals) numbering 50,000 received amnesty and returned to South Africa. Periodic outbursts of violence, particularly between ANC and Inkatha supporters, interrupted the talks. Political sniping from the conservatives led de Klerk to have a national referendum on his policies. His efforts were supported by 70% of whites, who thus for the first time voted to share power peacefully with the black majority.

The discussions were delicate, at times awkward. The ANC had to exercise caution, because blacks distrusted the idea that whites would genuinely negotiate away their control of South Africa. Outside the conference room, Mandela was careful to level gross insults at de Klerk calculated to reassure his own supporters that he was not giving in to white pressures. Behind the scenes, the parties worked towards consensus, led by the chief negotiators, Roelf Meyer of the NP and Cyril Ramaphosa of the ANC. The parties finally agreed that an interim government had to be elected to draw a permanent constitution and to govern, and

Soweto Township

it would have to provide minority (i.e. white) protection. The ANC senior leadership (but not its membership) quietly discarded black power.

A New Constitution

Agreement on the interim constitution was signed on November 17, 1993, the result of months of painstaking negotiations. The substance of the document was a fundamental victory for the ANC. The constitution provided for elections and specified that the 400-member National Assembly would not represent any specific constituency. Lists prepared by each national party would contain possible representatives. The party's percentage of the total (national) vote would determine the number of seats for each party. A Senate of 90 people would consist of ten members selected by each of the nine provinces of South Africa. In effect, this placed virtually all decisionmaking power in the hands of the national parties. After the constitution's adoption, plans proceeded for elections on April 26, 1994.

A Last Minute Accord

Because of increased political violence and apprehension over the imminent elections, President de Klerk declared a state of emergency in KwaZulu-Natal on March 31, 1994, which infuriated Chief Buthelezi and made him even more adamant. Buthelezi demanded amendments to the constitution that would secure the position of King Goodwill Zwelithini and the historic Zulu kingdom. On April 5, 15,000 Zulus armed with spears and clubs marched through the town of Empangeni; the SADF forces considered them too dangerous to disarm.

The election commission said balloting in KwaZulu necessitated postponement. Mandela rejected this, and international mediators, including Henry Kissinger from the U.S., finally secured a breakthrough on April 19 after two days of talks. The Zulus would participate in the balloting, abandoning demands for amendment of the constitution. There was a guarantee to the continued status of the monarchy and the kingdom of KwaZulu-Natal.

The real nature of the settlement was not apparent until almost a month after the elections. Zwelithini received the promise of more than a million acres of KwaZulu-Natal land. Buthelezi (jobless after the elections) would become home affairs minister in the new government lead by Mandela.

The 1994 Election

Election officials made elaborate and painstaking preparations for the first popular balloting including all races in South Africa. The problem of illiteracy was immense—50%—so election officials placed pictures of the leaders of each party listed above that choice on the ballot. Overcoming well-grounded fears, and waiting in line for hours on end, more than 70% of those registered voted.

Other Political Parties and Groups

Other groups participating in the election included the Freedom Front (FF)—formed in March 1994. The Freedom Front was headed by former defense chief General Constand Viljoen whose less than right-wing approach appealed to many conservatives.

White conservatives formerly belonged exclusively to the Conservative Party (CP). Its principal objective was the creation of an all-white state by the interim constitution, a proposition few ever took seriously. It refused to register as a political party for the elections.

The Democratic Party (DP) was the successor of two liberal parties popular among English speakers who opposed Apartheid. Tony Leon served as leader of the party.

The Pan Africanist Congress (PAC) and its militant wing, the Azanian Peoples Army, was a radical black party which adopted a slogan "one settler [a white], one bullet."

As predicted, the ANC demonstrated nationwide appeal and secured a majority of Assembly seats. The National Party and the Inkatha Freedom Party found their support more localized in Western Cape Province and KwaZulu-Natal. The National Party did well among Coloured and Asiatic Indian voters. The Freedom Front did well in areas dominated by rural whites.

The ANC in Power

Once in power the ANC demonstrated the balancing of ideology and practicality, required by the responsibility of governance. Its initial budget envisioned a million new housing units and a million new jobs over a five-year period, without the necessity of new taxes.

The government adopted the Restitution of Land Rights Act, a very controversial measure, in late 1994 and established a Land Claims Commission and a Land Claims Court. The act directs "balancing the desirability of remedying past human rights violations against . . . the need to avoid major social disruption."

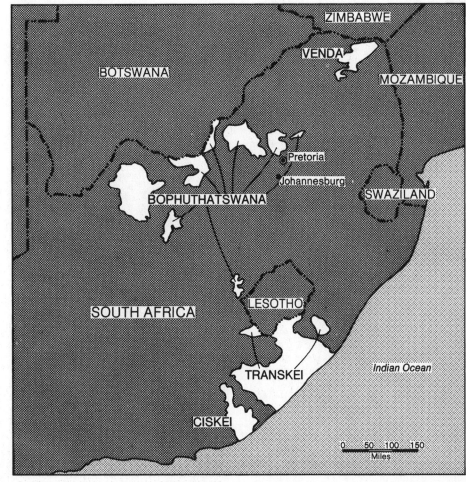

Black "homeland" republics

South Africa

Former President Thabo Mbeki

To the chagrin of those who preferred a state-controlled economy, foreign investment was encouraged and the government announced plans for a significant privatization of state-owned companies. The two policies were interrelated, for privatization could assure the international business community that the state was moving towards a more liberal economy.

So great was President Mandela's moral authority, that he could successfully say "No" to the more outrageous demands from various sectors of the liberation struggle. When the leader of former guerrilla forces threatened to return to armed struggle over problems arising from the integration of these forces into the South African army, Mandela warned against a "suicidal plot."

Social Discontent
Tensions ran high among South Africa's black population. During the election campaign, the ANC promised far, far more than could be realistically delivered to blacks. As the months wore on after the contest, their lives experienced minimal change. Symptoms of this malaise included a high crime rate, corruption, squatting on land, moving into nearby homes after ousting the occupants, and illegal strikes.

President Mandela strongly condemned all of this in his February 1995 speech that opened parliament. He criticized what he termed "a culture of entitlement," and accused blacks who "misread freedom to mean license." He condemned those guilty of murdering police officers, taking hostages, rioting, looting and other crimes.

The Constitutional Commission completed its work on a new governing document in May 1996. One notable provision paves the way for the purchase and transfer of land back to black Africans. It calls, however, for market-based compensation, which the government cannot afford. The Senate changed to a Provincial Council of premiers of the nine provinces and others chosen provincially. The new constitution has a Bill of Rights that is far more liberal than that of the U.S., but essentially continued the structure of government without change—maintaining a strong central authority, with the powers of provinces and smaller areas being strictly limited.

From Transition to Transformation
The ANC party congress chose Thabo Mbeki as party president in December 1997. President Mandela increasingly relinquished governmental affairs to Mbeki in preparation for the 1999 presidential elections.

Thabo Mbeki grew up groomed for leadership. Son of one of the principal ANC leaders, Govan Mbeki, Thabo early earned distinction for potential leadership from his father and his father's friend and colleague, Nelson Mandela. He left South Africa in 1962 for England where he studied economics at Sussex University; his Master's thesis was on small businesses in Ghana and Nigeria. Like his father, Mbeki was a member of the Communist Party, and in 1970, he went to Russia for military training. On his return to South Africa in 1990, he pragmatically resigned from the party.

Chief Mangosuthu Buthelezi

Mbeki's brief biography captures the ambiguity of the man. Steeped in Marxism, he also trained in Western economics. Nurtured in the idealism of a revolutionary movement and well versed in its Stalinist organizational style, he is practical and pragmatic. The breadth of his intellectual background later became necessary to hold together his coalition partners and to get a handle on a legacy of problems created by Apartheid.

Mbeki's accession to power marked a change in tone and language in the ANC's relationship with South Africa's white minority. Nelson Mandela signaled the shift in his valedictory speech to the 1997 ANC party conference. In this speech, reportedly prepared by Mbeki, President Mandela departed from the soothing rhetoric of multiracialism that had eased the transition to majority rule. Whites had "demonstrated consistently" a desire to cling to the privileges they enjoyed under Apartheid, he said. He accused some of being involved in a "counterrevolutionary conspiracy." The speech contained vintage Marxist rhetoric, stylistically out of character, highly controversial, an affront to those white South Africans who had long opposed Apartheid.

During his first term as president, Mbeki would repeatedly return to the theme. "Racist" would become a potent political charge leveled against white critics of his policies. The term also had the added advantage of undermining black support of any such criticism. Thabo Mbeki's emphasis on race was one indication of how difficult the transition from liberation movement to political party would be for the ANC.

The ANC soon discovered being the party of power is quite different from being in opposition, and this has deeply affected its relationship with its traditional partners, the Congress of South African Trade Unions (COSATU) and the South African Communist Party (SACP). Membership in the three groups often overlaps. Leadership of the two partners is frequently co-opted and interlocks with ANC leadership. After the 1999 election, for example, COSATU had to replace four of its principal officers elevated to parliament by virtue of membership on the ANC lists.

COSATU's new president, Willy Madisha, developed his career in the teachers' union and the SACP. Its new general secretary, Zwelinzima Vavi, was a National Union of Mineworkers (NUM) organizer as well as a member of the SACP.

Both COSATU and the SACP remain deeply socialist in orientation. They were not part of the process that created a major piece of the government's economic legislation, GEAR (Growth, Employment and Redistribution), and both feared GEAR leaned much too much towards a liberal capitalist economy. Both seem to prefer nationalization to privatization. The collision of the three partners seems inevitable, though "unity of the movement," at least in the short term, trumps the obvious divisions among them.

Big election issues for the ANC in 1999 were jobs and crime. Estimates put unemployment at 50%, making it one of the country's most urgent problems. An estimated 4.7 million people were unemployed and looking for work. GEAR had set a goal of 252,000 new jobs for 1997, but this did not adequately take into account the continuing recession in mining where the industry had to cut 50,000 mining jobs.

The 1999 Election

South Africa's second multiparty democratic election took place in early June 1999. Some 42 political parties participated. They ranged from God's People Party, dedicated to fighting Satan, to Keep it Straight and Simple (you work out the acronym). The ANC overwhelmed all comers, nearly winning a two-thirds majority with 266 seats. The National Party, burdened with the historical weight of Apartheid and deprived of forceful leadership, fell to a fourth-place finish. Not even calling itself the New National Party (NNP) helped to slow its decline; it won only 28 seats in the legislature.

The Democratic Party, a distant second-place finisher with a mere 38 seats, assumed the role of official opposition. White liberals congregated in the Demo-

Clifton Beaches near Cape Town   Photo by Rita Arendt

cratic Party. The DP also benefited from defections from NNP, especially in the Western Cape Province. Its leader, Tony Leon, was articulate and fiery as an orator. As leader of the opposition, he provided some of the best and much-needed criticism of the ANC. Chief Buthelezi's IFP won 34 seats.

South African voters do not vote directly for their representatives and have no idea who will represent them because of the country's proportional representation system. Parties create national and provincial lists and individuals enter parliament in terms of their ranking on those lists, which represent internal politicking. In 1999, for example, Winnie Madikizela-Mandela was number ten on the ANC national list, guaranteeing her a position in parliament.

In June 2000, the Democratic Party (DP), under the leadership of Tony Leon, merged with the New National Party (NNP) to form the Democratic Alliance (DA). In many ways, it was a merger of fish and fowl. The DP had inherited South Africa's white-minority liberal tradition. The NNP was, of course, the recently rebaptized National Party, which had created and enforced Apartheid for 46 years.

In many ways, the merger seemed to represent a voluntary death for the NNP. Loathed by black Africans as the party of Apartheid, the NNP had little to offer, and its cosmetic name change proved of little value in the last election. (It won less than 7% of the votes cast.) The question that remained was how long this awkward merger of DP and NNP would last.

According to the South African constitution, MPs lose their seats in parliament if their party dissolves. Therefore, the NNP and DP continued to exist in parliament until the 2004 national election. Such was not to be, however, for leadership disputes in Western Cape Province at the end of 2001 shattered the alliance was shattered. Grasping to keep the party and his own political career alive, the NNP leader, Marthinus van Schalkwyk, withdrew from the DA, negotiated a new relationship with the ANC, and transformed the face of South African party politics.

The alliance was attractive for the ANC because the governments of Cape Town and its province, which previously excluded the ANC, were now open to their politicians. At a national level, the ANC's political partners, COSATU and SACP, seemed left out of the loop regarding the new relationship, and some of their members expressed discomfort, adding to the strains within the triple alliance. Chief Buthelezi's IFP seemed to question its own relationship with the ANC, especially since an alliance between the ANC and the NNP could easily topple Inkatha's control of the KwaZulu-Natal provincial legislature. President Mbeki and the ANC quickly moved to use the new alliance to strengthen their domination of South African political space.

Sitting representatives passed legislation to permit "floor crossing"—allowing a representative to change parties without the unpleasant democratic necessity of resigning from office and standing for re-election on a new party list. The opposi-

King Goodwill Zwelethini

South Africa

Penguins, Boulders Beach, False Bay

Photo by Judi Iranyi

tion, with little more than a thin line of lawyers to defend themselves against the ANC juggernaut, challenged the legislation's legality and South Africa's Constitutional Court gave them partial victory. Municipalities permitted floor crossing, but at the provincial and national levels, the constitution required amendment before members could change parties. With more than a two-thirds majority in parliament, this posed no impediment for the ANC and its NNP partner.

Constitutional amendments to permit party changes at the national and provincial levels passed in February 2003. When the 15-day window in which lawmakers could change their political identities ended on April 4, the party changers reshaped the South African political landscape. Nine members of parliament crossed over to the ANC, giving the party 275 seats in the 400-seat body—a two-thirds majority of its own.

Mbeki and Transformation

Thabo Mbeki's presidency inaugurated a new phase in South African politics. From the transition years of Nelson Mandela, the system moved to transformation. Nelson Mandela had used his moral au-

thority to convince his fellow Africans to accept the new political system. His moderation and restraint similarly convinced whites to support the new dispensation. A Truth and Reconciliation Commission sought to soothe the emotional pains on both sides of the racial divide. Acceptance and reconciliation seemingly gained, the new government moved to transform the legacy of injustice that characterizes contemporary South Africa. Symptomatic are four laws passed early in the year 2000: the Promotion of Access to Information Bill, the Promotion of Administrative Justice Bill, the Preferential Procurement Policy Framework and the Promotion of Equality and Prevention of Unfair Discrimination Bill.

Two of the bills give ordinary citizens the right to make the government—at all levels—accountable. The Promotion of Administrative Justice Bill forces government to create mechanisms to explain its decisions, such as cutting welfare grants to affected members of the public. In theory, bureaucrats will think before acting, realizing they may have to justify any action they take.

The Promotion of Access to Information Bill is a reaction to the secrecy with which

the former white regime shrouded state affairs. The bill affirms a right of access to "any information held by a public or private body." The bill excludes defense, security and foreign affairs information.

The two remaining bills seek to transform Apartheid's legacy of racial injustice. The Preferential Procurement Policy Framework Bill gives preferences in gov-

Nelson Mandela

302

Busy downtown Durban   Photo by Nancy Sprotte

ernment contracts to companies that have actively hired workers disadvantaged based on race, gender or disability. Many South Africans ironically refer to the program as "positive discrimination."

The Promotion of Equality and Prevention of Unfair Discrimination Bill seeks nothing less than an end to discrimination, that is, aside from the "positive discrimination" of the previous bill. Its scope is vast. Discrimination is defined in the broadest possible terms and applied to 17 prohibited areas: race, gender, sex, pregnancy, marital status, ethnic or social origin, color, sexual orientation, age, disability, religion, conscience, belief, culture, language and birth or any other recognized ground.

The ambiguities of provisions in the four laws suggest that lawmakers expect years of legal wrangling before full implementation occurs. In the meantime, the government has to deal with issues more pressing.

Crime

South Africa is awash in a wave of crime that threatens to sink the state's capacity to protect its citizens and diminish its international reputation. (One study found that 60% of emigrants cited violent crime as a reason for leaving South Africa. North African states vying against South Africa to hold the soccer World Cup finals repeatedly stressed its insecurity.)

Car theft has long been one of the most common crimes in South Africa. The worst

of these resulted in violence, even murder. Johannesburg ranks as the world's carjacking capital. Located in Gauteng province, Johannesburg's vehicles all bear license plates with the initials GP. Local cynics persist in saying it means "Gangster Paradise." With focus, the police have succeeded in reducing the carjacking rate. For the 2004–2005 reporting year there were 12,434 cars hijacked in all of South Africa, down nearly 10% from the previous year's 13,793. Gauteng province is still the principal site for the crime; in 2004–2005 there were 6,902 auto hijackings—55% of the national total.

As police worked to reduce one type of crime, however, criminals adapted and upgraded. Rather than individuals in cars, thieves began to target armored vehicles moving large cash shipments. In a typical attack, four cars would surround and stop the vehicle; some 20 hijackers would leap out with assault rifles, bringing traffic to a halt, while their associates ripped open the vehicle's roof. In the 2002–2003 reporting period, there were 374 such attacks.

ATMs are now the target of criminal violence. South Africa is experiencing a wave of ATM attacks by gangs armed with sticks of dynamite, whose indiscriminate use, police fear, will ultimately end up in the loss of human life. The South African Bank Risk Information Center reported that more ATM attacks occurred in the first two months of 2007 than all of 2006.

The latest efforts to battle crime in Johannesburg have resulted in the placement of closed-circuit television cameras at nearly all traffic intersections in the huge metropolis. This has reduced police response time and is reported to have reduced violent crime rates in the city.

According to Interpol statistics, South Africa's murder rate is one of the highest in the world. South Africans, black and white, rich and poor have been victims of crime, a fact made evident to South Africans when the country's former first lady, Marike de Klerk, was found murdered in her Cape Town apartment in December 2001. In September 2002, police reported the murder rate had "stabilized," with 59 people a day being murdered. That was 21,535 a year. Police statistics show a slowdown of the country's murder rate. Nationally, 18,793 murders occurred between April 2004 and March 2005, but that is still 51 people murdered every day. South Africa remains one of the few countries in which one is more likely to be murdered than die in an automobile accident.

Rape attacks are more than double the annual murder rate in South Africa, making it the rape capital of the world. The 2001–2002 statistics showed six women were raped in South Africa every hour of every day—52,560 annually. A woman born in South Africa has a greater chance of being raped than learning how to read, while one in four girls faces the prospect of being raped before the age of 16. Some experts estimate that at least 60% of all rapes go unreported, and it is a crime where the police have made no progress. It continues to increase. Reported rape cases were up nationally in 2003–2004 (52,733), and increased yet again in the latest reporting period—55,114 in 2004–2005.

Charlene Smith, an ANC activist and rape victim herself, has highlighted the

Winnie Madikizela Mandela

South Africa

President Jacob Zuma

deeply embedded cultural values that create a culture of rape in South Africa. Surveys of public attitudes support her analysis. In Johannesburg, which has the highest incidence of rape in South Africa, a survey conducted among 1,500 school children in Soweto township found that a quarter of all boys interviewed said that "jackrolling"—a South African term for recreational gang rape—was fun. Weaknesses in the criminal justice system also contribute to the culture of rape. Only about 7% of reported rapes result in convictions, leaving most rapists with little fear of punishment.

The rape trial of former Deputy President Jacob Zuma brought the crime of rape and South Africa's culture of rape under the klieg lights of publicity. Zuma allegedly raped a family friend—an HIV-positive woman in her 30s—at his Johannesburg home in November 2005. In responding to the allegations, Zuma claimed he had consensual sex, while the woman, a 31-year-old AIDS activist, claimed she had been violated by a father figure, a man she had known since she was five years old. Despite one of the world's most progressive constitutions that guarantees gender equality, operative law remains anachronistically biased against women. The country's Sexual Offenses Act, passed during the Apartheid era, narrowly defines the crime and court procedure often requires the woman prove that she did not provoke the rape. In his defense Zuma was thus allowed to claim the woman wore a short skirt and sat "inappropriately," indicating she wanted sex with him. Following the norms of his traditional Zulu culture, he argued, to leave a woman in a state of arousal untouched would have been unacceptable and vilified.

Supporters of both accuser and defendant organized street demonstrations. Those supporting Zuma showed his political base in KwaZulu-Natal Province and among the most leftwing elements of the ANC tripartite alliance. Women's groups focused on the social and legal problems faced by the survivors of sexual violence. One of them, People Opposing Woman Abuse (Powa), estimated that one woman is raped in South Africa every 26 seconds, but only one in nine incidents is ever reported. Additionally, victims suffer further in a culture of silence and denial that surrounds the crime.

The case generated a tsunami of commentary. The president of the National Union Mineworkers seemed to express the values of an unreconstructed patriarchal culture when he justified Zuma's adultery. "We are not Christians," he told the union's national congress. "We don't listen to the Ten Commandments and we don't have to listen when Christians tell us adultery is wrong." (Zuma is a polygamist with three wives and at least 18 children.) Archbishop Desmond Tutu, South Africa's Nobel Prize-winning Christian cleric, thought the trial was "one of the worse moments" in the life of the country's democracy. "I've been saddened," he said, "by the reinforcement of the stereotype that when a woman accuses a man of rape, she is made out to be the guilty one, and her sexual history is brought up—whether true or not." That made it difficult for a woman to bring charges, he noted, because "she'll nearly always end up being the accused."

Tutu reserved some of his sharpest words for the behavior of Zuma's supporters, who insulted the accuser and, shouting "burn the bitch," burnt her photograph outside the court. It was, he said, "abominable," and a sad day for the country's nascent democracy "when we can use our freedoms in such a way that it stomps all over the dignity of the accused."

In early May 2006, Judge Willem van der Merwe ended the sordid trial by declaring the state had not proved the accused's guilt "beyond doubt." The accuser lived under heavy police protection during the trial due to threats against her life. She now lives anonymously in exile in a non-African country.

Education

Among the most important issues facing the Mbeki government are the distribution of social services, particularly education. The crisis in education has been ongoing, a consequence of Apartheid policies on curriculum and funding. President Mbeki has spoken often and with conviction of an African Renaissance. His new African century must produce doctors, engineers, and scientists, but the education system has been a shambles. Its desperate state is evident in the results of the 2000 matriculation exams—only 48.9% passed. The results were a shock and a call to arms.

Since then, the government has poured money into schooling, effected change, and produced improved results. Matriculation (final school year) exams were successfully passed by 61.7% of those taking them in 2001 and 68.9% in 2002. The 2005 pass rate dropped slightly, to 68.3%, suggesting progress had reached a plateau. Indeed, in 2006 the pass rate fell even more, to 66.5%.

Mitigating the seeming success of improved matric scores was the fact that the number of those passing the exam represented only 32% of those who entered the secondary school system two years before. South Africa's dropout rate is huge—more than 50%. (In 2005, 508,363 pupils took the matric exam, fewer than half of the 1,096,214 students who had been in grade ten two years before.)

The legacy of Apartheid's inequalities and disparities is still apparent. A pattern of regional inequality in results reflects long-term inequality of resource distribution. The best-endowed provinces (Northern Cape, Western Cape and Gauteng) performed best. The lowest pass rates occurred in the poor provinces with huge black and rural majorities. In 2006, Limpopo's pass rate, for example, dropped a huge 9.2%, from 64.9% in 2005 to 55.7%. Angry parents in the province burned ANC T-shirts emblazoned with President Mbeki's face to highlight problems with the educational system. Among the complaints: teachers working as municipal counselors, thus failing to fulfill their teaching responsibilities.

The causes of the crisis in education are manifold, though an obvious problem is the unequal disbursement of the basic material provisioning, classrooms and books, among schools across different areas of South Africa. KwaZulu-Natal, for example, faced a shortage of 14,000 classrooms (2003), which would take nine years to eliminate. Beyond the physical, however, the whole delivery system—an educational bureaucracy, too many of whom are unqualified, unprepared and unmotivated—remains a challenge. A culture of learning has yet to be cultivated, and individual classrooms remain sites of threat and intimidation against both staff and students. Those who can afford it send their children to private schools.

Eastern Cape province demonstrates the deplorable conditions in which education must function in South Africa's poorest areas. In 2000, 17% of the schools had no toilets, 45% had no electricity, and 28%

Providing improved services: building a water-treatment facility

©IRIN

no water. In 2003 the provincial legislature's standing committee on education still complained about the shortage of classrooms, dilapidated mud structures, absence of toilets, electricity, telephones and water. Worse, it found a high degree of poor discipline among both teachers and students after visiting 157 provincial schools. "Drunkenness, absenteeism, truancy and use of drugs within the school premises could be cited as most striking examples," it said.

In his 2004 state-of-the-nation speech, President Mbeki promised that no children would learn outdoors by the next time he described the state of the nation. In early 2005, however, Minister of Education Naledi Pandor openly wondered, in a parliamentary briefing, why children continued to learn under trees when the provinces had the money to build classrooms. For the government the issue is critical: education remains at the heart of its plans for social transformation. Parliament had apportioned more than twenty percent of the country's budget toward education, and the absence of constructed classrooms too openly displayed the government's inability to deliver services.

In May 2006, Education Minister Naledi Pandor claimed that in the last 30 months the government had built 179 new schools and would be spending $1.5 billion, or 21% of the national budget, on education in the fiscal year. Still, the shortfall is over-

whelmingly apparent. In early May 2006 nearly 900 students were attending high school in Orlando, a suburb of Soweto Township, but there was only one qualified teacher to teach three basic science subjects; the library had no up-to-date books and the "computer lab" had no computers. According to the educational research unit at Witwatersrand University, 43% of all South African schools still have no electricity; 27% have no running water, and a staggering 80% have no library.

Of the many proposals for educational reform, perhaps the most controversial issue has been the question of language. The 2005 education reform plan makes the teaching of English and Afrikaans optional, instead offering learners the choice of studying any two of the country's 11 official languages. According to official statistics, Zulu is the mother tongue of 23.8% of the population, followed by Xhosa, the natal tongue of 17.6%. Only about 8% of South Africans speak English as their first language. The proposal accords with the government's desire to develop the other nine official languages into media of instruction. Ultimately, the plan is to have universities teach in indigenous languages.

Truth and Reconciliation Commission

Racial tensions still exist in South Africa, but given the bitterness of past experience, it is remarkable that any harmony at all is possible. One important institu-

tion that helped advance the reconciliation process is the Truth and Reconciliation Commission (TRC) established by act of parliament in 1995. Its purpose was to investigate crimes committed during the Apartheid era, and as commission chairman, President Mandela appointed Archbishop Desmond Tutu, the 1984 Nobel Peace Prize winner. Tutu had been the first black Anglican Dean of Johannesburg and had led the church in South Africa into an active struggle against Apartheid.

The TRC heard some 21,300 witnesses and compiled a dossier of human rights crimes committed by all sides during the Apartheid era. A 3,500-page report submitted to President Mandela in October 1998 marked the conclusion of its investigative work. There was guilt aplenty in the report. The most serious culprit was the South African State itself. The commission's analysis of why this came about was simple and direct: Racism was at the center of state action designed to protect the power and privilege of a racial minority. Consequently, white citizens adopted a dehumanizing attitude towards black citizens. They ceased to think of them as citizens and this "created a climate in which gross atrocities committed against them were seen as legitimate."

The commission also held the opponents of Apartheid—the ANC and other liberation movements—morally and politically accountable for human rights violations. Thabo Mbeki, for example, had told the TRC that a number of ANC members—including 34 in Angola when the party was in exile—were executed by the movement's own security officials. At least one of those was wrongly executed by two ANC cadres who themselves were later put to death.

Important political figures did not escape the commission's condemnation. The commission found Winnie Madikizela-Mandela accountable for crimes committed by the Mandela United Football Club (MUFC). Killing, torture, assault and arson were all MUFC activities, the commission found, and Madikizela-Mandela herself was aware of this criminal activity, but chose not to address it.

The commission held Mangosuthu Buthelezi accountable as leader of the Inkatha Freedom Party for all the violence committed by its members. Between 1982 and 1994, IFP supporters caused the deaths of about 3,800 people in KwaZulu-Natal province alone, against 1,100 caused by the ANC. It was, the commission thought, a "systematic pattern" of murder and attacks by the IFP against its opponents, often in collusion with state security forces.

The commission was empowered to grant amnesty to those who asked for it

South Africa

and a separate panel existed to hold these hearings. Applicants were required to prove their crime had a political motive or was performed acting under direct orders. They were also required to offer full disclosure of their crimes and demonstrate genuine contrition. The commission received some 7,100 applications for amnesty and granted close to 1,000. It rejected the killers of Chris Hani—it was not a political crime according to the panel. It also rejected the amnesty application of five policemen involved in the death of Steve Biko and refused a blanket amnesty to ANC leaders, arguing that the amnesty was for repenting individuals.

The legislation establishing the TRC entailed the idea that victims of state-sponsored violence deserve compensation from the state for their suffering. Since the conclusion of hearings, a third of the commission's panels have dealt with reparations to the victims.

It received some 20,000 requests for financial reparation. Of these, 17,000 claimants received initial payments totaling $3.7 million. However, a special government fund existed to give the bulk of financial reparations. President Mbeki announced the government would be making a one-time payment of 30,000 Rand ($3,800) to the 22,000 victims of Apartheid designated by the TRC.

Testing Thabo

President Mbeki and his government came under increasing scrutiny as they confronted a number of issues and problems, many of their own making. Both the president's judgment and action on these have raised questions about his capacity to lead the nation. Part of the problem lies in the president's own style and personality.

Mbeki demonstrated a governing style more restrained than that of Mandela. He is seen as cool, distant and lacking a common touch. His rapport with the masses, that ineffable quality some like to call "charisma," pales beside that of more popular and populist leaders. Indeed, it is widely reported that Nelson Mandela preferred Cyril Ramaphosa, the mineworkers' leader and principal negotiator of the transition from Apartheid to majority rule, as his successor.

Lacking fundamental popularity and charisma and surrounded by those who have them can, one assumes, lead to a certain nervousness. Enemies can lurk and conspiracies abound, but the organizational and ideological traditions of the ANC stress internal discipline and external solidarity. Historically the movement could enforce discipline by rough revolutionary justice justified as necessary to the achievement of its goals—an elimination of the Apartheid system.

Once Apartheid ended and the movement had attained control of the apparatus of the state, divergences over the use, direction, and speed of government action to improve the everyday life of South Africans became evident. Managing those differences and the personalities and factions that have gathered around them tested Thabo Mbeki's judgment and leadership.

In foreign policy, the issue of Zimbabwe has loomed large. President Mbeki claimed the efficacy of "quiet diplomacy" before critics who demanded he condemn Zimbabwe's state-sanctioned violence against its opponents. The wisdom of that approach became ever more dubious as Zimbabwe collapsed economically under an increasingly dictatorial Robert Mugabe. The ANC and President Mbeki consistently refused to condemn comrade Mugabe and his thuggish antics. In this refusal, Mbeki abandoned moral leadership and jeopardized a visionary project for African development by alienating Western governments asked to finance the project.

Disgusted with President Mbeki's moral flaccidity and lack of leadership on the Zimbabwe issue, South Africa's Nobel Prize-winning cleric Desmond Tutu unleashed a withering criticism: Mbeki, he said "would be booed in the street" if he were ever to ask ordinary Zimbabweans what they thought about his views on their country. "The people of Zimbabwe have no respect for Mbeki. They don't know why he is supporting Mugabe. They don't understand it."

The 2004 Elections

Over the years, the ANC's democratic traditions have eroded. In the early days, the national executive committee conducted lively debates on important issues, but its ultimate authority waned to a concentration of effective power in an increasingly autocratic executive. Nothing better demonstrates presidential dominance in the South African political system than President Mbeki's decision to send an entire aircraft filled with weapons to rescue a beleaguered Jean-Bertrand Aristide in Haiti. The decision was single-handed, personal, and illustrative of the system's executive dominance.

Despite acquiescent silence on Zimbabwe that plunged millions of Zimbabweans into irreversible misery, and despite obtuse obstructionism on the AIDS issue that shortened lives and increased suffering of South Africans, Thabo Mbeki was effectively master of the South African political universe as the 2004 elections approached. Reelected ANC president in 2003, Mbeki led the party to a smashing victory—nearly 70%—in the legislative polls of 2004, surpassing the 1999 results and gaining more than a two-thirds majority in parliament. The victory assured his election to a second four-year term as president of South Africa by the National Assembly.

The ANC entered the poll allied with the New National Party (NNP) of Marthinus van Schalkwyk, but it hardly needed support. It won 279 seats in the 400-seat assembly, while its coalition partner won

Township housing, Gugulethu

Photo by Judi Iranyi

306

Goat herding in remote Northern Cape province
©IRIN

provincial governance. Four of the nine new ANC premiers would be women.

Zuma Corruption Trial

Mbeki got an opportunity to deal with corruption at the national level in June 2005, when courts convicted Schabir Shaik, the financial advisor to South Africa's deputy president, Jacob Zuma, of fraud and corruption. The case, which riveted the entire country's attention, involved some $200,000 in payments to Zuma to help secure business deals and negotiating a bribe for the deputy president with a French arms manufacturer. In his judgment, Justice Hilary Squires described as "overwhelming" the evidence of a "corrupt relationship" existing between Zuma and Schabir Shaik, his advisor.

Shaik exhausted his appeals and entered prison in November 2006 to serve a 15-year term; the Court also required Shaik to surrender some $4.7 million in illegal gains to the state.

Zuma reacted to the judgment by declaring his conscience clear because "I have not committed any crime," but within two weeks President Mbeki bowed to the pressure of public opinion. The court's ruling, he announced before parliament, had "raised questions of conduct" and it would be in the best interests of the country to "release" Zuma from "his responsibilities as deputy president of the republic and member of the cabinet." Zuma remained deputy president of the ANC.

The delay of 12 days between the conviction of Schabir Shaik and President

a mere seven. The Democratic Alliance, shorn of all connection with the NNP, gathered support as the principal voice of opposition to the ANC; it won 50 seats in the legislature, 12 more than in 1999. Its electoral partner, Chief Buthelezi's IFP, lost representation, dropping from 34 to 28 seats.

With Marthinus van Schalkwyk's self-serving alliance with the ANC, the NNP lost virtually all credibility with voters. They rejected its candidates massively, and the party emerged with nine assembly seats, down from 28 in 1999. The Freedom Front Plus party won support from the NNP's white Afrikaner support base, and Coloured NNP voters in Western Cape fled to the Independent Democrats (ID).

The ID, led by Patricia de Lille, was barely a year old when she left the Pan African Congress during the Assembly floor crossings of early 2003. De Lille's was often the most vigorous voice of critical opposition in the assembly where she combined roles of gadfly and moral conscience to devastating effect. She becomes the first woman to lead a political party in parliament and promises to be the most interesting and provocative of Thabo Mbeki's critics.

The ANC's electoral victory confirmed its conquest of South Africa's political space. It secured a majority in all but two provinces, Western Cape and KwaZulu-Natal. In each it became the dominant party, and having entered each province with a coalition partner, it emerged with a majority in the two provinces that had previously eluded it.

President Mbeki asserted his party's will over its coalition partners with no-compromise. In a display of personal confidence and power, he nominated premiers in all nine of South Africa's provinces. It provided an opportunity for a general housecleaning. ANC replaced incumbents in all but one of the premierships, Mbhazima Shilowa in Gauteng. It was a firm presidential message: the ANC will not tolerate incompetent, corrupt or inefficient

Cape Town harbor development with Table Mountain in the background
Photo by Rita Arendt

South Africa

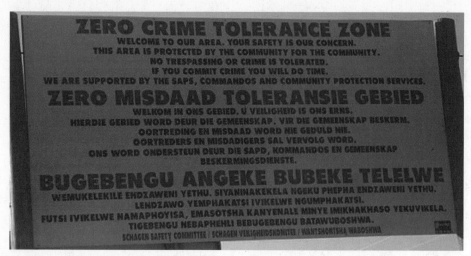

One township declares its opposition to crime.

Photo by Char Glacy

Mbeki's firing of his deputy suggested Zuma did not go easily or willingly. He was widely seen as Mbeki's successor as both the ANC's and the Republic's next president, and he had powerful support within the tripartite alliance, especially among youth groups and labor's left wing. He also remained enormously popular in his native KwaZulu-Natal province. (His father was reportedly a Zulu chief and advisor to the Zulu king.)

The firing of Zuma earned Mbeki much praise from both home and abroad. Opposition leader Tony Leon offered elegant praise for President Mbeki: "He faced a choice between two difficult paths. Each had its political costs. Yet in the end, he chose to uphold principle over politics. By so doing, he has led us to a great victory for our young democracy." *Business Day* delineated a similar profile in courage: "South Africans must be grateful for what Mbeki did. When it can sometimes seem as if S[outh] A[frica] is becoming mired in corruption, its leader acted against the hardest possible target. If that didn't take courage then the word has lost its meaning."

The *Mail and Guardian* moved the commentary from the personal to the political, calling the Zuma affair the country's "gravest post-Apartheid political crisis." It was a crisis that highlighted developing divisions within the ANC, between those who supported President Mbeki's economic liberalism and those who thought Zuma, seen much more as a man of the people, might better return the party to its socialist ideals. Indeed, everything that followed the Zuma sacking seemed to reveal the down and dirty politics of succession, both to the presidency of the ANC (decided in 2007) and to the presidency of the republic (decided in 2009). Zuma is now ANC president.

Byzantine, nasty, and complex, there would be enough intrigue to fill multiple spy novels as contending forces struggled for the soul of the ANC. Numerous hoax e-mails, the use of National Intelligence Agency personnel to spy on opponents, and the mysterious death of a mining magnate, accused of stealing millions, with close ties to the ANC, were the mere tips of the icebergs. When the accuser filed rape charges against Jacob Zuma, his supporters immediately saw it as a plot by Mbeki supporters, and his acquittal in June 2006 gave inspiration to his followers and stimulus to his campaign to become ANC president.

Zuma Corruption Trial and the End of Mbeki

In November 2005, the courts indicted Zuma on two counts of corruption, but the case collapsed when the prosecution was unprepared. Over the next three and a half years, Zuma's lawyers delayed any attempt to secure evidence and move the case ahead. On September 12, 2008, the Courts ruled that the charges against Zuma were invalid because the prosecution had repeatedly followed incorrect procedure. Just over a week later, Mbeki resigned as president of South Africa after pressure from the ANC National Executive Committee, regarding his possible role interference in the trial. On January 12, 2009, the Supreme Court officially overturned the accusations against Mbeki, but his resignation stood.

The interim president was Kgalema Motlanthe, a Zuma crony, who at the time of his appointment to the Presidency served as Deputy President of the ANC.

On April 6, 2009, the National Prosecution Authority (NPA) announced that it dropped all charges of corruption, racketeering, tax evasion, money laundering and fraud against Zuma.

Despite a sentence to serve time through November 2021, Shaik walked out of prison in March 2009. The courts released Shaik on medical parole, a distinction for the terminally ill, expected to die within a rather short period. He only served 28 months of his 15-year sentence. Controversy surrounds his release, for Shaik has not commented to the media any specific explanation of any terminal illness, and most reports indicate that he appears healthy. *The New York Times* wrote an article indicating that Zuma played a role in the release of Shaik.

A poll released at the Davos World Economic Forum in January 2007 showed that 63% of South Africans think their leaders are dishonest.

The 2009 Elections

In April 2009, over 17 million South Africans voted in the national and provincial elections, electing Jacob Zuma the new President of South Africa.

As expected, the ANC overwhelmingly dominated the vote, though they narrowly lost the two-thirds majority they previously held, necessary to amend the constitution. Compared with the 2004 election, the ANC lost 3.79% of the popular vote. The ANC now has 264 of 400 seats in Parliament.

The mostly White Democratic Alliance, led by Cape Town Mayor Helen Zille, increased their contingent in Parliament to 67, after winning 16.66% of the vote.

Following the resignation of Mbeki, defectors from the ANC formed a new party, Congress of the People (COPE), with the aim of creating a viable black-led competitor to end the ANC's quasi-monopolistic dominance of national politics. COPE was founded by former ANC luminaries, namely former ANC Chairman Mosiuoa "Terror" Lekota (who earned his nickname on the football pitch, not the battlefield) and former Premier of Gauteng province Mbhazima "Sam" Shilowa. COPE appointed Bishop Mvume Dandala as their candidate, a man with a squeaky-clean past compared to the controversial Zuma. Though analysts predicted COPE to make a significant impact on the election's playing field, the new party won 7.42% of the vote, taking 30 parliamentary seats.

The Present: Contemporary Issues

By regional standards, and even continental ones, the South African economy is huge. South Africa dwarfs its neighbors and represents as much as 40% of the entire economy of the continent. Nevertheless, the giant is sluggish.

On February 5, 2009, Tito Bowen, governor of South Africa's central bank, predicted that the country would experience "a rough patch or the next three to four years." South Africa's moderate growth over the past several years has stagnated, and its openness to the global economy has made it vulnerable to the worldwide recession.

A March 2002 survey, partially funded by South Africa's Department of Labor and conducted by the Norwegian Institute for Applied Social Science, found 45% of the population is unemployed—much higher than official figures. For youths aged 16 to 25, a 2005 report estimated an employment rate of 52%. Three-fourths of South Africa's unemployed are black Africans, the principal constituency of the ANC. The government estimates that the economy must achieve a minimum of 6% growth to offset unemployment.

South Africa is rich in natural resources, but the mining sector is in decline. It has, for example, the world's largest reserves of manganese (80%), chromium (68%), and platinum-group metals (56%). At least 40% of the world's total recoverable gold reserves are in South Africa.

Even with gold fetching over $600/oz by mid-2006, the industry was facing difficulties. Costs are rising and production is declining. Labor costs keep rising (remaining gold reserves lie deeper and deeper, requiring greater amounts of labor) and worker militancy has cut production through strike action. In August 2005, some 100,000 members of the National Union of Mineworkers put aside their tools. The union demanded a 12% wage hike and rejected the offer of a 4.5%–5% wage increase coupled with bonuses tied to any rise in the domestic price of gold. It was the first industry-wide stoppage in 18 years and cost companies $12 million a day in lost revenue. After four days, the crippling strike ended when the miners accepted a revised offer of 6%–7% wage increases.

As other producers in developing countries have come on line, South Africa's share of world gold production has dropped to 14%, down from 80% in 1970. In 2004, gold production declined by 9%—to 342 tons—the lowest since 1931, and employment in the industry has dropped from 530,000 to just 187,000 in the past decade. Overall, the sector contributes 2% to the country's gross domestic product.

South Africa is the world's fourth largest diamond producer, after Botswana, Russia and Canada, but like gold, this luxury industry experiences difficulty during worldwide recession. Some 13.7 million carats were produced in 2004, but De Beers, the foremost international diamond concern, reported that five of its seven South African operations were loss-making, owing mainly to the strength of the rand. The company, once a virtual cartel, faces stiff competition from Russia. Alrosa, the state diamond company which controls nearly the entire Russian production, plans to increase its output by 20%.

Party	Percentage of Vote	National Assembly Seats Won
African National Congress	65.90	264
Democratic Alliance	16.66	67
Congress of the People	7.42	30
Inkatha Freedom Party	4.55	18
Others	5.47	21
Freedom Front Plus		4
Independent Democrats		4
United Democratic Movement		4
African Christian Democratic Party		3
United Christian Democratic Party		2
Anzanian People's Organization		1
Pan Africanist Congress of Azania		1
Minority Front		1
Total		400

National Assembly Following the April 2009 Election

The government is shaping a new regulatory framework for the mining industry. In 2002, it enacted a law that formally transferred ownership of the country's resources to the state. Henceforth, companies exploiting those resources will have to pay royalties to the government. The initial percentages proposed by the government (around 3%) ran into stiff resistance. Most companies saw the proposed royalties as too high, especially since the government based the royalties on revenues rather than profits. The government and energy firms further negotiated the final wording of its Mining and Petroleum Royalty Bill. The planned royalty tax was to drop to 1% to encourage offshore oil and gas exploration.

The government is also targeting the mining industry in its drive for Black Economic Empowerment (BEE). Part of the government's plans to transform the economy by giving black Africans a significant share of major economic sectors, initial legislative drafts caused panic selling of mining shares in October 2002 when first released. Some shares dropped by 40% when it was learned the government was proposing that 51% of mining assets should be controlled by black South Africans within ten years. Negotiation reduced the amount transferred to black shareholders to 26% of equity by May 2014. As an incentive to the hard-pressed mining industry, empowerment requirements can drop to 16% if the company does enough to promote "benefaction"—increasing worker benefits.

BEE is a central goal of the Mbeki government. By 2014, it would like to see that South Africa's black majority holds major (largely unspecified) stakes in the economy. Whites, about 12% of the population, still control the economy, the mines, banks, factories and farms. Whites own more than 70% of the land and dominate the banking, manufacturing and tourism industries. According to government figures, white-run companies control 95% of the country's diamond production, 63% of platinum reserves and 51% of gold reserves.

As BEE deals have unfolded, however, the Mbeki empowerment model has come under increasing attack as enrichment of a few well-placed black businessmen, which has done little to improve the conditions of average South Africans. In October 2004, Kgalema Motlanthe, who then served as ANC Secretary-General, condemned the program as "narrow based." "It seems," he said, "that certain individuals are not satisfied with a single bout of empowerment. Instead, they are the beneficiaries of repeated bouts of re-empowerment. We see the same names mentioned over and over again in one deal after another." Indeed, Cyril Ramaphosa and Mathews Phosa (a former premier of Mpumalanga province), both members of the ANC's highest decision-making body, the national executive council, have signed numerous empowerment deals, as has Tokyo Sexwale, the former Premier of Gauteng province. Ramaphosa's brother-in-law, Patrice Motsepe, became a very rich man after signing several major empowerment deals in the gold sector worth around $503.4 million. The opposition Democratic Alliance claims that Motsepe and Sexwale were involved in 60% of the $6.4 billion empowerment deals done in

South Africa

Cape Point, the tip of the Cape of Good Hope, where the Indian and Atlantic Oceans meet.
Photo by Connie Abell

on a powder keg," the Nobel laureate said recently. While millions of South Africans live in "grueling, demeaning, dehumanizing poverty," he said, black empowerment "seems to benefit not the vast majority but an elite that tends to be recycled."

Unlike neighboring Angola, South Africa lacks rich oil resources. Coal is the primary fuel produced and consumed in South Africa. Estimates of the nation's recoverable coal reserves, the sixth largest in the world, are around 53.7 billion tons (about 5% of the world reserves). Coal is also the country's second most important foreign exchange earner, after gold, contributing 7% of export earnings.

Production is concentrated in a few regions, with Mpumalanga Province accounting for 83% of total output. South African coal mining produced 268 million (short) tons in 2004, with nearly one-third of total coal production exported—primarily to the European market. The bulk of domestically used coal generates electricity.

According to Interpol, South Africa is the fourth-largest cannabis producer in the world. An estimated 205,000 acres yield 387.2 million pounds of the drug. First introduced into the region some 500 years ago by Arab traders, cannabis (called "dagga" locally) is widely regarded as a traditional crop in many rural areas, particularly the Eastern Cape and KwaZulu-Natal. South African cannabis is some of the most potent in the world. Around a quarter of seizures worldwide involve the South African product. In some rural areas, farms produce up to three crops per year. While the producers are usually subsistence farmers for whom cannabis is a unique cash crop, the U.S. State Department reports that there are more than 100 drug syndicates operating in South Africa.

The current recession has taken its toll on the stability of the South African rand. Because the value of the nation's currency depends so heavily on the prices of gold, platinum, diamonds, and other luxurious commodities traded, the rand fluctuated greatly against the US dollar toward the end of 2008, eventually settling back in June 2009 almost exactly at the same value it held in June 2008.

South Africa now has one of the highest rates of HIV infection and in terms of absolute numbers, the greatest number of HIV-positive people—around 6.3 million—in the world. Unlike Uganda where the rate is dropping, South Africa's keeps rising. The government was slow to recognize the problem and slower to respond.

The statistics are appalling: one in five people is already HIV positive. The national Health Ministry estimates that HIV infects another 1,600 South Africans daily. Five thousand babies are born each month

2003. The benefits to BEE tycoons can be obscene, given the poverty in which most black South Africans live: When Standard Bank chose Saki Macozoma and Cyril Ramaphosa as empowerment partners, the deal netted each man around $30 million. Little wonder Secretary-General Motlanthe suggested the ANC should declare that once an individual had been empowered, he or she should no longer "be regarded as a historically advantaged person," eligible for further empowerment benefits.

Much of the BEE criticism reflects internal ANC politics. Rivals for future party leadership are more than happy to see

Cyril Ramaphosa criticized. Left-wing opponents of the ANC's move to liberal economic policies still press for a rethink on the issue. The COSATU leader, Zwelinzima Vavi, has threatened to obstruct a pending $18.6 billion deal in the finance sector to bring in more black partners. It will only help; he says "a narrow group of individuals . . . already rich through transactions of this type." The banks, he argues, should use their cash to build houses for poor blacks, fund small black businesses, and subsidize black farms. A similar line of criticism has also come from Desmond Tutu, increasingly the regime's moral conscience. "We are sitting

infected with HIV. Patients with AIDS-related infections already occupy 70% of South African hospital beds. There were 360,000 AIDS deaths in 2001 alone, and in 2006, 1000 persons a day were dying of the disease. As parents die, an estimated 700,000 children will become AIDS orphans by 2010. In February 2005, the government released statistics showing annual deaths in the country had risen 57% from 1997 to 2003, with common AIDS-related diseases like tuberculosis and pneumonia fueling much of the increase. The mortality spike was greatest in the 15 to 49 age category.

The impact on population growth will be significant. In 2015, South Africa's population will only reach 49 million, instead of 61 million—one-fifth less than earlier predicted because of AIDS. Life expectancy will decline accordingly. By 2010, it could be as low as 33 years in provinces like KwaZulu-Natal, which has one of the highest numbers of HIV/AIDS cases in the country. With more than 60% of new infections occurring in people 15 to 25 years old, the pandemic is expected to wipe out large segments of the very people who are needed to fight it—teachers, health professionals and government workers.

Until subjected to a court order, the government refused to employ vaccines known to reduce the incidence of mother to child transmission of the HIV virus. In December 2001, the Pretoria High Court ordered the government to provide antiretrovirals (ARVs) to all HIV-positive pregnant women. Treatment Action Campaign (TAC), a militant AIDS lobby group, brought the case that has significantly ratcheted up techniques of public embarrassment for a foot-dragging regime. The Constitutional Court rejected the government's appeal in April, saying the government was violating the constitutional rights of women and their babies by not supplying Nevirapine, a drug by now long proved to reduce mother-to-child HIV transmission.

At an international conference in July 2002, South Africa's health minister, Dr. Manto Tshabala-Msimang, said on record that the antiretrovirals were "poisons" killing "our people." She had also once suggested that those infected with HIV should eat beetroot and garlic.

When parliament reopened in February 2003 and the government had not yet signed on to an AIDS treatment and prevention plan, advocacy groups descended on it in protest. TAC volunteers occupied government ministries and defied police to arrest them. By April 2003 TAC protesters had taken their cause international, demonstrating outside South Africa's diplomatic missions abroad to demand the government supply antiretroviral drugs to

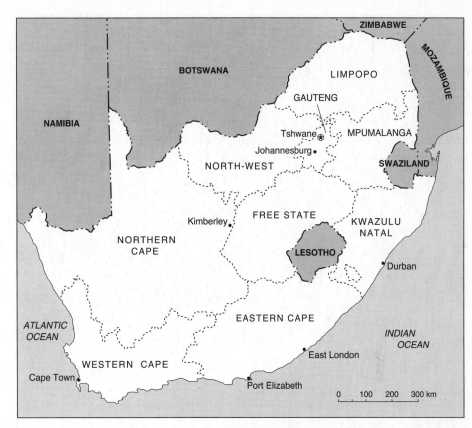

Provinces of South Africa

AIDS sufferers. Finance Minister Trevor Manuel announced in February 2004 that the government allocated an additional $305 million to fighting HIV/AIDS over the next three years, but it was not until two weeks before the April 2004 elections that the drugs began to appear. By the end of 2004, the World Health Organization estimated that 837,000 South Africans urgently needed antiretroviral drugs, but only 78,000 received them through government programs. By November of that year, the government had already spent $6.3 million on the legal costs of defending the government's policy against activists in the courts.

Government delay on HIV/AIDS is directly attributable to President Mbeki himself. He has criticized ARVs for both their costs and their toxicity, a notion picked up from his reading of the scientific dissidents, those who refuse to admit a relationship between HIV and AIDS. His attitude only worsened the situation, for while his government delayed, people died and infections increased.

The currently accepted fashion is to describe President Mbeki's views on HIV/AIDS as "unorthodox." They go well beyond that, suggesting at times the kind of paranoia that has led to acceptance of "conspiracy" accusations in other areas. In October 2000, for example, he told a

gathering of ANC officials that the CIA was part of a "conspiracy to promote the view that HIV causes AIDS."

According to South Africa's *Mail and Guardian* newspaper, Mbeki told the group the CIA was also working with big U.S. pharmaceutical manufacturers to undermine him. The reason for this, he explained, was the fear that his questioning of the HIV/AIDS link would lead to reduced profits in the sale of antiretroviral treatments.

President Mbeki reappointed his fellow AIDS obstructionist, Dr. Manto Tshabala-Msimang—"Dr. No" to AIDS activists—as health minister in April 2004. From that position she continued to urge people to follow a more healthful diet—lots of garlic and beetroot. Both Mbeki and Tshabala-Msimang came in for withering criticism from Kofi Annan's special envoy to Africa on AIDS, Stephen Lewis. In late 2005, Mr. Lewis published *Race Against Time* (Toronto: House of Anansi Press) a compilation of his lectures delivered as a private citizen. In the book, Mr. Lewis, a Canadian, singled out the South African government and its president for what he called "bewildering policies and a lackadaisical approach to treatment of the nation's HIV-positive citizens."

If Desmond Tutu thought the 2006 rape trial of Jacob Zuma was a disaster for

South Africa

The coastline near Cape Peninsula

South African democracy, for the country's AIDS activists it was worse. On the witness stand Zuma, who had headed the National AIDS Council when he was South Africa's deputy president, told the court he "took a shower" immediately after having sex with his HIV-positive accuser to "cut the risk of contracting HIV." TAC campaigners called the comments "ill-informed" and noted that there was no evidence that supported the idea that showers reduced the risk of HIV infection.

Proof of the disastrous consequences of misinformation came from the ANC's national health secretary, Dr. Saadiq Kariem, who admitted his concern that young people were misinterpreting Zuma's prevention claims. Following the trial, Kariem said, he had fielded calls from "ANC comrades enquiring whether a shower cap could help get rid of HIV." For her part, health minister Tshabala-Msimang un-

helpfully accused the press of misleading the public by publicizing Zuma's comments. In his final judgment, Justice Willem van der Merwe pointedly called Zuma's failure to use a condom with a woman whom he knew to be HIV-positive "inexcusable." For his part, the ANC president sought redemption through apology. Going on national radio after the courts acquitted him of rape, the 64-year-old Zuma apologized to the nation for having unprotected sex with an HIV-positive woman. "I should have been more cautious and more responsible," he told his interviewer. "I erred on this issue and on this, I apologize."

With Health Minister Manto Tshabala-Msimang sidelined with serious health concerns (she would ultimately undergo a liver transplant), the government finally formulated a major policy shift and announced it in March 2007. The five-year (2007–2011)

National Strategic Plan (NSP) marks a watershed in government thinking. ARVs are now a central tool in fighting HIV/AIDS, and the plan envisions a five-fold increase in the number of HIV-positive people receiving the drugs by 2011.

NSP's primary goal is to reduce new HIV infections by 50%. One means to that end is another key target of the plan: ensuring that 70% of all adults have an HIV test at least once in their lifetime. Ambitiously, the plan calls for 95% of pregnant women to take HIV tests by 2011, and HIV tests for 90% of their babies at six weeks. For those already afflicted, NSP aims to get antiretroviral medicines to 80% of the adults who need them; only 24% of those in advanced stages of the illness were receiving ARVs by mid-2006. The plan could cost up to $6.2 billion, but delivery, not cost, may be a more difficult problem to overcome.

South Africa experiences a critical shortage of healthcare workers, especially in rural areas. A recent report by the French chapter of Doctors Without Borders concluded the country (and its neighbors) could not contain the disease without an increase in the number of doctors, nurses and medical assistants available. South African health officials are enlisting traditional healers, called *sangomas*, to detect signs of HIV and persuade their patients take HIV tests and ARVs.

A recent issue in South Africa is the influx of Zimbabwean refugees fleeing their home country. The collapse of Zimbabwe (for which the South African government itself takes considerable blame as the one country that had the leverage to stop President Robert Mugabe) has generated social difficulties in South Africa. This has resulted in xenophobic attacks on the refugees in South Africa's cities.

The Future

The world will turn to South Africa in 2010 as the country hosts the FIFA World Cup. The government has been spending generously—over two trillion rand, or $258 billion—on infrastructure and social services, to ensure a successful games. The 2009 Confederations Cup, a trial run of sorts for the actual event, was by most accounts a success, but critics contend that the event lacked the influx of tourists expected with the World Cup. With a year to go, most of the host cities still lack clean, safe mass transport that most soccer fans will be expecting. The success or failure of the World Cup will likely determine the trajectory of South Africa in the global economy.

As violent crime continues, many of the mostly white educated elite are leaving the country. This "White Flight" is leading to a "Brain Drain," leaving many areas without doctors, lawyers, engineers, and other necessary professionals. Early demographic studies reveal that the whites are not the only people leaving the country; educated blacks are also leaving in droves.

In May and June 2008, xenophobic violent attacks against refugees from Zimbabwe and other nations in sub-Saharan African made headlines worldwide. With already high levels of unemployment, many South African natives viewed the refugees as "leeches" who would only contribute to problem. Though as of June 2009 the violent xenophobic attacks have mostly ceased, anti-immigrant sentiment remains high.

The ANC remains South Africa's dominant political party. Zuma's presidency thus far has surprised critics, for his appointments and actions have not been particularly radical. Zuma moved the highly respected Finance Minister Trevor Manuel from his previous post to be head of a new national planning commission, from which Zuma claims Manuel will have more power.

The future of South Africa may come down to how the government handles the HIV/AIDS epidemic going forward. While it is already too late for many millions of South Africans, it remains crucial to address the problem with aggressive measures. Failure in this area could turn Africa's greatest triumph of the 1990s into its greatest tragedy in the 21st century, by literally destroying the population; conversely, stopping the epidemic could enable South Africa to remain the motor for much of the continent's development.

Three rondavels, Blyde River Canyon, Mpumalanga

Photo by Nancy Sprotte

The Kingdom of Swaziland

King Mswati III

Basic Facts

Area: 17,364 sq. km. = 6,705 sq. mi. (about the size of Hawaii)

Population: 1,100,000 (UN 2007 est.)

Capital Cities: Mbabane (administrative); Lobamba (legislative).

Climate: Temperate, with chilly nights during the winter months.

Neighboring Countries: Mozambique (northeast); Republic of South Africa (north, west, south).

Official Languages: siSwati, English

Other Principal Languages: Zulu, Afrikaans

Ethnic Groups: Swazi, a small number of other Bantu groups; European

Principal Religions: Christian 60%, indigenous beliefs 40%

Chief Commercial Products: Sugar asbestos, wood and forest products, citrus, cotton, iron ore

GNI Per Capita: $2,280 (World Bank 2006 est.)

Currency: emalangeni (at par with the South African rand)

Former Colonial Status: Under South African protection (1894–1906); British Protectorate (1906–1968)

Chief of State: King Mswati III (b. 1966)

Independence Date: September 6, 1968

National Flag: Horizontal stripes of dark blue, red and dark blue, divided by thin yellow bands. A shield and spear design is in the center of the red stripe.

Land and People

High plateaus and forested mountains are found in western Swaziland, gradually descending from a maximum of 4,500 feet to a central region of an average height of 2,800 feet. These highlands give way to a lowland in the east, and the Lubombo Mountains rise at the eastern-most border. The temperate climate is warm enough to permit large quantities of sugar cane to grow, but at the same time it is ideally suited for forest growth of excellent hardwoods.

About 80% of Swazis live as peasant farmers on Swazi national land, "king's land," distributed through local chiefs. Deeply conservative, rural Swazis are fully aware that had not foreign ideologies been resisted by kings past, there would be no Swazi nation today. Modern urbanites talking of human rights and democracy are in many ways out of touch with Swazi reality.

The king, by custom the father of all his subjects and the embodiment of the nation, has stated that he would never recognize "anyone who comes to me saying he represents other Swazis." It's a statement that dramatizes the tensions between tradition and modernity that bedevil the kingdom.

The Past: Political and Economic History

For early history, see *Historical Background* and *The Colonial Period: The British.*

The British granted independence to Swaziland on September 6, 1968, which was done in formal ceremonies in Mbabane. Many foreign representatives were present, along with King Sobhuza's 112 wives.

All 24 seats of the National Assembly were held initially by King Sobhuza's National Movement. Reigning since 1921 until his death in 1982, he was the world's oldest ruling monarch. Elections in 1972 reduced the party to 21 seats; Dr. Ambrose Zwane's National Liberatory Congress Party won three seats and six additional members were appointed by the king. Within weeks the king abolished the constitution, dismissed the Assembly, and announced he would rule the old-fashioned way—by decree. Later, in 1979, a new bicameral parliament was opened consisting of a 50-member lower house and a 20-member upper house. Ten of each were chosen directly by the king.

King Sobhuza died in August 1982. Intrigue and plotting among the wives and 70 sons of the dead monarch began before he was buried. The struggles revolved around (1) The queen regent, (2) the *Liqoqo* (National Council), (3) the "Authorized Person" (4) the prime minister and (5) the House of Assembly and the Senate.

The young crown prince, the second–youngest son (and 67th child) of the late king, studied in Britain until 1986, when he reached the age of 18; his coronation was held on April 25, 1986. The young king quickly moved to assert his power, reshuffling the cabinet, dismissing the *Liqoqo*, and replacing the prime minister.

The Swazi king is Africa's last absolute monarch. While the country has a bicameral legislature, the king appoints a number of its members, has the power to dissolve it, and can rule by decree. Political parties have been banned in Swaziland since 1973, and it is the king who appoints the cabinet.

Legislative elections were held in September and October 1998. As a result of the ban on political parties, parliamentary candidates emerged through the three-tiered *Tinkundla* system. Tinkundlas, or traditional assemblies, nominate candidates—generally conservative and loyal to the king—in all the chiefdoms of Swaziland. These hopefuls are pared down in primary elections, with the remaining candidates vying in secondaries for 55 seats in the House of Assembly. Candidates run as individuals and cannot run on a party platform. The king appoints a further ten members of the Assembly.

From the Assembly, the king appoints his government, the cabinet. In 1998 King Mswati III reappointed his prime minister, Sibususo Dlamini. Of the 16 members of the cabinet, only three had been elected. All the others had been appointed to the Assembly by the king. Electoral accountability is irrelevant in an absolute monarchy.

The Swazi senate has 30 members, none of whom is directly elected. Twenty members are royal appointees. The remaining ten are selected by the Assembly. The whole system is designed to keep the king and his relatives in positions of power.

The Swaziland Federation of Trade Unions (SFTU) and the unofficial opposition, the Swaziland Democratic Alliance, are the most vocal opponents of Swaziland's absolute monarchy. With their leadership subject to arrest and intimidation, however, the groups have not yet been able to turn the monarchy to a more open and pluralist political system.

The SFTU did pressure authorities to create a commission on a new constitution in 1994, after a series of strikes and firebombs of unknown origin, but royalists and traditionalists made up the bulk of committee members. Actual work did not begin until 1996, and the commission was to have completed its work in 1998, but the king, finding it easier to rule by decree, postponed the commission's deadline indefinitely.

In December 2001, the hearings having concluded, Mswati appointed a constitutional drafting committee and ordered it to complete work within the next 18 months. By May 2003 the drafting process had still not been completed. Pressure built up, and Mswati announced in March 2004 that the country would have a constitution by the end of the year.

A traditional "Peoples Parliament" was summoned in September at the royal cattle kraal to discuss the constitutional drafts, and the king announced that all debate must end, including parliament's review and passage, by mid-November. The calendar was strictly followed; the Senate approved the document in mid-November, completing the process, but there was still more palaver and dithering to come as Mswati objected to certain provisions regarding the taxation of his family and the place of Christianity as an official religion.

King Mswati did not sign the document—164 pages long—until July 2005 after the changes he sought had been made. The whole process had taken ten years (1966–2006) and cost millions. The new constitution affirmed the king's absolute authority—over the legislature, security forces, and other institutions of government. The ban on political parties, in force for over 30 years, was retained. In one notable concession to democratic participation, the constitution allowed for the popular recall of members of parliament. It also made a break from tradition by declaring "Women have the right to equal treatment with men, including equal opportunities in political, economic and social activities."

In recent years Swazi absolutism has lurched from crisis to crisis, and from one public relations disaster to another. In November 2002 the prime minister said the government would ignore a Court of Appeal ruling that denied the king's power to issue laws by decree. A second decision by the court was also rejected, provoking a rule-of-law crisis: All six South African judges (on loan to Swaziland) who make up the Court of Appeal—the country's highest court—resigned to protest the government's decision to ignore their rulings.

The king found himself the object of legal action when the mother of a teenager he had chosen to be his tenth wife sued for the return of her daughter. The attorney general went to the judge hearing the case and threatened to have him fired if he did not drop the case. The judge refused and soon resigned, presumably under great pressure.

Even Swaziland's parliament, filled with royal relatives, decided to resist the king. It refused to approve purchase of a $48 million luxury plane for his majesty, proving once again how much easier it is to rule by decree. The debate was intense, and one MP (Marwick Khumalo, the king's cousin) noted the kingdom could ill-afford such extravagance while 140,000 of the king's one million subjects were currently starving.

In political parlance, Mswati II is tone deaf. While his countrymen faced drought-induced starvation, the king asked parliament for money to build palaces for his 11 wives in January 2004. The request amounted to $15 million—almost as much as the country's 2002 health budget. Two more wives have since been added to the royal seraglio.

In April 2004, the king celebrated his 36th birthday with a profligate expenditure of more than $612,000. Ten thousand guests gathered in the national football stadium to devour a portion of the national treasury. Included in the festivity's costs were ten new BMWs. By December, these proved insufficient to royal need, and the king purchased a luxury vehicle for a princely half million dollars. Among the car's creature comforts: a TV receiver, 21-speaker surround sound system, refrigerator, telephone, heated steering wheel, interior pollen and dust filter, golf bag and silver champagne flutes. Pictures of the vehicle have been prohibited, by royal decree.

Little changes in traditional Swaziland, except royal profligacy in the face of popular suffering. Mswati's birthday expenses in 2007 were well over two million dollars. Elsewhere in the kingdom Swazi farmers were overwhelmed by natural disaster. Poor rains at the beginning of the year, followed by freak hail storms, destroyed the year's maize crop; food rationing had to be introduced and nearly 300,000 Swazis were living on food rations from the donor community.

Political activists decry both royal profligacy and the new constitution, but seem to gain little traction in a situation where survival is more important than politics to most people. The banned Peoples United Democratic Movement (PUDEMO) has already announced its refusal to participate in next year's legislative elections because only independent candidates (not party-affiliated candidates) will be allowed.

A spokesman for PUDEMO's even more radical youth wing, the Swaziland Youth Congress (Swayoco), has declared 2008 "the year of liberation." In early February 2007 Swayoco's secretary-general, Mamba Mduduzi, was quoted as saying the future role of the monarchy would be decided in either of two ways: "the monarchy will call us in to some negotiations or the monarchy is pushed to abdicate through mass insurrection."

The conflict between government and PUDEMO took on a more sinister tone in 2008 as a bomb attack occurred near a royal palace in September, the same month in which elections were held, without parties permitted. (The King again appointed former Sibususo Dlamini to the post of Prime Minister, to which the SFTU and PUDEMO objected.) The authorities detained and held PUDEMO leader Mario Masuku for questioning regarding the incident.

The Present: Contemporary Issues

Swaziland has the dubious distinction of the world's highest adult HIV/AIDS infection rate, but there are signs the epidemic may be leveling off. From 42.6% of the adult population in 2004, HIV prevalence dropped to 39.2% in 2006. Campaigns to change male sexual behavior seem to have had some impact; more men are using condoms and more are seeking circumcision. Still, the consequences of the disease are devastating. At least five skilled workers in Swaziland's manufacturing sector die weekly, and the death of farm laborers and bread-winners has exacerbated the nation's food shortage. There are some 80,000 AIDS orphans in the country and 10% of all Swazi households are headed by children. A decade ago life expectancy was 61. Now it is just 41.5 (2005).

King Mswati III has declared HIV/AIDS a "national disaster," but enlightenment on the subject is not necessarily found among his advisors. One described HIV/AIDS sufferers as "bad potatoes"

An Outdoor Laundry   Photo by Rita Arendt

Swaziland

and said they must be removed from society lest "all will go rotten." His solution was an isolation camp for victims of the disease. Since HIV testing is not mandatory, most Swazis do not even know they are infected.

Swaziland's economy has been anemic for years, with a growth rate hovering around 2%. In 2001, however, real economic growth slumped to 1.5%—an all-time low. In 2005 it was an unimpressive 2.1%, and again dropped in 2006 to 1.8%. Worse, the country's population grew by 2.9%, pushing even more Swazi well below the poverty line. About 70% of the population lives on two dollars a day or less.

A major contributing factor the country's economic malaise is a continuing drop in agricultural productivity, compounded by drought. Seventy percent of Swazis earn their living from agriculture, but the sector's contribution to the national economy has dropped from 10.6% in 1999 to 8.6% in 2005. The prospects for Swazi agriculture are not promising.

One relative bright spot in the agriculture sector, until recently, had been Swaziland's principal export, sugar. The country is one of the world's lowest cost producers of sugar, and the industry has been its biggest employer, creating an annual turnover of $1.5 billion and generating more than $637 million in export revenues. Swaziland's sugar belt runs through the areas most affected by drought, however, and prevailing weather conditions have reduced production.

The whole industry has been artificially subsidized by the European Union, which purchased an annual quota for more than the international market price for sugar. The EU slashed its subsidy price by 36% beginning in 2007, and the Swaziland Sugar Association expected to lose $3.8 million annually between 2006 and 2008. The loss is expected to increase to $12.5 million in 2008/2009.

Because cotton requires little water, unlike sugar, the government has contemplated resuscitation of local cotton production as a cash crop. Some 16,000 farmers were growing the crop in the 1990s, but by 2004, that number had dropped to 4,500. Ideally, any increased production was to be bought by the textile factories that opened as a consequence of America's African Growth and Opportunities Act (AGOA).

Built largely by Taiwanese interests to take advantage of special benefits for Swazi manufactures offered by AGOA, the factories added some 28,000 new jobs to the Swazi economy. With the removal of import quotas on textiles as of January 2005, under terms of the Agreement on Textiles and Clothing (ATC), even this bright spot has dimmed. When ATC eliminated all quota restrictions on clothing worldwide, manufacturers found it more cost effective to move their operations to China and India, abandoning their Swazi workers. Eighteen of the country's 31 textile companies shut their doors by the end of 2005; industry employment halved in the same period, from 31,000 in June 2004 to 15,000.

The Swazi economy is highly dependent on neighboring South Africa, which surrounds it on three sides. Its currency is pegged to the South African rand; all its oil is imported from South Africa, as is nearly all its electricity and 85% of its consumer goods.

Fifty percent of government revenue currently comes from customs receipts from the Southern African Customs Union (SACU), but these will be lost when the union is dissolved as part of a larger regional trade reform. To compensate for the loss, the government has embarked on an ambitious program to develop transportation and tourism. A new international airport, international conference center, new highways, luxury hotels, an industrial park and an amusement park, were launched in mid-2000 as part of King Mswati's Millennium Projects initiative.

Swaziland's mountainous northern region is one of Southern Africa's prime marijuana (or "dagga" as it is known locally) growing areas. "Swazi Gold" is internationally known for its potency and has been a real money earner for Swazi farmers. The advantages of the crop are obvious: a ten-kilogram bag of maize can be sold for $11; a ten-kilogram bag of dagga can be sold for $405. International crime syndicates provide what elsewhere might be called "agricultural extension services" to fund and organize large-scale production.

The Future

Swaziland's future looks worse even than many of its African neighbors. The HIV/AIDS epidemic is a tragedy and an economic catastrophe. It is little surprise that the country's economy was estimated to have grown only about 1.6% in 2007, better only than a handful of states in Africa (some of which are conflict-ridden, such as Chad and Zimbabwe). The country will continue to rely on its South African and Mozambican neighbors for its markets and economic opportunities.

Politically, the situation seems little better. Even for a deeply traditional society, the Swazi absolute monarchy seems antiquated with its ostentatious and polygamous monarch. King Mswati has a royalist following, but is deeply unpopular with the other main political organizations in the country, the banned party PUDEMO and the SFTU trade unions. Declining economic conditions are likely only to exacerbate further the political tensions in the country.

Moving sugar cane from field to factory

©Mujahid Safodien/IRIN

The Republic of Zambia

Victoria Falls

Photo by Joe Joyner

Basic Facts

Area: 745,920 sq. km. = 288,000 sq. mi. (The size of Nebraska, South Dakota, Iowa and Minnesota combined.)

Population: 11,900,000 (UN 2007 est.)

Capital City: Lusaka

Climate: Temperate, because of its altitude, although Zambia lies close to the Equator. There is a wet season (October–April) and a dry season (May–September).

Neighboring Countries: Angola (west); Congo-Kinshasa (northwest); Tanzania (northeast); Malawi (east); Mozambique (southeast); Zimbabwe and Botswana (south)

Official Language: English

Other Principal Languages: Over 30, including Bemba, Kaonde, Lamba, Lozi, Lunda, Luvale, Mwanga, Nsenga, Nyanja Nyiha, Tonga, and Tumbuka

Ethnic Groups: African 98.7%, European 1.1%, other 0.2%

Principal Religions: Christian 50%–75%, Muslim and Hindu 24%–49%, indigenous beliefs 1%

Chief Commercial Products: Copper, cobalt, zinc, lead, and tobacco

GNI Per Capita: $490 (World Bank 2006 est.)

Currency: 1 Zambian Kwacha (ZK) = 100 ngwee

Former Colonial Status: British South Africa Company administration (1895–1923); British Colony (1924–1964)

Independence Date: October 24, 1964

Chief of State: Rupiah Banda, President (since November 2, 2009, previously interim president from August 19, 2009)

National Flag: Green, with an orange eagle in flight over a square block of three vertical stripes, red, black and red, on the right side.

Land and People

The Republic of Zambia is located in south-central Africa, stretching 750 miles west from the mountains of the great Western Rift. This is a high plateau country with an average elevation of 3,500 feet above sea level, which modifies its otherwise equatorial climate. It is only in the low river valleys that any oppressive heat and humidity are encountered.

The gently rolling country alternates between the waving grasses of the plains and forests of widely spaced trees. Great numbers of wildlife are supported by the vegetation, which grows rapidly during the rainy season of the year. The country is drained by two major river systems: the tributaries flowing north to the Congo River, and the Zambezi River, which flows southeast through Mozambique to the Indian Ocean. One of the greatest sheets of flowing water in the world is found at incomparable Victoria Falls, near Livingstone in the south. Swampy Lake Banguelu spreads its great width in the north-central part of the country; the deep blue sparkling waters of Lake Mweru and Lake Tanganyika are found in the North.

Zambians tend to be conservative and closely knit within their communities—the majority are Christian, particularly in the more densely populated south and west, but many in the rural section of the north retain their traditional beliefs.

The Past: Political and Economic History

For early history, see *Historical Background* and *The Colonial Period: The British*.

Northern Rhodesia became fully independent in 1964, taking the name Zambia from the Zambezi River. A republican form of government was established with a single legislative house initially composed of 75 members, but later increased in size. Until 1969, ten seats were reserved for white voters. The president is chosen by direct election; Kenneth Kaunda was selected as the first president in 1964.

Initially there were two major parties—the United National Independence Party (UNIP), led by Kaunda and the African National Congress (ANC), led by Harry Nkumbula (who died in 1984 in neighboring Zimbabwe). After winning a large majority in 1968, Kaunda abolished the opposition party in the name of "national unity."

Racial, religious and tribal frictions have been frequent in Zambia since independence. Political repression added to dissatisfaction with Kaunda by many. Massive nationalization of every major enterprise was started in late 1970, and state-owned and managed businesses and marketing facilities were instituted. Because of poor planning and lack of technical skills, the economy, particularly in the agricultural sector, suffered.

In the early 1970s, Kaunda silenced all organized political opposition. Zambia was officially made a one-party state, with UNIP the sole party. The Assembly was dissolved in 1973 and new elections were set. A "primary" election was first held; before a successful candidate could run in the general election he had to have the approval of the UNIP Central Committee; several who won in the primary were eliminated in this way. Twenty other candidates were announced as "official candidates" of the party, insuring their election.

To receive desperately needed funds from the International Monetary Fund and the World Bank, austerity programs were instituted in the 1980s. Unpopular, they failed to improve economic conditions. Zambia broke with the IMF in May 1987 and decreed that only 10% of its export earnings would be used to repay and service external debt. External assistance was frozen just as the country was again gripped by drought.

Unopposed, President Kaunda was reelected to a sixth five-year term in 1988. Voter turnout was substantially lower than in prior elections, indicating increasing dissatisfaction with the regime.

By 1990 pressures for change peaked. UNIP continued to endorse the single-party system, but increased food prices provoked riots and an attempted coup. Bowing to intense dissatisfaction, President Kaunda announced multiparty elections would be permitted.

On October 31, 1991, Zambians voted in the first multiparty elections in 23 years. The campaign was hard-fought. Kaunda was accused of being out of touch with

Zambia

the people and failing to control an economy that had produced an annual inflation rate of 400%. His opponent, Frederick Chiluba, a labor leader and head of the Movement for Multiparty Democracy (MMD), stressed the need to eliminate nearly universal corruption and theft in the government.

Kaunda, who had been in power for 27 years, was soundly defeated. Chiluba's MMD gained 125 of the 150 legislative seats. During his first term President Chiluba managed to reverse socialist policy: 140 state-owned, unprofitable industries were privatized. The government monopoly on foodstuffs was ended, resulting in higher prices for commodities, but the country's high external debt was lowered by $2 billion.

Old problems—inflation and currency devaluation—continued. Bureaucratic corruption was notorious. As November 1996 elections drew near, it became apparent that Kenneth Kaunda ("KK") would attempt a comeback. To prevent this, President Chiluba pushed through two constitutional amendments specifically designed to eliminate Kaunda. The first required that both parents of a candidate be Zambian. (Kaunda's parents were both from Malawi.) The second removed the requirement that a candidate win more than half the ballots to be declared president, making it possible to be elected president with a plurality of votes. Furious but helpless, Kaunda's followers boycotted the election.

With only 40% of registered voters turning out, Chiluba and his Movement for Multiparty Democracy won, gaining 131 seats in the legislature. Kaunda threatened continued civil disobedience and strikes, but was muted by a threat of criminal prosecution.

President Chiluba, elected to office as a reformer and committed to term limits, spent most of 2000 and 2001 seeking ways

to secure himself a third term. Teams of lawyers and parliamentarians were sent to Namibia to see how it had been done there. MMD members were prohibited from announcing candidacy for the 2001 elections, and when one cabinet member, Ben Mwila, violated the edict, he was summarily dismissed.

Chiluba coyly refrained from expressing any public desire for a third term, but everywhere his minions busily pursued the president's ambition. It was an aspiration that divided cabinet, party, and country. Those who opposed a third term were ruthlessly dispatched. Political frustration was ventilated in the streets. Violent protests erupted, and police had to intervene with tear gas. Finally, the president listened. In early May 2001 he announced that he would not seek a third term.

Thwarted but undaunted, Chiluba handpicked his successor, plucking a former vice president, Levy Mwanawasa, out of political retirement to be the MMD presidential candidate. (Mwanawasa had switched parties to join the MMD only a day before his appointment, angering MMD heavyweights who sought the job for themselves.) One of Zambia's leading lawyers, Mwanawasa had once served as solicitor general under Kenneth Kaunda and had been the first MMD vice president in 1991. He resigned the office in 1994, criticizing the MMD's tolerance of corruption and drug trafficking and gaining a reputation as a man of integrity. It was something President Chiluba and the MMD sorely needed, but the way candidate Mwanawasa had been chosen made it appear he was little more than Chiluba's puppet.

The December 2001 presidential and parliamentary elections were overtly rigged by the Chiluba government; the EU's chief official observer described the results as both untrue and unreliable. The Electoral Commission of Zambia (ECZ) nevertheless declared the MMD's Levy Mwanawasa the victor after he won 28% of the ballots against Anderson Mazoka, the outgoing head of the Anglo-American Corporation's East African operations who had only recently founded the United Party for National Development (UPND). As a political newcomer, Anderson received a remarkable 27% of the vote. Nine other candidates split the remaining votes.

In parliamentary elections the MMD won 66 seats in the 158-member National Assembly. UNIP won 11 seats, while the Forum for Democracy and Development (FDD) took nine and the Heritage Party four. The remaining seats were attributed to minor parties.

The opposition quickly launched a series of legal challenges to the elections with Zambia's Supreme Court. The court

annulled results in four district elections and stripped the MMD of its deputies, reducing the president's majority in parliament to a slender three votes. Mwanawasa said he would resign as president if the court invalidated the election results, but that proved unnecessary when the court finally rejected the opposition challenge in February 2005. Voting was flawed, it said, but the errors did not affect the final result.

Elected by the slimmest of margins, President Mwanawasa gained some popularity by a vigorous anticorruption campaign. He appointed a special task force to investigate and prosecute corrupt officials, and the biggest fish netted thus far have been ex-President Chiluba and numerous officials from his regime. The task force identified office buildings and houses which the suspects owned in Britain, Belgium and other countries and announced it planned to seize those believed to have been purchased with state funds.

Because public monies had been used to acquire assets in Britain, Zambia's attorney general lodged a civil suit against Chiluba and four of his associates in a London High Court. In May 2007 the judge found Chiluba and company had conspired to misappropriate around $46 million from Zambia's coffers. The money went to purchase property and luxury items ranging from motorcycles to jewelry. The judge somewhat caustically noted that Chiluba, who earned about $105,000 in salary over ten years, managed to pay an exclusive men's shop in Geneva $1.2 million. Of that, $500,000 was spent on clothes for Chiluba. Much to the consternation of the former president, the Zambian government had seized a full warehouse of wardrobe items: 349 shirts, many of them with the presidential monogram; 206 jackets and suits; and 72 pairs of shoes, many handmade in Switzerland with special high heels to help raise his

Former President Levy Mwanawasa

stature, physically at least. None of the defendants appeared in court, refusing to recognize its jurisdiction.

The indictment of ex-President Chiluba deeply divided the MMD, weakening President Mwanawasa's base of support, particularly in the north. To balance this loss the president reshuffled his cabinet, bringing in politicians from traditional opposition areas in the south. The new cabinet (besides expanding significantly) broadened ethnic and regional representation in the government, and threw the opposition into disarray as members crossed the aisle to join the government benches.

Since taking office President Mwanawasa has been hammered from every side. Ex-President Chiluba, determined to play the spoiler, backed the formation of a new party (the Party for Unity, Democracy and Development with its somewhat infelicitous acronym PUDD), which helped erode Mwanawasa's support in the MMD. Mwanawasa has also had to fire two vice presidents and face impeachment proceedings.

He survived the impeachment threat, but then had to face paralyzing strikes by government workers. The IMF withheld $100 million in aid when the government could not stanch budgetary hemorrhaging. Western donors followed suit, leaving the government with nothing to offer its angry workers but future installment payments.

The government was under enormous pressure to get its financial house in order. Budgetary deficits prevented Zambia from moving forward in the Highly Indebted Poor Countries initiative (HIPC), a program designed to reduce its crippling debt service costs. The impact on social services was devastating: in 2004, for example, it spent $156 million more on debt repayment than it did on education.

An austerity budget was presented in February 2004. The government promised to increase revenues by increasing taxes and to cut costs by freezing the salaries of public employees, a move that set off immediate protests. The political gamble paid off. By early 2005 Zambia attained the HIPC completion point, and in April the World Bank approved a $3.8 billion debt relief package. A few months later, the world's richest countries, collectively called the G-8, agreed to cancel the multilateral debt of 19 of the worlds poorest, Zambia included. About 95% of the country's $7 billion external debt disappeared by the end of 2006.

Civil society NGOs and opposition groups have called for a new constitution. In response, President Mwanawasa appointed a Constitutional Review Committee in 2002, and it reported out a draft in August 2005. Among its principal recommendations: presidential election by 50% plus one, the vice president elected as the running mate of the presidential candidate, and elimination of the controversial Chiluba-instigated amendment requiring both parents of a presidential candidate be of Zambian birth.

Government, opposition, and civil society remained at an impasse as to what the new text should say, how it should be adopted, and when it should be implemented. The Oasis Forum, an umbrella group composed largely of lawyers and church bodies, demanded a constituent assembly be summoned to approve a new text before the 2006 general elections. President Mwanawasa said "No," the 2006 elections would be held under the existing constitution. Time favored the president.

Controlling the electoral calendar, Mwanawasa set the elections for late September, giving his opponents a relatively short time to campaign. He went into the elections with a strong record of economic accomplishment: GDP growth was a solid 5.1%; inflation had dropped to 8% from 30% in 2001, and international lenders had agreed to write off a large chunk of Zambia's foreign debt to reward "good economic management." With surging commodity prices, export earnings had grown and once-closed copper mines had been reopened.

It was a record more appreciated abroad than at home. The practical benefits had yet to seep down to the average Zambian, and the president's opponents exploited the disconnect between statistics and life reality. His most formidable rival was the fiery populist, Michael Sata, leading the Patriotic Front (PF). Like most populists, Sata promised much—like slashing the 35% to 37% tax rates paid by government workers—and found outsiders to blame. Chinese and Indian businessmen, described as "poor paying," came in for particular abuse. More brimstone was added to the political fires when he vowed to recognize the independence of Taiwan.

Despite Beijing's lofty principals of "non-interference," the Chinese ambassador was moved to tell the local media that Chinese investors had put further investments in the country on hold until "the uncertainty of our bilateral relations" is clarified. The remarks only fueled a growing resentment against the Chinese presence in the country.

The only other candidate given a meaningful chance against President Mwanawasa was Hakainde Hichilema, a successful businessman chosen to lead the United Democratic Alliance (UDA). The UDA had brought together the three largest parliamentary opposition parties—the Forum for Democracy and Development (FDD), the United National Independence Party (UNIP), and United Party for National Development (UPND). Its intended candidate was UPND's Anderson Mazoka who had barely lost the controversial 2001 election to Mwanawasa, but Mazoka's untimely death in May 2006 altered electoral calculations.

When all the ballots were counted, President Mwanawasa emerged victorious, receiving 43% of the vote. His nearest rival was Michael Sata, at 29%. UDA's Hakainde Hichilema, strongly supported by ex-President Kaunda's UNIP, tallied a respectable 25%. Simultaneous parliamentary elections gave his MMD a solid bloc of 74 seats in a 150-seat legislature. In a move that would prove to be of greater consequence than expected, Rupiah Banda was appointed as the vice president.

Mwanawasa's suffered a stroke in June 2008 (his second) and never fully recovered. After several false reports of his demise in July, he died in August 2008. In his final years, Mwanawasa gained considerable international respect for his willingness as the chairman of the Southern African Development Community (SADC), to take a firm stand against the dictatorial Robert Mugabe in Zimbabwe. While controversial in Africa, this was appreciated overseas, especially given the relatively weak statements of South African president Thabo Mbeki on the matter. Mwanawasa was succeeded by Vice President Rupiah Banda, who took the presidency on an interim basis until an election was held. Mwanawasa's death was mourned even by his rival Michael Sata.

Rupiah Banda of the MMD was declared president by the electoral commission after the vote in October 2008. Banda had earned just over 40% of the vote, while Michael Sata of the Patriotic Front came in close behind with 38%. Hakainde Hichilema took most of the remainder with 20%. Sata rejected the results and Banda's presidency, calling the election fraudulent. In November, violent protests and post-election riots broke out in Lusaka and Kitwe.

The Present: Contemporary Issues

In March 1999, the Ministry of Health reported that 73% of Zambia's estimated nine million people were infected with tuberculosis, and 30% of that was related to the HIV/AIDS pandemic. Some 21.5% of all adults are HIV-positive and 200 a day die of the disease. As a consequence of the epidemic, life expectancy has dropped to 38.4 years (2005)—among the lowest in the world.

UNICEF estimates there are 75,000 street children in the country, many of them AIDS orphans. Many wind up on the streets of Zambia's cities, especially the capital, Lusaka, begging or eking out a living washing cars or carrying groceries. Females are exploited and treated as sex ob-

Zambia

jects, often raped, abused, and abandoned. Street boys tend to live in groups and survive by forming a gang to protect themselves. Though they don't get raped, there is a good deal of "compassionate sex" among themselves, which produces the inevitable sexually transmitted diseases.

In 2003 the government introduced heavily-subsidized antiretrovirals (ARV) for 10,000 HIV-positive people at around eight dollars a month—a significant reduction from the regular $250 a month cost. Greater availability and treatment success have led to additional problems.

With insufficient awareness that ARV treatment is lifelong, patients have gone off the drug once feeling better. Zambian health officials now warn of the emergence of strains of HIV that are resistant to current drug treatment. In August 2004 the government announced that it had begun the manufacture of cheap generic antiretroviral (ARV) drugs with Cuban assistance. By 2006 some 75,000 people were currently taking the drugs, now distributed free of charge, but that's a small percentage of the estimated 1.2 million people living with the disease.

A good deal of thinking about AIDS in Zambia is influenced by religion. Safe-sex messages are often worded in moral terms. One AIDS mural proclaims "One Zambia. One Nation. One Husband. One Wife," suggesting that the disease can be prevented by marital fidelity.

Zambia is one of sub-Saharan Africa's most urbanized countries. Nearly one-half the population is concentrated in a few urban zones, and rural areas are underpopulated. While agriculture supports half the population, with corn the principal food crop and money earner, it is copper that dominates the Zambian economy.

Zambia has long been copper-dependent. The metal traditionally produced 80% of national export revenues, and one mining company, Zambia Consolidated Copper Mines (ZCCM), contributed 25% of GDP. Socialist-style planning and administration during the Kaunda years did not help the industry develop. Two decades of under-funding and a shortage of capital investment in new mines dragged copper production from its peak of 720,000 tons in 1969 to 320,000 in 1996.

The economy deteriorated rapidly as copper revenues sank. State enterprises, already bureaucratically inefficient, became heavily indebted. Deficit budgeting increased debt and inflation. Goods and services were in short supply. Business confidence disappeared and consumer frustration mounted. The pressures forced the authoritarian Kaunda to open the political system to competitive multiparty elections. Given a voice, electors tossed him out in 1991.

The Chiluba government introduced far-reaching market reforms. Prices were determined in the market place, not the bureaucratic office. More than 300 state enterprises were privatized; about 82% of them were sold to Zambians, most of them well within the ambit of Zambia's governing party.

Economic reform has not meant improvement in the lives of most Zambians. At least 70% live below the poverty line of less than a dollar per day, according to the World Bank. Less that 10% of working-age Zambians work full time in the formal sector; thousands have taken to selling whatever they can find in petty-retailing markets. Prostitution, a good indicator of social breakdown, has skyrocketed.

The state mining conglomerate, ZCCM, was broken up and its constituent parts sold off after much hesitancy and delay on the part of the government. This only diminished the value of what was being sold. New management and capitalization failed to halt production declines in copper. Uneconomical, the mines were shut down by the new owners and remained closed for almost a year while the government sought a new buyer.

India's Vedanta Resources purchased 51% of KCM shares for a rock-bottom price of $25 million in August 2003. Since then burgeoning economies in China and India have driven commodity prices, especially copper, to lofty heights. The boom in prices has fired the Zambian economy, bringing higher profits, tax revenues, and foreign investment in its mineral sector.

In contrast to Chilean copper, which is mined near the sea, copper mined in landlocked Zambia has expensive added transportation costs. Konkola, for example, ships all its output by rail to Durban, South Africa or Dar es Salaam, Tanzania. Both ports are over 1,200 miles away and the journey takes several days. The poor state of road maintenance means that truck transport is prohibitively expensive. The Southern Africa Development Community (SADC) is planning a $200-million railroad line connecting Zambia's copper mines to the Benguela railroad. The 400-mile connector is expected to reduce transportation costs.

Given the spike in commodity prices projects hitherto thought too expensive are now deemed feasible. Vedanta is investing $400 million into the massive Konkola Deep project, which had been studied and restudied for two decades. When completed in 2009 it will extend the mine's life another 22 years and represent Zambia's single largest investment. The government, which owns 20% of Konkola, expects copper production to increase from 350,000 tons to 800,000 tons in the next three years.

There are signs of promising diversity, allowing Zambia to move away from its copper dependence. The country annually earns some $20 million from the sale of gemstones, mostly emeralds. Zambia now produces 20% of the world's emeralds, and one geologist believes that with modern technology and management annual gemstone earnings could rise to $250 million. In addition to high-quality emeralds, Zambia is also endowed with rich deposits of amethysts, aquamarines, and red garnets.

China has had a long-term interest in Zambia, establishing diplomatic relations only five days after independence. It has offered assistance in a variety of areas, ranging from telecommunications, medicine, education, and tourism (designating Zambia "Approved Destination Status" for Chinese tourists) to infrastructure improvement.

The Future

Since independence, Zambia has gone from one of Africa's wealthiest states to one of its poorest, but it may be turning a corner once again. The outlook was more promising through the mid-decade due to high commodity prices that benefit this economy based on mining. Of course, this makes the economy especially vulnerable to the global economic downturn. Economic growth in 2007 was estimated at about 6% (or roughly the continental average), and probably below that in 2008. On the positive side, reform would seem to have the country on a somewhat better trajectory than previously, though there is no reason to expect significant over-performance.

Politically, Zambia has some modicum of free political contestation and some reasonable degree of civil liberties. Though democracy is incomplete, the 2006 elections were widely viewed as an improvement upon prior presidential elections. The passing of Levy Mwanawasa triggered the more discordant election of 2009 between Rupiah Banda and Michael Sata. While the greatest post-election strife seems to have passed, there is little doubt that the response to this year's election was something of a setback for Zambia.

The Republic of Zimbabwe

Bridge at Victoria Falls connecting Zimbabwe and Zambia

Land and People

Zimbabwe is hot and humid in the southern river basin areas. Cluttered forests of hardwood predominate in these lowlands, with both teak and mahogany towering above the scrub vegetation that is the breeding ground of the tsetse fly, carrier of dreaded sleeping sickness. In the central areas, the altitude rises in a series of fertile plateaus, with corresponding modification of the tropical climate. During the winter, the land sometimes gives off enough heat at night to allow the intrusion of a thin frost by dawn. Most land not forested by tall trees, growing in less densely vegetated woodland, is under cultivation.

Victoria Falls, located on the Zambezi River is one of the greatest sights of Africa—they are more than twice as high as Niagara Falls and have a width of about one mile. The sparkling waters of Lake Kariba, downstream from the Falls, stretch narrowly to the northeast, held back by the 420-foot-high walls of the Kariba Dam that provides electric power to both Zimbabwe and Zambia.

Zimbabwe's social and political problems, like the spread of AIDS, have long been the subject of song by Zimbabwe's foremost musician, Thomas Mapfumo. Born in colonial Rhodesia in 1945, Mapfumo has a personal history that reads like a biography of Zimbabwe. Early recognizing how colonists exploited Africans in their native land, he sympathized with those fighting against white rule and wrote songs in his native Shona that uplifted the hearts and sustained the action of Zimbabwe's guerilla forces. It was *chimurenga* music, or music of the struggle. The music articulated the concerns of those who had no voice, or as Mapfumo says, it gave voice to the voiceless. Since the heady days of the liberation struggle, the musician has become increasingly disenchanted with Zimbabwe under Robert Mugabe. His music

Basic Facts

Area: 391.090 sq. km. = 151,000 sq. mi. (slightly larger than Montana)

Population: 13,300,000 (UN 2007 est.)

Capital City: Harare

Climate: Hot and humid in the southern Limpopo and Sabi River regions; temperate in the central and northern highlands. A rainy season normally lasts from October to April and there is a dry season from May to September. Drought conditions reoccur regularly.

Neighboring Countries: Zambia (north); Namibia (west); Botswana (southwest); Republic of South Africa (south); Mozambique (east)

Official Language: English

Other Principal Languages: Shona, Sindebele (the language of the Ndebele, sometimes called Ndebele)

Ethnic Groups: Shona 82%, Ndebele 14%, other African 2%, mixed and Asian 1%, white less than 1%

Principal Religions: Syncretic (part Christian, part indigenous beliefs) 50%, Christian 25%, indigenous beliefs 24%, Muslim and other 1%

Chief Commercial Products: Tobacco, gold, ferroalloys, and cotton

GDP Per Capita: $340 (World Bank 2007 est.)

Currency: Zimbabwean dollar

Former Colonial Status: Administered by the British South Africa Company (1889–1923); Autonomous state within the British Commonwealth (1923–1965); unilateral independence as *Rhodesia* (1965–1980), recognized independence (1980).

Chief of State: Robert Mugabe, President

Independence Date: April 18, 1980

National Flag: Seven horizontal stripes (top to bottom) of green, gold, red, black, red, gold, green. A white triangle at the staff contains a red star in which is centered the gold Zimbabwean bird.

Zimbabwe

still gives voice to those who suffer most, but it now criticizes the regime that betrayed their hopes for a better life. "Chaunorwa" criticized Zimbabwe's pervasive corruption under Mugabe, and was duly banned from state-controlled airwaves. Other songs have criticized the farm invasions and Zimbabwe's involvement in the Congo War. *Chimurenga Explosion* (aNOym reCOrds, 2000) had at least one of its cuts, "Disaster," denied airtime. "Disaster" is Thomas Mapfumo's description of Zimbabwe under Robert Mugabe. "I'm very disappointed," he says. "After all our struggle, I never expected our own black government was going to destroy our country." Mapfumo has moved his family to the United States and vows not to return to Zimbabwe while President Mugabe remains in office.

At least one other popular musician has courageously taken up the role of regime critic. Hoseah Chipanga daringly chose the 2006 pre-Independence Day ball, attended by regime bigwigs and diplomats, to unleash his critical thunderbolts. Unspared were leaders who used their privileged access to maize, flour and fuel to profit personally by selling them on the black market, or those who amassed multiple farms for themselves.

The Past: Political and Economic History

For early history, see *Historical Background* and *The Colonial Period: The British*.

By 1923, white settlers had gained self-rule for Rhodesia. In that year, white electors confirmed this by rejecting the possibility of joining South Africa. Instead, Rhodesia became an autonomous member of the British Commonwealth. British settlers chose a parliament; with very few exceptions, Africans could not pass the educational tests required to gain voting rights.

Whites further solidified control in 1931 with the passage of the Land Apportionment Act. About 150,000 settlers received exclusive rights to roughly one-half of the choicest land; the 3,000,000 native Africans could live on the remainder. Land would always be central to Zimbabwean politics.

In 1953, Southern Rhodesia was joined with Northern Rhodesia and Nyasaland to make the Central African Federation. The federation was dissolved in 1963, and Northern Rhodesia and Nyasaland earned independence as Zambia and Malawi respectively. Fearing a similar development, white Southern Rhodesians rejected the governing United Federal Party and replaced it with the more conservative Rhodesian Front (RF). By 1964, Ian Douglas Smith led the RF, and in 1965, the party swept the elections. After several attempts to persuade Britain to grant independence, the Smith government announced the Unilateral Declaration of Independence (UDI) on November 11, 1965.

After UDI

African nationalist organizations began to flourish after 1953, a development greeted with hostility by colonial officials. The first commanding nationalist figure was Joshua Nkomo. In 1961, Nkomo (an Ndebele) joined with Robert Mugabe (a Shona), and Reverend Ndabiningi Sithole (an Ndau) to form the Zimbabwe People's Union (ZAPU). By 1963, however, Sithole, Mugabe and other Shona intellectuals, disappointed with his leadership, split from Nkomo and formed the Zimbabwe African National Union (ZANU). The split shattered what had been a multiethnic and multiregional anti-colonial movement. It shaped political rivalries well into the post-independence period. Two movements claiming nationalist goals would each become ethnically specific and regionally localized. At the declaration of UDI in 1965, African anti-colonial forces had already experienced division.

UN resolutions condemned white rule in Rhodesia, and one forbade any member nation to trade with Rhodesia. Since Rhodesia was one of the very few sources outside the U.S.S.R. of chrome ore vital to the manufacture of hard steel, the U.S. Congress allowed the resumption of Rhodesian chrome purchases in 1971, infuriating many African nations. Faced with international sanctions, Rhodesia turned to the development of import-substitution industries, ironically providing the basis for one of Zimbabwe's greatest economic strengths: a richly diversified economy.

Negotiations with the Smith regime came to naught. Within Rhodesia Smith allowed the creation of a third nationalist movement, the United African National Council (UANC) led by Abel Muzorewa, a bishop of the American United Methodist Church. Anxious to deal with moderate nationalist elements, Smith opened talks with Bishop Muzorewa and two other black leaders, Chief Jeremiah Chirau and Reverend Sithole, who had lost out in a ZANU leadership struggle with Robert Mugabe. Smith excluded both ZAPU and ZANU from the talks, for both groups had already established their presence in neighboring Zambia and had launched minor guerrilla attacks against the white led regime since 1965.

All-out guerrilla war began in 1972 against isolated white farmers in northeastern Rhodesia. With the collapse of Portuguese authority in 1974, ZANU guerrilla forces found a permanent base of operations in Mozambique under Robert Mugabe. Joshua Nkomo and his ZAPU sup-porters raised their own guerrilla army, largely Ndebele speakers from southwestern Rhodesia, and opened a second front in the guerrilla war, operating out of Zambia. Both Mozambique and Zambia suffered terribly as targets of Rhodesian retaliation. By 1976, Mozambique and Zambia pressured the two guerrilla movements to fight the Smith regime jointly. This resulted in the creation of the Patriotic Front of Zimbabwe.

When the guerrilla war took on serious economic consequences in 1978, and whites began to flee the country at the rate of 1,000 per month, Prime Minister Smith signed an "internal settlement" with Muzorewa, Sithole and Chirau providing for qualified majority rule and elections with universal suffrage. Mugabe and Nkomo scoffed at this internal settlement and branded the other black leaders "Uncle Toms." Patriotic Front leaders rejected an offer of total amnesty. In the parliamentary elections of 1979, Muzorewa's UANC won 51 of the 72 seats allotted to African candidates, beating the ZANU splinter led by Reverend Sithole, which won only 12 seats. Muzorewa became Rhodesia's first black prime minister, but whites retained key positions within the government and the army.

The guerrilla war continued and the U.N. lifted none of their sanctions. Britain decided to end the crisis by creating a government that included all nationalist elements. The Lancaster House Conference began in London in September 1979 with Muzorewa, Nkomo and Mugabe. After endless weeks of fruitless discussions against a background of continuous fighting back home—an average of 100 lives were lost each day—the white minority finally consented to hold multiracial elections, supervised by the British, in 1980. These, it was agreed, would lead to independence for Zimbabwe.

The Lancaster House constitution would operate from 1980 to 1990, guaranteeing whites representation in parliament and protecting white economic interests. The new constitution established a bicameral legislature, with reserved seats for whites in both houses. Also, the new government prohibited compulsory land acquisition, as well as the establishment of a one-party state, before 1990. The three leaders accepted the draft constitution, and a total of nine political parties prepared for the upcoming elections. Both elements of the Patriotic Front, Nkomo's PF-ZAPU, Mugabe's ZANU-PF, ran separate candidates, as did the Muzorewa and Sithole organizations.

The election resulted in a stunning triumph for Mugabe. ZANU-PF won 57 of 80 black seats in the House of Assembly. Nkomo's ZAPU was successful in 20 contests, mostly in Matabeleland, while Bishop Muzorewa won only three victories, a humiliating performance. The white minority was badly frightened at the prospect of having the Marxist Mugabe as prime minister, but acting with conciliation he assured them equal treatment as with all other Zimbabweans. With representatives of 100 nations on hand, Zimbabwe achieved recognized independence on April 18, 1980.

Post-Independence Period

President Mugabe's politics of practical reconciliation was initially successful. Mugabe appointed Nkomo to a high-ranking cabinet position. Two prominent white Zimbabweans were also included.

The tasks of the new government were enormous. It had to integrate what were essentially three armies—the guerrilla forces of ZAPU, ZANU, and the Rhodesian Defense Forces. It had to reestablish social services and education in the rural areas, and resettle a million refugees, displaced by nearly 15 years of civil conflict. Mugabe adopted a cautious approach to socializing the economy. Farmers were placated when the government raised prices for cash crops. Despite populist pressures for land reform, he assured white farmers that the government would not confiscate their property. These incentives produced surpluses that allowed Zimbabwe to weather draught-caused crop failures of 1982–1984 better than most of her neighbors.

Fissures within the Patriotic Front soon developed. Authorities allegedly found a cache of arms on Nkomo's farm and accused him, along with his closest aides, of trying to overthrow the government. Mugabe expelled Nkomo and his aides from the cabinet in 1981. Nkomo's followers began a loosely organized campaign of dissidence. Centered in Matabeleland, the dissidence involved attacks on both white farmers and government targets.

The government responded with the full force of emergency powers first granted

the Smith regime and renewed annually ever since. They conducted sweeping raids in Matabeleland after 1981. An imposed, strict curfew on the area withheld food shipments in order to starve the area into submission. In 1983, the Mugabe sent the notorious Fifth Brigade, trained by North Korea, to suppress the dissidence. The brigade, known as *Gukurahundi*, or "storm that destroys everything" accomplished its goal with ghastly violence. According to the Catholic Commission for Justice and Peace, the Fifth Brigade was responsible for the deaths of an estimated 20,000 people between 1983 and 1987. The Matabele campaign demonstrated the regime's willingness to use violence and terror against its own people to consolidate its power.

In the 1985 general election, held at the height of the Matabeleland conflict, ZANU increased its parliamentary majority by eight seats and garnered 76% of the vote. Two years later parliament eliminated seats reserved for whites. In November, amendments to the constitution created the post of executive president with enhanced powers, combining the roles of head of state and head of government. Mugabe then won a new election to the presidency for a term of six years.

In the same month, the two main political parties agreed to unify. Nkomo's ZAPU was absorbed into the ruling party, ZANU-PF. It marked the triumph of the Shona branch of Zimbabwean nationalism and the creation of a de facto single-party state. Later amendments to the constitution provide a second vice-presidency, a post to which Nkomo earned appointment. ZANU-PF asserted it would "seek to establish a socialist society, on the guidance of Marxist-Leninist principles, and to establish a one-party state."

Despite state repression of political opposition, four opposition parties contested the March 1990 general election. Mugabe won 78% of the vote. The Catholic Com-

mission for Justice and Peace claimed that preelection violence and intimidation had been so great that it was "calling into question the freedom and fairness of the general election." Voter turnout was low—54%.

President Mugabe proved out of touch with his own party when he proposed to institutionalize the one-party state later that year. Churches, trade unions, and students all strongly opposed the proposal, which led to strains within the party. Ultimately, a majority of the Politburo rejected the Mugabe plan. With the collapse of the Soviet Union and the decline of communist ideology in Eastern Europe, enthusiasm for Marxist-Leninist doctrine and rhetoric declined in Zimbabwe. In June 1991, ZANU-PF's central committee decided to drop references to "Marxism-Leninism" and "scientific socialism" from the party's constitution.

Economic issues dominated Zimbabwean politics in the 1990s. With the expiration of the Lancaster House prohibition on forced land purchases, President Mugabe announced that the government would amend the constitution to speed up land redistribution. The Land Acquisition Act, finally passed in 1992, allowed for the compulsory purchase of 13,585,000 acres of predominantly white-owned land. The commercial farming community fiercely opposed the plan and was able to delay its implementation. A regional drought in 1992 brought great suffering, and the Mugabe government, blamed for inadequate planning for the anticipated crop failure, became increasingly unpopular.

With popular discontent rising, fear of the regime diminished. As it seemed to weaken in popular support, the government returned to one of Zimbabwe's genuine hot-button issues: land redistribution. The government published a list of farms it would be compulsory purchasing in May of 1993. The list included seventy farms, some of them the most productive in the country, amounting to 469,300 acres. A year later, news broke that a government minister was leasing the first farm seized under the Land Acquisition Act. Many came to believe the government was more concerned with self-enrichment than the needs of its constituents.

The April 1995 parliamentary elections did nothing to change the political landscape. ZANU-PF won its fourth successive electoral victory, winning 118 out of 120 seats. Zimbabwe was, in essence, a single-party state.

Mugabe won an overwhelming reelection to another six-year term in March 1996, but less than one-third of the electorate bothered to vote. A seeming triumph, the figures suggested ZANU's diminishing legitimacy. Emboldened by the example of President Mandela's moral leadership to

Sorting tobacco   Photo by David Johns

Zimbabwe

the south, legislators reacted vigorously to a series of corruption scandals that tainted the government. The media broke stories of high ZANU-PF officials looting of the veterans' compensation fund, leading 100 ZANU-PF legislators called for an official audit of the fund. Legislators also rejected a contract for a new terminal at the Harare International Airport when government planners awarded it to an inexperienced Cypriot company with close ties to President Mugabe's nephew.

Public demonstrations against the regime rose. Civil servants, railway workers, doctors and nurses, among others, protested wages and work conditions. Veterans of the liberation struggle, mostly poorly educated peasant farmers living in poverty, demanded payment and pensions for service. Food riots in January 1998 forced the government to send in the army when the police could no longer control the situation. The regime seemed to be unraveling.

A Regime of Personal Rule

By 1998, Robert Mugabe's control over party and state in Zimbabwe had little credible and effective opposition. Every constitutional amendment since independence had concentrated authority in his hands, and there were no checks to assure accountability. Robert Mugabe henceforth subjected Zimbabwe to his regime of personal rule, and the nation suffered the consequences.

Mugabe's economic mismanagement resulted in an economic meltdown. The value of the Zimbabwe dollar plummeted. Inflation soared. Prices on basic commodities rose beyond the affordability of most Zimbabweans. Mass "stay-aways" organized by the unions almost paralyzed the nation. The government acquiesced to populist demand, Rescinding fuel price increases, and introducing price controls on basic commodities. With government control over the economy accentuated, the International Monetary Fund withdrew its support.

Intensifying the domestic political crisis was President Mugabe's personal decision to intervene on behalf of Laurent Kabila when a second rebellion convulsed the Congo in August 1998. Mugabe's claim to be supporting a "legitimate" leader was pure sophistry, but then, one of the victims in any war is language. In this case, one authoritarian simply came to the rescue of another. This action demonstrated the lack of accountability for leadership in Zimbabwe. The government went on an arms-buying spree. China, Zimbabwe's main arms supplier, became the source of fighter aircraft. In addition, Zimbabwe added Swiss-designed cluster bombs to its arsenal. Defense costs skyrocketed.

Polls indicated that 70% of the citizenry opposed Zimbabwe's presence in the Congo. Faced with criticism, President Mugabe abused his critics left, right and center. The few independent newspapers remaining in Zimbabwe experienced ferocious criticism and threats of much closer control. Mugabe, in attempt to crack down on his critics, subjected labor unions, which had led demands for political reforms and articulated public anger over economic hardship, to a six-month ban on strikes.

Since 1999, Zimbabwe has continued its downward spiral, driven by the ambitions of one man: Robert Mugabe. Whenever there were problems, Mugabe found a scapegoat. When fuel shortages occurred, he accused white industrialists and farmers of hoarding it. In reality, the fuel crisis reflected all the ills of 20 years of authoritarian rule. Economic mismanagement was evident everywhere. Corruption and cronyism ran rampant and unilateral decision-making was disastrous.

President Mugabe's decision to assist Laurent Kabila was a major factor in the country's tale of economic woe. The daily tab for keeping 11,000 troops in Congo was $1 million. Despite acute shortages and massive lines at the gas pumps, the National Oil Company of Zimbabwe (NOCZIM) continued shipping available fuel to support the war. To pay for its costs, Zimbabwe signed a variety of deals that tended to treat the Congo as a neo-colony, rich in exploitable resources. The deals suggested less public policy to amortize war costs, than a means to engage the loyalty of the army and provide enrichment opportunities for officers, cronies, and supporters.

Perhaps the most outrageous concession Zimbabwe secured from the Kabila government was the one to log some 84 million acres of Congo's rain forest—15% of the Congo's territory. The concession went to a company that was part of the ZANU-PF business empire controlled by Robert Mugabe's right-hand man in financial matters, Emmerson Mnangagwa, Zimbabwe's parliamentary speaker. Though intended to generate and protect revenue streams for the country's political elite, Zimbabwe's Congo ventures failed miserably without the requisite expertise. In mid-2003, the army announced it was not involved in any commercial activity in the DRC.

Ineptitude, loss, and mismanagement in the Congo mirrored the general deterioration at home. Foreign exchange nearly disappeared. Inflation soared, as did the unemployment rate. Interest rates rose and the Zimbabwe dollar further declined. Increasingly larger numbers of people fell below the poverty line. This was the legacy of Robert Mugabe. Worsening con-

President Mugabe (early photo)

ditions gave rise to two major political movements.

In September 1999, the Zimbabwe Confederation of Trade Unions (ZCTU) launched a new political party, the Movement for Democratic Change (MDC). The confederation's dynamic and effective secretary-general, Morgan Tsvangirai, was designated party leader. In the months to come, the MDC would provide the kind of opposition the Mugabe regime had never seen before. Preexisting grassroots organizations enabled the MDC to mobilize opposition.

The second movement sparked by deteriorating conditions was one to amend Zimbabwe's constitution. President Mugabe appointed an official Constitutional Commission to recommend changes. It held hearings and learned that Zimbabweans overwhelmingly wanted to limit Mugabe's power.

The whole process ended in farce. A draft, which actually strengthened and consolidated the president's powers and allowed confiscation of white-owned farms without compensation, went through the final meeting of the 400-member constitutional commission. No vote took place. Despite delegates screaming their opposition, Constitutional Commission chairman, Judge Godfrey Chidyausiku, declared, "the draft is adopted by acclamation."

The MDC and commercial farmers organized a "No" campaign in the February 2002 referendum on new constitutional amendments. The government, which had never lost an election in 20 years, used its power to make its opponents' lives as miserable as possible. State print and broadcast media rejected all opposition advertising and virtually all statements critical of the draft constitution.

Despite governmental intimidation, the opposition handed President Mugabe his first defeat since independence. Fifty-five percent of those voting rejected the proposed amendments. Even the promise of white lands for Africans could not silence a populace suffering 20 years of misrule.

Like the wounded and cornered lion he was, Mugabe lashed out with special ferocity, orchestrating a storm of violence that reduced Zimbabwe to governance by thuggery and fear. The country witnessed "spontaneous" invasions of white-owned farms by self-styled "war veterans," "disillusioned," they said, by rejection of the constitutional amendment allowing confiscation and redistribution of lands. The reality was somewhat different.

Many of the so-called "war veterans" were far too young to have ever served. They were in fact part of the mass of urban unemployed, carefully organized and dispersed throughout the country with logistical precision. The farm invasions began within a week of Mugabe's referendum defeat in February and ultimately involved 50,000 squatters invading up to 1,400 farms. London's *Sunday Telegraph* reported the man coordinating the land seizures and organizing food and transport for squatters was General Perence Shiri.

The head of Zimbabwe's air force, General Shiri had also commanded the Fifth Brigade massacres in Matabeleland in the 1980s—probably the most notorious example of the state employing coercion against its own citizens. General Shiri's name also appeared on a list of 28 senior government and military figures given farms seized from whites.

The campaign was, quite simply, a program of state-sponsored terrorism. Its victims were initially white farmers who had been active in the campaign against the referendum and their black employees. Whites were humiliated and killed. Black farm workers had their homes and property destroyed, and most were forced to participate in the depredations of the next farm to be invaded. A state of law ceased, replaced by fear, intimidation, and violence.

In this environment, the June 2000 parliamentary elections took place. They were less about "landless veterans" than about ZANU-PF maintaining power. Fearful of losing power and perquisites—a whole network of ZANU-controlled corporations, for example—Mugabe and his minions resorted to force and terror to silence rural supporters of the MDC.

Zimbabwe's electoral geography explained the rural strategy. Rural parliamentary seats outnumber those in urban

Human rights demonstration ©IRIN

districts where opposition is greatest. Every rural victim of the regime's terror campaign became a living reminder of ZANU-PF's ability to destroy those who did not support it. Government-sponsored violence resulted in the deaths of some 30 people. Thousands were beaten, raped and intimidated, but MDC voters courageously made their way to the polls and handed ZANU-PF the surprise of its life. Out of 120 seats available through the election, the MDC won a remarkable 57; ZANU-PF won 62; the remaining seat went to Rev. Sithole's ZANU-Ndonga.

MDC made the best showing by any opposition party in Zimbabwe's history. Several ZANU-PF bigwigs were defeated, including Mugabe's right-hand man, Emmerson Mnangagwa. Zimbabwe's constitution allows the president to appoint an additional 30 members to parliament, and using this option Mugabe returned Mnangagwa to the House of Assembly, where he won election as speaker.

The EU characterized the election as neither fair nor free, and the MDC challenged nearly 40 results in court. Justices annulled election results compromised by violence and intimidation, putting the judiciary squarely in President Mugabe's rifle sights. Outright assault on justices started when courts ordered black squatters to end their illegal occupations of white-owned farms. War veterans, who had become the regime's storm troopers, invaded judicial premises and threatened judges. The police did nothing, and the regime informed the justices that it was unable to protect them or their families.

Under coercion, the chief justice of Zimbabwe's Supreme Court retired early. Mugabe appointed one of his cronies, Judge Godfrey Chidyausiku, to fill the vacancy. (Judge Chidyausiku had chaired the notorious constitutional commission that had proposed constitutional amendments to increase President Mugabe's authority and allow confiscation of white-owned farms without compensation.)

Mugabe and the Media

The regime's intimidation of judges was part of a campaign to destroy its opponents and those who abetted them in any way. The media, especially the *Daily News*—the only remaining independent newspaper in Zimbabwe and an outspoken critic of the Mugabe regime—faced much harassment and intimidation.

War veterans, now the regime's enforcers, assaulted *Daily News* journalists, fired steel bolts into its offices, and set up road blocks outside Harare to confiscate copies of the newspaper and prevent its distribution to outlying areas—where 70% of the population lives. An explosion rocked the paper's printing works with such force that the blast rattled houses five miles away. The attack destroyed five of the *Daily News's* six presses.

Investigators later determined five Soviet made anti-tank land mines, favored for their ability to toss a ten-ton tank into the air, caused the destruction. Those who set them off knew how to place them for maximum effect. In other words, it was not an affair of street-crazies with a few pipe bombs.

Zimbabwe

The Media Institute of Southern Africa (MISA) consistently ranks Zimbabwe as the worst offender of media freedom in the region. Journalists working there have found it increasingly difficult to gather news given the raft of anti-media laws enforced by the regime. Equally inimical to press freedom is the strategy of the country's Central Intelligence Organization (CIO) to own papers through shell companies or silent shareholders. In May 2006, the Paris-based international media watchdog, Reporters Without Borders, classified Robert Mugabe as a "predator" of press freedom, right up there with King Abdullah, Fidel Castro, Hu Jintao, and Vladimir Putin.

Radio, far cheaper than newspapers and more effective in reaching a rural audience, has been a major concern of the regime since Zimbabwe's Supreme Court declared the state's broadcasting monopoly unconstitutional in September 2000. Since independence in 1980, there has been no private broadcasting station in the country. Shortly after the court's decision, Capital Radio, financed by foreign charities, started operations broadcasting music, but its life was brief. Within days, armed police swept into the station's office, seized its equipment, and accused it of being a "pirate" station.

Averse to alternative voices, President Mugabe has used ZANU-PF majorities in parliament to pass a range of legislation designed to destroy free expression. A broadcasting act rushed through parliament in April 2001 with little debate, even after criticism from one parliamentary committee alleged it to be unconstitutional.

The bill required broadcasters to have a license, but licenses would be severely limited, and radio stations could not operate if financed by foreign interests. The government retained the power to shut down broadcasters if they did anything that was, in the words of the legislation, "prejudicial to the defense, public safety, public order, public morality or public health of Zimbabwe." This legislation served as the minister's license to kill independent broadcasters, and there was no doubt the minister would use the license to that effect. Zimbabwe's then information minister, Jonathan Moyo, made the government's position clear: "If there is a court which allows [independent broadcasting] in Zimbabwe, we [the government] will not allow it. It compromises our national security." So much for the rule of law. . .

In the spring of 2001, Chenjerai Hunzvi (nicknamed "Hitler" Hunzvi) and his "war vets" brought their circus of chaos to the cities. Businesses and charitable institutions were subject to veterans' raids, which amounted to little more than an ex-

cuse to steal, kidnap, and extort. When they threatened to invade embassies, the outcry was so great the regime pulled the plug on their depredations. The regime made its point: it could destroy the source of support for the MDC within the business community. For Hunzvi, it was a last hurrah of sorts. He died in early June 2001, reportedly of malaria of the brain.

President Mugabe's assault on courts, media, and opposition following the referendum defeat of 2000 was part of a strategy to ensure victory in the presidential election of March 2002. He mobilized police, army, and youth militia to intimidate and terrorize a hapless population. According to official figures, Zimbabweans cast nearly three million ballots, with Mugabe winning 56% of the vote. Morgan Tsvangirai, his most formidable opponent, won only 42%, with three minor candidates taking the remainder. ZANU-PF spokesmen claimed Mugabe won because people supported his seizure of white-owned land and saw the MDC and Tsvangirai as the stooges of white colonialists.

In reality, Mugabe won the election through massive fraud, manipulation, and terror. Beforehand, suspected MDC supporters were brutally beaten, bullied and robbed of their voter registration cards to prevent them from voting. Much of this occurred while police looked on. The government implemented the Public Order and Security Act to prohibit MDC rallies and to ban loudspeakers at the few permitted meetings. Further fraud occurred when officials finagled electoral rolls to reduce urban voters and augment rural ones. In the cities the usual number of polling places was halved; zealous officials at the stations that did open meticulously lengthened the wait of voters who were forced to stand in the hot sun for hours, or go home without voting. The lines became so long the courts had to order an additional day of voting in the urban centers.

Rural districts, in contrast, had an overabundance of polling stations. In areas suspected of being sympathetic to the MDC, ZANU-PF set up militia camps near polling stations to better threaten potential voters. The government rejected the use of see-through ballot boxes and prevented election monitors from even getting near polling stations. Widespread disparities in various voting reports further delegitimized the election. In its petition to the courts to invalidate the election, the MDC showed there were nearly 186,000 "missing" votes and perhaps as many as 246,000 "additional" votes.

The Crisis in Zimbabwe Coalition—a consortium of Zimbabwean NGOs—concluded that the "process of the presiden-

**Morgan Tsvangirai,
Prime Minister and MDC Leader**

tial elections has not enabled the will of the people to be expressed freely and fairly." It was a consensus opinion shared by every Zimbabwean civil society group charged with assessing or supporting the electoral process.

The Politics of Survival

Zimbabwe under Robert Mugabe is a handbook for those whose single goal is political survival. First: decapitate opposition leadership. Mugabe put Morgan Tsvangirai and two other pro-democracy leaders, Welshman Ncube and Renson Gasela, on trial for treason. The charge: concocting a plot to assassinate President Mugabe. The evidence: a four-hour fuzzy, often inaudible, secretly videotaped meeting between Tsvangirai and Ari ben Menashe, an international fraudster who admits to receiving $100,000 from the Mugabe regime as a "retainer fee." The judge: Paddington Garwe, a Mugabe appointee, installed after Mugabe had purged the higher courts of judges who had ruled that seizures of white-owned farms were illegal. Judge Garwe has taken possession of one of those farms. The possible sentence: if convicted, the three face the death penalty. The decision: In October 2004, Judge Garwe cleared Tsvangirai of the treason charges, saying the state had failed to prove its case against him. The follow up: in early December, the state appealed Judge Garwe's decision, and in May 2005, it reinstated a second treason charge over Tsvangirai's call for mass protests in June 2003. Finally, the courts dropped the charges in August 2005.

Second: maintain a semblance of democratic form by holding "elections," but win them by force, violence, and fraud. There were at least nine parliamentary by-elections (to replace a member who had died, or in one case, an opposition MP who fled the country in fear for his life). Each election consisted of bitterly fought races and violence. For ZANU-PF, the stakes were high: If it could reduce the MDC's representation below 50, it would regain a two-thirds majority, necessary to make any constitutional change it desires. The first seven races ended in victories for Mugabe's ZANU-PF after violent campaigns. The MDC's parliamentary delegation reduced to 50.

Third: if the opposition should elect a candidate to local executive office, appoint someone over him to render him ineffective and powerless. Zimbabwe's two largest cities, Harare and Bulawayo, both had MDC mayors until Mugabe appointed new governors to run the cities. Mugabe required the mayors to report to the governors, effectively reducing the MDC's authority and political activity.To avoid any future opposition victories in mayoral elections, the government announced it would gerrymander the cities' boundaries, folding districts part of urban Harare or Bulawayo into rural areas, traditionally ZANU strongholds.

Fourth: reward and punish supporters and opponents with all means available. Torture and arbitrary imprisonment are routine for regime opponents, and also for some who remain silent. As political misrule, economic mismanagement, corruption, and drought combined to create catastrophic food shortages in early 2003, more than half Zimbabwe's 12 million people were at risk of starvation. The government used its monopoly of grain imports to channel food to friends and supporters, and interfered with international food aid intended for distribution to others. ZANU controlled shopping centers often turned MDC supporters from bread lines. (Some people put principle aside and bought ZANU-PF cards in order to eat.)

Lest one have any doubt that starvation was policy, listen to Didymus Mutasa, ZANU-PF's organizing secretary, speaking at an August 2002 rally: "We would be better off with only six million people, with our own people who support the liberation struggle. We don't want all these extra people."

Fifth: muzzle and silence the press—there should be no witnesses. Since the presidential election, both local and foreign reporters have been intimidated, beaten, jailed or deported. The government has tried to destroy the *Daily News* financially (by prohibiting all government advertising on its pages) and physically (with those antitank mines). The government forcibly deported a correspondent for the British newspaper, *The Guardian*, despite court orders prohibiting his de-

portation. Chillingly, the government celebrated World Press Freedom Day (May 3, 2003) with the slogan "The media we have is not the media we need."

Sixth: intimidate members of the judiciary to accord their judgments with regime policy, and when they do not, ignore them—law serves the state exclusively. Despite the regime's "indigenization" of the judiciary, men of principle still, but infrequently, deliver independent rulings.

Judge Benjamin Paradza, a black judge on Zimbabwe's High Court, was such an independent voice. The government warned Paradza, a former fighter in Mugabe's guerilla army, when appointed to the bench, "not to embarrass the government with his court rulings." In mid-February 2003, Mugabe's police arrested Paradza, (despite constitutional prohibitions against the arrest of sitting jurists) and subjected him to a campaign of personal vilification.

At his arrest, Paradza said he was told: "You have been appointed to look after the government's interests, but you have embarrassed the government and now we are going to embarrass you." (Judge Paradza was the one had overturned state eviction notices against white farmers whose land the government was trying to seize.) The courts convicted Judge Paradza, widely regarded as the last independent judge in Zimbabwe, of alleged corruption in January 2006. Before sentencing, he fled the country and was believed to be seeking political asylum in the United Kingdom. In absentia, the courts sentenced him to three years in prison.

This strategy functioned to entrench Robert Mugabe and exhaust the opposition. The MDC's leadership found itself busy in court, disorganized and dispirited. The MDC's supporters grew disappointed and disillusioned as Zimbabwe's March 2005 parliamentary elections approached. The MDC leadership seemed unable to consolidate previous gains, and its support base waned as survival became the main concern for most. The threat of starvation, from a regime relentless in its pursuit of survival and power, tempted many MDC supporters to put their politics aside for the duration of the election.

A year before the election, the government announced a bumper harvest of maize and told the international donor community it would not need emergency food, but it refused to let United Nations staff assess the state of the country's crops and food stocks. The global community dismissed the food production figures. The Catholic archbishop of Bulawayo went so far as to say the government was "not telling the truth," noting that much land was lying fallow.

The run-up to the March 2005 legislative elections saw a great deal of nervous politicking among ZANU bigwigs jockeying to succeed Zimbabwe's aging dictator. As the succession competition heated up, ZANU-PF's internal politics got down and dirty. In late 2004, political guns aimed at the front-runner, Emmerson Mnangagwa, the speaker of parliament and long Mugabe's link to ZANU-PF's economic empire, after he seemed to have sewed up the support of provincial leaders in the race for party vice president. His enemies in the politburo convoked an emergency meeting, and a faction led by the influential former defense chief, General Solomon Mujuru, bulldozed through a resolution calling for a woman to fill the vice presidency position. The obvious candidate was Water Resources and Infrastructural Development Minister Joyce Mujuru, wife of General Solomon Mujuru.

Because most saw the contest for the vice president's post as putting the victor in line to succeed President Mugabe, ZANU's internal battle was ugly. Information Minister Jonathan Moyo, who had tried to rally provincial leaders to Mnangagwa, received reprimand for opposing Mujuru, dropped from his party position, and ultimately denied the party's nomination in the March 2005 elections. He successfully ran as an independent, suggesting ZANU continued in deep disarray.

The March 2005 parliamentary election conformed to the usual Zimbabwean standards: victory achieved through fraud, intimidation, ballot stuffing, and active participation of the dead. Official results gave ZANU-PF 78 of 120 contested seats; MDC managed to eke out 41 seats, and one lonely independent—Jonathan Moyo—would take his seat in the next parliament. There was never any doubt about the election outcome. ZANU-PF leaves nothing to chance.

Rural villagers were threatened, cajoled, and denied food if there was any possibility they might support the MDC. The Catholic Archbishop of Bulawayo, Pius Ncube, condemned the "evil and systematic denial of food to hungry people," and called for civil disobedience. Well before the election, the government was predicting "an above-average national harvest," even a bumper harvest of 2.75 million tons of maize. The prediction was all posturing and prevarication. By May 2005, five million Zimbabweans were in urgent need of food aid.

May 2005 also saw the regime launch yet another lethal assault on its citizens. Secure with an unassailable parliamentary majority, the government began Operation *Murambatsvina*, a Shona word meaning, "clean out the garbage." The "garbage" was, at least initially, the poor and

Zimbabwe

marginal population of Harare's shanty-towns. The government designed the program to rid the shantyowns of illegal structures and illegal business activities; the *Murambatsvina* bulldozers leveled everything in their path: cardboard shacks and solid cinder block homes, lives and livelihoods. Direct police action killed at least six people. Many of the more vulnerable—children, AIDS victims, the aged—succumbed to exposure in Zimbabwe's midwinter cold. Hundreds of thousands of people were displaced as *Murambatsvina* was extended to other cities—often a stronghold of opposition supporters.

The regime's callous disregard for its own citizens was no secret. Their *Gukurahundi* campaign of the 1980s sought to kill its opponents. Didymus Mutasa (see above), had said three years earlier that the country would be better off with only six million people (out of an estimated population over 12 million). And of those affected by *Murambatsvina*, Police Commissioner Augustine Chihuri claimed they were a "crawling mass of maggots bent on destroying the economy . . ." Many analysts saw the operation as a means of forcing potential opposition supporters out of the cities into rural areas where the government's control of food would make them more subject to control.

The regime moved to firm up its control elsewhere. With the 30 seats President Mugabe appointed to the House of Assembly, ZANU-PF had a two-thirds majority in parliament; the party could change the constitution at will, and it did so in late August 2005, amending the constitution for the 17th time since independence. With its 22 clauses, the Constitutional Amendment Bill stripped landowners of the right to appeal against government expropriation of their lands and allowed the government to deny passports to its enemies if deemed in the national interest.

The amendment bill also created a 66-seat Senate, which seemed to have no other purpose than to provide comfortable sinecures for aging ZANU-PF politicians. The body has 50 elected members and six appointed by President Mugabe; traditional chiefs would fill the remaining ten seats. Elections were quickly called (allowing senatorial salaries to begin as soon as possible), but almost no one cared. A record low turnout of 15% sent 43 ZANU-PF faithful to the new body, and only seven from the MDC. The senate election revealed latent cleavages within the MDC and further eroded its effectiveness as an opposition party.

Party leader Tsvangirai called for a boycott, arguing the regime had never and would never permit a free and fair election. Others, largely Ndebele from the Southern provinces—savagely repressed

Artists at Shona Sculpture Park near Harare with sculpture of an AIDS victim
Photo by David Johns

by the Mugabe regime in the 1980s—refused to have ZANU-PF senators represent them and urged participation. In February 2006, the pro-senate faction elected as its leader Arthur Mutambara, a former student leader who had gone on to be a NASA research fellow and lecturer at the Massachusetts Institute of Technology. Mutambara said he returned to Zimbabwe after 15 years of exile in South Africa to provide new blood and leadership to the opposition. As the rancorous division unfolded, ZANU politicians gloated and rumors surfaced of the country's security services dispersing millions of Zimbabwean dollars to destabilize the opposition.

Factional division within ZANU-PF by 2007 allowed Mugabe to seize the agenda, once again, sidelining political rivals and further concentrating power. To ensure an absence of opposition, Mugabe sent his security forces against the MDC and the physical assault landed many, including Morgan Tsvangirai, in hospitals. His bashed and bandaged head became the iconic image of Mugabe's repression. At the same time, Mugabe supporters trashed MDC offices. In addition to his MDC opponents, Mugabe also launched a crackdown on lawyers, the last defenders of basic freedoms in the country. Mugabe's police arrested and charged two of Tsvangirai's defense attorneys with "defeating the course of justice." When colleagues protested the arrests, the police beat them up as well.

Some brave Church officials were some of the last standing opponents of the regime. Zimbabwe's Catholic bishops called the situation "extremely volatile" and worded strong letters about how "the state responds with ever harsher oppression through arrests, detentions, banning orders, beatings and torture." Even more remarkably, they supported Morgan Tsvangirai's refusal to participate in the 2008 elections if they were conducted under the present constitution. "In order to avoid further bloodshed and avert a mass uprising," they wrote, "the nation needs a new people-driven constitution that will guide a democratic leadership chosen in free and fair elections." For Mugabe, the bishops were on a "dangerous path." Given the recent brutalizing of the political opposition, Mugabe's next words were ominous: "Once [the bishops] turn political, we regard them as no longer spiritual and our relations with them would be conducted as if we were dealing with political entities."

The Present: Contemporary Issues

Since 2007, Zimbabwe's situation has deteriorated further. Besides Morgan Tsvangirai, several other prominent Zimbabweans in both the ruling ZANU-PF and the opposition MDC attempted to counter Mugabe as the country moved towards presidential elections. From within the ZANU-PF, Mugabe faced a potential battle for the party nomination from one of his former ministers, Simba Makoni. Mugabe supporters within the ZANU-PF managed to exclude Makoni from the vote by citing obscure qualification rules; this led Makoni to declare as an independent in the presidential election. Makoni was then menaced with violence by Mugabe backers (including the loose group of "war veterans" that had occupied farms across the country), who trotted out the usual accusations that Makoni was a pawn of the West and a stooge who was hoping to split the ZANU-PF vote to give the presidency to Tsvangirai.

In the first round of the presidential election, Tsvangirai took the largest share. The Zimbabwe Electoral Commission, however, tallied this share at 47.9%, under the 50% needed to win the presidency outright. Mugabe was purported to win 43% of the vote, and Makoni over 8%. This result would ensure the necessity of a second-round runoff between Tsvangirai and Mugabe. The MDC cried foul, with Tsvangirai saying the presidency was being taken from him in a "scandalous daylight robbery."

Tsvangirai insisted he was the outright winner, but did not (for some time) rule out competing in the runoff. Makoni threw his support behind Tsvangirai, and it seemed clear the MDC candidate would receive the majority vote, if there were a free and fair election. At the same time, however, the clear support for the MDC heightened repression by the government and its allies. Tsvangirai faced threats to his life and attacks on his office and person, in addition to legal impediments, such as accusations of treason. Similarly, MDC Secretary-General Tendai Biti was accused of treason in June 2008 upon his return to Zimbabwe from South Africa, and is threatened with the death penalty for (among other trumped-up charges) alleging that Tsvangirai had won the presidency outright in the first round of voting. Elsewhere, open support for the MDC put many ordinary Zimbabweans on the receiving end of state violence.

Finally, at the last minute, just before the runoff scheduled for June 27, 2008, Tsvangirai pulled out, claiming that Mugabe and his supporters had made a credible election impossible. Tsvangirai asserted that violence and threats against his supporters had made it impossible for them to participate in the electoral process. He further maintained that the election was rigged (and indeed that preventing his victory in the first round of voting allowed the ZANU-PF time to manipulate the results).

Mugabe won the sham election uncontested; most international observers did not recognize the result as legitimate. Tsvangirai denounced the result, occasionally from his refuge in the Dutch Embassy, where he fled on at least two occasions in fear for his life. African countries attempted to reconcile the two parties and craft a government of national unity. Mugabe was defiant, but he agreed in August 2008 to share some power.

Zimbabwe's contemporary crisis is political in origin, but has a wide range of consequences beyond the political sphere. The economy has essentially collapsed. From 2000 to 2008, the GDP of Zimbabwe dropped over 54%, the worst performance of any African economy. Surprisingly, the IMF estimates that, despite worldwide recession, Zimbabwe might grow by 2.8% this year. (One should note that this growth would be mostly because the economy has dropped so greatly that the only direction to go is up.)

Hyperinflation in Zimbabwe almost certainly set world records. Unable to stop the hyperinflation, the government now pays employees in American dollars, the most widely accepted currency in Zimbabwe. Most stores quit taking Zimbabwean dollars over the end of 2008, and now list prices in US Dollars, South African Rand, and Euros. An estimated 95% of the population lacks employment in the formal sector. At least 80% of the population lives on less than a dollar a day.

Traditionally, Zimbabwe earned its principal revenues from agricultural exports. Tobacco was the principal commercial export, but mineral resources, like gold and various ferroalloys, also made a significant contribution. The economy is currently in free fall. Social violence orchestrated by ZANU-PF has disrupted the agricultural sector, especially food and tobacco. The government's confiscation of commercial farms for distribution to the landless has destroyed the most vibrant component of a desperate economy. The big farms not only kept Zimbabwe fed, but produced 30% of its total exports. Tobacco alone was the single biggest earner of foreign exchange—about 35%—and traditionally contributed at least 15% of Zimbabwe's GDP.

The effects of the regime's disastrous economic policies are apparent in exports of tobacco and gold, until recently Zimbabwe's principal sources of foreign exchange. In 2001, tobacco brought in $584 million, but by 2004, earnings had fallen to $240 million; from contributing 35% of all foreign exchange earnings in 2001, tobacco contributed only 20% in 2004. The 2005 crop was the "lowest since 1980," according to the Zimbabwe Tobacco Association: around 55,000 tons, down from 260,500 tons in 2000. Gold has traditionally been Zimbabwe's second most important source of export earnings, but production is generally declining. According to the Chamber of Mines, 2004 production was around 19.7 metric tons. The figure represents a 57% increase over 2003's production of 12.6 metric tons, but is still well below the all-time record of 28 tons in 1999.

Since 1994, when it was first mined, platinum has emerged as one of the country's major foreign exchange earners, and has probably replaced tobacco and gold as the country's top source of foreign currency. Zimbabwe, which produced some 150,000 ounces of platinum in 2005, is the world's second largest producer of platinum after South Africa. The government considers platinum vital for the economy's recovery, but misguided black empowerment policies will very likely strangle even this silver goose. In March 2006, the minister of mines announced that 51% of all foreign mining shares would go to the government, half of them without compensation. Given the enormous capital investment required to increase mine production, it is unlikely the government, in its present parlous circumstances, will have the money to invest, and equally unlikely the companies will wish to foot the entire capital investment cost for only 49% of the profits. The government extended this confiscation of assets to all foreign-owned business in mid-2007. Zimbabwe's trade and industry minister defended the takeovers, proclaiming, "Our people need a stake in the running of the economy." The takeover would be without compensation.

As part of President Mugabe's "Look East" policy, the government has turned its attention to Asia, and particularly China. Apparent in the tourism sector, China, which is now Zimbabwe's biggest investor, has granted it "Approved Destination" status for Chinese tourists. Some 24,500 intrepid Chinese visitors made the trip in the first nine months of 2004—hardly the flood of tourists promised by officials when Air Zimbabwe launched a twice-weekly round-trip flight to China. Most press reports indicate the flights are nearly empty. So too were the flights to Dubai inaugurated in May 2005.

Central to Zimbabwe's economic implosion is the fact that the centerpiece of its economic program, fast-track land resettlement, has been an abject failure. President Mugabe has said his often-violent land reform program would stimulate economic growth, but the opposite is true. First, there was corruption in the program. Top government officials and the well-connected, the ZANU-PF elite grabbed some of the best and richest farmland at the expense of the landless poor. Second, there was the decline in production. Some 300,000 to 350,000 families have been resettled, but without adequate experience, equipment or resources (to buy fertilizer, for example), only a small percentage of the land listed has been cultivated, and that in rudimentary circumstances. Once

Zimbabwe

productive lands have languished, leaving the country without food or the cash crops needed to purchase imports. Third, there was the decline in farm employment, with several hundred thousand jobs—black farm workers for the most part—disappearing.

The government has accumulated a growing external debt. Much of this comes because of the regime's system of patronage and pre-electoral payoff. Party faithful win lucrative appointments in state corporations, which almost inevitably lose money. Unbudgeted spending sprees usually precede tough elections.. To avoid action by disgruntled civil servants, laid low by skyrocketing inflation, the government granted huge salary increases—between 200% and 300%—in April 2006. The government's wage bill is now well over 50% of GDP. The only way to pay for it is to borrow, increasing the domestic debt, or print more money. Either way, inflation continues to rise as a result.

In March 2004, Mugabe congratulated himself for his presidential performance with a salary increase of 436%—from Z$20 million to Z$87.2 million (including a broad range of allowances). This will help pay for his retirement cottage: a three-story palace on 42 acres in Harare's most affluent suburb. It has 25 bedrooms, an apartment for each of Mr. Mugabe's three children, swimming pools, Jacuzzis, and servants' quarters. Sensors to warn of poison or germ attack and radiation detectors are part of palace security, and full-time riot police monitor the grounds in luxury barracks.

Capital has flowed out of Zimbabwe in recent years. Without investment, there has been no job creation, and old jobs are being disappearing as business shrinks. Inflation has destroyed domestic savings as a possible source of investment. In these circumstances, the Mugabe regime has increasingly relied on Chinese investment assistance, generally divorced from any political or human rights concerns.

Alongside all of Zimbabwe's other social tragedies, AIDS takes its own horrific toll. In less than 15 years, AIDS has gone from isolated occurrence to pandemic. In 2001 UNAIDS estimated that 2.3 million Zimbabweans were living with HIV/AIDS and the country had the third highest infection rate (33.7%) in the world, just below Swaziland and Botswana. A later study looking at more recent statistics, from the Health Ministry and the United States Centers for Disease Control and Prevention, reported that about 35% of the country's adults were infected. At least 3,000 individuals a week were dying because of HIV/AIDS, and life expectancy fell from 44.5 years in 1997 to 37.3 in 2005, among the lowest in the world.

The social consequences are devastating. Zimbabwe is well on its way to losing an entire generation. Left behind are the orphans—an estimated one million since the 1980s—deprived of traditional family support and often abandoned to life on the streets of the country's larger cities. There they turn to the only life available: begging and crime. In the rural areas, the surviving elderly people have to care for the country's AIDS orphans. UNICEF estimates that one Zimbabwean child out of five will be an orphan by 2010, 80% of them because of AIDS.

In addition to the AIDS crisis, a recent cholera outbreak infected over 60,000 people and killed almost 4,400 Zimbabweans. Cholera is a curable disease, but most Zimbabweans cannot afford the (relatively inexpensive) treatment.

The Future

Zimbabwe's immediate future is one of the bleakest of any country in Africa, despite an expected $1 Billion in foreign humanitarian aid over 2009.

After years of recrimination and violence towards Mugabe's opponents from military and paramilitary personnel, power-sharing negotiations surprisingly culminated in an accord between the MDC and the ZANU-PF on August 16, 2008, with Tsvangirai agreeing to serve as a Prime Minister alongside President Mugabe.

After almost six months of delay, on February 11, 2009, Morgan Tsvangirai was sworn in as Prime Minister, though it remains unclear how much actual authority the Prime Minister will have, given that Mugabe has kept his Presidential title. Tsvangirai has attempted to leverage his position to build a power base within Zimbabwe's political system, and continues to burnish his reputation on the international scene as the country's most promising political hope, although the international

The sophisticated architecture of ancient Zimbabwe   Photo by David Johns

community will continue to resist accommodating any Mugabe-led regime. Mugabe almost certainly has no interest in ceding real power as part of the "Unity Government," but rather hopes allowing Tsvangirai to become Prime Minister will enable him to contain his opponent and shift blame if Zimbabwe spirals further. (The suspicion between Mugabe and Tsvangirai was epitomized by the supposed highway accident that injured Tsvangirai and cost the life of Tsvangirai's wife in early 2009. While Tsvangirai openly suggested there was no foul play, the MDC is conducting its own investigation into the incident.)

Economic and political refugees fleeing the Zimbabwe crisis have poured into neighboring South Africa (sometimes braving crocodile-infested waters to do so), over the mountains into Mozambique, and elsewhere. In late 2008, many of these refugees suffered at the hands of a wave of xenophobia throughout South Africa, though in 2009, that appears to have mostly ceased.

The majority of those affected in Zimbabwe are black Zimbabweans who have suffered the agonies of hyperinflation, economic collapse, and arbitrary dictatorial rule. For the remaining white Zimbabweans, the future looks unwelcoming as well. At his 85th Birthday in February 2009, Mugabe spoke again of land reform: "the few remaining white farmers should quickly vacate their farms, as they have no place there. . . I am still in control and hold executive authority." Whereas Zimbabwe had 5,600 white-owned farms in 1980, as of March 2009 only 250 are left, and that number continues to decline quickly. Violence continues as land reform stays at the top of the nation's political agenda.

From one of the most promising countries in Africa, called the "Bread basket" of the continent, at moments in the 1980s, Zimbabwe has become one of the continent's most disastrous polities and economies. Hyperinflation, the destruction of the productive (real) economy, and increased violence and scapegoating are the realities.

The advent of the unity government is just the start of possible positive change. The government has still not ensured the rule of law and secure property rights for individuals. One suggestion for monetary stability is reintroducing the Zimbabwean dollar, tied to the South African rand (as done with the currencies of Namibia, Lesotho, etc.) to inject economic stability.

Most likely, Zimbabwe will not change in a positive direction until Robert Mugabe is no longer in a position of power. Until then, Mugabe's Zimbabwe will remain an ideal example of the consequences of absolute power and corruption.

Web Sites and Selected Bibliography of Key English Language Sources

General Web Sites:

Africa South of the Sahara: Selected Internet resources http://www-sul.stanford.edu/depts/ssrg/africa/guide.html. Prepared by Karen Fung for the Information and Communication Technology Group (ICTG), African Studies Association, USA. A comprehensive introduction.

African Studies Internet Resources. Prepared by Joseph Caruso, Columbia University. http://www.columbia.edu/cu/lweb/indiv/africa/cuvl/

An A–Z of African Studies on the Internet. Prepared by Peter Limb, Michigan State University. http://www.lib.msu.edu/limb/a-z/az.html

International Governmental Agency Sources:

UN Conference of Trade and Development http://www.unctad.org/. Statistical data on Least Developed Countries and discussion of poverty strategies.

UN Development Programme. *Human Development Reports.* http://hdr.undp.org. Provides important material on country achievement on life expectancy, educational attainment and adjusted real income.

UN Economic Commission for Africa. http://www.uneca.org/. ECA is the regional arm of the United Nations, mandated to support the economic and social development of its 53 member states. Its annual economic reports are useful.

Integrated Regional Information Networks (IRIN), part of the UN Office for the Coordination of Humanitarian Affairs (OCHA): http://www.irinnews.org/. Current news on humanitarian issues. Its focus reports and specials often contain useful political insights.

The International Monetary Fund (IMF). http://imf.org/external/country/index.htm. Useful material on country projects and debt alleviation.

World Bank in Africa. http://www.worldbank.org/afr/. Useful statistical material and poverty alleviation projects.

U.S. Government Sources:

Central Intelligence Agency (CIA) *The World Factbook* http://www.cia.gov/cia/publications/factbook/index.html. Basic material on land, people, government and economy for each country.

Department of Energy. Energy Information Agency. http://www.eia.doe.gov/. Country analyses provide useful material on energy resources of producing states.

State Department:

Bureau of African Affairs: http://www.state.gov/p/af/. Particularly useful are its *Background Notes* for individual countries.

Bureau of Democracy, Human Rights, and Labor: Annual *Human Rights Reports* for each country: http://www.state.gov/g/drl/hr/.

Annual *International Religious Freedom Reports*: http://www.state.gov/g/drl/rls/irf/.

Bureau for International Narcotics and Law Enforcement Affairs Annual *International Narcotics Control Strategy Report*: http://www.state.gov/g/inl/rls/nrcrpt/.

Counterterrorism Office. Issues the annual *Patterns of Global Terrorism* report: http://www.state.gov/s/ct/

Non-governmental Organizations (NGOs)

Amnesty International http://amnesty.org/. The human rights situation country by country.

Global Witness. http://globalwitness.org/. The group is dedicated to breaking the links between natural resources, conflict and corruption. Its reports on trafficking conflict diamonds and illegal timber cutting provide in-depth studies those linkages.

Human Rights Watch. http://hrw.org/. Excellent reports on a range of human rights issues.

Institute for Security Studies. http://www.iss.co.za/. A South African research institute. Excellent studies, mostly on Southern African issues.

International Crisis Group (ICG). http://www.crisisweb.org/. An independent, nonprofit, multinational think tank. Its reports on Central, Southern, and West Africa, as well as the Horn of Africa are packed with information and insight.

Transparency International. http://www.transparency.de. A German NGO. Its annual *Global Corruption Report* is in English.

News Agencies

http://news.bbc.co.uk. BBC news—better than the *New York Times*, *Washington Post* or *Los Angeles Times* for major news events. North African news is often covered under its "Middle East" rubric.

http://allafrica.com/. Republishes current news stories and topical features from some 100 African newspapers and agencies. For detailed African news, the best site.

Miscellaneous

http://www.xe.com/ucc/. The Universal Currency Converter. For the more obscure African currencies, go to http://www.xe.com/ucc/full.shtml.

http://www.banknoteworld.com. To see what a country's currency looks like.

http://www.embassy.org/embassies/. To locate a country's embassy in Washington.

Books: General

Adams, William and Andrew Goudie, eds. *Physical Geography of Africa.* New York: Oxford University Press, 1999.

Ali, Taisier M. and Robert O. Matthews, eds. *Civil Wars in Africa: Roots and Resolution.* Montreal: McGill-Queen's University Press, 1999.

Anshan, L. *A History of Chinese Overseas in Africa.* Beijing: Chinese Overseas Publishing, 2000.

Ayittey, George B. N. *Africa Unchained: The Blueprint for Africa's Future.* New York: Palgrave, 2005.

Bayart, Jean-Francois, Stephen Ellis, and Béatrice Hibou. *The Criminalization of the State in Africa.* Oxford: James Currey, 1999.

Bayart, Jean-Francois. *The State in Africa: The Politics of the Belly.* New York: Longman, 1993.

Boardman, Henry G. *Africa's Silk Road: China and India's New Economic Frontier.* Washington: World Bank Publications, 2007.

Bøås, Morten, and Kevin C. Dunn. *African Guerillas: Raging Against the Machine.* Boulder, CO: Lynne Rienner, 2007.

Chabal, Patrick and Jean-Pascal Daloz. *Africa Works: Disorder as Political Instrument.* Oxford: James Currey, 1999.

Chabal, Patrick, et al. *The History of Postcolonial Lusophone Africa.* Bloomington: Indiana University Press, 2002.

Cowen, Michael and Liisa Laakso, eds. *Multi-Party Elections in Africa.* New York: Palgrave, 2002.

Easterly, William R. *The White Man's Burden: Why the West's Efforts to Aid the Rest Have done So Much Ill and So Little Good.* New York: Penguin, 2006.

Ellis, Stephen and Gerrie Ter Haar. *Religious Thought and Political Practice in Africa.* London: Hurst, 2004.

Englebert, Pierre. *State Legitimacy and Development in Africa.* Boulder, CO: Lynne Rienner, 2002.

Fietzek, Gerti. *Under Siege: Four African Cities—Freetown, Johannesburg, Kinshasa, Lagos.* Ostfildern-Ruit, Germany: Hatje Cantz, Verlag, 2002. (Distributed in USA by Art Publishers).

French, Howard W. *A Continent for the Taking: The Tragedy and Hope of Africa.* New York: Alfred A. Knopf, 2004.

Gikandi, Simon, ed. *Encyclopedia of African Literature.* London: Routledge, 2003.

Good, Kenneth. *The Liberal Model and Africa: Elites Against Democracy.* New York: Palgrave, 2002.

Guest, Robert. *The Shackled Continent: Power, Corruption and African Lives.* Washington, DC: Smithsonian Institution Press, 2004.

Herbst, Jeffrey. *States and Power in Africa: Comparative Lessons in Authority and Control.* Princeton, NJ: Princeton University Press, 2000.

Hunter, Susan. *Black Death. AIDS in Africa.* NY: Palgrave, 2003.

Kalipeni, Ezekiel, Susan Craddock, Joseph R. Oppong, and Jayati Ghosh, eds. *HIV and AIDS in Africa: Beyond Epidemiology.* London, Blackwell Publishers, 2004.

Karl, Terry Lynn. *The Paradox Of Plenty: Oil Booms and Petro-States.* Berkeley: University of California Press, 1997. [Though the work focuses on Venezuela, it is abundantly relevant to Africa's petro-states.]

Keppel, Gilles. *Jihad: The Trail of Political Islam.* Cambridge, MA: Belknap Press of Harvard University Press, 2002.

Kevane, Michael. *Woman and Development in Africa: How Gender Works.* Boulder, CO: Lynne Rienner, 2004.

Larémont, Ricardo René, ed. *Borders, Nationalism, and the African State.* Boulder, CO: Lynne Rienner, 2005.

Larémont, Ricardo René, ed. *The Causes of War and the Consequences of Peacekeeping in Africa.* Portsmouth, NH: Heinemann, 2002.

Le Vine, Victor T. *Politics in Francophone Africa.* Boulder, CO: Lynne Rienner, 2004.

Lindsay, Lisa A. and Stephan F. Miescher, eds. *Men and Masculinities in Modern Africa.* Portsmouth, NH: Heinemann, 2003.

Mamdani, Mahmood. *Citizen and Subject: Contemporary Africa and the Legacy of Late Colonialism.* Princeton, NJ: Princeton University Press, 1996.

Meredith, Martin. *The Fate of Africa: From the Hopes of Freedom to the Heart of Despair. A History of 50 Years of Independence.* New York: Public Affairs, 2005.

Miers, Suzanne and Martin A. Klein. *Slavery and Colonial Rule in Africa.* Portland, OR: Frank Cass Publishers, 1999.

Miles, William F.S. *Political Islam in West Africa: State-Society Relations Transformed.* Boulder, CO: Lynne Rienner, 2007.

Morris, James. *Butabu: Adobe Architecture of West Africa.* NY: Princeton Architectural Press, 2004.

Moss, Todd J. *African Development: Making Sense of the Issues and Actors.* Boulder, CO: Lynne Rienner, 2007.

O'Connor. David and Andrew Reid, eds. *Ancient Egypt in Africa.* London: University College London Press, 2003.

Olivier de Sardan, Jean Pierre. *Anthropology and Development: Understanding Contemporary Social Change.* London: Zed Books, 2005.

Renner, Michael. *The Anatomy of Resource Wars.* Washington, D.C.: Worldwatch Institute, 2002.

Reno, William. *Warlord Politics and African States.* Boulder, CO: Lynne Rienner Publishers, 1999.

Rosander, Eva Evers, and David Westerlund, eds. *African Islam and Islam in Africa: Encounters between Sufis and Islamists.* Athens, OH: Ohio University Press, 1997.

Rotberg, Robert I., ed. *State Failure and State Weakness in a Time of Terror.* Washington, DC: Brookings Institution Press, 2003.

Schatzberg, Michael G. *Political Legitimacy in Middle Africa: Father, Family, Food.* Bloomington: Indiana University Press, 2001.

Segal, Ronald. *Islam's Black Slaves: The Other Black Diaspora.* New York: Farrar, Straus and Giroux, 2001.

Singer, P. W. (Peter Warren) *Corporate Warriors: The Rise of the Privatized Military Industry.* Ithaca: Cornell University Press, 2003.

Visonà, Monica Blackmun, et al. *A History of Art in Africa.* New York: Harry Abrams, Inc., 2001.

Vogel, Joseph O., ed. *The Encyclopedia of Pre-colonial Africa: Archaeology, History, Languages, Cultures, and Environment.* Walnut Creek, CA: Alta Mira Press, 1997.

World Bank. *Breaking the Conflict Trap: Civil War and Development Policy.* New York: Oxford University Press, 2003.

World Bank. *World Development Report 1997: The State in a Changing World.* New York: Oxford University Press, 1997.

World Bank. *World Development Report 2003: Sustainable Development in a Dynamic World: Transforming Institutions, Growth, and Quality of Life.* New York: Oxford University Press, 2002.

World Bank. *World Development Report 2005: Investment Climate, Growth, and Poverty.* New York: Oxford University Press, 2004.

Young, Crawford. *The African Colonial State in Comparative Perspective.* New Haven, CT: Yale University Press, 1994.

Zartman, I. William, ed. *Collapsed States: The Disintegration and Restoration of Legitimate Authority.* Boulder, CO: Lynne Rienner, 1995.

Zeleza, Paul Tiyambe, ed. *Encyclopedia of Twentieth-Century African History.* London and New York: Routledge, 2002.

Zell, Hans. *The African Studies Companion: A Guide to Information Sources.* Third Edition. Locharron, Scotland, Hans Zell Publishing Consultants: 2003.

Coastal West Africa

Beah, Ishmael. *A Long Way Home: Memoirs of a Boy Soldier.* New York: Farrar, Straus and Giroux, 2007.

Clapham, Christopher S. *African Guerrillas.* Bloomington, IN: Indiana University Press, 1998.

Clark, Andrew Francis and Lucie Colvin Phillips. *Historical Dictionary of Senegal.* Lanham, MD: Scarecrow Press, 1994.

Daniels, Morna. *Côte d'Ivoire.* Santa Barbara, CA: ABC-CLIO, 1996.

Decalo, Samuel. *Historical Dictionary of Benin.* Lanham, MD: Scarecrow Press, 1995.

Decalo, Samuel. *Historical Dictionary of Togo.* Lanham, MD: Scarecrow Press, 3rd ed. 1996.

Dunn, D. Elwood. *Historical Dictionary of Liberia.* Lanham, MD: Scarecrow Press, 2001.

Eades, J.S. and Christopher Allen. *Benin.* Santa Barbara, CA: ABC-CLIO, 1997.

Farah, Douglas. *Blood from stones: the secret financial network of terror.* New York: Broadway Books, 2004

Ferme, Mariane C. *The Underneath of Things : Violence, History and the Everyday in Sierra Leone.* Berkeley: University of California Press, 2001.

Forrest, Joshua B. *Lineages of State Fragility: Rural Civil Society in Guinea-Bissau.* Athens, OH: Ohio University Press, 2003.

Gifford, Paul. *Ghana's New Christianity: Pentecostalism in a Globalising African Economy.* Bloomington: Indiana University Press, 2004.

Hirsch, John L. *Sierra Leone: Diamonds and the Struggle for Democracy.* Boulder, CO: Lynne Rienner, 2001.

Huband, Mark. *The Liberian Civil War.* Portland, OR: International Specialized Book Services, 1998.

Hughes, Arnold. *Historical Dictionary of The Gambia.* 3rd ed. Lanham, MD: Scarecrow Press, 1999.

Human Rights Watch. *How to Fight, How to Kill.* New York: Human Rights Watch, 2004.

International Crisis Group. *Guinea: Change or Chaos.* Brussels: ICG, February 2007. Available online at http:// www.crisisweb.org/

Kourouma, Ahmadou. *Waiting for the Vote of the Wild Animals.* Translated by Carrol F. Coates. Charlottesville: University Press of Virginia, 2001.

Lobban, Richard. *Cape Verde: Crioulo Colony to Independent Nation.* Boulder CO: Westview Press, 1995.

Lobban, Richard. *Historical Dictionary of Cape Verde.* Lanham MD: Scarecrow Press, 3rd ed. 1995.

Mbacké, Khadim. *Sufism and Religious Brotherhoods in Senegal.* Interpretive translation by Eric Ross; edited by John

Hunwick. Princeton, NJ: Markus Wiener Publishers, 2005.

Mundt, Robert J. *Historical Dictionary of Côte d'Ivoire (the Ivory Coast)*. Lanham, MD: Scarecrow Press, 1995.

Pham, John-Peter. *Child Soldiers, Adult Interests: The Global Dimensions of the Sierra Leonean Tragedy*. New York: Nova Science, 2005.

Richards, Paul. *Fighting for the Rainforest: War, Youth and Resources in Sierra Leone*. Portsmouth, NH: Heinemann, 1996.

Söderling, Ludwig and J. Clark Leith. *Ghana-Long Term Growth, Atrophy and Stunted Recovery: Research Report No. 125*. Uppsala, Sweden: The Nordic Africa Institute, 2003.

Central West Africa

Achebe, Chinua. *Home and Exile*. Oxford: Oxford University Press, 2000.

Amadi, L.O. *Dictionary of Nigerian History: from Aba to Zazzau*. Bethesda, MD: International Scholars Publications, 1998.

Bocquené, Henri. *Memoirs of a Mbororo: The Life of Ndudi Umaru: Fulani Nomad of Cameroon*. New York: Berghahn Books, 2002.

DeLancey, Mark W. *Historical Dictionary of the Republic of Cameroon*. Lanham, MD: Scarecrow Press, 3rd. ed. 2000.

Falola, Toyin. *The History of Nigeria*. Westport, CT: Greenwood Publishing Group, 1999.

Fegley, Randall. *Equatorial Guinea*. Santa Barbara, CA: ABC-CLIO, 1992.

Gross, Jean-Germain, ed. *Cameroon. Politics and Society in Critical Perspectives*. Lanham, MD: University Press of America, 2003.

Harford, Tim. *The Undercover Economist: Exposing Why the Rich Are Rich, the Poor Are Poor—and Why You Can Never Buy a Decent Used Car!* New York: Oxford University Press, 2005. [Despite the title, an insightful look at how corruption undermines development in Cameroon can be found in chapter eight.]

Human Rights Watch. *Chop Fine: The Human Rights Impact of Local Government Corruption in Rivers State*. Nigeria. New York: Human Rights Watch, 2007.

Human Rights Watch. *The Price of Oil: Corporate Responsibility and Human Rights Violations in Nigeria's Oil Producing Communities*. New York: Human Rights Watch, 1999.

Human Rights Watch. *Revenge in the Name of Religion: The Cycle of Violence in Plateau and Kano States*. New York: Human Rights Watch, 2005.

Human Rights Watch. *Rivers and Blood: Guns, Oil and Power in Nigeria's Rivers State*. New York: Human Rights Watch, 2005.

International Crisis Group. *Nigeria's Faltering Federal Experiment*. Brussels: ICG, October 2006. Available online at www.crisisweb.org/

Kalck, Pierre and Thomas O'Toole. *Historical Dictionary of the Central African Republic*. Lanham, MD: Scarecrow Press, 2nd ed. 1992.

Liniger-Goumaz, Max. *Historical Dictionary of Equatorial Guinea*. Lanham, MD: Scarecrow Press, 1998.

Liniger-Goumaz, Max. *Small Is Not Always Beautiful : The Story of Equatorial Guinea*. London: Hurst, 1988.

Maier, Karl. *This House Has Fallen: A Journey Through Nigeria's Heart of Darkness*. New York: Public Affairs, 2000.

Obi, Cyril I. *The Changing Forms of Identity. Politics in Nigeria under Economic Adjustment: The Case of Oil Minorities Movement of the Niger Delta*. Report No. 119. Uppsala: Nordic African Institute, 2001.

Okonta, Ike and Douglas Oronto. *Where Vultures Feast: Shell, Human Rights, and Oil in the Niger Delta*. San Francisco: Sierra Club Books, 2001.

Paden, John N. *Muslim Civic Cultures and Conflict Resolution. The Challenge of Democratic Federalism in Nigeria*. Washington: Brookings, 2005.

Roberts, Adam. *The Wonga Coup: Guns, Thugs and a Ruthless Determination to Create Mayhem in an Oil-Rich Corner of Africa*. New York: Public Affairs, 2006.

Rotberg, Robert I., ed. *Crafting the New Nigeria: Confronting the Challenges*. Boulder, CO: Lynne Rienner, 2004.

Suberu, Rotimi T. *Federalism and Ethnic Conflict in Nigeria*. Washington, DC: United States Institute of Peace Press, 2001.

Equatorial West Africa

Adelman, Howard and Govind C. Rao, eds. *War and Peace in Zaire/Congo: Analyzing and Evaluating Intervention: 1996-1997*. Trenton, NJ: Africa World Press, 2004.

Ballentine, Karen and Michael Nest, eds. *The Democratic Republic of Congo: Economic Dimensions of War and Peace*. Boulder, CO: Lynne Rienner, 2005

Cilliers, Jakkie and Christian Dietrich, eds. *Angola's War Economy: The Role of Diamonds*. Pretoria, SA: Institute for Security Studies, 2000.

Dallaire, Romeo. *Shake Hands with the Devil: The Failure of Humanity in Rwanda*. New York: Random House, 2003.

De Witte, Ludo. *The Assassination of Lumumba*. Trans. Ann Wright and Renée Fenby. New York: Verso Books, 2003.

Doom, Ruddy and Jan Gorus, eds. *Politics of Identity and Economics of Conflict in the Great Lakes Region*. Brussels: VUB University Press, 2000.

Dunn, Kevin. *Imagining the Congo: The International Relations of Identity*. NY: Palgrave, 2003.

Eggers, Ellen K. *Historical Dictionary of Burundi*. Lanham, MD: Scarecrow Press, 1997.

Gondola, Ch. Didier. *The History of Congo*. Westport, CT: Greenwood Press, 2002.

Global Witness. *Digging in Corruption: Fraud, abuse and exploitation in Katanga's copper and cobalt Mines*. Washington, DC: Global Witness Publishing, 2006. Available on line.

Gourevitch, Philip. *We Wish To Inform You That Tomorrow We Will Be Killed With Our Families: Stories From Rwanda*. New York: Farrar, Straus, Giroux, 1998.

Hatzfeld, Jean. *Into the Quick of Life*. London: Serpent's Tail, 2005.

Hatzfeld, Jean. *Machete Season*. New York: Farrar, Strauss, Giroux, 2005.

Hochschild, Adam. *King Leopold's Ghost*. New York: Houghton Mifflin Co., 1999.

Hodges, Tony. *Angola: Anatomy of An Oil State*. 2nd edition. Oxford: James Currey, 2004.

Human Rights Watch. *The Curse of Gold*. New York: Human Rights Watch, 2005. [On the exploitation of gold resources in the northeastern Ituri district.]

Human Rights Watch. *Leave None to Tell the Story: Genocide in Rwanda*. New York: Human Rights Watch, 1999. Reissued April 2004 with update.

Human Rights Watch. *Some Transparency, No Accountability: The Use of Oil Revenue in Angola and Its Impact on Human Rights*. New York: Human Rights Watch, 2004.

International Crisis Group. *Burundi: Democracy and Peace at Risk*. Brussels: ICG, November 2006. Available online at http://www.crisisweb.org/

Jefremovas, Villia. *Brickyards to Graveyards: From Production to Genocide in Rwanda*. New York: State University of New York Press, 2002.

Lemarchand, René. *Burundi: Ethnocide as Discourse and Practice*. New York: Cambridge University Press, 1994.

MacGaffey, Wyatt. *Kongo Political Culture: The Conceptual Challenge of the Particular*. Bloomington: Indiana University Press, 2000.

Mamdani, Mahmood. *When Victims Become Killers: Colonialism, Nativism and the Genocide in Rwanda*. Princeton: Princeton University Press, 2001.

Melvern, Linda. *Conspiracy to Murder: The Rwanda Genocide and the International Community*. London: Verso Books, 2004.

Nzongola-Ntalaja, Georges. *The Congo. From Leopold to Kabila: A People's History*. New York: Palgrave, 2002.

Peterson, Dale. *Eating Apes*. California Studies in Food and Culture, 6. Berkeley: University of California Press, 2003.

Peterson, Scott. *Me against My Brother: at War in Somalia, Sudan and Rwanda*. New York: Routledge, 2000.

Pottier, Johan, et al. eds. *Re-Imagining Rwanda: Conflict, Survival and Disinformation in the Late Twentieth Century*. Cambridge: Cambridge University Press, 2002.

Review of African Political Economy, 29:93/94 (September/December, 2002). Special issue devoted to "State Failure in the Congo: Perceptions & Realities."

Trefon, Theodore, ed. *Reinventing Order in the Congo: How People Respond to State Failure in Kinshasa*. London: Zed Books, 2004.

Walker, John Frederick. *A Certain Curve Of Horn: The Hundred-Year Quest for The Giant Sable Antelope of Angola*. New York: Atlantic Monthly Press, 2002.

Wallis, Andrew. *Silent Accomplice: The Untold Story of France's Role in the Rwandan Genocide*. London: I.B. Tauris, 2006.

Wrong, Michela. *In the Footsteps of Mr. Kurtz: Living on the Brink of Disaster in the Congo*. New York: HarperCollins, 2001.

Southern Africa

Allen, John. *Rabble-Rouser for Peace: The Authorized Biography of Desmond Tutu*. New York: Free Press, 2006.

Ashforth, Adam Philip. *Witchcraft, Violence and Democracy in South Africa*. Chicago: Chicago University Press, 2004..

Barber, James. *Mandela's World: The International Dimension of South Africa's Political Revolution 1990-99*. Athens, OH: Ohio University Press, 2004.

Bauer, Gretchen and Scott D. Taylor. *Politics in Southern Africa: State and Society in Transition*. Boulder, CO: Lynne Rienner, 2004.

Beck, Roger B. *The History of South Africa*. Westport, CT: Greenwood Publishing Group, 2000.

Blair, David. *Degrees in Violence: Robert Mugabe and the Struggle for Power in Zimbabwe*. London and New York: Continuum Books, 2002.

Bond, Patrick. *Elite Transition: From Apartheid to Neoliberalism in South Africa*. 2nd edition. Scottsville, SA: University of KwaZulu-Natal Press, 2006.

Booth, Alan R. *Historical Dictionary of Swaziland*. Lanham, MD: Scarecrow Press, 2000.

Boraine, Alex. *A Country Unmasked: Inside South Africa's Truth and Reconciliation Commission*. New York: Oxford University Press, 2000.

Bowen, Merle L. *The State Against the Peasantry: Rural Struggles in Colonial and Postcolonial Mozambique*. Charlottesville: University Press of Virginia, 2000.

Campbell, Catherine. *Letting Them Die: Why HIV/AIDS Prevention Programmes Fail*. Oxford: James Currey, 2003.

Chan, Stephen. *Citizen of Africa: Conversations with Morgan Tsvangirai*. Cape Town: Fingerprint Co-operative, 2005.

Crais, Clifton. *The Politics of Evil: Magic, State Power and Political Imagination in South Africa*. Cambridge: Cambridge University Press, 2002.

Crosby, Cynthia A. *Historical Dictionary of Malawi*. Lanham, MD: Scarecrow Press, 1993.

Eades, Lindsay Michie. *The End of Apartheid in South Africa*. Westport, CT: Greenwood Publishing Group, 1999.

Englund, Harri, ed. *A Democracy of Chameleons: Politics and Culture in the New Malawi*. Uppsala: The Nordic African Institute, 2002.

Forester, Peter G. and Bongani J. Nsibande, eds. *Swaziland: Contemporary Social and Economic Issues*. Aldershot: Ashgate Publishing, 2000.

Galli, Rosemary. *People's Spaces and State Spaces: Land and Governance in Mozambique*. Lanham, MD: Rowman & Littlefield Publishers, 2003.

Gillis, D. Hugh. *The Kingdom of Swaziland: Studies in Political History*. Westport, CT: Greenwood Publishing Group, 1999.

Giliomee, Hermann. *The Afrikaners: Biography of a People*. Charlottesville: University of Virginia, 2003.

Graybill, Lyn S. *Truth and Reconciliation in South Africa: Miracle or Model?* Boulder, CO: Lynne Rienner, 2002.

Grotpeter, John J. *Historical Dictionary of Zambia*. Lanham, MD: Scarecrow Press, 1998.

Gukurahundi in Zimbabwe: A Report on the Disturbances in Matabeleland and the Midlands 1980-1988. Johannesburg: Jacana Media, 2007.

Gumede, William Mervin. *Thabo Mbeki and the Battle for the Soul of the ANC*. Capetown, SA: Zebra Press, 2005.

Hall, Margaret and Tom Young. *Confronting Leviathan: Mozambique since Independence*. Athens, OH: Ohio University Press, 1997.

Hammer, Amanda and Brian Raftopoulos and Stig Jensen, eds. *Zimbabwe's Unfinished Business: Rethinking Land, State and Nation in the Context of Crisis*. Harare: Weaver Press, 2003.

Hansen, Karen Tranberg. *Salaula: the World of Secondhand Clothing and Zambia*. Chicago: University of Chicago Press, 2000.

Harrison, Graham. *The Politics of Rural Democratization in Mozambique: grassroots governance in Mecúfi*. Lewiston, NY: Edwin Mellen, 2000.

Hassan, Fareed M.A. *Lesotho: Development in a Challenging Environment: a Joint World Bank-African Development Bank Evaluation*. Abidjan: African Development Bank; Washington, D.C.: World Bank, 2002.

Henning, Melber, ed. *Reexamining Liberation in Namibia: Political Culture since Independence in Namibia*. Uppsala: Nordic African Institute, 2003.

Human Rights Watch. *Deadly Delay: South Africa's Efforts to Prevent HIV in Survivors of Sexual Violence*. New York: Human Rights Watch, 2004.

Human Rights Watch. *Not Eligible: The Politicization of Food in Zimbabwe*. New York: Human Rights Watch, 2003.

Huddlestone, Sarah. *Face of Courage: Morgan Tsvangirai*. Cape Town, South Africa: Double Storey Books, 2005.

Hyam, Ronald amd Peter Henshaw. *The Lion and the Springbok: Britain and South Africa since the Boer War*. Cambridge: Cambridge University Press, 2003.

International Crisis Group. *Zimbabwe: An End to the Stalemate?* Pretoria/Brussels: ICG, March 2007. Available online at http://www.crisisweb.org/

International Crisis Group. *Swaziland: The Clock is Ticking*. Pretoria/Brussels: ICG, July 2005. Available online at http://www.crisisweb.org/

Jackson, Ashley. *Botswana 1939–1945: an African Country at War*. New York: Oxford University Press, 1999.

Jacobs, Sean and Richard Calland, eds. *Thabo Mbeki's World. The Politics and Ideology of the South African President*. NY: Palgrave, 2003.

Johnston, Deborah. *Lesotho*. Santa Barbara, CA: ABC-CLIO, rev. ed., 1997.

Lodge, Tom. *Politics in South Africa: from Mandela to Mbeki*. Bloomington: Indiana University Press, 2003.

Melber, Henning, ed. *Reexamining Liberation in Namibia: Political Culture since Independence*. Uppsala: Nordiska Afrikainstitutet, 2003.

Meredith, Martin. *Our Votes, Our Guns: Robert Mugabe and the Tragedy of Zimbabwe*. New York: Public Affairs, 2002.

Newitt, Malyn. *A History of Mozambique*. Bloomington, IN: Indiana University Press, 1995.

Pitcher, M. Anne. *Transforming Mozambique: The Politics of Privatization, 1975–2000*. Cambridge: Cambridge University Press, 2002.

Raftopoulos, Brian and Tyrone Savage, eds. *Zimbabwe: Injustice and Political Reconciliation*. Capetown, SA: Weaver Press, 2005.

Ross, Robert. *A Concise History of South Africa*. New York: Cambridge University Press, 1999.

Saunders, Christopher C. and Nicholas Southey. *Historical Dictionary of South*

Africa. Lanham, MD: Scarecrow Press, 1999.

Schoeman, Stanley and Elna Schoeman. *Namibia*. Santa Barbara, CA: ABC-CLIO, rev. ed. 1997.

Sheldon, Kathleen E. *Pounders of Grain: A history of women, work and politics in Mozambique*. Portsmouth, NH: Heinemann, 2002.

Tekere, Edgar. *A Lifetime of Struggle*. Harare: Sapes Books, 2006.

Temkin, Ben. *Buthelezi. A Biography*. Portland, OR: Frank Cass Publishers, 2003.

Terreblanche, Sampie (Solomon Johannes), *A History of Inequality in South Africa, 1652–2002*, Scottsville, SA: University of KwaZulu-Natal Press, 2003.

Tomlinson, Richard. et al. eds. *Emerging Johannesburg: Perspectives on the Post-Apartheid City*. London: Routledge, 2003.

Walker, Liz, et al. *Waiting to Happen: HIV/AIDS in South Africa—The Bigger Picture*. Boulder, CO: Lynne Rienner, 2004.

Woods, Anthony. *The Creation of Modern Malawi*. Boulder, CO: Westview Press, 1998.

East Africa Island Nations

Allen, Philip M. *Madagascar: Conflicts of Authority in the Great Island*. Boulder, CO: Westview Press, 1995.

Bennett, George and Pramila Ramgulan Bennett. *Seychelles*. Santa Barbara, CA: ABC-CLIO, 1993.

Bradt, Hilary. *Madagascar*. Santa Barbara, CA: ABC-CLIO, 1994.

Metz, Helen Chapin, ed. *Indian Ocean: Five Island Countries*. Washington, DC: U.S. GPO, 3rd ed. 1995.

Dick-Read, Robert. *The Phantom Voyagers: Evidence of Indonesian Settlement in Africa in Ancient Times*. Winchester: Thurlton Publishing, 2005.

Ottenheimer, Martin and Harriet Ottenheimer. *Historical Dictionary of the Comoro Islands*. Lanham, MD: Scarecrow Press, 1994.

Scarr, Deryck. *Seychelles since 1770: History of a Slave and Post-Slave Society*. Lawrenceville, NJ: Africa World Press, 1999.

Storey, William K. *Science and Power in Colonial Mauritius*. Rochester, NY: University of Rochester Press, 1997.

Eastern Africa

Aboubaker Alwan, Daoud. *Historical Dictionary of Djibouti*. Lanham, MD: Scarecrow Press, 2000.

Ali, Ayaan Hirsi. *Infidel*. New York: Free Press, 2007.

Baltimore, The Walters Art Museum. *Ethiopian Art: The Walters Museum*. Lingfield, UK: Third Millennium Publishing, 2001.

Crummey, Donald. *Land and Society in the Christian Kingdom of Ethiopia: from the Thirteenth to the Twentieth Century*. Champaign, IL: University of Illinois Press, 1999.

Darch, Colin. *Tanzania*. Santa Barbara, CA: ABC-CLIO, rev. ed. 1996.

De Waal, Alexander. *Islamism and its Enemies in the Horn of Africa*. London: Hurst & Co., 2004.

Elkins, Caroline. *Imperial Reckoning: The Untold Story of Britain's Gulag in Kenya*. New York: Henry Holt, 2005.

Fegley, Randall. *Eritrea*. Santa Barbara, CA: ABC-CLIO, 1995.

Forster, Peter G. and Sam Maghimbi, eds. *Agrarian Economy, State, and Society in Contemporary Tanzania*. Brookfield, VT: Ashgate Publishing Company, 1999.

Fozzard, Adrian. *Djibouti*. Boulder, CO: Westview Press, 1999.

Gregory, Robert G. *South Asians in East Africa: An Economic and Social History, 1890-1980*. Boulder, CO: Westview Press, 1993.

Heldman, Marilyn with Stuart C. Munro-Hay. *African Zion: The Sacred Art of Ethiopia*. New Haven: Yale University Press, 1993.

Henze, Paul B. *Layers of Time: A History of Ethiopia*. New York: Saint Martin's Press, 1999.

Henze, Paul. *Eritrea's War*. Summerset, NJ: Transaction, 2002.

Killion, Tom. *Historical Dictionary of Eritrea*. Lanham, MD: Scarecrow Press, 1998.

Levine, Donald N. *Greater Ethiopia: The Evolution of a Multiethnic Society*. Chicago: University of Chicago Press, 2000.

Little, Peter D. *Somalia: Economy Without State*. Oxford : International African Institute in association with James Currey, 2003.

Maathai, Wangari. *Unbowed*. New York: Knopf, 2006

Maloba, Wunyabara O. *Mau Mau and Kenya: An Analysis of a Peasant Revolt*. Bloomington, IN: Indiana University Press, 1998.

Marcus, Harold G. *A History of Ethiopia*. Berkeley, CA: University of California Press, 1994.

Maxon, Robert M. *Historical Dictionary of Kenya*. 2nd ed. Lanham, MD: Scarecrow Press, 2000.

Menkhaus, Kenneth John. *Somalia: State collapse and the threat of terrorism*. New York: Oxford, 2004

Mukhtar, Mohamed Haji and Margaret Castagno. *Historical Dictionary of Somalia*. Revised edition. Lanham, MD: Rowman & Littlefield Publishers, 2003.

Munro-Hay, Stuart and Richard Pankhurst. *Ethiopia*. Santa Barbara, CA: ABC-CLIO, 1995.

Negash, Tekeste. *Eritrea and Ethiopia: The Federal Experience*. New Brunswick, NJ: Transaction Publishers, 1997.

Neyko, Balam. *Uganda*. Santa Barbara, CA: ABC-CLIO, rev. ed. 1996.

Oded, Arye. *Islam and Politics in Kenya*. Boulder, CO: Lynne Rienner Publishers, 2000.

Ofcansky, Thomas P. and Robert M. Maxon. *Historical Dictionary of Kenya*. Lanham, MD: Scarecrow Press, 1999.

Ofcansky, Thomas P. and Rodger Yeager. *Historical Dictionary of Tanzania*. 2nd ed. Lanham, MD: Scarecrow Press, 1997.

Pankhurst, Barbara. *The Ethiopians*. Malden, MA: Blackwell Publishers, 1998.

Pausewang, Siegfried, et al. *Ethiopia Since the Derg. A Decade of Democratic Pretension and Performance*. New York: Palgrave, 2003.

Peterson, Scott. *Me against My Brother: At War in Somalia, Sudan and Rwanda*. New York: Routledge, 2000.

Prouty, Chris and Eugene Rosenfeld. *Historical Dictionary of Ethiopia and Eritrea*. Lanham, MD: Scarecrow Press, 2nd ed. 1994.

Rotberg, Robert I., ed. *Battling terrorism in the Horn of Africa*. Washington: Brookings Institution, 2005.

Schraeder, Peter J. *Djibouti*. Santa Barbara, CA: ABC-CLIO, 1991.

Woodward, Peter. *The Horn of Africa. Politics and International Relations*. Rev. ed. New York: Palgrave, 2003.

Wrong, Michela. *I Didn't Do It For You: How the World Betrayed a Small African Nation*. New York: HarperCollins, 2005.

South Sahara Africa

Amnesty International. *Sudan: The Human Price of Oil*. London: Amnesty International, 2000.

Azevedo, Mario. *Chad: A Nation in Search of Its Future*. Boulder, CO: Westview Press, 1997.

Burr, J. Millard and Robert O. Collins. *Africa's Thirty Years' War: Chad, Libya, and the Sudan, 1963–1993*. Boulder, CO: Westview Press, 1999.

Burr, Millard and Robert Collins. *Revolutionary Sudan: Hasan al-Turabi and the Islamist state, 1989-2000*. Leiden; Boston, MA : Brill, 2003.

Coalition for International Justice. *Soil and Oil: Dirty Business in Sudan*. Washington: CIJ, February, 2006. Available online at www.cij.org

Decalo, Samuel. *Historical Dictionary of Chad*. Lanham, MD: Scarecrow Press, 1997.

Decalo, Samuel. *Historical Dictionary of Niger*. Lanham, MD: Scarecrow Press, 1996.

Deng, Francis Mading. *War of Visions: Conflict of Identities in the Sudan*. Washington, DC: Brookings Institution Press, 1995.

Human Rights Watch. *Entrenching Impunity: Government Responsibility for International Crimes in Darfur*. New York: Human Rights Watch, 2005.

Human Rights Watch. *"If We Return, We Will Be Killed" Consolidation of Ethnic Cleansing in Darfur, Sudan*. New York: Human Rights Watch, 2004.

Human Rights Watch. *Sudan, Oil, and Human Rights*. New York: Human Rights Watch, 2003.

Human Rights Watch. *"They Came Here to Kill Us:" Militia Attacks and Ethnic Targeting of Civilians in Eastern Chad*. New York: Human Rights Watch, 2007.

International Crisis Group. *Darfur Rising: Sudan's New Crisis*. (Africa Report No. 76). Brussels: International Crisis Group, 25 March 2004. (http://www. crisisweb. org/)

Johnson, Douglas H. *The Root Causes of Sudan's Civil Wars*. Bloomington: Indiana University Press, 2003.

Khalid, Mansour. *War and Peace in Sudan: A Tale of Two Countries*. New York: Kegan Paul, 2003.

McFarland, Daniel M. *Historical Dictionary of Burkina Faso*. Lanham, MD: Scarecrow Press, 1998.

Mosely Lesch, Ann. *The Sudan: Contested National Identities*. Bloomington, IN: Indiana University Press, 1998.

Packer, George. "The Moderate Martyr: A radically peaceful vision of Islam," *New Yorker*, September 11, 2006, 60-69.

Peterson, Scott. *Me against My Brother: At War in Somalia, Sudan, and Rwanda*. New York: Routledge, 2000.

Petterson, Donald. *Inside Sudan: Political Islam, Conflict, and Catastrophe*. Rev. ed. Boulder, CO: Westview Press, 2003.

Popenoe, Rebecca. *Feeding Desire: Fatness, Beauty, and Sexuality among a Saharan People*. New York: Routledge, 2004.

Prunier, Gerard. *Darfur: Ambiguous Genocide*. Ithaca, NY: Cornell University Press, 2005.

Reeves, Eric. *A Long Day's Dying: Critical Moments in the Darfur Genocide*. Toronto: Key Publishing House, 2007.

Rovine, Victoria L. *Bogolan: Shaping Culture through Cloth in Contemporary Mali*. Washington: Smithsonian Books, 2001.

Schutyser, Sebastian. *Banco: Adobe Mosques of the Inner Niger Delta*. Milan: Five Continents Editions, 2003.

Scroggins, Deborah. *Emma's War*. New York: Pantheon, 2002.

Sudan Divestment Task Force. *PetroChina, CNPC, and Sudan: Perpetuating Genocide*. Available online: http://www.sudan divestment.org/docs/petrochina_cnpc _sudan.pdf

Warburg, Gabriel. *Islam, Sectarianism, and Politics In Sudan Since the Mahdiyya*. Madison: University of Wisconsin Press, 2003.

Zamponi, Lynda F. *Niger*. Santa Barbara: ABC-CLIO, 1994.

North Africa

Abdo, Geneive. *No God but God: Egypt and the Triumph of Islam*. New York: Oxford University Press, 2000.

Adamson, Kay. *Algeria: A Study in Competing Ideologies*. Herndon, VA: Cassell Academic, 1998.

Ahmida, Ali Abdullatif. *The Making of Modern Libya: State Formation, Colonialization, and Resistance, 1830–1932*. Albany, NY: State University of New York, 1994.

Arnold, Guy. *The Maverick State: Gaddafi and the New World Order*. Herndon, VA: Cassell Academic, 1996.

Beattie, Kirk J. *Egyptian Politics During Sadat's Presidency*. New York: Saint Martin's Press, 2000.

Borowiec, Andrew. *Tunisia: a Democratic Apprenticeship*. Westport, CT: Greenwood Publishing Group, 1998.

Bouqia, Rahma and Susan Gilson Miller, eds. *In the Shadow of the Sultan: Culture, Power and Politics in Morocco*. Cambridge: Harvard University Press, 1999.

Burr, J. Millard and Robert O. Collins. *Africa's Thirty Years' War: Chad, Libya, and the Sudan, 1963–1993*. Boulder, CO: Wesview Press, 1999.

Ciment, James. *Algeria: the Fundamentalist Challenge*. New York: Facts on File, 1997.

Daly, Martin W., ed. *Modern Egypt from 1517 to the End of the Twentieth Century*. New York: Cambridge University Press, 1999.

El-Kikhia, Mansour O. *Libya's Qaddafi: the Politics of Contradiction*. Gainesville, FL: University Press of Florida, 1997.

Findlay, Anne M., et al., *Morocco*. Santa Barbara, CA: ABC-CLIO, 1995.

Gould, St. John. *Morocco*. NY: Routledge, 2002.

Howe, Marvine. *Morocco: The Islamist Awakening and Other Challenges*. New York: Oxford University Press, 2005.

Human Rights Watch. *Egypt: In a Time of Torture*. New York: Human Rights Watch, 2004.

Jensen, Erik. *Western Sahara: Anatomy of a Stalemate*. Boulder, CO: Lynne Rienner, 2004.

King, Stephen J. *Liberalization against Democracy: The Local Politics of Economic Reform in Tunisia*. Bloomington: Indiana University Press, 2003.

Lawless, Richard I. *Algeria*. Santa Barbara, CA: ABC-CLIO, 1995.

Long, David E. and Bernard Reich. *The Government and Politics of the Middle East and North Africa*. 4th ed. Boulder, CO: Westview, 2002.

Murphy, Emma C. *Economic and Political Change in Tunisia: From Bourguiba to Ben Ali*. New York: Saint Martin's Press, 1999.

Naylor, Phillip Chiviges and Alf Andrew Heggoy. *Historical Dictionary of Algeria*. Lanham, MD: Scarecrow Press, 2nd ed. 1994.

Niblock, Tim. *"Pariah States" & Sanctions in the Middle East: Iraq, Libya, Sudan*. Boulder, CO: Lynne Rienner Publishers, 2001.

O'Conner, David and Andrew Reid, eds. *Ancient Egypt in Africa*. London: University College of London Press, 2003.

Park, Thomas K. *Historical Dictionary of Morocco*. Lanham, MD: Scarecrow Press, 1996.

Pazzanita, Anthony G. *Historical Dictionary of Mauritania*. Lanham, MD: Scarecrow Press, 1996.

Pennell, C.R. *Morocco Since 1830: A History*. Millwood, NY: Labyrinth, 2000.

Perkins, Kenneth J. *A History of Modern Tunisia*. Cambridge: Cambridge University Press, 2004.

Quandt, William B. *Between Ballots and Bullets: Algeria's Transition from Authoritarianism*. Washington, DC: Brookings Institution Press, 1998.

Rubin, Barry. *Islamic Fundamentalism in Egyptian Politics*. New York: Palgrave, 2002.

St. John, Ronald Bruce. *Historical Dictionary of Libya*. Lanham, MD: Scarecrow Press, 3rd ed. 1998.

Stora, Benjamin. *Algeria, 1830–2000: A Short History*. Ithaca, NY: Cornell University Press, 2001.

Sullivan, Denis J. *Islam in Contemporary Egypt: Civil Society vs. the State*. Boulder, CO: Lynne Rienner Publishers, 1999.

Takeyh, Ray. *The Origins of the Eisenhower Doctrine: The U.S., Britain and Nasser's Egypt, 1953–57*. New York: Saint Martin's Press, 2000.

Vandewalle, Dirk. *Libya since Independence: Oil and State-Building*. Ithaca, NY: Cornell University Press, 1998.

White, Gregory. *A Comparative Political Economy of Tunisia and Morocco: On the outside of Europe looking in*. Albany, NY: State University of New York Press, 2001.

Willis, Michael. *The Islamist Challenge in Algeria: A Political History*. New York: New York University Press, 1997.